Britannia's Burden

To
The Kangaroos of Tidbinbilla

Britannia's Burden

The Political Evolution of Modern Britain 1851–1990

Bernard Porter
Professor of Modern History
University of Newcastle upon Tyne

Edward Arnold
A member of the Hodder Headline Group
LONDON NEW YORK MELBOURNE AUCKLAND

The weary Titan, with deaf
Ears, and labour-dimm'd eyes,
Regarding neither to right
Nor left, goes passively by,
Staggering on to her goal;
Bearing on her shoulders immense,
Atlantean, the load,
Wellnigh not to be borne,
Of the too vast orb of her fate

    Matthew Arnold, 'Heine's Grave'

First published in Great Britain 1994

Distributed in the USA by Routledge, Chapman and Hall, Inc.
29 West 35th Street, New York, NY 10001

British Library Cataloguing in Publication Data

Available on request

ISBN 0-340-56196-3 (boards)
ISBN 0-340-56197-1 (paper)

Produced by GreenGate Publishing Services, Tonbridge, Kent
Printed and bound in Great Britain for Edward Arnold,
a division of Hodder Headline plc,
338 Euston Road, London NW1 3BH,
by Mackays of Chatham, plc

Contents

Preface

An awful lot of nonsense has been spoken and written about British history over the last few years, usually to bolster particular political points of view. Most of it is not demonstrably wrong, but worse: only half-right, or superficial, or taken out of context, and consequently misleading. It was my irritation at this which spurred me to write this book; which covers the main developments of Britain's political history over the past century, and attempts to explain them. By so doing I hope it may also contribute to an understanding of the country's present predicament.

It has a theme. I am afraid it is a rather deterministic one. Britain's fate since the middle of the nineteenth century has been largely beyond her control. The origins of it lie back at the beginning. Almost everything that has happened to Britain since 1850 grew from the embryo that was present in the body politic at that time. That gave birth to her rise, but also her decline, and the twists and turns of her political progress from that time onwards – from whiggism *via* imperialism and then socialism to right-wing free marketism – each stage of which grew inexorably from the one before. I shall try to explain how that worked in the following pages. Of course not everything was predetermined. Each stage could have been handled differently, in ways that might have had an important impact on people. The main current could not have been diverted, however. That was beyond the power of anyone.

That (in a nutshell) is the book's argument. It will involve a number of revisions of common assumptions about Britain's past. Among these are the following: that Britain was a free-market society in the mid-nineteenth century; that her success was due to that; that she strayed from this path later on due to a revival of aristocratic values; that the 'new' imperialism of the end of the nineteenth century was an aberration; that it was popular in any real sense; that it fulfilled the aims of capitalism; that imperialism and socialism were mutually antagonistic; that her empire estranged Britain from continental Europe; that its going helped the political left; that the left was dominant in Britain at any time during the twentieth century; that consequently its defeat in the 1980s was any kind of achievement; and that the result of that defeat was to return Britain to anything like the 'values' of the point in time where this book begins. Most of these reappraisals are not original, but are based on the work of other historians. What I have tried to do is bring them together in a pattern that makes more sense of Britain's recent history (in my view) than some other more popular accounts.

The book can also be read as a narrative. I have tried to write it so that it comes over as such. The overall arrangement is chronological. It includes some material that is meant simply to give the 'flavour' of a time. It also features one or two little literary indulgencies, which I trust I will be forgiven for: in particular the device of beginning each section with a description of a royal visit somewhere. This may be felt to be artificial; but the aim of each is to make a point. I have also indulged my interests in architecture and cricket somewhat. The down side of all this, of course, is that an enormous amount of information has been left out; but that is inevitable in a work of this size covering so long and eventful a period. Certain omissions may well be more significant than what has found its way into the book. (Some are burning in my mind now; but it is too late: the book has to go to the printers.) It is up to others, however, to compensate for this, and write alternative histories of Britain based on what *they* believe to be the significant events.

I owe debts to a number of people. The biggest is to Ian Hancock of the Australian National University in Canberra, who arranged a six-months-long visiting fellowship for me in 1989, which enabled me to get started on this book. The ANU provides the ideal atmosphere for relaxed research: good libraries, good weather, good company; a kind of All Souls in the Outback, plus Democracy. Three other libraries merit special thanks for their help: the Brynmor Jones Library at the University of Hull; the Robinson Library at the University of Newcastle; and the Literary and Philosophical Society of Newcastle upon Tyne, which any scholar who has visited it will tell you is the Platonic ideal of a library. Many friends and colleagues have helped, in these three places and elsewhere. (I hope they will forgive this general and anonymous acknowledgement.) Christopher Wheeler at Edward Arnold has been exceptionally encouraging, and patient when I ran over my deadline. He also seems to know what is in the book better than I do. (He wrote the 'blurb'.) My children helped mainly by growing up but still not growing away. My wife Deirdre has tolerated living with half a husband (mentally, that is; the other half besotted by the book) for four and a half years with better grace than I deserve. I'll try to make it up to her now that the devil has been exorcised.

Bernard Porter
Newcastle upon Tyne
February 1994

Part I

A period of most wonderful transition
(1851–80)

Chapter 1

The Great Exhibition (1851)

On the morning of Thursday 1 May 1851, in a light drizzle, Queen Victoria set out from Buckingham Palace to open the 'Great Exhibition of the Works of Industry of All Nations' in Hyde Park. With her were her husband Albert, who had taken a prominent part in arranging the Exhibition, and two of their children. Their carriage was accompanied by a troop of mounted Life Guards 'in scarlet coats, bright cuirasses, and glittering helmets' trotting magnificently beside them;[1] but she still – as she confided later to her diary – felt nervous.[2] That may have had something to do with the potential danger of the occasion. The previous year she had been attacked in a London street by a mentally deranged ex-Hussar called Robert Pate. The crowd then had not been nearly as large as this one, which could easily have hidden a dozen more such assailants. Alternatively, she could have been concerned for the success of the Exhibition, for which Albert had been cruelly pilloried in certain quarters for months. What if it turned out to be a flop?

In the event she need not have worried on either score. The occasion was a wonderful success. 'You should have heard,' wrote one observer, recounting it for a very young readership, 'how the crowds huzzaed and shouted when they saw the Queen, who looked very much pleased,' as well she might. When she entered the building – Joseph Paxton's great 'Crystal Palace', made of glass and iron – she was greeted by 25 000 'Ladies waving their handkerchiefs, the gentlemen their hats', and cheering her to the skies. 'Even the sun popped out his head from the clouds,' wrote our children's author, 'and poured a flood of golden light through the glittering dome.'[3] It must have been dazzling, because none of the surviving pictures of the Crystal Palace shows a dome. Whatever it was, below it was displayed 'a girdle of female beauty' in the galleries: 'The Englishwoman, calm in the possession of her chaste and aerial loveliness, the animated

Parisienne, rich in her indescribable grace, and the daughter of the South, with her restless and impassioned gaze.'[4] That must have been a sight. Many of those present likened it to 'fairyland'. A huge organ, augmented by a band of 200 and a choir of 600 souls, struck up the National Anthem, followed by the Hallelujah Chorus from the *Messiah*. They could hardly be heard above the cheers. Every face gleamed with joy; some wept with emotion; a Chinaman became so moved and excited that he rushed through the cordon of nobles surrounding the Queen to perform 'a grand salaam' before her;[5] even Frenchmen could be heard shouting 'Vive la Reine!' It was, wrote the Queen after it all, 'one of the greatest and most glorious days of our lives;... a day which makes my heart swell with thankfulness.'[6]

For Victoria all this was a delight. For her ministers it must have come as something of a relief. It could have turned out otherwise. Many people had been warning that it would. The most vocal in Britain was the eccentric and ultra-xenophobic Tory MP Colonel Charles de Laet Waldo Sibthorp, who foresaw widespread robbery, murder, epidemics of strange diseases, and a 'piebald generation' as the outcome.[7] The 'piebald generation', presumably, would come about as the result of liaisons between all those chaste and aerial Englishwomen and foreigners. It hardly bore thinking about.

Some continental Europeans predicted even worse. This had a lot to do with their recent experiences. In 1851 they were still recovering from their terrible 'Year of Revolutions' (1848), which Britain had by and large managed to avoid. That clearly made them chary of large crowds. They knew what crowds could turn into. As a result continental ministers wrote to Britain's foreign secretary, Lord Palmerston, warning him. They sent him reports from their police spies in London, showing the mayhem that was being planned. Some of them were chilling. One Prussian report claimed to have evidence that Karl Marx was plotting to assassinate the Queen.[8] Another putative conspiracy had continental socialists joining in Britain with American Roman Catholics, of all people, with the object of installing Bishop Hughes of New York as Pope. A third involved 200 000 Irishmen led by their priests disguised as match-sellers and allying with 90 000 continental visitors to set London alight by means of 'inflammatory balls' blown into shop doorways through hollow walking-sticks. Perhaps the most ingenious plan involved disguising the assassins as trees. (The Exhibition, remember, was held in a park.)[9] The whole idea, claimed continentals, was foolhardy. It could re-ignite the embers of revolution, which would then spread to them. Britain would be best advised to call the whole show off.

It was out of concern for prognostications like this that the British authorities originally planned to have the Queen open the Exhibition privately, with just themselves and a few trusted friends present in the Crystal Palace.

In the end public pressure forced them to let the crowds in. It was a risk, but it worked. The Cassandras were proved ludicrously wrong. Not only did the Queen open the Exhibition safely in public; she also opened it without – as it seemed – protection of any kind. 'The military were nowhere to be seen,' reported the *Daily News* the next day (presumably the Life Guards did not accompany her into the building); 'the police required a close and searching scrutiny to find them out.' That, it concluded proudly, was a 'lesson' for foreign absolutists.[10]

The lesson was a simple one: though not simple enough, apparently, for the absolutists to grasp. Queen Victoria was safe not because she was protected by armies, police, spies and repressive laws – all the normal paraphernalia of state security on the Continent – but because she ruled beneficently, and within a framework of liberal government. That, at any rate, was how many of her subjects saw it. Liberalism was its own best defence. By not oppressing people, it gave them nothing to rebel against. So they would not rebel; so there was no need to take precautions against them. In fact such precautions were usually counter-productive. Armies, police, spies, repressive laws, were precisely what made people feel oppressed. They were the causes of unrest and rebellion, therefore, and not their cures. This was something of a paradox, but it was generally believed. It helped explain why Britain had escaped the revolutionary turmoil of 1848. It was also one of the things that made Britain such a happy place in 1851, by contrast with the Continent. More important, because there was no reason for Britain to want to keep this to herself: it was one of the things that eventually would make the whole world happy too.

A similar idea lay behind Britain's material supremacy in 1851, which the Great Exhibition exemplified even more obviously. Every country in the world was invited to display its goods there. Most of them did. The space – 800 000 square feet in all – was divided amongst them by a committee. The smallest area, a mere 25 square feet, went to the Falkland Islands, which were Britain's least significant colony at that time. (The display consisted of some drawings of natural features, a few stones, and 'specimens of grasses, sheep's wool, &c., produce of these islands'.)[11] The largest area for a foreign country went to France, which ended up with 65 000 square feet. Britain's exhibits, however, took up over 400 000 square feet of floor space, or about half the whole. This was considered fair because it was, after all, *her* Exhibition; and also in view of the fact that she was indubitably the leading industrial power of the world.[12] If anyone doubted this, there was ample proof of it in her section: a forest of machines and engines of every shape and size, including railway engines, portable steam-engines, oscillating engines, steam-pumps, weighing machines, hydraulic presses (one huge one for raising tubular bridges), steam cranes, sea-water regenerators, filtering pumps, power-looms, self-acting mills, carding machines, mechanical throstles, a slubbing and roving frame, a rotary disc scutching machine, a heckling machine, a gorse-cutting and bruising machine, an Archimedean root-washer, a globe-roaster for coffee, several self-acting bolt-head and nut-shaping machines, and hundreds more.[13] They dominated the show, and in turn reflected Britain's dominance in this field of heavy manufacture. What was the reason for that supremacy?

It may have been racial. That was suggested by a contemporary children's guide to the Exhibition, which pointed out that the kinds of exhibits differed according to whether their producers were 'Germanic' people, or 'Celts'. Germanic people were a 'matter of fact' folk, concentrating on 'those things which they are *quite sure* are "real" – the matters which they can handle, feel, see, and hear'; whereas 'Celts' were 'matters of fancy' people, less 'understanding' than the Germanics, but more 'imaginative'. The English, of course, were Germanic; the French were Celts. That was why Britain was ahead of France in the production of useful objects, and France ahead in the decorative arts. It was largely in the blood. But there was another reason too.[14]

That was a matter of policy. Britain's industry was *liberated*, just as her polity was. Her people were not naturally more talented than other people (most contemporary comparisons, indeed, made them out to be duller),[15] but they had maximized the return on what talents they had by deliberately freeing them from government interference and control. This applied as much to controls designed to assist industries as it did to controls designed to obstruct them: which repeated the paradox in the political field. The best judge of what should be produced, by whom, where, and at what price was the 'market', or the natural mechanism of supply and demand, which should consequently be the only arbiter of these things. This was called *'laissez faire'*, or 'free trade'. The idea behind it was that the healthiest economy – like the securest polity – was the least pampered and protected one. *That* was why Britain needed 400 000 square feet of floor.

In this sort of way the idea of 'freedom' pervaded the Exhibition, albeit only implicitly. There are, of course, many kinds and conceptions of 'freedom'. The one exemplified by the Exhibition, and popular in many influential circles in early Victorian Britain, was distinctive in a number of ways. One was its negative emphasis, its view of freedom as simply an *absence* of constraint; another was its conception of this absence mainly in relation to the *State*. The idea, very broadly, was that the State's powers in nearly every sphere of activity should be kept to a minimum, in order to enable individuals to realize their full potentialities. Another way of putting it was that political relationships between people, which nearly always produced friction, should give way to economic ones, which (because economic transactions always benefited both sides) did not. An important rider to this was that the *general* good of the community would follow automatically. There are problems with this scenario, some of which were pointed out at the time, and many of which are still contentious today. But it was a seductive notion, all the same.

There are obvious reasons for this. The idea was very simple. It all seemed to fit. It short-circuited many of the trickiest problems of political and economic theory, by reducing them to a negative. Where should the line be drawn between private and public good? Answer: nowhere, because private and public good were complementary. Who should govern the country, or elect the governors? Answer: it did not *matter*, if the governors were given no significant powers. This, incidentally, is why early Victorian liberals were very seldom democrats, and must not be confused with them: because they only believed in freedom *from* government, not the freedom of people to participate *in* it. (Democrats at that time were generally not liberals, but socialists, because only socialists believed in the State enough to care who ran it.) Another attraction of the idea was that it gave moral sanction to material self-interest, which will have helped self-interested people to sleep at night. It also allowed them to be political as well as economic liberals, and hence to place themselves in what was regarded at the time (rightly) as the 'progressive' camp.

This mid-nineteenth century confluence between the two sorts of liberalism – political and economic – is worth noting. It was important to the early Victorians, many of whom would have been very uneasy if they had thought there could be any tension between political and economic liberalism – that the free market was incompatible with other freedoms, for example. It was also important because we shall find the two separating and dividing later on. But that was in the future. For the present, the connexion between economic and political liberalism seemed straightforward. Economic prosperity depended on (among other things) low taxation, which in turn meant minimal public expenditure in areas, such as certain kinds of policing, that might be considered to restrict political liberties. Restrictions on political liberties were less necessary when people were contented, which meant (again, among other things) materially well off: which they would be under a free system of economic production and exchange. In short: economic liberty made people prosperous, hence happy, hence unlikely to rebel, hence easily kept in order, hence *cheaply* kept in order, hence lightly taxed, hence productive, hence prosperous... and so on. It was a perfect circle. That was one of the beauties of the system.

Its greatest beauty, however, was the *optimism* it implied. This was exemplified in the Great Exhibition, too. It partly derived from the 'self interest'

thing. Most optimistic theories of human social development rely on a
faith that men's and women's more altruistic side will ultimately triumph over their selfishness: a prognosis which may possibly be sound, but
at some periods of history seems hard to credit. Mid-nineteenth century liberalism's optimism had very different roots. Altruism did not come into it.
People would progress and improve in the future – stop fighting, killing,
wasting resources, tyrannizing – simply because they would come to see
that none of these activities *gained* them anything. The basis of it, therefore, was individual human selfishness. That made a difference.
Selfishness seemed a far more dependable trait than altruism. If this was to
be the foundation for Utopia, even the deepest-dyed cynic could help in the
building of it.

This was the moral and idealistic side of British liberal capitalism in the
mid-nineteenth century. It probably found its ultimate expression in the
international field. There free commerce was believed by some to be the
salvation of the world, no less. It would work quite simply. The exchange
of goods amongst peoples, to everyone's benefit, would break down
animosities between them, and hence between their governments.
Boundaries between nations – like political restrictions on the domestic
level – would wither away. The world would become one. That, for example,
was the prospect that the age's leading free trade campaigner, Richard
Cobden, held out. Here was how he put it, to a Manchester audience on the eve
of the repeal of the Corn Laws (imposing tariffs on imported corn) in 1846:

> I have been accused of looking too much to material interests. Neverthe-
> less I can say that I have taken as large and great a view of the effects of
> this mighty principle as ever did any man who dreamt over it in his own
> study. I believe that the physical gain will be the smallest gain to humanity
> from the success of this principle. I look farther; I see in the Free-trade
> principle that which shall act on the moral world as the principle of
> gravitation in the universe, – drawing men together, thrusting aside the
> antagonism of race, and creed, and language, and uniting us in the bonds
> of eternal peace. I have looked even farther. I have speculated, and prob-
> ably dreamt, in the dim future – ay, a thousand years hence – I have
> speculated on what the effect of the triumph of this principle may be. I
> believe that the effect will be to change the face of the world, so as to
> introduce a system of government entirely distinct from that which now
> prevails. I believe that the desire and the motive for large and mighty
> empires; for gigantic armies and great navies – for those materials which
> are used for the destruction of life and the desolation of the rewards of
> nature – will die away; and I believe that such things will cease to be
> necessary, or to be used when man becomes one family, and freely
> exchanges the fruits of his labour with his brother man.[16]

There is a visionary quality about that. This was undoubtedly another of the characteristics of mid-nineteenth-century liberal capitalism which commended it to people of goodwill.

That same vision informed the Great Exhibition, at every level. Henry Cole, its main organiser, hoped that visitors would come away from it with two dominant impressions. The first was pious: a feeling of 'deep thankfulness to the Almighty for the blessings which he has bestowed'. The second was 'the conviction that they [the blessings] can only be realized in proportion to the help which we are prepared to render to each other – therefore, only by peace, love, and ready assistance not only between individuals, but between the nations of the earth.'[17] Others took up this theme. A children's writer thought that visitors would be impressed by the marvellous display of the *peaceful* applications of human ingenuity in the British section, which would, he predicted, soon have all the foreigners following England's example and beating their swords into ploughshares too. Once that was done, there would be no turning back. 'Men have learned once for all the proper use of iron and steel. They know now what God sent it for.'[18] According to another children's author this was the whole idea behind the enterprise:

> The Great Exhibition is intended to receive and exhibit the most beautiful and ingenious things from every country in the world, in order that everybody may become better known to each other than they have been, and be joined together in love and trade, like one great family; so that we may have no more wicked, terrible battles, such as there used to be long ago, when nobody cared who else was miserable, so that they themselves were comfortable.[19]

In the same spirit Queen Victoria called the Exhibition a 'peace festival'.[20] That was its purpose: to help spread peace upon earth.

By another way of looking at it, however, that was hardly necessary. Progress would come anyway. That seems to have been Prince Albert's belief, for example, in the months leading up to the Exhibition, which he regarded more as a celebration of a crucial and very exciting but nonetheless inevitable and already irreversible historical stage, than as a means of achieving it. At a banquet to raise funds for the project, he talked rhapsodically of the 'period of most wonderful transition' in which they were then living, which had been made possible, he said, by increasing international trade, and which was about to lead 'rapidly to the accomplishment of that great end to which, indeed, all history points – the realization of the unity of mankind'. The Exhibition's place in this was 'to give us a true test and a living picture of the point of development at which the whole of mankind has arrived in this great task, and a new starting point from which all nations will be able to direct their further exertions.'[21] That was its main significance. The Great Exhibition was a marker, a milestone along the road the world was taking – with Britain in the lead, guiding it forward – towards the ultimate liberal-capitalist millenium. As if this were not enough, it also made a tidy profit (£186 000),[22] which will have pleased the harder-headed liberal capitalists.

Chapter 2

Britain in 1851

I

The Great Exhibition was never of course intended to reflect the totality of life in mid-nineteenth-century Britain. It was seen as a display of her material achievements, and as an expression of her hopes. The achievements were genuine, though to make proper sense of them we shall need to set them against some contemporary failures, which were also real. As for the hopes: most of them have been dashed in the long term, but we should not infer from this that they were unreasonable in the context of their time. Many of them were not.

It is easy to see why contemporaries were hopeful. Quite apart from the events in Hyde Park which dominated it so thoroughly, 1851 was a good year. The *Annual Register*, looking back on it, described the 'general condition of the country, so far as regards revenue, commerce, employment, and the circumstances of the labouring population,' as 'prosperous and hopeful', with 'pauperism' diminished, and a marked 'absence of complaint', except in the agricultural sector.[1] That was a fair summary. The economy was expanding, with the country growing richer (both absolutely and relative to the increase in its population) year by year. Industrially Britain was way ahead of any of her rivals, and in some areas (textile manufacture, merchant shipping, overseas trade) ahead of most of them put together.[2] There were more well-off people in Britain, and fewer paupers, than ever before in the century.[3] The fiscal state of the country was healthy, with a large surplus of revenue over expenditure, despite successive reductions of taxation and the virtual abolition of import duties over the past few years. Income tax was levied at only 7 old pence in the pound, or 3 per cent.[4] What made this possible was the low level of public expenditure, which stood at only £54.7 million in 1851, most of it spent on defence (27%) and servicing the national debt (52%), and virtually nothing on areas like education and health, which were regarded as no business of governments.[5] That, it was said, left industry and commerce free to prosper: which they did.

It may also have contributed to Britain's social and political stability at this time. There were no significant riots in Britain in 1851, for example, which would have been scarcely credible even ten years before. At the level of 'high' politics things were almost boringly stable, despite a ministerial 'crisis' in February when Lord John Russell's entire Whig cabinet resigned, but only to reconstitute itself a few days later when it became clear that there was nothing to take its place. The only lively political issue of the year was the matter of the 'Papal Aggression', when Pope Pius IX tried to restore Catholic bishoprics in Britain; but even that was never *controversial*, because nearly every Briton took the same (anti-Catholic) side. All this made for a dull, negative sort of parliamentary session, which the *Annual Register* admitted was unlikely to leave any 'signal trace on the records of history'.[6] That in a way could be regarded as another good sign, because it went to show how little needed to be done to keep Britain happy and secure. On the foreign front the prospects seemed good too, with no wars anywhere in the world involving Britain, and no realistic prospect of one. The sky was cloudless. Nothing looked likely to spoil the party. That was why the visitors to the party – the Great Exhibition – enjoyed it so much.

What made it all the more enjoyable was the contrast it afforded with the rest of the world. Middle-class Britons were fascinated by events abroad around 1850, partly because of the lack of political excitement in their own country, and partly because so many events overseas pandered to their prejudices. Foreigners, of course, were not generally liberals or free traders; and it was this that was supposed to explain most of the dreadful things that had happened to them recently, like the 1848 revolutions and their aftermaths. Economically no continental European country could match Britain at this time; politically they were all either weak, divided, unstable, tyrannized over or tyrannies themselves. The biggest tyrannies were Russia and Austria, who had both been at loggerheads with Britain very recently when they had demanded the extradition of the Hungarian national leader Lajos Kossuth from Turkey, where he had fled after the failure of the 1848–49 Magyar revolt, only to find Palmerston rooting for him. Austria was mainly unpopular for being one of the oppressors of Italy, together with the Pope and a particularly nasty Bourbon nicknamed 'King Bomba' in the south, at a time when Italian nationalism could draw on a great deal of sentimental support in Britain, mainly from the liberal educated elite. France combined tyranny with a chronic incipient instability, exemplified when its President, Louis Napoleon, made a bloody pre-emptive strike to put down what he claimed threatened to be yet another French revolution in December 1851. As well as these big events, travellers came back to Britain with countless tales of small persecutions, like being spied on by invisible

agents and affronted by *gensd'armes* and *douaniers*, all of which served
the purpose of making most of their readers grateful (if they were not
already) to be British, and 'free', and with a comfortable strip of water
between them and the non-British world.[7]

The contrast with abroad was highlighted further by the presence in Britain (especially London) of several thousand Continental political refugees,
who had sought asylum there after the failure of their revolutions in 1848.
Britain admitted them because she admitted *anyone* who came to Britain at
this time; indeed, for most of the nineteenth century she had no laws that
would have enabled her to turn them back. This underlined her superiority
over the Continent graphically. Britons in general did not like the refugees.
Most of them were poor, some of them were socialists (Karl Marx was
one), and all of them were foreign. The point was, however, that Britain
could tolerate them, whereas the Continent could not. The Continent was
afraid of them. Britain was afraid of no-one. Palmerston used a vivid metaphor to explain why.

> A single spark will explode a powder magazine, and a blazing torch will
> burn out harmlessly on a turnpike road. If a country be in a state of sup-
> pressed internal discontent, a very slight indication may augment that
> discontent, and produce an explosion; but if the country be well gov-
> erned, and the people be contented, then letters and proclamations from
> unhappy refugees will be as harmless as the torch upon the turnpike
> road.[8]

The refugees could be a confounded nuisance sometimes, and in October
1851, for example, were the occasion for the most serious diplomatic row
between Britain and the Continent of that year.[9] But it was almost worth
having them in the country nevertheless, just to enable Palmerston to make
that point.

The refugees, then, proved that Britain was on the right liberal lines. By
the same token they could also be said to show that the Continent was not.
Things seemed to have gone into reverse there, back towards tyranny and
repression and all the rest. This was a worry. But it was not yet a serious
one. Some sort of reaction was only to be expected, after all, in the wake of
the traumatic shock of 1848. The Continent should soon get over it. The
way for Britain to combat the reaction was to ignore it, and continue to
trade. That was the Cobdenite liberal path: to trust in peaceful traffic
between individuals worldwide to chip away gradually and relentlessly at
the political barriers that constrained them, so that eventually those barriers
would collapse.

The first part of that process was already under way. Britain was a phe-
nomenally expansionary society in the mid-nineteenth century, as if she
could not contain her energies within her own domestic bounds. Her trade

with the world outside came to £200 millions worth in 1851, a figure which represented 38% of her national income, and even then did not include 'invisibles', which are more difficult to compute.[10] That was far larger than any other country's foreign trade, and it was also spread much *wider* than theirs: not just to Europe, but through all the most distant regions of the earth. The signs of this were visible nearly everywhere: Britain's goods and capital in the most unlikely places, her ships plying every ocean, and her people – hundreds of thousands of them – scattered all over.

Some of the people were there on official business: as diplomatists, for example, or colonial governors, or the military; but most were private entrepreneurs. There were merchant seamen, of course, and traders, on the coasts of Asia and Africa; planters in the Indies, east and west; fortune seekers in California and New South Wales, where 1851 saw the first strike of gold; settlers in the most temperate parts of southern Africa and Australasia; explorers and missionaries in the least temperate regions; adventurers and rogues everywhere. Britons also infested the European continent, with 20,357 living in France in 1851, for example,[11] and goodness knows how many elsewhere. They included tourists, who were already numerous, and sometimes quite adventurous; and longer-term residents, plying an amazing variety of trades: especially connected with engineering projects – railways, mines and the like – where they invariably went out with the hardware. In Russia they were also highly sought after as doctors, gardeners, mechanics, governesses, nursery maids and jockeys; and as manageresses for the English boarding houses that sprang up along the Galernoi Oulitza in St Petersburg to provide proper tea, cooked breakfasts and week-old *Times* newspapers for the British tourists who passed that way.[12] All over the continent – notably in Florence, and Pau in southern France – there were little communities of British people who had settled permanently, often for the climate, but who had shipped out with them their English customs and lifestyles, like social life-support systems in an alien environment.[13] This was what Cobden meant by internationalism. All these people were working to extend liberalism throughout the world, whether they intended it or not, or even realised it. They were a much more powerful proseletizing force than governments could ever be.

II

So: it all looked to be going to plan. The British economy, liberated, was soaring high, and spreading the message of liberation across the world. That was one, quite plausible, way of looking at the situation both at home and abroad in the year of the Great Exhibition. But it was not the only one. There is another side to the picture: some less happy features of early Victorian society which, approached from a different ideological starting point, might have suggested a less optimistic prospect.

Contemporaries were aware of most of these failings and flaws. Some of them they were happy to tolerate, in the interest of a greater good. An example was their poor showing in the fine arts – painting, sculpture, music and so on – and in higher education, which were not early Victorian Britain's strongest suits. Artistic judgments, of course, are generally supposed to be subjective; but few objective critics would dispute that, apart from some novels, the Scottish universities, a handful of gothic-revival buildings and possibly a pre-Raphaelite painting or two, mid-nineteenth-century Britain was something of a cultural and intellectual desert in this period by comparison with the Continent. The Great Exhibition may have obscured this, because the fine arts were supposed to be excluded from it: perhaps in order not to show Britain up.

Some contemporaries regretted this. Others took comfort in the thought that, with all their money, they could always buy in their artistic pleasures from abroad. A few seem to have positively revelled in their philistinism, regarding it as a mark of superiority over the Continent, a product of the higher stage of civilisation that came with liberal capitalism, and consequently to be cherished. A fictional personification of this attitude is Dickens's Thomas Gradgrind in *Hard Times* (1854), the cold utilitarian who rejected what he called 'fancy' and insisted on 'nothing but facts', and who has often been dismissed as a caricature, but had one or two real-life contemporary counterparts. One, an Orcadian entrepreneur and writer called Samuel Laing, looked forward eagerly to the day when the spread of liberal-capitalist values throughout Europe would have killed the artistic muse, which he regarded as effeminate and elitist, stone dead.[14] That attitude was not universal, but it was widespread enough to do damage. Even science suffered. In 1851 Charles Babbage, who is credited with inventing a very early forerunner of the computer, complained that he was starved of resources to build it by government parsimony, and the general anti-scientific ethos of the time.[15] That appears in retrospect to have been a serious loss. Most early Victorians would probably have argued, however, that their lack of a Flaubert or a Wagner was not.

They could live with that. What they could not live with was widespread *material* deprivation, under a system whose main justification was supposed to be that it created wealth. There certainly was material deprivation in Britain in 1851: not as much, perhaps, as there had used to be, but still too much for more tender-minded liberal capitalists to feel easy about. The impression given by the Exhibition was clearly misleading here. 'You must not think, from all this, there are no poor people in London', children visiting it were told,

> for unfortunately there are thousands. Some beg, others steal, and those who are honest and able to labour, work. But those who cannot obtain

work are very badly off; and persons die from starvation.

In Ireland it was the same:

> Sometimes the crops of potatoes fail, and then the unfortunate peasants die by hundreds from hunger. The favourite dance of the common people is called a jig.[16]

That last observation may betray a certain lack of sensitivity; but at least the point had been made. It was made again, and far better, by a score of mid-nineteenth-century writers, ranging from novelists like Elizabeth Gaskell, Charles Kingsley and Charles Dickens, whose grimmest industrial novel, *Hard Times*, first appeared at around this time, to social reporters like Henry and Augustus Mayhew, and a German visitor called Friedrich Engels, who was a bit of an industrialist himself.[17] Some of the conditions they described, in Engels's Manchester and Dickens's 'Coketown', for example, were just about as far removed from the glitter and warmth of the Crystal Palace as it was possible to imagine. Such accounts may have been exaggerated, for effect, but not by much. In workhouses, where the poorest went, things were usually even worse.

Contemporary optimists got around this in one of two ways. The first was to assume that poverty was in most instances the fault of the poor themselves, except in a very few cases of genuine misfortune, which were taken care of by the 1834 Poor Law safety net. Those cases had a hard time of it, because the workhouses *had* to be spartan in order to deter scroungers; but at least they were better off than if they were dead. Others were poor out of improvidence, or intemperance, or simple choice. If they wanted to get on, they could. That was the severe response to poverty.

It was probably unreasonable. Most of the evidence indicates that there was a chronic surplus of labour around 1850, which is why it commanded so low a price. Unemployment was serious in some areas, casual work was common, and a quarter of a million people emigrated abroad to find jobs each year.[18] That suggests that at least a part of the blame for poverty should be put on the economic system, which for some reason was not working at full capacity. The second optimistic response took this on board. There was a flaw somewhere. This was how it appeared to the philosopher John Stuart Mill, for example. Mill thought that the situation was so iniquitous that even 'communism' was preferable. Coming from an early Victorian liberal that must have raised some eyebrows. The passage – in the second edition of his *Principles of Political Economy* (1849) – is worth quoting at length.

> If, therefore, the choice were to be made between Communism with all its chances, and the present state of society with all its sufferings and injustices; if the institution of private property necessarily carried with it as a consequence, that the produce of labour should be apportioned as

we now see it, almost in an inverse ratio to the labour – the largest portions to those who have never worked at all, the next largest to those whose work is almost nominal, and so in a decreasing scale, the remuneration dwindling as the work grows harder and more disagreeable, until the most fatiguing and exhausting bodily labour cannot count with certainty on being able to earn even the necessaries of life; if this, or Communism, were the alternative, all the difficulties, great or small, of Communism would be but as dust in the balance.

The point was, however, that this was an unfair comparison. To make it fairer you had to pit communism against 'the regime of individual property, not as it is, but as it might be made'. Mill claimed that the system had 'never yet had a fair trial in any country', including even Britain.[19] The industrial and capitalist revolutions were still relatively young. Survivals from older economic regimes, and certain problems peculiar to the early stages of the new one, meant that their benefits were slow to trickle down. Trickle down, however, they would. Then things would get better, and even – according to some more radical free marketeers – more egalitarian.[20]

That was all very well; but it was still just theory. There were few reliable signs yet that this upturn, from the point of view of the *workers* in capitalist industry, had begun. Most of the statistics that modern historians have gleaned from this period suggest that it had not. Wage rates in industries like house building, shipbuilding, engineering and textiles appear to have been stable, or rising only marginally, for the past 20 or 30 years. In agriculture (except in Scotland) they had substantially declined.[21] This contrasts markedly with most other economic indices for this period, which as we have seen were all rising, often spectacularly. This suggests that whoever was benefiting from the recent liberation of industry in the market it was not the workers. That was not to say that they would not benefit eventually. But that was a matter of faith, not experience.

If many of the British working classes were badly off in 1851, the Irish were doing much worse. Here salvation looked even further away. Ireland's population had actually declined by 20% over the past ten years, through famine and emigration, and was to continue decreasing steadily from then on.[22] This indicated that something was wrong with the system, surely: if it was able to support progressively fewer people, and in no greater comfort, as time went on. It also had political implications. The Irish were a rebellious people, albeit sporadically, and often brutal in the ways they chose to rebel. In July 1848 the south of Ireland had been the scene of the only genuine revolutionary outbreak on British soil of that year. Three years later there was no immediate danger of a recurrence of this, possibly because the people were too demoralised and weak with hunger; but the country was by no means safe. On 4 December 1851 Lord

Templeton's estates manager in County Monaghan was murdered by a gang who cracked his skull open in several places; and there were several assassinations of Irish magistrates during the same year.[23] Violence was never far beneath the surface in Ireland, yet always too deep, it seemed, for liberal reason to penetrate.

Back in Britain violence was also common, but not in so overtly protesting a form. Most of it was simply criminal, or else accidental. There were some horrible murders in early Victorian Britain, for example, and terrible disasters. 1851 had its fair share, with probably between 200 and 300 homicides all told, 214 people killed on the railways (excluding suicides), and 113 men killed in the two worst pit accidents.[24] Of course it is possible to argue that many crimes and accidents have political implications. Some Victorian ones could be attributed to parliament's reluctance to hinder commercial competitiveness. The opposition to Samuel Plimsoll's efforts to legislate to prevent merchant vessels being overladen, for example, argued along these lines. As a result the 'Plimsoll line' was successfully resisted until 1876. How many lives that political decision took is impossible to say. F.B. Smith has suggested that one reason for the macabre nature of many Victorian inner-city murders was the drinking of beer laced with strychnine to give it an extra kick, justified, in the alleged words of Cobden's free trade ally John Bright, on the grounds that 'adulteration is an acceptable form of competition'.[25] That may give these events a political dimension. But they were not seen like that. Almost without exception they were universally regarded as acts of God, of human wickedness, or of carelessness. In most cases that may have been fair.

Overt political violence was rarer. Even some of that was passed off as criminal. That was not difficult. Most of the popular protests of the 1850s had no clearly focussed political objective, or else were only political in a reactionary and essentially loyalist way. Examples of the former were the 'bread riots' of the mid-1850s, which caused great damage in London and the north of England; and a demonstration in Hyde Park against restrictions on Sunday trading in 1855. The latter (reactionary) category included some exciting anti-Catholic and anti-Irish riots in the 1850s, which were directed far more against the 'Papal Aggression' than against anything the government had done. So they were safe. As well as this, all were characterised by the middle class press as involving only 'youths of the very lowest and dirtiest class, and dirty women and girls',[26] which made them a social problem rather than a political threat.

That was probably fair. But it did not entirely dispose of the danger. How could it? Just three years earlier, middle-class Britain had *felt* herself threatened, at any rate, by the biggest working-class democratic mass movement ever in British history: Chartism. That had involved hundreds of thousands of men and women, with very clearly focussed political objectives indeed. They could not have just disappeared. They had to be there somewhere. Consequently the authorities still needed to be on their guard.

That may explain the latter's nervousness at another event of 1851. In October that year the Hungarian leader Lajos Kossuth, recently snatched from the jaws of Austria and Russia, visited England on his way from Turkey to America. At Southampton, where his ship docked, he was given a tumultuous popular reception, which was repeated elsewhere when he made a tour of the country over the next couple of weeks. On the surface none of this looked threatening. Most of the warmth shown to Kossuth clearly derived from the popular mood of liberal xenophobia – hatred of autocratic foreign regimes – which was prevalent at that time. It was also implicitly pro-Palmerston, for the stand he had taken at the Turkish stage of the affair. Nevertheless it was unpopular in high circles. Queen Victoria, especially, was reported to be miffed by reports of Kossuth's reception in Manchester, which had been warmer than hers when she had favoured the city with a royal visit just the week before.[27] She also had in mind an incident the previous autumn when Kossuth's military adversary, the Austrian general Julius von Haynau, who was also rumoured to have ordered women to be flogged, had been given a very different reception when he had made a trip to a brewery in London, only to be set upon by the workforce there.[28] Both these incidents were perceived as involving mainly the working classes, who on this issue were acting entirely separately from the middle-class radicals they were supposed to share most of their interests with. 'This movement,' said *The Times* of the Kossuth demonstrations, 'has only touched the scum of the nation'. If that was so then the size of the crowds involved suggested that the scum went disconcertingly deep.[29]

All this may have had domestic implications. That was the worry. What seemed to have happened was that the class solidarity which Chartism had engendered in the 1840s had now been diverted into these internationalist channels. That lifted the domestic threat for a while, but for how long? Occasionally glimpses of a more dangerous radicalism appeared. One example was this broadsheet of 1854.

OUT WITH
ABERDEEN
LET OUR MONEY BE GIVEN FOR
FREEDOM NOT DESPOTISM
THE
BLOOD OF BRITONS
Shall not be Shed to Prop up the
RASCAL ROYALTIES

OF THE WORLD.
The Polish, Hungarian, Italian,
and German People are our Natural Allies.
MAZZINI AND KOSSUTH
ARE OUR FRIENDS, AND
NOT THE FANATIC
NICHOLAS!
NOT
The Drunkard, Frederick William!
NOR
THE BOY-TYRANT, FRANCIS JOSEPH![30]

'The People' against 'Rascal Royalties': there was a revolutionary sentiment, if ever there was one. It may not have been significant; but at the very
least it indicated that the potential was still there for serious politically
directed working-class protest, if liberal capitalism should ever fail to
deliver the goods.

It was something to put on the other side of the balance, against the optimists' view that dissent had simply been killed with liberal kindness, and
consequently no longer required to be feared or legislated against in those
enlightened times. That was a useful idea to put about, if it made people
feel trusted and 'free'; but it was not one that many of the men in authority
in Britain relied on too heavily, and it may not have been true. The state,
after all, was not entirely bereft of instruments of domestic repression in
1848, and occasionally – in the 'year of revolutions', for example – brought
them out for putative troublemakers to see. It also had its police forces,
spearheaded by the new state-run London Metropolitan Police, which were
widely regarded by the working classes as being aimed against them, and
as a result had actually provoked riots in the midlands and north of England
in the 1840s.[31] From the authorities' point of view, however, the beauty of
the police was that they were not *too* provocative: that you could use them
to contain protest without *killing* people, which was the danger when you
called the military in. John Saville has demonstrated the extent to which
strong police action, mass arrests, and sentences which were heavy yet
always fell short of the ultimate (and most provocative) sanction of hanging, were used to put down the Chartist troubles of 1848.[32] Likewise in
1851, despite the trouble the *Daily News* had in spotting them, the police
were there in considerable force at the Great Exhibition, including a little
detachment of plain-clothes men newly formed for the occasion to keep a
watch on foreign refugees.[33] According to the Commissioner of the Metropolitan Police this was the main reason why the first of May had gone off as
peacefully as it had: the strong and skilful measures *he* had taken to avert

trouble, and not the inherent loyalty of the people at all.[34] Mid-nineteenth century Britain, therefore, still needed her police. That sullied the liberal-capitalist dream a little.

More serious was the fact that she still needed her army: not only to keep in the wings to deploy against domestic rebellion if it ever came, but also to further her commercial interests abroad. This too was a disappointment. Free trade was supposed to be a pacific enterprise, not requiring force. That was because no one could rationally object to it. Unfortunately some benighted foreign races did. One notorious example was the Chinese, with whom Britain fought a series of little wars between 1839 and 1860 in order to compel them to keep to agreements they had made earlier to admit British imports. One of those imports was Indian-grown opium, which the Chinese had compelling reasons for wanting to exclude; but in Britain's view it was the principle that counted. Elsewhere what the *indigènes* objected to was Britain's imposition on their societies of another fundamental liberal capitalist principle: that of individual ownership (and consequently sale) of land. That provoked bitter struggles in New Zealand in the 1850s and early 1860s, for example, and in India from the 1820s through to the great mutiny of 1857. Worse was to come. Free trade was supposed to be anti-colonialist as well as anti-military. Yet in the 1840s and 1850s British governments were still annexing colonies, including Hong Kong in 1841 (arising out of the 'Opium Wars'), Natal in 1843, the Punjab in 1849 and Lower Burma in 1852, to add to the already extensive empire they had inherited from their less enlightened forebears.[35] Usually they were annexed in order to stabilize Britain's commercial relations with them, or with bordering states. In effect what she was doing, in most of these cases, was to force the benefits of free trade on folk. That seemed wrong.

III

This was one of the many inconsistencies and irregularities that riddled Britain's situation at this time, and indeed for years afterwards. It partly derived from the fact that Britain was not yet a fully fledged liberal-capitalist society, but was still at a transitional stage. The empire exemplified this: particularly the older parts of it, which made little sense in nineteenth-century liberal-capitalist terms, and would almost certainly not have been originally acquired under a liberal-capitalist regime. Back home the picture was similar. Liberalism, capitalism and industrialisation were the dynamic and 'progressive' forces of the time, but they had not yet swept the board. They shared that board with institutions and values rooted in other traditions, often rival or even contradictory ones, but with which they nevertheless managed somehow to co-exist.

For example: at least half of Britain's population still lived in villages and small towns in 1851, many of them in the south of England, which was still scarcely touched by industry. Most of the working classes, wherever they lived, did not work in factories, or with machinery, but in far more venerable occupations – 1.3 *million* as domestic servants, for example[36] – and with their hands. Certain jobs were highly mechanized – especially textile manufacture – but most were not. As J.F.C. Harrison reminds us:

> A vast amount of wheeling, dragging, hoisting, carrying, lifting, digging, tunnelling, draining, trenching, hedging, embanking, blasting, breaking, scouring, sawing, felling, reaping, mowing, picking, sifting, and threshing was done by sheer muscular effort, day in, day out.[37]

Millions of men and women were engaged in work of this sort, whom the industrial revolution had, essentially, passed by.

Likewise relatively few of the middle classes were 'capitalists' in any real sense, beyond possibly owning a few safe shares. Most of them worked in professional and 'genteel' occupations, and spurned the 'entrepreneurial' values which were supposed to infuse them, apart from a small unrepresentative minority in the industrial North. They were not, for example, particularly 'competitive', especially in the labour market, where many of them still depended on the old pre-capitalist institution of 'patronage' to shelter them from the most bracing competitive winds.[38] Above them, the aristocratic and gentry classes, which were supposed to have no place at all under the new dispensation, continued to flourish, and indeed to run the country, through their dominance in government. At the beginning of 1851 Lord John Russell's cabinet was made up of eight peers, four baronets, and a mere couple of commoners. Even the House of Commons itself was peopled largely by 'gentry' and sons of lords.[39] So far as the personnel of government in the mid-nineteenth century was concerned, the bourgeois played a very minor role.

Not too much should be read into any of this. A liberal-capitalist society does not need all or even most of its middle-class members to be capitalists in order to merit the description; and certainly does not require to be directly administered by them. Because a man is a lord it does not follow that he only thinks in lordly ways, and is impervious to the values of the classes below. So far as the middle classes were concerned it did not really matter who ruled them, as long as they did not rule them too much. They themselves preferred not to do it, because ruling was not considered to be a 'productive' occupation: one, that is, which increased wealth. They did not think that any good could come of it, which is why they wanted to see it cut back. If the gentry would agree to go along with all this, there was no harm in letting it do the job. The Chancellor of the Exchequer was always a member of the Commons, because he had charge of the middle classes' money and so had to be their man. Beyond this, however, if it made them feel important and wanted – why not let the aristos appear to be in charge?

It was never put as bluntly as that, but this was how things broadly turned out. Most mid-century governments did most of what the middle classes wanted – the repeal of the Corn Laws was the latest and best example – and very rarely acted against their wishes or interests. Even the Foreign Office, which was the most aristocratic and exclusive of all government departments throughout the century, usually did what it was told. Much has been made of the fact that it was indifferent to British commerce, out of aristocratic snobbery, and unwilling therefore to 'push' it very vigorously abroad; but orthodox middle-class free-market doctrine was against 'pushing' trade anyway, so that was all right.[40] Palmerston – Russell's Foreign Secretary – was middle class himself in many ways. His peerage was merely an Irish one, which meant he sat in the Commons; he had been educated at Edinburgh University at the feet of a disciple of Adam Smith (Dugald Stewart), so knew his 'political economy'; and he shared much of the liberal xenophobia of the middle classes, which is why he was their darling most of the time, and also, incidentally, Queen Victoria's pet hate. In a way Palmerston could be said to personify the *hybridity* of the times.

This hybridity was a crucial feature of early Victorian society. A number of inferences can be drawn from it. One is this: that insofar as the most impressive features of Britain in 1851 – like the Great Exhibition – spelled 'success' for liberal capitalism, it was a success for a *degree* of liberal capitalism only, and not for the whole hog. The same, of course, can be said for its failures. What seemed to be doing well in many ways, and less well in others, was a particular mixture of liberalism and social control, machines and muscle, capitalism and paternalism, efficiency and waste, free trade and empire, new and old; not just one single ideology or system of government or economics, but a highly uncomfortable (from an ideologue's point of view) muddle of two or three. That is indisputable. The moral, however, is less clear.

Contemporary free marketists assumed that once the muddle was sorted out, and the mix became purer, things would get better still. If there were deficiencies in Britain's economic and political situation in the mid-nineteenth century, as of course there were, this was the reason. Britain was not yet free marketist enough. Pre-free market survivals were holding her back, like the aristocracy, whom Cobden blamed for war and imperialism, and institutions like patronage, which retarded development by encouraging job security and therefore sloth. According to Mill, as we have seen, this also explained some of the economic iniquities of the day. The assumption behind all this was that this half of the hybrid was a brake on the rest. Breed it out of the creature, to produce a purer strain of liberal capitalism, and it would really then be able to spread its wings and fly. This was how the free marketists kept their spirits up, in the face of all these inconsistencies and flaws. None of the latter reflected on liberal capitalism itself. All would disappear when liberal capitalism triumphed, as it was bound to. Hence the prevalent optimism of the time.

It was a rational point of view, and not inconsistent with the evidence. Neither was it, however, the only interpretation the evidence would bear. Because Britain had never had a fully working liberal-capitalist economy and culture, there could be no empirical proof that such an economy and culture would work in the way the optimists claimed. To come to that conclusion, you needed to approach the evidence that was available – all of it partial, confused and ambivalent – from a particular theoretical standpoint. If you did not – if you favoured a different theoretical standpoint, for example, or had none at all – then the situation could appear less rosy.

For example, Britain's widespread poverty might look unsettling if you had no theoretical reason for believing that eventually wealth would trickle down. What would the employment situation be like when industry became less labour intensive: again, if you put aside the theoretical argument that new technology always replaces lost jobs? Was the British economy's dependence on exports healthy? The huge lead it had in this area was greatly to Britain's credit, of course, and thoroughly deserved in view of her pioneering efforts; but had it not all been rather too *easy*? Could it be sustained? What would happen when other countries started competing? Theoretically competition benefited everyone; but what if in reality it did not? What if foreign markets became closed to Britain, because they began supplying their own wants, or deliberately kept imports out? What would happen to Britain's surplus production then, if yet another free-trade axiom proved faulty, and supply did not automatically create its own demand? Even one or two maverick economists were starting to worry along these lines, and in particular about what they suspected might be the long-term tendency in a free market for profits to fall.[41] That again contradicted orthodox theory; but if there was anything in it, it conjured up a vision of progressive trade depression which was almost too awful to contemplate.

All these scenarios had political implications too. If wealth did not trickle down, technology did not create jobs, the surplus could not be sold, and industry became less profitable, then the people would not like it, and would withdraw their consent. Liberal capitalism simply could not cope with that. If it tried to enforce compliance it would become less liberal; if it did not then the capitalism would come under threat. In either case the circle would be broken, and the whole great edifice be reduced to dust. It was a nightmare, though it probably did not trouble the sleep of many middle-class people at the time.

Nevertheless it was an alternative. It looked at the same evidence as the free marketists did, but through a different theoretical lens. In particular, it did not assume that liberal capitalism worked best when it was 'pure'; from which it followed that it might not be advisable to try to purify it. Perhaps some of its 'hybrid' features actually *helped*, especially early on. Without them, the transition to liberal capitalism might have been too abrupt to bear. The transition was a revolutionary one, and consequently painful. The pain might have provoked dangerous reactions, if it had not been *softened* by factors like these. John Bourne has suggested that this was an important latent function of patronage, affording some security to middle-class groups who in a fully competitive environment might have become 'dangerously alienated' by their sufferings as a consequence.[42] The same might be said of some of the other 'reactionary' features of the time. In the short term they seemed to hinder the process of change, but in the medium term they may have made it easier.

The important question, however, concerns the longer term. For this 'hybridity' in Britain's economic and political structure turned out to be not merely a transitional feature, but a persistent one. The aristocracy and gentry retained a leading role in British society, from which they continued to radiate an alternative and in some ways antagonistic set of values to the entrepreneurial one. Towards the end of the century those values may even have started pushing the entrepreneurial ones back. That would have horrified the early Victorian free marketists if they could have foreseen it. Perhaps it would have made them think twice about tolerating the the upper classes as much as they did. The revolution had not been drastic enough. The victors had been too kind to the vanquished. The French had had the right idea in 1791: guillotine the lot. On the other hand that had not done France much good in the long term. Perhaps a milder French revolution would have lasted better. This is a matter of controversy still. Was the survival of pre-capitalist values in Britain an incubus, threatening the health of her capitalism thereafter? Or would it help preserve it, by muzzling it in order to restrain its natural propensity to bite?

Chapter 3

The Golden Years
(1851–70)

I

In 1851 doubts were still expressed about Britain's economic and political prospects. Over the next 20 years, however, most of those doubts subsided. The optimists – however tenuous the original grounds for their optimism had seemed to be – were vindicated. Things got better on a wide range of fronts. The third quarter of the nineteenth century is generally reckoned to have been one of Britain's most 'successful' periods. A common appellation for it is the 'Golden Years'.

This is an odd description in some ways, but also highly revealing. It is odd because the 1850s and 1860s did not display most of the features usually attributed to golden ages in the past. Mid-Victorian Britain was unimpressive militarily, for example; feeble diplomatically; and relatively barren culturally and artistically. Some foreigners despised her for these reasons. For Britain, however, that just went to show how backward their criteria for measuring 'goldenness' were. She was way ahead of them. She had passed through the stage of historical development where military glory and artistic achievement were considered marks of national merit or greatness. She now acknowledged a different and superior *measure* of greatness: commercial prosperity allied to political freedom, in which she excelled.

There could be no doubt about the prosperity. The figures spoke for themselves. In 1855 the national income (according to modern calculations) totalled £636 million, or £22.90 per head of the population; in 1873 it had risen to £1149 million, or £35.70 per head. In other words the average person had become 55% (45% if we allow for inflation) better off. Most of this rising prosperity was due to increasing industrialisation. Coal production – which in a largely steam-driven industrial system is probably the best indicator of this – doubled over the same period, to 128.7 million tons a year. So (roughly) did iron output, the railway network, and shipping tonnage. Foreign trade more than trebled between 1850 and 1873, with exports being worth £255.2 million and imports £371.3 million a year by the end of the period. 'Invisible' earnings, again, bridged the trade gap, so that Britain's overall balance of payments surplus rose from £10 millions to £81 millions over these years. Britain's staple exports, cotton and woollen manufactures, increased from 1508 million yards in 1850 to 3830 million yards in 1873. All this had an effect on employment and on wages. The numbers working in woollen mills and cotton factories expanded from 485 000 to 730 000; average wages are reckoned to have risen by about 30% in real terms. The rate of income tax, which stood at 7 old pence (3 new pence) in the pound in 1850, had dropped to 2 old pence (0.83 of a new penny) by 1875. That was its lowest point during the whole of our period.[1] These figures are tedious, but the mid-Victorians would have pored over them with great pride. They were the quantitative measure both of their national greatness at this time, and of the essential rightness of the economic system in which they reposed their trust.

Of course the economic climate was not as entirely cloudless as this implies. For a start the improvement was not smooth and continuous. It started off very slowly, and only really launched itself in the early 1870s, after a couple of decades which were not really very much more dynamic than the years before. During that couple of decades there was one serious depression in the textile industry, during the 'cotton famine' caused by the American Civil War; and at least two fairly grave financial slumps, in 1858 and 1866, the latter sparked off by the collapse of the great banking firm of Overend and Gurney on 11 May. That put in train a series of further bankruptcies which caused 'embarrassment and distress among thousands of families,' as the *Annual Register* put it, 'and cast a gloom over the surface of society'. The immediate impact, of course, was borne by the investing classes, many of whom 'found themselves reduced from affluence to poverty' in no time at all, and to a 'lower position in society', which was worse. But the working classes also suffered as a result of the effect of the crisis on demand, which 'was felt through all the channels of trade', and caused abnormally high levels of unemployment for two or three years.[2] This was sometimes forgotten afterwards.

It was forgotten, of course, because slumps like this were always fairly quickly recovered from, which was a tribute to the *resilience* of the mid-Victorian economy. The 1866 slump in particular was followed shortly afterwards by what was probably the most impressive little boom of the whole nineteenth century, when iron output leapt by about 50% and total exports by 25% in just three years (1870–73), and the level of unemployment among trade-union members – the only figures we have – plummeted from nearly 8% in 1868 to less than 1% in 1872. Wage rates reflect the same pattern: bobbing and dipping during the 1850s, improving slowly in the 1860s with a slump after 1866, and only really taking off between 1871 and 1875.[3] That trend mainly benefited skilled workers; the unskilled may have fallen behind. By the end of this period, however, after that amazing little spurt at the finish, most classes of people felt better off, and almost certainly were so. This is why these are called the golden years. At the time the gold seemed to be solid all through. That, of course, may have been a trick of the light.

II

If it was, it was not spotted by many contemporaries. Opposition to the new order melted away. The Conservative party abandoned its resistance to free trade in 1852. Lower in the social scale Chartism died, to be replaced by no other significant working-class democratic movement for thirty years. Bronterre O'Brien, one of the old Chartist leaders, came to the despairing conclusion that 'the people always appear doomed to be humbugged'.[4] That was one way of looking at it; another was to regard them as having come to their senses. It happened quite suddenly. 1848 saw the final mass challenge by labour to the economic and political system of the day. After its failure, working-class radicals travelled other paths. They left the 'system' alone, and sought alternative ways of improving their lot. Some did it individually, typically by striving to climb out of their class into the one above. Others continued to act collectively, but piecemeal, in trade unions, co-operative societies, friendly societies and the like. The point of these was to compete in and with the system, but not to overturn it. Members tended to stress the 'moderation' of their ambitions and methods, and their 'respectability': both words defined in a middle-class way.[5] Most of the rest of the working classes simply deferred to the new capitalist order, and settled down to their jobs. That left only a very tiny minority whose radical democratic fires still burned, in little isolated patches; quite safely while the vast expanse of bushland between them was so well doused. Most of them became inactive, or else theoreticians, which came to much the same thing.

What this betokened was that the system had now become accepted: by some people approvingly, by others merely perforce. One of the latter was the Chartist Ernest Jones. In the 1840s he had been one of the most radical of them, a socialist to his bootstraps; but by 1867 this had changed. In a speech that year he claimed that he had not altered his basic view of capitalism, certain aspects of which he still felt were 'very terrible and very wrong'. But he had resigned himself to the fact that they were ineradicable, at least for the time being. The workers could no longer, he said, hope to return to 'what men call first principles'. 'I am about to take the world as I find it, and see whether we cannot make the best of it, such as it is, without any violent and sudden disruptions of Society.' The next year Jones was selected as *Liberal* parliamentary candidate for Manchester.[6] That was a common radical metamorphosis.

The broad reasons for this were clear. The new-found resilience of British capitalism, giving it an air of permanence, had much to do with it; together with Chartism's obvious failure in 1848. Another key factor was the slow but steady improvement most workers were now experiencing in their material situation, and the prospect of further advance which the system held out. These created favourable conditions for social stability, which were then exploited skilfully (which is not to imply cynically) by some employers, middle-class humanitarians and the state.

Employers did their bit by recognizing 'moderate' trade unions and behaving paternalistically in many instances, thus softening the most potentially abrasive edges of the system they operated. Recognition of trade unions spread widely in the 1860s, though there were isolated examples earlier.[7] Paternalism took a number of forms: the provision of decent housing, schools and churches for employees, for example; 'works dinners and treats, trips to the countryside and the employer's residence, libraries, reading rooms, canteens, baths, lectures, gymnasia, burial societies and the like', all of which, claims Patrick Joyce, 'were to become the rule rather than the exception among the big employers'.[8] Most of the latter were impelled towards this sort of behaviour by their religion, and by a very human, if ideologically suspect, reluctance to deal with their 'hands' as if they were mere commodities. 'He was not indifferent to the teachings of political economy,' said an Ashton-under-Lyne newspaper of a local employer, Hugh Mason, in 1868; 'but he should be very sorry if the rigid and abstract rules of political economy alone prevailed in his workshops.' Apart from anything else, it would prevent his exerting the *moral* tyranny over his workers which was the other face of this mid-Victorian industrial paternalism. But it worked. Mason's was a happy firm with a 'family' atmosphere and a loyal workforce, kept that way, and also profitable, as were many other such enterprises, by this deliberate deviation from the true economic faith.[9]

Outside the factory gates there were countless other agencies, mainly middle-class led, designed to assist the working classes towards 'respectability'. Most of them originated in the first half of the century, or even earlier: Societies for the Propagation of various kinds of Knowledge, for example (Christian, Scientific, Useful); committees formed to build free museums to enlighten the people further, such as the one which – under Prince Albert's aegis – began the construction of the great South Kensington site in London after the 1851 Exhibition; and bodies to improve the morals of the workers, by stopping them drinking, or betting, or desporting themselves on Sundays, or anything else they found pleasurable. Another kind of example is the Trustee Savings Bank movement, whose 'father' is generally taken to be a Scottish Christian minister named Henry Duncan, who had formed one of the earliest banks for working-class savers in 1810. Duncan was another deviant from the economic orthodoxy of the day: a man who once admitted that he had 'no relish for more money than will support myself, or be useful to my friends', which was hardly the right capitalist spirit, and whose own bank, therefore, was founded on entirely different lines: owned by its depositors, and run by directors who were expressly forbidden to profit thereby. By 1861 – the movement's nineteenth-century peak – there were 645 Trustee Savings Banks in Britain, with 1 609 852 depositors, and £41 735 467 of deposited savings:[10] a solid tribute to what a much later President of the Trustee Savings Bank Association called his movement's 'disinterested desire to serve the people, all working together with the spirit of brotherhood'.[11]

Those sentiments and principles were to spell the death of the Trustee Savings Bank movement eventually, in the more rigorous individualist climate of the 1980s;[12] but in mid-Victorian times trusteeship, together with co-operation and paternalism, were accepted as welcome additions to the varied tapestry of the country's economic and social life. This acceptance, or toleration, marked a significant recent mellowing of attitudes on the part of the employing classes from the 1840s, which had been another period of ideological chill. That was probably due to the fact that economic conditions had eased for them, too, as well as for the working classes, so that business was no longer the same grim struggle it had used to be in industrial capitalism's earlier formative stage. The ideological ice was melting in the warm economic glow of the Golden Years. Security and prosperity made for moderation and generosity on both sides, the outcome of which was a degree of social peace – almost harmony – which had not been seen in Britain for very many years.[13]

Another important element of that harmony was the resonant note of libertarianism that ran through it, impressing nearly everyone, including those who were never likely to benefit from it in any direct and tangible way. People believed they were free, which encouraged them to be content. By 'free' they generally meant free *politically*, by comparison with the Continent. That comparison, which was frequently made at the time, was a potent one, because it added the pride of *nationality* to people's consciousness of liberty. Liberalism and patriotism – even xenophobia – were allies, each bolstering the other and both together reinforcing people's feelings of well-being. That was a great source of strength.

In a nutshell, Britain was felt to be better than Continental countries because her government was less authoritarian and intrusive than theirs.[14] It did not, for example, interfere in politics – even radical politics – like foreign regimes did, with their active persecution of certain political doctrines, and their networks of spies. Victorian Britons (outside Ireland) took great pride and comfort in the knowledge that they could discuss politics confidently, without any fear of eavesdropping, unlike abroad. This may have been an almost unique situation in the history of modern civilized societies: a government which deliberately abjured 'secret-service' methods in nearly every field of activity, and especially domestically, where there is no sign of its ever having tried to glean intelligence about native socialism, for example, except by the most open and above-board means.

In 1871 those means consisted mainly of writing to Dr Charles Marx, who was living in London, to ask. That was in order to be able to respond to a German request for information about the socialists. The sequel is illuminating. Marx obliged by sending reams of communist propaganda back to the Home Office. The conclusion the latter drew from it was that although *he* might be a bit of a firebrand, there was nothing to be feared from *British* socialists. That was reassuring. The animal existed, but it was harmless. Socialist ideas had taken 'no root' in England. At present they were 'purely speculative'. No socialist had any idea of propagating them 'otherwise than by peaceable discussion'.[15] That justified the liberty the socialists had been given to air their ideas. It was also supposed to be a fruit of that liberty: the moderation with which British radicals pursued their aims, by contrast with the less free Continentals.

III

All these signs were immensely encouraging; but of course they did not tell all. No age in history has ever been Golden all the way through. This one was no exception. Nearly everyone acknowledged flaws in it. One was the degree of social unrest that still existed in it, though in less dangerous forms than before. Mid-Victorian Britain may have been a moderate and harmonious society, relatively speaking; but it was not a particularly orderly one.

Rioting, for example, was a common occurrence still. 'Bread riots', of poor people simply demanding food to subsist on, continued well into the 1860s, with one of the worst occurring at Stalybridge in Lancashire in 1863. Anti-Catholic riots were also a feature of the 1860s, led by a rabble-rouser called William Murphy, who managed to mobilise tens of thousands of bigots to wreck churches and attack priests' houses, with tales of young virgins being seduced in the confessional, monastic sodomy, and nuns bricked up alive in convent walls. Another favourite target of the 'Murphy riots' was the Irish immigrant community in Britain, probably for racial reasons as well as religious ones. An interesting variant of this was the clashes that took place in 1864 between Irish and Italian immigrants in

Holborn in London, with the Irish attacking the Italians – mostly republican refugees – for daring to oppose the Pope. Elections were a regular occasion for disorderly behaviour, which was one of the reasons given for not subjecting the fairer sex to the risks of having to vote. Industrial disputes quite often turned violent, provoking a parliamentary commission of inquiry in 1866, for example, when strikers in Sheffield blew up a blackleg's home. The years 1866–67, in fact, were two of the roughest of the whole of the nineteenth century, with the first ever Irish bombing campaign in mainland Britain, claiming about a dozen victims; and a huge and spectacular riot in and around London's Hyde Park in July 1866, when perhaps a quarter of a million people went on the rampage to demand the parliamentary franchise.[16] These are just the highlights. There was plenty more of the same. What did it all signify?

It may have signified no more than that some people could not be trusted to behave. They were simple hooligans, whose salvation lay in moral reform, perhaps, or education, or stiff punishment, if there was any hope for them at all. This was probably true of some of them: young irresponsibles who just enjoyed rioting, for instance, whatever the ostensible cause. That was a common initial reaction by the non-rioting classes, partly because it placed all the blame on the disorderly, and none at all on the order they disturbed.

On the other hand it was not a very optimistic response, if the inference to be drawn from it was that this sort of behaviour was always to be a feature of British society; nor was it, in many cases at least, fair. Bread riots indicated real poverty. You could blame that on inadequacy and imprudence if you liked, or rest assured that the Poor Law could cope with it. But there were other indications that genuine economic distress was more widespread than it theoretically should have been at this stage of Britain's capitalist development: when things had gone well enough for long enough, surely, for the wealth created by the free market system to have really begun 'trickling down'. Charles Dickens's 'social novels', which he continued writing right up to his death in 1870, were one such indication; though it may have weakened his 'message' to dress it up as fiction, which his readers could consequently legitimately discount if they wanted to. Others avoided this risk by reporting factually on their observations of the lower orders of society: Henry Mayhew, for example, in four thick volumes on *London Labour and the London Poor* in 1861–62; and the journalist James Greenwood in a celebrated series of newspaper articles describing 'A Night in the Workhouse' which he had spent, disguised as a pauper, in January 1866.[17] These, and a few other works like them, pictured a side of mid-Victorian society which must have jarred against the accepted liberal wisdom somewhat.

Yet they do not seem to have shaken that wisdom seriously. The problem was that very few of the middle classes could *relate* to this kind of thing. The poor were an alien world. That was a point the writers themselves often made. Later the latter came to be called 'social explorers', to emphasize the parallel between them and the men who were just then opening up *entirely* different worlds in Africa and elsewhere.[18] The poor rarely impinged, except as beggars, which the middle-class 'Mendicity Society' existed to hound off the streets, to be then locked away – hopefully – out of sight behind the workhouse walls. Indirectly they made an impression through the expense this process involved: the poor rate (or tax) which supported the workhouses, and which increased by an alarming 48% (from £7.7 millions to £11.4 millions) between 1860 and 1872.[19] That may have struck home. In general, however, there was very little general awareness of poverty, at least as a persistent problem, in mid-Victorian times; and even less of a perception that this poverty might have implications for the way the British economy was run.

There were critics of the latter. John Stuart Mill became more of one as time went on, describing himself in the 1860s as a 'Socialist', in the sense of an egalitarian, though without any idea of how and 'by what precise form of institutions' his socialist ideals might best be realised.[20] Another contemporary heretic was John Ruskin, the art critic-turned-economist, whose *Unto This Last*, first serialised in 1860, castigated the whole 'bastard science' of political economy on mainly moral grounds. There were others too; including, of course, Karl Marx, the first volume of whose *Capital* first appeared (in German) in 1867. Needless to say, very few British economists read that. The same applied to the others. Few people of any kind read the Ruskin book, which was a publishing failure;[21] and Mill's *Autobiography* did not appear in print until after his death in 1873. So almost nobody was in a position to learn of the doubts about contemporary British society expressed by these great men. If they had been, they would have found two important questions being posed.

The first concerned the quality of life in mid-Victorian Britain. That was questionable on several levels. No one could doubt that the quality of the bread rioters' life was likely to be poor. It was probably not much better for millions of others, who could afford food, and roofs over their heads, but little else. Hours of work in mid-Victorian factories were long and arduous, and living conditions in the cities spiritually as well as materially bleak. One of the aspects of industrial life which most appalled contemporary critics was the literal inhumanity of it: that is, the way the patterns of life of human beings were subjected to the impersonal discipline of the machine. A famous passage in Dickens's *Hard Times*, describing 'Coketown', put it vividly:

It had a black canal in it, and a river that ran purple with ill-smelling dye, and vast piles of building full of windows where there was a rattling and a trembling all day long, and where the piston of the steam-engine worked monotonously up and down, like the head of an elephant in a state of melancholy madness. It contained several large streets all very much like one another, and many small streets still more like one another, inhabited by people equally like one another, who all went in and out at the same hours, with the same sound upon the same pavements, to do the same work, and to whom every day was the same as yesterday and tomorrow, and every year the counterpart of the last and the next.[22]

'Coketown' was a fictional name, but everyone knew it stood for Preston. There was not much 'quality' there.

It was also arguable that there was not much 'freedom', either. This was obscured for contemporaries by their obsession with freedom from *government*. Freedom from government, of course, does not necessarily mean freedom in absolute terms. There are other tyrannies besides state ones. Some of them are merely strengthened when the protection of the state is taken away. How truly 'free', for example, are unprotected workers in a market situation in which there is underemployment, and they depend on selling their labour to live?

That was not all. Other kinds of 'unfreedom' were occasionally remarked on at the time. Many middle-class folk could be regarded – as one contemporary put it – as 'slaves to convention': to the elaborate and rigid, albeit invisible, structure of precepts and taboos which permeated British society during the nineteenth century, often with no formal legal base to it, but no less tyrannical for that.[23] (Some of its victims fled to the Continent, to form the nuclei of the little expatriate communities we have already remarked on there: refugees, if you like, from *social* persecution in their own land.)[24] Matthew Arnold, another great mid-Victorian dissident, also took up this question of 'freedom'; this time in order to berate the pride his contemporaries took in Britain's freedom of *expression*, when for him the important thing was the *quality* of what was being expressed.[25] That led Arnold on to a vigorous defence of 'culture' in society, which was another quality he claimed the mean utilitarian spirit of the age was eroding away. Really it all came down to the same basic point. No one, in any social environment, could really be called 'free' who was not free to choose the best, or at least the good.

'Culture', defined in conventional artistic and intellectual terms, does seem to have been a loser during these British 'Golden Years'. A quick trawl of the leading fine arts yields very few fishes most of us would not want to throw back. England had two contemporary poets – Browning and

Tennyson – who might just have made it to the Continent's second rank. Pre-Raphaelite painting was an interesting little side-eddy of the European romantic movement, producing perhaps a dozen pictures of quality. There were no major British musical composers in these years, though William Sterndale Bennett did try. The best products of the Gothic revival movement in architecture were yet to come. The narrative semi-art of the novel went through a moderately good period, but not as good as the quarter-centuries immediately before and after this one. The universities were in the doldrums. Outside the universities, science, being practical, fared better. Charles Darwin published his *Origin of Species* in 1859, and *The Descent of Man* in 1872, though most of the work for them had been done long before. They give this period some scholarly distinction. On the artistic side, however, it has very little. Was this simply fortuitous? Or did it have something to do – as Arnold suspected – with the ethos of the time?

That was the first big minus that could be put against liberal capitalist Britain's 'Golden Age'. The second one was entirely different. It took the 'Age' on its own terms, even accepting its own measure of 'goldenness', but questioned whether it was really as securely based as it seemed. In those days you had to be a real Jeremiah to doubt this. Scarcely anyone did, until they could look back on the period from later. It was only then that one or two hidden features of the 1850s and 1860s began to emerge.

One was that it was a very *artificial* time in many ways, most of which favoured Britain. The most important artificiality arose from Britain's relations with the world outside, which because she was so cosmopolitan a country, and so abnormally dependent economically on foreign trade, were not merely incidental to her but vital. So far as Britain was concerned the world outside was divided into two sectors. The first comprised the continent of Europe; the second – the 'wider world' – took in the rest. Both sectors were in positions of what might be regarded as unnatural – certainly unusual – disadvantage in relation to Britain during these years.

Europe was going through a kind of revolution. Between 1859 and 1871 many of its boundaries were quite drastically adjusted, and several new nations (Germany, Italy, Roumania, Hungary) were formed. This process was accompanied by a number of wars, both between nations – Franco-Austrian, Prusso-Danish, Austro-Prussian, Franco-Prussian – and civil. It was all very unsettling and debilitating, at least while it was going on. It undoubtedly held up the Continent's economic development. Britain all this time was politically stable, with no serious threat or challenge to her territorial integrity, even in Ireland, which was relatively quiescent; uninvolved in any major foreign wars after 1858; and able therefore to concentrate on the more peaceful and profitable arts. It was not simply a question of their following separate paths. The paths crossed. Britain actually profited from the Continent's difficulties. That remarkable little economic boom of 1870–73, for example, can be partly explained in terms of the opportunities the Franco-Prussian war of 1870–71 gave to British industry to supply the combatants both during it, and in the years of recovery afterwards. Europe's preoccupation with its own internal problems in this period of national formation and territorial shift also had the effect of allowing Britain almost a free run in the wider, extra-European world.

That made up the major part of Britain's huge overseas market in mid-Victorian times: around 57% of it, in fact, in 1860, and 62% in 1880.[26] No other country did anything like as much trade as this in Asia, Africa, the Americas and Australasia. Britain had no serious commercial rivals, therefore, from Europe or anywhere else. Nor did she meet with much resistance in the countries she traded with: either because they were happy to trade with her, or because they were too weak to object. Some could not object because they were ruled by Britain anyway, like her vast Indian empire, which year after year – and with ruinous effects on its native textile industry – soaked up 18–24% of Lancashire's exported cotton goods.[27] Others, like China, were coerced into satisfying some at least of the voracious demands of Britain's growing manufacturing machine. There was a great deal to be said for this extra-European trade, which was not usually 'exploitative' in any pejorative sense, and did a great deal to spread the benefits as well as the evils of European civilisation in mid-Victorian times. It was also a source of enormous profits for Britain. That, however, was part of the problem. The profits came too easily. She did not really have to compete for them. This was a situation that was unlikely to last; which might be ominous if she ever came to *depend* on it.

Another hidden danger was domestic. The social peace of the 1850s and 1860s was not, as we have seen, entirely unruffled. Most of the disorder and rioting of those years was impotent politically, which is why the mid-Victorians felt more secure about it; but it was not invariably so. Those who took comfort from the apolitical, atavistic and indeed often overtly racist (that is, anti-Irish) forms it usually took, which Neville Kirk has rightly diagnosed as another significant factor behind the contemporary deradicalization of the mid-Victorian working classes,[28] may have been deluding themselves. Rioting of any kind indicated an underlying volatility which might not always be so harmlessly diverted. On 23 July 1866 this was demonstrated suddenly and unexpectedly. Radical political rioting returned. Tens of thousands of supporters of parliamentary reform assembled in London's Hyde Park in defiance of a Home Office ban, pushed over the park railings, trampled down the flower beds, and then took to the streets, rampaging through the West End hurling stones at the 'toffs' and their clubs and villas, and eventually having to be put down by troops. It was hardly surprising that, for a fleeting moment at least, many of the upper and middle classes feared that the Terror had crept up on them again.[29]

We shall see the government's response to this in a later chapter. In a word, it was to concede. At the same time we shall find concessions being made on other fronts – social and economic – too. They had the effect of prolonging the truce between the middle and working classes which is such a feature of these mid-Victorian years. But it was at a price, the full cost of which became clear just a few years later; when Britain at last sailed out of the unnatural little harbour that was her 'Golden Age', and into the rougher seas beyond.

Chapter 4

Political Flux
(1851–66)

I

The Reform riots of 1866 were a shock, but only because of their ferocity. The issue itself had been around for many years. In the 1840s the main torch bearers had been the Chartists, with their cry for universal manhood suffrage. After their defeat the flame was dimmed a little, but never completely doused. Franchise reform on a less ambitious scale was a live issue throughout the 1850s and early 1860s. The Whig leader Lord John Russell was in favour of it. The Tory leader Lord Derby came out in support of it as prime minister in 1859. Bills to try to effect it were debated in the House of Commons nearly every alternate year. The difference now was that there was no longer any great heat or passion surrounding the question, before 1866; partly because there was very little heat or passion in politics at all.

The heat had been taken out of them by the resolution of the two major political conflicts of the 1840s, and the consensus which prevailed over most of the other great domestic issues of the time. The two major conflicts had been over Chartism and free trade, the first of which evaporated after the collapse of the Chartist movement, and the second of which ended when the Conservative party finally decided to ditch protectionism in 1852. Thereafter there was general agreement among the parties over most major questions. As late as 1865 *The Times* claimed that the only difference between Conservatives and Liberals was the question of the malt tax.[1] One or two religious issues might be added to that. Otherwise everyone took the same view of the direction to be travelled. Broadly speaking, it was along the same line on the political map they had been travelling up to then.

Most of the legislation of the period – and there was plenty of it, despite the mild political climate – was in this mould: conservative and progressive at the same time, advancing forward carefully from a base and on principles that were already established and agreed. There were no great leaps forward, and no deviations or changes of course. This applied whatever kind of government – Whig, Tory or coalition – was in power. Free trade was extended by abolishing more and more import duties in successive budgets, thus continuing and completing the work of the repealer of the Corn Laws, Sir Robert Peel. In 1856 it was made compulsory for counties to form police forces, which consolidated another of Peel's achievements. At the same time the criminal legal code was alleviated in stages, making it more humane. The trend towards 'toleration' was furthered by the admission of dissenters to the universities of Oxford and Cambridge in 1854 and 1856, and of practising Jews to parliament in 1858. A number of administrative reforms was instituted in the civil service which cut down the extent of aristocratic patronage there and opened most branches of the service (apart from the Foreign Office) to entry on meritocratic lines. It was all good middle-class liberal stuff, removing impedimenta from the market place, with the exception of the police, and so enabling individuals to fulfil themselves, to the benefit of society as a whole.

There was another reason for the relative lack of political passion in mid-Victorian times. Government was supposed to be minimal. Few of the legislative reforms of the 1850s altered this. Minimal government was bound to arouse less controversy than the interfering kind. Hence the relative unimportance then attached to parliamentary reform, even by its supporters: on the grounds that as parliament had few powers over people it did not much matter who participated in it. By the same token, of course, it made those who already participated in it less important and maybe less serious than they would have been otherwise. This is a marked feature of mid-Victorian parliaments. Very few men sought to become MPs in order to 'get things done'. (Some became civil servants for this reason, in an age when there was more scope for reformist initiative in Whitehall.)[2] People who stood for parliament more often than not did it simply to be able to put the letters after their names. Their political allegiances were governed by family ties, personal loyalty or mere habit, more than by principle. Once in parliament, unless a clear local interest was at stake, they were simply lobby fodder. Most of them had no ambitions to rise. Those who did rise, to become ministers, did so on merit, rather than because of their political views. It was rather like the officers of a ship being recruited for their professional competence, rather than for the course they intend to sail. If they were too set on a particular course, in fact, it was likely to go against them. Conviction – 'enthusiasm' – was not considered a virtue in mid-Victorian politics.[3] They were all Church of England in this sense.

One effect of all this was to remove one of the adhesives which usually binds a political party together, and consequently to make the party situation in Britain in the 1850s abnormally fluid. In fact it may be wrong to talk in terms of 'parties' at all at this time. MPs were divided into a number of different camps, whose boundaries were blurred and changing all the while. It is possible to distinguish four main ones. There were Lord Derby's Conservatives, whose chief distinguishing characteristic was that they had used to be protectionists, but were not any longer. Then there were the Peelites, who had broken away from the Conservatives over this issue in 1846, when the latter had still been protectionist. (Peel himself had died in 1850.) Thirdly there were Lord John Russell's Whigs, who had always been against protectionism; and lastly the Radicals, who were also against protectionism, but more so. Between these groups there was much wheeling, dealing and transferring of allegiances, in a way that generated great interest and excitement; for minimal government does not necessarily mean minimal *politics*, and certainly did not at this time. In fact people seemed to enjoy the game more in these conditions, possibly because less was thought to rest on the outcome.

One of the outcomes, however, turned out to be an important one. This was the creation of the Liberal party, whose birth is generally dated to a meeting of MPs in Willis's Rooms in St James's Street, Westminster, on 6 June 1859, but which had been a twinkle in the eyes of its several progenitors for many years before. It was made up of most of the Whigs, some Peelites (including William Ewart Gladstone), and all the Radicals. Its first leader was Palmerston, who gave it a very different flavour from the one it was to acquire eventually.

Palmerston had the reputation of being a Radical in foreign policy, which was why the people loved him and the Queen detested him so much; but he was as rank a reactionary as the latter could have wished for at home. He was, for example, implacably opposed to parliamentary reform, on the grounds that it would 'virtually disenfranchise the middle classes', and give the country over to 'a small clique of socialist agitators', who he believed held the proletariat in thrall.[4] He shared this view with many other Whigs and Peelites, whose opposition to parliamentary reform was usually stronger than the supporters' support for it was, for one simple reason. If you believe in minimal government, it will not help much to have a wider franchise; but it could *hinder* dreadfully if you think there is a risk that the new voters might try to *maximise* the government again. This was the fear; and the reason why many Whigs and Peelites were unhappy to see the reformer Russell, who would have been a more natural choice in many ways, at the head of a party composed partly of pro-reform Radicals. Palmerston reassured them. He also reassured the Conservatives, who for this reason do not seem to have worked very hard to topple him while he was in power. Lord Derby described him as 'a conservative minister working with Radical tools, and keeping up a show of Liberalism in his foreign policy'.[5] That turned out to be the ideal formula for political survival in these years.

Palmerston in fact dominated British politics from 1850 until his death (in harness) in 1865: as Foreign Secretary until he was sacked in December 1851; later as Home Secretary in Lord Aberdeen's coalition government of 1852–5; and finally as Prime Minister from then until – with a short break in 1858–9 – October 1865. His personal influence must be counted another factor behind the relative political quiescance of these years. According to the Conservative Lord Salisbury his main domestic achievement was to lead Parliament to do 'that which it is most difficult and most salutary for a Parliament to do – nothing'.[6] That was not meant ironically, but as a real tribute to his judgment and skill. It may also have been a mark of the stability of the society he was leading; because there was, in truth, no overwhelming pressure on him to do more.

II

That was the home front. Abroad things were more eventful. They were also more interesting to the majority of politically-minded people between 1850 and 1865, and quite rightly, because they were every bit as important to them as anything happening at home. That was because of the extent to which Britain, as we have seen, depended on her foreign trade, uniquely among European nations at that time.

This had two implications. The first, obviously, was to give Britain political interests abroad. The second was to make those political interests different from other countries'. This in turn affected Britain's foreign relations fundamentally. The latter can only be properly understood, in fact, in the light of the enormous divergence of aims – almost cross purposes – that existed between Britain and most other nations then. Other factors contributed to it, including geography – Britain's insularity – and her relative stability as a nation at this time of nation-*building* elsewhere. By far the most important considerations, however, were the spread of her interests in the world outside Europe, and her liberal-capitalist ethos and ideology.

Both these things were sometimes difficult for Continentals to appreciate. This created misunderstandings between them, right up to relatively recent times. For most European countries in the 1850s and 1860s, Europe and its fringes – north Africa and the Near East – effectively constituted their whole world. It was where most of the vital international issues that concerned them arose, and were played out. National security, for example, was conceived purely in European terms. It was a question of making sure that other European countries did not become ambitious or powerful enough to attack you, either directly or by threatening smaller states. Attacks were likely on a number of grounds: expansionist pretensions, disputed frontiers, fears of being attacked by the other fellow first. Most intra-European diplomacy during the nineteenth and the first half of the twentieth centuries was devoted to trying to prevent this, often unsuccessfully. Sometimes Continentals blamed their lack of success on Britain's failure to pull her weight. If she could have underwritten a guarantee here, for example, or joined an alliance there, or stood firm somewhere else, one or other of Europe's succession of aggressors would have been deterred. That was the complaint. It may have been justified. But it took no account of Britain's side of the question, which was just as rational, from her point of view and even possibly the world's, as the Continent's.

Britain's situation *vis-à-vis* Europe was entirely different. Her trade and empire made sure of that. Europe was not her whole world. Her's was larger. Her chess pieces were more widely scattered than any Continental country's were, which was bound to affect the way she moved them. (The chess analogy was popular with contemporary diplomatists too, probably because it was such a clever game.) Some of those pieces were more valuable and also more vulnerable than the ones in the European corner of the board. She had to keep them well covered. It was possible that a situation might arise in which they would have to be given priority over Europe. Europe, of course, was also of interest to Britain, but in different ways. Britain had economic interests there, but nothing that needed to involve diplomacy. Usually they were perfectly secure without diplomatic help; if not then they were not worth insisting on, at the risk of conflict. Britain had no acquisitive or aggressive ambitions on the Continent, and no significant territorial disputes there. (The only exceptions were over Heligoland in the North Sea and the Ionian Islands in the Aegean, which were expendable, and Gibraltar, which was not a live issue at this time.) Her only direct political interest in Europe was defensive: to guard against unprovoked attack. That, as we have seen, had to vie for priority with defensive interests elsewhere, and also with Britain's calculations of the *cost*.

Britain's concern for cost arose from the emphasis she placed on national wealth as the main objective of governments. Not every nation shared this view. Some regarded Britain's priorities as low and mercenary. Bismarck, for example, sneered at her preference for money-making over national 'greatness'. He tended to measure greatness in terms of size, military strength and diplomatic clout.[7] Others saw it in terms of cultural achievement. Britain, as we have noted before, thought she had outgrown all this. 'Greatness' was a chimera, a kind of fool's gold, if you could not eat it; and worse if your means of achieving it were at the expense of your eating well. Wars certainly were; as were great armies, which drained money *via* taxation from wealth-creating enterprises. Concern about national frontiers – size – was simply irrelevant, or should be, in Britain's ideal world in which those frontiers would make no difference to *trade*. It only needed this way of thinking to catch on more widely for war eventually to become obsolete. In the long run, therefore, it was simply not true to say that Britain was putting wealth before greatness or even security. The three were complementary. The problem was what to do in the meantime, while the Continent was still playing its silly games.

The danger was that if Britain got too involved in those games it could be to the detriment of her own ultimately peace-inducing economic growth. It was a difficult calculation; and a different one, it is worth reiterating, from the one the Continentals were faced with. Britain's only direct interest on the Continent was to avoid being invaded from there. That suggested two practical strategies. The first was to station troops to repel invaders: in Britain's case mainly *naval* troops, because of the strip of water any invading army would need to cross. The second was to try to prevent any Continental state or alliance of states growing powerful enough to be able to mount a convincing invasion. One way of doing this was by threatening intervention, probably in conjunction with others, if that seemed to be on the cards. In that case the intervention would need to be military.

The naval precaution seemed sensible to most Britons, partly because they needed a navy to guard their extra-European interests anyway. Navies were also cheaper than armies, chiefly because the competition at that time was not great. During the 1850s, for example, the Royal Navy cost the British taxpayer under £10 million a year, which was excellent value for the biggest navy in the world in a decade that saw it involved in one major and several minor wars. That presented no problem.

The other option, however, was less attractive. Armies were very expensive. Britain's cost her more than £13 million a year in the 1850s, not counting the forces that were paid for out of Indian and colonial revenues.[8] For that she got only the fourth or fifth best army in Europe, whose sole remembered achievement in this decade was a fiasco: the charge of the Light Brigade. To strengthen it in order to be able to intervene in Continental affairs more effectively would have been prohibitively expensive: not because her economic system could not afford the taxes which would have been necessary to pay for it, but because it would not *tolerate* them. It was against its whole ethos: to pay for the protection of the hen that laid the golden eggs, in effect, by cutting back on her feed.

The worst thing would be if the hen got involved in a European war. That was the danger of entering into alliances with other countries which, as part of the arrangement, might oblige Britain to fight over issues that were not really her direct concern. Other countries feared and detested war, of course, but none quite as much as Britain, who had less to gain from one, and more to lose. (We are referring here to large wars which involved her directly; not to other people's wars, which could be a source of short-term profit for her, or to little one-sided ones.) Again, it was a matter of priorities. Britain's top priority, arising from her liberal- capitalist interests and ethos, was to avoid wars, whereas for most of her neighbours the top priority was to *win* any wars they might become involved in. The difference, though it was only one of emphasis, was important. It affected the risks they were prepared to take. A continental country might be prepared to risk war in order to avoid being defeated, for example; Britain would go further in the direction of risking weakness in order to avoid being involved. That being so, it is not surprising that Britain was chary of allying with governments which were more willing – albeit marginally – to risk what she most feared.

That was her basic position during most of the second half of the nineteenth century. Clearly it was not altogether satisfactory. By her reluctance to become involved in the problems of European security Britain was risking allowing a situation to develop – the domination of Europe by an aggressor – in which that security, and ultimately her own, might come under threat. People were aware of the dilemma. At the beginning of our period there looked to be a possible way out. That was the device known as the 'balance of power'. The idea was that if all five great Powers in Europe (including Britain) were roughly equal, any sign of aggression by one of them would be immediately snuffed out by the other four ganging up on her. That was the theory. It was attractive to Britain because it limited her liability to providing just a quarter of the force needed to stop an aggressor, at worst. At best it could mean that Britain was not called upon at all: for who could fail to be deterred by odds of four to one against? So it met both of Britain's main short-term diplomatic needs. It combined security with lack of commitment. That was probably its appeal to Lord Palmerston, who at the beginning of 1851 was still Britain's Foreign Secretary, though not for long.

III

The foreign policy of any country is rarely entirely and exactly in tune with that country's interests and principles. It can be swayed by powerful individuals or pressure groups, nullified by sheer incompetence, or distorted by circumstances – especially the policies of other countries – outside a government's control. This happened occasionally in Britain's case in the decade and a half after 1851. In general, however, her responses to the diplomatic events of these years conformed very closely indeed to her special interests, as the first developed industrial and commercial capitalist economy in Europe.

Early on this was obscured slightly by the reputation of Lord Palmerston as a far more positive and active European statesman – 'high profile' would be the expression used today – than would seem to be appropriate to Britain's underlying position in relation to the Continent then. This worried some of his colleagues. He was regarded as too much of a risk taker. He seemed to delight in irritating and antagonising foreign countries, in ways which delighted his popular constituency but in diplomatic terms were gratuitous, and could even provoke wars. His support for Kossuth was one example, accompanied as it was by grossly insulting lectures to the Austrian government on how it should order its internal affairs. Another was his stand on the principle of asylum in Britain for political refugees, which led nearly all the Continental governments to gang up ominously against Britain in the autumn of 1851.[9] The most notorious instance was the 'Don Pacifico' affair of 1850, in which Palmerston risked war with the whole of Europe by bullying Greece to accede to a quite outrageous reparations claim on behalf of a Gibraltarian whose house had been attacked by a Greek mob. Later he defended this in Parliament on the grounds that British citizens, like the ancient *cives Romani*, should be entitled to the protection of their government anywhere in the world.

None of this seems to fit the pattern of a Britain seeking to distance herself as much as possible from European affairs, in the interests of a quiet life to pursue her trade outside. But impressions can be misleading. Palmerston was generally as concerned as anyone else was to avoid war. He also, however, seemed to enjoy sailing close to the danger of it, for the thrill it gave him, and the way it demonstrated his fine judgment of a safe course. For the rest, Karl Marx may have had the measure of him. 'He exults,' he wrote in his American newspaper column in 1853, 'in show conflicts, show battles, show enemies... What he aims at is not the substance, but the mere appearance of success.'[10]

So it was all bluff and bluster. Some of Palmerston's more radical critics believed it was also rank hypocrisy. The liberal rhetoric was simply meant to pander to the populace. When the chips were down Palmerston showed his real, deep-dyed reactionary side. Hungary was supposed to illustrate this. Palmerston helped save Kossuth from the Austrians once he had been defeated, and was all over him when he visited England in 1851; but he had not lifted a finger for him when his support had been most needed: in 1848–9, when Russia had intervened to crush the Hungarian revolt. In Italy he was a little more forthcoming, coming out in favour of an Austrian evacuation, for example, and even working clandestinely at one point to further reform in Sicily.[11] Even there, however, he always set his face against full Italian nationalism, until it was a *fait accompli* and he trimmed to the wind. His Near Eastern policy was to uphold the integrity of the Ottoman (Turkish) empire, which at that time was the most illiberal and corrupt in Europe by a very long way. In December 1851 he supported the French president Louis Napoleon's bloody *coup d'état* against his own parliament. That was so outrageous that it provided the opportunity for Russell to sack him as Foreign Secretary, which he had been itching to do for some time. All these policies were of a kind. It was difficult for most people to square them with Palmerston's liberal pretensions. Even his supporters were confused.

In fact these policies were defensible, even to liberals, if they bore in mind one thing. The overriding liberal desideratum was peace. It followed from this that anything which maintained the peace was a desideratum too. Simply keep countries from each other's throats, and liberalism would develop naturally and much more enduringly there. Wars could only breed reaction: even wars for liberal ends. Nationalism was illiberal for the same reason – because it was destabilizing – and also *irrelevant* to liberalism, because national boundaries would be of no significance in a truly (that is economically) liberal world. This was where the balance of power came in. It was the thing that ultimately preserved the peace. It required all the Powers to be kept equal. That meant, as well as restraining their expansionary tendencies, not letting them *contract*. In the last resort this might well involve bolstering up a tyrannical regime against some very untyrannical, indeed even liberal, rebels. This was the rationale for all Palmerston's 'reactionary' policies; which were designed to keep France stable, Austria on her legs, and Russia contained, in the interests of balance and therefore of security and peace.

The trouble with the idea of the 'balance of power' in the 1850s was that it did not have much longer to run. The last time it was a factor in British policy was in 1854, when it was one of a number of motives for the war against Russia in the Crimea. Palmerston was a prime mover here, though by this time he was no longer at the Foreign Office. (He was the Aberdeen coalition's Home Secretary.) It was the one occasion when he actively courted war in Europe, in order to prevent Russian expansion into the Balkans and eastern Mediterranean. This sits uneasily with Britain's main national interests and principles as they have been described here. The Crimean war looks like an aberration in many ways. If one examines the detailed diplomacy leading up to it, it appears to have been avoidable. Why was it not avoided?

One can tack together a number of reasons, but even all together they hardly seem convincing. The balance of power was one. Russia, the power that needed to be curbed in this instance, was a potential threat to British India's north-west frontier too. As well as that, her claims over the 'Holy Places' and in the Balkans took her dangerously close to Britain's overland and riverine routes to India – the lifeline of the Empire. 'Wider world' interests were involved, therefore, as well as strictly European ones. One historian has tried to prove that local economic interests were also crucial.[12] Britain had an ally in France, and the promised neutrality of the other two great Powers, which made war safer. These are 'rational' reasons for Britain's bellicose policy. There were also, of course, rational reasons against. Richard Cobden expressed many of them forcefully at the time.[13] The argument was fairly evenly balanced. What may have made the difference – pushed Britain into the war finally – may have been irrational factors: like simple bungling, or Russophobia and war fever stoked up by the press.

Whatever it was, the Crimean war marked a watershed. Britain and France won it, but mainly through France's military prowess. Nothing about the performance of her own army will have encouraged Britain to contemplate doing that sort of thing again. She was just not a military power. France was, and thoroughly enjoyed her war, which added splendidly to her battle honours. For Britain it just brought frustration and immense suffering, not least to the soldiers who through War Office incompetence died in their thousands not of gunshot wounds, but of disease. As it went on people turned against it, and the anti-war feeling persisted afterwards. It was one of the reasons why Britain never fought in Europe again, for more than half a century after the end of the Crimean war in 1856.

Another reason was the utter collapse of the 'balance of power' as a means by which Britain could achieve European security on the cheap. There was a simple reason for that. The balance would only work smoothly if all the parties to it shared the same interest in preserving the European status quo. In fact few of them besides Britain did. They were all dissatisfied with their present boundaries, and with the terms of the treaties (Vienna 1815, and now Paris 1856) which had settled them. France had territorial ambitions in Savoy, for example; Prussia in Schleswig-Holstein; and Austria and Russia in the Balkans. It only needed two or three of them to agree together to turn a blind eye to each other's aggressions in these areas for the whole balancing mechanism to fail. It would then be a question not of four to one against, but of three to two against, or even – if they were lucky – odds on. This is what happened during the course of the 1850s and 1860s. It took Britain – and especially Palmerston – a little time to twig on to it, partly because Palmerston really was a very old dog to be learning new tricks at this stage (he was 75 in 1860), but mainly because of the particular convenience of the idea of the balance for Britain. When that went, it was as if her European crutches had been snatched from her. For years she found nothing adequate to replace them. Hence the diplomatic walking difficulties she experienced in the 1860s, which are generally reckoned to have been the most humiliating period ever for Britain in Europe before 1938.

Its highest point was at the beginning, but that had little to do with diplomacy in the conventional sense. On 23 January 1860 a commercial treaty was signed between Britain and France which reduced the duties on a range of goods exchanged between the two countries, and established the rule that no duties either of them imposed against the other should exceed the duties on the same sorts of goods they imposed against any of their other trading partners. (Later this came to be called the 'most favoured nation' principle.) It is often known as the 'Cobden Treaty', because the main negotiator on the British side was Richard Cobden, who was not even a member of the government. He saw it as the first major step towards a new kind of diplomacy, which eventually would render the old kind obsolete. He died in 1865, probably mercifully, because later events were to prove him sadly wrong.

In the meantime the old – and to free traders like Cobden unnecessary – Continental quarrels continued, with Britain almost powerless to influence their outcomes. She gained credit in October 1860 by finally accepting the fact of Italian unification, in a speech by the Foreign Secretary (Russell) which *may* have had an important practical impact by dissuading other powers from stepping in to break Italy up again. Thereafter it was downhill all the way. Rock bottom was reached in 1863–66, when Britain threatened intervention in two cases of great-power aggression on the Continent, but then, when the powers failed to be deterred, backed down.

The first case involved Poland, where high-handed treatment by her Russian masters in 1863 provoked a spirited rebellion, which gained widespread sympathy in Europe. France wanted to march in with Britain against Russia, and thought Britain had agreed. Britain, however, got cold feet at the last moment, mainly because she suspected France – rightly, as it happened – of only wanting the opportunity to do a little aggressing on her own account. The result was that France was denied another moment of military glory, at the very least, and the Poles their freedom, much to the resentment of both. The following year a similar thing happened. Prussia and Austria invaded the Danish duchies of Schleswig and Holstein, despite a clear warning from Palmerston that if they did then Britain would step in. He reneged on that, too. The reason was probably a good one: Britain had an available army of only 20 000, Palmerston pointed out, 'and more could not be got together'; what could conceivably be the point of pitting that against 'the hundreds of thousands which Germany, if united, could oppose to us'?[14] By this time the alternative, of the 'balance' coming into play, was a dead duck. France might have been persuaded to help. If so, however, it would only have been in order to grab the Rhineland. That would not have restored the balance, but only upset it in another way. The logic of all this was inescapable. The criticism that can be made of Russell and Palmerston is not that they succumbed to it, but that they ought to have borne it in mind before they started issuing their threats.

Britain's contortions over these issues had some unfortunate results. They undoubtedly raised the Poles' and the Danes' hopes, for example, and so prolonged what turned out to be hopeless resistances. They also encouraged the German Chancellor Bismarck – if he needed any encouragement – to go on with the next stages of his scheme to unite Germany without bothering about how Britain might react. As those particular events unfolded – Prussia's defeat of her erstwhile ally Austria in 1866; her victory over France in 1870–71 followed by the transfer of Alsace-Lorraine; the final consolidation of the existing German states; the proclamation of the new *Deutsches Kaisserreich* at Versailles in 1871 – Britain remained on the sidelines, diplomatically almost completely inactive (apart from measures she took to safeguard Belgium), and essentially impotent. In 1870 another great international crisis underlined that impotence. Russia unilaterally revoked the clause of the 1856 Treaty of Paris which forbade her to station warships in the Black Sea. Britain's response was not to try to stop it, but merely to fudge the issue, transparently, by getting all the other signatories to the Treaty to pretend that they had freely agreed *multi*laterally to let Russia do this. It was pathetic. But it was better than bluffing. And it was arguably necessary, in view of the sort of nation Britain was at this time: liberal, capitalist, and world-wide in the range of her interests and responsibilities.

IV

That gave her a different perspective on things from her neighbours on the Continent, from which issues like the status of Schleswig and the neutrality of the Black Sea appeared almost parochial. Outside Europe Britain had far more on her plate, enough to keep any government's hands full to overflowing: including, for example, the most serious challenge to her imperial sway ever mounted since the American colonies had rebelled in 1776.

That was in India. In 1857, at a barracks at Meerut near Delhi, native Indian soldiers ('sepoys') staged a mutiny against their British officers, which spread to other regiments and to some civilian groups mainly in the northern and central regions of India. It was put down, but only after 14 months of bitter and often savage fighting on both sides. It was a strain for Britain in more ways than one. It tied up troops, to an extent that made any other substantial military commitment on Britain's part virtually unthinkable during the course of it, and something to be considered very carefully even after it was over, when the British element in the Indian army was, for obvious reasons, increased. It greatly injured Indo-British relations and attitudes, undermining the trust and warmth that had often existed between the two communities before 1857, and engendering a powerful white racism in some quarters, both in India and in Britain, which was to endure. It involved the British government in new imperial responsibilities, when after the Mutiny parliament took the country over from the East India Company which had been its intermediary before; a change that was not quite as radical as it appears on paper – the East India Company had not been a *commercial* company in the usual sense for years, and most of its personnel were kept in post – but which nevertheless seemed to be a step in the wrong direction, according to the dominant dogma of the day. It was a worrying time; and excuse enough on its own for Britain's air of distraction, so far as the affairs of her European neighbours at that time were concerned.

It also highlighted a general problem, which was to create the most lasting strain of all for Britain in her relations not only with India, but also with the rest of the extra-European world. The Indian Mutiny was not the only colonial rebellion of this period. There had been dozens of relatively minor ones in India before it; and there were scores in other colonies both before and after. The most serious were the Kaffir wars of the 1850s and 1860s in southern Africa, the Maori wars of 1860–63 in New Zealand, and a major rebellion – almost as traumatic in some ways as the Indian one – on the West Indian island of Jamaica in 1865. At the root of most of these conflicts was a clash between the traditional values of the natives (or in the Jamaican case the Afros), and the unfamiliar values associated with the quite fundamental changes the British interlopers were trying – often forcibly – to introduce to them. Most of these were economic in nature, especially those which related to the tenure of land. All these changes pointed in the same direction: the incorporation of more and more countries into the great world-wide free market which would ultimately be the salvation of them all. So they should have been good news.

The fact that they were not always received as such was a blow. It was a practical blow because it forced the guardians of the market to act out of character in some instances: *hardening* their political control when they should theoretically have been able to relinquish it. The change in India's status came in 1858. In 1865 Jamaica was taken out of the hands of its local white and mixed-race electorate to become a Crown Colony, ruled directly from Whitehall. British Kaffraria was annexed to Cape Colony in 1865, followed by Basutoland in 1871. As well as this, it might also have been seen as an ideological blow: if it had been thought to be a permanent thing, not just a passing phase; and if it had not been balanced on the other side by some very much more favourable auguries.

For at the very same moment that the tide of colonialism was lapping at these shores, it was receding very gratifyingly elsewhere. In the colonies of European settlement, in particular, imperial apron-strings were snapping one after another during the 1850s, leaving most of the colonies and provinces of Canada, Australia and New Zealand effectively in the hands of their set-tlers (excluding, that is, their aboriginal inhabitants) by 1860. Self-governing colonies, of course, were expected to look after their own local defence, as well as everything else. Consequently British troops were progressively withdrawn from Canada and Australia during the middle 1860s, and even from New Zealand, despite its recent troubles with the Maoris; and had all gone by 1870. The same was attempted in South Africa, but the continuing vulnerability of the white-settler communities there made that impossible yet. In 1865 a parliamentary committee recom-mended the decolonisation of three of Britain's possessions on the west coast of Africa. (The fourth, Sierra Leone, was to be kept as a refuge for fugitive slaves.) That also came to nothing; but at least the intention was there.

All in all, then, and despite some sad disappointments, the 15 or so years after 1851 were moderately hopeful ones for people in Britain who held the orthodox mid-Victorian liberal view of the world. Their humiliations over Poland and Schleswig-Holstein did not matter. Britons were big enough – *mature* enough – to disregard them. The Crimean war was a blow, as was the Indian rebellion: for much the same reason, which was that they demon-strated – in different ways – the thickness of the barrier of irrationality that the liberal gospel still had to penetrate. On the other side there were its gleaming successes: the Cobden treaty, Canada, the demilitarization of Australia, and the fact that after 1856 Britain remained at peace in Europe for 58 years. These were no mean achievements, and certainly proof against the sneers of such as Bismarck, who probably could not comprehend them anyway.

The 15 years from 1851 to 1866 were dominated by foreign and impe-rial affairs. This was mainly simply the way things turned out: the turmoil on the Continent, the Indian and Jamaican revolts, prosperity and stability at home. A secondary reason, however, was the personality of Palmerston, who was chiefly interested in foreign policy, and very much against almost any kind of progress or even activity on the domestic front. In October 1865, while out driving, Palmerston caught a chill, and a few days later died. Whigs, especially elderly ones, predicted that this would make a dif-ference. As one of them came away from the funeral in Westminster Abbey on 27 October he was heard to remark, apprehensively: 'Our quiet days are over; no more peace for us'.[15] He did not have to wait long – just one or two years – to have his worst fears born out.

Chapter 5

Reform
(1866–75)

I

The domestic lull of the 1850s and early 1860s was not natural. Liberal capitalism – the dominant ideology of the period – is not usually a static system. It needs to grow, progress, change, in order to prosper and survive. Dynamism is inherent in it, and with it a degree of economic instability. This creates social pressures, which are bound eventually to translate into political ones. The fact that few such political pressures were apparent in Britain in the 1850s may only have meant that they had not reached the surface yet. Discouraged by the recent failure of Chartism, disarmed by relative prosperity, distracted by foreign adventures, and obstructed by the parliamentary situation of the time, they nevertheless continued simmering away deep down, ready when any of these factors was removed or weakened to erupt, and to spill through on to the political crust once again.

In fact around 1865 all these obstructive and apparently stabilizing factors weakened together, to one degree or another. The demoralising effect of the defeat of Chartism simply receded as time went by. Prosperity proved a disappointment to many of the working classes, as they realised how little of it was actually filtering down to *them*, even before the economic slump of 1866 dented it. Foreign adventures came to a stop in the later 1850s, when Britain withdrew into diplomatic isolation, at least so far as Europe was concerned. Lastly, the parliamentary political situation changed out of all recognition around the middle of the 1860s, when not only Palmerston but also Russell and Derby, who between them had more or less run Britain since 1832, quit the political scene almost together.

Two things happened as a result of that. Younger men (by comparison) took over, dominant among them William Ewart Gladstone and Benjamin Disraeli, who between them were to run Britain for the next 15 years, when Disraeli died, leaving Gladstone dominating for a time on his own. The second result of the removal of Palmerston, in particular, was to release the log-jam that had been building up behind him previously. Important political and social legislation poured out of Parliament in a rush, giving the inevitable impression that something more positive must have happened then to give rise to what some saw as a veritable revolution. In reality it was probably simply no more than that people had got tired of waiting.

This seems to be especially true of the major political measure of the period, which was Disraeli's great Parliamentary Reform Act of 1867. That – or something like it – had been *expected* for years. This may have been one reason why there was so little popular agitation for it, to compare for example with the often very violent agitation which had preceded the first reform bill of 1832. An alternative explanation is sheer public apathy. If so, then the root of that was generally felt to be prosperity. In 1859 Cobden wrote to his ally John Bright that folk seemed 'too well-to-do in the world to agitate for anything'.[1] Others made similar diagnoses right through the 1850s and early 1860s. As late as March 1866 Bright was still bemoaning the fact that while people were willing to turn out in their thousands to cheer the Italian revolutionary leader Garibaldi when he had visited Britain in 1864, they refused to demonstrate on their own behalfs. If they would simply do that, he went on, 'Parliament would have to take notice of them'.[2] Four months later, to Bright's gratified surprise, that happened. The Reform riots of July 1866 came almost out of the blue. But nothing in this sort of politics ever really comes out of the blue. What probably occurred was that people who had been expecting Reform to come about naturally, got impatient when it did not. That helped force the issue.

The auguries for parliamentary reform seemed good right through the 1850s and early 1860s. It did not look as though the middle classes needed to be pushed. 'Even if there were no wish on the part of the people for organic change of any kind,' wrote the third Earl Grey in 1864, 'the time is coming when it will be impossible that things should remain as they are.'[3] A further extension of the franchise was a natural sequel to that earlier one in 1832, and a natural consequence of the progress the disenfranchised classes had made – under the beneficial influence of liberal capitalism – since that time. The Liberal MP Edward Baines made this point in 1861, to a Reform conference of working men. In 1832 it had been right to exclude them from the franchise, he told them, because they had been 'destitute of education and intelligence'; but times had changed since then. 'The older men amongst the audience', he went on, 'knew in what great variety of ways the amount of cultivated intelligence amongst working men now was immensely greater than it was when they were lads', so that their 'good conduct', as he put it, could no longer be in doubt.[4] Ironically this was felt to be borne out by the lack of working-class agitation on behalf of Reform, which Gladstone in 1864 claimed simply proved how safe it would be to concede it to them.[5] They had *earned* the vote, through their wise abandonment of their old Chartist excesses, and their moderation generally. Another way of putting it was that they had accepted the system. They would no longer threaten the ship if they were taken aboard.

It is this way of thinking that marked the Parliamentary reformers of the mid-nineteenth century off from the Chartists, and from 'democrats' both then and today. The difference, which we have noticed before, was crucial. For democrats the popular will is sacrosanct. For Victorian liberals it was not. Other things came before it: generally individual 'freedom', both economic and political. It followed from this that the right to participate in the government of one's country was not a basic human right, as it is for a democrat, but a privilege to be granted only to those people or groups who had shown that they would not use it to undermine those higher priorities. That does not sound very liberal, but it was in a way. In the first place, although the vote was a privilege to be earned, it was one which anyone (or at least any man) *could* earn: which gave everyone an equal opportunity. Second, many mid-Victorian liberals believed that everyone *would* earn it in time, as liberal-capitalist enlightenment spread. Then liberalism might become democratic too. But that was not for basically democratic reasons; and it was not to be *yet*.

There was widespread support in Parliament throughout the later 1850s and early 1860s for a measure of reform along these limited lines. It came to nothing because the supporters could not agree on the details, and because (for reasons we have already touched on: mainly their belief that government should be minimal anyway) it was not a high priority even for them. It became a high priority partly for party political reasons. Palmerston's death in 1865 put the Liberal party back into Russell's hands. It also meant that Tory support was less likely for a Liberal government. This made it necessary for the Liberals to woo the Radicals to gain a majority. The Radicals, of course, supported Reform. So did Russell, and also (since 1864) his deputy, Gladstone. That made it inevitable that the post-Palmerston Liberal party would be a Reforming one.

More surprisingly, it had a similar effect on the Conservatives. They had been out of effective power for years now. That was partly because of their 'reactionary' image in an age of 'progress', which was an electoral liability. Some of them started thinking of ways to reverse this. 'The task before our leaders,' said one prominent Tory backbencher in 1856, 'ought to be to shew that Toryism is not necessarily antagonistic to Progress.'[6] In the early 1860s Derby's deputy, Disraeli, had become convinced that if the Conservatives remained anti-Reform they would simply die out. Such was the momentum generated by mid-Victorian progressivism: no one could afford to resist it, not even those who called themselves Conservatives. Another calculation was also involved. If Parliament was to be reformed anyway, as seemed likely, then would it not be better for *them* to do it, rather than the Liberals? That way they would get the electoral credit, and could ensure that any new distribution of seats favoured the Tory shires.

By the autumn of 1865, therefore, and for all kinds of reasons (*except* pressure from below), most leading parliamentarians had come over to the idea of Reform. The main barrier was Palmerston. But then he died. As soon as he was safely in his grave, Lord John Russell trotted round to the Queen and told her that he intended bringing in a Reform bill as soon as one could be drawn up. From that point events moved forward to their predicted conclusion: which was the second great Reform Act of 1867.

The route chosen, however, was not quite so predictable. It was full of unexpected turns. In March 1866 Gladstone presented Russell's bill to the Commons. It was a very moderate measure, but still managed to frighten the more diehard Tories and Whigs, who voted it down. A redistribution bill designed to appease the Tories by shifting some seats from the boroughs to the counties also failed. The Liberal government thereupon resigned, and a Conservative minority took over.

It was then that the unexpected happened. The Conservatives, having defeated a mild Reform bill on the grounds that it was too strong, then went ahead and passed one that was stronger still. It added about 900 000 new electors to the roll, many of them working-class. It may be that the Conservatives did not realize what they were doing. About 300 000 of the new voters came as the result of a backbench amendment to the bill which Disraeli accepted precipitately, without doing his sums. He seems to have been desperate to push the measure through at almost any cost, in order, as Derby put it, to 'dish the Whigs'.[7] Politically he thought the cost could be offset by tapping what he believed to be a rich reservoir of natural working-class Tory support. He also saw that the bill would be more likely to gain his party electoral credit if it could be seen to be magnanimous, and not forced on it. If it was to have that effect, however, it would have to be done quickly. Prevaricate any longer and it would be too late.

That was because of the new situation created by the Reform riots of 1866–67, which started after the defeat of Russell's bill. Many Conservatives were deeply shocked by them, and some even feared revolution. What concerned them most was the apparent powerlessness of the authorities in the face of them. The main one, in Hyde Park on 23 July 1866, had gone ahead despite a ban by the Home Office, and then was only brought to order not by the police or troops, but by the organisers themselves – the officers of the Reform League – after parleying with the Home Secretary, Spencer Walpole. Rumour had it that the League's offer of help had brought tears to Walpole's eyes.[8] The following May another illegal demonstration was allowed to proceed unhindered, while 10 000 Hussars, Horse Guards, Life Guards, police and special constables stood impotently by. These events infuriated the bloodthirstier Tories, who felt that a touch of cold steel could easily have put an end to all this nonsense in no time at all, if only Walpole had shown more spunk. (He resigned after the May 1867 affair.) That was one response to the riots. But it was not the most common one, even among Conservatives.

The most common one was probably also the most rational. The riots were an indication of the necessity for Reform. They put paid to the notion that the middle and upper classes had any significant choice in the matter, and consequently that the concession of reform was really an act of generosity: though if they were clever they might still be able to give this impression. 'Events had become too strong for them,' said a Tory backbencher in May 1867; and even the Queen warned Derby, a little earlier, that if he did not do something soon on the Reform front, 'very serious consequences may ensue'.[9] Again, it showed that there was no baulking 'progress'. If you tried, you ran the risk of provoking something worse. Everything in Britain's recent history and in that of the European continent pointed this lesson: that obstruction, and especially repression, simply fanned the revolutionary flames to more menacing heights. Ever since 1848, at the latest, Britain's domestic stability had rested on other foundations entirely: on the consent of her people, based in its turn on their trust in their rulers' liberal intentions towards them. 'To have used cutlasses on 6 May,' writes Royden Harrison, 'or to have shown prolonged resistance to the League, would have been to squander an immense fund of valuable social and political capital.'[10]

By delaying as long as they did they may have squandered a little capital, but that was soon recouped by the extent of the concession when it ultimately came. The Reform Bill became law on 15 August 1867. It was famously described by Disraeli as 'a leap in the dark'. He seems to have found it exhilarating. Others, however, did not like the sensation one bit.

This was because the Act raised a spectre. Not everyone saw it. It concerned the behaviour of all those new working-class voters. Most Liberals seemed confident that they would not cause much trouble. That was because the workers were good liberals underneath. 'Look at the savings banks and the trade unions,' said one MP in 1866. 'Are not the working classes learning the value of capital? Look at the co-operative building and manufacturing societies. Are they ignorant of the value of property?'[11] If they were not won over yet, they would be soon. This was the way of 'progress', which could be relied on to bring every voter to his liberal senses in time. Disraeli also trusted the workers, but for a different reason.

It was because they were, as he put it, as 'interested' as any other class in 'the stability and even in the glory' of Britain.[12] In other words, they were natural conservatives. That was reassuring. But it was not the universal view.

Others were less sanguine. Most of them were Conservatives, but they included the banker and writer Walter Bagehot, who once stood for election as a Liberal. In a new introduction to the second (1872) edition of his most famous book, *The English Constitution*, he expressed his fears about the effects of the 1867 Act. His problem was that he did *not* trust what he called 'the ignorant multitude of the new constituencies'. In fact he was 'exceedingly afraid' of them. This was because he expected them to use their powers to try to create a 'poor man's paradise', which anyone with a smattering of political economy knew must fail disastrously. It would happen in one of two ways. The workers might 'combine... as a class together', in a new political party, to force their demands through parliament. Alternatively, the traditional parties might seek to forestall this by buying them off. That was the most likely outcome, and something to be deplored.

> In plain English, what I fear is that both our political parties will bid for the support of the working man; that both of them will promise to do as he likes if he will only tell them what it is; that, as he now holds the casting vote in our affairs, both parties will beg and pray him to give that vote to them. I can conceive of nothing more corrupting or worse for a set of poor ignorant people than that two combinations of well-taught and rich men should constantly offer to defer to their decision, and compete for the office of executing it. *Vox populi* will be *Vox diaboli* if it is worked in that manner.[13]

That view was typical of many. It got short shrift in Bagehot's time, but it was to endure. Later it was to exert a significant influence on British politics, as we shall see.

II

The rot – as Bagehot perceived it – may have set in very soon after the Reform Act. Much of the legislation which came in its wake could be regarded as the product of working-class pressure. Some of it also offended against 'political economy'. Consequently the period was seen by some later malcontents as a turning point.

It is not difficult to see why. A listing of the major 'social reforms' of this period reads impressively. In 1866 and 1872 two new Public Health Acts compelled local authorities to furnish certain basic sanitary and other services in towns and cities. Another Act of 1872 was directed against the adulteration of food. The Metropolitan Poor Act of 1867 inaugurated the first state-run medical service (outside the armed forces), for the inhabitants of workhouses. A Factory Act of 1874 limited hours of work for women and children in textile factories to 56^1/$_2$ a week, and raised slightly the age at which children could be employed in mills. An Artisans and Labourers Dwellings Act of 1875 began what later came to be called 'council house' building. The most important new measure of this period was probably W.E. Forster's Education Act of 1870, which provided universal schooling, subsidized by the state, and often in directly-run 'board schools', for children up to the age of 13. Then there were a number of important trade union Acts: the first, passed in 1871, giving trade unions legal status for the first time, and two more, both passed in 1875, going some way towards legalising strikes by exempting them from certain breach of contract and conspiracy laws. All strikes, of course, involve breaking contracts, and a kind of 'conspiracy', which made this latter legislation in particular a real breakthrough.

Later it came to be seen as the thin end of the socialist wedge.[14] Yet it was passed by a Conservative government. The first trade union Act was passed by the Liberals. The other social measures of this period were divided roughly equally between them. Did this not bear out Bagehot's fears? The parties were pandering to the people: against their own better judgments, and to the detriment of the nation as a whole.

That was probably unfair, for all kinds of reasons. In the first place you would need to be a very rigorous free marketeer indeed to believe that making councils dig drains, or giving teenage children a couple of hours off on a Saturday, or stopping sweet manufacturers colouring their aniseed balls with poisons like copper arsenate, undermined freedom of contract and self-reliance and the rest *significantly*. Few politicians in the later 1860s and early 1870s were that extreme. Consequently they did not need to be bullied by their constituents into making 'concessions' along these lines.

This is particularly true of the Conservative party, which adhered to political economy broadly during this period, but not yet *strictly*. This is scarcely surprising, in view of its Tory paternalist roots. Disraeli himself was highly pragmatic on these issues, despite acknowledging publicly on more than one occasion 'those inexorable rules of political economy to which we must all bow'.[15] That may have been designed to appeal to the industrial middle classes. Early on in his career he wrote novels which suggest that he was something of an old-fashioned Tory paternalist himself. Most of his later professions of faith in political economy came as caveats to speeches advocating social reform nonetheless. Historians differ over whether Disraeli was ever a 'genuine' social reformer (or indeed, a genuine *anything*); but none has ever suggested that he was a genuine free marketeer, in the sense of a committed and rigid one. In this he reflected his party, which tended to distrust commitment to any kind of ideology at all. That has always – until recently – been the Conservatives' great strength.

The Liberals contained more dogmatists, which is one reason why their record of social reform in these years is less impressive than the Conservatives'. They generally remained truer to their liberal capitalist consciences, except over Ireland, where it *is* possible to argue that they were thrown off course by pressures from below. In 1870 an Irish Land Act was passed giving a measure of security to tenants there, right against the free marketist grain. That showed that even the Liberal party could be flexible when it needed to be; but this flexibility was not reflected in its mainland legislation yet. Of all the social measures passed by the 1868–74 Liberal governments only one – Forster's Education Act – made a really big difference to people's lives, and that had overwhelming support from both sides. (The only significant controversy surrounding it centred on the thorny question of whether Church of England schools should be subsidized out of rates paid by nonconformists.) The other Liberal measures were generally weak. The 1872 Public Health Act plugged a few gaps in the 1866 one, but left many more open; the Adulteration Act was permissive only, not widely implemented, and backed up by derisory fines on offenders where it was; and the 1871 trade union legislation disappointed trade unionists more than it satisfied them by neglecting to free them from the grip of the conspiracy laws. (That was left for the Conservatives to do later.) If anyone was pandering to the proles, therefore, it was not the Liberals. They were too busy pandering elsewhere.

In the context of the total legislative activity of this period, in fact, social reform – whichever party carried it out – was relatively insignificant. Disraeli was uninterested in it, had no constructive ideas about it, and left most of the running on it to his underlings.[16] Much the same could be said of Gladstone, except that he more often tempered *his* apathy with downright obstruction. His prime domestic concern at this stage of his career was to enlarge liberal freedoms, in an entirely orthodox way. Hence, for example, the *meritocratic* achievements of his first spell: like the Order in Council of 1870 making entry into the Home civil service competitive rather than dependent on patronage; Edward Cardwell's Army reforms of 1870–72, which among other things stopped officers *buying* promotions; and the University Tests Act of 1871, which abolished the requirement for Oxbridge college fellows to be practising Anglicans. The Married Women's Property Act of 1870 – allowing women to retain their ownership rights after marriage – was another giant step in the same direction. During his government and the subsequent (Conservative) one, income tax was brought down to almost absurdly low levels – two old pence in the pound in 1875, for example, or 0.83% – which took some more constraints off individuals. As well as this, society was humanized somewhat by the abolition of transportation in 1867, and of public executions in 1868. (People were still hanged, but discretely now.) This set the tone for the period, far more than all those marginally retrogressive little 'social' reforms could hope to do.

This was where most of the reforming energies of the time were concentrated: against abuses surviving from the aristocratic past, rather than against the new perceived evils of the present time. Britain was still mainly engaged in casting off her feudal fetters, and too preoccupied with them, perhaps, to realize where the next set of fetters was coming from. Her rulers had the same broad vision of progress they had had for 20 years or more: the eradication of institutional injustices, the maximisation of individual liberty, unblocking the channels of advancement for men of merit; and maybe one day unblocking them for women of merit too. All these affected and benefitted the middle classes far more than the lower. So far as *their* 'social problems' were concerned – chiefly poverty, and its concomitants of vice and crime – the legislation of the 1860s and early 1870s had almost no direct bearing on them.

This was because poverty, above the level of destitution (where the Poor Law came in), was still not regarded as a proper area of concern for the state. Vice and crime were: but only in the state's capacity as enforcer of the law. Poverty was the responsibility of two sorts of people: the poor themselves, of course; and the charitable rich, who should be allowed to dispense their charity as they saw fit. This kind of approach has always presented problems. One is that rich people are sometimes mean. (That may be why they are rich.) They also have particular views about who deserves their charity, which may not accord with other people's, and do not necessarily relate to justice or real needs. Some of those views are rooted in prejudice; others reflect the contemporary state of knowledge about social suffering, which in its turn is affected by the publicity which different groups of social sufferers can command. Certain groups are bound to have fewer problems in this regard than others. It depends on the image they can project. Tear-stained children's faces have always been a potent one; with the result that Dr Barnardo's, for example, was never badly off. Some charities in mid-Victorian times got far too much money. Other worthy ones got scarcely any at all.[17] This unevenness was one of the main flaws in the contemporary charitable system. The mid-Victorians' solution to it, however, was not to bring the state in, but to try to rationalise it privately.

That was the purpose behind the formation in April 1869 of the voluntary 'Charity Organisation Society', which in many ways was the most characteristic social agency of the time. The Queen became its patron in 1873. The original plan for it had the whole country divided into regions patrolled by 'Charity Agents', who would investigate the incidence of poverty in their areas, the extent to which it was being relieved by existing agencies, and any cases of what the COS called 'the maladministration of charity': by which was meant over-generosity, or helping the wrong people. Then the really needy were to be directed to the appropriate charities, and the flaws and imbalances would disappear. In the 'last resort', if local agencies were inadequate, the COS might dispense aid out of its own funds. In either case it had to be done discriminately. Everyone in the COS agreed that giving money or even food to poor people did 'inevitably more harm than good' in the long run. Consequently care had to be taken to ensure that aid was only given in 'deserving cases', not for example to scroungers or imposters; and secondly that even in those cases it was dispensed in such away as to encourage – as the COS's Annual Report put it in 1875 – 'habits of prudence and self-reliance, and of those social and sanitary principles, the observance of which is essential to the well-being of the poor and of the community at large'.[18]

It never worked quite as smoothly as that, partly because the Poor Law Board and many private charities were not as co-operative as they really needed to be. The COS did not, therefore, solve the problem of poverty. Relief continued to be dispensed haphazardly. Widespread social distress remained a feature of British life, hidden to an extent in the 1860s, but still there to be highlighted, as we shall see, in future years. Perhaps it could have been significantly reduced if the COS had had its way. The price for that would have been a system of investigation into the circumstances and lifestyles of claimants which would inevitably have been highly intrusive, but probably no more so (by the society's lights) than the poor deserved. On the credit side it would have helped people materially, eradicated the stain of poverty, reconciled the poor to the 'system', reassured some of the more concerned middle classes about that system, and so helped *preserve* the system in the years to come. That was if the COS had been more successful than it was.

Its lack of success did not seem to matter at the time, however, because the system was under no obvious threat. Nothing that had happened in Parliament threatened it seriously, despite Bagehot's fears, with the possible exception of Disraeli's trade-union legislation, which gave unions privileges which in strict free-market theory they probably ought not to have. Both the main political parties adhered to the system in essentials, and there was no anti-system party – no distinctive grouping of the new working-class electorate, for example – in sight. Compared with the Continent, where in 1871 the workers were busy building the first communist state in history, the British proletariat seemed years behind. When that experiment – the Paris Commune – was smashed in May 1871, therefore, and thousands of 'Communards' fled to Britain to escape reprisals, scarcely anyone feared that the virus would catch on there. We have seen already how relaxed the Home Office was.[19] So was *The Times*. English socialists, it claimed (and there were a few), were harmless. When they ranted on about class war and the rest, 'they know quite well they are using hyperbolical verbiage which has no reference to the state of their own country, or to the opinions of their own class'. *The Times* listened to all this not in alarm, but with 'a satisfied confidence' that even the socialists must come to their moderate senses 'in the sober light of day'.[20] That was a typical response. Britain was *different* from foreign countries. She was safe. This was because liberal capitalism was working. Twenty years on from the Great Exhibition, there were no domestic signs of danger to it yet.

Chapter 6

Auguries
(1873–80)

I

Britain's 'golden years', of increasing prosperity, social peace, moderate reform and above all optimism, drew to a close in the early 1870s. The social peace continued for a while after that, which may be one reason – the lack of pressure – why the flow of moderate reforms dried up. Increasing prosperity took a knock from a trade slump after 1873 which turned into what came to be called the 'Great Depression'. That had an obvious effect on the optimism. Another cause for worry was events abroad. The world was coming to seem less friendly in a number of ways. Some of them were new, and unpredictable; but an old foreign threat also flared up again in the mid-1870s. That came from Russia. It landed on Disraeli's plate, at the beginning of his second government, which ran from 1874 to 1880.

Disraeli's Russian (or 'Eastern') policy was spectacularly successful at the time. It was also probably the wrong policy, and certainly a failure in the long term. This was because it was incongruous with Britain's real interests in the 1870s, and the underlying problems which beset them. It is possible that it was intended to distract attention from some of those problems: from people's domestic grievances, for example, in order to divert pressures for reform. That must always be a suspicion with regard to adventurous foreign policies pursued by Conservative governments. Get the plebs hating an external enemy, and they will forget to hate you. It is usually an unfounded suspicion, and is particularly unconvincing here. Even if Disraeli had been experiencing domestic difficulties in the mid-1870s – and it is difficult to see this – the 'Eastern Question' involved a plausible threat to Britain, which is quite enough to explain his intervention on its own.

The threat came – as it had at the time of the Crimean war – from one of Russia's recurring bouts of aggressive expansionism, which was thought to endanger Britain's interests in three ways. It threatened the 'balance' in Europe, and consequently European peace; it threatened India, to which the Russian central Asian empire was by now perilously close, especially on its north-west frontier with Afghanistan; and it threatened Britain's *routes* to India through the Ottoman empire, which in 1876–78 was invaded by Russia and forced into a treaty (San Stephano) which Britain regarded as compromising its 'integrity'. This was a reasonable way of looking at it.

What may have been less reasonable, however, was the practical response Disraeli chose to make. On India's north-west frontier he went to war with Afghanistan in 1878–79 in order to force her Amir to accept British control over his foreign policy, and keep the Russians out. Gladstone regarded that war as 'unjust' and 'frivolous'.[1] In the middle east Disraeli's policy was even more controversial. That was to insist on restoring the Ottomans' integrity, as a buffer against Russia. He nearly came to war over that, too, this time against Russia herself; but in the end (in 1878) he succeeded in frightening her into a compromise. That was a tremendous diplomatic victory. But was it the best sort of victory, from Britain's point of view? Lord Salisbury, who was Disraeli's secretary of state for India at the time, thought not. His instinct was that by bolstering the Ottoman empire in this way Disraeli had, in his words, 'backed the wrong horse'.[2]

There was an alternative policy to Disraeli's. That was quite simply to give up the Ottoman empire as a bad job and *partition* it among the interested European powers. There was a lot going for this. The Ottoman empire by this time was a pretty rickety structure, corrupt at its centre and plagued by rebellions nearly all over, which probably could not have stood upright for a moment if it had not been for the presence of its European allies propping it up. Many people in Britain were uneasy about propping it up, not only for this practical reason but also for the moral reason that it was currently engaged in slaughtering (and supposedly worse) many of its Christian subjects. Some people got quite worked up over this, in a famous popular campaign against the 'Bulgarian atrocities' which was taken over by Gladstone in September 1876. That irritated Disraeli, who at first did not believe the 'atrocity' stories that were retailed to him, and in any case did not think that foreign policy should be affected by sentimental considerations like this.

Even he, however, might have allowed himself to be moved by another consideration: which was that Britain did not really need to defend this unpopular regime in order to secure her interests. The integrity of the whole Ottoman empire did not matter to her. The only bit of it that did matter was Egypt, because it was through Egypt that the only short route to India – the Suez canal, opened in 1869 – now ran. As long as that was secured, she could abandon the rest. Disraeli may have seen some sense in this at one stage. In November 1875 he bought 44% of the shares in the Suez Canal Company for the British government with the help of his banker friend Lord Rothschild, in a novel kind of *coup* which was widely interpreted as the prelude to a switch of eastern policy. A year later, however, he had changed tack. Anyone who thought Suez only needed to be defended locally, he said, must be 'utterly ignorant of geography', because it would be an easy matter for Russia to attack Egypt from Constantinople through Turkey and Syria.[3] Most commentators since have thought that he must have been looking at too small-scale maps. Either that, or he had other reasons for favouring the Ottoman strategy.

That is likely. One reason may have been simply to achieve a diplomatic victory, in order to acquire *kudos* both for himself and for his country. That is what Lord Derby, his foreign secretary, who resigned twice over the Eastern question, suspected. 'He believes thoroughly,' he wrote to Salisbury in December 1877, 'in "prestige", as all foreigners do, and would think it (quite sincerely) in the interests of the country to spend 200 millions on a war if the result was to make foreign states think more highly of us.' He added that he imagined that this was not Salisbury's way of looking at things.[4] Disraeli's victory was certainly a prestigious one. He had stood firm, turned Russia back, stolen a march on Germany, smashed her '*Dreikaiserbund*' with Austria and Russia, and gained a new possession: the island of Cyprus, ceded to her by Turkey in return for a secret British promise to defend the latter if she were attacked again. By doing this he felt he had finally restored Britain's reputation in Europe after all those humiliating diplomatic climb-downs of the 1860s, and in particular Gladstone's cave-in to Russia over the remilitarization of the Black Sea in 1870. He even believed he had gone some way – as he wrote to his ambassador in Vienna in 1879 – to make Queen Victoria 'the dictatress of Europe'.[5] The 'jingoes' – the term was actually coined during the Eastern crisis – loved it. So did the dictatress.

Nevertheless, Disraeli's triumph was short-lived. It came to almost nothing even in the short run. He lost the next election to Gladstone, who almost immediately set about caving in again, as we shall see: in South Africa, the Sudan, and even Ireland (though he held on in Afghanistan). Over on the Continent Bismarck recovered. His *Dreikaiserbund* re-formed in 1881. The following year Britain bombarded and occupied Egypt, which in effect meant that she had switched her bet in the near eastern stakes from Salisbury's no-hoper to a horse which at least looked as if it could run. All Disraeli's achievements ended either in tatters, or else (like Cyprus) merely burdens to her, of no positive benefit.

Of course Disraeli's own defeat in 1880, and his death a year later, had something to do with this. No one else in the Conservative government had

his flair, or even his commitment to the strategy he had chosen. We have
seen how lukewarm Derby and Salisbury were towards it, for practical reasons; others – like the colonial secretary, Lord Carnarvon, who resigned
over the issue – were positively against it on Christian grounds. But it was
not simply a matter of personalities. The fact that his policy needed someone as brilliant as Disraeli to sustain it is significant in itself. The reason
was that it ran right across the grain of all Britain's most vital national interests at that time, which were mainly commercial, and far too vulnerable to
be put at risk merely in order to assert national pride. Britain was a shopkeeper nation, with a shopkeeper's priorities. Picking fights with the local
gentry over matters of sheer hubris was not one of them.

II

The nature of Britain's underlying weakness in the world after the mid-
1870s is very easily stated. She was over-extended. That is to say, her
interests were spread much more widely in the world than it was comfortable for her to defend. The reasons for this are instructive. They also
underline the intractability of the problem, which was not to be solved
simply either by contracting her interests, or by committing more to their
defence.

At the root of the problem lay the fact that when Britain had extended
her interests originally, it had been into a virtual power vacuum, in which
she had few powerful competitors or enemies. It was then that she built up
her network of international (and especially extra-European) trade, on
which she very soon came to *depend* to a far greater extent than any other
country depended on its overseas trade. She was able to do this firstly
because of her early start as an industrial nation, ahead of all her rivals; and
secondly because most of her potential rivals were too distracted – by revolutions, for example, and civil wars, and the business of forging themselves
into nation states – to have much time or energy for the world outside. This
meant that Britain was able to achieve her expansion with only the minimum of force. This was important to her for a reason that has been spelled
out already: force cost money, which had to be raised from taxes, which
ultimately fell on wealth-producers, who – the theory went – produced less
wealth, and consequently less trade, the more they were taxed. In this
somewhat roundabout and paradoxical way, defending trade also had the
effect of undermining it.

Sometimes force *had* been needed even before the 1870s, to deal with
rebellious natives, for example, and with the Russians in 1854. That was
regrettable, but not devastating, because of the confident belief many mid-
Victorians had that this kind of thing would become progressively less
necessary as liberal enlightenment spread. As other nations cottoned on to
the fact that trade benefited everyone, and benefited them more than – for

example – territorial imperialism could do, they would slowly stop pursuing policies which hampered trade, which would mean that expensive measures to defend it would no longer be required. Then Britain could trade really cheaply. The conditions would be ideal.

That was the hope that began to be dashed in the 1870s. Europe had changed a lot by then, often for the better. It had shaken itself down into a tidier state structure, for example, shed some of its grossest anachronisms, and started 'modernising'. Most of the old distractions had disappeared. This was good. But none of these developments seemed to have made the Continent very much more *liberal* than before, in the British sense of the word. Economically the main trend after 1870 was reactionary, with Continental states tending to develop their economies in narrow, nationalistic ways. There were no more Cobden treaties; only new exclusive tariffs, and the German *Zollverein*, or customs union, whose purpose was deliberately political. There were even fewer signs of progress on the diplomatic front. European states still squabbled with one another over territory, and over one piece of territory in particular – Alsace-Lorraine, which Germany had taken from France in 1870 – in a way that certainly did not lessen the likelihood of general war. They also started looking abroad for colonial conquests: especially France in north Africa and south-east Asia, partly in order to compensate her for the loss of Alsace-Lorraine. The world in general seemed to be taking a step or two backwards in the 1870s, away from the promised liberal millennium.

That presaged an uncomfortable future for Britain. It was likely in the first place to be a far more competitive one. Germany and France, in particular, were industrialising rapidly, and looking to send more of their industrial production abroad. Germany's steam-engine capacity – which was a fair rough index of the extent of any country's industrialisation in a steam-driven age – rose dramatically from 260 000 to 5 120 000 horsepower between 1850 and 1880, which still did not establish her on a par with Britain (7 600 000 h.p.), but at least now put her in the same league.[6] By 1880 she was doing nearly half as much foreign trade as Britain. France was close behind Germany (a little ahead in imports), with Austria, Belgium, the Netherlands and even Russia catching up too.[7] 'The singularity of our position has gone', observed one commentator in 1870, which was a good way of putting it; others ventured the thought that this ought to be a cause of alarm.[8] Strictly speaking it should not have been. In free-market theory everyone is supposed to gain from everyone else's prosperity, simply because competitors are customers too. Some felt, however, that this only held true if they competed fairly. In view of the Continent's recent record on free trade and protection, there were bound to be doubts over that.

This was one cause for concern. Another was political. Increasingly prosperous rivals, who had not yet grasped the connexion between prosperity and peace, for example, and were beginning to look beyond the confines of Europe to new pastures abroad, could pose threats to Britain's interests overseas which she just could not cope with without – as we have seen – grave damage to the source of her own prosperity. Russia already had an empire which abutted dangerously on to Britain's, as the events of the late 1870s had made everyone aware, and which showed no signs at all of being dissolved by the warm waters of capitalist affluence. France had also had some minor brushes with Britain in the wider world recently. Germany had not yet; but there were signs of it, with German predators nosing around the western Pacific and the African coasts suspiciously. If foreign powers started competing with Britain colonially as well as commercially – going for colonies as a matter of deliberate policy, that is, rather than stumbling into them reluctantly, which was Britain's way – it had serious implications. It had undertones of what was called 'imperialism', which at that time Britain identified with the aggressive political expansionism of the Bonapartes. In Britain's past history it was also associated with the 'colonial system', of protectionism, which no one wanted to see back. The prospect, then, was of all the major naval powers of Europe competing with one another to partition a world which Britain would have liked to see kept open for everyone to trade in, into separate empires kept for each colonial power's exclusive use. Such a development would gravely impoverish and could even ruin her: both through the trade she lost in the course of it, and through the expense of defending the trade she was able to keep.

This fundamental problem appears to have been entirely beyond Disraeli's understanding. Conservatives often like to see themselves as the only 'realists' in politics. Some historians have followed them in this. 'The right have the advantage over the left,' claims one of the latter, 'of seeing the world as it is.'[9] That was not true of Disraeli. He saw the Russian threat clearly, but *narrowly*, without taking account of its broader context, and of the reality of Britain's fundamental weakness. As a result he was cavalier with his country's interests, which could have turned out disastrously if he had been more successful in the longer term. The alternative policy – of hedging, trimming, cutting losses, even occasionally giving in – was inglorious, and bound to enrage the 'jingoes'. Nevertheless, as the next Conservative prime minister after Disraeli – and a far wiser one – put it in 1877: 'perhaps it is what suits our nation best'.[10]

III

Lord Salisbury was uncommonly far-sighted in the 1870s. Very few others in Britain – either statesmen or laypeople – saw as much to worry them in the international situation as he did. The only aspect that was beginning to cause general concern was foreign trade rivalry. This was because it was commonly supposed to be one of the factors behind what came to be known as the 'Great Depression' of the later nineteenth century, one of whose features was a sudden and spectacular drop in British exports (from £255 million to £191 million worth) between 1873 and 1879. After 1879 exports recovered, but were still pretty sluggish in their growth right to the end of the century. Prices and profits declined, and there was high unemployment in some years (1878–80, 1884–87). On the surface this seemed to indicate a certain decline in competitiveness, both in the home market, where imports rose fairly steadily, and abroad.[11] It was another possible sign of underlying weakness; though it was not an unambiguous one.

There are problems with the 'depression' of 1873–96. Some contemporaries denied it was happening at all. When a Conservative government set up a Royal Commission to inquire into it in 1885 they could not find a single Liberal to serve on it, because Liberals did not like to think it was possible for a free-market economy to become 'depressed'.[12] Whatever kind of depression it was, it certainly did not merit the adjective 'Great'. Most economic indices continued rising during the course of it: including industrial output, national income, average wages and earnings from foreign investments. The 1873–79 plunge in exports was freakish, and explained by the equally freakish little boom of 1870–73, which was a response to the short-term demand triggered by the end of the Franco-Prussian war. If that blip is disregarded, it is difficult to see any very great contrast between the 'golden years' of 1850–70 and these 'depression' years. The graph levelled off a little. There were periods of relative stagnation. Britain's economy was not expanding as fast as foreign economies were. Industry was becoming slightly less important relative to finance, which was just then beginning its long climb to the dominant position in the British economy it was later to achieve. But there was no long-term absolute decline, such as the word 'depression' normally implies.

In a way, however, that hardly mattered. What did matter was the public perception of what was going on. Roughly the same economic situation that Britain had been in during the 1850s and 1860s was now being regarded rather less sanguinely than it had been then, mainly – probably – because it was coming to seem more of a *struggle* than before. Foreign competition and diminishing profits were the outward signs of this. This may well have been the normal condition of competitive capitalism – it probably was; but the Victorians had got so used to seeing the almost fortuitously favourable conditions of the 1850s and 1860s as 'normal' that they over-reacted to this fall from that happy state when it came. In fact Britain's economic performance in the 1870s and 1880s was about what one would expect of an ordinary, mature capitalist system in the real world, as opposed to the commercial lotus land she had inhabited before. Nevertheless many people did not see it that way. All they noticed was decline. Some of that decline was due to foreign rivalry. But that begged the question: why had Britain buckled in the face of it? So began the hunt – which has lasted to the present day – for the *domestic* causes of Britain's modern deterioration as an economic power.

One favourite quarry almost from the start was the upper classes. That was not surprising. They (or many of them) had always been against the ethos of the new bourgeois age, and seldom missed a chance of letting the bourgeoisie know it, often unkindly. This rankled with the likes of Richard Cobden, for example, who as early as 1865 thought he could detect a recrudescence of what he called 'the spirit of feudalism... in the midst of the antagonistic development of the age of Watt, Arkwright, and Stephenson'.[13] He may have been right; though the problem had always been there to some extent. It was the price to be paid for allowing the upper classes to keep their heads. While they did, many of their old traditional values were bound to remain attractive to those 'beneath' them, either for bad reasons – like snobbery – or for good. From the beginning the phenomenon was noticed and remarked upon whereby successful entrepreneurs became dissatisfied with the usual fruits of entrepreneurial success – mainly money – and started hankering after the higher social status that was still associated with the aristocracy and gentry. Thomas Love Peacock has an example in *Crotchet Castle* (1831): Ebeneezer MacCrotchet, who we are told was 'ambitious of founding a family, and of allying himself with nobility', and to this end would 'throw away thousands for a gewgaw' – a gaudy trifle – in a most unbusinesslike way.[14] MacCrotchet – under a hundred other names – was a real historical phenomenon.[15] The drawback to his kind of conduct was obvious. It diverted both entrepreneurial energy and capital into unproductive channels, in ways that were bound to be detrimental to the generation of wealth.

Apparently this got worse in the 1870s. One of the villains of the piece was the public schools. They had undergone a revolution just before, chiefly in the direction of cleaning up their previous reputation for anarchy and immorality, and as a result had become attractive to the middle classes for the first time. This was their great growth period, with all the existing schools expanding, and new ones being founded (including one or two famous ones) to take the overspill. They were the seminaries for the newly affluent bourgeoisie; the criticism that is sometimes made of them, however, is that they did not inseminate them with bourgeois values, but with the rival 'feudal' ones. In at one end went the sons of the nineteenth century's thrusting entrepreneurs; out at the other came superior young snobs who turned up their noses at solid mercenary endeavour, and wasted their lives instead on unproductive occupations like politics, public service, colonial government or the Church. Hence – according to one fashionable school of thought – Britain's subsequent economic decline.

In fact it was almost certainly less simple than this. The public schools were probably responding to a demand. That is what one would expect in an educational 'free market', which is what the late Victorians had. People wanted the education they provided, because it led on to jobs which really did exist. The country still needed governors, bureaucrats, colonial rulers and (arguably) priests. Indeed, it needed some of them rather more than before. More aspects of life were coming within the ambit of the state; the civil service and local government were growing; the empire was expanding and looking for men to police and run it. Richard Cobden once claimed that this latter development was *caused* by the pressure from the upper classes for jobs of this type, but that is plainly ludicrous. None of this extension of the state came about as the result of a surplus of public-school-educated paternalists. The schools were simply reflecting contemporary society. The task therefore is to account for the demand for paternalists, not the supply.

The upper classes may have been merely a scapegoat. They diverted attention away from another and more unnerving possibility: which was that liberal capitalism was simply not working as it should. That was certainly true in one sense. Under liberal capitalism the state, in nearly all its forms, was supposed to wither away, as people saw how much better off materially they were without it. That was clearly not happening. Abroad it was proving unexpectedly difficult to persuade foreign countries of the advantages to them of unfettered trade, and of the harm that would be done to that trade – and consequently to themselves – if they allowed nationalistic or imperialistic motives to intervene. At home people were more sensible; but many of them were finding their free-market faith slipping just a little, as they contemplated the obduracy of the problem of poverty even in a free society, for example; and then later this alarming apparent tendency of industrial and commercial profits to fall. It was these considerations that put pressure on governments to intervene more, which enlarged the state, and which consequently created the need for more state employees.

Of course these problems may have been simply temporary. In that case they did not need to do any serious harm to liberal capitalism's ultimate prospects. Foreign states would come to their senses in the end. Profits would recover at home. The 'trickle-down' effect would reach the poor eventually. Then the state could recede again; and presumably the public schools would either adapt to the new market situation, or else go to the wall. That was a reasonable position to take in the 1870s. There was no compelling reason – nothing so very terrible happening in Britain or the world recently, for example – to shake a really committed free market ideologue out of his beliefs.

For those who were less firm in their faith, however, the pressures and responses of the 1870s had highly unsettling implications. If the trends of the later 1870s turned out to be permanent, it could mean one of two things. One was that there was a serious flaw at the heart of the capitalist system. Capitalism was not being welcomed with open arms because it was not, in fact, good for everyone. People – some people, at any rate – were reasonable to reject it. That was not a widely held belief at this time, but it did chime in with the ideas of one or two contemporary maverick economists: like Marx and the later Mill, whom we have met already;[16] and the Manchester-based economist Stanley Jevons, who was working in the 1860s to undermine the classical labour theory of value. Each of these men in different ways questioned whether, in some respects, free marketism actually *worked*. The broad argument was that it might in some circumstances, and at a certain *stage*, but that it became less and less successful as time went on. The 'Great Depression' could be read as an augury of this. If so, then the ramifications were dire.

The alternative, however, was scarcely less so. Even if the sceptics were mistaken, and the free market could be counted on to work perfectly for ever, it was unnerving that more people in the world had not jumped to this yet. They should have done. The health and even the survival of the system depended on it. Certainly its association with political liberalism depended on it. The idea had originally been that capitalism could afford to be liberal because eventually no one would want to challenge its obvious veracity, and hence pose a political threat. Consequently they could be left politically free. If more and more people did come to challenge it, as they seemed likely to do in the 1870s, and then began doing in a serious way in the 1880s, it created a different situation entirely. It posed a dilemma.

Something had to give. Either one had to compromise: chip away at the edges of the free-market system, as Britain had begun doing on the domestic front recently; or one had to try to force the system on people regardless. For a Victorian liberal this was obviously a deeply unattractive choice. Each alternative involved betraying a firmly held conviction. Either you compromised your economic liberalism, or you found yourself employing illiberal political means. There was the further complication that if you did the latter it would eventually – because of the expense – react adversely on the economic liberalism too. The two sorts of liberalism no longer seemed to be mutually supportive. It was at this point, in fact, that the first hairline fissure between them began to appear.

Part II
A Great Parting of the Waters
(1881–1910)

Chapter 7

Home to Roost
(1881–87)

I

On Saturday, 26 March 1881 Queen Victoria, who had been at Windsor for the past three weeks, prepared to board the royal train back to London. This was not unusual. What was unusual was that 15 minutes before her train left, another train looking very much like the royal one, but empty apart from the driver and fireman, made the same journey from Windsor to Paddington. One assumes that the crew were volunteers, and well paid, for the purpose of the empty train was to make sure that if there was a bomb on the line it would not harm the Queen.[1] If there had been a bomb (and there turned out not to be), it would probably have been the work of Irish-American Fenians.

The authorities' precautions were reasonable. There had already been a number of Fenian outrages earlier in the year. On 14 January, for example, a bomb had exploded in the meat store of Salford barracks, killing a boy and gravely injuring a woman who were passing by. Shortly before the Queen's happily uneventful train journey from Windsor, on the evening of 16 March, another bomb had been discovered in a window of the Mansion House in London by a woman who spotted the flickering glow of its fuse. She called the night watchman, who bravely pulled the fuse out.[2] Another of the Fenians' targets was rumoured to be Windsor Castle itself. On 10 February, the *Annual Register* tells us,

> Two strangers, supposed to be Irish, called at the cottage of Mrs Blay, in Lammas-avenue, Windsor, and asked which was the east or south side of the cavalry barracks. She said that she could not tell them, and one of them then asked, 'Will you allow me to leave this in your washhouse till we can call for it?' and placed upon the ground a bag containing something like a 4½ gallon cask. He added that she must not be inquisitive or

interfere with the bag. She refused, and they then asked if she knew where they could find an empty house to stay in till it got dark, as they were strangers there. After asking for some matches, which they did not obtain, both left the cottage, one of the strangers carrying away the cask on his shoulder, under his cape. The police and the military were informed of the incident, and every effort was made to trace the men, but nothing has since been heard of their movements. The Queen was not at Windsor but at Osborne, but she was expected to return a few days subsequently.[3]

If that story is true, it may indicate why the Fenian campaign was not more successful than it was. But it was clearly something that had to be taken seriously.

These were relatively trivial events, but indicative of some important changes that had taken place in the tenor of British life recently. Thirty years before, when the Queen had made that journey from Buckingham Palace to Hyde Park to open the Great Exhibition there, very few people had seriously feared for her safety. But now they were bound to. These were violent times. Irish violence was new to Britain, but had been plaguing Ireland herself for years. On 6 May 1882 the chief secretary for Ireland and his under-secretary, Lord Frederick Cavendish and Thomas Burke, were stabbed to death while walking in Dublin's Phoenix Park by members of an Irish secret revolutionary society called the 'Invincibles'. There were renewed Fenian outrages on the British mainland in 1883–85, whose targets included the Houses of Parliament, the Tower of London and the hind quarters of the lions in Trafalgar Square.[4] The lions were the only ones of these to escape.

Abroad things were no better. In June 1878 the German Kaiser was the target of an assassination attempt by a socialist, Karl Nobiling, which laid him low for two or three months with more than 30 small shot wounds in his face, head, arms and back. He survived.[5] Tsar Alexander II of Russia was less fortunate, perishing horribly after a bomb was hurled at him by 'nihilists' in a street in St Petersburg on 13 March 1881. In July the same year President Garfield of America was shot at in Washington by Charles Guiteau, a lawyer, for a reason which seems to have been political, if obscure. He died from his wounds six months later.[6] Assassinations in foreign countries had used to be disregarded as of no relevance to Britain, because of her superior liberalism, which innoculated her from such things; but no longer. The United States was not one of your backward Continental tyrannies, and even Alexander II was liberal by Russian standards. Then there were the Irish. Britain might still not be quite as vulnerable as the worst foreign autocracies; but she could no longer be regarded as immune.

II

Bombs and guns and knives were of course not typical of British political life in the 1880s. Only a tiny number of people resorted to them: the most irreconcilable of the malcontents, or the most mentally deranged. Nevertheless they could not be dismissed out of hand as simply isolated acts of criminality or madness. They were also symptomatic of an uneasy political situation underneath.

It was most uneasy in Ireland. That had nothing to do with the Fenians, who were little more than an irritant. On the whole they were treated rather lightly by the British public: 'It is very curious,' noted one top civil servant at the time, *à propos* of an explosion in St James's Square, 'how calmly people take these outrages as matters of course!'[7] Certainly no one felt 'terrorised'. The real Irish threat to the government lay not there, but in the much more effective popular campaign that was being waged in Ireland itself to refuse what were regarded as 'unfair' rents to landlords, and protect tenants who were threatened with eviction as a result. That agitation grew fierce around 1879–80. In September 1880 Captain Charles Boycott, Lord Erne's land agent in County Mayo, found himself suddenly deprived of servants, labourers, and even the services of shopkeepers, blacksmiths and the like, in an impressive demonstration of tenant strength from which the verb 'to boycott' derives. That was highly effective. There were also mass demonstrations, and a few murders. The government responded with 'coercion' and arrests. But that merely added to the long-term problem. It did not make for a happy union between Britain and Ireland. 'We all know,' wrote the Home Secretary, Sir William Vernon Harcourt, to Gladstone in December 1883, '...that we hold Ireland by *force and by force alone.*'[8] For a Liberal, that was an shameful confession to have to make.

In mainland Britain the situation was not so serious; but there were signs of a similar sense of alienation there too. One was the re-birth of socialism. The British 'Social Democratic Federation' (*social* democratic to distinguish its ideology from that of simple *political* democracy) was founded in June 1880 by H.M. Hyndman, a Cambridge graduate and journalist who had been converted to socialism by reading Marx's *Kapital*. It was the first significant native socialist party in Britain for 30 years, and probably the only one ever to be headed by a former county cricketer.[9] The Fabian Society, which is generally regarded as more 'moderate' but included nationalisation without compensation as one of its policy planks, began life four years later, in 1884. Neither was ever a mass movement, or anything approaching one; but they both exerted an influence disproportionate to their numbers.

This was because they clearly touched a chord. There was a great deal of working-class distress at this time. Some of it was retailed to the middle classes in 1883 in a famous pamphlet by Andrew Mearns, a Congregationalist minister, called *The Bitter Cry of Outcast London*. That described in graphic terms a visit he had made to the 'pestilential rookeries... reeking with poisonous and malodorous gases' and 'swarming with vermin', in which the poorest had to live.[10] It was also at around this time that William Booth's Salvation Army was mobilised, to provide both spiritual and material succour for this under-class. A little later the researches of the shipowner Charles Booth (no relation) in London's east end revealed for the first time the extent of the problem of poverty, even among those with jobs. Charles Booth had begun his great statistical survey of the *Life and Labour of the People of London* (1889–1903) in order to be able to refute what he regarded as Hyndman's wildly exaggerated claim that a quarter of London lived in poverty; only to find, to his discomfort, that the true figure was nearer a third. Booth's discomfort arose mainly from his humanitarian feelings. Even for the more stony-hearted, however, poverty on this scale could give pause for thought. A follower of Booth's, the chocolate manufacturer Benjamin Seebohm Rowntree, whose *Poverty: A Study of Town Life* (1901) extended the latter's methods to York, suggested that 'no civilisation can be sound or stable which has at its base this mass of stunted human life'.[11] People as poor as this clearly had no stake in society. That made them a likely source of danger to it.

Listening to the socialists was one step towards this. And listen the working classes did. They may not have become card-carrying socialists themselves in large numbers, but they could always be counted on to give the new creed a sympathetic ear. This became increasingly so in the mid-1880s, when the socialists – partly because they were refused halls to speak in – began holding meetings out of doors. The meetings got steadily larger, especially after the police started trying to stop them, so that 50 000 or 60 000 became a regular gathering in Dod Street, Limehouse – a favourite venue – by the autumn of 1885. Many of them saw skirmishes, which led to arrests. Then on 8 February 1886, during a very hard winter of heavy unemployment, the inevitable full-scale riot broke out in Trafalgar Square when two rival political demonstrations – one protectionist, the other socialist – met head on. After the demonstration a part of the crowd went on the rampage in the west end of London, looting shops and hurling paving stones at gentlemen's clubs, apparently because the gentlemen were leaning out of the windows jeering at them. That was called 'Black Monday'. 'Bloody Sunday' followed on 13 November 1887 in the same place, when a procession of unemployed who had marched from Clerkenwell was charged by police and a battalion of Grenadier Guards. Three men were killed, and about 200 more injured. Nothing quite like this had been seen since Chartist times. The 1866 Hyde Park demonstration came nearest to it: but that had been quickly defused, by a simple dose of parliamentary reform. These new rioters did not look as though they would be so easily bought off.

There were no more serious unemployed riots after 1887. One of the reasons for this was an upturn in trade, which cut the rate of unemployment dramatically. But it did not remove the danger. In the first place it was obvious that riots could return if there were ever another slump. Secondly, *employed* malcontents could be just as menacing as out-of-work ones. Instead of taking to the streets they organised in trade unions, to exploit the advantages which economic prosperity invariably brings to organised labour. (Trade unions are always more powerful at times of high employment, when their bargaining power is greatest.) The later 1880s saw the rise of what was called the 'new' (or unskilled) unionism, and some spectacular strikes. The threat had not come to an end, but merely changed tacks.

As if all this was not enough, Britain was also faced with crises abroad. There were two major ones in the early 1880s. The first was in South Africa, where her new colony of the Transvaal asserted its independence and defeated a British military force at the battle of Majuba Hill in February 1881. That was a shock. The second came in September 1881, when Egypt's national leader Arabi Pasha ousted a puppet khedive who had been forced on her two years earlier by her French and British creditors. Both these reverses threatened some vital British interests. One important one was Britain's sea routes to India and the east, which passed through Egypt (at Suez) and around southern Africa. In other words, they put at risk her *trade*.

At the same time Britain was suddenly confronted by pressure from Germany overseas. After haughtily disclaiming any desire for colonies for years – 'I will have no colonies,' Bismarck had said in 1871; 'For Germany to possess colonies would be like a poverty-stricken Polish nobleman acquiring a silk sable coat when he needed shirts'[12] – he suddenly started grabbing them in handfulls. By 1886 Germany had annexed South-west Africa, the Cameroons, Togoland, Tanganyika, north-eastern New Guinea and dozens of smaller Pacific islands, in one of the fastest imperial snatches in history. That also could be regarded as menacing.

The most worrying factor, however, was the way all these crises *converged*. This contrasted markedly with the apparent lull of the decade or so before, when at least the problems had lined up behind one another to attack Britain in turn, and the domestic scene had on the whole been pretty calm throughout. Now, in the early 1880s, that had changed. All the blows were falling together: the land war in Ireland, Fenian terrorism in Britain, a resurgent socialism, popular riots, colonial rebellion, German rivalry; all set against a general background of trade stagnation and unemployment.

This compounded the danger. Harcourt gave an example, in a letter he wrote to the Queen just after leaving office in June 1885. It was about Ireland, whose situation, he wrote, was 'dark and dangerous', and – worse still – had repercussions elsewhere.

> It affects not only our domestic condition but our foreign relations. States unfriendly to us calculate on this source of internal weakness. They know what we know: that the condition of the Irish question, especially having regard to the Fenian organisation in the United States, makes a foreign war for England a danger so great as to render it practically impossible.[13]

That could have been said of any of Britain's other problems in the early 1880s. Crises could not be isolated. They had knock-on effects. Statesmen had to bear this in mind, when responding to any of them.

III

Why did all this happen *then*? One reason was sheer bad luck. Another was the fact that the Liberals were now in power. The Irish and the Transvaalers, for example, undoubtedly calculated that they were more likely to wrest concessions from them than from the Tories, and planned their tactics accordingly. But it would be wrong to put all or even most of the blame on the new government. These crises had been gestating for ages. They were the culmination of a much longer historical development. What was happening now, in fact, was that some of liberal Britain's oldest chickens were coming home to roost.

We have met these chickens already. They were the mid-Victorian free-range variety, who had grown fat by foraging all over the farmyard in the 1850s and 1860s, with only very weak fences to protect them from the foxes who were then too busy bickering among themselves to notice them, and seemingly unaware – because of their belief that other animals were bound to behave like chickens once they saw the sense in it – of the potential danger to them once the foxes had sorted out their differences and begun to notice the holes in the fence. Once that happened, as it did in the 1870s and 1880s, it was too late. Britain had already become too dependent on free trade overseas. She could not withdraw without depriving her economy of vital markets. She could not defend those markets adequately without undermining her economy at its heart. The problem was fundamentally insoluble, once the original liberal solution to it – the hypothesis that enlightenment would spread and convince everyone of the virtues of free market capitalism, so that Britain would not have to defend her corner of it – collapsed.

It was this collapse that was at the root of most of her problems. Neither abroad nor at home were the assumptions of liberal capitalism being accepted as they should. Most of the crises of the early 1880s involved challenges to those assumptions of one kind or another. The Irish, South African and Egyptian revolts, for example, did. They were – at least in embryo – *nationalist* uprisings, which dented the liberal capitalist notion that economic *inter*nationalism would soon supersede all that. Two of these revolts also took more direct issue with capitalism. The Irish Land League was against the idea of an 'economic rent', which of course lies at the heart of any free market; for which it was branded at the time as 'communist'.[14] Arabi's rebellion in Egypt was basically a revolt of debtors against those who owned their assets. Both, therefore, can be regarded as anti-capitalist reactions, at least in part.

The same was true nearer home. The Trafalgar Square riots were implicitly anti-capitalist; the SDF and Fabian Society, of course, overtly so. There was little sign here of that spread of liberal enlightenment the mid-Victorians had so confidently expected – and actually seen something of in their own time – as the demonstrable benefits of the free-market system trickled down. Free marketists were in retreat, as the socialists now started gaining ground. It was this trend which made things appear more ominous – or promising – than perhaps they really were. Socialist societies might be small, but until very recently they had been nothing. 'Few movements surely,' wrote William Morris at the end of the decade, 'have made so much progress during this short time in one way or another as Socialism has done.'[15] They were on the up. That gave them confidence. Another morale-booster was the knowledge they had that they were – quite simply – bound to triumph in the end. This, said Morris again, was what Marx and Engels had taught them: 'that, whether Socialism be desirable or not, it is at least inevitable'.[16] That is always nice to know.

This represented quite a reversal. In the past it had been the economic liberals who had thought they were on history's side, and drawn strength from this. Now that strength was ebbing away. Doubts were creeping in, and spreading. They reached the Congregationalist church, for example, in 1885, when after a heated discussion its annual assembly passed a resolution which bade Christians remember that 'the so-called laws of trade and economics' – 'so-called', note – were 'not the only rules which should direct the transactions of manufacturers, traders, labourers and purchasers'.[17] There were other straws in the same wind. George Auldjo Jamieson, a businessman and member of the 1886 Commission of Inquiry into the 'Depression', maintained in a minority report that 'No system of human politics or economics can be *absolutely* true; it can be true only *relatively* to the circumstances and conditions of the society to which it is applied.'[18] To an orthodox free trader that was rather like saying that gravity only worked sometimes, and that in certain situations you might have to fit suction pads to your shoes.

This kind of heresy was becoming more common. It did not always take a socialist form. Another ideology undergoing something of a renascence in the 1880s was protectionism, organised from 1881 onwards in a pressure group with the seductive title of the *Fair* (as opposed to Free) Trade League. Fair Traders blamed 'unfair' foreign commercial practices – tariffs, bounties and the like – for most of Britain's current economic ills. It was a plausible point, and one that affected British workers as well. Unfair competition was undercutting their jobs. That was what one of the founders of the League told his own workers in 1891: that 'It is the foreign blacklegs, and not the home, you have to face.'[19] It followed, of course, that fair trade would also be a useful counter to socialism, if it were true that it was *free* trade that was creating the conditions in which socialism grew. That may have been one of the motives for the attack the SDF launched on the Fair Traders in Trafalgar Square on 8 February 1886, which was the spark that fired the 'Black Monday' riot of that day.

The socialists won that skirmish. By the end of the 1880s they also seemed to be on their way to winning the much more important battle for people's minds. 'Socialism' was no longer a dirty word. Politicians vied to appropriate it either for themselves, or for their champions. This was a sign of the times. 'Why, sir,' a Tory MP told an audience in Exeter in 1889, 'the greatest Socialist (in its true sense) of this century was that great and illustrious leader to whom our party must always feel in bonds of deepest gratitude – Mr Disraeli.'[20] A few years earlier that would surely have been something to keep quiet about.

All this – the reaction, the heresies – was worrying for liberals whichever way they looked at it. The worst way of looking at it was to suspect that it might indicate some flaw in the system itself. Perhaps free-market capitalism was not all it was cracked up to be. Maybe its benefits did not trickle down, or not to the extent that had been hoped. That would explain and indeed might be felt to justify the resistance to it of those waiting at the end of the pipe for the drops to dribble out. Another possibility was that the market was not free enough yet for one to be able to tell: still hampered by protectionism abroad, for example, and various restrictive practices (like those associated with trade unions) at home. That would mean that some of the pipes could still be clogged up, which was another possible explanation for the trickle's not getting through. A third option was that the system *was* working, but that people were too stupid to see it: too stupid, that is, to be able to make a rational calculation of their own best interests. That could either be because of some deficiency in their mental capacities, or perhaps because of a tendency to be gulled by plausible agitators. These were all somewhat unsettling alternatives. A less unsettling one was that this was just a bad patch, a temporary squall, which Britain merely had to battle through as best she could before sailing into the calm seas and balmy breezes of all those old-fashioned liberal expectations again. That was reassuring, because it did not undermine any liberal assumptions fundamentally. Unfortunately, however, it also came to look less and less credible as time went by.

Liberals, however, were not too downhearted. Few of them accepted that liberal capitalism was doomed, or even at crisis point. If they suspected it was flawed, then it was only at the edges. It could be preserved – not pristine, but in essentials – with a few modifications here and there. In order to achieve that they could not afford to be too dogmatic; but then most of them were becoming less and less inclined to dogmatism in any case. This was certainly true of their gurus – economists like W.S. Jevons and Alfred Marshall, and the philosopher T.H. Green – whose position was coming to be that though free-market forces were preferable to state intervention generally, they should not be assumed to be so in every situation, and that if a good case could be made out for state intervention in a particular area in terms of broader liberal aims, like freedom and opportunity, then it should not automatically be ruled out for ideological reasons. Liberal capitalism, that is, was coming to be less a creed than a preference: a matter of choice rather than of faith, not to be rejected, by any means, but supported now – and by implication able to be modified – on *pragmatic* grounds. This gave liberals room to manoeuvre, and so possibly to save themselves.

Adapt and survive: that was the only way out. It was also fraught with difficulties. The problem was the choices that had to be made: *where* to adapt, compromise, give way, intervene; which were bound to arouse controversy in the liberals' own ranks, and indeed – as we shall see – often did. Many of the choices touched deep liberal principles, especially in Ireland, where the most drastic compromises with what had always been understood to be fundamental economic liberties were made. Others involved national interests abroad, where three different conflicting elements – principle, patriotism, expediency – had to be juggled, often in more than one part of the world at once, with the result that in some cases one or perhaps two of them dropped and broke. Ministers were sometimes charged with making bad choices from all these alternatives; but in many instances there were no good ones to be made. This was not their fault, but the result of the situation they had inherited, from the 'golden years' of British liberal capitalism, which were what had got them into this mess.

Chapter 8

Gladstone at Bay
(1880–85)

I

The man who found himself saddled with all these choices on 23 April 1880, when his second government took over from Disraeli's, was William Ewart Gladstone. He was well past retirement age (or would have been if such a concept had existed in the nineteenth century), and indeed had already retired from political life more than once. He said he liked retirement, when he could immerse himself in his hobbies, which were theology and the Greek classics, and had only returned to the leadership of the Liberal party reluctantly, out of a sense of duty. That was the kind of man he was. Not everyone at the time appreciated his high-mindedness, or even credited it. 'His hypocrisy makes me sick', was Lord Salisbury's reaction – a not unusual one – in 1885.[1] Bismarck too suspected him of cant. 'It is very convenient,' he once said of him, 'to have principles which can be made to fit in with and justify your conduct.'[2] What probably annoyed them both was that Gladstone's high mindedness did not stop him being practical. When a thing needed doing, in the merely material interest of his country, he did it. Generally one expects more of high-minded people than that.

His practicality arose from his genuine feeling for what really were the material interests of his country then, which was far more highly developed than we have seen Disraeli's was. This was despite his age (he was 70 at the beginning of 1880), which may in fact have been an asset, because it meant that his political career stretched back to the time when those interests had first crystallised. Another factor was his mercantile background (his father had been a prosperous Liverpool trader), the influence of which seems not to have been entirely erased from him by his education at Eton and Oxford, and by his Tory political origins. His transfer to the Liberal party had come *via* Peel's free trade faction of the Conservatives, and his early ministerial reputation rested on his progressive reductions of import duties and income tax in two spells as Chancellor of the Exchequer between 1852 and 1866. In foreign policy he had tended to be a non-interventionist, though not in every case. All this placed him solidly in the middle of the strongest current of British politics in the later nineteenth century: the one, that is, which was most responsive to the broad economic imperatives that ran beneath.

In the 1880s those imperatives were shifting slightly, in ways that have already been described. Gladstone was responsive to the shifts too. This was his other great political asset: his *flexibility*, which again belied his years. He was not an opportunist. Opportunists are those who sail with a prevailing eddy, for short-term political advantage. Disraeli was an opportunist. Gladstone, by contrast, stuck with the underlying currents, and only turned when they did, because his boat had a deeper draught. He did not change tack often, and never capriciously or cynically. When he did so it was only after long and agonising thought, and doubtless also a good deal of prayer: for he was a deeply religious man. This gave to his policies a solidity which was not always politically successful, in the face of a more fickle electorate, but which truly reflected the needs of his time. The effect of it was to enable him to navigate his ship between rocks which might easily have scuppered both more stubborn and more impulsive politicians, and with very little damage to it apart from some rather ugly scratches to the exterior paintwork.

II

Gladstone never rated paintwork – the outward appearance of things, reputation, prestige – very highly. Others, however, did. This accounts for the obloquy his policies attracted in certain quarters, especially with regard to foreign and imperial affairs, where Disraeli had so recently stimulated in some people, at any rate, an appetite for 'prestige'. Gladstone could not satisfy that appetite. His view of it was the traditional British liberal one. Prestige was a chimera. You could not eat it, get energy from it, make it into things.[3] It was not worth fighting over. Almost nothing, in fact, was worth fighting over, including even territory, which was at the bottom of most wars at this time. Wars – whatever their pretexts – diminished wealth; none of the objects for which they were fought ever increased wealth; all nations' best interests were served by free and peaceful trade *across* territorial boundaries, which made the existence of those boundaries unimportant, and so their disposition a matter of indifference too. Considerations like these – based on first economic principles, coupled with Britain's situation as a great commercial power pre-eminently – were bound to make any military victory essentially hollow, whatever it might do for a nation's self-esteem, and for its reputation among other similarly military-minded powers.

Hence Gladstone's abject surrenders, as his critics saw them, on a number of international issues of the day. The two worst were in South Africa and in the Sudan. In South Africa Gladstone responded to a humiliating military defeat at the hands of a rebel Transvaal republic in February 1881 not by going in with a larger force to bring the Transvaalers to heel, which would have been the prestigious course of action, but by caving in. The 'South African Republic' was told it had won. In the Sudan the situation was slightly different. Britain took over control of Egypt in 1882. Egypt was *de jure* ruler of the Sudan. The Sudan, however, was claiming independence under a fanatical Muslim leader known as the 'Mahdi'. Gladstone thought Egypt could not afford to run the Sudan, and so did nothing to back her claim. He did do one thing, however. In 1884 under pressure from the press he sent out General Charles Gordon, who was a bit of a fanatic himself, though on the Christian side, to rescue an Egyptian Army detachment trapped in Khartoum. Gordon exceeded his orders, tried to save the whole town from the Mahdi, and got heroically slaughtered as a result. Gladstone was consequently much vilified back home for not rescuing *him*. In fact he had sent out a second force to do so, but it had dawdled, and so got there too late. But that was not taken into account.

Together with his proposals for Ireland, of which more anon, these events branded Gladstone as what today would be called a 'wimp'. The rationale behind them was sound, and consistent with Britain's interests at that time. Britain had no *moral* claim to the South African Republic, and could expect no material advantage from ruling it that would justify the outlay involved in trying. (This was before it was realised that there were massive deposits of gold there, which were bound to colour things later on.) This was even more true of the Sudan. Even if that had not been so, there was a general principle involved here. Gladstone had fought the 1880 election partly on the platform that interference in the affairs of other countries was wrong in any case. Nations were equal. 'You may sympathise with one nation more than another. Nay, you must sympathise in certain circumstances with one nation more than another.'[4] But that did not give you *carte blanche* to intervene. It was a matter of fundamental national *rights*. It was also, he might have added, a matter of convenience – even possibly of survival – for Britain. Britain could not *afford* to intervene widely. She was not equipped to. If she tried to take on the necessary equipment, it would be a drain on her wealth; more so even than in the past, because of the huge continental European military forces with which she would now have to compete. She was already dangerously over-stretched. It would not do to pull the elastic out tighter still. Hence Gladstone's much vaunted 'anti-imperialism', which was one of the main points of difference between him and his arch-rival at this time.

There is a problem here. Gladstone was proud of his resistance to imperialism, in the usual (aggressive) sense of that word. He attacked it when he thought he saw it in Disraeli, especially in the case of Afghanistan. He abjured it in South Africa, and then a little later in the Sudan. His Irish policy, in the eyes of his critics, was equally anti-imperialist, in almost the most crippling way possible. But there were inconsistencies. Sudan was only a problem for him in 1884 because of his takeover of its formal suzerain, Egypt, two years before. What on earth was an anti-imperialist doing bombarding Alexandria, and then occupying and governing the country, as Gladstone did in July 1882? Later on he did much the same, though less dramatically, elsewhere. North Borneo, much of New Guinea, and large chunks of eastern and southern Africa were all annexed to the British Crown during Gladstone's second ministry. This was a far bigger bag than Disraeli could claim. (His consisted of Cyprus.) And yet Disraeli was supposed to be the one who liked colonies. It was this kind of thing, of course, which gave rise to the charges against Gladstone of 'hypocrisy'.

The true explanation, however, is straighter and simpler than that. The fact is that what looks like imperialism was not imperialism at all. Gladstone certainly did not intend it as such. In the case of Egypt he saw Britain as intervening on behalf of what he called the 'Concert of Europe'. That made it all right. It was not a case of Britain going after more territory, but representing the whole European community in defence of international law. (He had taken the same view of the Crimean war.) He would have preferred France to be involved as well, but she had dropped out. That did not alter the situation. Britain was doing Europe's work for her, in rescuing Egypt from anarchy. When she had accomplished that, and restored a stable and solvent government, she would withdraw. She never annexed the country formally. It continued to be ruled by an Egyptian: not the Egyptian most other Egyptians wanted, true, but they would soon grow to love him; with the top British man there – Sir Evelyn Baring, later Lord Cromer – merely 'advising' him, especially with regard to his country's financial affairs. That was the official line.

It did not convince everyone at the time, least of all the French. Later it came to look even less plausible. This was because of the way things turned out. The longer Britain stayed in Egypt, the more she became enmeshed. Her 'puppets' depended on her presence to survive. 'Anarchy' still looked the likeliest outcome if they toppled. Her interests in Egypt – especially the Suez canal – were so vital as to make it difficult to contemplate leaving while that remained a risk. And so the impression gained ground that this – a permanent occupation – was what Britain had been after all along.

Gladstone's Egyptian adventure was a piece of naked imperialism, whose skimpy coverings – all that talk of European concerts and ultimate withdrawal – only a simpleton could fail to see through.

The same applied to Britain's other imperial acquisitions at this time. Few of them, either, were annexed outright as 'colonies'. Most went under the name of 'protectorates' or 'spheres of influence'. Many were not properly ruled by Britain at all, but were either neglected, or given over to commercial companies, 'chartered' for the purpose, to rule and exploit at the same time. With hindsight this too came to look simply like colonialism in another guise. In many ways, indeed, it was. It was imperialism *in effect*. What was missing was the full panoply of an imperial state apparatus in these countries; but it is only a very narrow definition of 'imperialism', surely, which would regard that as a necessary prerequisite. Commercial companies and even financial advisers could be as domineering as any formal colonial administration; indeed, it can be argued that they were likely to be *more* domineering than if they were restrained by certain kinds of colonial administration, as we shall see. Looked at from this perspective, Gladstone's continued professions of anti-imperialism seem hollow.

But they were genuine. There can be little doubt about this. Gladstone simply could not conceive that bringing backward countries into the embrace of the world market could be regarded as imperialism at all. This was a definite limitation on his part. It arose from his mid-nineteenth-century ideological upbringing. Freedom meant freedom to buy and sell. Tyranny – and by extension imperialism – arose when governments interfered in that process. All Gladstone's efforts in the colonial field therefore were directed to avoiding imposing governments on the countries he took over, and minimising the effects of the governments other European governments imposed elsewhere. By that means he assumed he was avoiding imperialism too.

The Berlin Africa Conference of 1884 is a good example. It is generally regarded as a crucial stage in the late-nineteenth-century European 'scramble for Africa', but so far as Britain's motives were concerned was nothing like so acquisitive and competitive as that implies. Gladstone did not mind other European countries grabbing bits of Africa in the least. When he learned that Bismarck was after colonies in West Africa he retorted: 'If Germany is to become a colonizing power, all I say is "God speed her!" She becomes our ally and partner in the execution of the great purposes of Providence for the advantage of mankind.'[5] (That must have puzzled Bismarck, who was under the impression that Britain would feel threatened by this new initiative, and may in fact have taken it partly in order to put Britain under threat.) Gladstone's line was that if other countries were willing to share the burden and cost of bringing these benighted regions into the world market, that was all to the good. The important thing was to ensure that it *was* the *world* market they brought them into, and not just a cosy little exclusive arrangement with themselves.

To this end he made it his main priority at the Berlin Conference to secure freedom of trade over the whole of the area in dispute, however it was carved up among the Powers. That became Article 1 of the Berlin Treaty which settled the issue, though not every Power kept to the letter of it subsequently.[6] Britain also gained some territory by that treaty; but not as much as she could have got if she had wanted to, and always simply in order to prevent existing British commercial or strategic interests falling into unfriendly hands. This essentially negative motivation explains her subsequent neglect of her new acquisitions. The very words 'protectorate' and 'sphere of influence' are significant in this regard. They are not the same as 'colony', and they were not meant as euphemisms for the latter. A colony is a territory occupied and ruled by a foreign power. A protectorate or sphere of influence is a territory which it is agreed cannot be occupied or ruled by any *other* foreign power. The words define a negative rather than a positive status. The difference is crucial. It was what enabled Gladstone to avoid being sucked into the contemporary 'scramble for Africa'. That at least was his own perception. He had come through the whole affair a little politically dishevelled, perhaps, but with his anti-imperialist virginity still essentially intact.

Of course he was fooling himself. He was also showing himself to be out of touch with some powerful new trends of the time. Virginity, even in Gladstone's technical sense, was beginning to lose its appeal. Imperialism was proving to have seductive charms. Among those who succumbed to them were a number of intellectuals, including two professors of history, J.R. Seeley and J.A. Froude, who both wrote influential books in the 1880s seeking to remind their countrymen of what they regarded as Britain's proud imperial past.[7] There was also pressure from other quarters. Businessmen suffering from the trade depression started looking to colonies as a way of getting them out of their difficulties.[8] Lower down in the social scale (usually) 'jingoes' hankered after the vicarious excitement a 'forward' imperial policy would provide. Gladstone was deaf to all of this. Later, when the imperialist clamour grew so loud as to drown out all other sounds, it was this which made him appear so hopelessly out of tune with the modern age.

In fact he may merely have been out of *fashion*; for despite the endorsement given to it by our two professors, it is arguable that imperialism – in their sense – has never been as solid a tradition in British history as they maintained. We shall see later how superficial a phenomenon it was even at its supposed late-nineteenth-century peak. There were good reasons for this, stemming from Britain's situation as a world-wide free-trading nation. Free trade offered the prospect of trading with everyone, at minimal expense, and so to everyone's benefit; dividing the world into empires restricted trade, at great cost, and at the risk of war. It cut right across the liberal-capitalist grain. It was bound to be unprofitable, and could be perilous. It was reasonable, therefore, for a power in Britain's position to seek to avoid it if she possibly could.

This is what Gladstone did. He thought he was succeeding, though he did not altogether, as we have seen. That was where his flexibility came in. It was forced on him by changes in the currents flowing beneath his keel: a general regression in Europe away from the free marketism which had seemed to be its destination earlier, back to the protectionism and imperialism of the past. No one could be certain yet whether this regression had set in for good. If so, then it was ominous both for the ideology of free marketism – which in its mid-nineteenth-century British form had been thought to carry within it the seeds of its own inevitable triumph – and for Britain's interests in the world. If those interests now had to be defended imperially it could be disastrous for her. This is in fact what transpired. Britain eventually collapsed under the weight of the imperial responsibilities she was forced to take on. In retrospect that might be thought to justify Gladstone's resistance to this trend in the 1880s, however hopeless that resistance really was.

III

The third of Gladstone's imperial 'surrenders' in the 1880s, after South Africa and the Sudan, was Ireland. Ireland was supposed to be an integral part of the United Kingdom, with MPs sitting in the British House of Commons, which strictly speaking made her a domestic issue rather than an imperial one; but there are also ways in which she qualified as a colony, including an increasingly vigorous 'nationalist' movement which aimed at her liberation from what it regarded as alien rule. This movement, and its repercussions, dominated Gladstone's political life from early on in the 1880s until his eventual (final) retirement in 1893.

Irish nationalism was another great disappointment for liberal capitalists. We have seen already[9] that nationalism had no place in most British liberals' intellectual baggage in the mid-nineteenth century, mainly because their ideal was a world in which national frontiers would have no great material significance. It did not matter who governed countries, so long as they governed them minimally, in which case the bonds of government would be too light to be noticed, and consequently to be perceived as an imposition. This was the way Britain thought she was governing Ireland. If anything Ireland was *over*-represented at Westminster, with slightly more MPs than its population warranted by comparison with the rest of the Kingdom.[10] Any serious civil discrimination against Irishmen that had once existed, usually on account of their Catholicism, had been legislated away long before. Even the most protestant of British governments had leant over backwards to be fair to the Irish in the field of education: subsidizing a Catholic seminary in Maynooth out of taxation, for example, and establishing a Catholic university in Ireland to rival the traditionally protestant Trinity College Dublin in 1862. There was little cause for Irish complaint. Most formal channels for advancement were open to everyone. For the rest, the economic fortunes of the country were left to the free market, unhindered in any way by British government interference; as they were, of course, in mainland Britain too.

That, however, was the root of the trouble. For liberals this was the most dispiriting thing of all. It was not British state tyranny the Irish mainly objected to, but what they saw as the effects of the precisely opposite policy of economic *laissez-faire*. Most Irish resentment against the British in the later nineteenth century originated in disputes between native tenants and their Anglo-Irish landlords, of a kind which was not unknown on the mainland – especially at this time in Scotland – but was given greater force in Ireland by the depth and extent of rural poverty there, and the way it could be harnessed to the nationalist cause. From the point of view of the dominant classes in Britain there was nothing at all wrong with the existing relationship between Irish tenants and landlords. If tenants were being evicted, it was because they could not pay the 'economic' rent for their holdings: the rent, that is, that the owners could get elsewhere. That was nature's way. Landlords had every right to maximise the profits on their property. It would be wrong – indeed tyrannical – to try to prevent them. The problem was far more intractable than those stemming from sectarian differences had been, because it touched a far deeper spiritual nerve. In the former case all the British needed to compromise was their religious convictions. What was under threat here was the principle of the free market, no less.

Gladstone was enormously exercised over this. He was not altogether happy with Britain's religious concessions to the Irish, either: in 1877 he had visited Maynooth and confided to his diary that he found it a 'saddening' experience;[11] but he could live with that. The land question was something else. Initially he allowed himself to wonder whether the Land League's campaign of non-payment of rents really was due to distress, or to 'conspiracy'. He wished the landlords would stick up for their rights more.[12] His first legislative response to the 'land war' was a new Coercion bill to whip the Irish into line. That was passed in March 1881, but only in the teeth of unprecedented parliamentary obstruction by the Irish MPs, and the severe misgivings of Gladstone's own Radicals, some of whom voted against the measure, and others (like John Bright) only went along with it reluctantly, on the understanding that coercion would not be the government's only tack.

Most Liberals, indeed, agreed that it was no solution to the problem in itself. Hence Gladstone was also forced to consider tackling the land question. That filled him with misgivings. According to one of his cabinet colleagues, Lord Carlingford, he seemed 'very averse to interference with "freedom of contract"' even while they were drafting the new legislation; and on introducing it to parliament he still insisted that in theory 'there is no country in the world which, when her social relations come to permit of it, will derive more benefit than Ireland from perfect freedom of contract in land'. At one point he wondered whether a clause might not be inserted in the bill allowing 'a future return to free contract' once the present emergency was over.[13] In the end, however, the deed was done. The new Irish Land Act was passed in August 1881, giving tenants substantial rights against their landlords, including fixity of tenure, and 'fair' rents established by a commission. Tories and even some of the more Whiggish Liberals saw it as the end of freedom as they knew it. Earl Grey (the son of the great one) accused Gladstone of 'mocking' at the 'economic laws which it has been the object of the wisest men for many ages to discover and explain'.[14] That must have made him wince.

It might have softened the blow if the Land Act had worked. In the event, however, it did not: Gladstone thought because Parnell, the nationalist leader, was determined that it should not.[15] The trouble in Ireland got worse, culmimating in the Phoenix Park murders of May 1882, and then at the beginning of 1883 spreading over into Scotland and England at the hands of the Fenians and their bombs. To counter all this Parnell was arrested and imprisoned for six months from October 1881; a new Coercion Act was passed in June 1882; and Britain's first mainland 'political' police agency for many years – the 'Special Irish Branch' – was set up, secretly, in March 1883. Liberals hated this. John Morley, a future Irish Secretary and Gladstone's biographer, called the Coercion Act 'odious'.[16] Gladstone once apparently absented himself from one of his own cabinet meetings in order to avoid finding out from his own Home Secretary what his new police spies were up to.[17] It was all very distasteful. But it had to be done.

It was this, plus political exigencies, which led Gladstone to begin contemplating a *political* solution to the Irish question in the winter of 1881–82. In April 1882 he mused to his Irish Secretary that maybe the trouble with his Land Law, and with most other efforts to conciliate Ireland over the past dozen years, was that 'every plan we frame comes to Irishmen, say what we may, as an English plan'. That – and not its demerits –

was why they rejected it. This was quite a thought. It may not seen a very remarkable one to us today; but John Morley spotted its significance. To him, it illustrated 'the depth to which the essence of political liberalism had now penetrated Mr. Gladstone's mind'.[18]

The crucial word here is 'political'. Gladstone had not been a *political* liberal heretofore. He had been a fairly typical mid-nineteenth-century *economic* one. He believed, in other words, that it did not much matter who governed people; only to what degree. We saw this in relation to his colonial policy. He also thought that, logically, this was how the 'people' should feel themselves. Now, in Ireland, he was seeing that piece of logic confounded before his eyes. People were rejecting every degree of government – minimal, interventionist, coercive, benevolent – simply because it was being imposed on them by someone else. It seemed irrational, even perverse; but it also had its bright side. It could be thought to rehabilitate 'political economy', if the only reason the Irish were rejecting *that* was atavistic national pride. There was nothing intrinsically wrong with it. Gladstone was right to persist in his theoretical defence of the 'perfect freedom of contract in land'. Perhaps this was why he continued to dwell on the political side of the Irish question, right through to December 1885, when it became known (through a 'leak' to the press by his son) that he had been won over to the policy of Irish 'Home Rule'.

IV

Gladstone may have kept true to his free market faith in his heart; but it was what he *did* that mattered, and alarmed countless of his co-religionists both in the Conservative party, and among his own Whigs. Two members of his cabinet, the Duke of Argyll and W.E. Forster, together with a junior minister, Earl Cowper, resigned over what they saw as appeasement of the Irish in 1881–82. Ordinary backbench Whigs were terribly perturbed. It was the anti-free-contract side of the new legislation that most upset them. In 1881 Earl Grey said he saw the philosophy of the French revolution behind it;[19] others, looking forward rather than back, thought *they* discerned in it the spectre of 'socialism'.[20] That was the perceived significance of the 1881 Irish Land Act, seen as it was against the background of some other highly disturbing recent trends.

Some of those trends were democratic. That was always something the Whigs had feared. Their view of the matter was that the popular will was all very well in its way, and of course had to be listened to, but was also fickle, crude and potentially dangerous, and so had to be moderated by a superior political class. That was how they saw their own role for most of the past century: restraining and channelling popular demand in Britain, so that liberal progress could be achieved in an orderly way. Now that role was threatened: by an urban electorate which seemed to be more susceptible to the Radical wing of the party, and by certain developments in party organisation – especially the emergence of what was called the 'caucus', initially in Birmingham civic politics – which were seeking to make MPs answerable to local party committees rather than to their own consciences. Gladstone tried to compensate for this, and at the same time to reassure the Whigs, by over-representing them in his first two governments. (Nine out of 15 of his 1868 cabinet were Whigs, and seven out of 14 of his 1880 one.)[21] But they still did not feel they could trust him. He had never, after all, been a Whig himself; he was a bit of a populist; and he had *convictions*, which for a Whig of the old school was almost as disagreeable as democracy was. All this worried the Whigs no end. As a result they may have exaggerated the significance of what parliament and Gladstone actually did in the domestic sphere.

Not that this was negligible. Gladstone's second government had some very real legislative achievements to its name. One was the Reform Act of 1884 (and its related Redistribution Act, passed the next year): the third of the great nineteenth century series of Reform Acts, which had the effect of increasing the electorate by 80 per cent. The Whigs did badly out of that, losing a number of what Donald Southgate calls 'biddable boroughs': small constituencies, that is, which Whigs could effectively 'buy'.[22] That was another reason for anxiety. On the other hand it was difficult for the Whigs to complain. The 1884–85 Acts were not as radical as they might have been, with plural voting retained, for example, nearly half of the adult male population still disfranchised, and women excluded, despite quite an impressive effort on their behalf. Besides, it would clearly not be good for Whigs – the successors of Lords Grey and John Russell – to be seen to be defending the late nineteenth century equivalent of 'rotten' boroughs (Southgate's 'biddable' ones), simply in order to cling on to their own seats. The other major legislative feather in Gladstone's cap in the 1880s was the Married Women's Property Acts of 1882 and 1884. The first of these gave women rights over their goods and chattels, which until then had passed automatically into their husbands' hands on marriage. The second stopped wives being regarded as 'chattels' themselves. Again, neither was a measure that any self-respecting Whig would be likely to want to be seen objecting to. Both were pretty Whiggish, in fact, in essence.

The measures they really fussed over were the ones that seemed to them to be ideologically suspect. Some of them may not seem to be that significant in retrospect; but then one needs to be sensitive to the implications that lay beneath. One such was the Employer's Liability bill of 1880, which made employers liable in certain circumstances to compensate workmen accidentally injured while in their employ. That was supposed to interfere with the former's contractual and property rights, and in a strict sense probably did. Even more tyrannical was supposed to be the Hares and Rabbits bill of the same year, which allowed tenant farmers equal rights with landowners to slaughter any small furry animals with long ears they found encroaching on their lands. That provoked a furious opposition: not on behalf of the hares and rabbits especially (though some critics did raise the question of what the working man and also poor Renard was going to do for his favourite Sunday dinner if the effect of this bill was to exterminate it), but more out of a sense of outrage at the 'radical and revolutionary tendencies of the Government in interfering with freedom of contract and trespassing on the rights of property' in this way.[23] When a supporter of the bill cited the 1870 Irish Land Act as a precedent, it did not mollify the critics one bit.[24] This was one of the reasons they had objected to Irish land reform in the first place. It was seen as an augury of the Radicals' intentions for mainland Britain too. Ireland was a kind of laboratory, for the social revolution which was to be foisted on all of them if the 'caucus' got its way. This was why they were so curiously solicitous over the question of who had the right to shoot the genus *Leporidae*.

In reality, though both the Employer's Liability Act and the Ground Game Act (as it was later re-named) undoubtedly did offend against the most rigid of free-market principles, neither was as apocalyptic as it was taken to be. The Whigs were getting things out of proportion. The reason for this was probably the *rhetoric* of their rivals, the Radicals, who did have a knack of alarming the Whigs gratuitously. The man who offended most in this regard was Joseph Chamberlain, a Birmingham caucus man, and an advocate of state intervention for social purposes, with a populist bent, and a greater contempt for the aristocratic classes than many of his fellow bourgeois had been able to hang on to in these more 'gentrified' and deferential times. (He once compared them to the biblical 'lilies of the field: they toil not, neither do they spin'; which did not go down at all well.)[25] In January 1885 he launched a strong direct attack on the 'rights of property' which was received with horror in most political circles. He then followed that up with what became known as his 'Unauthorised Programme' – unauthorised, that is, by Gladstone – which embraced, besides such extreme political measures as universal manhood suffrage and a form of federal home rule for *all* the constituent nationalities of Britain, proposals for subsidizing housing out of property taxes and death duties, and the creation of a new smallholding class in Britain on lands compulsorily purchased from some of the greater landowners. The general opinion among those landowners themselves was that this was the sheerest socialism. Chamberlain did not deny it. Instead he talked ominously of their need to pay a 'ransom' to society, in return for society's allowing them to continue to grow fat on their unearned, undeserved wealth.[26]

All this was dire. The auguries were not encouraging for strict economic liberals in 1885. Whiggery was profoundly demoralised, the Radicals cock-a-hoop. Gladstone was unreliable. Even if you credited him with more sense than Chamberlain, he was getting very old indeed now, and was universally assumed to be on the way out. Who or what would follow him no one could tell. It could be something even more Radical. In that case liberalism (the economic variety) might not be at all secure. So far it had only been eroded at the edges; but that could be the beginning of a long slide. 'If you once desert the solid ground of individual freedom,' wrote the jurist A.V. Dicey in October 1885, 'you can find no resting place till you reach the chasm of Socialism.'[27] That was the danger. One can see why the Whigs were discontented. That discontent was to have profound repercussions. The short-term ones will be the subject of the next chapter. The long-term ones will take us through almost to the end of this book.

Chapter 9

The Revolt of the Whigs
(1886)

I

1886 was a pivotal year in British history. What made it pivotal was a mass defection from the ranks of the Liberal party in the late spring and summer. It is usually called the 'Home Rule' split, but few historians believe that Irish Home Rule was the only or even the main reason for it. The men who seceded were a motley bunch, with a complex array of motives. Most of them were on the Whiggish wing of the party, and had been growing progressively more disenchanted with a whole range of Liberal policies for years. Gladstone's Home Rule proposal was the occasion for the final crisis, but the significance of it runs wider and deeper than that.

What happened, in a nutshell, was this. Gladstone's second government – divided, demoralised, and deserted by its erstwhile Irish Nationalist allies, who had lost patience with it – was defeated in the Commons over a minor issue in June 1885, and resigned. After a short interval of minority Conservative rule the Liberals won the ensuing election in November, but with the Nationalists holding the balance. Meanwhile Gladstone had come out for Home Rule, with the result that several members of his second ministry refused to serve in his third. He pushed ahead regardless with a Home Rule bill, which the Commons threw out on its second reading in June 1886 by a majority of 343 votes to 313. Among the 343 were 93 Liberals,[1] the bulk of whom then joined with their fellow anti-Home Rulers in the Lords, led by the Marquess of Hartington (elder brother of the Phoenix Park victim Lord Frederick Cavendish), to hive off and form the 'Liberal Unionist' party. In the next election, in July 1886, the Liberals lost heavily, with 191 seats to the Conservatives' 317, the Liberal Unionists' 77 and the Nationalists' 85. That ushered in a period of Conservative and Unionist hegemony which – apart from a brief ineffective interlude in 1892–94 – lasted for 20 years.

These events were significant in two main ways. In the first place – and most obviously – they delayed self-government in Ireland for 34 years. On the other hand, even if Gladstone had been able to rustle up the 30 extra votes he needed to pass his bill in the Commons, it is certain that the Lords would have rejected it: which makes that effect less drastic than it seems. Secondly, these events split the Liberal party grievously. The Unionist group never returned to the Liberal fold (though some individual members did), but on the contrary remained a separate and competing political entity until the mid-1890s, when it allied with the Conservatives, and then in 1912, when those two parties formally merged. The effect of this was crippling for the Liberals, and also of critical importance to the longer-term evolution of the Conservative party, as we shall see.

II

The issue of Home Rule itself was important to these developments, but probably not crucial. The opposition to it was genuine. There was outrage at the idea that the government was giving in to terrorism; concern for the protestant minority in Ireland; and misgivings about the effect of this act of separation on the unity of Britain's farther-flung empire. Some absentee landlords were worried about their Irish rents. Others simply did not trust the Irish to behave decently once the hand of their master was taken away. Lord Hartington drew a horrifying picture of an independent Irish parliament riding roughshod over every civilized value – suspending trial by jury and Habeas Corpus, reneging on contracts, setting tariffs and bounties, even establishing 'public works on a great scale' – with Britain powerless to do anything to stop it, short of conquering the island again by force.[2] Such fears were real. In very few cases – perhaps none at all – were they exaggerated or feigned.

On the other hand they were not bound to incite the amount of opposition that they did. In many ways Gladstone's scheme for Ireland, after all, was quite moderate. It fell far short of full national independence. Even after Home Rule, according to the terms of the 1886 bill, Britain was to retain control of Ireland's foreign policy, her defence, her customs service, her post office, her currency and much else. The rest was to be devolved to a parliament in Dublin, which nevertheless would still owe allegiance to the Queen. Most unionist Liberals, and even some Conservatives, were in favour of some measure of devolution for Ireland, at least. Even self-styled imperialists were not invariably on the anti-Home Rule side. Some thought that what they called 'Home Rule all round' – for Britain's regions and colonies, that is, as well as Ireland – would strengthen imperial unity, rather than the reverse. (Cecil Rhodes was one of these.) It was not a simple question of being for or against Home Rule, therefore, but rather a matter of degree.

That being so, there should have been room for manoeuvre and compromise. Gladstone made considerable efforts in this direction. He offered a very good deal to Anglo-Irish landlords, for example, guaranteeing a 'fair' price to those who wished to sell their lands to their tenants after Home Rule, underwritten by a loan from the Treasury. In April 1886 Joseph Chamberlain, who had left the cabinet in March, thanked Gladstone for some other 'very considerable modifications' he had made since then, and predicted that with just a few inches more movement 'I shall be delighted to be relieved from an attitude which I only assumed with the greatest reluctance, and which I can only maintain with the deepest pain and regret.'[3] In the event Chamberlain found himself among the 93 who were still resisting in June. But the impression given, both by him and by others, was that the difference between them and the party on the question of Ireland was not really *that* deep.

But there were other obstacles to a reconciliation. In Chamberlain's case sheer opportunism may have been a factor. He was one of very few Radical Liberals to make the jump over to the Unionists, and almost the only one not to return to the Liberal fold in time.[4] His presence among all those Hartingtonian Whigs, like a thistle among the untoiling lilies, appeared anomolous to say the least. If one of the reasons for the Liberal Unionist rebellion was to escape from the Radicals in the Liberal party (as we shall see it was), then it must have been unnerving to land on the other side of the fence and find the fiercest Radical dog still clinging to your trouser leg. The usual explanation for this is that it was a cynical calculation on Chamberlain's part. He had voiced no strong views about Home Rule before 1886. In his 'Unauthorised Programme' he had even sketched out a scheme of his own. When he resigned from the cabinet in March 1886 it was not over the major issue, but because he objected to the generosity of Gladstone's Irish Land Purchase bill – the one which guaranteed a fair price to Irish landlords – on the grounds that the British taxpayer would eventually have to pick up the tab.[5] When he joined the major rebellion in June it was because he reckoned it would help get Gladstone defeated, which would make it easier for himself to jump into his shoes when he retired, as after such a defeat he surely must.[6] Eventually he was stymied because Gladstone refused to retire, but hung on long past the time when Chamberlain could hope to be welcomed back. He was stranded on the Unionist beach. Later on we shall see what became of him there.

Chamberlain, however, was a special case. He was an 'advanced' state-interventionist Radical, whereas most of his Unionist allies were the opposite. They represented that older tradition of Liberalism, going back at least to the 1850s, which sought the salvation of mankind in the free play of individual economic self-interest, which nothing in the world should be allowed to constrain or tamper with: not even the consent of the majority of the people to such constraints. Their quarrel with Gladstone over Ireland largely centred on the fear that if Ireland were given self-government, she might use it to govern herself in non-free-market ways. Lord Hartington's catechism of the ills that were likely to follow in the train of Irish Home Rule, which we have met already, makes this clear. He started with the threat – as he saw it – to civil liberties in an independent Ireland, but then quickly went on to itemize all kinds of economic impositions – interference with contract, the extension of the land laws to house property, protective tariffs, bounties, public works, high taxation – which he obviously regarded as tyrannies of the most repressive kind.[7] These were his reasons for object-ing to Irish self-government. They clearly were not exclusively Irish reasons. They grew out of concerns which were general, and applied to a range of contemporary British government policies, all of which were just as abhorrent to Hartington as was Home Rule.

They were also concerns which went back quite a long way. In this sense Home Rule was not a new issue, and the crisis it gave rise to not an isolated one. It was one of an almost continuous line of Liberal upsets and defec-tions which began in the 1870s, reached one little peak around 1880 when whole families of prominent Whigs moved over to the Conservatives,[8] and continued – as we shall see later – into the 1890s and beyond. It was a con-tinual process of leakage, for lots of different *specific* reasons, but also one main broad one.

There can be no doubt as to what that broad one was. The darkest cloud the Whigs perceived looming over them in 1886, and for several years before that, had little to do with Ireland, and even less to do with the empire, but was the prospect of 'socialism'. This was at the front of nearly every politi-cian's mind then, however he defined it, and whether he feared it or not. We have seen some of its manifestations already: socialist parties springing up like mushrooms; municipalities organising people's lives for them; par-liamentary legislation which seemed to strike at the edges – if not at the very heart – of property and freedom of contract. The latest instance in 1886 was a new Railway and Canal Traffic Act which empowered govern-ment to intervene to lower railway companies' freight charges: 'autocratically', in the eyes of some Whigs.[9] For those of us who have experienced a much greater degree of socialism in the years since the 1880s all this may seem all rather small beer, nothing much to get worked up about; but people did get worked up about it at that time. 'The Irish diffi-culty, though bad, is not the worst of it,' wrote the Liberal Goldwin Smith to Lord Selborne in 1886; '...worse still is the state of the nation, which is loose from its old moorings of principle, much shaken in moral fibre, and in a fever of revolutionary excitement.'[10]

The 'moorings of principle', of course, were the old Liberal virtues of economic freedom, which Liberals themselves now seemed to be turning away from in droves. For some of them this was a voluntary change of direction, taken out of conviction; but others seemed to be simply swept along by the crowd. 'The liberalism of today,' wrote Gladstone, '...is far from being good. Its pet idea is what they call construction – that is to say, taking into the hands of the state the business of the individual man.'[11] Yet Gladstone was supposed to be leading them. One of A.V. Dicey's reasons for leaving the Liberal party was that he felt he could not trust it 'to resist socialism'.[12] That was a common feeling among Unionists. It is also why so few of them – even when the Home Rule question had receded – returned to the Liberal party, which continued to flirt with these social and economic heresies for the rest of its life.

It explains too why they did not join the Conservative party straight away. For the first few years, in fact, they remained genuinely independent of the Conservatives, except on the issue of the Union: more often than not, for example, voting with the Liberals in divisions in the Lords.[13] The reason for this was that the Conservative party was no sounder on political economy than the Liberals were. It had some collectivist skeletons in its own cupboard, as Lord Wemyss pointed out in 1883; examples he cited were legislation preventing ships being dangerously overladen, and enforcing compulsory attendance at school.[14] It also had a Radical wing of its own, in the form of Randolph Churchill's 'Fourth Party' of 'Tory democrats', which in Donald Southgate's words 'equalled Chamberlain in rabble-rousing demagogy and excelled him in vulgarity'.[15] If Gladstone was unreliable as a prophylactic against this sort of thing, the Conservative leader Lord Salisbury looked scarcely better. As a life-long Tory, he did not have the principles of the free market bred into him. He had acquired a good veneer of them in the 1860s, but veneers tend to peel in certain climes. In 1881, sure enough, he was heard suggesting that there might be times when 'the policy of *laissez-faire* can no longer be pursued without disaster to the state'; and two years later he came out with the disturbing idea that 'freedom of contract' was 'not on a level with the Ten Commandments'.[16] This meant that the Conservative party was no safer a refuge for economic purists than the Liberal party was. Hence the Liberal Unionists' continued independence, until organisational and electoral difficulties made this impossible.

'If these men had not left us on Home Rule,' concluded Robert Spence Watson, later president of the National Liberal Federation, 'they must have gone whenever any Liberal principle had to be put into practice.'[17] That was probably true; so long as it is borne in mind that what Spence Watson understood by a 'Liberal principle' was very different from how it will have appeared to 'these men'. That confusion itself is significant. There were now two varieties of Liberalism. Each claimed it was the One True Church. They had managed to co-exist happily in mid-Victorian times, but had grown increasingly antithetical since. The 1886 Home Rule crisis was the catalyst which pulled them apart institutionally. Now Liberals had to choose between them. Broadly speaking, the choice was between a mainly economic liberalism, and one which emphasized political democracy more. The Liberal Unionists after 1886 were those who stuck firm to their economic faith, whatever the political implications of that might be.

III

The political implications were in fact profound. Free market liberalism, once so dynamic and confident, was now an embattled creed. It was surrounded by enemies, and undermined by traitors – the new breed of Radical – within. Leaders who should have known better seemed unwilling or powerless to stand up for what they believed. In some cases this looked like sheer cowardice in the face of terrorism: in Ireland most obviously, but also – after the 'Black Monday' riots of February 1886 – in England. At other times it was done simply in order to curry votes. That was scarcely less reprehensible: a case of public men cravenly deferring to public clamour, in the teeth of their better judgment; just as friend Bagehot had warned they would all those years ago.[18]

Hedgers and trimmers were an obvious target for aggrieved free market purists in the 1880s; but it may have been unfair to place all the blame for this situation on them. They were clearly under pressure from an electorate which had been greatly expanded recently, and which seemed to the Liberal Unionist George Goschen to be – to put it mildly – 'less favourable to political economy' than in the past.[19] If this was so, then it made the problem worse. It was not faint-hearted politicians who were undermining 'freedom', but the people themselves. The democracy was rejecting it. Did this mean that 'freedom' would need to reject democracy in its turn? That was the inference many Whigs drew.

In fact it was not a new one. Free marketeers had never been particularly keen on democracy, as we have seen. At best it seemed irrelevant to the kinds of individual freedoms they espoused; at worst – and as seemed to be transpiring then – it could actually injure them. Votes had been granted to groups of people in the past – in 1867 and 1884 – on the understanding, or in the hope, that they would not use them too positively. Even on those occasions there had been a number of Whigs who worried that they would. These worries seemed to be borne out in the mid-1880s. You could not trust democracy with liberty. They were not only distinct from each other, but – as the *Edinburgh Review* put it in July 1885 – 'radically opposed'.

Liberty is based on the free action of co-ordinate powers, mutually checking and controlling each other; Democracy claims an absolute supremacy and undivided authority, which is the soul of despotism. Liberty respects and protects all personal and corporate rights, even when they are opposed to the action of the State; Democracy crushes all resistance to its own pleasure. Liberty is the child of law, Democracy of lawlessness. Liberty is patient, tolerant, and enduring; Democracy arrogant and impetuous. Liberty can only exist with order and peace; the path of Democracy is stained with blood, for it leads to deeds of violence and civil war.

From this it followed, the *Review* concluded, that 'Liberty has more to fear in this age from Democracy than from any other cause'.[20]

That stated the problem. What was the solution? It was no use hoping to reverse the democratic tide. No one – no Liberal, at any rate – suggested returning the franchise to what it had been in 1883, or 1866. That being so, they had to try to protect freedom *from* democracy somehow. The *Edinburgh Review* thought a lot could be done simply by building the Whigs up again in Parliament as a barrier against the Radical foe. The Radicals after all were only a tiny minority. They looked more only because they clamoured and agitated a lot – techniques they had learned from the French Jacobins – but their bubble could be pricked. Most middle-class Liberals were still moderate people. If they would only choose as parliamentary *candidates* 'men of character, independence, and principle', the electorate would rally to them, and the Radical danger would evaporate.[21] That was one answer. It was something to be going on with. But it may not have been enough.

It rather assumed that Radical 'agitation' was the only source of the problem, whereas it plainly went deeper than this. Agitators after all had no difficulty in finding real grievances to exploit. Working-class people were better off now than they had been 20 years previously; but they were not *that* much better off. There was still poverty and destitution in Britain, and as much inequality as there had ever been. Free marketism therefore was not self-evidently working to everyone's advantage. Assuming that it would do so eventually – as you had to if you were a Believer – that still left a problem. People may have been wrong to pin their hopes on state intervention to improve their lot, but it was easy to see why they did. Even without Radicals to agitate them they could come to these views for themselves. They arose out of their material situation. Consequently it would require a positive effort to constrain or counter them. A simple old-style Whig barrier might not hold very long.

A number of free marketeers gave some thought to this in the 1880s, followed by more later on. Among the early ones was a distinguished set of intellectuals, including the philosophers Herbert Spencer and Henry Sidgwick, the jurists A.V. Dicey, J.F. Stephen and Henry Maine, and the historians J.R. Seeley, J.A. Froude and Goldwin Smith. Their contribution to the cause was to write books and articles for the Reviews.[22] Another prominent group of activists consisted of high-born large-scale landowners, for the simple reason that the onslaught on contract and the rights of property at this time seemed to be particularly targetted at them. Some businessmen also joined in the fray. They tended to be more practical. In 1882 some of them clubbed together to form the 'Liberty and Property Defence League', to counter collectivist ideas in a number of ways. They included parliamentary lobbying against bills the League disapproved of; issuing popular pamphlets; lecturing in working men's clubs; and later organising 'free' (or 'blackleg') labour to break strikes.[23] Most of these activities were not ineffective. They were a promising first salvo in what looked likely to be a long-drawn-out defence.

Long drawn-out; and also rather grim. It is difficult of course to measure this kind of thing; but there can be little doubt that the crusade for economic freedom from 1882 onwards was more joyless than it had been 40-odd years earlier, when the Anti-Corn Law League – a kind of precursor of the NPDL – had run its campaign to establish free trade originally. The reasons for this are obvious. The ACCL had been riding the crest of a wave of history, not struggling against the current, as seemed to be the case in 1882. It had been sustained in its exhilarating progress by certain hopes and expectations, some of which still remained 40 years later, but many of which had been cruelly dashed. One such expectation was that once established, free trade would carry all before it in the world, inaugurating such an era of international peace and domestic social harmony that no further struggle would be required. That had not happened. Consequently many of the attitudes associated with free marketism in those earlier days, but which in fact derived more from the optimism that had surrounded it, wilted and died.

The main casualty was liberalism, in just about every meaning of the word apart from the economic one. *Liberality* was one, according to the novelist John Galsworthy, one of the most percipient observers of upper-middle-class life in the closing years of the nineteenth century, who had one of his characters remark (in *The Man of Property*, set in the 1880s) on the 'movement against generosity, which had at that time already commenced among the saner members' of that class.[24] Another victim was the hope of greater *equality*, which some of its early afficionados had seen as one of the main benefits of free-market capitalism, levelling people up in the economic scale, and so adding to their sense of social contentment, but which by the 1880s had been more or less completely ditched. By now free-market capitalism had come to be much more firmly associated with out and out *in*egalitarianism, which the *Edinburgh Review* for example went so far as to proclaim was one of the 'inseparable consequences of civilisation', and the thing that distinguished 'higher' from 'savage' social states.[25] One consequence of that was to make free marketism that much more difficult to sell to men and women at the foot of the economic scale. A longer-term casualty of the decline of liberal optimism was the collection of *civil liberties* which had surrounded economic liberalism in the past. A particular casualty was mainland Britain's freedom from 'political policing', which could be said to have been theoretically compromised by the formation of the Special Irish Branch in 1883, though the first serious inroads began a little later.[26] All this, plus the struggle, almost completely blotted out the sun that had warmed the free-trade cause in earlier times, and made its champions severer sorts of women and men.

Most crucial of all in this connexion was the thought that must have been in every free marketeer's mind that they could *lose* this particular engagement, with appalling consequences both for themselves, and for the whole of the country and even the world. 'It would seem,' wrote the editor of the *Edinburgh Review* in July 1885, 'as if this nation was approaching a crisis of its history – a great parting of the waters – a chasm between the past and the future – a passage from death to life, *or possibly, from life to death*.'[27] That captures the mood precisely. Everything depended on the coming battle for the soul of the Liberal party, which could prove the last. That accounted for the furrowed brows of the Knights of the Market in the 1880s. No such fears had ever troubled the minds of their forebears, in that heroic age when the first great crusade for free trade had been fought and won.

IV

The second crusade was nothing like so successful in the short and medium terms as the first. It was always a strictly defensive movement, against forces which seemed overwhelming for most of the next 90-odd years. Those forces included not only socialism, which was its original enemy, but also two others: imperialism, which Lord Salisbury claimed Gladstone's Home Rule campaign had 'awakened the slumbering genius' of, by reminding people of the value of the empire whose integrity Irish devolution appeared to threaten;[28] and the much broader current of that sheer political pragmatism which was the main obstacle to the establishment of any kind of 'pure' doctrinal state in Britain then, as afterwards. These three contemporary trends, each of them in different ways alien to the genuine free-market spirit, dominated British politics for the 25 years after 1886, and ensured that the direct and positive contribution of what came to be regarded as a comparatively reactionary creed – always a crippling handicap for any political grouping to carry in an age of self-conscious 'progressivism' – was minimal.

Its main impact, in fact, was indirect and negative. The Unionist defection of 1886 did little for the cause it represented; but it had an important effect on the future history of the two main parties in Parliament, albeit after short delays. In the case of the Liberal party the delay was caused by its continued distraction by the Irish issue until 1893, after which the fact that its Whiggish ballast was now so much lighter than in the past may have encouraged its development in exactly the direction the Whigs had abandoned the ship in protest against originally. It became, in other words, more state interventionist and Radical. That in turn deterred the Unionists from rejoining it, and frightened others of a similarly Whig disposition out of it. The chief beneficiary of this (again after a delay) was the Conservative party, which became – what it had emphatically not been for most of the nineteenth century – the main refuge and home for free-market ideologues. That was a major realignment, a kind of sudden reversal of the political polarities of the time, to which the events of 1886 contributed in no small measure.

Political polarities in Britain, however, are rarely as straightforward as this. The Liberal party always retained some Whigs. In the Conservative party the situation was more complicated still. Free marketeers who fled there to escape the social interventionism of their erstwhile Liberal colleagues found themselves almost immediately rubbing shoulders with imperialists of an equally interventionist kind. Some of them were even protectionists. It was this tendency, every bit as much as the 'socialist' one, which prevented Britain's return to free-market purity over the next few years. At the very least it created something of an ideological strain on the British political right. On the one hand there was this new imperial enthusiasm, which fitted in well with many Conservatives' authoritarian and also paternalistic instincts. On the other hand there was the even newer creed (so far as the Conservative party was concerned) of individual economic liberty. In many ways the history of modern British Conservatism can be seen as a struggle between these two opposing nests of ideas, with the former generally dominant until recent times, when the empire itself and consequently the imperialists' whole *raison d'etre* vanished, leaving the individualists with a relatively clear field. But that is to run ahead.

All this had its origins in the split of 1886, which was itself part of a more general crisis that had begun some years before and was not fully over yet. That crisis grew out of the difficulties experienced by the Liberal party, and by extension the system of liberal capitalism, in the face of some new circumstances of that time: notably the 'Great Depression', resurgent socialism, and imperial rivalry and colonial nationalism abroad. The drama of the split reflected the gravity of the crisis, but without indicating any clear underlying cause. It could have been simply a transient problem. Perhaps if the mass of the Liberal party had stood firmer they could have weathered it. It may have been more serious than this, and pointed to a weakness in democracy. Alternatively it may have signified a basic flaw in the logic and practice of liberal capitalism itself. That, of course, was the least welcome hypothesis to most Liberals at the time.

Chapter 10

Capital versus Labour
(1886–95)

I

It was several years before all the ramifications of the split of 1886 were
fully worked out. In the meantime politics continued confusedly, and on
the whole ineffectually. The Conservatives won the July 1886 election by
default, and for six years governed more or less by default as well. The Liberal party came back in 1892, but in such a state of ideological confusion
still that it hardly knew what to do with its victory, and so shortly afterwards succumbed again. For much of this period most of the interesting
and innovative political developments took place outside parliament. Only
later did mainstream parliamentary politics manage to catch up with them.

Some of them were happening outside Britain. It is symptomatic of the
uncertainty of the age we are coming into now that people were beginning
to look to foreign countries for indications of what the future held for them,
rather than assuming – as they had in mid-Victorian times – that Britain
was in the vanguard, and so had nothing to learn from anywhere else. The
country that attracted the most interest was Germany, whose recently un-
banned socialist party was making startling progress in the later 1880s,
polling well over a million votes in the *Reichstag* elections of February
1890. More significant than this for some folk were the concessions Bismarck was making to the socialists in the form of social welfare provisions,
designed to forestall the great class war which a number of commentators –
by no means all of them Marxists – predicted if something like this were
not done. The picture abroad definitely suggested that socialism was on the
up. In May 1891 the Pope attacked it in an encyclical, which he would not
have bothered to do if it had not seemed to pose a threat. He also – to be
even-handed – criticized the tyranny of the marketplace, which showed
how far the current anti-capitalist mood had got through to him too. (His

main objection was to the employment of women in factories, which was not, he believed, where God intended the natural mother and home-maker of the species to be.)¹ Capitalism was on the moral defensive in Europe around 1890. This was not a trend anyone in Britain could ignore.

Few of them did. The socialist-capitalist dichotomy overshadowed all other topics of public debate in Britain at this time, including Ireland, until the later 1890s when imperialism took over for a while. Much of the debate took the form of predictive essays and novels, with the predictions being based on trends their authors thought they could detect at that time. Most of them were utopian, like the American Edward Bellamy's state-socialist *Looking Backward*, published in 1888, and William Morris's more anarchistic *News from Nowhere*, which came out in 1891. Non-socialists also joined in: like the Salvationist William Booth, who dreamt up what must be one of the most aesthetically pleasing utopias of the day: a society in which want, crime, disease, war and cruelty to animals have all been banished by the 'angels of industry and Economy', and everyone spends at least part of every day worshipping God in great crystal temples – the London one covering the whole of Hyde park – presumably with tambourines. (Some of the details are a little vague.)² On the other hand there were the *dys*topias: very often the selfsame visions, but seen through different eyes. In May 1890, for example, Mrs Florence Fenwick Miller (a well known women's suffragist) looked a little further ahead than Bellamy and Morris, and saw their ideal socialist states leading to – among other things – 'The almost total extinction of the male sex', and the reduction of the female to a mere breeding machine.³ The popular romantic novelist 'Ouida' (Marie Louise de la Ramée) painted a picture of 'a community taxpaying, decree-obeying, uniform, passionless, enduring as the ass, meek as the lamb, with neither will nor wishes; a featureless humanity practising the goose-step in eternal routine and obedience' under socialism.⁴ Before that stage, however, many dystopians predicted bloody civil wars between the classes, which according to one American professor, writing in 1890, would climax in a general European conflict around 1915. That last prediction was uncannily accurate; but its effect is rather spoiled by all his others, which were way out. (Queen Victoria, for example, was supposed to suffer an 'apoplectic shock' and go comatose in 1891; which was kept well hidden if it was true.)⁵ That was the debate at its most imaginative.

On the mundane level it pervaded every form of serious literature. Books were written for and against socialism, including *Fabian Essays in Socialism* (1889), edited by George Bernard Shaw, and *A Plea for Liberty* (1891), edited by Thomas Mackay, which has not worn so well, probably because Thomas Mackay was not G.B. Shaw. The Fabians also produced cheap 'tracts' which were widely read, and articles in the monthly reviews.

They in turn were met with counter-articles by anti-socialists, often appearing side by side in the same journals, so that readers could compare the arguments. Occasionally a review devoted a whole issue to this kind of debate.[6] The newspapers carried features on socialism, which those who were really interested could follow up in the Labour movement's own flourishing press: *Reynolds's Newspaper*, the *Labour Leader*, Robert Blatchford's *Clarion*, the *Labour Prophet*, *Justice*, the anarcho-communist *Commonweal*; all of which except *Reynolds's* were started up in this period. Again, the antis fought back, with Frederick Greenwood's new weekly *Anti-Jacobin* in 1891, for example, but without quite the same edge or spark. Socialists were taking all the initiatives, stimulating people's interest, setting the terms of the debate, throwing down the gauntlet for the future. It was a heady time for them. 'The hour of Labour, it is said, has now arrived.'[7] All its adversaries could do was try to defend and contain.

Labour was making a certain amount of headway in the real world too, especially in the industrial sphere. The early years of the 'New' (that is, unskilled) trade unionism, after 1888, saw a clutch of famous strikes, most of which were successful, including the Bryant & May matchgirls' strike of 1888, and a great London dock strike the following year. In 1893 there was violence at a miners' strike near Featherstone in Yorkshire, when troops were brought in and two men were killed. That year saw more than 30 million working days lost through strikes overall, which figure was not even approached again until the 'Great Labour Unrest' of 1911–14.[8] Socialists were involved in many of these strikes, inevitably.

They did not always have it their own way. As early as April 1891 the journalist W.T. Stead thought he saw 'signs that the employers are now going to have their innings'.[9] One of their tactics was to form federations, in order to counter the unionists' solidarity with a solidarity of their own. They then organised 'lock-outs'; or mobilised strike breakers, with the help of an offshoot of the Liberty and Property Defence League called the 'National Free Labour Association' formed in 1893.[10] The Shipping Federation, set up in response to the London dock strike of 1889, succeeded in overturning the gains won by the strikers within three years. Conditions turned in the employers' favour after 1891, with a sharp rise in industrial unemployment which undermined the unions' bargaining strength.[11] In 1893 the latter suffered another little setback when a court case (Temperton *versus* Russell) cast doubt on one of their supposed immunities by ruling that union leaders could be prosecuted if their unions interfered with freedom of contract. That was the first of a series of adverse legal decisions. So the industrial battle ebbed and flowed.

Another battlefield was local government, especially in London, where county council status had been conferred for the first time in 1888. The

London County Council immediately became – as towns like Birmingham and Glasgow had been for an earlier generation – a proving ground for 'collectivism'; or at least, for as much of it as the powers granted to the council would permit. That did not turn out to be very much: a direct labour agency, a minimum wage for workers involved in council projects, some slum clearance, a few tramways municipalised; but at the beginning the collectivists on the LCC were full of great hopes. Lord Salisbury loathed its 'new revolutionary spirit',[12] but others welcomed it with open arms. This, surely, was where the national future also lay. More significant still was the *way* it was all done: by means of a new alignment on the left of politics, which reflected most people's wishes and interests far better than the contemporary Liberal party seemed to do. Most of the 118 London county councillors were divided into two parties: a 'Moderate' minority, which roughly corresponded with the Conservatives; and a ruling 'Progressive' party which was made up of Radical Liberals, socialists, Fabians, Labourites, and even the odd Liberal Imperialist, including the chairman Lord Rosebery. They seemed a motley crew, but in their common belief in constructive measures in the pursuit of social justice they were not. On the other side, the Moderates generally stood by the principles of freedom from municipal interference, and low rates. The battle lines were clearly drawn, therefore. That was more than could be said for the parliamentary parties at that time.

It was in these kinds of areas – the London docks, the Yorkshire coalfield, the LCC, even the monthly reviews – that by common consent the crucial political struggles and debates of the day were going on. It was not clear yet which side was winning; or even that either side would need to win outright. A widespread view, on both sides of the Parliamentary political fence, was that social*ism*, in its most extreme sense, could be bought off by discriminating measures of social *reform*. The Conservative *Quarterly Review* believed that this was the only way to 'justify to the people the existing basis of society', and so maintain stability.[13] A maverick Liberal Unionist – the Roman Catholic Sir Rowland Blennerhassett – accused those who obstructed reform of unwittingly furthering the cause of revolution.[14] A Tory added another angle: 'Not until our lower ranks are comfortable and contented here in Britain,' he wrote in January 1890, 'can we expect them to be imperialists.'[15] Of course not everyone agreed with this. Frederick Greenwood thought that the only proper response to popular discontent was to tell the people the 'truth', which was, in a nutshell, 'that the wrong way of satisfaction is to seek it by State interference with liberty and property'.[16] Others (usually women) warned of the dangers of wasting too much 'pity' on the poor, which was apt to 'relax the moral fibres'; and of any kind of charity – state or even private – which tended to 'support...

the meanest at the expense of the noblest of the race'.[17] There was no una-
nimity on these matters. Everyone did agree, however, that like it or not
'the social question will constitute the politics of the future';[18] which meant
that they would have to come to terms with it in one way or another before
long.

II

Why then did Parliament not take it up more vigorously in the 1890s? One
reason was undoubtedly its social composition. Nearly all MPs were still
landed, business or professional men. None ran very much risk of starving,
going homeless, being thrown out of work, or having to wet-nurse other
mothers' babies in order to survive. Since 1874 a trickle of working men
had managed to get into the Commons, but always under Liberal auspices.
In the early 1890s there were around a dozen, including James Keir Hardie,
who had been returned for West Ham South in 1892. When (following an
earlier Scottish precedent) a British 'Independent Labour' party was
formed in 1893, with Hardie playing a leading role, all its first candidates,
including Hardie, were defeated in the election of 1895. Labour made
almost no impression in Parliament in the 1890s, except symbolically.
Hardie's arrival to take his seat on 4 August 1892, 'in a cloth cap and tweed
jacket, conveyed on a two-horse break with a trumpeter on the box',[19]
caught the eye, but very little else. When a few days later he asked the
Speaker to consider bringing the House back during the hunting and shooting season to debate ways of easing the condition of the working classes he
got nowhere. Parliament was still not really for the likes of him.

Still, one might have expected it to bow a little to *pressure*. That was
usually how these things had worked out the past. You do not need to experience suffering in order to be moved by it: either through humanitarian
empathy, or through fear of its effects. These were what had motivated the
last great tranche of social reforms in Britain, in the 1830s and 1840s: a
time when the House of Commons had been even more exclusive than it
was in the 1890s. Some people hoped for the same now: not so much from
the Conservatives, but from Gladstone's fourth Liberal government, which
took office in August 1892. The signs of social awareness were there. In
September 1891 the National Liberal Federation had come out with a list of
policy objectives (the 'Newcastle Programme') which included some
social reforms. The LCC election results of March 1892 seemed to bode
well, with the ruling Liberal-backed Progressives boosting their majority.
Looking at the July *general* election results, the Fabian Sidney Webb
thought he saw in them a clear swing to the 'progressive' wing among successful Liberal Parliamentary candidates. On the basis of that he urged the
new government to go for collectivism in a big way.[20] If he really expected
this, however, he was to be disappointed.

The government was not totally inactive in the social sphere. One of Gladstone's first executive acts was to appoint a working-class MP – the ex-miner Thomas Burt – to a junior ministerial post. Among the government's legislative achievements were a measure empowering the government to reduce railwaymen's hours of work; a new Factory Act; and a famous budget by the Chancellor, Sir William Vernon Harcourt, which introduced death duties for the first time and was the occasion for his famous remark that 'we are all socialists now'. Webb, however, who was a real socialist, was impressed by none of this. Any advance had been reluctant, and the minimum any government – of whatever political persuasion – would have had to concede. None of the big hoped-for measures had materialised: a new, stronger Employers' Liability law, for example; strong parish councils; or a bill reducing the statutory working day to eight hours, which was the major Labour demand of the day. Webb blamed these failures on the obstruction of the remaining Whigs in the cabinet, and the pusillanimity of most other ministers.[21] That was in the face of the government's defence that it had too little *time* for social measures because of the Irish problem; and that it was frustrated at every turn by the House of Lords.

Both these excuses were plausible. The Lords were certainly a nuisance. They were responsible for the ditching of the Employers' Liability bill, for example, by their insistence that employers should be allowed to contract out of it, which undermined its whole point. They emasculated a Parish Councils bill. They also contributed towards the Liberals' other, Irish, excuse. Ireland did take up a lot of parliamentary time in 1893. A second Home Rule bill – slightly more moderate than the first – was introduced in the Commons in February, debated in 81 separate sittings, and passed all its readings by 1 September. The majorities for it never went much over 40. That meant that if the 102 Irish votes were disregarded it did not get a majority of mainland British votes at all. It was on this ground – or pretext – that the Lords, when it came to them, immediately rejected it by the enormous margin of 419 votes to 41. That was an awful waste of Gladstone's efforts; and also, other Liberals pointed out, of time that could have been devoted to (among other things) an Eight Hours bill.

That last point, however, was hardly convincing. Of course the Irish issue and the Lords *were* obstructive, but there are reasons to suspect that some Liberals rather welcomed them as such. For those who wanted progress they were frustrating. They were less so, however, for those who did not. Lord Ripon, for one, secretly hoped that the Irish issue would not go away too soon, because 'if it were displaced a whole series of Labour questions would come to the front'.[22] Those questions were bound to be divisive. This was because the Liberal party was still riven between Radicals and free marketeers. Not all the latter had fled in 1886: only those whose free market principles had set them against Home Rule. But of course there was no necessary logical reason why they should. Free marketeers could be Home Rulers too. Those who were stayed behind in the Liberal party, where they found themselves just as much at odds with their Radical colleagues over other issues as they had ever been. John Morley is one example: an extreme individualist who thought the LCC was being run by 'blatant democrats' whose 'anarchic follies' were driving away the small shopkeeper vote; but also Gladstone's closest ally on Home Rule.[23] Gladstone himself could be said to be another. Many of these men were unhappy enough about what their own government was actually doing in the social field: especially for instance Harcourt's 1894 budget, which Gladstone found a little too 'violent' for his taste.[24] Anything more radical was out of the question; certainly an Eight Hours bill, which struck at the very root of liberty as the free marketeers saw it. The journalist W.T. Stead pointed out that even the most tyrannical and arbitrary Russian Tsar had never sought the power 'of denying to every citizen the right to labour more than one-third of the day'.[25] Liberal opinion had already been tested once on this – on a private member's bill in February 1892 – and had, predictably, divided into two camps. (Even the ex-miner Burt was against it.) The party could not risk exposing these differences in government. Hence the advantage of the Irish issue, which was just about the only thing keeping the Liberal party together in the early 1890s; ironically, in view of the role it had played in 1886.

The truth of this could be seen after the autumn of 1893, when the Irish and House of Lords issues both died, and the Liberal government stood revealed for the aimless and confused body it really was. It still had no social policy to speak of. It lost Gladstone in March 1894, in protest against his own cabinet's naval estimates. His successor was Lord Rosebery, chosen – gossip had it – after the Queen had vetoed Harcourt for being too radical. In fact Harcourt was in most ways far less genuinely radical than Rosebery, who was just then in the process of trying to overhaul Liberal ideology fundamentally. Unfortunately for the party his new line managed to antagonise both of its main wings: the Whigs by favouring social reform, the Radicals by harnessing it to imperialism. He and Harcourt also quarrelled a great deal, which added to the party's general sense of demoralisation.

In June 1895 the government was ambushed and defeated in a snap vote in the Commons. The occasion was a surprise, but not the defeat itself. Everyone had been expecting it: if not on this, then on some other contentious issue, like Welsh church disestablishment, local option (for the sale of alcohol), or a government proposal to erect a statue of Oliver Cromwell in Parliament square. (The Irish would have found it difficult to vote for that.)

No one was too shocked. Some ministers seemed relieved. 'Do not condole with me,' one was reported to have told a sympathiser afterwards: 'what I have been praying for for months has at last come to pass.'[26]

Gladstone blamed all this on a tactical error he reckoned he had made in September 1893, after the Lords' defeat of his Home Rule bill, in not going to the country straight away on a 'People *versus* the Peers' ticket. (He had been advised that Liberal party funds would not stretch to it.) Thus, he wrote in 1895, was 'let slip an opportunity... nothing less than splendid' for getting the Liberals a solid majority for one or even two more terms.[27] This was almost certainly a delusion. In the first place he could not have been at all sure that the people would have supported him wholeheartedly against the peers. There is no sign at this time of any widespread feeling of outrage against them he could have tapped. (A contemporary cartoon in *Judy* – *Punch*'s Conservative rival – shows Gladstone trying vainly to put a match to a barrel of gunpowder marked 'popular indignation' placed against the gates of the House of Lords, with the caption underneath: 'Damp!')[28] In the second place even if public opinion had rallied, and Gladstone had managed to curb the Lords and pass the bill, he would not have known what to do next. His party would still have been at odds on the other pressing problems of the day. It had not yet worked out which side of the capital/labour fence it should be sitting, or even whether (for this was one of the options) it should be taking a position somewhere in between. There were still some old-fashioned liberal issues it could take stands on, but even they were beginning to run dry. Disestablishment was one of them. It was highly unlikely that *two* terms of office could be spun out of that.

In the event it was the Conservatives who picked up those two terms. After the June 1895 defeat Rosebery went to the country, and got trounced. The Conservatives and Liberal Unionists together won a majority in the House of Commons over their Liberal and Nationalist opponents of 152 seats. At the next election, in 1900, they preserved that majority almost intact. That gave them continuous power for a little over ten years; and the Liberals the same period of time to sort themselves out.

III

The early 1890s were a time of disappointment for many people in Britain, therefore; but not usually of despair. The only political tendency which was prone to despair was the extreme free-market one, which saw everything going downhill. 'They are not improving, these domestic affairs of ours,' wrote Frederick Greenwood; '...and by every sign and token we must fear that they will grow worse.' His 'signs and tokens' included the 'success of robbery associations', by which he meant trade unions, and the 'competition of statesmen in the bribery of lawlessness', or promises of social reforms; from which it is easy to calculate his position on the political

map.[29] An impartial observer might think that on the contrary his like were
doing pretty well at this time, considering everything; but that just goes to
show how pervasive the *impression* of inexorable progress by the socialists
was. Either that, or the free marketeers were already preparing their alibi
for the failure of the British economy in the future. When that happened it
would not be the market that was responsible, but all this socialism introduced into it in the 1880s and 1890s. We shall see a lot of this argument
later on.

Those who were not quite so close to this particular political edge, but
still regarded themselves as old-style Liberals, tended to be apprehensive,
but not quite so gloomy as that. An example is James Bryce, a distinguished historian and a member of Gladstone's fourth cabinet, who in
November 1890 gave an address at the Brooklyn Library in New York
which summed up well the contrast between the new Liberal mood and the
old.

> Thirty years ago there was... a greater confidence in the speedy improve-
> ment of the world, a fuller faith, not only in progress, but in rapid
> progress, a more pervading cheerfulness of temper, than we now dis-
> cern. Men acknowledged the presence of great evils, but expected them
> to be soon removed. They saw forces at work in whose powers they had
> full confidence – the forces of liberty, of reason, of sympathy; and they
> looked forward to, and were prepared to greet, the speedy triumph of the
> good. To-day we in Europe have by no means ceased to believe in and to
> value these same forces. They are at work, and their work is visible. But
> it is slower than the men of 1850 expected; and because it is slower, we
> are less disposed to wait patiently for the results. We are less sanguine
> and more unquiet; less resolute and more querulous.

That was salutary, but it did not have to be disillusioning. Bryce himself
refused to be disillusioned. He took comfort in history, which taught that
'though depression and discouragements frequently overshadow its path'
the 'general progress' of mankind was always 'upwards', so that 'in each
age it gains more than it loses and retains most of what it has ever gained'.[30]
That was something to hold on to, and to sustain a *guarded* liberal optimism, at least.

The pleasant thing about the 1890s, in fact, was that nearly everyone
then could be guardedly optimistic, whatever political views he or she held.
This was because the situation seemed so nicely balanced. Most political
options still appeared to be open, in a way they are not in every period and
place. Everyone, therefore, had some reason for *hope*. Socialists, as we
have seen, were buoyed up by the knowledge that history was on their side:
though this was clearly a different sort of history from the one that buoyed
up Bryce. Women suffragists had some very material achievements to

cheer them: like Lord Salisbury's conversion ('in principle') to their cause in 1890–91, and the grant of the vote to some of them in local government elections in 1894. Conservatives and moderates of all kinds must have been encouraged by the lack of serious disorders in Britain after 'Bloody Sunday' (13 November 1887), apart from strike riots which were easily if somewhat crudely put down, and the occasional 'anarchist' scare. The latter were nothing in Britain compared to the Continent, where people were being blown up all over the place by a new violent strain of anarchist, which the British environment clearly did not suit at all. This was another encouraging sign. Only at the two extremes – which in a way were the same extreme, because anarchists are basically individualists – do we find the kind of desperation that is often provoked in people by a lack of hope. For everyone else there was – or seemed to be – everything to play for still.

The same was true abroad. No one of course could be entirely confident of anything that might happen there. Misgivings were voiced in some quarters about Britain's ability to maintain her position in the world in the future, against the rising military strength of Germany, for example, and the long-term potential of the United States of America to become something more than an ordinary power.[31] Nevertheless there were signs of hope there too. Europe and even the wider world were unusually – almost uncannily – peaceful during the years around 1890; leading Lord Salisbury, who was not a natural optimist, to admit that even he could not detect 'a single speck of a cloud' on the international horizon in November 1891.[32] There was plenty of colonial activity, but most of it by agreement between the different colonising powers, which meant that it did not threaten anybody; unless you wished to count the people who were being colonised, which was ridiculous because all this was being done for their good. An example is the Anglo-German treaty concluded in 1890 by which Britain gave Heligoland to Germany in return for the latter's recognition of Britain's right to seize Uganda. That was unpopular with Queen Victoria, because it broke her First Rule of Diplomacy: 'Giving up what one has is always a bad thing';[33] but most other people saw it as a model of how disputes could be settled amicably. Other potential conflicts too were being settled either by negotiation, or by international conferences, or by arbitration; which was clearly promising for the long-term peace and stability of the world.

There were other hopeful trends. One was the development of new weapons, which it was felt must make international conflicts impossible in the future: like the armed submarine, which an American scientist confidently expected would soon make naval warfare obsolete.[34] Another heartening development was the current enthusiasm for federations; in Australia, for example, where in the course of the 1890s the separate colonies all came voluntarily together into a single 'Commonwealth'. To some commentators that suggested similar arrangements elsewhere: a single Balkan state, perhaps, or a continental European union, or a reconciliation between the British empire and America; with Tennyson's *Locksley Hall* (1842) vision of 'the Federation of the world', no less, as the ultimate goal.[35]

There were of course a few cynics and doubters around, who were not convinced by any of this. Some people are never completely happy with a silver lining until they can see the cloud behind it. One such was a French observer writing in 1891, who had deduced from *his* study of history, which went right back to King Menes, that 'storm has succeeded to calm in constant rotation, and the profoundest calm has ever been the forerunner of the most terrible storm.'[36] That will have wiped the smiles off some faces. The point was, however, that this was still just one of many possibilities. Things might get worse, but they could also get better. Both at home and abroad no good cause seemed lost yet; with the possible exception of pure free marketism, which no one gave much of a chance.

Chapter 11

Imperialism
(1890–1902)

I

From most people's points of view – though not of course from everyone's – the 1890s got worse as they went on. There was certainly more pessimism about at the end of the decade than at the beginning. It was sparked off by a nasty little depression which struck around 1892–93, causing industrial and commercial stagnation, if not an actual recession, and high levels of unemployment. That passed over; only for Britain then to become assailed by threats from abroad, which blew up quite suddenly around the middle of the decade, ruffling the relatively placid diplomatic waters Britain had been sailing through before then, and climaxing in a major colonial war in 1899. It was a disappointing finish to the century; especially as the decade had started off so well.

The foreign threat was the most depressing one, because it reminded Britain of her essential vulnerability. For a short while in the early 1890s that had been hidden by the unexpected outbreak of peace and concord that had taken hold of Europe then; untypically, as it came to appear in December 1895, when the first of a series of potentially serious conflicts arose between Britain and some of her European colonial rivals. This involved a 'raid' on the independent Transvaal Republic in South Africa by a posse of British freebooters, which was trivial enough in itself (the raiders were easily stopped and captured), but which had the more worrying side-effect of provoking the German Kaiser into a form of intervention – a telegram of congratulation to the President of the raided republic – which Britain chose to regard as hostile in intention. Another potential conflict arose later, in the summer and autumn of 1898, when a tiny French and a large British force both arrived at Fashoda on the upper Nile to claim the Sudan for their respective countries, and looked for a while like fighting over it, until France very sensibly backed down. The third crisis actually drew blood: the 'Boer war' between Britain and the Transvaal, which grew out of the threat which the latter was supposed to pose to British supremacy in southern Africa by virtue of its new wealth from the goldfields recently discovered there, and which ran for two and a half years from October 1899. This last event in particular turned out to be a struggle for Britain, and underlined a fact that had been only too clear to some alarmists for years: that her situation in the world was extremely precarious, in view of the wide spread of her interests, her relatively small military forces, the structure of her economy, which seemed to rule out much higher military spending, and the increasingly aggressive designs and capabilities of her rivals in continental Europe and north America.

For the threats in South Africa and the Sudan could not be seen in isolation. In the first place they were only a selection from among a number of challenges to Britain's position all over the world which surfaced in the later 1890s: elsewhere in Africa, for example; in central Asia; in China; and in the South Seas. The 'selection' was made by the British government, which, confronted by threats on so many fronts, was forced to pick and choose: to arrange priorities, cut its colonial coat according to its military cloth, concede an interest here in order to be able to stand firmer on a more vital one somewhere else; all in order to avoid having too many fires blazing at the same time.[1] One very specific example is the build-up to the Boer war of 1899, during which a whole series of conciliatory arrangements was made with other powers to try to ensure that they did not exploit Britain's military entanglement in South Africa; illustrating that even the engagements Britain won usually involved losses elsewhere.[2] British imperialism in the 1890s used at one time to be portrayed as a display of strength by Britain, an *expansive* episode in her history, the peak of her power in the world, a time of confidence; but it was in reality none of those things. Every time she seemed to be expanding it marked an overall contraction: because of the adjustments that had to be made elsewhere in order to make this gain possible, and also because, in the light of her fundamental interests in the world, whenever she had to secure one of those interests forcibly it marked a defeat of another kind.

It was a defeat because it generally denoted that she had failed to secure her interests by more 'informal' means, which was the way she preferred. That was becoming impracticable in the 1890s. No one else shared Britain's ideal vision of a great free world market of independent nations trading openly with every other nation equally, which was what the 'informal' method required. Instead the world was travelling in an entirely opposite direction. It was rapidly being carved up between great competing empires, with the stronger countries snaffling up all the territories of the smaller ones: presumably in order to make them even stronger in the future, and so fit them for a great 'struggle for survival' between the hugest of these new leviathans which was widely thought to be the next (and last) act of the international drama being played out then. Lord Salisbury spelled this out in a speech in 1898, in which he divided nations into 'the living and the dying' (which caused some flutters among the sicklier members of the world community); predicted that the former would eventually gobble up all the latter; and then warned ominously of the danger of the situation that would have been created at that point, when the 'mighty armies' of the remaining 'living' nations 'stand opposite threatening each other'.[3]

The contrast between this scenario and the old British liberal ideal was absolute. It was particularly worrying for Britain, for two reasons. The first was that – assuming that she was one of the 'living' nations which would make it to the semi-final stage – there was a danger that she might be defeated in the final rounds. The second was that even if she *won*, the kind of effort which would be necessary to allow her to win would cripple her in other ways, especially economically and in respect of the liberal freedoms she presently enjoyed. At the very least it would transform her so fundamentally that no mid-Victorian, if he or she were still around, would recognize the shape that emerged. Britain could not possibly survive as she was.

The years around 1900 were full of predictions of this kind, and other clearly related manifestations of pessimism about the future, which indicate how deep in some quarters this feeling went. It was a great time for 'invasion novels', for example: novels, that is, purporting to describe *future* invasions of Britain, and usually designed to arouse national vigilance against a threat that was believed to be really there. It is a genre which goes back a long way,[4] but which peaked in the 1890s and early 1900s, when the leading practitioner was one William le Queux, a kind of professional paranoiac, who published two invasion stories. The first was *The Great War in England in 1897*, which first came out in 1893 and described Britain being overrun by a Franco-Russian army aided by a German Jewish spy (le Queux was also paranoid about Germans, Jews and spies). The second was *The Invasion of 1910*, serialised in the *Daily Mail* in 1906 (with the route of the invading forces cleverly chosen to take it through the *Mail*'s best markets), this time with the Prussians wearing the jackboots.[5] Another famous contemporary invasion novel, of a sort, was H.G. Wells's *The War of the Worlds* (1898), where it was the Martians who held southern England in thrall. Between the Prussians and the Martians other putative invaders to look out for were the Americans, whose rise to superpower status (though it was not yet called that) was widely predicted at this time; the Japanese, who beat mighty Russia in war in 1905; Islam, stirrings of whose future rise were detected as early as the 1900s; and the Chinese.[6] There seemed to be no end to it. The future was seen as a series of battles, as each successive wave was beaten back; or not beaten back, as the case might be.

Much of this was sheer sensationalism, whipped up in le Queux's case, for example, by the new yellow press for cynical profiteering motives, and taken seriously by very few even of those who read it. Nonetheless it did reflect, in a distorted kind of way, some widespread anxieties which were more sober and sensible, and were also based on sound evidence: like the inescapable facts that foreign countries *were* becoming more imperially-minded, including even the United States, who had a bracing swim in these waters in 1897–98, annexing Hawaii, the Philippines and Puerto Rico along the way; and that at one or two points (like Fashoda) they were start-ing to collide. Even if you confined yourself to that, and looked no further ahead, there was clearly an urgent problem here. Around 1900 that prob-lem dominated the political debate in Britain; either pushing out of the limelight the other problems that had seemed to beset Britain before then, or else dragging them further into the limelight, harnessed to this wider imperial issue.

II

One of the problems it harnessed – in debating terms only, for nothing very practical came out of this in the short run – was that of social reform. Until now social reform had generally been discussed in terms of its advantages for those it would immediately benefit, and its potential contribution to domestic peace. Britain's apparent vulnerability in the world in the later 1890s added another dimension to this. Social reform came to be seen as an imperial interest too.

The argument went like this. In a world of great competing empires, Britain needed to look after her own great competing empire in order to survive. That was no easy task. Britain's was a difficult empire to defend. At that time it covered nearly 12 million widely scattered square miles, which was about a fifth of the world's habitable land. A census of its popu-lation in 1901 counted some 398 401 404 heads. (Even that was probably an under-estimate, because in some colonies it apparently never occurred to heads of households that the enumerators wanted them to include females too.)[7] Most of these people were 'aliens', and consequently not to be depended on to defend the empire if the chips were down. A lot therefore rested on the shoulders of the small minority of patriotic Anglo-Saxon adult males in the empire, most of whom lived in Britain, and cannot have numbered more than about ten or eleven million there at most.[8] Those ten or eleven million had to be *fit*; for as the social imperialist Arnold White put it apho-ristically: 'the Empire will not be maintained by a nation of outpatients'.[9]

They also needed to be loyal, which once again was thought to be more likely if they were comfortable. A depressed population was an easy prey to socialism, which would be fatal to the empire in view of most socialists' antipathy to it. It followed that the people had to be nurtured, into what Lord Rosebery called 'an Imperial Race'.[10]

For many imperialists this involved constructive measures of social reform. It did not invariably. Some thought that the problem with the 'Race' at present was that it was being mollycoddled: people were not being allowed to starve if they were lazy, for example, or perish if they were sickly, thus diluting the general stock. John St Loe Strachey, editor of the *Spectator*, drew a lesson here from the fall of the Roman empire, which he attributed to its adoption of what he called 'State socialism' long before the barbarians came on to the scene.[11] That was one approach. The other, however, was more common. The state needed to intervene *more*, in order to strengthen the sinews and spirits of men and women who could not be blamed for their own weaknesses, but were simply the casualties of the economic system of the time. 'All this sounds terribly like rank Socialism,' admitted one 'social imperialist' in 1905; '...but I am not in the least dismayed. Because I know it also to be first-class Imperialism. Because I know Empire cannot be built on rickety and flat-chested citizens.'[12] That was the crux of the matter, and one of the ways in which imperialism and social reform could be regarded as – in Lord Milner's words – 'inseparable ideals'.[13]

The range of mooted reforms was wide. Some were identical to the ones non-imperialist social reformers also advocated: free medical treatment, for example; slum clearance; free school meals; advice and help for mothers-to-be. Others will not have appealed to them at all. Compulsory military drill in schools was one, together with rifle training in schools and workplaces, and military conscription for all young adult males. These were seen as ways of toughening boys and men, and also injecting them with habits of discipline which it was hoped they would then carry with them to their factories, as well as for their purely military advantages. Others advocated compulsory sterilization for 'unfit' subjects, so that they would not defile the Race, and immigration controls – which did not exist at all before 1906 – aimed primarily against east European Jews. Many imperialists wanted to ban or at least discourage women from working outside the home, so that they could concentrate on their natural and patriotic duty of breeding and rearing the next generation of the Imperial Race. Away from strictly social measures, there was some pressure to reform Parliament, usually by abolishing political parties, which were seen as divisive; and there was a movement to unite the empire in a great '*Zollverein*' or tariff union, which of course would involve setting tariffs against other

countries first.[14] That was the most strongly urged of these reform measures. Many imperialists believed that it was essential to Britain's survival in
the future: that the 'alternative', as one of them put it in 1909, 'is union or
death'.[15]

'Death', of course, meant curtains for the working classes too. This was
the other side of the social/imperial equation. The relationship between the
two things was supposed to be symbiotic. The empire needed fit men (and
indirectly women); but fit men needed the empire more. This was because
they needed the *markets* the empire provided for the goods they made in
their factories. Britain still depended massively on her trade abroad, which
in 1900, for example, was worth 46.5% of her estimated national income;[16]
and also increasingly on her capital investments overseas. About a third of
her exports and probably much more of her investments went to the empire;[17] a proportion which was likely to grow if – as seemed likely – the rest
of the world went protectionist. People's *jobs*, therefore, depended on it; as
well as the general prosperity of the country, without which, of course, no
really effective scheme of social reform was even affordable.

That was why it was in every class's interest to strive to defend the empire
against its enemies. If they failed, the prospect was almost too depressing to
contemplate. Imperialists had nightmares about this, some of which they
published afterwards. One of the best known is Cecil Rhodes's vision in
1895 of a country wracked by 'bloody civil war' as its colonial markets
shrivel, the surpluses pile up, and unemployment soars.[18] Other predictions
were only marginally less terrible. One anonymous commentator in 1908
painted a picture of a post-imperial Britain reduced to 'a practicable clear-
ing-house, a good banker, a playground for the rich, a hell for the poor'.[19]
Lord Curzon predicted a similarly 'sordid existence' for the working
classes, and a descent into 'a narrow and selfish materialism' for the rest.
The nadir would come when foreign tourists flocked to Britain to see her
cathedrals, castles, country houses and other 'relics of a once mighty sovereignty', like they flocked to the ruins of Athens then. That was when the
British would know they were finished.[20] Some of this is quite impressive
as prophesy. At the time, however, it was intended rather as a warning, of a
future state to be avoided if possible, in everyone's interest and with everyone's help.

For a short time around 1900 the prospects for this seemed encouraging.
On every level 'imperialism' seemed to be catching on. In politics the 'social
imperialist' idea suddenly became fashionable, taken up by self-styled
'progressives' who believed they had outgrown what Lord Rosebery
memorably (if obscurely) called the 'fly-blown phylacteries of obsolete
policies',[21] especially *laissez-faire* liberalism, and were looking for a bright
new creed to suit the times. It appealed across party boundaries; giving

some social imperialists the idea that perhaps a new centre party could be founded on the basis of it, to break the existing two party mould. In the meantime, social imperialists were to be found everywhere: in the government party, including Joseph Chamberlain, the ex-Radical, who was now Colonial Secretary; among the Liberals, led by Rosebery and a group in the party called the 'Liberal Imperialists' (sometimes shortened to 'Limps'); and even in the ranks of Labour. In 1900 the Fabian Society – after an almighty row over the issue – came out in favour of a kind of welfare imperialism, which may have been partly motivated by the calculation that they were more likely to achieve their socialist aims by working with rather than against the imperialist grain.[22]

One of the things that suggested this was the way the grain was running was imperialism's reception by the people generally. They seemed to be going for it in a big way. The evidence for this lay all around. Much of the popular press (especially the *Daily Mail*) was rabidly imperialistic. Imperial and militarist propaganda was drummed into boys at school, and into adults in music halls, the cinema, churches, poster campaigns and a dozen other ways.[23] Working-class men flocked to join the colours at the start of the Boer war.[24] There were pro-imperialist riots during the course of it: for example in the Yorkshire seaside town of Scarborough in March 1900, when the homes of the Quaker (and therefore pacifist) Rowntree family were attacked, anti-war meetings were broken up, 'pro-Boers', as they were called, were beaten up in the streets, and order had to be restored eventually by the military. A couple of months later came mass 'mafficking' demonstrations in London and elsewhere when it was learned that the Boer siege of Mafeking in northern Cape Colony had been broken: better-tempered demonstrations in general than the Scarborough riots, but still an impressive display, as it seemed, of raw working-class 'jingoism'. The Conservative government was confident enough of this feeling to decide to call a 'Khaki' general election to exploit it in October 1900, which it won comfortably. Non-imperialists *felt* outnumbered. Most of them therefore kept their heads down.

III

They may have been too timorous. Impressions can be misleading. This one was thoroughly so. Imperialism was never a popular ideology in Britain, in any significant sense. This was in spite of all the propaganda efforts that were put into making it popular, which by themselves of course only tell us what the propagandists *wanted* folk to think. The riots and demonstrations of 1900 are not much more helpful. The most famous of them – 'Mafeking night' – took place in the *City* of London, the banking area: which was an odd place for the proletariat to choose to congregate. There is evidence – albeit tenuous – that many of that particular crowd were not working class at all, but medical students and lower-middle-class clerks. That was the *Daily Mail*'s main readership, too. The working class's own press, with one temporary exception, was highly critical of the war. Discussions in working men's clubs appear to have been detached and balanced. Most Labour MPs kept clear of the question, or actively opposed the war.[25] In the 'Khaki' election of 1900 Labour did better than it had in the previous one, despite being smeared by its opponents as 'pro-Boer'. Even the Liberal party gained marginally, with anti-war candidates experiencing no greater difficulties in getting elected than the 'Limps'. None of this suggests that imperial fervour carried everything before it, even at its peak. It may well have been merely a minority movement; though it was difficult to tell this from the noise it made.

Even if it was more widespread – and we can never know for sure – it seems to have been a very brief and shallow phenomenon. All the biggest demonstrations came during the Boer war; there were none at all before it, after it, or even towards its end. Before 1899 Chamberlain was not at all confident of the public mood on imperialism, and havered over whether to go to war in South Africa, in case he had no support.[26] When it came to it he got a great deal of very vocal support, as we have seen, but little of any great consequence in the longer term. Many of the Scarborough rioters were simple hooligans. For the rest, most of their enthusiasm was for the British troops out there in Africa, and not for any wider policy or ideal. They supported their own side when it was shooting and being shot at by foreigners, but that was as far as it went. When the war was over they would probably transfer those feelings back to Blackburn Rovers or Aston Villa, not to 'imperialism'. That was the sort of support it was.

This is usual with jingoism. It is never very reliable. It usually denotes two things: an underlying sense of weakness, and a questionable cause. Britons do not 'maffick' when they feel secure, or if they are clearly in the right. (There were no jingo demonstrations, for example, during the second world war.) It rarely indicates any solid, constructive support for a cause or ideology, and it often harms any cause it is associated with in the long run. That is why so many genuine imperialists were embarrassed by the scenes they witnessed or read about in 1900. One of them, searching for the most disparaging adjective he could find to describe it, called it 'a very *American* outburst'.[27] 'Nothing could be more repugnant to some kinds of Imperialist than some kinds of Imperialism', wrote another. 'The Imperialism which squeaks through the penny trumpets and swaggers in the music halls, is of all the sentiments masquerading in the name of patriotism anywhere in the world the most vulgar, blatant and inept.'[28] It was also fickle. John Galsworthy's fictional Soames Forsyte, a financier, caught up in the

'Mafeking' crowd in May 1900, took no comfort at all from it, but only fright that 'one of these days' the mob would turn against his kind.[29] That was another and probably more rational way of looking at popular jingoism; not as proof of the underlying imperial patriotism of the British working man at all.

That was during the war. After it the jingo storm very quickly blew itself out. The mood changed visibly. The war itself was partly to blame for this. It turned out to have been a longer haul than expected. 5774 British troops were killed in it, which is not a very great number by the ghastly standards of many twentieth-century conflicts, but was more than had been killed in battle, for example, in the Crimean campaign.[30] It was expensive, pushing income tax up to 14 old pence (5.83p) in the pound at one stage.[31] It showed up some grotesque military deficiencies on the British side, which would have been fatal against a bigger enemy. In the end Britain had only won by sheer weight of numbers, and by means of tactics – farm burning, herding women and children into insanitary 'concentration camps' – which few Britons could take any pride in. In June 1901 the Liberal leader Sir Henry Campbell-Bannerman described these tactics as 'methods of barbarism': which was strong language for any politician to use against his own nation's army while it was under fire.[32] It was not the most glorious of victories.

The moral aspect was important. The Boers attracted widespread moral sympathy abroad, partly because they were so clearly the underdogs. Britain was cast in the role of bully. She was also accused of having provoked the war in the first place, for motives of sheer mercenary gain: to grab the fabulously rich gold fields of the Rand in the Transvaal for the benefit of 'stock-jobbers' in the City. That idea fitted many of the facts, and was widespread in Britain too. J.A. Hobson, a liberal economist, incorporated it into a general theory he was formulating at the time which explained all modern imperialism in terms of capitalist greed.[33] Labour, of course, lapped this up; as did many Liberals, who were genuinely shocked by the whole episode. This is one reason for the reaction against imperialism which set in even before the war reached its end. People simply did not feel good about it.

What they felt worst about was the notion that this sort of thing might become the norm. The Boer war was a shock, something new in the experience of most contemporaries: the first war for 43 years – and the first *colonial* war for more than a hundred – in which Britain was pitted against men of European origin. (The *first* Boer war in 1882 – little more than a skirmish – hardly counts.) All the way through it the fear nagged in the background that other European powers might intervene. That seemed to augur the beginning of a new stage in the history of modern competitive imperialism: the stage when, as Salisbury had put it in 1898, all the 'dying nations' had dropped out of the running and the 'mighty armies' of the 'great nations' met head on.[34] That was not a pleasant prospect.

The imperialists had shown them how to cope with it; but that was not a pleasant prospect either. This was the nub of the problem. Even if the imperialists were right, and the future did lie with great land powers and empires, there was no congenial way in which Britain could adapt to this. 'Methods of barbarism', militarism, protectionism: all offended against liberal principles which had become embedded far too deep in Britain's national culture to be prised out easily, or even at all. It was not just a question of morality. Nineteenth-century liberalism had never assumed that morality and self-interest were necessarily at odds. This was what made the imperialists' prescriptions doubly difficult to accept. 'Methods of barbarism', for example, were not only wrong: they undermined the potential loyalty of the Boers. Conscription was not only wrong: it damaged prosperity by diverting healthy young labour from productive work. An imperial *Zollverein* was not only offensive: it was a restraint on trade. Imperialism as a whole was not only immoral: it was also *self-destructive*, in all these ways. These notions, rooted as they were in Britain's recent history, and bolstered by the economic structures created by that history, could not be toppled overnight. This is why it is virtually impossible to conceive of any contemporary British government accepting the imperialists' nostrums. If they had, it might possibly have saved Britain as a Great Power; but it was never really on.

This explains why imperial enthusiasm in Britain at all levels was as thin and fragile as it was. It had no deep *roots*, and so could bear no great weight. Jingoes for example were happy to yell and dance and break the odd anti-imperialist window for the sake of the empire, but were not prepared to make *sacrifices* for it. In the 1906 general election they were asked for one small sacrifice: a dearer loaf of bread, which the Liberals claimed would be the effect of the policy Chamberlain was urging of 'tariff reform' as a first stage towards an imperial *Zollverein*. Jingoism soon quailed before that. The result of the election was a landslide victory for the Liberals, pro-Boers and all. It more than wiped out the effect of the 'Khaki' election, and any encouragement the imperialists had drawn from that.

They were bitterly disappointed. But it was not only the 'people' who had let them down. Their political leaders also lacked imperial conviction. Most of them were fair-weather imperialists only. Even Lord Rosebery, who at one time looked the likeliest man to form the imperialists' longed-for 'centre party' by hiving the Liberal Imperialists away from the main Liberal rump, dithered disastrously until it was too late, and then left politics altogether to indulge his interests in the Turf. Joseph Chamberlain, who was probably the only real 'ideological' imperialist in the government of the day, resigned from the cabinet in 1903 because it would not follow him on the question of an imperial *Zollverein*. Most ministers were pragmatic on these issues, to a greater or lesser extent. The greatest pragmatist of them all was their leader, Lord Salisbury, whose whole foreign policy was founded on the twin ideas that, firstly, no one could tell for sure what would happen in the future, so that it was pointless to plan for it; and secondly, governments were powerless to do much about it in any case. 'It is all pure drifting. As we go down stream, we can occasionally fend off a collision; but where are we going?'[35] That earned him a rebuke from Lord Curzon, who accused him of behaving like an ostrich.[36] An ostrich, however, is probably not a bad thing to behave like, if you have a large capitalist body and long thin liberal legs.

IV

Britain's resistance to the full effects of the imperialist virus did not mean that she avoided infection altogether. On the contrary she suffered a hefty dose of it, from which it took her years to recover. The fact that it only partially affected her probably meant that it did her more damage than it would have done if it had taken her over completely, simply because of the continual battles that raged between it and the antibodies which were there to protect the main functions of the system. That system, in the terms of this metaphor, was the liberal capitalist structure which Britain had inherited largely intact from the nineteenth century, and whose relationship with imperialism had always been somewhat uncomfortable.

This was in spite of the fact that essentially imperialism was an outcome of capitalism. Neo-Marxists maintain that it was an inevitable 'stage' in its development. Be that as it may, it is clear that most of Britain's new colonial possessions in the second half of the nineteenth century were taken in order to protect the commercial and financial interests in the world that her capitalist system had established for her. Those interests included sources for the raw materials which her factories made into products, markets for those products, and fields in which to invest the profits from the sale of them. Sometimes colonies were taken not because they were valuable intrinsically, but for strategic reasons: because they lay on the routes to valuable markets elsewhere. South Africa exemplified all these factors: a source of food and raw materials, a market for British goods, a highly profitable field of investment (in gold and diamond mines), and an essential naval base (at Simonstown) protecting Britain's long-haul shipping lanes to the markets of the Far East. There can be no real doubt that these were the main reasons why Britain defended and extended her South African and other colonial possessions in the later nineteenth century. At any rate – though this is not conclusive – no-one at the time ever disputed it.

This is because these were considered to be perfectly respectable motives for taking colonies at that time. They only became disreputable later on. That was when the 'economic theory' of imperialism, attributing colonial expansion to capitalism, was taken over by anti-imperialists in order to discredit it. It is usually assumed that this was how it originated. In fact it started out as an argument in *support* of imperialism, dreamt up by imperialists themselves in order to persuade capitalists to support them on the grounds that imperialism was profitable.[37] Some of them – like Cecil Rhodes – claimed that it was also *necessary*, in order to secure foreign markets in which to sell the surplus goods produced by the capitalist machine. This, of course, went right against the traditional view that imperialism was a *restraint* on capitalist development. J.A. Hobson, who is generally credited with inventing or discovering the 'economic theory' of imperialism, maintained this still. His argument was that colonies only *seemed* to be necessary to capitalism, and would not be if the 'surplus' could be soaked up at home. That could be done by giving the creators of that surplus – the workers – more purchasing power, by paying them higher wages. Then there would be no pressure for markets abroad, hence no imperialism, and things would return to their free-marketist norm. That was one view. Other people took the more realistic one that foreign markets were indeed necessary for British capitalism, and in the conditions of that time might have to be secured imperially: but that this was regrettable all the same. In other words: you could accept that imperialism was a consequence of capitalism, but still regard it as an unwelcome one. The relationship between the two was close, but incongruous.

The incongruities ran very deep. For a start there was the question of cost. Free-market capitalists disapproved of state expenditure. Imperialism normally entailed enormous state expenditure: for the armies necessary to subjugate colonies, and then for the bureaucracies needed to run them. The fact that this expenditure was usually ultimately recovered from the colonies themselves made little difference, because the effect then was to impoverish British capitalism's customers. That was one incongruity. There were others. Imperialism was a statist system, almost by definition; capitalism tended, as we have seen, to anarchy. That led to differences of emphasis. Imperialists were interested in governing people; capitalists by and large were not. Imperialists set much store by the qualities of leadership and loyalty in men and women; capitalists valued enterprise and individual initiative more. Imperialism was associated with paternalism, especially abroad but also (as we have seen) at home; capitalism preferred sturdy self-reliance. Imperialists were often warriors; capitalism was supposed to be the way of peace. In 1919 the Austrian sociologist Joseph Schumpeter characterised imperialism as a kind of throw-back to a previous and more primitive stage of political and social development.[38] That was how it appeared to some contemporary capitalists too.

The systems diverged to this extent, therefore; and yet they existed together. Imperialism had been grafted on to what was in effect an alien structure of institutions and values. The results were confusing. The graft did not 'take' equally everywhere. It was most successful, as one would expect, in the colonies. This was because the people who ran the colonies were almost bound to be men who shared the imperialists' value system, and not the capitalists'. This was ironic, if they were supposed to be running the empire for the capitalists' benefit. It arose from the fact that capitalists – active capitalists – could not be bothered with this sort of thing themselves, because governing people was considered to be an 'unproductive' pursuit. Consequently they had to find others to take on the burden for them. (The same had applied in Britain for years.) The best place to find them was among the classes who had so far resisted the capitalist ethos in Britain: the aristocracy and gentry, and the gentri*fied* middle classes, who still for example believed in the notion of 'service' to people less fortunate than themselves. One of the functions of the public schools at this time was to instil such ideas into young men, in order to meet the increasing demand for colonial administrators from the 1890s on. (This is why it is such nonsense to blame the schools for turning out people like these.) When they reached the colonies, they found the situation there and the company they kept confirmed and strengthened this ethos. They saw their role as almost entirely paternalistic. In most colonies there were rules categorically forbidding them to have financial interests in the country, which was another barrier to their acquiring commercial values. The whole colonial experience, in other words, both drew on and nurtured *anti*-capitalist traits in British society.

This is why it is wrong – or at least simplistic – to regard British imperialism as a 'capitalist' phenomenon, and nothing more. It may have been capitalist in origin, but it was not in the way it worked out. Colonial governments often actively obstructed capitalist development in what they saw as the interests of their native subjects. A good example is Nigeria in 1910-11, where the local Governor, supported by the Colonial Office, refused to give the Liverpool soap manufacturer William Lever permission to set up factories whose effect would have been to turn small peasant proprietors into 'wage slaves' working for him.[39] That went right against the free-market grain. Capitalists usually got on better in colonies which were only loosely controlled by the Colonial Office, like the ones given over to 'chartered companies' to rule in the 1880s, or 'settlement' colonies like Australia and South Africa where the local whites were in control. They got on best of all in 'informal' colonies of the old type, where the writ of the Colonial Office did not run at all. As a general rule the more formal an imperial relationship was, the less capitalist or exploitative it was likely to be. If imperialism really was a consequence of capitalism, therefore, it seems in many respects to have been a counter-productive one.

The same contradiction could be seen in other colonial situations after 1905, when a Liberal – and reputedly less imperialistic – government took over from the Conservatives. In India it took the form of a struggle between a somewhat authoritarian local government (there is no necessary conflict, of course, between authoritarianism and paternalism) and a Secretary of State for India, John Morley, whose strong liberal antecedents should have inclined him more towards Indian self-rule. That was resolved by means of a series of administrative changes announced in 1909 (the 'Morley-Minto Reforms') which could be represented as a step towards self-government, but so small as not to worry the authoritarians unduly. A similar clash of principles in South Africa was resolved by getting rid of Sir Alfred (now Viscount) Milner, the British High Commissioner, who had wanted to rule the Boers despotically until they were clearly outnumbered by loyal Britons; and then by granting the two newly-conquered Boer states immediate self-government within a new Union of South Africa under the British flag. That seemed remarkably generous at the time. Conservative imperialists (including Milner) predicted disaster from it, but were confounded in the short and medium terms. The result was highly satisfactory for British capitalists in South Africa, simply because self-government was less expensive, and less likely to put obstacles in the way of their exploitation of the vast – and mainly black – cheap labour market which was one of the attractions of the place.[40]

Imperialist values usually won out in the dependent empire, therefore, but had to give way to more liberal ones in the white-dominated colonies. Back in Britain they had – as we have seen already – less success. Few of the more radical imperialists' suggestions were taken up, except those that suited the interests of other parties too. They included the Alien law of 1905, enacted as a sop to London East Enders who felt threatened by cheap immigrant labour, as well as to anti-semitic prejudice; and Lloyd George's social reforms of 1906–10, which owed something to imperial considerations – in particular revelations about the poor physical condition of many of the men who had volunteered for military duty in the South African war – but which also, of course, had the Labour party's backing.[41] A certain amount was being done by voluntary agencies – pressure groups, rifle clubs, imperial youth movements like the Baden-Powell Boy Scouts – but not enough. Imperialism had made scarcely any impression on the domestic social scene, which one writer described in 1906 as still dominated by the 'pseudo-liberal policy of drift, neglect, and mammonism, miscalled non-interference, individualism, and free trade'.[42]

This dichotomy, between old-fashioned capitalist and new-fangled imperialist principles, continued to dog British politics for many more years. It affected all three main parties, but the Conservatives most seriously. During the Boer war the Liberals became the first casualties, as they were bound to be with their free-market and anti-imperialist traditions; but they soon recovered as those traditions came to be put behind them in the early twentieth century, and as they found liberal ways of ruling the empire (like the South African one) which reconciled the critics in their ranks to the fact that they were ruling it at all. Labour of course had none of the Liberals' hang-ups about state intervention, which is what made them the imperialists' best allies over social reform; and were too far away from government as yet to feel the need to formulate policies for the empire itself. The Conservatives, however, were less fortunate.

They were sorely afflicted. The new phenomenon hit them at a bad time. They were just then in the process of becoming the main capitalist party in the state, in succession to the Liberals who seemed to be abandoning that ground for new social-radical pastures, and in response to all those fugitives from the Liberal party who were looking for somewhere else to cultivate their free-market ideas. Imperialism upset all that. It did not appeal to those ideas at all, but to more traditional Tory ones: authority, patriotism, militarism, *noblesse oblige*. That tendency in the Conservative party was given a boost, therefore, to the detriment of the free-market one, which now found it had a new rival on its hands. The first big battle between the two came over the issue of tariff reform (linked with Chamberlain's *Zollverein* project), which raged within the party from 1903 onwards, helping to lose the Conservatives the 1906 election along the way. Later the party was able to cover up its differences more decorously, but without ever finally settling the issue between the two competing creeds. For most of the next half-century or so the Right remained split along these lines, with the imperialists probably having the edge. That may have done far more to obstruct and undermine free-enterprise capitalism in Britain before 1979 than 'socialism', which is usually taken to be the villain of the piece.

Chapter 12

Progress and Reaction
(1900–1910)

I

The effect of the half-grip that imperialism held Britain in from around 1900 onwards was to keep her permanently suspended between two different paths of social and economic development. The first was the free-market capitalist path which Britain had first nervously set out on in the early nineteenth century, then sauntered along increasingly confidently later, until the closing couple of decades of the century, when stones and pot-holes underfoot made the going less easy. The other had started off years before as the paternalistic Tory path, almost petered out in the mid-nineteenth century, when many Tories came off it to join the walkers on the other track, but then got clearer and a little smoother later on, with the help of some renovation work done on it by imperialists and others. The two paths ran very close together, so that it was possible to hop from one to the other, or even at times to walk on both at once, albeit uncomfortably. That was what Britain did, perforce, in the 1900s.

Most of her journey took her along the free-market path. We must not lose sight of this, or exaggerate, as some contemporaries were wont to do, the incursions made by the state in Britain before 1914. The crusade for 'tariff reform' which Chamberlain launched in 1903 failed completely, and never recovered from Chamberlain's own disablement (by a stroke) in 1906. Free trade survived (apart from emergency wartime measures) until 1932. Britain's industry was nearly all in private hands until even later, very loosely regulated, and with no significant pressure at all as yet for any of it to be taken over by the state. Public expenditure was higher in the 1900s than in the 1890s (£163 million as against £107 million per annum), necessitating a rise in income tax from around 7 pence in the pound to one shilling; but the latter only represented a rate of 5%, which was still very low by post-World War I standards.[1] That is probably as good a guide as any to the extent of state intervention in the economy in these pre-war years, which was so slight as to be hardly worth mentioning; were it not for the fact that some of it was felt to constitute an important new departure at the time.

That departure was the famous clutch of social reforms carried out by the new Liberal government between 1906 and 1911. They included Acts to provide free school meals and medical examinations for needy children in 1906–7, and the first state insurance schemes for old age, sickness and unemployment in 1909 and 1911. The latter were very minimal, with old-age pensions limited to five shillings a week (or 7s 6d. for a couple) for those over 70 years of age and with annual incomes of under £31 10s., and unemployment and sickness insurance restricted to certain industries. All were contributory. They had a dual genesis. The first was imperialism, which we have mentioned already;[2] in particular imperialist concern about the poor physical condition of working-class recruits for the Army during the Boer war, analysed in the report of an 'Interdepartmental Committee on Physical Deterioration' published in 1904. The second was the growing influence of organised Labour in British politics, after the foundation of the Labour party (originally the Labour Representation Committee) in February 1900, and its winning of 29 parliamentary seats, with the help of an electoral pact with the Liberals, in 1906.

The Labour party itself can be seen as a sign of a shift away from free marketism in British politics, though it was perhaps not quite as significant a shift as it came to seem later on. In a way it was a reluctant response to provocation. The 1890s had seen a powerful reaction against the trade unions in particular, spearheaded by employers' organisations and the extreme free-marketist Liberty and Property Defence League. One of their weapons was legal actions against unions involved in industrial disputes, which with the help of a generally sympathetic judiciary succeeded in chipping away many of the immunities trade unionists believed Disraeli had granted them in 1875. Picketing was limited, for example; strikes were banned in certain situations; and in 1901 a famous case brought on behalf of the Taff Vale Railway Company ruled that unions could be made liable for losses suffered by employers as the result of some strikes. The unions found they could do nothing about this. The courts seemed congenitally biased against their more collectivist view of liberty. The only authority above the courts was the legislature, which enacted the laws the courts enforced. It was this that brought a significant number of trade unions (but not two of the biggest, the Miners and Cotton Spinners) round to agreeing to finance a new body which would work for direct Labour representation in the Commons. Finance was the crucial ingredient, in order to be able to pay not only for electoral campaigns, but also – in these days before parliamentary salaries – any Labour MP's living expenses while he was away from his work. Because it was crucial, and the trade unions the source of it, they were given a predominant role on the executive committee of the new party. The minority represented various Labour political groups like the ILP, the SDF and the Fabians.

The party's origins and composition ensured that it was never *socialist* in any unequivocal sense. The main socialist element in it initially was the Marxist SDF, which soon got fed up with it and (in the autumn of 1901) left. Thereafter there remained a number of members who were 'under a vague Socialist influence', as Henry Pelling puts it, but usually liked to stress their nonconformist Christian backgrounds more.[3] A review of Labour MPs' reading habits in a contemporary journal revealed what Kenneth Morgan calls 'a reassuring bias in favour of the Bible, Shakespeare and Dickens, Ruskin and Carlyle, but no reference to Marx or other alien ideologues.'[4] Ramsay MacDonald, the party's first secretary, preferred the word 'socialist*ic*' to describe it,[5] which was presumably intended to indicate something less red-blooded than socialism pure. Its founding conference explicitly rejected a resolution (moved by the SDF) calling on it to embrace socialism and the class war, in favour of a much milder amendment which defined its function as to promote and support 'legislation in the direct interests of labour', whatever they might be. Even undoubted socialists like Keir Hardie took this line. The reasons were that the dominant trade unions were not invariably socialist; and that the electorate was feared to be even less so. Exactly the same considerations determined that the Labour party before the war was not generally seen or intended as a party of *government* – a rival to the Conservatives and Liberals – but simply as a working-class pressure group.

This was why no one was frightened of it. The foundation of the party in 1900 was scarcely noticed outside Labour circles: hidden away on page 12 of *The Times* of 1 March, for example, in a report only five column inches long. In 1903 the Liberal chief whip Herbert Gladstone was quite happy to agree (secretly) to the electoral pact with MacDonald which gave Labour most of its 29 seats in 1906. In retrospect this seems like a case of deliberately making room in the Liberal nest for a cuckoo's egg; but Labour never looked like a cuckoo before 1918. It caused no trouble for its Liberal allies, once the latter had given it most of what it asked for, which was not really very much. The social reforms of 1906–11 were part of the bargain, though Labour would have preferred old-age pensions to have been non-contributory. A Trades Disputes Act of 1906 reversed the Taff Vale judgment, and a new Trade Union Act of 1913 reversed another one which had come up in the meantime (the Osborne case, 1908), which had put a block on trade-union political funds. In 1911 a clause in the budget allowed for the payment of MPs. That was about all. Labour's demands were narrowly conceived, and hardly revolutionary ideologically, except to the most zealous of free marketeers. They complemented perfectly the ideas of the new post-Boer war Liberal party, which was itself far less zealous on the free-market issue than it had used to be.

It had been slowly losing that zeal, as we have seen already, over the past 20-odd years, mainly in response to what were perceived to be the shortcomings of the market in the social sphere: the persistence of poverty and the failure of the 'trickle-down' effect. Socialism, of course, was one suggested means of curing these problems, usually through varying degrees (according to how socialist you were) of intervention by the state. Liberals were nervous of this, in case it went too far and destroyed some of the desirable features of 'liberty', but were beginning to take on board the point that absolute non-intervention might not necessarily conduce to real individual liberty if, for example, it had the effect of allowing certain individuals to aggregate powers over others. An example of this, cited by the Liberal social scientist L.T. Hobhouse, was the typical relationship between employer and employee, which in free-market theory was supposed to be a free and equal one, on the grounds that either party could choose to look elsewhere for employment or labour if he or she was unhappy with the contract between them, but which in fact in most situations was heavily loaded towards the employer, because he had a wider choice of workers than the worker did of jobs.[6] That was an argument for the *collective* weight that a trade union could put into the other side of the scale. In other circumstances the *state* might need to be called in to redress the balance; which was difficult to stomach as long as one persisted in regarding the state and individual liberty as antithetical. This is where the 'New' Liberals, as they came to be called, differed from the old. In 1896, through the medium of a new monthly organ called the *Progressive Review*, they set themselves the task of 'exposing the pernicious fallacy' of that assumption, and so laying the foundation for a new type of liberalism which would aim to use the state positively in order to extend people's liberties beyond the narrow limits which they felt the free market imposed.[7]

The *Progressive Review* collapsed very quickly, but its philosophy prevailed. Not only was the Liberal party affected by it, but also the new-born Labour party, whose secretary and then leader from 1911, Ramsay MacDonald, helped edit the *Review*, and was a close colleague of these New Liberal trend-setters for many years: closer, probably, than he was with most of his own Labour party men. Together they forged a new consensus on the moderate Left of British politics, which was far more influential over a longer period than socialism was. One of its explicit purposes was to pre-empt the danger of socialism gaining support in Britain, by sanding down the roughest edges of the capitalist system which might provoke that effect. The ultimate object was peace between the classes.[8] For that reason this general approach was supported by many businessmen, especially a new Edwardian strain of 'model' or paternalist employers: William Lever in Liverpool and George Cadbury in Birmingham, for example, who both built healthy new towns for their workers to live in; and by imperialists who wanted a fit and loyal proletariat to defend their empire for them when the chips were down. Needless to say it was not supported by the older kind of Liberal (now more often a Conservative), who could not accept that the way to stop socialism was to appease it, and who by now must have been feeling miserably isolated and ineffective in the face of all these trends.

II

A certain amount of 'progress' was made on the domestic front in the 1900s, therefore; and yet most self-styled 'progressives' found the going hard. Most of the main trends of the period either seemed to be against them, or else 'progressive' in the wrong direction: like certain contemporary commercial developments, of which more anon. In politics the rise of the Labour party and the Liberal election victories of 1906 and 1910 gave an impression of progress – that is, of growing democratization – which may have been misleading, in view of the conservatism of both parties, and certain indications pointing the other way. One such indication is the failure over these years of the cause of women's suffrage, which was all the more surprising in view of the progress it had been making up to then.

Female enfranchisement, especially as it was advocated by most of its champions – not women's suffrage universally, but only on the same terms as men – was essentially a Victorian liberal cause. It grew out of the same body of ideas that had produced the great Victorian reform bills of 1832, 1867 and 1884, and should have followed on naturally, one would have thought, from them. It was first espoused in parliament during the debates on the second of these bills by the doyen of Victorian liberal philosophers, J.S. Mill, and had a good run in the Commons in the debates on the third. It made steady practical progress at local government level from 1869, when women ratepayers were given the vote in municipal elections, through to 1894, when a Local Government Act allowed them to vote for parish councils too. If this curve had continued it would soon have reached parliament. But it stopped. No further progress was made for the next 20 years, apart from an Act of 1907 confirming (after it had been challenged) that women could *become* county and borough councillors as well as voting for them. The reason, of course, was that men, who had the power to grant women the parliamentary vote, thought they were not fit for it. But opinion on this

– as on the question of male working-class voters – had been softening for some time. Some reason has to be found for the fact that it suddenly hardened again then.

The main one is clear. The 'hardening' coincides exactly in time with the upsurge of interest in and concern for the empire which suddenly revealed itself in the later 1890s, and was a reactionary influence in other contemporary areas of British life too. Its most important feature in this context was the feeling of national vulnerability which accompanied it, and which bore on the question of women's suffrage in two ways. The first was the idea that Britain had become too soft, or feminine, to survive in a masculine (today we would say 'macho') world; which was a good reason for not allowing the softer sex any say in her government. It was also a cause for worry, incidentally, about the 'lack of virility' which some imperialists detected in the male half of the population, especially in the light of all the publicity surrounding Oscar Wilde's trial for homosexuality in 1895. Dirty postcards and other sources of 'impurity' were feared to have the same kind of effect.[9]

The second way in which the 'woman question' affected the empire was in diverting women from their proper duties towards it, which mainly consisted in breeding imperial males. In the past, wrote one imperialist in 1908, they had performed these duties nobly: obeying their menfolk always, marrying, and then facing 'the obligations of the marriage tie and the sufferings and dangers of childbirth... with as much coolness and courage as was expected of the man on the field of battle', in order to 'produce children who should carry on worthily the traditions of... the race'. Now that had all gone. Girls were too interested in other things. Many were declining to marry, or if they did marry refusing to share their husbands' beds: 'an act of cold-blooded treachery and of heartless cruelty', whose effects could be seen in a declining national birth rate. 'Does this not mean,' our critic went on, 'that women are showing the white feather, and are shirking one of the duties of their sex?'[10] Another imperialist agreed. 'Women's true place is in the background,' not out on the streets 'passing their lives in rowdyism, and agitating for things they would be better without.' 'Patriotism is what we want in women..., not suffragism.'[11] 'The root of the evil', wrote a third imperialist, '...the cause of the deterioration of our population, lies almost solely in the fact that our women know nothing about the duties which Nature intends them to perform.'[12] Two of these imperialists, incidentally, were women themselves, so they should have known.

Throughout the battle over the question of women's suffrage imperialists took leading parts on the anti-suffrage side. Its leader – and president of the National League for Opposing Women's Suffrage – was Lord Curzon. His lieutenants included Rudyard Kipling, Lord Cromer, Joseph Chamberlain and Lady Jersey, president of the Victoria League, a women's organisation dedicated to upholding the empire. The old Queen-Empress herself was very much against 'this mad, wicked folly of "Women's Rights"', and thought its ringleaders ought to be whipped.[13] The imperial connexion is patent. It may have made the women's suffrage cause a hopeless one before the war, despite all the efforts of both the main pro-suffrage groups: Millicent Fawcett's National Union of Women's Suffrage Societies, and the Pankhursts' more militant Women's Social and Political Union: the one that broke the law. The latter may have alienated some male support, or alternatively given some males an excuse to withdraw it. On a couple of occasions suffrage bills seemed to come close to victory in the Commons, especially in 1910, but were lost on technicalities, or because the Irish, for example, opposed them on tactical grounds. If a bill had passed the Commons, however, the 'Antis' took comfort from the thought that the Lords would assuredly stop it. That was where the imperialists were at their strongest. And until 1911 the constitutional position was that the Lords could block any Commons legislation they wanted to, though it was generally understood that they would not interfere with finance bills.

The reactionaries saw that as their ultimate defence not only against women's suffrage but also against other liberal measures they felt bound on patriotic or imperial grounds to resist. The main one – as it had been back in 1893 – was Irish home rule, though that was never tested in this decade. The eventual test case was another issue entirely: David Lloyd George's so-called 'People's Budget' of 1909, which aimed to raise the money needed for old-age pensions and other expenditure from new or increased taxes, many of which (higher death duties, an estates transfer tax, a 'super-tax' on incomes over £5000) were deliberately targetted at the landed and the rich. Lloyd George did not expect the Lords to reject it, but they did. That set in motion a constitutional crisis which – after two further general elections, both in 1910, and the threat of a mass creation of Liberal peers to overwhelm the reactionaries – resulted in a significant clipping of their lordships' wings. In April 1910 they passed the budget; the following year they accepted a bill prohibiting them from blocking finance bills again, and allowing them only to *delay* other bills, until the Commons had reconsidered them twice. The reactionaries were bloodied, therefore; but so were the progressives. The price they had to pay was a massive reduction in their Commons majority after the 1910 elections, the second of which saw the Liberals and Conservatives tie with 272 seats each, and the Liberals holding on to power only by virtue of their alliance with 84 Irish Nationalists and 42 Labour MPs. Overall it did not look too bad for the reactionaries. The electoral tide seemed to be flowing with them. Their main fear, home rule for Ireland, had not yet come to pass. All kinds of ways remained to scupper it. In the meantime they still had the House of Lords, with its remaining powers of obstruction, as a useful long-stop.

Placing a long-stop, however, is usually the sign of a defensive field. The reactionaries did fairly well in preventing the progressives from scoring as highly as they might have done; but they were not very penetrating in attack. This was not entirely their fault. For the first half of the decade they had a Conservative government taken up with the Boer war, and then divided and demoralised over the issue of tariff reform; for the second half the Liberals were in power. Consequently the reactionaries, of all varieties, had few opportunities to achieve anything positive in the domestic field. Free marketeers were boxed in. Imperialists got their next generation of military recruits fattened up with the help of the School Meals Act. They also won a partial ban on Jewish immigration with the 1905 Aliens Act, which the Liberal government watered down but did not repeal. Beyond that they had to rely on voluntary efforts, especially organisations like rifle clubs and the Baden Powell Boy Scouts (started up in 1907), to strengthen the fibre of the race. In view of the national and imperial dangers which the imperialists anticipated for the future – shrewdly as it turned out – none of this was enough. That built up frustrations on the right of British politics; some of which were to surface, as we shall see, in the immediately pre-war years.

III

Politics, of course, are not everything; and are almost nothing in a situation in which they are allowed to interfere as little in the *economy* of a country as they were in Britain before the first world war. Very little that any British government did in this period greatly affected material fortunes of any group of people in the country then. There were exceptions to this, but all on the edges of society: individuals the government directly employed, contracted, gave pensions to, imprisoned, hanged or shot, and who would not have been employed, imprisoned, hanged or any of those other things otherwise.

Britain's economic fortunes in the 1900s were almost entirely determined by her situation then: as a relatively small country, crowded, with limited and diminishing natural resources, a mature capitalist economy, a still powerful non-capitalist upper class, over-producing, dependent on her foreign trade to survive, with a very widespread *pattern* of trade, especially in 'underdeveloped' countries, consequently imperialist whether she liked it or not, over-extended, and also militarily vulnerable at home. All these things have to be emphasized, in order to avoid being tempted into unfair comparisons with the economic performances of other countries, whose circumstances were usually very different. America was one example often brought up at the time. Her progress was remarkable: with an economic growth rate double that of Britain's, for example, and its benefits seeming to trickle down to all.[14] Contemporary critics of Britain's economic performance often contrasted her entrepreneurial lethargy with America's 'irresistible vigour' and 'marvellous business instinct',[15] in a way that implied that these were the root causes of America's superior performance; but they may not have been. America had enormous natural advantages over Britain. She was far more favoured both with natural resources, and with room to expand. She had a huge domestic market, which obviated the need for markets abroad. She did trade abroad, but only marginally, and mainly in the relatively 'developed' markets of the Americas and Europe. She did not depend on her trade as Britain did, and so was less under pressure to become imperialistic. When in the 1890s and 1900s she did have a couple of imperial flings nonetheless, for reasons no historian has quite been able to fathom, she did not become in any way dependent on the empire that ensued.[16] She was secure from attack at home. She could *afford* therefore to be individualist, materialist, acquisitive and all the other qualities that were supposed to make the capitalist wheels turn more smoothly, to a far greater extent than Britain could at this time. Britain's situation required at least an admixture of different qualities, in order to enable her to keep her very different vessel, in very different seas, afloat. At its simplest level: acquisitive individualists do not make the best imperialists. Hence Britain's alternative course.

That course may – unavoidably – have damaged her economy. If so the damage was not spread evenly. In some areas the figures for Britain's economic performance in the 1910s look quite impressive. Foreign trade, for example, increased by 36% between 1900 and 1910, especially exports, which rose by 47%. Net earnings from capital invested abroad increased by 64%. All this contributed to record balance of payments surpluses between 1906 and 1913, which in most circumstances would be an obvious sign of health.[17] Away from the figures, appearances seemed to confirm this. The country *looked* prosperous. One obvious sign was the tremendous amount of public and corporate building that was going on, usually in the grandiose neo-baroque style characteristic of the Edwardian period which simply exuded economic confidence. New buildings erected between 1900 and 1910 included a new War Office, the Old Bailey, the British Museum's Edward VII Galleries, the main front of Buckingham Palace, Selfridges, and most of Regent Street and Piccadilly Circus in London; plus the Mersey Docks and Royal Liver buildings in Liverpool, and Belfast and Cardiff City Halls. In the shops a range of exciting new products – plastics, artificial silks, gramophones, sewing machines, typewriters, telephones, motor cars – added to the image of affluence. Companies were expanding through mergers and takeovers.[18] New kinds of enterprise like multiple stores (Liptons, Boots) were springing up. The number of extremely rich people was increasing.[19] That in particular should have boded well for everyone; for was it not a fact, as the extremely rich Scots-American Andrew Carnegie once put it, that 'the condition of the masses is satisfactory just in proportion as a country is blessed with millionaires'?[20]

In this case, unhappily, the answer seemed to be No. This was the other side of the Edwardian economic picture. Despite all the signs of prosperity, people in general did not appear to be doing well. The main problem was with industry, where growth – especially in the traditional staples of iron and steel – simply stopped. One of the reasons for this was foreign competition, mainly from Germany and the United States, which already by 1900 had pushed the British iron, steel and coal industries into second or third place.[21] Germany and America were also showing more enterprise in new areas like chemicals, plastics and motor cars. In compensation for this Britain was forging ahead *financially*, which benefitted the middle classes, but did much less for those members of the working classes who could not edge into at least the white-collar category.

This is reflected in the statistics that describe *their* situation at this time. Unemployment for example reached high levels in 1904 and then again in 1908–9, when nearly 8% of trade unionists were out of work.[22] In 1910 the number of paupers in workhouses reached its highest level of all time: 256 000 in England and Wales, compared with 188 000 in 1900.[23] Hence the current demands for unemployment and old age insurance, which when they were granted did help: elderly people in particular were grateful to Lloyd George for saving them from the workhouse. But they did not affect the underlying economic malaise. Average wages, which seem to have risen quite steadily over most of the later nineteenth century, declined slightly after 1899, and never really recovered until the Great War. In America, by contrast, they increased by about 2% a year in real terms. Estimated figures for the British national income show the same trend: rising from £18.3 to £44.1 per head in real terms between 1855 and 1899, then hovering just below the latter figure for the next ten years.[24] If these figures were accurate, but the rich were getting richer, it must mean that the gap between them and the poor was widening. In 1905 the Liberal MP Leo Chiozza Money did some sums on this, and worked out that a third of Britain's national income was in the hands of only 3% of the population, while a half had to be shared among the poorest 88%. He thought this was worrying. Could it be 'a good thing', he asked rhetorically, 'or an honourable thing, to be one of the few whose bark is borne upon the waters of wretchedness, whose fortunes float upon a sea of unfathomable depths of despair?'[25]

Rhetorical or not, Carnegie might have had an answer for this. He would probably have blamed the Briton's own lack of enterprise and energy. Many native Britons did too. 'Our weakness compared with our two greatest competitors,' wrote one commentator, 'is our different view of work.' The main difference was that while they 'live to work', Britons only 'work to live'.[26] This tendency was encouraged by the trade unions, which another critic *defined* as 'organisations... directed to the shirking of work'.[27] Other targets were drink, lack of parental discipline, the national obsession with sport, immigration, emigration, too little education, and too much education. ('A store of undigested knowledge robs us of an open mind.')[28] Similar criticisms were made of the employing classes, which had become slothful, stupid, content with an easy life and unacquisitive. In other words, they were not playing the game well enough. That was one view. But there was also another: that there was something fundamentally wrong with the rules of the game.

This of course was the socialist line. For Marxists especially, Britain's economic development in the 1900s was going entirely according to the script. It was just what they had always predicted for the stage in its evolution which British capitalism had reached now, when its internal contradictions were finally beginning to take hold. As competition became more cut-throat and profit margins fell, capitalists were forced into increasingly drastic measures, including wage cuts, mergers, searching further afield for markets, and – when all else failed – shifting their capital to less intensively developed economies abroad. That explained everything: the wage stagnation of the 1900s, the trend to bigger and bigger businesses, the increase in Britain's exports, and – most of all – the spectacular growth of her overseas investments. Imperialism was probably an offshoot of this: the latest (and hopefully the last) resort of a desperate capitalist system seeking to defer its inevitable end by forcing the government to seize the commodity and capital markets which would enable it to carry on for a few more years before the great collapse. Lenin, who elaborated this theory in his *Imperialism, the Highest Stage of Capitalism* in 1917, thought he had it from the horse's mouth itself, when he stumbled on Cecil Rhodes's words – cited in our last chapter – predicting 'bloody civil war' if Britain did not find colonies in which to sell her surpluses.[29]

The man Lenin acknowledged as his original source for this idea was J.A. Hobson, who as a 'New Liberal', however, could not be expected to take it this far. His version was different. The problem could be solved short of socialism. The way to do it was for Britain to pay her workers higher wages, thus increasing the *domestic* market for the goods she produced. That would have two effects: it would stimulate growth and prosperity all round at home; and it would marginalise the role of foreign trade (like in America), so abolishing the pressures for imperialism. Capitalism would be rescued from its own internal contradictions. Cobden's vision of wealth at home and peace abroad could be revived. The trickle down effect would start working again. All it needed was a nudge, to remove the blockage. The 'unseen hand' would do the rest.[30]

It looked very simple; but of course there was a practical flaw. Struggling to sell his goods in an increasingly competitive environment, the last thing a manufacturer would normally think of doing was increase his own labour costs, which he would have to do in order to boost domestic demand. For this reason the idea made no headway in Britain at all until much later, when John Maynard Keynes took it over from Hobson and suggested other, more sophisticated ways of putting it into effect. (In this way Hobson can be regarded as the progenitor of not one but two of the twentieth century's most influential ideas: the theory of capitalist imperialism, and Keynesian economics.) Nevertheless the notion that unrestrained capitalism was not necessarily in the best interests of everyone caught on widely in Britain, far beyond the ranks of the socialists, whom one would expect to take this attitude, and of the New Liberals. It was equally strong among many of the reactionaries of the time, for a variety of reasons, some bad (and pilloried mercilessly by historians since), but others understandable, and even perhaps in their own ways reasonable.

IV

The worst reason for the anti-capitalist hostility of the 1900s was probably class snobbery and the racism that often went with it. Upper-class people did not generally mind capitalists, but did mind it when those capitalists tried to buy themselves into their 'society', and minded it most of all when they found themselves forced to aid the process when they fell on hard times, typically by marrying American money or selling their country seats to rich upstarts who would not know what to do with an escutcheon if it fell into their laps. Apparently this was happening a lot then. According to one account the worst offenders were 'Jews, solicitors, American millionaires of the humblest birth and the crudest behaviour, stock-jobbers, Afrikanders, [and] Company promoters'.[31] That list itself sets the tone. Jews were especially resented, particularly at the time of the Boer war, when 'cosmopolitan financiers', as they were sometimes euphemistically called, were pictured on the floor of the Stock Exchange callously speculating on the fortunes of the conflict – on the lives, that is, of British Tommies – or even blamed for its outbreak. Later their hand was seen whenever a financial scandal broke.[32] Anti-semitism was rife in the upper reaches of British society in the 1900s (as well as lower down). Resentment against other kinds of interlopers – Americans, solicitors and the rest – was usually milder, but just as prejudiced. Feelings like these undoubtedly fuelled contemporary hostility towards the *nouveaux riches*, but should not distract us from the serious import of the issues that lay beneath.

At bottom, the controversy over 'the rich' in Britain was between two rival value systems. The new system – the threatening one – represented the latest stage in the development of competitive capitalism, and turned on the simple principle (summarised here by a critic) that 'Business is business,... and cannot be conducted on the rules of the Sermon on the Mount'.[33] Money-making was its only purpose, and consequently a sufficient justification on its own for anything a capitalist did. Opposing that was the British industrialist's more traditional approach, which did not despise money-making, but acknowledged that in certain situations it should be subordinated to other considerations, like the need for probity and a concern for the welfare of the people he employed. That tied in with even older-fashioned paternalistic traditions in British society, which we saw in the last chapter received a great boost from the contemporary upsurge in imperialism. This created a need both for governors and the values appropriate to governing, and also for defenders of the empire and the qualities (leadership, loyalty, discipline) appropriate to *that*. All these values and qualities were thought more likely to come from a paternalistic than from a commercial ethos, which added considerable weight to that side in the debate.

More weight still may have come from people's moral feelings against what were seen as some of the excesses of the new commercial approach. In a nutshell, that approach seemed to be based on sheer *dishonesty* to a degree that was not yet widely tolerated in Britain, possibly because of the hold that all those old-fashioned paternalistic ideas still had on her, but for reasons that are nevertheless fairly easy even today to understand. A contemporary novel by H.G. Wells, *Tono-Bungay* (1909), expressed many of these feelings, against its anti-hero, Ponderevo: who becomes fabulously rich by making a quack tonic cheaply and then selling it expensively by persuading people – through advertising – that it is a miracle cure for everything. Taxed with the morality of this, he replies that 'I'd like to know what sort of trading isn't a swindle in its way'. Commenting on the climate of opinion generally in Britain Wells remarks that 'There can be little doubt that men infinitely prefer the appearance of dash and enterprise to simple honesty'.[34] Others made the same point in even stronger terms. 'Throughout our industries there is corruption, deceit, knavery, trickery, in innumerable shapes,' wrote another critic in 1902. 'The great bulk of our business men have become tricksters, and believe deceit is necessary to success in business.'[35]

It is not difficult to see how this impression arose. The 1900s saw a spate of particularly shocking financial scandals in Britain, beginning with the collapse of the fraudulent company promoter Edward Hooley's empire in 1898, and continuing with the Kynoch affair during the Boer war, which involved a lucrative government contract going to a firm chaired by the brother of a member of the Cabinet. Others followed at regular intervals, climaxing in the most notorious of them all – the 'Marconi scandal', again involving government ministers – in 1912.[36] At the same time suspicions surrounded some grants of knighthoods and peerages to capitalists, allegedly in return for money for Liberal party funds.[37] How widespread this sort of thing was, or how novel, is difficult to say. Most commercial corruption both then and earlier was probably covered up. Nevertheless the evidence is almost irresistible that there was a decline in commercial probity at this time. At the very least there was a much stronger *smell* of corruption in the 1900s than there had been earlier; which did little for the reputation of the wealth-creating (or manipulating) classes in Edwardian times.

That however was only part of the picture. Critics of 'commercialism' objected to some of its legitimate manifestations too. Oft-cited examples were advertising, and the new 'yellow press'. Advertising enjoyed a considerable boom in these years, ending up with an estimated annual turnover of at least £15 million and 80 000 employees by 1914. It was almost entirely unregulated (apart from an 1889 Act prohibiting the promotion of cures for venereal disease and sexual impotence), and consequently quite unscrupulous in its methods, as a glance through almost any contemporary popular newspaper will confirm.[38] The press was a sadder case. Advertising had never had a high reputation. The mid-nineteenth-century British newspaper press, by contrast, was one of the glories of that age. Even at the 'lowest' end of the market, in the weekly tabloids produced for the skilled working classes, it was varied, informative and intelligent. That began to change with the advent in 1896 of Alfred Harmsworth's *Daily Mail*. The *Mail* was the first newspaper to be produced entirely according to market principles: that is, to satisfy a demand. If that demand was for sport, gossip and sensation, then that was what the *Mail* would provide. It would not preach to people, or try to stretch them, which would be elitist and arrogant. Everything in the paper had to be attractive, exciting and easy to swallow. 'Do not forget,' *Daily Mail* journalists were told, 'that you are writing for the meanest intelligence.'[39] These were the main journalistic criteria, not 'truth', which came a very poor fourth. For Harmsworth himself the overriding criterion was profitability. Because the *Mail*'s editorial line was usually imperialistic, some people saw him as having a political aim. In fact a 'famous Englishman' (unnamed) was probably nearer the mark when he described him in 1901 to the Liberal journalist H.W. Massingham as 'only a tradesman speculating in the reaction'.[40] The 'yellow press' in other words was a product not of the political but of the commercial morality of the day. That was what its critics objected to. They objected even more when Harmsworth was raised to the peerage (as Lord Northcliffe) in 1905;

which so far as they were concerned simply compounded one scandal with another.

One more manifestation of the new commercial morality gave cause for concern. Some of the new rich seemed to be inordinately fond of *flaunting* their wealth: their cars, yachts, great houses, wives' jewellery and the rest. That was socially insensitive, to say the least. Upper-class snobs attributed it to their low origins; but it may have had another source. The trend from industry to finance, and to a lesser extent from small- to large-scale firms, was almost bound to create a less socially aware capitalist class. Most *nouveaux riches* were not employers of labour in any direct sense. That may be why – as one contemporary observed – so many of them adhered to the rather cold view that the 'only and proper bond' between masters and men was the 'cash nexus'.[41] You would not find Lever or Cadbury saying that. The same factor – social distance – explained their vulgar ostentation. Mr Toad, in Kenneth Grahame's clearly cautionary *The Wind in the Willows* (1908), is a fictional example of this: a *parvenu* whose vulgar display of wealth to the neglect of his social duties (as squire of Toad Hall) provokes resentment all around him, and near-disaster when the working classes (the Stoats and Weasels) use the opportunity to stage a revolution, from which he is only saved when the traditional gentry (Mole, Ratty, Badger) bring him to a realisation of the social responsibilities which attach to his new position in life. This pointed another danger of the new spirit of the age.

That new spirit nevertheless seemed to be everywhere. Nothing was sacred. Even cricket was beginning to be affected. Cricket, of course, is the game it is better to play sportingly than to win, and which amateurs, or 'gentlemen', play simply for the love of it. By the 1900s it was not, in fact, entirely like that. E.M. Grace, the former Gloucestershire player, lamented at the time how *competitive* the game had become recently, especially with the advent of the County Championship (or league); how mercenary even some 'gentlemen' now were, with the most famous ones commanding large appearance fees; and how the recent emphasis on what he called 'profit and averages' was undermining the true spirit of the game.[42] He might have added – though he did not, probably out of familial loyalty – that one of the worst offenders in all these regards was his own more famous brother W.G., who was also not above a bit of cheating if he thought it would help to win a match. That seemed well up with the times.

But there was also another side to the picture: both in cricket and in the world outside. W.G. Grace was not yet typical. Cricket retained many of its old moral principles. It also clung tenaciously – and notoriously – to its old *social* values, with 'players', or professionals, rigidly segregated from the upper-class 'gentlemen' off the field of play, for example, and the relation-ship between them on it resembling the hierarchical and paternalistic structure of the earlier nineteenth century far more than the egalitarian individualism of modern times. In this respect (as in so many others) cricket mirrored the society it was rooted in pretty exactly. Both were affected, but never taken over completely, by the new commercial spirit of the age.

People always exaggerate new things. They did so during the industrial revolution, for example, when from some contemporary accounts you would have thought that one could hardly move in Britain for dark satanic mills. We have seen how they exaggerated the strength and significance of popular jingoism around 1900. In the later 1900s the impression that the new commercial morality and its pioneers were sweeping everything before them in Britain was natural, in view of the publicity accorded them, but nonetheless mistaken. Britain was still a laggard in this area. To appreciate how laggardly she was, one only needed to cast a glance across the Atlantic to America, which in respect of most of the phenomena described here – the number of really rich people, the merger movement in industry, vulgar ostentation, corruption, advertising, the 'yellow' press – was far ahead of her.

In Britain the resistance to all this held up really very well. The new commercial spirit was always struggling. Condemnations of it greatly outnumbered justifications in the influential periodical press. Most literature was unsympathetic.[43] Britain's most powerful institutions remained largely impervious: the public schools, ancient universities, Church, civil service, trades unions, upper-class 'society', even many businesses. The empire and nearly everything associated with it, as we have seen, were fundamentally opposed. The dominant political consensus of the day was for a modified form of 'commercialism', with the poorest victims of it being helped from the public purse. Another sign of the strength of the resistance was the pattern of employment in Britain, which seems to have been shifting away slightly from the 'productive' towards the 'non-productive' sector. Between 1891 and 1911, for example the Census's category of 'Public Service' occupations rose by 97%, the armed forces by 65%, and other 'professions' by 44%, at a time when the population as a whole increased by only 9%.[44] Another flourishing non-productive area was the arts, which were then enjoying quite a remarkable little renaissance in Britain, after the arid utilitarianism of the mid-nineteenth century. Not since the very early nineteenth century had Britain been able to boast such a constellation of artistic talent as is represented by the names of Shaw, Wilde, Hardy, Yeats, Beardsley, Morris, Mackintosh, Lutyens, Parry, Elgar and Delius, among others; all of whom found it possible (if sometimes only barely) to pursue artistic careers in Britain, in Delius's case in deliberate preference to a promising business one. A few of them, calling themselves 'Aesthetes', preached a doctrine of 'Art for Art's sake', which was just about as 'unproductive' as you could get. All this may have been symptomatic not merely of resistance to the inroads of commercialism, but of a more aggressive fight back. Capitalism's outer ramparts were falling, to a combined socialist, New Liberal, imperialist, moralist, artistic, gentlemanly, snobbish and racist attack.

We have seen, however, that there was more to it than that. Britain's relative capitalist decline in the 1900s was not just a matter of hidebound prejudices obstructing progress, though hidebound prejudices undoubtedly helped. Behind them, and behind all the other social and moral values which *may* have held Britain back economically from this time onwards, was something far more solid and rational: her material interests in the world, and especially her dependence on foreign trade with underdeveloped markets in a hostile international environment, which made her situation entirely different from that of any of the countries with which she was sometimes unfavourably compared. Of course this does not excuse all her failings. She could have coped better, and no doubt would have done, if she could have seen as clearly as historians can exactly what was going on. But it explains why the general attitude or ethos with which she approached her problems differed from that of, say, the United States. The main bugbear – though it was not the fundamental one, because in itself it was merely the effect and visible sign of her underlying difficulties – was the empire. If Britain had been able to do without her empire, she might have followed America's example. The qualities and values which prevented her following that example would have died out naturally. When many years later she was forced to do without her empire, they did.

Part III
A Very Great Danger
(1911–40)

Chapter 13

Pre-War Crisis
(1911–14)

I

On 11 November 1911 George V, King of Britain and Ireland and Emperor of India in succession to his father, Edward VII, who had died in May 1910, embarked at Portsmouth on the P&O steamer *Medina*, bound for India. By doing so he became the first reigning British monarch to venture outside Europe 'since Coeur-de-Lion set forth on his Crusade'.[1] The idea – the king's own – was for him to be crowned Emperor of India at a great 'Durbar' (or public audience) near the ancient Hindustan capital of Delhi. At first he had wanted to crown *himself*, Napoleon-style; but the Archbishop of Canterbury, who reckoned that he was the one who ought to do any crowning that came up, objected, and so it was agreed that George should arrive at the Durbar with the crown – a new one, paid for out of Indian taxes, but then taken home to London, where it still is – already on his head.[2] This was how it was done, on 12 December 1911, amid scenes of splendour certainly unmatched ever in Britain, and probably in India too. Here is how *The Times* described the climax.

> Enthroned on high beneath a golden dome, looking outwards to the far North whence they came, their Majesties the King-Emperor and Queen-Empress were acclaimed by over 100 000 of their subjects. The ceremony at its culminating point exactly typified the oriental conception of the ultimate repositaries of Imperial power. The Monarchs sat alone, remote but beneficent, raised far above the multitude, but visible to all, clad in rich vestments, flanked by radiant emblems of authority, guarded by a glittering array of troops, the cynosure of the proudest princes of India, the central figures in what was surely the most majestic assemblage ever seen in the East. It was a sight which will remain indelibly engraved upon the memory.

No one who was there, *The Times* concluded, 'not even the poorest coolie who stood fascinated and awed upon the outskirts of the throng', could have been 'unresponsive to its profound significance'.[3]

That significance was supposed to be that it symbolised the close – even symbiotic – historical ties that existed between Britain and India, and also their permanence. As if to emphasise the latter the King-Emperor announced at the end of the Durbar, to everyone's surprise, that the capital of the British *raj* in India was to be removed forthwith from Calcutta to Delhi, with the help of a huge £4 million programme of great public buildings, starting with a new official residence for the Viceroy. Work on that began very quickly. It was designed by Edwin Lutyens, not (thankfully) in Edwardian baroque but in a 'stripped classical' style with Indian features,[4] spacious and imposing, and clearly intended to house British viceroys for decades or even centuries to come. It was a tangible expression of faith in the greatness and resilience of the British empire in India, and by extension elsewhere.

Unfortunately the landscapes of the world are littered with the ruins of great buildings which at the time were thought to reflect the strength and glory of the regimes which put them up, but turned out to presage their fall. New Delhi comes into this category. Thirty-six years after the Delhi Durbar, and a mere 16 after the Viceroy's Residence was completed, Britain's rule in India was at an end. That does not mean that this could or should have been foreseen in 1911. Between then and 1947, when Britain left India, a number of things happened – most notably two world wars – which are likely to have diverted the course of history into channels that could not reasonably have been predicted at the earlier date. Nevertheless there were signs of weakness even then. The British grasp on India was less secure than the success of the Durbar suggested. The same was true of some other parts of the empire, including its heart, where it was questionable in 1911 whether Britain even had a proper grip of herself.

So far as India was concerned the other side of the picture was revealed by an incident which took place at Barisal in East Bengal on the evening before the Durbar, when a police inspector was shot by a gunman, presumably for political motives.[5] He was just the latest in a string of victims of the serious terrorist campaign which had been going on for a few years now, especially in Bengal since its partition by the last viceroy, Lord Curzon, into separate (Hindu and Moslem) states. The incident which aroused the most outrage was one which claimed the lives of a Mrs and Miss Kennedy of Muzaffarpur, whose carriage was mistaken for that of the local judge and bombed in April 1908. In the following year the arm of the terrorists reached London, where Sir William Curzon Wyllie, political aide-de-camp to the Secretary of State for India, was assassinated by an Indian nationalist at the Imperial Institute on 1 July. Rigorous policing ensured that there was no serious trouble during the King-Emperor's visit. Then, almost exactly a year after the Durbar, the viceroy himself (Lord Hardinge) was gravely injured by a picric acid bomb thrown at his elephant as he made his first state entry into New Delhi on 23 December 1912. This was discouraging. It was also, incidentally, the very good reason why the imperial crown was shipped back to England after the Durbar, instead of being left in Delhi, where it would have been a standing temptation to nationalist firebrands.[6]

India was not the only part of the empire where there were strains. Egypt had a comparable nationalist movement. So did Ireland, which was promised limited home rule as a result in 1911. In South Africa Britain's problems were of a different kind. There the white population had *de facto* control. Sometimes they exercised that control in ways that Britain deplored, especially with regard to blacks. Theoretically Britain could intervene, but in important cases that was never on. A notorious example came up in 1906, when the Natal government sanctioned the execution of 12 African rebels after a travesty of a trial, Whitehall ordered a stay of execution, the local government resigned *en masse*, and Whitehall – faced with the prospect otherwise of resuming direct rule and perhaps provoking another South African war – caved in.[7] That illustrated the weakness of her imperial sway. 'Empire' usually implies the domination of one country by another. In the case of the 'white' dominions – Canada, Australia and New Zealand were in the same boat in this regard – there was no question of that.

Elsewhere Britain had to tread carefully in order to avoid dangerous protest from those she was supposed to dominate. This was the situation in tropical Africa, for example, where her rule was much more absolute, but not as absolute in practice as it was theoretically. This was because she had so many Africans to rule, and so few Britons on the spot to do the ruling, which made the latter always potentially vulnerable if they rubbed the Africans up the wrong way. It was probably for this reason, rather than because of any innately superior sense of humanity on Britain's part, that her colonial record at this time was not quite so bloody as some other colonial powers'; though there were exceptions, like an incident at Denshawai in Egypt in 1906 when British troops over-reacted to a justified protest demonstration by villagers, killing and wounding a number of them. It also helps to explain one distinctive British approach to the problems of colonial government in the early twentieth century, which was to leave the natives alone as far as possible to organise themselves both politically and economically along their own customary lines, however 'unprogressive' those lines might be from a European capitalist point of view. The name given to this was 'Indirect Rule'. One of the casualties, which we have met already, was William Lever's scheme to develop the Nigerian palm-oil extracting industry in a modern way,[8] which was blocked on the grounds that it would be too disruptive of traditional African patterns of land tenure, and hence unsettling socially. Indirect Rule, as it worked out in practice, was an easier and cheaper way of running an empire than trying to reform or 'raise' or 'improve' it. There was a much better chance that the natives would remain docile if they were not interfered with too much.

In every kind of colony, therefore, Britain compromised and conceded in order to avoid provoking dangerous unrest. Whom she compromised with depended on who (apart from herself) was the dominant or potentially dominant group. In the more recent and 'backward' colonies of tropical Africa and the Pacific that tended to be the traditional ruling elites; in the dominions it was the white settlers; and in India it was the 'moderate' middle-class nationalists, in deference to whom, for example, the partition of Bengal was eventually revoked. (This was George V's other great surprise announcement at the 1911 Durbar.) The object of this strategy was to enable Britain to hold on to the empire. By the same token, however, it made it difficult for her to do what she might have wanted to do *with* it. She had little freedom of action there. Everywhere she was cabinned and confined by the need to appease local opinion. This made the empire less of an *asset* to her than it could have been otherwise. In fact it is possible to argue that by this time the empire had become a liability to her overall.

It is impossible to compute this accurately, though some have tried. There are too many imponderables involved. The basic purpose of the empire was to protect Britain's trade and capital investment in the wider world. In 1911 about 33–35% of both was done with the empire, which was a large proportion, but not a majority.[9] How much of Britain's colonial trade would have remained if the colonial tie had been broken, and how much of her *non*-colonial trade depended on the existence of colonies and the imperial Navy nearby, no one can say. On the other side there were some clear economic disadvantages arising from the empire from Britain's point of view. Two American historians, Lance Davis and Robert Huttenback, point to the vast hidden 'imperial subsidy' (like naval expenditure) which Britain paid to Australia, New Zealand, Canada and South Africa in this period, for example, without the financial gains she made from those countries apparently ever covering her costs. (Davis and Huttenback go on from that to claim that Britain lost out generally as a result of imperialism, but the calculations on which they base this are highly problematic, and do not, for example, take account of *trade*.)[10] Then there were certain other possible indirect effects. The empire may have blunted Britain's competitive edge, by providing her exporters with relatively 'soft' markets; or distorted the home market in the way J.A. Hobson described;[11] or helped bolster a paternalistic ethos which was corrosive of the capitalist 'spirit' at home. It is hopeless to try to draw up an imperial 'balance sheet' accurate and sensitive enough to take all these factors into account. All we can say is that imperialism had its economic drawbacks as well as its advantages. And even if the latter outweighed the former, they may not have done so sufficiently to compensate for certain other burdens the empire brought in its train.

The main one was diplomatic. From the point of view of Britain's foreign relations her empire was an almost unmitigated liability. Looked at strategically it was a monster. It had thousands of miles of land frontiers, some of them almost inviting attack. Most of its 400 million subjects considered themselves alien to Britain, and so had to be regarded as potentially disloyal if ever they got the chance. It provoked jealousies outside from strong and heavily-armed rivals, especially France, Russia and Germany (in that order). It was only very thinly guarded by British troops, perforce. It was constantly vulnerable, in a dozen different ways. No other European power had quite so many distractions and potential weaknesses outside Europe. This put Britain at a great disadvantage, therefore, in her European diplomacy. Other powers – relatively speaking – had only themselves to consider. Britain had to consider the effects of any decisions she took on all these other responsibilities too.

The empire consequently dominated her diplomacy throughout the later nineteenth and early twentieth centuries, in ways which were often highly damaging. Initially it inclined her to a policy of 'isolationism', or keeping clear of European alliances, whose disadvantage was supposed to be that they could drag Britain into wars over questions that were of no direct concern to her, and which then might have dangerous repercussions on her interests overseas. The drawbacks of that policy were that it left her with no friends to help her if she were attacked; and that it left continental Europe to organise itself into a new alliance system in the 1890s (Germany plus Austria *versus* France plus Russia) without any kind of input or influence from her. In the 1900s, as that alliance system hardened, became more and more militarized, and created tensions of its own, the dangers of isolation from it became more apparent, and Britain eventually had to change tack. When she did so it was the empire – again – which determined the way she went, with possibly drastic effects. We shall come on to this later.[12] The point to stress at this stage is that the empire's contribution to all this was to restrict Britain's choices, stay or force her hand; to dominate *her*, in fact, to a far greater extent than she can be said to have dominated it. This of course was not the impression given by the King-Emperor and Queen-Empress as they sat enthroned on high beneath their golden dome, 'looking outwards to the far North whence they came', in the hot sun on that dusty plain outside Delhi on 12 December 1911. But it was far closer to the reality.

II

It was also closer to the reality back home. Many imperialists realised this. 'Whether England will appreciate its momentous character,' wrote our *Times* reporter at the Delhi Durbar, 'we cannot tell.'[13] Almost certainly it would not. Ordinary Britons had never been imperialistic in this sense. This, of course, was another of the empire's weaknesses. It had long been a worry to dedicated imperialists, who knew how difficult it was going to be in almost any foreseeable circumstances for the empire to pull through the next few years without a much greater measure of what they called 'imperial patriotism'. There were few signs of this in 1911. (That may help to account for the fact that George V's first coronation – the one in Westminster Abbey on 20 June – was something of a popular flop: though a light drizzle and the fact that people could now see coronations on film in the comfort of their local picture-houses will have had something to do with that too.)[14] The underlying reason for this relative imperial apathy, as we have seen, was the fundamentally *un*-imperialist nature of the society to which the dedicated imperialists' form of imperialism was attached, as a kind of accretion. But there were also some additional reasons for it in 1911. That was a very eventful year. A lot of exciting and worrying things were happening nearer home. It is not really surprising that people's attention was distracted by these away from the empire, where little apart from the great Delhi Durbar appeared to be going on.

The most exciting events were on the industrial front. The coronation itself took place during a seamen's strike. Other groups striking at around this time were dockers, railwaymen, miners, cotton operatives and even (briefly in August 1911) schoolboys demanding an extra half-day holiday and the abolition of homework.[15] Altogether there were 903 strikes in 1911, 857 in 1912, and 1497 in 1913, compared with an average of 464 a year in the 1900s. Ten million working days were lost through them in 1911, and a staggering 40 million in 1912.[16] Many strikes gave rise to violence, which had to be put down by troops. The most notorious occasion was at Ton-y-pandy in South Wales in November 1910. This was followed in the summer of 1911 by serious riots in Liverpool and Hull, where one town councillor, who had been in Paris during the 1871 Commune, claimed they exceeded even that event in ferocity: 'women with hair streaming and half nude, reeling through the streets, smashing and destroying... he had not known that there were such people in Hull'.[17] In the course of the Liverpool disturbances two men were shot dead by artillery. A few days later (on 19 August) another two were shot in Llanelly, and five more killed when rioters accidentally set fire to a railway van containing detonators. The rioters then, for some reason, turned on the Jews, who started pouring out of Wales in droves. Nothing like this had been seen in Britain for nearly 30 –

perhaps even 70 – years.

It was clearly a grass-roots thing. Trade-union membership soared from two and a half million in 1910 to more than four million in 1913.[18] Many strikes were called when the militant membership of a union turned down agreements negotiated with the employers by its more moderate leaders. The new leaders who came in to displace them – Ben Tillett of the Dockers' Union, Tom Mann of the new all-embracing 'Workers' Union' – often had political as well as purely industrial aims. Those aims were far to the left of the Labour party, which Tillett and Co. regarded as a nest of traitors to their class. In 1912, for example, Mann called for a full-scale class war in Britain; Parliament, he said, was 'a farce and a sham, the rich man's Duma, the employer's Tammany, the Thieves' kitchen and the working man's despot', so that the only way the proletariat could hope to win its rights was by taking up arms in 'the most brutal' and 'pitiless' kind of war.[19] Many railwaymen and South Welsh miners, in particular, called themselves 'syndicalists', advocating direct worker control of industry. To achieve their aims, in the summer of 1914 three of the biggest unions – miners, transport workers and railwaymen – formed a 'triple alliance' with a plan to strike *simultaneously* at a given moment, to maximise their impact. That did not happen before the war; but it was, as Basil Thomson, the new head of Scotland Yard's Special (Political) Branch, put it: 'a threat... held *in terrorem* over the nation for several years'.[20]

Thomson believed that a revolution might be brewing, which only 'a European war to divert the current' could prevent.[21] The King also thought he saw revolutionary signs.[22] That was probably alarmist. The men charged with restoring order on the spot, the military commanders, who had better intelligence than Thomson, took a calmer line. Major-General Nevil Macready in South Wales, for example, put most of the blame for the trouble there on to the mine owners, who he thought were positively spoiling for a fight. They were the ones who needed to be held back.[23] Few government ministers seem genuinely to have feared the worst. Few of the strikers expected it. Those who claimed afterwards that they had been cheated out of their revolution by the War were probably fooling themselves. But it is impossible, of course, to know for sure.

What is much clearer is that *something* was going seriously wrong. Consensus in Britain – what there was of it – was breaking down. On top of this industrial trouble were other manifestations of anomie: like this one.

The 'Votes for Women' Movement was at its hysterical worst about this time. The 'Wild Women' were behaving like demented idiots in order to prove to the nation that they were fit and proper persons to have a hand in government affairs. The most insane deeds of sabotage were being carried out by the fanatics of the movement, and women who a short while before had been courteous and charming specimens of English feminity were prancing and howling in the streets, chaining themselves to railings outside Number 10 Downing Street, slashing the nation's art treasures to pieces in our galleries, and setting fire to the residences of politicians, statesmen, and national leaders.[24]

That is the account of a contemporary policeman, writing as if he could still feel the scratches from the suffragettes' nails. Another source of unrest was Ireland. In this case the threat came from the political Right, after the Irish had definitely been promised home rule, and were simply waiting for the inevitable Lords veto on it to be overridden under the terms of the 1911 Parliament Act. The right, of course, objected to this, and even contemplated resisting it (some of them) by force of arms. An added problem here was that many British Army officers shared their views. In March 1914 the main army detachment in Ireland, stationed at the Curragh in Dublin, staged a 'mutiny' by announcing that they would resign or disobey if ordered north against the anti-home rule 'Ulster Volunteers'. Again, the war intervened. If it had not, this might well have turned out to be a more serious threat to domestic stability in Britain than the one from the left.

Overshadowing these threats there was another, much bigger one. The prospect of European war was in the air continually in the early 1910s, and especially during July 1911, between the two coronations, when the arrival of a German gunboat, the *Panther*, off Agadir in Morocco seemed to presage a clash between France (who had claims there) and Germany. No one would have been surprised if that had been the trigger for a general European conflict. Everyone expected it. A trivial feature of George V's first coronation may illustrate this. Sir Edward Elgar provided a number of musical compositions for the occasion. One was a 'Coronation Ode', which in fact was not a new work but one he had originally written for Edward VII in 1902, with a couple of changes to suit the new circumstances. One of those changes was significant. In 1902 the penultimate section had been a gentle invocation to 'Peace, Perfect Peace', for soloists and unaccompanied chorus; in 1911 that was dropped. Now the Ode went straight into its fully-orchestrated climax – 'Land of Hope and Glory', with stirring words by A.C. Benson – without any pause before it for thoughts of peace.[25] The simple reason for this was that Britain was not actually at war in 1911, as she had been at the beginning of 1902; but it could be considered an unfortunate omission all the same. If you were superstitious you might think that it boded ill. It certainly seemed to reflect – probably unwittingly – the widespread mood of resignation in the face of war at that time.

It affected people in many ways. There was a great spy scare, whipped up largely by the popular newspapers, which had people scouring the country for the thousands of German agents who were supposed (wrongly) to be stationed all over Britain, usually disguised as waiters and barbers, waiting for '*der Tag*' when, at a given signal, they would bring Britain to a standstill by sabotage.[26] That was the negative side. More positively, military pressure groups like the Navy League and the National Service League flourished, each boosting its membership to around 100 000 by 1914. More than 150 schools and 20 colleges and universities had Officers' Training Corps by 1910.[27] Sir Robert Baden-Powell's Boy Scout movement caught on wonderfully, probably for all sorts of entirely extraneous reasons, but partly too in response to the nervous patriotic feelings stimulated by the war fever of the time. 'I am sure that if you boys will keep the good of your country in your eyes *above everything else* she will go on all right,' wrote Baden-Powell in the 1911 edition of *Scouting for Boys: A Handbook for Instruction in Good Citizenship*. 'But if you don't do this there is very great danger, because we have many enemies abroad, and they are growing daily stronger and stronger.'[28]

For Baden-Powell 'good citizenship' was the key. This was what linked the foreign threat to Britain's domestic problems. Many Britons were playing into the hands of the Germans – for the most part unintentionally – by their general social habits and attitudes. *Scouting for Boys* is peppered with historical parallels (usually false ones) to illustrate the harm of this. 'Another cause of the downfall of Rome', for example,

> was that the people, being fed by the State to the extent of three-quarters of the population, ceased to have any thought or any responsibility for themselves and their children, and consequently became a nation of unemployed wasters. They frequented the circuses, where paid performers appeared before them in the arena, much as we see the crowds now flocking to look on at paid players playing football.[29]

Welfarism and professional football were common targets, signs of what was widely coming to be regarded as Britain's 'national deterioration' at that time. Others included mental illness, suicide, self-abuse, homosexuality, dirty postcards, stunted growth, Jewish immigration, commercial corruption, 'shirking', suffragism, trade unions, strikes, socialism and art. These all undermined the general social fabric of Britain, it was felt, in ways which could be disastrous from a national and imperial point of view.[30]

It is almost incredible how in retrospect people can sometimes get the mood of an age completely wrong. After the Great War this pre-war period was often portrayed as a golden era of contentment and peace. In reality it was nothing of the sort. Nearly everyone lived in fear of something: poverty, unemployment, strikes, riots, assassinations, Rome rule, national deterioration, foreign spies, war. Dreadful, spectacular things happened one after the other. One of the most dramatic was a spate of ugly incidents in London featuring Jewish immigrant anarchists, culminating in January 1911 in the grisly death of three of them by shooting and burning in a besieged house in Sidney Street in the East End. Another depressing event came on 15 December 1911, when the Norwegian explorer Roald Amundsen pipped his British rival Robert Falcon Scott to the South Pole, which was a blow to national pride: though the British made as much as they could of his heroic failure, as is their wont. (Other examples are the charge of the Light Brigade, Rorke's Drift, Gordon at Khartoum, Dunkirk, and England's semi-final against West Germany in the 1990 World Cup.) Then on 15 April 1912 a much more terrible event occurred: the sinking of the great White Star ocean liner *Titanic* on its maiden voyage, with the loss of 1513 lives because the company had not considered it economic to provide life-boats for all of them. Most of the casualties were *men*, because they had chivalrously let the women and children into the boats before them, and *lower class*, because they were in a more dangerous part of the ship. That could be taken as a kind of allegory of the economic and social *malaise* of Britain then.

III

How the *malaise* should be treated depended, of course, on one's diagnosis of it. Another problem of the time was that there was no agreement over this. There was some agreement over what constituted the most serious symptom of ill health. That was the labour unrest. An immediate cause of that was almost certainly the gap that was opening up at this time between the very rich, and the great mass of the fairly poor. Wage stagnation, together with narrowing opportunities for social mobility, took away the poor's hope of improvement, which had kept them relatively docile before. At the same time the rich were getting richer, and some of them less socially responsible than in the past. This indicated some kind of economic malfunction. Inequality was one thing; but not even the frankest inegalitarian could be happy with a situation in which the general prosperity of the country was growing with no advantage at all to the poor. This much was fairly widely accepted in Britain. The differences arose over what underlay *that*.

Broadly speaking there were two possibilities. One was that capitalism was not working; the other was that it was not being *allowed* to work. The first was the view, naturally, of Marxian socialists, who had been expecting something like this to happen for years, as a prelude to capitalism's inevitable collapse. In a much diluted form it was also the view of 'New' Liberals like J.A. Hobson, who believed that capitalism needed to be saved from some of its own worst tendencies in order to continue to benefit folk and so to survive.[31] Social imperialists, old-fashioned Tories and tariff reformers agreed with them on this, if on nothing else. It was the most common explanation of events, and underlay the Liberals' social reforms of 1906–11, which were intended to reconcile the workers to the liberal capitalist system by rubbing down its roughest edges.

The other version was the opposite of this. It put the blame elsewhere entirely: not on capitalism but on its enemies, including New Liberals and paternalists as well as the socialists. Their continual tamperings with the mechanisms of the market meant that the system was no longer being given a fair chance. Recently this had got worse. British opinion and policy, claimed the old free marketist A.V. Dicey, had 'run vehemently towards collectivism' at a headlong rate. The New Liberals with their social and trade-union legislation were the main offenders. The effects of all this had been to stifle the market, encourage a dependency culture and sap individual enterprise, with the results they could see all around them then.[32]

This latter analysis was not of course new, though it had – as we have seen – gone out of fashion recently. In the 1910s it was fighting against daunting odds. One of its biggest obstacles was the clear preference that the 'democracy' seemed to be showing for collectivism, which created problems for individualists who did not want to be seen as anti-democrats. Usually they got round this by insisting that the British people – even the stagnant workers – were individualists underneath, but gulled into errors by the socialists. Dicey conceded that some of those errors were very plausible ones, which made it necessary to counter them with some even more plausible truths.[33] It was this that lay behind the formation in 1907 of a new body, the Anti-Socialist Union, explicitly in order 'to collect facts and figures and train public speakers to counteract the fallacious statements so persistently put out by socialist writers and speakers'. It did this by means of propaganda: more than a million pamphlets distributed in the course of a single campaign in Durham and north Lancashire in 1911, for example; and through a college in London run to teach right-minded people the techniques of public speaking, from which 771 graduates, including more than a hundred women, had emerged by January 1910.[34]

It was an impressive effort; but was it enough? Some people feared not. There was a great deal of pessimism on the anti-socialist front. Socialism was seen as a great incoming ocean tide, against which older values were as vulnerable as a sandcastle on a beach: all the more so if the sandcastle was an individualist one, whose builders therefore were forbidden to dig a social-reformist moat around it to divert the full force of the waves. A few of them saw even greater dangers: of covert subversion by the socialists, for example, and help from Britain's enemies abroad. The Anti-Socialist Union claimed that socialists had already 'infiltrated the civil service' in order to 'capture... the machinery of state for the social revolution' in advance.[35] That was like tunnelling beneath the sand. There were also persistent rumours of German spies egging on strikers, and subsidising the suffragettes with

'German gold'.[36] According to the patriotic Imperial Maritime League the Labour party and even the radical section of the Liberals were not what they professed to be, but were in fact the 'advance agents of a Foreign Power'.[37] That helped explain their success.

Few people in authority believed this nonsense. But it had some effect. The government became more vigilant. In 1909–11 it took a range of measures to protect Britain against domestic subversive threats. The first was the creation in 1909, under pressure from the military and from sensationalist newspapers, of Britain's first counter-espionage agency for a hundred years, later known as MI5; though it was on a scale – a lone asthmatic Army captain in a tiny room with a filing cabinet – which clearly shows that the government was not as impressed by the spy menace as the military and the newspapers were. Two years later, at the height of the Agadir crisis, it rushed the second and most infamous of Britain's Official Secrets Acts through Parliament, so swiftly that almost no MPs noticed how draconian it really was. At the same time a 'register' of foreigners in Britain was started up; the Home Office resumed intercepting and opening people's mail on a large scale; and the Metropolitan Police Special Branch – previously directed mainly against Irish-American dynamiters and foreign anarchists – was put on to watching native British dissidents for the first time.[38] Compare this with the situation in Victorian times, when no such measures were felt to be necessary on the ground that the only polities that could be subverted were those that deserved to be, and one can see how far Britain had come since then.

It was no coincidence that these developments took place at exactly the same time as the Liberals' two major social reforms: old-age pensions and national insurance; and also at roughly the same time as some comparable developments in India. There were similarities between them. Each involved an unprecedented degree of state interference with the liberties of individuals. On the other hand they could also be claimed to *augment* those liberties by safeguarding them against threats from other sources, like poverty, illness, subversion and foreign attack. The main difference between them was that they related to different kinds of liberty: political in the one (counter-subversive) case, economic in the other. And the reason why they all happened at this time was that it was then that the tensions which had been growing *between* these two different conceptions of liberty for years seemed to be coming to a head.

In mid-Victorian times, as we have seen, they had appeared to be entirely compatible, and indeed even symbiotic. This was why there had been so little interference in both kinds of liberty then. Now that no longer seemed to be the case. Political and economic freedom were separating into different ideological camps. Absolute economic freedom, it appeared, could no longer co-exist with absolute political freedom, or democracy. Voting patterns in 1906 and 1910 seemed to indicate this. Something had to be done, therefore, to ease the tension. There were a number of possibilities: to cut down one kind of freedom in order to preserve the other pristine, for example; or simply to abandon both. Asquith's government preferred a third way. That was to cut pieces off the edges of both kinds of liberalism, in roughly equal measure, in order to try to make the remainder fit together again. This was what was done around 1910. A little of each was sacrificed, in order to preserve as much as possible of the rest. It was almost as simple as that.

In a way it was a revolutionary turn of events; though the full extent of the revolution was not appreciated at the time, because so much of it (the counter-subversive side) was hidden from view. It might have worked. Liberals seemed confident that it would, both in India and in Britain. They had found the antidote to popular revolution: carrots for 'moderate' progressives, combined with vigilance over the rest. In India this took the form of reasonable concessions to non-violent nationalists (Morley-Minto, the Bengal U-turn),[39] together with a strengthening of the 'Political Crime Branch' of the police. At the same time that Branch was deliberately kept on as tight a rein as possible, to avoid alienating the moderates, who on this kind of issue – inspired by older British values – were probably even more sensitive than the British.[40] In Britain the concessions took the form of social reforms, while the vigilance was exercised by the Special Branch, MI5 and the rest. Again, those agencies were kept relatively gentle, and mostly hidden, in order not to give liberals the idea (which would have been an entirely false one) that Britain was anything approaching a 'police state' yet.

That preserved a kind of stability, though a somewhat restless one. How long it could last was problematical: probably for quite some time. We shall never know, because in August 1914 the normal political and economic development of the country was interrupted, rudely though not entirely unexpectedly, by the outbreak of what later came to be known as the 'Great' War.

Chapter 14

The Great War (1914–18)

I

Britain entered the war on 4 August 1914: the day after Germany had invaded Belgium, which Britain was pledged to defend. That pledge, however, was not her reason for going to war, but rather the need to prevent German hegemony in Europe, which would pose a direct threat to herself. It was an ominous step for Britain to have to take. There was no conceivable positive advantage she could gain from it. She had no territorial ambitions in Europe, or anywhere else for that matter, that a war could help her achieve. She was already overburdened with colonies, which could be put in jeopardy by a conflict which would be bound to draw British troops away from them, and could be taken advantage of by native trouble-makers egged on by enemy agents in their midst. She was not very good at fighting European armies, as the Boer war had shown only recently. Most important, all her national material interests militated against war: the wide spread of her foreign trade and investment, her dependence on it, and her dependence too on a system of generating that trade and investment which required peace to allow it to prosper. On top of this, of course, there was the risk that she might lose. That was probably the best reason of all for Britain not to want to go to war; but it was not the only one. This is what had long distinguished her in this regard from most of her neighbours. They were anxious to avoid wars – naturally enough – if there was a danger they might be defeated in them. Britain, uniquely in Europe, was almost as anxious to avoid wars she could win.

This difference was a source of disappointment for Britain. It dashed the hopes she had used to have, that other powers would come to share her pacifism in time. International free trade would chip away at the importance that had used to be placed on national frontiers and even sovereignty,

making them less worth fighting over, and consequently less likely to provoke fights. At the same time commerce would give everyone a positive
interest in peace. That was the theory. Sadly it had not worked out like that.
Countries still quarrelled over territory, and armed themselves to the teeth
in order to acquire or defend it. Alsace continued to be an irritant between
France and Germany; the Balkans between Austria and Russia. The expanding British empire – despite Britain's scrupulous adherence to the principle
of the 'open door' over the whole of it – was an object of jealousy from
every quarter. As such it was probably one of the factors that provoked the
Great War: needlessly, in Britain's consistent and perfectly rational view. If
it had not been that, however, it would have been something else. The Continent, because of the greater premium it put on territory, was always more
war-orientated than Britain was. That accounts for Britain's main foreign
policy priority in the years leading up to 1914: which was to avoid any
commitments in Europe that might have the effect of dragging her into conflicts which arose out of other countries' interests, or their perception of
those interests, but could have no conceivable rationality for her.

Paradoxically, that policy may have contributed towards her involvement in the Great War in the end. In the 1890s, when the great armed
alliances which eventually confronted each other on the battlefield in 1914
started forming, Britain kept studiously clear of them, for exactly this reason.
This was despite insistent pressure from Germany to join the alliance she
had at that time with Austria, which Germany felt Britain would be bound
to adhere to eventually in order to protect herself against the threat to her
colonial interests posed by the rival alliance of France and Russia. That
threat was a real one. It was highlighted by Britain's obvious vulnerability
during the Boer war, when it was possible to conceive – and the Continental powers apparently contemplated – two or more rivals taking advantage
of her situation to attack her on other exposed flanks. In the 1900s Germany herself added to it by building a navy which in Britain's eyes could
not possibly be justified in terms of her existing overseas interests, and consequently must have been designed to challenge Britain's. In this situation
'isolationism' came to seem more precarious than it had used to be. Still,
however, the prime minister Lord Salisbury insisted that it was 'much less
danger than being dragged into wars which do not concern us',[1] which may
have been right.

In 1904 an alternative turned up. France suggested a settlement of the
colonial disputes she had with Britain, which would relieve that particular
pressure for both of them. That became the basis of the Anglo-French *entente*
of that year. Three years later a similar arrangement was reached with Russia. No European commitments attached to either of these: no British
promise, for example, to come to France's or Russia's help if either country

was directly attacked. That was the joy of an *entente*, as opposed to the fuller-blooded alliance that Germany had been angling for. For Britain it seemed a way of safeguarding her overseas interests while still avoiding a European war. But of course it did not work out like this.

That was because in German eyes the *ententes* appeared entirely differently. Britain insisted that they carried no European implications, but in fact they did. Even before them Germany had felt vulnerable: 'encircled' by two great hostile military powers, France and Russia, and with only feeble and decadent (albeit lovely) Austria by her side. She had been banking on Britain to redress the balance. Now Britain's incentive to join the central powers had been removed. She had her extra-European security, and needed nothing more that another alliance could give. It is just possible that this – the closing of the circle around her – was one of the factors pushing Germany towards war in 1914.

If so, then it was more than just a paradox: it was a tragic irony. Britain's policy looked to have been counter-productive. There may be a general lesson here: that trying to avoid wars is not necessarily the best way of preventing them. On the other hand this was certainly not the main cause of this war; and we cannot be certain that jetisoning isolation earlier – entering into an alliance with Germany, for example – would have been any more likely to stave it off. It might simply have encouraged German aggression instead of provoking it. That made isolation still a rational choice. Right up to the last moment, in fact, it could have worked for Britain. If war was inevitable, as it may have been, it did not follow that it would need to involve her. If it had been more limited in its scope – restricted to the Balkans, for example, or even the Franco-German border – Britain could and probably would have kept out. That was the other reason why it made sense before 1914 to keep aloof. Germany's invasion of Belgium, however, put paid to that. The war that followed was bound to be a general European one. Britain had to join in, despite the risks, which as we have seen were greater for her than they were for any of the other combatants: certainly if she lost, and probably even if she emerged victorious.

II

Among the reasons for fearing a war were its possible repercussions on the domestic front. These made many people in Britain nervous, though not everyone. Some on the political Right, for example, positively welcomed the war, as a way of bucking the country up. Years of peace, they argued, had made the British materialistic, lazy and soft. The best way of pulling them out of this was by a good bracing war: lots of healthy marching and fighting and obeying orders, especially for the working classes, to lick them back into proper patriotic shape.[2] This may have been in Basil Thomson's mind too when he spoke of a war diverting the workers from revolution.[3]

But this was a minority view. For anyone with an ounce of common sense the idea that a war would 'brace' the nation was clearly problematical, at best. After all, if 'national deterioration' had gone as far as some rightists claimed it had, there should be little left to brace. A.V. Dicey, for example, claimed that one of the results of what he called 'collectivism' was an all-pervading moral flabbiness in Britain which would be bound to collapse at the first German prod. The country was essentially 'indefensible'.[4] That was a worry.

Others were concerned at the strains a war would place on the loyalty of the working classes, and the opportunities for mischief it might afford political agitators among them. That was an alternative and much more common way of regarding the relationship between war and revolution than Thomson's. To guard against this danger drastic contingency plans were drawn up some time before 1914 to put down 'Civil Trouble in the Metropolis in Time of War'. They included drafting two army battalions into likely 'centres of discontent' in London, and empowering soldiers to shoot suspected trouble-makers on sight.[5] Hopefully these powers would not be needed, but you could never tell for certain where the working classes were concerned.

The workers in fact remained a source of worry to their betters throughout the war. In December 1915 a *Times* reporter wrote in his diary of 'members of the poorer and more discontented working-classes who ask why should they fight? What has the country done for them? Would they be worse off under the Germans?' He added that these were only rumours, for 'no such expressions have reached my ears';[6] but there was little comfort in this. One of the government's many problems at this time was that it had no reliable means of knowing what the working classes thought of the war, except *via* trade union leaders, who were not necessarily representative.[7] The workers' antics before the war, often in defiance of their leadership, suggested alarming political currents beneath. Other rumours had enemy agents stirring up those currents for their own ends, financed by plentiful 'German gold'.[8] That added immensely to the peril.

Talk of 'German gold' and the like was part of a general mood of fear of treachery and subversion in the early years of the war, which was not always rationally based. It had other manifestations too. Even the royal family came under suspicion because of its German origins, and was forced to change its name from Hanover to Windsor in 1917. Prince Louis Battenburg became translated into 'Mountbatten' at the same time. Lord Haldane was forced out of the government in 1915 because he was known to admire German literature and science. At one time a rumour was going round that he had been imprisoned and then shot as a spy in the Tower. Other rumours surrounded German pastrycooks resident in Britain, who were supposed to be putting slow poison into their strudels, and German barbers, who had taken to cutting English throats rather than beards. Anyone with a German-sounding name was liable to be attacked as a spy, including a London pub landlord called 'Strachan', who had his windows smashed in May 1915.[9] Another Scot, the architect and water-colourist Charles Rennie Mackintosh, was expelled from his holiday cottage on the Suffolk coast by local police who could not distinguish a Glaswegian accent from Low German, and suspected that his intricate drawings of local wild flowers concealed maps of estuaries to aid enemy landing craft.[10] Our *Times* reporter diagnosed all this as a kind of 'hysteria': people's 'nerves', he wrote, were 'jangling, and they are subject to hallucinations. They seem to be enveloped in a mysterious darkness, haunted by goblins in the form of desperate German spies.'[11] Another diagnosis would be mass paranoia. It bore no relation to the facts. The home front turned out in fact to be surprisingly solid and secure, bearing in mind the horrors and the long duration of the war.

There were exceptions. There was a tenacious 'No Conscription' movement, for example, especially after April 1916 when universal compulsory military service came in, which waged subversive war against the authorities by sheltering conscientious objectors and helping them to escape abroad. Altogether 16 500 men refused the draft, of whom a hard core of 1298 rejected every alternative form of war work offered to them (on the grounds that it would merely release others to do the killing), and landed up in gaol.[12] There were also some damaging industrial strikes, especially in the spring of 1917 when at one time 200 000 men all over the country – mostly in munitions and munitions-related factories – downed tools.[13] Ireland was a continual problem, its loyalty never to be relied on (which is why military conscription was not risked there), and the scene of a serious revolutionary outbreak in the spring of 1916 – the Easter Rising in Dublin – which had to be put down by troops. There was even some disaffection in the army: occasional murmerings of mutiny, for example, culminating in a famous insurrection at Etaples base camp in northern France in September 1917, which is estimated to have involved more than 1500 men.[14] Apart from Ireland, however, none of this ever got out of hand. The army got its conscripts. There were no serious mutinies where it mattered, at the front. War production, including munitions, continued. The working classes by and large stood up better to the stresses of war in Britain than in most other combatant countries. None of the early pessimists' fears was ever borne out.

One of the reasons for this was undoubtedly the workers' fundamental loyalty. What exactly they were loyal to is uncertain: but it was clearly enough to bond them to their leaders during the war. 'King and country' –

basic, unthinking patriotism – was probably part of it. Loyalty to a *cause* was another; the cause in this case being a typical English mixture of decency, fair play and the protection of underdogs, against the 'evil Hun' who, by his onslaught on 'poor little Belgium' on 3 August 1914, and then by a whole string of 'atrocities' attributed to him by propaganda thereafter, not always fairly, was considered to have transgressed all these principles. Another target – an odd one, for a military machine – was Prussian 'militarism'. A third binding factor was class loyalty. This could have been dangerous if it had been directed against other classes in Britain, which is what the pre-war pessimists had feared, but that appears not to have happened on the whole. Soldiers were loyal to their comrades; workers to their workmates; widows and bereaved mothers to other women in their unhappy situation: not divisively, but in such a way as simply to strengthen their solidarity in the task that was given to them. Hence, for example, the widespread revulsion shown in working-class circles against 'conshies' (conscientious objectors) throughout the war, not primarily because of their views, but because they were seen to be avoiding their share of a burden which no one relished, but which it was felt had to be borne evenly to make it fair.[15]

This was one factor. But it was not the only one. The government was gratified by the degree of loyalty shown by the working classes during the war, but never took it for granted. It punished dangerous dissent rigorously, to deter other potential dissenters. Deserters and mutineers in the army were court-martialled and then shot: probably around 300 of them all told.[16] Conscientious objectors were treated a little more kindly. They were allowed to plead their cases before tribunals, whose task was to rule on whether or not their objections were 'genuine'. That was merciful, and also unique among the major combatants in the war, but it did not always work out fairly, mainly because of the rampant prejudices of those who sat on the boards. Many good men were imprisoned unjustly, and then maltreated, 70 dying as a result.[17] Agencies dedicated to helping 'conshies' were hounded mercilessly; including one in Derby which was put out of commission in 1917 by a government spy who probably trumped up a charge against its leader – Alice Wheeldon – of plotting to murder Lloyd George by hammering a poisoned nail through his boot, in order to discredit the anti-conscription movement generally.[18]

On the industrial front the government legislated in 1915 to prevent strikes in munitions factories; and backed that up with an array of more covert controls. One was the widespread use of spies (again) to detect dangerous subversion on the factory floor, some of whom used *agent provocateur* tactics, like calling for volunteers to help them sabotage production lines or bomb Parliament.[19] Men were deterred from leading strikes by draconian punishments for those who dared to, and the threat which many of them *felt* hung over them – whether or not it really did – that if they were troublesome their work could be re-classified as non-essential, which would mean being sent to the front.[20] Finally, a new system of press censorship was used to prevent news of strikes – and hence the contagion itself – spreading.[21] The authorities were taking no chances.

That was one way of keeping the workers in line. The other – because coercion might not work, and could even be counter-productive – was to try to *persuade* them of their community of interest with the government. The government in fact was quite good at this. One of its approaches was to appeal to members of its own upper class to set an example, which by and large they did. Early on the King set the tone by announcing that for the duration of the war his household would eat the same sort of rations as his subjects, and would be giving up alcohol. That undoubtedly helped. A little later on society ladies were to be seen arriving at recruiting stations with motor-car loads of surplus footmen, butlers and gardeners, as their personal contribution to the war effort. The gentlemen of the Athenaeum released their waiters, and agreed for the first time in the club's 90-year history to have their brandies and sodas brought to them by girls.[22] More impressively, the upper classes also volunteered for the front themselves in large numbers, and in fact suffered greater losses, proportionate to their numbers, than any other British social class.[23] That will have appealed to the workers' sense of 'fairness', which Bernard Waites has convincingly argued was their main 'standard of judgment' of these things.[24]

The government also cultivated the workers more directly. It needed to. Labour shortages caused by army recruitment gave a great boost to the workers' bargaining powers. They could not be simply bullied, without great risk. Anti-union legislation like the 1915 Munitions Act was deeply resented, partly because of the implication it was felt to carry that the workers could not be trusted to behave themselves patriotically otherwise; and was not wholly effective anyway. Co-operation was clearly preferable: for example over the thorny issue of 'dilution', or the replacement of skilled labour by unskilled, often women, which was vital if the factories were to continue functioning while the skilled men were at the front. That was achieved by means of concessions. One concession was the firm government action that was taken against 'profiteering' – capitalists charging excessive prices for goods in short supply due to the war – which was probably the thing that offended the workers' sense of 'fairness' most. Food rationing was introduced in February 1918 for the same reason. Strikes were generally settled by the government's stepping in to give the strikers what they wanted.[25] Labour was also appeased in other ways. Trade-union leaders were taken into the innermost councils of government, with one of them – the Engineers' ex-general secretary George Barnes – even making it to war cabinet rank in August 1917. That was part of the bargain: a means of unifying the classes that made up the embattled nation, in this instance by satisfying the material demands of the class that was considered to be the least dependable.

This it was which gave rise to one of the most surprising effects of the war: which was to improve enormously the material condition of one part of the British population. For another part, of course, its effect was disastrous. More than 720 000 British servicemen died in the war, 500 000 under the age of 30; plus another 15 000 merchant seamen, and 1266 civilian victims of German naval bombardment and Zeppelin raids. Millions more were wounded. The conditions for those who survived – the horrors of the trenches – are well known. For most people and families that probably outweighed everything. Nothing could compensate fully for it. Yet there *were* compensations. On the home front things were different. There was widespread worry, fear, bereavement, the occasional bomb falling out of the sky; and there were shortages, due to war exigencies and German naval blockades. In general, however, most people who stayed at home during the war found themselves substantially better off. Poverty was abolished for the duration. There was plenty of work at good wages, as a result of the unions' market strength. Prices were kept within acceptable limits, as a result of government curbs on the *profiteers'* market strength. There was less food than before, but it was better distributed, so that everyone had enough and some had far more than ever in the past. One result of this was that the incidence of most diseases diminished (except respiratory ones, because of long hours spent working in munitions and other factories), infant mortality decreased, and life expectancy generally (that is, excluding soldiers) went up. This was despite (surely not because of?) a mass exodus of doctors to the battle front, which left some areas chronically short of professional medical services.[26] Contemporaries noticed this and were impressed. 'More has been done for the social betterment of the labouring classes by three years of this frightful War,' wrote our *Times* man in May 1917, 'than by the garnering of the harvests of peace for many generations!'[27] To him this was a wonder. Others, however, saw disturbing implications to it.

For the fact was that it had been achieved only at a price. That price was a kind of revolution in Britain: not the revolution that had been predicted by the pessimists before the war – a socialist one – but a more limited kind, controlled from the top, and designed mainly to pre-empt the socialists. The change really had been immense. It had been heralded before 1914, but could never have been achieved on this scale without the war. Its main beneficiaries were the state, which was more powerful and intrusive than it had ever been in Britain – 'We are now living under a Government that rules practically by dictatorship', mused the *Times* diarist in July 1918 [28] – and organised labour, which had become almost an estate of the realm. The main victim was old-fashioned liberalism, which had simply shrivelled in the heat.

The transformation can be traced in the changing political complexion of these years. When the war began it was with Asquith's Liberal ministry – minus just two resignations on account of the war – at the helm. Over the next four months that ministry became progressively leavened with non-Liberals, who eventually ousted the old guard. By the end of 1916 Asquith had gone, and the new streamlined 'war cabinet' consisted of just six men, only one of whom – the new prime minister, Lloyd George – had been there originally. Lloyd George was an ex-Radical, and one of the heralds of the new statism before 1914. George Henderson, another of the six, was Labour. The others were all Conservatives, and Conservatives of a particularly illiberal stamp. Three of them – Bonar Law, Milner and Curzon – were leading adherents of the doctrine of 'social imperialism', which we have seen had posed the main threat to *laissez-faire* liberalism in the past. (The other was Neville Chamberlain, about whom almost nothing was known as yet, except that he was the son of an even more leading imperialist.) They saw little wrong with the new state of affairs. It was just what they had always advocated: a strong state harnessing socialism to a national and patriotic end. The upshot was a fitter people, a victorious army and (as we shall see) an expansion of the British empire to its greatest ever extent. To social imperialists this must have seemed like a little bit of utopia: if social imperialists had been the kind of people ever to think in utopian terms.

Some of them had their doubts, especially over Labour, of whose lasting loyalty they were never completely confident. Those doubts were shared by others. Few economic liberals, for example, were at all reassured by the workers' co-operation during the war, in view of the price (or ransom) that had been exacted for it. If anything that seemed to bear out their pre-war fears. The unions were too powerful. That was why the government had had to buy them off, with the result that now they were even more powerful and menacing. One index of their strength was their membership, which increased during the course of the war by well over 50%.[29] Another, of course, was their entree into the government. That was greatly resented by many on the other side of industry, who in 1916 set up their own 'Federation of British Industries' (FBI) to try to redress the balance against the TUC. The following year the FBI extended its activities into covert intelligence and propaganda in order to tackle the new trade-union and socialist menace at its roots.[30] It was joined by other smaller private anti-socialist groups,[31] and by the official secret service – Basil Thomson's Special Branch – which by the end of the war had shifted its attention almost entirely away from German espionage and subversion (which there had always been precious little of in any case) to this new threat from the Left.[32] That was how concerned they were.

Of course it was not only events on Britain's own labour front which provoked this. In October 1917 came the bolshevik revolution in Russia, which had a huge impact. The pessimists were thoroughly alarmed. One of them, Britain's main secret agent on the spot, cabled back desperately to try to persuade his government to stop the war with Germany immediately, in order to turn its defences against this much greater menace. 'Gracious heavens,' he wrote, 'will the people of England never understand? The Germans are human beings; we can afford even to be beaten by them. Here in Moscow is growing to maturity the arch enemy of the human race.'[33] Back home there were rumours (some of them true) of secret 'soviets' being set up in Leeds and Tunbridge Wells, bolshevik 'cells' among the trade unions, and communism taking hold in such key areas as the armed forces and the police, who came out on strike in London in August 1918.[34] The cancer seemed to be spreading. Russia showed where it could lead. Of course there were special circumstances there which had probably aided the revolution, and which did not pertain in Britain. On the other hand there were other circumstances in Britain which theoretically, at least, seemed to make her even more vulnerable.

One was the fact that in Marxian terms – and the bolsheviks did after all purport to be Marxists – Britain was far riper for revolution than Russia was. This was one of the odd things about the Russian revolution. It may help explain much of the history of the Soviet Union since. Marx had insisted that you could only have successful socialist revolutions where the conditions for them were right. That meant that a country had to have passed through all its 'natural' stages of *capitalist* development first, so that the contradictions inherent in that system could come to the top. Revolution would arise out of that situation. Russia was nowhere near that stage in 1917. She was probably the most backward capitalist economy in Europe at that time, save in one or two industrial centres; scarcely yet out of her 'feudal' wraps. To put it simply: the revolution should not have happened there. It was seriously premature (which might account for the totalitarian incubator that was found necessary in order to keep it alive after 1917). Britain and Germany in particular were far more pregnant with socialism than Russia was. One contemporary Special Branch man was very much alive to this: aware of how much closer conditions were in Britain 'to those laid down by Communist philosophers as necessary before a Proletarian Dictatorship could be imposed'.[35] He had clearly read his Marx. Others probably had not (anti-Marxists do not usually), but intuitively sensed something of the sort. It was not a comfortable feeling.

For many people it took away much of the pleasure they might have felt otherwise at the prospect of an end to the war. That would not solve anything on the domestic front. Britain's fundamental domestic problems went back long before the war. The main one was the growing alienation of many of her working classes from the economic system of the time, which may have been one of Marx's 'internal contradictions' showing through, or not. During the war it had been contained by a combination of coercion and concession, which had worked. That however was merely temporary. When the war ended the coercion would be lifted, and the concessions withdrawn. That would return the situation to the way it had been in 1914, which was bad enough. In fact, however, it would be far worse than this. If Marx was right it would be worse because British capitalism would have moved that much further on towards its crisis. Even if he was not, it would be worse because of the gains Labour had made during the war, and the encouragement (and maybe material help) it could expect from its comrades in the east. All this suggested that there would be very little peace at home after the guns had stopped barking in Flanders. This was the overall effect of the war on the British domestic scene: to highlight its problems and allow drastic solutions, which would then leave the problems worse when the solutions were taken away.

III

That was the domestic front. Abroad things followed a similar pattern. The British empire survived the war, but only at a cost. Just as there was a potentially unreliable class in Britain, so there was also in many of her colonies, which needed to be appeased in order to secure its loyalty. That was the price of the empire's survival in the short term, which did nothing for its prospects later on.

This however was not how it appeared initially. Most of the early signals emanating from the empire gave no hint at all of trouble to come. Everyone rallied to the flag. Even before the war the governments of the self-governing dominions pledged support for Britain however things turned out. Australia handed her navy over to her as a token on 3 August 1914. Canada sent a million bags of flour.[36] Then came the soldiers, paid for and trained by the colonies: a steady stream of big, keen, healthy lads, as the romantic view of them had it, filing into the trenches from the bush and the plains and the veldt. The numbers were impressive, especially considering that most of them were volunteers. (Canada and New Zealand both adopted conscription in 1917, but in very mild forms.) Canada sent 458 218 men in all, Australia 331 814, New Zealand 112 223, and South Africa 76 184. New Zealand's was the best figure proportionately, representing nearly one-fifth of her adult males. (South Africa's was the worst.)[37] They were used in every theatre of war, including the western front and the middle east, where they impressed the British troops mightily by their physical fitness, their bravery, their ways with the womenfolk, and their refreshing lack of respect for the British officer class.

That was heart warming. Even more so was the response of many of the non-self governing colonies. Out of India, for example, came almost extravagant professions of support from the princes, especially, and a gift of £100 million – a whole year's revenue – from its coffers (not that the ordinary Indians, of course, had any say in that). Nearly a million and a half native Indian troops were raised, mostly to guard their own north-western frontier or serve in the nearby Persian Gulf, but many of them finding their way to Mesopotamia, for example, and German East Africa. Britain also recruited soldiers from her own colonies in East and West Africa; and tens of thousands of non-combatant auxiliaries from Egypt, the West Indies, Mauritius, Fiji, Malaya and elsewhere. Some colonies gave gifts of money, presumably voluntarily: like the £200 sent to the Treasury by the nomadic Galla people of northern Kenya, who could hardly spare it.[38] Everyone was chipping in.

The other way the empire seemed to be turning up trumps was commercially. Britain badly needed imports during the war years, especially of foodstuffs, to compensate for the loss of supplies from Europe and the diversion of her own productive resources to the war. The empire spectacularly obliged. From 1910 to 1914 Canada had exported an average of £29 millions' worth of goods to Britain a year; between 1915 and 1919 that figure rose to £86 millions' worth a year. Other colonies showed similar rises: India for example from £46 million to £80 million a year over the same period, Australia from £38 million to £60 million, and so on. In the meantime British exports to the colonies slumped. So the increase was one-sided; but it served to emphasize the material importance of the empire to Britain at this time. She had other sources of imports too, notably the United States and Latin America, whose trade with Britain showed a comparable trend;[39] but it was the foison of the colonies that impressed. Some people thought its importance far transcended the war situation, and might be used as the basis of something splendid afterwards.

What they had in mind, of course, was a revival of Joseph Chamberlain's old 'imperial *Zollverein*' idea, for a self-sufficient empire developed rationally as an economic unit, and surrounded by tariff barriers against foreigners. Closely related to that scheme in the past had been proposals for an imperial defence union, which had also clearly come closer recently; and for some kind of political union, to bind the whole together formally. On 20 March 1917 a significant step was taken towards that when Lloyd George set up what he called his 'imperial war cabinet', which included all the dominions' premiers, plus the Indian and colonial secretaries (representing the dependent empire), as well as the members of his war cabinet proper. The immediate purpose of that was to involve the colonies more closely in war-time decisions; but it was also seen as a possible nucleus for a centralized imperial executive afterwards.[40] A couple of months later the South African premier Jan Smuts (despite the relative laggardliness of his own dominion's war effort) was co-opted into the ordinary domestic war cabinet. His colleagues there included, as we have seen, Curzon and Milner, who were two of the most ardent British imperial federationists around.

Other imperialist federationists could not fail to be encouraged. For them this was the positive aspect of the war. It had forged the empire together; brought its value home to people; and pushed its charismatic leaders to the fore. All that was required now was for these advantages to be held on to when the war came to an end. An immense effort was put into trying to ensure this, therefore, through propaganda and other means. Scores of pro-imperial pamphlets were issued. Some of them emanated from a new 'Empire Resources Development Committee', founded in January 1917, whose particular line was to urge the methodical exploitation of the empire after the war by a great state-supported and tariff-protected consortium of capitalists.[41] Workers were enlisted to the cause *via* a 'British Workers National League' set up in May 1916, which was endorsed by W.M. Hughes, the renegade Australian Labour prime minister.[42] Especially active in many of these enterprises (including that one) was a group called the 'Round Table': a set of younger proteges of Milner which for some years now had been dedicated to imperialism with a quasi-religious zeal. A number of them found their way into government, in subordinate but influential posts. They also worked to influence the press, the universities and dominions' governments. Some of their methods were secretive, and they have been seen as a malign conspiratorial influence on events in Britain right through to the time of appeasement;[43] but they could not have been influential at all if they had not had at least one current of history running with them, and support from other quarters outside their own little clique. Hence their success during the war years, and their hopes of what could be done with and by means of the empire when the war was over.

Sadly for the imperialists, those hopes may have been misplaced. They took little account of certain weaknesses that the war also revealed in the empire; and they may have misinterpreted its strengths. The willingness of the dominions to place their troops under British command in the war, for example, certainly did not indicate a desire for closer unity in the longer term; indeed in Lord Beloff's judgment 'the main effect of the war upon the dominions' was 'to increase their own self-reliance and to diminish the prestige of the British government'.[44] The Anzacs' experience of their British officers may well have strengthened that. As well as this, a couple of the dominions were deeply split over the issue of the war: Canada over the need for conscription, and South Africa over whether to support the war at all, with one group of Afrikaners resorting to force to protest against what they regarded as Smuts's toadying to British imperialism. (Hence South Africa's relatively poor showing on the western front.)[45] Even the colonies of settlement, therefore, were not completely sound.

In other parts of the empire the problems were worse. India was the most problematical. True, many of the disasters that might have been expected there never transpired. Britain was able to siphon her own troops away from India to the war fronts, replacing them with territorials or natives, without too much damage resulting. Those who stayed behind (a mere 15 000 at one point) were vastly outnumbered by the Indians recruited to serve outside, which probably made India a military asset on balance. (The doubt arises over the efficiency of the Indian army, which on one or two occasions turned out to be disastrously ill-organised for service overseas.)[46] On the other hand the war certainly stirred things up politically. Terrorist groups used the opportunity to step up their violence, especially in the Punjab and Bengal, which at one stage apparently 'threatened to become ungovernable'. Germany helped, as was only to be expected, through her agents in nearby Persia and Afghanistan, and through an 'Indian National Party' of exiled extremists attached to the German general staff in Berlin.[47] That was on the far edge of nationalist politics. Nearer to the moderate centre things were calm initially, but then grew more ruffled as the war progressed. By the summer of 1917 the secretary of state for India, Edwin Montagu, saw nationalist agitation as 'a seething, boiling political flood raging across the country', which in his view required to be appeased.[48] The viceroy, Lord Chelmsford, agreed that any delay would be 'fatal'.[49] Hence the 'Montagu declaration' of July, which conceded to the nationalists most of what they wanted: 'the increasing association of Indians in every branch of the administration, and the gradual development of self-governing institutions with a view to the progressive realisation of responsible government in India as an integral part of the British empire'. It was the most liberal statement of intent for India ever uttered; borne of the necessity, as Montagu later put it, to keep 'India quiet for six months at a critical period of the war'.[50]

Similar pledges were given elsewhere, for similar reasons. The most notorious, and the most troublesome later on because they were contradictory, were those given to Arabs and Jews in Palestine. Palestine was part of another empire at this time – Turkey's – but was fair game because Turkey was one of the belligerents in the war on the German side. It was important to defeat her because of the threats she posed to the Suez canal and Britain's oil interests in the Persian gulf. Straight military attempts to do this met unexpected obstacles, including the humiliating failure of the Dardanelles campaign in 1915. Looking around for other means, Britain came across a nascent Arab national movement, which she thought could be harnessed to her cause. As her part of the bargain she promised the Arabs their independence after the war. The latter understood, reasonably, that this promise embraced Palestine; which however European and American Zionists also had their eyes on for a Jewish 'national home'. To secure *their* support, and in particular that of American Jews for United States participation in the war, the famous 'Balfour declaration', backing this aspiration, was issued in November 1917. Another document, the 'Sykes-Picot' treaty negotiated secretly with France in April 1916, gave Palestine to Britain. Maybe all these promises were technically compatible, if you juggled a little with the words of them; but the expectations they aroused among Arabs, Jews and British imperialists were certainly not.

Others shared those expectations, even without any such specific promises to give them weight. One general result of the war was to make Britain's colonial subjects everywhere realise how important their collaboration had been to her, which adjusted their perception of the balance of power between them a little. At its lowest it undermined the British myth of omnipotence in some colonies, making dissidents just a little bolder as a result. They were also encouraged by the general appeals to 'freedom' that were bandied about with increasing frequency as the war went on, as a justification for it on the *entente* side; especially after the entry into the war in April 1917 of the United States, who considered herself (not altogether consistently) as the leading anti-imperialist power, and was damned if she, at any rate, was going to put herself out in this way merely to prop up the decaying empires of a corrupt old world.[51] There was hope here not only for the Serbs and the Belgians (who were the ones the British mainly had in mind when they talked of national freedom), but also possibly for Indians and Arabs and Africans, if liberty was as indivisible a principle as the Americans claimed.

All this had implications for the empire; just as the growing confidence and influence of organised labour had implications for the British state on the domestic front. Both had managed to come through the war unscathed in any serious way, but only at the price of concessions – both overt and implicit – to the forces that had threatened to scathe them at one time. The long-term impact of those concessions was not yet clear. Some believed they could reverse them: renege on the Montagu declaration, for example, and return things to the *status quo ante* after the war. Progressive imperialists (like the Round Table group) thought they could work with them, to create a new sort of empire based on federalism abroad, social reform at home and efficient economic development all over, for which they had already coined a new word: the 'commonwealth'. A third alternative was that these concessions marked the beginning of the end of the empire in any form. Which of these it would be only time would tell; and would depend not only on the legacy of the war on Britain and the empire, but also on the effects of the very different conditions of more 'normal' times, when they returned.

Chapter 15

Post-War Crisis (1919–21)

I

Some wars in history have been successful, in the sense of solving more problems than they have caused. The Great War was emphatically not one of these. It failed in its main declared purpose, which was to curb German expansionism permanently, and so prevent a future European war. It created new problems both in Europe and elsewhere in the world, particularly the middle east, most of whose later crises can be traced back to this time. It contributed indirectly to the success of the Russian bolshevik revolution, which was probably the single most destabilizing event of the twentieth century. Of course not everyone was a loser from the war. Among nations, the United States gained immensely in wealth and prestige. Most British dominions profited economically. Some people at the time thought the Russians had benefitted politically. On balance, however, the war was a disaster. So far as Europe was concerned, and also many other parts of the world, it left people significantly less secure, prosperous and happy after it than most of them had been before.

For her part Britain came out of it better off, probably, than if she had been defeated in it, but worse off than if she had not been involved in it at all. That was predictable, and indeed had been widely predicted before the war had started. For years now Britain had had far more to lose from a major war than she could possibly gain from one, irrespective almost of whether she won or lost. Most British statesmen before 1914 had felt this instinctively. Hence their concern to avoid war if possible. The upshot of the Great War, which they had not been able to avoid, proved their instincts sound.

There were some contrary signs. At first glance the after-effects of the war on Britain did not look all bad. She had after all won it, which presumably meant something, if only that her power relative to Germany – her main military and economic rival before 1914 – was greatly increased. Her national independence was still intact. So was her empire; which could even be said to have been extended by the war, if one ignored – as many did – the fact that most of the extensions took the form of what were called 'mandates', which were territories given into a country's care to be looked after on behalf of the whole world community (represented by the new League of Nations) until they were fit to rule themselves. Mandates were not supposed to be colonies. On the other hand they did not differ all that much in practice from the colonies Britain already had. 'I do not think that that mandate is likely to impose upon us any conditions which we would not impose upon ourselves,' the Colonial under-secretary told the House of Commons in July 1919. 'We have always in very large measures treated native territories under our rule as a mandate to us in the interests of the in-habitants and of the world at large.'[1] So that was all right. Counting these new acquisitions, Britain's empire was now at its greatest extent ever. The most significant addition was the great swathe of territory Britain now con-trolled in the middle east, stretching from Egypt in the west to the Persian Gulf, and taking in Palestine, Transjordan, Mesopotamia (Iraq) and the Gulf states on the way. In August 1919 a treaty concluded with Persia gave her a dominant influence there, and consequently up to India's western border. This was something that imperialists had dreamed about for years.

There were other pluses. Britain was no longer under immediate threat from Germany, who lay defeated, impoverished and mostly disarmed. For the future, high hopes were placed on the League of Nations and various other new diplomatic mechanisms to ensure that similar serious threats would not arise again. Statesmen seemed genuinely committed to this, includ-ing the British prime minister, Lloyd George, who promised that if his government were elected again in December 1918 it would 'try to initiate the reign on earth of the Prince of Peace', no less.[2] At home the country had suffered grievously in many ways, and yet had come through the war fairly solidly united behind its government, which was better than many had feared at the beginning of it, and a hopeful sign. This had been achieved in the main by sinking political differences, compromising over economics, and by this means welding the people into one. That, again, had been a pre-war social imperialist dream. Many people thought it could be sustained even after the war had come to an end. It was with this in view that plans for the post-war 'reconstruction' of Britain began to be drawn up as early as March 1916, culminating eventually in ambitious schemes for industrial conciliation, health, secondary education, poverty, unemployment and housing: probably the most extensive programme of social reform ever proposed for Britain, to be implemented as soon as peace came. Empire;

security; unity; welfare: if all this could be achieved now on a permanent basis, then something good, at least, could be said to have come out of the war.

Alas, it was not to be. This became plain almost immediately after the armistice was signed. Problems arose on every front: at home, in Europe, overseas. Few of them stemmed from the war alone. Most were familiar from long before, although usually in less acute forms. They derived from the fundamental and growing contradiction that had lain at the heart of Britain's situation in the world from around the middle of the nineteenth century onwards, between her economic and political needs as a nation and her means. We have explored the reasons for this already. Ultimately its roots go back to Britain's mid-Victorian capitalist and commercial expansion, which had taken place originally in a competitive near-vacuum, and on the assumption that no one would object, because it was based on free exchange between men. Later that assumption was exploded. Customers behaved badly and had to be taken in hand in order to maintain free market conditions, which was a kind of contradiction in itself. Foreign rivals threatened Britain's freedom to trade from another direction, and so had to be warded off. All this required money, men and methods for which no allowance at all had been made in the original plan. Things had been supposed to become easier as the benefits of free-market capitalism spread. Instead they became more difficult. Britain's markets overseas remained vital to her economically, but grew more burdensome to administer and defend. This was clear to most people by the end of the Boer war in 1902, and patently obvious in 1914. A similar pattern pertained on the British domestic scene, where free-market capitalism was also confronted by challenges requiring to be met in unforeseen and incongruous – that is, against the original spirit of free-market capitalism – ways. That was the situation before the war. The war itself did not improve matters. At best, it enabled Britain's underlying problems to be contained, but only temporarily, and in ways which exacerbated many of them in the longer term.

This was clearly so abroad. Here even Britain's colonial (or mandated) gains were two-edged. Before the war, as we saw, she had been grievously stretched imperially; afterwards with these new obligations added to her existing ones the fabric simply broke, at about half a dozen points. Old-established colonies demanded redemption of the pledges they believed had been made to them in return for their recent efforts and sacrifices; the new mandated territories resented merely exchanging one set of colonial fetters for another. Egypt was the first to rise, with a rebellion there in March 1919; followed by similar ones in the Punjab, Persia and Iraq. Nearer home, in Ireland, which could be regarded as a kind of colony, nationalists formally declared their independence from Britain in January 1919, and then set about trying to effect it with a bloody campaign of guerilla warfare. In the winter of 1920–21 that campaign was extended to the British mainland, in a short flurry of 'Irish Republican Army' attacks on farms, factories, arsenals, telegraph lines and railway signal boxes, mainly in the north of England, which left 14 people dead (including five IRA) at the end of it.[3] Then in May 1921 Palestine started giving trouble, of a slightly different kind: with Arabs, whose country it was, at violent odds with Jewish immigrants, who claimed that God and Arthur Balfour had promised it to them. There were also anti-western riots in China. Some of these problems were cannily exploited by Russia, who proved less enervated by her recent revolution and continuing civil war than Britain had hoped and expected, and whose propaganda struck chords among the victims of 'capitalist imperialism' everywhere.[4] This was what imperialists had feared for decades: a *combination* of punches on the British empire which could possibly have been coped with *seriatim*, but not all at once.

That would have been difficult at any time. It was made more so after the war by Britain's state of exhaustion as a result of it. This manifested itself in a number of ways. One was economic. The war had drained Britain of wealth, forced her to borrow massively, disrupted her industry, and devastated her trade. By 1919 her national debt had risen to £7481 million, which was ten times more than in 1914. The cost of servicing that debt alone – the interest on it – was the equivalent of nearly the whole amount raised by income tax, which between 1919 and 1922 stood at the unprecedented standard rate of 30%. In 1919 Britain's trade deficit was £660 million, or five times as high as on the eve of the war.[5] This was partly a result of her export markets falling to rivals who had been less hard-pressed than she during the war: especially America and the self-governing dominions of the empire. They gained economically, at Britain's considerable expense. One of the results was to limit Britain's options when it came to responding to crises abroad. Expensive ones were ruled out. In most cases that meant military ones. Other pressures had the same effect. The army was exhausted, too. Soldiers who were kept on after the war to police the colonies strongly resented it, sometimes to the point of mutiny. This led to wholesale cuts in the military in 1919–20. By 1920, according to the Chief of the Imperial General Staff, Sir Henry Wilson, Britain simply did not have the resources to cope with every threat. 'Our small army is far too scattered,' he confided to his diary in May; 'in no single theatre are we strong enough – not in Ireland, nor England, not on the Rhine, not in Constantinople, nor Batoum, nor Egypt, nor Palestine, nor Mesopotamia, nor Persia, nor India.'[6] That was ominous. It was also disappointing for imperialists like Wilson; who scarcely had time to welcome the materialisation of their dream before it seemed to be turning into a nightmare.

The nightmare also struck closer to home. Wilson included England and the Rhineland in his list of 'theatres' which might require the army's presence. The Rhineland was there not – at this stage – because of any fear of a German revival, but because of a new danger: communism. It was the Russian Revolution of October 1917, of course, which had sparked that off. From there it was seen to spread rather like a disease. One German army commander described how his battalion caught it simply by contact with soldiers returning from the eastern front. 'This Eastern Division had been infected with Bolshevism. It spread this poison among my men. It was like the breath of Hell. My men withered away.'[7] Most of the defeated countries experienced mini-revolutions during the winter of 1918–19. In March 1919 Lloyd George apparently seriously contemplated the prospect that 'In a short time we might have three-quarters of Europe converted to Bolshevism', with Britain alone standing firm 'for social order and common sense'.[8] Others suspected that even that might be optimistic. How could they be sure that the disease would not waft over the Channel too?

This for example was the fear at this time of Lord Burnham, the proprietor of the *Daily Telegraph*. 'He thinks that we cannot hope to escape some form of revolution... He says that revolution is in the air among all classes and that there will be no passionate resistance from anybody.' That was in October 1918.[9] Events in Britain over the next two or three years did nothing to allay this. As soon as the war ended – before, in some cases – the 'Great Labour Unrest' of the pre-war years resumed. In 1919, the first full year of peace, nearly 35 million working days were lost through strikes, which was only a few million short of the previous record of 1912. In 1921 that record was smashed, with 85 872 000 workless days.[10] The worst strikes were in mining, the docks and on the railways, but other groups of workers were involved too, including the police in Liverpool, London (again) and elsewhere. In January 1919 the Red Flag was hoisted over Glasgow Town Hall in the course of a strike there, and Army tanks were sent in. Many of the strikes were accompanied by violence. One of them – in the spring of 1921 – threatened to become *general*, when the old pre-war 'Triple Alliance' of powerful trade unions plotted to bring miners, railwaymen and transport workers out simultaneously, but was foiled on what later became known in left-wing Labour mythology as 'Black Friday', 15 April, by some union leaders' lack of stomach for the fight. That relieved the situation for the moment; but not before many conservatives had become convinced that they stood on the edge of an abyss.

This was where the Russian revolution came in again. It aggravated the danger in two ways. Firstly it provided a beacon of hope for native British revolutionaries, showing what could be done. Communism was no longer merely a theory, but had become a reality in conditions which seemed to be if anything less favourable than they were in Britain now. Secondly, it was thought to be providing direct advice and help: 'Moscow gold', for example; and trained subversives to help British comrades dig away at the sides of their abyss. That was not an unreasonable suspicion. Everyone knew that the Russians were anxious to export their revolution abroad. 'Comintern' – the Third Communist International – had been formed in 1919 with exactly that purpose in view. Soviet agents were known to be stumping Britain already, openly inciting the people to revolt.[11] A 'Hands Off Russia' movement, directed against British military intervention against the bolsheviks, was attracting impressive mass support. You did not need to be paranoid to see a hidden Soviet hand there. Another popular organisation, the National Unemployed Workers' Movement, formed in 1921, was led by avowed communists. In 1920 the 'Communist Party of Great Britain' was founded, with Moscow links. Then there was that hammer and sickle flying over Glasgow's George Square. The evidence was there. The Russians were in town. It did not require an enormous imaginative leap – though it may have been a mistaken one – to deem them responsible for most of Britain's ills at this time.

Those were some of the dangers that appeared to loom, even for victorious Britain, in 1918–21. The pre-war crisis had returned, with a vengeance. The empire was crumbling, and anarchy threatened at home. Behind all this lurked the blood-red form of the dragon of bolshevism, exploiting the situation where it could, or even manipulating it according to some analyses. All this made for an uncertain outlook: probably the most uncertain and exciting on the domestic and imperial fronts in any contemporary's living memory. How, then, was the government to cope?

II

Broadly speaking, there were two possible ways. One was simple intransigence, bolstered by repression; the other was more conciliatory, with a view to easing the pressures rather than containing them. Britain tried both methods in her empire, but in different proportions as time went by. Her initial response to colonial nationalist rebellion was swift, firm and often bloody. Later, however, she veered away from this approach, out of either moral revulsion, or necessity, or both.

In some places her first reactions gave the appearance of sheer panic. In April 1919 one Army commander, frightened by an unarmed independence demonstration in Amritsar in northern India, ordered his troops to open fire on it, and then to continue firing into the backs of the demonstrators as they tried to flee, until nearly 400 lay dead on the ground. Afterwards he claimed that his prompt action had saved the Raj from a re-run of the Indian Mutiny. In Iraq the next year the sore-pressed British military forces resorted to poison-gas shells and aerial bombing as a cheap way of keeping Iraqi and Kurdish tribesmen in check. Sometimes whole villages were blasted simply for not paying their taxes.[12] In Ireland nationalist violence was met by augmenting the local police with squads of recently demobilised British soldiers – the 'Black and Tans' – who very soon gained a reputation for brutality which was clearly deserved in many cases; and by sending in terror and even assassination gangs. These are only the most notorious examples of a general trend. More of what are conventionally regarded as 'atrocities' were probably perpetrated by the British authorities in these two or three immediately post-war years than at any other time of peace in modern British history. Two excuses were usually offered for them. One was that they were merely responding to 'atrocities' on the other side. In the Irish case that was true, although atrocities always look worse when they come from governments. The other was that they worked. Often they did. The question was, however: at what moral, political and financial *cost*?

It was this consideration which ruled the full repressive option out of contention for Britain in the end. People at home simply would not stand for it. Some were deeply concerned at the ethical implications of it, especially after Amritsar. Others resented the cost. Included among the latter was a large proportion of the normally imperialistic middle classes, groaning under their new 30% income tax burden, and looking everywhere they could think of – abroad as well as at home – for cuts. In 1921 an 'Anti-Waste League', the brainchild of the press magnate Lord Rothermere, which actually succeeded in getting three of its members elected to Parliament in by-elections in that year, singled out Iraq as one costly responsibility that should be dumped.[13] That should not surprise us. The British middle classes had been generally imperialistic for years, but only while imperialism seemed to pay for itself. Subsidizing it through taxation went right against their grain. It went even more against the grain of the working classes, who by and large felt no interest at all in maintaining costly colonial commitments, especially if part of the cost to them involved being kept on in uniform, as we have seen, to risk their lives. Loyal as the average Tommy was, his loyalty tended to evaporate somewhat the further his duties took him from hearth and home. In other words he was a patriot, but not an imperialist. Neither of these factors was new. Britain had never been totally dedicated to empire right across the social spectrum. She could not be, consistently with her character as a predominantly commercial nation, with predominantly commercial values which were fundamentally antithetical to empire in any tough, committed way. That was why she had rejected Joseph Chamberlain's imperialism in 1906, because of the price tag (tariffs) attached to it;[14] and why she refused to pay this new price for a fuller-blooded imperialism in 1918–21.

It was not only the blood that she rejected. In Iraq, for example, most of the expense was incurred not by the military, but by a new paternalist administrative structure on the Indian pattern which its Civil Commissioner, Sir Arnold Wilson, tried to impose on it in 1919 on the grounds that – as he telegraphed back to London in May the following year – 'Good administration, with consequent cheap food for the masses and security of property for all classes, is the only bulwark against Bolshevism that I know.'[15] That was undoubtedly a kinder way of controlling the Iraqis than bombing them from airplanes; but it was no less costly, and so no more acceptable to the anti-wasters. They just wanted out. That, in fact, was the strategem adopted by the government in the end. Confronted by all these revolting natives, chronically short of resources to contain them, and bereft of adequate support in Britain, it pulled in its horns. A series of withdrawals took place on selected fronts. That did not always stop the repression or the atrocities; but it did have the advantage of seeming to wash Britain's hands of them.

It was managed quite skilfully in the main. (Britain has always been good at strategic retreats.) One exception was Asia Minor, where Lloyd George's dogged support of Greek claims against the Turks nearly involved Britain in what would have been a highly damaging new war in 1922. His climb-down over that (the 'Chanak crisis') came rather late in the day. Elsewhere he read the signs earlier. One of his first foreign-policy decisions was to withdraw British troops completely from Russia, where they had been engaged since late in the war in a hopeless campaign to try to turn the tide of bolshevism back. By December 1919 they were all out; despite the vigorous protests of Lloyd George's own War minister, Winston Churchill, who regarded the communists as 'enemies of the human race' who 'must be put down at any cost'.[16] A little later Britain granted (southern) Ireland what she called 'Dominion status', which was a lot more than home rule though a little short of full independence, with effect from the beginning of 1922. That provoked protests too, especially from military and intelligence men on the spot who believed that with a little more repression they could have had the Irish licked.[17]

In the middle east there was a whole series of withdrawals: but with many of the blows softened by means of treaties whose purpose was to retain a kind of 'informal' British influence there still. So, for example, Egypt was conceded a form of independence in February 1922, but with certain functions – including the defence of the Suez Canal – remaining in British hands. In Iraq, Britain's brief 'Indian' experiment was abandoned in 1921, to be replaced by a 'native' government under the Emir Feisal (who got Iraq as a consolation prize after France would not let him have Syria) bound to Britain by a treaty which, for example, allowed the latter to retain some of her bomber aircraft there. (Bombing had been found to be a relatively cheap way of keeping order.) 'Transjordan' – which is what Britain decided to call the left-over bit of territory between Iraq and Palestine – was given to Feisal's brother Abdullah, on the same kind of terms. Persia was abandoned to the Persians and the Russians, who came to a separate arrangement between themselves in 1921. This allowed most British troops to be withdrawn from the middle east, apart from one or two areas of more direct and vital importance to her than the rest: Suez and Aden, because of the route to India; the Persian Gulf states, because of the oil; and Palestine, because no one could be found there – or anywhere else, for that matter – to sort out the rival claims of the Arabs and the Zionists. Britain marginally favoured the Jews at first, partly because she thought a future Jewish state would marginally favour her. That fitted in well with the general plan, which was for Britain to retain her dominant position in the middle east, but more subtly: 'in friendly and unostentatious co-operation with the Arabs', as Balfour put it in September 1919,[18] so as to disguise the degree of her control, and avoid the cost.

On the whole it worked: from Britain's point of view, that is, and in the short term. (Some of the long-term results for the people of the middle east were disastrous.) Britain had retained most of what she wanted in the area, at a saving of hundreds of millions of pounds in military expenditure, and nearly a million demobilised men.[19] She had stopped – or at least slowed down – the rot. She managed to hold on to all the rest of her empire, though not without a certain amount of trouble (a lot in India), and some more concessions – as we shall see – along the way. The crisis had been contained.

On the other hand that was clearly no cause for complacency. The immediate crisis had indeed been contained; but not before it had revealed some alarming weaknesses in Britain's imperial command. Colonial resistance movements were growing in confidence and strength, while Britain's ability and will to face them down weakened. It was possible that the latter trend might be reversed in the future, as Britain put the war behind her and recovered some of the prosperity and imperial morale she had lost in the course of it. On the other hand other circumstances might be even less favourable later than in 1918–21. One advantage she had then was that she was allowed to cope with her colonial problems on her own. No other great power was involved. Apart from Soviet Russia, whose intervention in British colonies was confined to moral influence, none of them was interested. Europe was recovering from the war. The United States had withdrawn into isolationism. This was a unique situation, which would probably never recur. In the past the most serious threats to the British empire had never come *from* it, but always from the outside. The same was true – probably much more so – in the post-war years. If Britain ever lost her empire it would be because another great power took it from her, or helped it to liberate itself, or dragged her into a war (like the last one) which would further loosen her grip. In this sense she could be said to hold her empire only on the sufferance of others. And those others had not yet revealed their post-war hands.

III

In the empire Britain coped with her crises, in the last resort, by opting out. That, of course, could not be done at home. If a problem became intractable on the domestic front she could not simply hand over power to native rulers and withdraw. Nor could she seriously contemplate the other extreme, of repression on the scale that Britain sometimes resorted to abroad. One or two men apparently did. In 1921, for example, Sir Hugh Trenchard, Chief of the Air Staff, thrilled by the successes of his bomber aircraft in maintaining order in Iraq, offered them to the government for use at home in suppressing 'industrial disturbances or risings' there; but he was never taken up on it.[20] Even at the height of the General Strike in 1926 there was no strafing of native villages in the coal fields of the West Riding of Yorkshire, for example, from the air. That was inconceivable. British men and women – even working class ones – were simply not the same as Iraqis and Kurds. Quite apart from anything else, most of them now (since 1918) had the vote.

That made a difference both to the nature of the crisis that beset Britain at home, and to the way it was met. Britain was now a democracy for the first time in her history. Just before the end of the war the parliamentary franchise had been extended to all adult males (with the usual exceptions: peers, prisoners, lunatics), and most women. This added *13 million* new names to the register for the election of December 1918, which was easily the largest proportionate increase (177%) of any of Britain's nineteenth or twentieth century parliamentary reform Acts.[21] The women, of course, were the great novelty; but it was the men who presented the problem. The women came from all social classes, with a slight bias if anything (because they had to be over 30 and ratepayers or wives of ratepayers) towards the uppers and middles. All the additional men, however, were working class. That altered the whole social balance of the electorate. The workers were now in a majority. Potentially, at any rate, they were – though the phrase was not used until later – 'the masters now'.

This, of course, was what many people on the right of British politics had dreaded for years. Their main fear (first clearly voiced by Bagehot in 1872)[22] was that the working classes might use this majority to vote *as* a class, against the interests of the whole nation as other classes might perceive them. After the war a trend seemed to be setting in that way. The workers' chosen vehicle was the Labour party, whose sectional function was clearly indicated by its very name. Labour was just about tolerable as a wing of the broader-based Liberal party in parliament, as it had been by and large before 1914. Now however, bolstered by all these new likely voters, it was raising its sights. The 1918 election was the first in which it fielded enough candidates to form a majority if they had all won. In the event it won 63 seats (excluding Coalition Labour), which was not bad against a 'khaki' ticket, and on the basis of a new party manifesto that was explicitly socialist for the first time. In by-elections over the next four years it added another 14 seats to these. In the 1922 general election it roughly doubled its representation, overhauling the Liberals in the process and thus becoming the official opposition for the first time.[23] That put it in line for government, which represented a remarkable rate of political progress over so short a period. The next stage might see the natives taking over completely; though in this case with no chance for the imperialists to withdraw.

That was bad enough, if you were not a working-class Labour voter yourself; but it could be even worse. This was where the crises of these early post-war years – the strikes, the demonstrations, the buzzing political activity on the left – came in. They indicated an alarming degree of class militancy among these people who now had the vote and in the future might form governments; and in particular their susceptibility to communism. Communists were the great new bugbear of this time. They were highly active in Britain, as we have seen, especially among the large pool (never less than a million) of unemployed. Two communists were elected to parliament in 1922. They were also suspected of having designs on the Labour party: by the head of the Special Branch, Basil Thomson, for example, who believed that Labour was a particular target for what he saw as a 'Moscovite Jew' conspiracy to rule the world. He cannot have been reassured about this when in 1921 he was given the sack from the Special Branch, due *he* believed to pressure on the Coalition government from Labour leaders who feared he 'knew too much' about their 'subversive activities'.[24] Thomson's view was extreme, but he was by no means alone in it on the Right or 'Die-hard' wing of British politics at this time; and in a milder form (shorn of its conspiratorial and anti-semitic aspects, for example) it reflected a widespread fear in Britain after the war.

One solution suggested by Thomson before he left was to privatize (in effect) the secret services, so as to enable them to maintain an independent watch on any Labour government that might come to power.[25] That did not happen (so far as we can tell); but even without it the secret services were able to pursue their prey pretty freely. On the domestic side their main prey – quite reasonably – was the political left, which was subjected to a degree of surveillance quite unlike anything that had been seen – or would have been permitted – before the war.[26] That was one response to the crisis. Another took the form of legislation enabling drastic action in situations the government defined as 'emergencies', which could include strikes. An example is the Emergency Powers Act of 1920, which revived some of the old wartime Defence of the Realm Act's provisions, especially in giving ministers an almost arbitrary authority ('such powers and duties as His Majesty may deem necessary for the preservation of peace') in certain circumstances.[27] In the same year the 1911 Official Secrets Act was strengthened, forbidding (among other things) the disclosure of privileged information injurious not only to the safety but also to the 'interests' – whatever that might mean – 'of the State'.[28] Another wartime innovation that was kept on was propaganda: in spite of the fact that the department formally responsible for it had been closed down in 1919, mainly to allay suspicions that it might be used for partisan purposes by the government.[29] In 1921, for example, £55 000 was spent in just three months on official propaganda against the national miners' strike, but channelled through bodies like the Middle Class Union and the Women's Guild of Empire to disguise its source.[30] All this was new in peacetime – certainly in the period covered by this book – and even in a small way revolutionary. It marks a crucial stage in the long slide from *relative* political liberalism to *relative* authoritarianism (both 'relatives' are important) which has been such a feature of British history in the twentieth century. One contemporary critic attributed it to what he called 'the war habit', which he said 'the Departmental mind finds it very difficult to get rid of';[31] but it was clearly more than merely a hangover from the war. Ministers certainly believed that these precautions were fully justified by the critical circumstances of *that* time too.

Nevertheless this was not the aspect of their response to the domestic problems of the time that they took most pride in. Much more important in the early months of the post-war Coalition government was supposed to be its social programme. That had an anti-socialist purpose too. The idea was to establish a fair and caring society that would leave workers and other potential subversion-fodder impervious to the blandishments of the Left. It was the equivalent on the home front to Sir Arnold Wilson's contemporaneous 'Indian' experiment in Iraq: the 'only bulwark against Bolshevism' that he knew.[32] The foundations had been laid during the war years, as we have seen. Then it was called 'Reconstruction'. One of the arguments for carrying on with Coalition government after the war, instead of reverting to party politics, was to carry out this policy. The Coalition would build on the experience of the war to forge Britain into a contented, united and efficient nation permanently. Then her troubles would melt away. That was the plan.

It might have worked. (It did for a time, after the *second* world war.) But it was not given a proper chance in 1918–21. Some early signs seemed promising. The new Coalition government contained a fair number of liberal interventionists and social imperialists.[33] They were the ones who would push reconstruction through. A few significant reforms were enacted in the early years, including an extension of unemployment insurance, a sharp rise in pensions, and an important Education Act. The big post-war promise, however, had been of 'homes fit for heroes'. In 1919 Dr Christopher Addison, the wartime 'Minister for Reconstruction', seemed to deliver on that with a brace of acts which subsidized both council and private house building from central funds. The target was for 300 000 houses within the year. But that was not to be. Only a fraction of them were built.[34] Some of the government's other measures also disappointed: like the Education Act of 1918, for example, whose provisions for compulsory part-time education for 14- to 18-year olds were simply not implemented. Worse was to come. In June 1920 the government decided not after all to place a special tax on excessive wartime profits, which had been widely canvassed in the country and would have been a real token of its genuine dedication to the principle of social equity.[35] That went hand in hand with a programme of swingeing cuts in just about every area of government social expenditure, which in August 1921 was put into the hands of a body – the 'Geddes Committee' – of penny-pinching businessmen. It was an almost complete turnaround, which embittered many genuine reformers in the government at the time – Addison, for example – and greatly damaged the subsequent reputation of the government, which was seen as having surrendered abjectly to people Stanley Baldwin once famously castigated as 'a lot of hard-faced men who looked as if they had done very well out of the war'.[36]

That was not entirely fair. Parliament probably did become more hard faced after the election of 1918. More businessmen were elected, and fewer paternalists.[37] That tilted the balance a little way against the social reformers. The main obstacle they had to face, however, was the economic situation of the time. In 1921 – when the reaction finally set in – that was particularly bad. Britain was hit by recession. Production dropped by 18% compared with 1920; foreign trade by 45%; unemployment probably approached two million; and income tax stood at six shillings in the pound for the third successive year.[38] The anti-wasters had their tails up. No one with any scheme that involved spending public money stood a chance. That was why reconstruction withered. It went the same way as Sir Arnold Wilson's great plans for Iraq, and for the same reason. Britain simply could not afford it then.

That left the domestic problem in Britain worse, if anything, in 1921 than it had been at the end of 1918. Britain could not withdraw; could not repress; and now, it seemed, could not appease. The same factor that was provoking the crisis at home – trade depression, leading to wage cuts and unemployment – was also preventing her from acting to defuse the crisis politically. All this played into the hands of the communists, who saw it, of course, as further evidence of the internal contradictions of British capitalism speeding it towards its inevitable final crisis and end. If they were right, there was nothing that anyone any longer could do. The next few years should show.

Chapter 16

Avoiding Extremes
(1922–31)

I

The British House of Commons does not often debate general principles. On 20 and 21 March 1923, however, it did. In *Hansard* the debate is labelled simply 'The Capitalist System'. The major protagonists were Philip Snowden, Labour MP for Colne Valley, and Sir Alfred Mond, Liberal MP for Swansea and managing director of the chemicals firm that later became ICI. Snowden moved that capitalism had failed in Britain, and consequently ought to be replaced by socialism. Mond, naturally enough, disagreed.

It was a curious debate in many ways. It was not important in any practical sense. Nothing hung on it. The outcome was a foregone conclusion, with socialists as overwhelmingly outnumbered in the House as they were. It could not achieve anything, and was not intended to; except perhaps – as Snowden said – to mark 'the extraordinary progress which socialist opinion has made in this country during the last 20 or 30 years',[1] and so give a kind of legitimacy to it. It probably did not change the views of anyone who attended either way. It certainly did not resolve the main issue. Whether capitalism in Britain could be said to have 'failed' in 1923 was still as contentious a question at the end of the debate as it had been at the start. Snowden reeled off a list of the imperfections of society under capitalism from child labour in the early nineteenth century through to slum overcrowding in 1921. Mond either denied them, blamed them on human nature or claimed they would be worse under socialism. Both positions were equally rational. When Snowden attributed 'most of the great inventions' of the world to a pre-capitalist stage of 'tribal communism', and Mond claimed that England was a free-enterprise economy under William the Conqueror, they were both being equally perverse.[2] (History was obviously not their strong suit.) That sort of evidence was inconclusive. And the contemporary economic evidence was hardly more of a help.

The problem with that evidence was that it was mixed. In some ways British capitalism did not do too badly in the 1920s. In March 1923, true, the economy was still fairly depressed on all fronts; but it picked up very soon afterwards, and from 1924 to 1929 is estimated to have grown as rapidly as in the 1890s, which is usually counted as a moderately prosperous decade.[3] The growth was especially marked in relatively new industries, like motor-car manufacture, electrical engineering and chemicals. The result was that Britain's national income started rising steadily for the first time since 1899, by about 10% (in real terms) during the five years 1925–29. Average real wages also rose, though by less.[4] Capitalism was pushing ahead again. But it was also leaving a lot of folk straggling behind. Foreign trade was in the doldrums. Several large manufacturing sectors were having a terrible struggle, especially textiles, iron, steel and shipbuilding, all of which produced appreciably less now than before 1914. The upshot of that was high levels of unemployment in certain areas: the docks, for example, because of the trade recession, cotton, wool, linen, shipbuilding, steelmaking and coalmining; most of which were concentrated in certain parts of Britain (Scotland, the north of England, Ulster, South Wales), which made the problem especially acute there. Overall the number of registered unemployed scarcely ever dipped below a million (or 10% of the insured labour force) throughout the 1920s.[5] This suggested that whatever failings capitalism might have could be chronic ones.

On the other hand it is obviously unfair to blame the rules of a game for the fact that some people do not play it well. What was clearly happening here was a partial failure of adjustment. Certain areas of the economy responded well to the new market demands and conditions of the 1920s, others did not. Overlying that was the fact that resources (including labour) were not being transferred from the unsuccessful to the successful sectors fast enough to eliminate waste. All kinds of reasons could be found to account for this. Management and labour in the old manufacturing areas were too conservative. Employers would not adapt; workers refused to move. Trade-union restrictive practices blocked change. Re-training facilities were poor. Financial institutions shied off investment in domestic manufacturing industry, and particularly in its older sectors. Interest rates were crippling, and the price of sterling – especially after it was tied to the gold standard in 1925 – was too high. That made it more difficult for Britain to sell goods abroad. This was a constant grouse by manufacturers throughout the 1920s, and touched on another, more serious complaint: which was that fiscal policy in Britain generally was too much influenced by the City of London – bankers and stockbrokers, who mainly benefitted from tight monetary policies – at the expense of the productive sector, which had to bear the brunt. In other words, British capitalism's problems in the 1920s were either of its own making, or due to wrong policies imposed from above. The corollary of this was that theoretically, at any rate, they could all be solved.

That was almost certainly true. The economy under capitalism could still flourish. In certain areas it already was flourishing. Sir Alfred Mond's own ICI – formed in 1926 from an amalgamation of Mond's family firm with three others – was a famous example: expanding from a capital value of £72.8 million in 1927 to £102.5 million in 1930; its profits rose continuously even into the depressed 1930s; and giving work to 42 000 people in 1930.[6] That showed what could be done. It also showed how to do it. In ICI's case it was through what was called 'rationalisation', which involved massive mergers and the introduction of American 'scientific management' techniques. In most cases where firms succeeded it was through such methods. This was the way of the future, capitalism's new path to recovery and progress. It was the best answer of all to those who claimed that capitalism was 'failing', or stumbling to an inevitable grave.

It also, however, had one or two unsettling implications. More was being changed by these new developments than mere methods and techniques. The whole *ethos* of capitalism was affected. One of capitalism's justifications in the past, for example, had been that it encouraged enterprise and endeavour in individuals, through the competitive opportunities it afforded them. In the age of large conglomerates, some of them becoming multinational, with enormous quasi-monopolistic powers, where were the competitive opportunities for individual enterprise and endeavour now? This was one of Snowden's more telling points in the March 1923 debate: 'Suppose a worker succeeds in saving £200 or £300, let him start business as a chemical manufacturer in competition with Brunner Mond'; and he would very soon see how he would get along. The interesting thing about Mond's reply to this challenge is that he conceded the argument readily. There was no point at all, he agreed, in small-scale rivals trying to compete with the big boys. 'What they want to do is to become shareholders in the [that is, *his*] company.' That was the extent of the opportunity now open to individuals. The reason for this, he claimed, was that capitalism had changed beyond all recognition from its early, pioneering days. 'The whole theory of capitalism, as expounded by some hon. Members, is entirely out-of-date. It does not exist in our modern industrial system.'[7] Consequently, Mond was saying, modern capitalism could be judged neither on the record, nor by the standards, of that earlier and more primitive version.

That answered Snowden's criticisms neatly. Modern capitalism had no connexion with any of the abuses of the past. Nor could it be censured for stifling many of the aspirations that had once been crucial to capitalism, but were no longer feasible or necessary in these times. It was a new creature; evolved from the old one, certainly, but different in many ways. For a start it was generally bigger, organised on a larger scale than before, often in near-monopolies or trusts (which Mond defended),[8] and usually capitalised *via* the stock market. The personal touch of the old capitalist-owner had gone, to be replaced by systems and methods and a professional managerial class, with the result (lastly) that its *values* had also changed, quite radically in many respects, and in ways that were bound to affect the values of society generally. Central to these changes was the new emphasis on the 'system'. Mond was very keen on this. Enterprise, initiative, freedom and the rest were all very well, he thought, but it was 'sound methods' that were the important thing. 'The real point of modern industrial enterprise' – again, he was drawing a contrast here with old-style capitalism – 'is management, and that is really the key.' Nothing else mattered: even ownership. 'I do not care whether you have privately-managed business or State-managed business. If it be badly managed, it will be a failure.'[9] That was another indication of the transformation that capitalism had undergone.

'Management' – in the sense meant here – may have been one of the most important new ingredients. Its origins go back to the turn of the century, and in particular to an American called Frederick Winslow Taylor, who devised the ground rules for what he first called 'scientific management' then. It started spreading to Britain after the war, often through American takeovers of British firms.[10] An early characteristic was a somewhat mechanistic approach to human organisations, justified by the need for efficiency. 'In the past the man has been first,' wrote Taylor in 1911; 'in the future the system will be first.'[11] This meant reducing most of the men and women working for it to mere drones, which Taylor thought would keep most of them happy, because their work would be undemanding and consequently unstressful, so long as they were paid moderately well. Later on management experts discovered some other human needs and ambitions which needed to be satisfied if workers were to be contented, which seemed to make it more human; but the underlying philosophy remained the same. The system came first. Man was secondary. If individual human needs were taken into account it was in the interests of corporate efficiency, and for no other reason: certainly not their intrinsic worth. There is an argument for that, of course, on human grounds. If the system benefits people ultimately, in the case of capitalism by maximising prosperity, for example, then even their subordination to the system must be to their greater good in the end. (That would have been the approach of Machiavelli; whose pinched features can be dimly made out behind much modern management theory in the labour relations field.)[12] But it still had unsettling implications;

not only for industry (where new scientific management techniques were fiercely resisted by some trade unions, for example, and in one case were only able to be imposed by means of a great national 'lockout', in the engineering industry in 1922),[13] but also in the wider community.

This was natural. People are very often influenced in their general attitudes by the values that surround whatever occupations they are in. Mid-nineteenth century capitalists were, for example, in ways which – as we have seen – greatly boosted political liberalism at that time. If the new breed of corporate manager was influenced in the same manner, it will have been in a very different direction. The very idea of 'managing' men and women is an intrinsically illiberal one, the more so the more deliberately 'manipulative' it becomes. It makes philosophical nonsense of the idea of 'democracy', by which people are meant to manage themselves. It undervalues human individuality, or even human needs, by comparison with the needs of the system or the corporation; which brings it close – ironically – to the sort of socialism that subordinates individuals to the state. It elevates 'leadership' – what Mond called 'the captain of industry'[14] – far higher than might be thought to be healthy in a truly liberal society. If notions like this did percolate through into the general ethos, they were bound to make a difference to the way society was run. What they did, in fact, was to aggravate the historical tendency we have noticed before for British capitalism to be prised away from the liberalism it had used to be associated with; and consequently to help with the long-drawn-out process of undermining society's liberal base.

In the final analysis, both Mond and Snowden could have been right in that famous Commons debate of 20–21 March 1923. Mond was undoubtedly right in general terms to point out how far capitalism had changed from the pattern of earlier days. By the same token, however, Snowden may have been justified in his strictures on the performance of that earlier pattern of capitalism, *before* it had changed. It was because it *had* failed, as he claimed it had, that it was having to be superseded. But of course that was not an end to the matter. The point to be addressed now was this: how much more successful and resilient would the new version be? Could large-scale, quasi-monopolistic, illiberal, scientifically managed capitalism make any better headway against its competitors abroad and its enemies at home than its predecessor had managed to do? Today of course we know at least part of the answer to this; but they could not at that time. So far as the domestic scene was concerned, the battle had only just begun.

II

Capitalism certainly believed it had a battle on its hands. The post-war crisis testified to that. Things were calmer now, in 1923, than they had been then. Days lost in strikes fell from 85 million in 1921, to 19 million and then ten million in the two following years. Trade union membership also slumped.[15] (Unemployment probably had much to do with that.) On the other hand ten million lost working days did not exactly indicate a state of industrial concord, and there was no guarantee that worse was not to come. That fear, as we shall see, was borne out very soon. Then there was the Labour party. In March 1923, when Snowden locked horns with Mond over the theoretical question of the survival of capitalism, he was one of 144 Labour MPs in the House of Commons, which was nearly twice as many as had sat there in the previous parliament, just four and a half months before. Every subsequent general election during the decade saw Labour increasing the size of its popular vote.[16] On two occasions it formed governments. That suggested that socialism was an enemy to be feared.

That problem was exacerbated for the capitalists by the fact that the anti-socialist opposition was split. It had not used to be. One of the main reasons for the continuation of the Lloyd George Coalition government after the war was to present a united front against Labour, who had withdrawn from it (apart from a handful, who were promptly expelled from the party) in November 1918. Lloyd George himself claimed that this was because Labour were a lot of 'Bolsheviks'.[17] As late as the autumn of 1922, when the Coalition appeared exhausted and demoralised, and tarnished by Lloyd George's reputation for 'corruption' (after a 'sale of honours' scandal that summer),[18] many Liberals and Conservatives felt that unity against Labour was still the wisest way. They included the Conservative leader Austen Chamberlain, who argued strongly along these lines at a famous meeting of the party to discuss the issue at the Carlton Club in London on 19 October 1922. The majority, however, disagreed. The result was that the Conservatives ditched the Coalition, and asserted their independence again. The main reason for that was the fear that the party might simply not survive another period under Lloyd George.[19] Against this, however, was the obvious danger that splitting the anti-left vote might let Labour in.

That was indeed what happened over the course of the next two general elections. Three roughly equal parties battled them out, leaving the issue entirely unpredictable under Britain's 'first past the post' system. In both elections the Conservatives polled 38% of the total vote, but with different results in each case. In November 1922 their 38% gave them an overall majority in seats: 345 out of 615 (or 56%). That should have made things safe for a while. But then an odd thing happened. The Conservative prime minister, Bonar Law, who was mortally ill, resigned in May 1923; Stanley Baldwin took over; and almost immediately called another election for December, entirely unnecessarily, in order to get a mandate for tariff reform. He won almost exactly the same number of votes, but distributed differently, so that this time they secured him only 258 seats. That was still the biggest share of any party, but did not constitute an absolute majority. The other two parties polled roughly 30% each in both elections, with Labour slightly ahead in seats. Its tallies were 142 in 1922; 191 in 1923. That made it the official opposition. In January 1924 it also made it the *government*, when Baldwin decided he could not govern on a minority basis, and the King summonsed Labour's Ramsay MacDonald, who agreed to have a go. Clearly MacDonald would not have been in this position if the Conservatives and Liberals had still been linking arms. From an anti-socialist point of view it all looked to have been a disastrous mistake.

In fact, however, it turned out surprisingly well: so well, indeed, that many Conservatives later came to believe that clever old Baldwin had planned it from the start. If so, then it would have made him the shrewdest political operator in Britain since Disraeli, at least. In the first place, the 1923 defeat put an end to tariff reform as a viable policy for the foreseeable future, which relieved the Conservatives of a commitment that was unpopular generally and divisive even among themselves. Secondly, it meant that the first ever Labour government, being also in a minority, would be powerless to effect any real socialism, and unlikely to survive for very long. That, thought Baldwin, they could live with. It was why he took no action to stop MacDonald's taking over in January 1924, for example by negotiating with the Liberals; and why he did nothing to bring him down in his first ten months.[20] In February 1924 – just a fortnight after the changeover – Baldwin justified these decisions on the grounds that if Labour had not come in then, it would have done so later with a majority, and hence the opportunity to do some real mischief.[21] At the very least, that was a consoling thought.

Thirdly, the situation allowed Baldwin to deliver the final *coup de grace* to the Liberal party. This – if he really did intend it all along – was a truly Disraelian stroke. One of the results of the Disraeli's extension of the franchise to the working classes in 1867 had been to attract nervous ex-Liberals into the Conservative camp.[22] Much the same happened in 1924. The spectre of a working-class government seems to have provoked a mass exodus of Liberal voters to the Conservatives – one of several since 1867 – presumably because Conservatism was seen as a more secure redoubt. That was certainly the line the Conservatives took. Baldwin himself may have felt fairly relaxed about Labour, but the voters were not allowed to be. Almost the whole Conservative campaign in the next election, in October 1924, was geared to persuading them that MacDonald's government was a hotbed of bolshevism. Hence the infamous 'Zinoviev letter': supposedly written by the president of Comintern, Grigori Zinoviev, to the British communists, suggesting that they already had their covert agents in the Labour party; intercepted by the secret services; passed on to Conservative Central

Office *via* its connexions in the secret services; and then 'leaked' to the *Daily Mail* just three days before the election, for maximum impact.[23] How effective that was is debateable. It probably did not lose Labour much support (they made a net gain of more than a million votes in any case). But it may have helped the shift from the Liberals to the Conservatives. In any event the strategy was successful overall. Labour gained a larger proportion of the vote but lost seats. That was because the anti-Labour vote was more effectively marshalled behind the Conservatives. They romped home with 419 seats, a gain of 161, mostly at the expense of the Liberals. The latter slumped to 40. They were never again to be a power in the land.

Whether this was part of a master-plan of Baldwin's going back to before the 1923 election is difficult to say. It is unlikely, to say the least, that he went into that election deliberately intending to lose it because he knew that it would set all these other events in train. That was a shock. On the other hand he was quick to spot and exploit its advantages. That was his genius (as it had also been Disraeli's): his ability to divine what he called the way 'things were shaping themselves' anyway, and then ride them, rather than trying to obstruct. In the 1920s he saw two inevitable (as he thought) trends. The first was 'the disappearance of the Liberal Party'; the second was the arrival of Labour as a permanent fixture on the political scene.[24] Both these trends had more or less worked themselves out by the autumn of 1924, to the Conservative party's great gain. That, however, was not the end of it so far as Baldwin was concerned. If there was a master plan, it was only Phase One.

III

Phase Two was more difficult. Labour was now established in the Liberals' old place on the Left of British politics. For some Conservatives – especially those who had believed their own propaganda in the 1924 election – this was a worrying prospect. For Baldwin it was not; but only so long as Labour and the working classes were kept moderate. The way to do that, he felt, was to avoid provoking them. That meant Conservative governments adopting a conciliatory or consensual approach to their opponents, even if it meant compromising some of their beliefs.

This was nothing new. It was another policy that went back to Disraeli, at least, and to the time in the 1870s when – as we saw – free-market capitalism seemed to falter a little, and hence re-aroused opposition, which was then defused by means of social and trade-union legislation, for example, which strictly speaking offended against free-market principles, but was believed to be a necessary and justifiable price for social peace nonetheless. Later on this approach took on a patriotic aspect, in the hands of 'social imperialists' who held that breaking free-market rules in order to protect workers was a means of binding all classes together in the interests of 'national efficiency'. In fact most of the dominant British political trends of the past 50 years had emphasised this 'consensus' approach: Tory Democracy, Chamberlainite Liberalism, municipal socialism, Fabian collectivism, social imperialism, the New Liberalism, wartime and postwar coalitionism; so that Baldwin had a strong historical tradition behind him, whether he realised it or not. Consensus also grew naturally from his character; from his upbringing by an industrialist father who prided himself on his friendly relations with his workers;[25] and from his experience of the early post-war years, when a more confrontational style of politics had, he believed, nearly brought the country to ruin. A more emollient approach would re-unite the nation; marginalise extremists; blunt the edge of the threat from the left to capitalism; and also, incidentally, broaden the Conservatives' electoral appeal.

There were problems with it, however. One was that Baldwin had little positive to offer the workers: no spare cash for the sort of social reforms that might emolliate them, for example, and no short-term panacea for the most pressing problem of the day, which was unemployment; bar protective tariffs, which he had advocated partly as a means to safeguard jobs in Britain, only to be rebuffed by the electorate in 1923. It was this that undoubtedly lost him the next election, in 1929. That left him with very little but the *reputation* or 'image' of a conciliator to offer the workers; and with certain negative proofs of that, such as his refusal to be positively provocative in situations where all the pressures were on him to be so. There were plenty of those, arising essentially out of the size of the Conservatives' victory in 1924, which could easily have been used as a means to flatten Labour if the Diehards had got their way. 'So large a majority creates dangers of its own,' Austen Chamberlain wrote to Baldwin shortly after that victory; 'Reaction would be fatal.'[26] The reactionaries were rampant, especially on the back benches. Baldwin could feel them baying at his ears.

Initially he was able to hold them back, in a way that did no end of good to his conciliatory image. A backbencher called Macquisten introduced a bill in March 1925 to curb both the trade unions and the Labour party, by altering the basis on which the former contributed to the latter's funds. It might have passed, if it had not been for an eloquent personal appeal from Baldwin to its supporters to show magnanimity and desist. He conceded that the bill was right in principle. They could pass it if they wished. They had their majority. But how had they won it? 'It was not by promising to bring this Bill in; it was because, rightly or wrongly, we succeeded in creating the impression throughout the country that we stood for stable Government and peace in the country between all classes of the Community.' Forsaking the Macquisten bill would confirm that. 'We know we may be called cowards for doing it. We know we may be told we have gone back on our principles. But we believe we know what at this moment the country wants'; which was neither retributive legislation, nor even principled legislation if the principles could be seen as divisive and partisan. People wanted neither a sectional nor a dogmatic government, but a 'national' one; which in Baldwin's view – and his words at the very end of his peroration – was the only way of achieving, on the domestic stage, 'peace in our time, O Lord'.[27]

It worked then, with the defeat of the bill; but sadly for Baldwin consensus did not fare so well after that. The Diehards had rallied loyally over Macquisten, but were still basically sceptical of the wisdom of Baldwin's approach. What he really needed, to justify it, was a placatory response from the other side. That, however, was not forthcoming. This was Baldwin's other great difficulty. Certain sections of the left were in no mood at all to meet him half way. Economic conditions were partly to blame for that; especially in the coal industry, whose managements announced their intention in 1925 to cut miners' wages in order to make their product more competitive. That, of course, was the 'correct' approach economically, but it threatened to provoke a strike. Other unions pledged support for the miners. That would take the country back to 1921, which was exactly what Baldwin was anxious to avoid. To that end he compromised again: this time by extending a Treasury subsidy to the mining industry which would enable it to sustain the higher wage level for another nine months. In the meantime they would all talk around tables to try to sort out the problems of the industry consensually. The Diehards regarded this as a humiliating surrender to threats. 'Red Friday' (31 July), the day when it happened, became the equivalent of Labour's 'Black Friday'[28] in their mythology.

Again, it did not work. When the nine months were up, in April 1926, the original dispute remained. An inquiry (the Samuel Commission) had proposed a compromise, but neither side would accept it. Baldwin tried to smooth things down, but was met with intransigence from the mineowners especially, who were probably the most unregenerately diehard industrial group in Britain then. The TUC also proved less flexible than it might have been, *possibly* because it, too, had taken 'Red Friday' as a sign of weakness, and thought the government would cave in. If Baldwin still had any inclinations this way, the majority of his cabinet did not. On Sunday, 2 May, it broke off negotiations, and the General Strike began. 'Everything I care for,' Baldwin told the Commons the next day – still carefully cultivating his image as a pacifier – 'is being smashed to bits.'[29]

Despite this, however, the outcome was not too bad for Baldwin in the end. The strike achieved the best of both Conservative worlds. For those who had been itching for a good class battle, it had almost everything. The

state, which the government insisted was itself under threat from the strikers, flexed its muscles impressively. The Emergency Powers Act
immediately came into force. Operations were co-ordinated with military
efficiency by a cabinet committee called the 'Supply and Transport Organisation', which had been preparing for exactly this contingency –
stockpiling food and coal, for example – for months. The BBC was more or
less taken over by the government side, and an emergency newspaper published – the *British Gazette* – with newsprint smuggled in from Holland,
while all the other Fleet Street presses lay idle.[30] The police went in in
force, arresting strikers and seditionists by the thousands. (7960 were eventually brought to trial.) Twenty-six Army battalions were called out, and
shifted about the country in convoys of armoured cars, to impress the natives.
Royal Naval battleships were sent to the Clyde, the Mersey and Rosyth,
and cruisers to other ports. The Special Branch and MI5 were used together
with Army Intelligence to sniff out plans and plots before they matured.
Probably the government's most successful ploy was its call for volunteers
to keep essential services going in what was presented as a 'patriotic'
cause. That struck a resounding chord. During the first week of the strike
114 000 people volunteered from London and the home counties alone,
together with 3350 Cambridge undergraduates who were given the time off
by their patriotic tutors: far too many, in fact, for the jobs available. (In particular very few got the opportunity to drive railway trains, which is what
most of them probably secretly hankered after.) All this gave a tremendous
boost to middle-class morale, and to the notion of the anti-strike cause as a
popular one.[31] The TUC was nothing like so well prepared (which suggests
that it had not really expected the strike), or served. After just nine days the
General Strike collapsed, though the miners struggled on, vainly, for
another six months. The government had won quite comprehensively.
There could be no doubt at all about this.

Afterwards the hardliners were cock-a-hoop. In May 1927 they capitalised on their victory by passing an Act very like Macquisten's, curbing the
unions, with Baldwin powerless to stop them. They also went on the rampage against communists, wherever they could be found. The Communist
Party of Great Britain was harried continually; with its headquarters in
King Street, Covent Garden, raided frequently, often on the flimsiest of
pretexts, and members arrested and imprisoned for 'seditious libels' which
would have been considered normal political currency in earlier and less
nervous times.[32] In May 1927 the London offices of ARCOS, the official
Russian trading agency, were the target of a famous raid by 150 police with
pneumatic drills and oxy-acetylene torches, to search for evidence of espionage which was never found; though enough communist *propaganda* was
discovered there to justify the government, it believed, in breaking off

diplomatic relations with the USSR.[33] All this was quite reactionary in its way. It could have been provocative. That was what the moderates had feared in October 1924. But it did not work out like that.

In fact the public response was mild. The 1927 Trades Disputes Act aroused fury and disorder in the House of Commons while it was going through, but scarcely a murmur outside.[34] All over the country industrial peace (where there was any industry left to be peaceful) returned. The tally of days lost through strikes swung from its record high of 162 million in 1926 to a record low of just over one million the next year, more than half of them accounted for by the continuing dispute in the coal mines.[35] Labour militancy evaporated to almost nothing. Communist party membership declined from its peak (10 730) at the time of the General Strike, to less than a third of that (3200) at the end of 1929.[36] Its electoral fortunes also waned. Moderates came to the fore in both the Labour party and the TUC. Quite suddenly, the domestic scene returned to calm. The socialist dragon had been slain, or temporarily immobilised, at least.

IV

That is, if it really was so fierce a dragon in the first place. There must be doubts over this. Even 10 000 card-carrying communists were not an enormous number: the equivalent of just one-tenth of an FA cup final crowd, or one-twentieth of the crowd that turned up to see the first Wembley final in 1923, which on that occasion had been able to be controlled, famously, by a single policeman on a white horse. That puts it into perspective. Of course it is not a very fair comparison. Football supporters, by and large, do not set out to subvert the state. Ten thousand probably did not represent the full strength of the CPGB, some of whose membership may have been covert, posing as members of other more mainstream parties in order to harness them to communist ends.[37] That was always a suspicion on the part of the right, who used to see dragon scales all over the Labour party, in particular. On the other hand it was probably an exaggerated one. There is no proof and little likelihood that this sort of thing happened to any great or very effective extent. The real Labour party was a far gentler creature: furry rather than scaly, with no fire-breathing capacity, and scarcely even any teeth.

It always had been, right back to its birth in 1900, as we saw.[38] In its first years it was merely a special interest group attached to the Liberals, and on the whole perfectly content to be there. In the war it stood in the same position *vis-à-vis* the Coalition, though with substantially more influence. Afterwards, in that somewhat confusing little postwar period in which anything looked possible, including even revolution, Labour wore a fiercer mask for a while; but it lost no time in trying to shed that when the situation calmed down. In the Capitalism *versus* Socialism debate of March 1923, for example, Philip Snowden was continually at pains to stress the moderate nature of the kind of socialism *he* espoused: that for a start there was 'no analogy between Socialism and Bolshevism'; that Labour advocated 'no revolution' and would resist 'any proposal of confiscation'; and that whatever a Labour government did in the direction of social reform would be done stage by careful stage, so that 'no further step forward' would be taken 'until the previous step we took has been justified by success'.[39] That was in order to consolidate and improve Labour's hold on the broad-left ground of British politics, which the Liberals were now vacating, leaving the vacuum into which Labour was now being sucked. We have seen how that happened. Labour's displacement of the Liberals made it look as though there had been a lurch towards socialism on the left, but that is not what had really happened at all. The Liberals declined not because leftists rejected their philosophy for something stronger, but because of the draining away of their anti-Labour support to the Right. That left them weak and vulnerable, and consequently no longer an effective vehicle for their own left wing: the social reformers in the party, 'New Liberals', 'Lib-Labs' and so on; who as a further result of this realignment – not a cause of it – abandoned the Liberal ship, just as their right-wing shipmates had done, but this time in order to jump to the vessel that was steaming past them on their other, larboard bow. That further leavened Labour's lump: broadening its base, diluting its socialism, and establishing, as a result, more continuity than seems apparent from the surface with the political situation before the war. In a way, in fact, the Labour party in the 1920s simply took up where the old Liberal party had left off. It *became* the old Liberal party; or rather, became very much like what the old 'New' Liberal party of the 1910s would probably have grown into, if it had survived intact. The label was different, but the line of development was the same.

The composition of the 1924 government emphasized this. Ramsay MacDonald himself had very strong ties with the Liberals, going back to the 1890s when he had been a founder member of a progressive political discussion group – the 'Rainbow Circle' – which was one of the main anvils on which the 'New Liberalism' was originally forged. He still kept in touch with it even when prime minister.[40] His first cabinet contained four ex-Liberals, including two (Haldane and C.P. Trevelyan) who had been ministers in Liberal governments; plus even two Conservative peers. The policies they pursued were moderate to a fault. On broad issues, for example, they were faithful to free trade, unlike the Conservatives; admirably internationalist in their foreign policy; and 'sound' financially. On the negative side they never even attempted to *nationalize* anything, despite an unambiguous commitment to 'common ownership' in their 1918 constitution; that was left, surprisingly, to the Conservatives, who took the electricity-supply industry under public control in 1926. The 1924 government's one solid domestic achievement, the Wheatley Housing Act, was built on foundations laid by the Liberal Addison in 1919, and further extended by the Conservative Edward Hilton Young in 1933. All this was intensely frustrating to left wingers, one of whom in 1924 openly accused MacDonald of 'trying to turn the Labour party from the party of the working class into a national party'.[41] That may well have been so.

Left-wing frustration was even more pronounced during Labour's second term of office. That came at a bad time, to put it mildly. Baldwin's government had come almost to the end of its natural five-year term, gone to the country in May 1929, and been narrowly beaten by Labour: probably because of persistent high unemployment rather than anything it had done or Labour promised to do. Labour however was still 20 seats short of an overall Commons majority, which made it dependent on other parties' votes. Five months later came the great New York stock-exchange crash, sparking off what was probably world capitalism's biggest crisis thus far. That was encouraging to socialists theoretically, but it was difficult to see how it could be exploited in practical terms. Depression hit British industry, doubling unemployment (from averages of 1 216 000 in 1929 to 2 630 000 in 1931),[42] which increased the need for social expenditure – for example on unemployment benefit – while at the same time, of course, depleting the public revenues from which that expenditure would need to be raised. That created an obvious tension. One way of resolving or avoiding it would have been to allow expenditure to exceed revenue for the time being; but that was thought likely to undermine foreign financial confidence in Britain, and consequently the country's financial stability if it caused a run on the capital invested there. In August 1931 the 'May Committee', set up to look into this, recommended £24 million worth of new taxes and £96 million worth of economies, in order to balance the books. Most of the economies would be in the form of cuts in the 'dole'. That would be unlikely to go down well with Labour backbenchers. On the other hand the other parties would accept nothing less.[43]

It was an impossible situation for MacDonald. He tackled it in the worst conceivable way for Labour: by proposing an all-party coalition, which Baldwin accepted and joined, but the bulk of Labour spurned. The result was that the latter were trounced in the election called in October 1931 to seek a mandate for the change, losing nearly two million votes and more than 200 seats, while the 'National' government won 554 seats overall, 473 of them Conservative, which was (and remains) an all-time record. The new government was dominated by Conservatives, though with MacDonald at its titular head and five other renegade Labourites with him in the cabinet. Afterwards Labour never forgave MacDonald for this, rightly from their point of view, but unfairly if it was thereby implied that his action had made any significant difference to the general situation. Labour would undoubtedly have fared better if it had stuck to the compromise its Chancellor, Snowden, proposed over the May Report, even if that had meant defeat and another period in opposition to the Conservatives; but it would not have been more effective, or socialism brought any nearer, than they turned out to be in the event. It was the circumstances of the time that determined that: the dilemma over public spending posed by the financial crisis, coupled with the people's clear reluctance to go for more radical solutions to that dilemma, which may have existed in theory, but only at great risk.

That reluctance was demonstrated beyond reasonable doubt by the overwhelming size of the National government's electoral victories both in 1931, when it polled 67% of the popular vote,[44] and then again when it next went to the country in 1935. People wanted financial stability, cautious social progress, industrial co-operation, avoidance of political extremes: in a word, consensus, which is by and large what they got. It was Baldwin's and MacDonald's sensitivity to this which brought them together in 1931, in the face of considerable resentment from some of their more extreme party colleagues, who in Baldwin's case saw him as little better than a 'socialist'.[45] The path they took was not a very heroic one, as heroism is generally conceived in this field. They went with the odds instead of battling against them; followed rather than led; let things slide rather than got things done; survived rather than were slain. On the other hand they did little harm, at least domestically, which at that particular period of European history must be counted a success. Continental Europe just then was full of heroes (as well as not a few cowards), which did not make it self-evidently a better place. That is certainly what Baldwin thought. Viewing the scene abroad in 1935, he told a film newsreel audience that they should all feel profoundly thankful to be 'living in this country, under a system of National Government... True to our traditions, we have avoided all extremes. We have steered clear of fascism, communism, dictatorship, and... shown to the world that democratic government, constitutional methods and ordered liberty are not inconsistent with progress and prosperity.'[46] Most contemporaries showed by their votes that they did, indeed, appreciate that.

In the final resort it is probably this factor above everything that enabled British capitalism to survive these Great Depression years. There was simply no deep or widespread revolutionary feeling (of any political complexion) in the country, but rather an overwhelming craving for what in contemporary America was called 'normalcy'. This operated at every level: not only political, but also for example in the industrial field. In 1928 the 'Mond-Turner' talks, between between a team of leading progressive industrialists led by our old friend Sir Alfred Mond, and representatives of the TUC, with Baldwin's blessing,[47] explored ways of replacing confrontation in industrial relations with a more co-operative approach. The following year the TUC General Council in 1929 announced that at last it was prepared to lend its help 'to promote and guide the scientific reorganisation of industry', despite a decade of resistance, on the highly realistic ground that 'The movement can find more use for an efficient industry than a derelict one.'[48] That was another manifestation of the consensual and collaborative spirit of the time, which could well have been the best prophylactic against 'extremism' in those circumstances that could have been devised.

Of course it was impossible to be sure. Some people still greatly feared communism, especially, even as late as 1930. Sir Wyndham Childs, recently head of the Special Branch, recalled that year in his memoirs how he had originally been engaged – as he understood it – specifically to 'deal with the menace of Communism', and yet 'during those weary years when Mr. Baldwin's Government held power' had simply not been allowed to strike the 'final blow'.[49] Others were more vigilant than Baldwin; including the semi-autonomous MI5, which took over the Special Branch's main responsibility for counter-subversive work in 1931; and private agencies like Conservative Central Office, which had its own little spy organisation under the control of an ex-MI5 man called Joseph Ball, and the 'Economic League', founded by an ex-head of Naval Intelligence in 1919, which kept a close – some would say paranoid – eye on potential subversives in industry.[50] This kind of activity increased in the 1920s and 1930s, indicating that not everyone was lulled into indifference by the success of consensus.

There were other malcontents too. That was inevitable. The consensus of the later 1920s and 1930s was curious in many ways. It was very unequal, heavily weighted towards the capitalist and Conservative side: reflecting perhaps the decisive victory which that side had achieved in 1926. It set the agenda; labour (and Labour) went along with it perforce. The former (the capitalists) could be seen in effect to be 'managing' the latter, though in a way – as with all the best management techniques – that made labour feel it had some positive input too. Socialists resented that. Others cavilled at other aspects. From the opposite end of the political spectrum free marketeers disliked the concessions that had already been made to labour to keep it sweet, to the detriment they believed of profitability and hence prosperity for all. They were the ones who called Baldwin a 'socialist'. Yet another group felt that he and MacDonald were *too* orthodox in this respect. They included a growing school of economists, among them J.A. Hobson and J.M. Keynes, and of maverick politicians of all parties, who believed that the best way of recovery from the depression was for Britain to *spend* her way out of it: by *raising* benefits and wages, and even artificially creating jobs through public works, in order to create a demand for goods which would then stimulate industry to produce them; instead of lowering benefits and wages to cut costs and so make industry more *competitive*, which was the accepted way. One Labour MP, Sir Oswald Mosley, impatient with his own party's obstinacy on this point, broke away to form a new 'Keynesian' group of his own – the 'New Party' – in February 1931. Others – and Mosley himself a little later – turned to Continental-style fascism as a means of rescuing Britain from what they saw as a form of government (democracy) which only encouraged mediocrity and torpor, and so threatened Britain's (or, more often, England's) national soul. So there was plenty of dissent. Unfortunately for it, it was too marginal and diffuse to be effective. For the time being consensus ruled; that is, if 'ruled' is not too bold a word to describe it.

Chapter 17

Security and Empire (1922–35)

I

If it was important that Britain avoid extremes at home, it was vital that she did so abroad. This was because of the underlying fragility of her international situation. That fragility went back decades, as we have seen. Fundamentally it arose from the contradiction implicit in the nature of her national economy, between her commercial and financial interests overseas and her ability to defend them. We have gone over all this before: the origins of the contradiction, and its effects on Britain's foreign policy. In a nutshell: it made her more *vulnerable* than most other powers, partly because she was open to attack on so many more fronts – colonies, spheres of influence, markets, trade routes and so on all over the world; and partly because it was less easy for her to divert economic and human resources into defending those fronts. That gave her a greater interest than most countries had in avoiding war – the ultimate 'extreme' in the realm of foreign affairs – if she possibly could. She had not been able to manage this in 1914; but the result of that war merely emphasised her wisdom in trying to. It had weakened her, even though she had won it. That left her even less fit to fight another, if one ever came along, than she had been to fight the first.

In the early 1920s that did not seem to matter, partly because the extent of Britain's weakness was obscured somewhat, and partly because hopes were high that another war could be avoided indefinitely. The obscurity was due to the understandable contemporary assumption that the winners of wars must also be gainers, and to the fact that the real gainer from this war – the USA – had left the scene. After 1920 the American people decided that they wanted nothing more to do either with Europe, or even with the League of Nations their own president (Woodrow Wilson) had done so much to bring about, and retreated into their isolationist shell. Russia, the only other power with the size and resources to compete with the USA in diplomatic terms, had left the scene earlier, for other reasons. For the next few years they constituted what Paul Kennedy has called the 'Offstage Superpowers'[1] in the great world drama that was being enacted: intrinsically greater than any of the other nations, and capable of dominating the latter if they wished, but preferring not to exercise that option, and so leaving lesser powers like Britain and France with most of the dialogue and an illusion of star billing that they did not really deserve.

The hope of peace sprang from the existence of the League of Nations, even without the Americans, and from the genuine progress that was made during the course of the 1920s in settling both current and prospective disputes between nation states. The ultimate aim of all this was 'collective security': a system by which peace would be guaranteed by every country agreeing to help resist aggression wherever it occurred. That would share the burden of peacekeeping around, and hopefully lift it altogether in practice, by deterring potential aggressors with the knowledge of the sure retribution that their aggression would bring. It was similar to the early nineteenth-century 'balance of power' idea in this regard, and beset by the same difficulties: that not every country shared the same interest (with Britain, for example) in outlawing aggression, and not all of those which did (like Britain) were happy about committing themselves to armed resistance in situations where other powers might not join in. Still, in the 1920s it looked as though it might be on. In the winter of 1921-22 the United States, Britain, Japan and other interested parties signed a series of treaties in Washington respecting each other's rights in the Pacific, guaranteeing China's integrity, and limiting naval tonnages. In 1924 the American 'Dawes Plan' lightened Germany's reparations load; Britain recognised the Soviet regime in Russia; and the 'Geneva Protocol' – to enforce compulsory arbitration in all disputes between nations – was *almost* signed. In 1925 at Locarno in Switzerland the European powers (including Britain) erected an impressive system of defensive alliances to secure boundaries, and persuaded Germany to renounce her claim to Alsace-Lorraine. From 1925 onwards talks went on to prepare the way for a great world disarmament conference; which got nowhere, but never gave up. In 1928 the representatives of more than 30 nations meeting in Paris signed the 'Kellogg Pact', solemnly renouncing aggression in all circumstances; a mere 'scrap of paper',[2] true, but at least it showed the right spirit. That was the encouraging thing about all these developments. Things were moving slowly, but generally along the right lines. For the moment, too, it seemed to be working. The 1920s were a relatively peaceful decade in world affairs: perhaps the most peaceful for a hundred years. Europe seemed particularly calm. That was also heartening.

Britain was indeed heartened; but only to a certain point. There were two main causes for concern. The first was that all this might only be a temporary respite: as indeed with hindsight we can now see it was. War remained a possibility, even if not an immediate one; especially in view of Germany's persistent feelings of grievance over the terms of the Versailles settlement, and some ominous muscle-flexing over on the other side of the world, by Japan. Then there were the Offstage Superpowers, who could not be ignored indefinitely, in view of their obvious potential strength, and the ideological threat posed by one of them – Russia – even while she took little overt part on the diplomatic stage. Of course to be aware of these possibilities you had to take a longer-term view of the geopolitical situation than the majority of people, who merely followed the more obvious signs of the time; but one or two people did think this far. One was Leopold Amery, Baldwin's Colonial Secretary in 1924–29, who predicted not only the rise of the United States and Russia – 'potentially capable of organisation on American lines' – but also, following them, of the 'Chinese Empire', and the creation in response to these three great super-economies of a 'European Economic Union' (his words, in 1928), which Britain would be in danger of being sucked into if she did not take evasive action then.[3] Thoughts like this were a useful corrective to the euphoria induced in other circles by Washington, Locarno and the Kellogg Pact.

The other worry concerned trade. Britain's record in this area was abysmal throughout the 1920s, with the exception of one little post-war export boom in 1920, which however soon fell away. Thereafter trade was sluggish, never quite (if we allow for inflation) reaching its 1913 level in any year between 1921 and 1939, for example, and declining steadily as a proportion of world trade too.[4] A number of legitimate excuses could be made for this: Britain's loss of markets during the war, the stagnation of world trade generally, foreign tariffs, the depression of the German market due to reparations; but all these began to look a little threadbare when the continental European economy, in particular, began reviving around 1924–25, and still Britain found herself unable to profit thereby. Industrial backwardness was partly to blame; together with the high price of sterling, maintained at that level for the benefit of the financial side of the economy, which flourished still. Britain was becoming less competitive. For a nation that depended on trade as much as she did – less than before, but still two and a half times as much as France, for example[5] – this was as deeply disturbing as the embryonic diplomatic threats from Germany, Japan, America and Russia were.

There did, however, seem to be one possible way out. Both these concerns pointed in this direction. The one area of British trade that seemed to be flourishing – relatively, at any rate – was *imperial*, which had always previously (as we have seen) counted for only a minority of her total commercial activity, but in the 1920s and 1930s began creeping up as a proportion. In 1910–14, 25% of Britain's imports had come from the colonies, and 36% of her exports had gone there. By 1930–34 the figures were 31% and 42%; and by the end of the inter-war period 40% and nearly 50% respectively.[6] The same trend could be seen in the pattern of British foreign investment.[7] One of the reasons for this was that the colonies were in the sterling area, which made the high price of the pound irrelevant; others were that most of them were mainly primary producers, and consequently easier for Britain to penetrate with manufactures; and that they did not by and large erect tariffs against British goods. For many people in Britain that made them much more worth cultivating than foreign markets, on the grounds that whereas 'Nothing this House can do will have the slightest effect on the amount of goods that the foreigner will purchase from us,' as an MP put it in 1925, they did have some control over the colonies.[8]

That also chimed in with the feelings of geopoliticians like Amery, with his auguries of American and Russian world-domination, European union, and Britain's colonies gravitating towards 'the great American Union' if she did nothing to prevent it soon. The empire was her only way out of this trap. It had the resources Britain did not have on her own to enable her to compete with the great power blocs that were forming on each side of her. All it needed was *consolidating*: Amery suggested by federating Britain and the self-governing dominions somehow, with the dependent colonies in Africa, Asia and elsewhere attached to the whole as a kind of vast tropical estate, providing mineral and vegetable products for it, and ruled firmly but kindly by whites. The first step to this – as it had been for a previous generation of imperialists – was an imperial customs union, which would unify the empire economically. That scheme, rejected originally by the electorate in 1906, and then again in 1923, took on a new lease of life around 1930, as indeed did the idea of the importance of the empire to Britain generally; which was ironic, in view of the fact that it was already then in the process of slipping from her grasp.

II

That, however, was by no means obvious – and may not have been inevitable – in the 1920s and 1930s. Things were apparently looking up for the empire. It was not *expanding* any longer: the days for that were clearly past; but it seemed to be progressing on other fronts. The idea of 'colonial development', for example – that is, developing colonial resources with help from the state: Joseph Chamberlain's plan initially – made great strides. An early initiative in this direction was the 'Empire Cotton Growing Association', set up by Royal charter in 1921 and funded by the government, mainly as a research facility for Africa. Others followed. In 1929 a general

Colonial Development bill was moved by the Labour government and passed almost *nem. con.*, pledging £1 million of taxpayers' money over three years to subsidize more research and the provision of infrastructure projects (railways, docks etc.) all over the dependent empire. In 1924 the great British Empire Exhibition was held at Wembley to publicize the colonies back home; two years later a new Empire Marketing Board was set up to encourage folk to buy colonial-made goods.[9] In 1932 came the big prize: which was Britain's final abandonment of free trade through an Act which levied a tariff of 10% on most imports, with the exception of those from the colonies, in order, obviously, to enable the imperialists at last to build their beloved imperial *Zollverein*. Not only did all this happen; it also happened with widespread public approval, which was encouraging for those who wished to see the empire becoming a really popular cause.

This was a breakthrough. Before 1914 the idea of giving state aid or preference of any kind to colonial trade and development had been political taboo. Hence Joseph Chamberlain's frustration and eventual failure then, simply because he had been ahead of his time. Now the time had caught up. The main reason for that was Britain's persistent economic difficulties during the war years and after, which seemed to call for drastic measures. In particular, unemployment was clearly the catalyst both for the introduction of tariffs in 1932, at the worst point in the inter-war slump; and for the Colonial Development Act of three years earlier. Everyone in the debate on that referred to the beneficial effect it was likely to have on employment at home, by stimulating demand in the newly developed colonies for British-made products. One MP claimed that this was the bill's whole 'genesis'.[10] Ministers denied that this was its only purpose; but it was by far its strongest selling point.

It also indicated a degree of national *consensus* over certain aspects of colonial policy which was new, and which fitted in with other domestic trends. As with those trends, it was forged over the dead (or dying) body of free-market economics. Britain's colonial rulers, as we have seen, were never so wedded to this as the middle classes at home had been, partly because it conflicted in an obvious way with their professional role. Free-market capitalism, and the values that surrounded it, had little place in them for formally 'ruling' other people at all, which wasted money, time and energies that would be far better spent on more productive pursuits. Hence the creation (in effect) of the public schools in the later nineteenth century, in order to preserve older, paternalistic values which *were* conducive to ruling, and to hand them on to those who went out to govern the empire (and elsewhere), against the main ideological grain of the time. In the twentieth century these were joined by another group of anti free marketeers: collectivists of various kinds, who shared with the old-style paternalists a belief that the 'cash nexus' should not be the only thing that governed the relations between people, and that society (in their case, the state) had positive obligations to its less advantaged members. The Fabians were especially active here, co-operating closely with progressive and constructive imperialists to forge the empire into a model of modern welfare socialism.[11] One leading Fabian – Lord Olivier – had even once been a colonial governor himself. It was a curious alliance, this: between the eighteenth and the twentieth centuries, in a way; but it was understandable in view of their common disapproval of the values of the intervening nineteenth century, which they effectively squeezed out.

This was highly promising to flexibly-minded imperialists: the kind that had been known as 'social imperialists' before the war, for example, and had used to dream of a time when the whole nation could put its whole strength behind the empire, and draw strength from it in return. To a certain extent that situation had now come to pass. In the 1920s and 1930s, for example, almost no one in Britain was an anti-imperialist in the strict sense: in the sense, that is, of believing that British colonial rule should be brought to an end there and then. (The only exceptions were the Marxists, and they did not think that was possible before the Revolution.)[12] Liberals tolerated the empire; Conservatives enthused over it; socialists tried to make it better than it was. All agreed that ditching it then would have detrimental effects on everyone concerned. Most of those who gave any thought to it saw its future in more positive ways: united still, if anything even more closely, but also evolving: either into a 'commonwealth' of self-governing dominions with Britain a mere *primus inter pares*; or into a great new international power bloc – depending on the degree of their imperialism. Everyone would benefit: colonists, the natives of the various dependencies, and native Britons back home. That would remove frictions and antagonisms, and make the whole great edifice stable and secure: possibly for all time, which if it could be achieved would buck what before now – with the decline and fall of every empire that had ever arisen in the past – had seemed to be an absolutely inexorable historical trend.

III

That was the hope. Whether it was ever on is hard to say. It seems unlikely. The empire was never on balance a source of strength to Britain between the wars. Some parts of it still drained her militarily, despite her new trick of using the RAF to police rebel areas from the air, which was admirably cost-effective, albeit somewhat barbarous. That was used in Iraq (as we have seen), Somaliland and Aden, mainly over thinly-populated desert terrain.[13] It was not so well suited to her other colonial trouble spots. They tied up troops endlessly, sometimes in hopeless tasks. Probably the most hopeless was Palestine, which flared into a bloody terrorist war between Jews and Arabs, with the British caught in the middle, around 1929. Palestine was difficult partly because it was so unique. It is difficult to think of another example in history of a people which has been separated from its homeland for centuries, fighting to reclaim it from the men and women who have settled there since. It was a little like the Welsh coming back to retake Warwickshire; except that the Welsh, of course, would not have the bible to prove their title to the land; powerful friends abroad (including some Britons who saw Zionism as a kind of substitute imperialism); or a history of the most horrendous persecution, which was just then reaching a peak in Nazi Germany, to make their pleas almost irresistible. That was the situation facing Britain in Palestine in the inter-war years. It made the normal problems facing a colonial power in the twentieth century – rebellions, strikes, boycotts, assassinations, bombs – seem almost trivial by comparison.

The worst case of the latter was India. In 1917 she had been promised progress towards self-government by a liberal Secretary of State under pressure of war.[14] Some imperialists regretted that now. Lord Birkenhead, the Secretary of State in Baldwin's second government, wrote to his viceroy in 1924 of 'a considerable reaction from the Montagu reforms' among his cabinet colleagues, who felt that 'too much has been given away'.[15] They tried to pull back, in part by exploiting the savage communal (Hindu *versus* Moslem) antagonism that wracked the country then, and which provided a convenient and in many ways reasonable excuse for delay; though there is no evidence that they ever deliberately stirred it up, in a cynical 'divide and rule' kind of way. But it was too late in any case. Expectations had been raised. Obvious attempts to renege on Montagu provoked India's most effective nationalist rebellion since the Mutiny, which was Gandhi's second passive resistance – '*satyagraha*' – campaign in 1930. A compromise was reached in 1935, with a Government of India Act which granted almost full responsible government in the provinces, but only a very limited degree of Indian self-rule – shared between the provinces and the conservative 'princely states', and excluding many vital matters – at the centre. That was never likely to satisfy the Indians for long.

No other parts of the empire were as troublesome as India. On the other hand few of them showed signs of turning into the positive assets the imperialists craved. Even the latters' much heralded achievements were often less impressive in reality than they were made out to be. 'Colonial development', for example, looked good in theory, but in practice usually turned out to be pretty meagre: especially after the slump of 1929–30, which made money as tight for this purpose as it was for anything else. Few colonies gained as much as they lost as a direct result of that slump. Improvements in social welfare were minute, if they happened at all; prompting one governor (of Tanganyika) to christen this whole interwar period in his colony's history its 'mothball' phase.[16] The other question with 'development' was how it should be implemented, especially in the newish colonies of European settlement in east-central Africa; where the settlers assumed that they were the best agents of progress, mainly by the simple expedient of taking the best land and employing the natives to cultivate it for them, whereas a powerful school of humanitarian opinion in Britain – which included many Colonial Office mandarins – thought that smacked too much of 'exploitation' for comfort. Kenya was the main battle-ground for these two rival approaches, and – unusually in this period – for a conflict on party lines between Labour, who took the humanitarian side, and the Conservative Amery, who mainly took the settlers'. One of the reasons for the latter's line was a grandiose scheme he had in mind to unite the whole of east-central Africa (Kenya, Uganda, Tanganyika, Northern and Southern Rhodesia, Nyasaland) into a new 'Great White Dominion' (that is, white-dominated), to rival and counterbalance South Africa, whose Afrikaner population still made it unreliable. That battle ended in a draw, which was a worse result for Amery than for his Labour adversaries, because time was not on his side. This kind of thing held up 'development' for years, while the political ground rules were sorted out.

Likewise the imperial visionaries' *Zollverein* did not in the end come to much. Almost directly after the Import Duties bill was passed in 1932, Baldwin and Neville Chamberlain (his Chancellor) went to Ottawa to negotiate 'preferences' between Britain and the self-governing dominions. But they hit two problems. The first was that the dominions were major exporters of foodstuffs, which would hit British farmers (Tory voters to a man) if they were let in free. The second was that many of the dominions were keen on building up their infant manufacturing industries, behind tariffs designed to protect them from competition from the likes of Britain. That gave little room for manoeuvre. A few bilateral agreements were signed, most of them heavily weighted to the advantage of the colonies. Very few dominions abolished their duties against British imports entirely. The whole package together did not really constitute a 'customs union'. (On the other hand it made up enough of one to upset the remaining free traders in the National government, most of whom – including Snowden – resigned: leaving the 'National' cabinet completely dominated by Conservatives after September 1932, by the ratio of 16:4.)

The sad truth of this, from the imperialists' point of view, was that the dominions simply did not have enough imperial patriotism to make them want to subordinate their own *national* interests (as they now regarded them) either to Britain's interests, or to what British imperialists saw as a common imperial interest, in any effective way. Maybe they had grown out of this. Paternalistic Britons often referred to them as 'daughters'; which metaphor itself should have prepared them for the likelihood that the daughters would grow away from their parents at a certain age. For the most part they still seemed fond of them, though with enormous regional variations (the Tasmanians had the reputation of being the most doting); but they also had lives of their own to lead. Their formal relationship to Britain was unclear. Efforts were made during the 1920s to try to define it, which the dominions always resisted if they thought they might cramp their style. Everyone agreed they were now free and equal with Britain; the disagreement came over whether this meant they were equally free to participate in common decisions, or equally free to go their own ways. There was a big difference between the two. In 1926 Arthur Balfour, who had had a certain amount of experience of drawing up 'declarations' which could mean all things to all men, came up with another one for the dominions; which he proposed should be regarded as

> autonomous Communities within the British Empire, equal in status, in no way subordinate one to another in any aspect of their domestic or external affairs, though united by a common allegiance to the Crown, and freely associated as members of the British Commonwealth.[17]

The ambiguity of that, of course, lay in the phrase 'common allegiance to the Crown', which was full of pitfalls: because for example it was the Crown which, in strict legal terms, declared war. That was what had happened on 4 August 1914, when George V had formally committed the whole empire to war against Germany without any proper democratic consulation in Canberra or Pretoria, let alone New Delhi or Lagos. The dominions would not stand for that again. In 1922 two of them (Canada and South Africa) made it crystal clear that they would not support Britain if she went to war over Chanak. Over the next few years most dominions evolved independent foreign policies, without recourse to London. When at last the relationship between them and Britain was finally codified in the Statute of Westminster (1931), it was in terms that left no doubt at all that the latter did not have to abide by anything the mother country did or enacted, unless their own legislatures chose so to do.[18] That was probably necessary, if the Commonwealth was to stay together at all; but it was not very *useful* to those who had hoped it might assume a form that would enable it to compete properly with the nascent – and far more closely federated – superpowers.

As if that was not enough, there were also bound to be doubts about the strength of imperial patriotism back home. A tremendous amount of effort was put into 'educating' the general public on this: hence the Wembley Empire Exhibition, and Empire Day (24 May), and *Boys'* and *Girls' Empire Annuals*, and even a great 'Empire Christmas Pudding' recipe, utilising ingredients from all the colonies, which was issued one year.[19] How much this actually struck home among ordinary, non-political sorts of people, however, is anyone's guess. Amery recalled overhearing a conversation between two 'well-dressed ladies' in the train coming away from the Empire Exhibition in 1924 which suggested that its educative effect was fairly minimal. One was saying how much she had enjoyed the 'Chinese' Pavilion; to which her companion replied: 'I think you mean Japanese my dear; China doesn't yet belong to us.'[20] If that was the state of knowledge among the better-dressed part of the population, what must it be like in what the chairman of the Royal Empire Society in 1931 called the 'many dark corners of Britain, especially in the industrial areas, where the rays of our Empire sun have been unable to penetrate'?[21] 'Who is for Empire?' asked Lord Beaverbrook, proprietor of the messianically imperialisic *Daily Express* in 1929. 'The answer is all men and no one. For while all men are willing to register the sentiment of goodwill towards the Empire, the practical side... has been forgotten.'[22] That had been the snag with popular imperial patriotism in Britain for years.

These were some of the problems of empire. They may not have been insurmountable. Two groups of imperialists felt not. The first were the Indian diehards, like Birkenhead and also Winston Churchill, whose stridently reactionary views on this subject were the main cause of his exclusion from office from 1931 to 1939. (He regarded Gandhi as a 'seditious' and 'half-naked' 'fakir'; thought Britain had 'as good a right to be in India as anyone there'; and believed the result of the 1935 Act would be to abandon 'our children [the Indians] to carnage and confusion'.)[23] The diehards wanted India retained and ruled as of old. Their attraction to the subcontinent seems to have been mainly emotional: Lord Birkenhead never went there, for example, but had apparently had his imagination fired in youth by tales 'of romance, of strident colours and the clash of virile peoples, of stately Indiamen riding at anchor in the mists of Gravesend, making ready for their six-month voyage, of the wild Maharatta hordes scouring the table-lands of the Deccan, and of the columns of the Company's armies winding through parched hills to the relief of distant fortresses';[24] which may have made them less than practical in the face of the irresistible pressures that were building up there. But they were *passe*. The influential school of imperialists in the 1930s was the other one.

These were the realistic imperialists; the ones with a broad and mainly sound grasp of the situation that faced Britain in the world in these years of her relative national decline, and with an imperial vision which was at least adapted and tempered to that situation, even if eventually – as we now know – it turned out to be beyond their reach. Adaptation meant compromise, even with 'half-naked fakirs' if that seemed necessary on long-term strategic grounds. Britain had to conserve her energies in defence of the possible, rather than chase off after nostalgic dreams. That was the view of the 'Round Table' group of imperialists, for example, who set the progressive imperial agenda between the wars. Britain's position was weaker than it looked. To survive as a great power she needed to build up her potential assets, which were the self-governing dominions and her tropical 'estates'; and tread very carefully elsewhere. That meant avoiding, if possible, unnecessary and certainly unwinnable wars. A war with the Indian National Congress was unwinnable; which accounted for what Churchill regarded as Britain's 'nauseating' climb-down there in 1935.[25] A war with Germany was also probably unwinnable, and would certainly be fatal for the British empire, and hence for Britain's remaining great power pretensions, however it turned out. Which brings us on to appeasement: supported strongly by this group of imperialists, as we shall see, but not by the other; and especially not by the romantic, impractical Churchill, whose whole trouble was that he never knew when he was beaten, thankfully.

Chapter 18

Appeasement
(1935–40)

I

Appeasement apart, the later 1930s were a moderately successful time for Britain. Her economic situation improved, though not by much. Between 1933 and 1937 industrial production grew steadily; foreign trade increased; unemployment fell; and incomes rose for those in work. On the other hand unemployment never fell below a million and a half even in the best year; 1938 saw another downturn; and Britain had a balance of payments (not only trade) deficit for most of this period.[1] That last phenomenon, in particular, was almost unprecedented, and indicated the basic weakness of her economy at this time.

The National government – 'national' in name, at any rate – carried on. MacDonald resigned the premiership in June 1935, to be succeeded by Baldwin, who in his turn gave way to Neville Chamberlain in May 1937. Each of these transfers was smooth and bloodless. Chamberlain was a suitable man to head a National government in one way: never, as John Ramsden points out, a real Tory, but an ex-Liberal Unionist (like his father Joseph), who spurned 'the odious title of Conservative', once called himself a 'socialist', and was certainly genuinely committed to social reform.[2] In another way, however, he was an unfortunate choice. Baldwin was a centrist politician because he was never absolutely certain of anything and tolerated honest disagreement; Chamberlain was a centrist out of conviction, and was impatient of other ideas. Consequently he was loathed both by Labour and in certain sections of his own party, as cocksure and arrogant people very often are. That may have affected his reputation at the end of his career, when his failure in one big thing – appeasement – blotted out his and his government's achievements in other ways.

In fact the latter were quite considerable. The 1930s were not the easiest of times to steer a polity through. On the Continent polities were veering out of control on all sides. Britain's ride was less exciting, but also safer. The route followed was a familiar one: moderate reform designed to placate the working classes, who might otherwise turn to socialist or other alternatives. The most notable reforms of this period included a whole series of measures to improve, centralise and extend unemployment relief, which prefigured the post-war welfare state in some respects; and two important housing Acts, in 1933 and 1935, which probably demolished more slums and got more new homes built – more than 300 000 a year from 1934 to 1937 – than any other piece of legislation in British history.[3] These dealt with what were seen to be the two most pressing problems of the day. Another part of the government's strategy was to cultivate moderate trade-union leaders, by having them represented on official inquiries, for example, and even knighting a couple of the vainer ones.[4] All this helped to keep the lid on protest, and so maintain stability.

That grew more difficult, however, as time went by. The National government survived, but lost ground steadily. In the 1931 election it had had the support of 67% of those who voted; by 1935 this had slumped to 54%. Over the same period Labour – now in unambiguous opposition – increased its share from 31 to 38%, and its representation in the Commons from 52 to 154 seats. By September 1939, after a string of by-election victories, another 11 had been added to that.[5] Outside parliament mass demonstrations, occasionally turning violent, indicated a growing impatience with 'consensus' on the left. It was a spate of such riots which forced one of the government's unemployment relief reforms on it, in January 1935. Communism was burgeoning again, both through the CPGB itself, whose declared membership had increased to nearly 18 000 by 1939, and in the growth of 'satellite' organisations with a significant communist input, like the British Soviet Friendship Society and the Left Book Club. That took them back almost to where they had been around 1920–24.

Another potentially destabilizing factor was the growth of fascism. That had started in Britain as far back as 1923, with the 'British Fascisti', founded by a Miss Rotha Lintorn-Orman to wage 'holy war' against the anti-Christ of communism. It also had an answer to the unemployment problem: lower income taxes so that gentlefolk could afford more servants.[6] Other rival groups followed, but none was of any great significance before Sir Oswald Mosley's 'British Union of Fascists' (BUF), which grew out of his 'New Party' after a visit Mosley paid to Mussolini's Italy in 1932. It mainly represented a reaction against the political caution and moderation of the time, exemplified both by the government and by the Labour party which had so recently spurned his bold plans for economic regeneration;[7] and had as its general aim a 'national renaissance', to be undertaken, Mosley later wrote, 'by people who felt themselves threatened with decline into decadence and death and were determined to live, and live greatly'.[8] Hence the marching and shouting and strutting which characterised it, and its emphasis on 'Action' – almost any kind of action – to stir the country out of the lethargy of the time. It was also, in common with its sister fascist parties on the Continent, anti-communist and anti-semitic; the latter mainly in order to tap existing anti-alien feeling in London's east end, which it succeeded in.

That did it no good in the end. Overt fascism made a lot of noise in Britain in the 1930s, but was never much of a threat to anyone, except possibly the Jews it attacked physically on one or two notorious occasions, and even they proved well able to look after themselves. 'Mosley and his pimpled followers' were little more than 'a joke to the majority of English people', claimed George Orwell at the height of the BUF's rise, in 1937;[9] though they had some significant support, for example from Lord Rothermere, who owned the *Daily Mail*; Lord Nuffield of Morris Motors; and probably – though only privately – King (later ex-King) Edward VIII. From 1937 the BUF's appeal began to pall, due to the improved economic climate; internal squabbles; the reputation for brutality it acquired, especially after one of its 'rallies' in the Olympia Hall, London, in June 1934 when its stewards were widely reported to have used sickening violence against hecklers; and its identification with Nazism at a time when Nazi Germany was clearly surfacing as Britain's next enemy. But it was probably supernumerary in any case. The right in Britain did not need race, or even 'action', as causes to rally to in the 1930s when it already had other, more potent ones, like empire. There was less of a *place* for fascism in Britain than there was on the Continent. That was why it always seemed faintly incongruous.

Nevertheless neither it, nor the CPGB over on the other extreme of British politics, was entirely inconsequential. Both were symptomatic of a growing frustration over the way nothing was being done about Britain's fundamental problems in the 1930s, which both groups saw as a failure on the part of capitalism to provide a decent standard of life – more specifically, employment – for millions of people who lived under it. The communists thought the solution lay in revolution and socialism; the fascists in disciplining capitalist energies to national and social ends. In contrast to this the National government seemed to be doing little more than alleviating some of the symptoms, leaving the underlying disease untreated and uncured. The longer that situation went on, the more people turned to this view of it. As a result the centre shrank, and the 'consensus' became more and more precarious. That explains another significant feature of the growth of political extremism in the 1930s: which was the counter-measures it provoked. The two most drastic of these were the Incitement to Disaffection Act of 1934, directed against communist propaganda; and the Public Order Act of 1936, aimed at fascist marches and uniforms. Both undermined what by now were coming to be called 'civil liberties', thus continuing what we have seen already was an established inter-war trend.[10] That itself could be taken as a symptom of insecurity.

That word, in fact, sums up the National government's whole outlook in many different areas of policy at this time. Britain was insecure. At home she was insecure in the face of a fragile economy, chronic unemployment, social unrest, the menace of socialism, rising demands on public expenditure, and threats from the right. All these were compounded by other sources of insecurity abroad: imperial over-extension, commercial vulnerability, the threat of a European war. Some of these problems could have been met head on, and so effectively countered; but usually only at the price of capitulating to another threat: like the threat to liberalism if one chose the fascist solution, or to public order if one went along with the free marketeers – who were a diminishing and endangered species at this time, but surviving, just – and gave liberal capitalism its head once more. The National government's approach was different. Rather than choose one or other nostrum, it thought it better to try to steer carefully between all of them, fending off, if it could, the rocks that appeared on either side. Keith Middlemas calls it a 'deep strategy of crisis avoidance'.[11] It achieved a mild success on the domestic front, as we have seen, in at least saving Britain from some of the European continent's excesses and disasters; though how long that could have gone on in the normal course of things is anyone's guess. Unfortunately the course of things stopped being normal from September 1939 onwards; partly due to the fact that the strategy of crisis avoidance turned out to be far less successful when it came to dealing with European dictators, than with socialists and trade unionists at home.

II

The main difference was that at least one of the dictators was bent on a crisis, whereas the socialists and trade unionists were not. In order to be pacified, or 'appeased', you need to prefer peace to other options, which Hitler apparently did not. 'I do not care whether there is a world war or not,' he told Chamberlain on one occasion; 'I am determined to settle it [Czechoslovakia] soon.'[12] That made things particularly difficult for Britain, who did care whether there was a world war or not, more than anything.

Appeasement was not a new strategy in British diplomacy, though it had been in abeyance for a while. Before 1914, for example, Sir Edward Grey had offered the Kaiser other people's colonies in Africa in order to placate him, which came to much the same thing; as did the string of concessions Britain had made to Prussia and Russia between 1863 and 1870 in order to duck out of wars which seemed to be looming otherwise.[13] These had been at times of particular ferment on the Continent, which Britain had good reasons for not wishing to become enmeshed in; though she would have preferred more dignified and civilised ways of preventing it. For a time after the Great War there had seemed to be some hope for that, as new methods of avoiding war, like negotiated disarmament and collective security, were tried. In the early 1930s, however, that hope collapsed. Japan invaded Chinese Manchuria in September 1931, without 'collective security' coming into play at all. Two years later Germany flounced out of the Geneva disarmament talks, effectively wrecking them, and withdrew from the League of Nations. Italy invaded Abyssinia in 1935 and got away with it. Countries began re-arming. International anarchy returned. Britain's response to that was the same as her response when anarchy had reigned previously: appeasement, in order to avoid what for her would be the unalloyed disaster of war.

It was unalloyed then for the same reasons it had been unalloyed for many years now, only more so. Britain had no ambitions on the Continent. Because of the kind of economy she had, she needed peace in order to trade and therefore live. Wars drained treasure, built up debts, and diverted resources into unproductive – indeed destructive – pursuits. That had been so for decades. What made it worse now was the precarious state of Britain's finances, leading the Treasury to warn the government in January 1939, for example, that she simply did not have the resources or the borrowing power to sustain a war of any length.[14] *Preparing* for war – rearmament – would only exacerbate that, by weakening her economic base still more. That was why the Treasury, for one, was so keen on appeasement.

Another problem was the wide spread of her interests and responsibilities overseas, which already overstretched her means of defending them. This situation was unique to Britain. Other countries had colonies, but not her degree of dependence on them. The effect of war on them would be unpredictable. Some would be sure to fall away. If the collapse became general, Britain might sink to the status of a colony herself: a German *gau* if she lost the war; an American or European or Russian one if she won. That was widely predicted, for example by the 'Round Table' group of imperialists, which was another powerful lobby for peace.[15] These were not unreasonable fears, especially after the experience of the first world war, which had nearly been the ruin of her economically and diplomatically. A second could finish her off.

There were other good reasons for appeasement. It was even possible to make out a moral case for it, on the grounds that the dictators – Hitler in particular – were only being conceded what was theirs by right. Many people in Britain believed that Germany had been badly treated at the Versailles

Conference, and deserved some recompense. That was partly because she was no longer regarded as solely responsible for the first world war, from which it followed that she should not have to shoulder the whole penalty. The reparations demanded of her (£6.6 billion) were seen as excessive, and as having had the effect – by depressing her economy – of preparing the soil for Nazism to germinate in. Some of the huge adjustments made to her eastern boundaries, mainly to the benefit of Poland, had been objected to by the British at the time as unfair. Most of the territories Hitler had his eye on before 1939 – Austria, the Sudetenland area of Czechoslovakia – were German speaking, and presented as anxious to become incorporated into the German *Reich* themselves. Hitler used the word 'self-determination' – a resonant one among liberals – to describe his ambitions for them. Of course he was lying; but it was impossible to know this for sure before March 1939, when his troops marched beyond the Sudetenland into (Czech speaking) Prague. That, of course, was the moment when Britain's resistance stiffened.

Before then, even if her leaders had been more prepared to resist they might have found it a hard job marshalling public support. Nearly all the press was pro-appeasement, especially Conservative papers but also, for example, the Labour *Daily Herald*.[16] When Chamberlain returned from his famous Munich Conference on 1 October 1938 brandishing the paper concessions over Poland he had extracted from Hitler, and proclaiming (unwisely) that they augured 'peace for our time', he was met with cries of 'Good old Neville' from the crowds in Downing Street, and a feeling of relief generally.[17] If he had called an election then, as some were pressing him to do, he probably – despite the gradual erosion of the National government's support before 1938 – would have won it comfortably. (That is what the earliest 'Gallup' polls in Britain predicted.)[18] The press could be blamed for this, or poor leadership, or wishful thinking; but it had the same effect. Public opinion might well not have backed a war before 1939, especially over a morally ambiguous issue like the Sudetenland. From that point of view it was worth waiting until Germany went that little bit further, thus clearly demonstrating her perfidy.

That was in Britain. In the dominions opinion was even firmer against war. Czechoslovakia was further away from Ottawa and Canberra, after all, than she was from London, and so of less concern to Britons overseas. If there was a contemporary threat to them it came not from Germany but from Japan; who at that moment was confining her aggression to the north and west of her, but could easily become a direct menace to at least three British dominions if she turned her attention east and south. If anyone needed to be resolutely resisted, in the dominions' eyes, it was her. That was another reason for appeasing the European fascists. 'We cannot provide simultaneously,' wrote Neville Chamberlain in 1934, 'for hostilities with Japan *and* Germany.'[19] All the pressure from the dominions was on Britain to choose Japan. Until 1934, at the earliest, that was the strategic choice she made. Even after that, when she began re-arming against Germany, the dominions used what influence they possessed to restrain her from any too drastic steps in Europe. In 1938 they let it be known, for example, that they would not support Britain in a war over Czechoslovakia.[20] That probably made no difference to Chamberlain, who was resigned to abandoning Czechoslovakia in any case; but it called attention to the vital imperial dimension to all this.

These are some of the good, wise, far-seeing excuses for appeasement. It does not follow, of course, that all appeasers were good, wise, far-seeing men. Some, for a start, were women; whom Richard Law (Bonar Law's son) held wholly responsible for appeasement in December 1939: 'They're the villains of the piece. How foolish our fathers were to suppose that women would ennoble and sanctify politics. The brutes, untouched as they are by any but the most crudely material considerations, they have brought nothing but degradation and dishonour to politics.'[21] Unfortunately there are no contemporary opinion polls to tell us whether or not that is true. Materialism, however, is by no means gender-specific, and was common among male appeasers too. The financial community was strongly in favour of appeasement, for good old-fashioned liberal-capitalist reasons – peace would bring prosperity which in its turn would melt the hearts of the dictators – as well as narrowly selfish ones. Many of them also feared war because of its likely effect on the domestic politics of the country, with workers and socialists having to be pandered to, as in World War I.[22] Others went for appeasement because, quite frankly, they preferred German Nazism to Russian communism, which – whatever else might be said about him – Hitler was commendably sound on. This was a consideration in government circles too. In 1937 Lord Halifax, soon to become Chamberlain's foreign secretary in succession to the anti-appeaser Anthony Eden, apparently told Hitler personally how appreciative he and his cabinet colleagues were 'that the Führer had not only achieved a great deal inside Germany herself, but that, by destroying Communism in his country, he had barred its road to Western Europe and that Germany therefore could rightly be regarded as a bulwark of the West against Bolshevism'.[23] In other words, appeasement was necessary in order to secure protection for a beleaguered capitalist system. That was the domestic dimension to it.

It was not an easy question, therefore. Against appeasement were numerous arguments from honour and principle ('aggression shall never pay'); some ambiguous treaty commitments; hatred of fascism; and the suspicion that Hitler had designs on Britain and her empire in any case. For it stood almost every consideration of British national interest, providing that last fear was groundless; Britain's long tradition of appeasement; some right-wing fascist and left-wing pacifist prejudices; and one or two moral points, arising from the treaty of Versailles. The material argument had to be in favour of appeasement, in view of the irreversible damage to Britain and her empire that any war, even a victorious one, was likely to do. It was the *rational* course of action. Hitler may have banked on that, in order to ensure that Britain kept out of the war he was planning on quite another front. In that case he clearly over-estimated even Chamberlain's rationality; just as Chamberlain did his, by acting on the assumption – or the hope – that Hitler could be appeased.

III

Formally speaking, appeasement came to an end on 3 September 1939, when Germany refused to withdraw from Poland, which she had invaded on the 1st against the terms of the Munich agreement, and so Britain (together with France, Australia and New Zealand) declared war on her. The man who issued the ultimatum was Neville Chamberlain, which suggests that even he was not an absolute appeaser: someone, that is, who sought peace at *any* price. Nor, to be fair to him, had he entirely neglected over the past few years to prepare for the war he hoped to avoid: in 1939, for example, despite Treasury doubts, Britain's military expenditure was nearly six times as large as it had been in 1934.[24] Nevertheless the moment, when it came, was a blow. 'Everything I have worked for,' Chamberlain told the Commons, '...has crashed into ruins.'[25] He knew what war would mean for Britain in the world. Sir Robert Vansittart, Chief Diplomatic Adviser at the Foreign Office, also knew what it would mean, but found himself able to come to terms with it: 'it is better that the temple should perish and be remembered,' he wrote somewhat apocalyptically in 1940, 'than be pre-served and turned into a pig-sty.'[26] Winston Churchill, the leading anti-appeaser, who regarded himself as entirely vindicated by the decision of 3 September, did not know what it would mean. Throughout the war he persisted in regarding it, unlike the majority of his compatriots, as a war for the survival of the whole British empire, rather than just for Britain's own security. That was probably just as well, if it kept him going during the course of it, to the immense benefit of the people he eventually came to lead. But it was a delusion all the same.

For those who both knew and feared the likely effects of the war, the ultimatum did not rule out all hope. The first few months of the war saw a British passenger liner and an aircraft carrier sunk in the Atlantic, and a bat-tleship – the *Royal Oak* – daringly attacked and destroyed by a U-boat while at anchor in Scapa Flow in the Orkneys, but little else in the way of direct confrontation between Britain and Germany. Germany was taken up elsewhere: in Poland, then Finland, then Denmark, then Norway, then the Netherlands, then Belgium, then France. British troops were involved in Norway and France, but failed to stem the tide. In France they hardly set sight on a German until May 1940, when the French army was overwhelmingly defeated in the Ardennes, and they all had to be brought back. That was the occasion of the famous Dunkirk evacuation, when almost the whole British expeditionary force, plus thousands of French soldiers – a third of a million men altogether – were ferried back to safety in Britain under constant German bombardment, by a motley collection of naval, passenger and merchant vessels, including small fishing boats and pleasure craft. That was one of the lowest points of the whole war for Britain; but it was before she had fought a proper battle yet. The first direct German assault on her did not come until August, with the 'Battle of Britain', between the rival air forces over the Channel, and the beginning of the German aerial bombardment of London: the 'Blitz'. Up to then it was often referred to as the 'phony war': not real, a kind of harmless sparring. While it remained like that, many appeasers believed they still stood a chance.

It was for this reason that the government – still with plenty of appeasers in it until May 1940 – slow-pedalled during the phony war, never gearing up to a proper total war footing until later, in order to continue exploring the possibilities for peace. Those possibilities certainly existed. Hitler was still open to negotiation. War with Britain had never been part even of his most grandiose pre-war plans. He was quite happy to let her (and the United States) share the world with him, so long as he was allowed to overrun northern and eastern Europe, and possibly Russia too. Britain's empire would remain intact. She should, he thought, be able to live with that. Consequently he put out feelers, *via* a number of intermediaries, to explore the feasibility of a settlement along these lines.[27] Unfortunately Chamberlain could not accept this after having made the invasion of eastern Europe his sticking-point in 1938. Instead he pinned his hopes on the chance of a *putsch* in Germany, with someone replacing Hitler – a general, say – who might shift a little on the question of Poland.[28] Sadly for him that never happened, mainly because Hitler's successes put him beyond the reach of his generals. There was a *putsch*, but it happened in Britain: on 10 May 1940, when Chamberlain, having lost the confidence of the House of Commons, resigned as prime minister, and Churchill took over. That buried appeasement for good. 'I would only have to lift my finger and I could have peace,' said Churchill in December; 'but I do not want it.'[29] So that was the end of that.

It was a brave line to take. The prospects for Britain looked grim in May 1940. Few members of the cabinet held out any great hope for victory. Even Churchill had his private doubts.[30] The Duke of Windsor – the former

King Edward VIII, sympathetic to Germany, and the focus of several trivial pro-appeasement plots even after May 1940 – was reported to believe that Britain had 'virtually lost the war already' in August 1941.[31] Old appeasers looked on with growing dejection as most of the other effects they had predicted from the war – impoverishment, socialism at home, diplomatic enfeeblement, imperial decline, Russian resurgence – came to pass. From a purely selfish national point of view they were entirely right. For Britain to persist in the war against Germany had to be ruinous. She might win it, but only by leaving her sting in her assailant, like a bee, and so perishing as a power. It was foolish. On the other hand it was also a glorious, altruistic, heroic way to go.

Part IV
Brave New World
(1940–70)

Chapter 19

World War II
(1940–45)

I

In July 1940 Churchill decided that the best position for the Duke of Windsor, who had been floating dangerously around Europe for some months, would be as Governor of the Bahamas, an insignificant British colony off the coast of Florida. Accordingly, the Duke set sail from Lisbon at the beginning of August. He did not like the new arrangement, and complained continually both about that and about a score of other petty slights he thought he detected towards him and his wife. One of them involved his manservant, Piper Alastair Fletcher of the Scots Guards, who was of military age and consequently according to the War Office was needed to defend his country, but who the Duke felt was much more essential to his own welfare and comfort. When on 17 August they docked at Nassau, the capital of the Bahamas, the couple immediately took a dislike to Government House, where they were expected to live, and insisted on lodging elsewhere until it was redecorated. That made them both unpopular; as did the Duke's open racism, and the Duchess's vanity and extravagance.[1] The Duke, of course, had been brought up to expect something better than this. Maybe if he had been allowed to stay on as King after December 1936 he would have grown into that job in the way that his younger brother, who had taken over from him as George VI, was to do. On the available evidence, however, it looks as though Britain was well rid of him.

Meanwhile back in Britain, where George remained, braving the German *Blitzkrieg* with his subjects and doing his bit to bolster morale, the Duke's defeatism seemed well founded for a while. In June 1940, with France capitulating and Italy entering the war on the German side, Britain stood alone against the Axis war machine. A string of disasters followed: the retreat from Norway, the loss of the Channel Islands, the bombing of

Coventry, defeat in Greece, and surrender to the Japanese in Hong Kong, Malaya, Singapore and Burma. Hitler controlled Europe from Finisterre in the west to Rostov in the east; Japan, who came into the war in December 1941, was mistress of eastern and south-east Asia and the Pacific down to the Philippines. That was probably Britain's nadir.

Things improved after that. The difference was made by the entry of the USSR and the USA into the war, in June and December 1941 respectively. Both were brought in unwillingly, as the result of invasions by Germany and Japan. Russia's involvement had the effect of tying up a vast proportion of the German army, which might otherwise have been used against Britain. After soaking up what was probably the most terrible punishment in the history of warfare, the Red Army then began slowly beating the Germans back from 1942 onwards. America's entry, after the Japanese attack on Pearl Harbour in Hawaii on 7 December, took much of the potential pressure off Britain's forces in the East, and led to massive military assistance in Europe from June 1942. It was shortly after that that Britain registered her first significant military victories against the German army, in north Africa in October–December 1942. Thereafter the war went mainly the Allies' way, with the German and Italian armies in retreat in Europe, and then Japan in the Pacific, leading to ultimate victory against Germany in May 1945, and Japan three months later.

So the pessimists' direst prognostications were confounded in the end. Britain was not defeated. On the other hand she did not win very comfortably, or without enormous sacrifices along the way. 265 000 British servicemen were killed during the course of the conflict, which was a much smaller figure than in the first world war, but still a tragic toll. The second war hit civilians far harder than the first, mainly through German aerial bombing, which killed 60 000 men, women and children and wounded many others. An immense amount of physical damage was done. Overall the war is estimated to have cost Britain more than £34 billion, which was the equivalent of nearly seven times her entire gross national income in 1939, and left her saddled with a national debt of £21.37 billion in 1945.[2] That was the material price she paid. But even that was not the sum of it. Britain suffered in other ways. She was transformed by the war – or at least, during the course of it – both as a world power, and domestically. This bore out the appeasers' other fears.

II

The impact on Britain's world position came mainly as a result of America's and Russia's intervention. They saved Britain's life, but at the expense of her status. No one doubts now that Britain owed her victory more to their efforts than to her own. That was not because Britain put less effort into it proportionately – far from it – but because America and Russia, being larger and richer, had far deeper reserves of effort to draw upon. That was why Churchill had been desperate for America's help, especially, from the start.

Whether he realised the full implications of this is difficult to tell. America's part in the war was decisive to the winning of it, but also had ramifications which went far beyond that. Though she was in the war she was far from the front line, and so relatively safe from enemy attacks on her industry. That enabled her to carry on producing war requirements uninter-ruptedly, which was an enormous boon for the other Allies but also a source of profit to herself. Britain grew thin as she fought; the USA grew fat. She also very soon became the dominant military and political partner in the alliance. All this left her top dog in the world when the war came to an end, by contrast with the sleeping dog (for she had had this potential for years) she had been before. Russia's intervention had similar repercus-sions. Like America, she had not pulled her full diplomatic weight before then: partly because of her economic problems, and partly because she was treated as a pariah by the rest of the world. The German invasion of 1941 changed all that. Russia's pariah status was lifted. As Britain's enemy's enemy, she immediately became her friend. Her brave resistance in the winter of 1941–42 drew admiration all round. Her progress thereafter, westwards across eastern Europe and then over the German frontier, extended her ter-ritorial power. The result of all this was that a war that had started off as a European one finished with Europe being squeezed between two great extra-European hegemonies, whose dormant potential it had unleashed. They had gained enormously, at Britain's (among others') expense.

This had implications for the British empire, in particular. Both the USSR and the USA were ideologically anti-imperialist, or claimed they were. (It really depends on how you define imperialism.) Neither of them was happy with the idea of joining the war with Britain in order to win her colonies back for her. 'One thing we are sure we are not fighting for,' pro-claimed *Life* magazine in 1942, 'is to hold the British empire together.'[3] Russia, we can be certain, felt the same. America, however, was the one who exerted the pressure. On 11 August 1941 for example, before she had entered the war, Roosevelt induced Churchill to sign a statement of war aims – the 'Atlantic Charter' – which among other things committed Brit-ain to the principle that 'all peoples' had the right 'to choose the form of government under which they live'. What Churchill had in mind was mainly east European peoples; colonial subjects, he told the House of Com-mons at the time, were entirely different, and not necessarily to be included in this at all. 'I have not become the King's First Minister,' he assured *The Times* in November 1942, 'in order to preside over the liquidation of the British Empire.'[4] That was quite unequivocal. But it was also futile.

America certainly saw no reason why non-Europeans should be exempted. In March 1942 Roosevelt urged Britain to hand India over to the Indians immediately. Two months later the American State Department suggested a new Atlantic Charter specifically directed to the colonies, and spelling out a timetable for imperial withdrawal. Later on American pressure eased a little,[5] but it was always there in the background. After the war it would have to be reckoned with. It was difficult to imagine Britain – by then clearly reduced to second-class status – holding on to her empire without the support or at least the indulgence of the two emergent first-class powers.

There were also pressures on the empire in the colonies themselves. Just as the Great War had done, the second world war stirred things up. Most of the self-governing dominions turned up trumps, contributing to the war effort heroically in many instances, though usually in theatres adjacent to their own frontiers and shores. Churchill took that as proof that 'the bonds which unite us, though supple and elastic, are stronger than the tensest steel.'[6] Initially the dependent colonies also remained loyal, which the Colonial Secretary attributed to the fact that they 'recognised instinctively' – implying that they could not have done so from experience – that Britain was the 'true guardian' of liberty in the world.[7] But that was not the whole story. Among the dominions, South Africa was (again) less whole-hearted in her support than most; and Ireland was a definite liability. India gave a tremendous amount of trouble, including a new civil disobedience campaign starting in October 1940 which paralysed parts of the country; bloody riots in August 1942; and some collaboration with the Japanese through a so-called 'Indian National Army' sponsored by them. There were also strikes, riots and subversion in Northern Rhodesia, Kenya, Nigeria, Palestine, Iraq and elsewhere. Worst of all was the apathy of some colonial subjects in the face of Italian and Japanese invasions of their territories, which compounded the damage that Britain's losses of her south-east Asian colonies and Somaliland (overrun by the Italians in September 1940) inflicted on her prestige.

This could not be ignored or brushed aside. Britain responded to it in two ways. Firstly, she put a great propaganda effort into defending her empire against its critics: not aggressively or complacently, but in ways to which she hoped they might respond sympathetically. The Australian historian W.K. Hancock, for example, began his contribution to the campaign – *Argument of Empire*, published as a 'Penguin Special' in 1943 – by affecting to welcome American criticism.

> The British have been rather too prone to treat the Empire as their own intimate family concern and to look upon its problems only from the inside. If the Americans will help them to see the shortcomings and errors of the

Empire – which is what the Americans themselves seem mostly to be noticing just now – that won't do any harm. Anyway, the Americans may later on discover one or two good points in the British Empire – things that the British themselves have taken a bit too much for granted.

One of the first 'good points' to which Hancock drew attention was the empire's similarity to the Soviet Union, of all places, in at least one thing: its multi-racialism. 'May it not be the destiny of both,' he asked, 'to play a part in building the bridge over which humanity will escape from the conflict and chaos of snarling nationalism and frantic racialism into a rational partnership of co-operating peoples?'[8] No doubt that was meant to appeal to the empire's Russian critics, too.

It was skilfully done. The empire was presented in these propaganda pieces as almost a liberal institution: tolerant, flexible, ever mindful of its subjects' welfare, a pioneer of federal self-government in its dominions, and dedicated to 'raising' all its peoples to that stage ultimately by gradual steps. Past mistakes were admitted, contritely, but not allowed to detract from the overall impression of good. The future, it was promised, would be even better. It was a seductive picture. It also, however, carried a price. To make it look convincing, Britain clearly needed to act consistently with it. For the authors of the propaganda, who were quite genuine in their feelings about the empire, that presented no great problem. Nor did it to many progressive practical imperialists, who for some years now had been pressing for more enlightened policies towards the empire, as we have seen.[9] They welcomed the new need for the empire to justify itself by its deeds. So did some of the empire's more constructive internal critics, like the Fabians, who in October 1940 set up a special 'Colonial Bureau' to research into colonial affairs, advise, and push for reform.[10] The Bureau was immensely influential; but only because the circumstances were right. The Colonial Office was receptive to its ideas in any case. There was pressure from the colonies for reform. And the empire had to be made to live up to the propaganda that was being put out on its behalf.

To do that it had to be shown to be pointing in the direction of self-rule, at least, and improving in material ways. In 1943 the Colonial Secretary, Oliver Stanley, pronounced that his government was 'pledged to guide colonial people along the road to self-government within the British empire', which would have been more helpful if it had given some idea of the *length* of the road to be travelled, but was at least a token of good intent.[11] In March 1942 Stafford Cripps was sent to India with a more specific proposal to set up an Indian assembly straight after the war to discuss with Britain the precise form of India's independence, which Britain would then enact. It was turned down by the Nationalists; but after it Britain could hardly deliver less. Promises of constitutional reform were also given to

Northern Rhodesia, the Gold Coast, Nigeria, Kenya, Ceylon, Malta, Jamaica, Trinidad and British Guiana, some of which were honoured even before the war came to an end. For the rest, two new 'Development and Welfare' Acts were passed in 1940 and 1945, the first of which broke 'new ground', as Malcolm MacDonald put it, by establishing the principle that British tax-payers should directly subsidize these things. He also insisted that the measure was not a result of the war – 'a bribe or reward for the Colonies' support' – but would have been enacted anyway.[12] It was certainly pre-pared before the war; whether it would have got through the miserly fingers of the Treasury without the pressures and opportunities offered by the war, however, is questionable.

None of these measures necessarily weakened the empire in theory. Churchill was unhappy that Cripps's Indian proposals might – and pleased, therefore, when they failed – but he was a notorious diehard in these mat-ters. Other imperialists managed to come to terms with them. The 'Round Table' group was the quickest to adapt, because it had already given some thought to these eventualities before the war. It could easily swallow pro-gressive self-government for the more highly developed colonies, for example, so long as they remained within the Commonwealth; and 'devel-opment and welfare' seemed a perfectly valid way of fulfilling Britain's 'trusteeship' obligations towards the rest. These were means of strengthen-ing the empire, not undermining it: relieving its tensions, smoothing points of friction, reconciling the contradictions that had dogged it for a century; and so adding to what Churchill had described as its 'tensile' strength.

They also had two other advantages. Reforms like this commanded widespread support in Britain, even among socialists, who rather warmed to the notion of the empire as a kind of gigantic welfare state. That could be a means of cementing the British people to their empire in a way that had not generally – despite appearances – been known before. Secondly, they might even reconcile the Americans to it; which would be invaluable in the future, with America as dominant in the world as she was bound to be, if she could be somehow induced to help defend Britain's liberal empire from communist predators. It would be rather like ancient Rome coming to the aid of Greece against the barbarians. That gave some grounds for hope. The empire might yet survive the war. But it would assuredly not remain the same.

III

Whether anything else would remain the same was a moot point. Many people assumed that Britain's domestic situation could not. 'You cannot hope to go through a world convulsion of this magnitude,' wrote the Con-servative MP Robert Boothby in November 1939, 'without fundamental changes in the social as well as the economic structure.' He predicted that one 'certain' result of the war would be 'the transition from monopoly capitalism to socialism' in Britain.[13] That, of course, was exactly why many Conservatives (though not Boothby himself) had been so keen to avoid war in the first place. It would stimulate people to rebel, just as they had in the Great War, against the social and economic *status quo*. The government would be unable to resist. Therein lay the danger.

This had nothing to do with people's views of the war itself. On the whole the British felt good about that. One sign of this, ironically, was the lack of any manifestation of extreme 'jingoism' throughout the conflict, such as had featured so prominently in the South African and first world wars. This was not because folk were more apathetic towards this one, but because they felt more secure in the justice of their cause. Appeasement may have helped here. As King George wrote to Neville Chamberlain on the occasion of his final resignation from the cabinet in September 1940: 'your efforts to preserve peace were not in vain, for they established, in the eyes of the civilized world, our entire innocence of the crime which Hitler was determined to commit.'[14] Britain's hands were spotless.

As a result few people opposed the war, in any sense. The only exceptions were outright pacifists, who were treated much more humanely in this war than in the last;[15] communists, who started by regarding it as a capitalist war until Russia entered it, when they changed their tune; a handful of fascists and fellow-travellers, who were interned *en masse* in 1940, unnecessarily in many cases; and a few unregenerate and mostly upper-class appeasers, like the Duke of Hamilton, whom Hitler's deputy Rudolf Hess (or someone very like him)[16] thought was worth flying to in Scotland to cultivate in May 1941. (He crash-landed and was captured.) But they were a minority. The vast majority of civilians were solid. So were the troops. Desertions, for example, fell from a rate of 1.26% of men per annum in 1914–18, to 0.7% in 1939–45. There was scarcely any mutiny. Only three men on the British side (all Ceylonese) faced firing squads for these crimes in the second world war, compared with around 300 in the first.[17] There may be other factors to explain these statistics, like a more humane military set-up in the 1940s and, of course, the lesser risks servicemen were expected to run. But whatever the reasons, the government had no cause to fear a popular reaction against the war on this occasion. That is not what provoked the social transformation of Britain.

In fact it was the reverse. People did not feel alienated from the war; they felt involved. The political events of 1940 had much to do with this. Chamberlain's resignation in May that year was widely seen as a response to pressure not only within parliament, but outside. So was his replacement by Churchill, who was regarded as the 'popular choice', over the head of Lord Halifax, who was preferred by Chamberlain, most Tory grandees, and the

King. The leading role played in the *coup* by the 'people's party' – when its leader Clement Attlee effectively sealed Chamberlain's fate by telling him that Labour would not support him – corroborated this. It also strengthened Labour's position in the Coalition ministry that ensued. Unlike in the first war, it was not just there at the invitation of the government; it had helped bring that government about. That made a difference. So did Labour's patriotism, which – unusually, perhaps – contrasted at this time with the Conservatives' equivocal attitude to the German threat over recent months.[18] All this boosted the position of the Labour minority within the cabinet. To the war itself the latter made an enormous contribution, especially on the home front. It also represented the people's social aspirations after the war, often against Churchill's more reactionary instincts. The wartime coalition was in every sense a partnership, between the people's choice as war leader, and the people themselves. This was something entirely new.

The conduct of the war itself reinforced this 'popular' dimension. The people were involved in it in a way not seen in Britain since the Norman invasion. Sometimes this was perforce. Everyone – every city dweller, at any rate – was vulnerable to German bombs, which rained down on the country intermittently from September 1940. Likewise everyone was affected by rationing, which was introduced at the beginning of the war to ensure that food and other essential goods were distributed equally and according to need. Others contributed their garden railings, requisitioned ostensibly to melt down and make into steel for fighter aircraft, but also with the object of making their owners feel they were doing their bit. People were encouraged to volunteer for non-combatant service in a variety of capacities: special constables, fire-watchers, air-raid wardens, Home Guards. Occasionally a mistake was made. One bad one was an idea of the Minister for Information, Duff Cooper, for a 'Silent Column' of citizens – 'Cooper's Snoopers', they came to be called – who would inform on people they overheard making 'defeatist' remarks. That was widely regarded as offensive and un-English, and very soon dropped.[19] The Home Guard was a much happier scheme. It was started up in May 1940 to encourage men ineligible for military service to feel that they, too, were contributing – as indeed they were – to their country's defence. That tapped a rich seam of enthusiasm and ingenuity. The story is told, for example, of how the Glamorgan coastal Home Guard dressed up one of their members, a 63-year-old descendant of one of the Zulu chief Cetewayo's *impis*, in his traditional war regalia and stuck him on the foreshore in the hope that if the invaders approached they would assume they had made a serious navigational error and turn back.[20] That may be apocryphal, but it is in keeping with the spirit of the whole enterprise. Everyone was chipping in, one way or another.

This had social implications. The war was a great leveller. German bombs, for example, were no respecters of class. On 12 September 1940, in a daylight raid on London which gutted scores of houses in London's suburbs, Buckingham Palace was also hit. The King thought this created 'a new bond' between him and his people, 'as Buckingham Palace has been bombed as well as their homes, & nobody is immune from it'. 'I'm glad we've been bombed,' said his Queen. 'It makes me feel I can look the East End in the face.'[21] It worked at other levels too. People were brought together physically, in neighbourhood air-raid shelters and underground railway stations, whither they fled to escape the bombs. Quite suddenly centuries-old habits of reticence broke down. 'It is quite common now to see Englishmen speaking to each other in public,' observed the Labour peer Lord Marley in 1941, 'although they have never been formally introduced.'[22] Middle-class people came into intimate contact with the poor for the first time when hundreds of thousands of mothers and children from vulnerable urban areas were evacuated to the country to be billeted on perfect strangers. That could be an eye-opener. 'I never knew that such conditions existed,' wrote Neville Chamberlain himself after the first wave of evacuations in September 1939; 'I feel ashamed of having been so ignorant of my neighbours.'[23] It was an education all round.

These effects should not be exaggerated. Not everyone did the public-spirited thing. Many billeters were simply irritated or revolted by the ill-mannered urchins they suddenly found disturbing their rural arcadias, and muddying their carpets with their boots. The best-off of the middle classes had their own private air-raid shelters, which they might allow their servants into so long as they kept to their places there, but not any old riff-raff from outside. There was a great deal of profiteering, despite genuine government efforts to stop it, and a flourishing 'black market' which vitiated the object of rationing somewhat. Duff Cooper's Silent Column did manage to discover a fair number of grousers, and bring them to book, before it was run down. Industry – even essential war production – was increasingly afflicted by strikes as the war went on, despite an Order passed in July 1940 (No.1303) outlawing them. They cost the country 3.7 million working days in 1944, for example, and the war effort much needed fuel and equipment.[24] That was not very patriotic. Nevertheless it was exceptional. The general tendency of events on the home front during the war years was to change people's attitudes on these things. At the very least, it made them think.

The popular writer J.B. Priestley believed they were modifying people's 'habits of thought' quite fundamentally. 'We are actually changing over,' he claimed in a radio broadcast in July 1940, 'from the property view to the sense of community,' which he predicted would outlive the war.[25] Other factors also encouraged this: the success of state direction in British industry, for example; and the heroic example of the Red Army in Russia, which seemed to give the lie to the proposition that communist methods were invariably inefficient compared with capitalist ones. Everyone loved the Soviets after June 1941; even the Athenaeum club, which elected the Russian ambassador, Ivan Maisky, a member in 1942.[26] Socialism was respectable. Individualism ('the property view') was discredited, partly because of its blatant inadequacy in a war context: much of the blame for the slow pace of rearmament at the beginning of the war, for example, was put on Chamberlain's reluctance to interfere with free industrial enterprise then;[27] and partly because of Britain's chronic economic and social problems before the war, which were associated with it. That was vital. People were becoming exasperated with capitalism in any case. Scores of academic and government economists, for example, led by Keynes, had already come to the view that the laws of the market had to be 'managed' somehow, in order to counteract what appeared to be their natural propensity to instability and inequality. The war gave them the perfect opportunity to promote their nostrums: to introduce a little socialism into the economy, if only to enable the main capitalist machine to work more smoothly than in the past.

Memories of the past also influenced workers and others who had suffered directly from the malfunctioning of the economy in the interwar years. For many of them the second world war – like the first – brought considerable benefits. Unemployment slumped to 75 000 in 1944, which was almost nothing, especially by comparison with the one and a half million out of work on the eve of the war.[28] Round about a million more women found employment outside the home than in 1939. There was far more overtime available in industry for both sexes, which more than compensated for the fact that average hourly wage rates did not quite keep pace with rising prices. Children and nursing mothers were cosseted with milk, blackcurrant juice and cod-liver oil provided cut-price or free. The disabled were looked after with new rehabilitation schemes, leading to guaranteed work.[29] It was all very satisfactory. It also showed how things could be, if only the will was there, and the dead hand of the Treasury taken away. (The 'Treasury view' collapsed almost as soon as the war began. You cannot run a war on a balanced budget. The country has to decide what is required, and then finance it in any way it can: by borrowing if necessary.) It gave people a glimpse of what seemed to be a better way of economic and social life. That was not something they would gladly abandon when the war came to its end. No one wished to return to the bad old days.

Nevertheless that is what many workers fully expected. This went back to another memory: which was of their disappointment after World War I.

That, too, had produced better living standards for workers, and expectations of better things to come – 'a land fit for heroes to live in' – which had been simply dashed afterwards. That experience affected public opinion in the early 1940s deeply. Surveys reported widespread cynicism among both workers at home and servicemen at the pledges for the future that emanated from Whitehall. The Conservatives were most distrusted, understandably, with the result that they did consistently badly in opinion polls; but many people felt that what they called the 'big vested interests' would have their way in any case, and see to it that the promised brave new post-war world would come to nothing, whichever party was in power.[30] One effect of this was to turn some of them to the Communist party, which registered its highest membership ever – 56 000 – in December 1942.[31] It also had an impact on industry, where workers were reluctant to accept labour 'dilution', for example, and other erosions of their working conditions in the interests of war production, simply because they feared that the effect of them would be to put them out of work again as soon as the labour market returned to 'normal' after the war. That was the reason for some of the strikes and lockouts of the time.[32]

They were right to distrust some of the politicians: especially Churchill. Others however were genuinely committed to a new post-war deal. They included all of Labour; most Liberals; and even many Conservatives, some (like Harold Macmillan) because they shared the prevalent sense of disillusion with unfettered capitalism, and others because they feared, as Quintin Hogg put it in February 1943, that 'If you do not give the people social reform, they are going to give you social revolution.'[33] All the main currents were running this way. Forging ahead resolutely with the flow of them were the 'experts' who were actually responsible for translating these vague aspirations for social reform into concrete proposals for post-war 'reconstruction'. In December 1942 many of the latter were brought together in Sir William Beveridge's report on *Social Insurance and the Allied Services* – usually known simply as the 'Beveridge Report' – which envisaged a future in which the state would ensure full employment, comprehensive social insurance and free health care for all. That laid out the ground plan of what a little later came to be known as the 'welfare state'.

The Beveridge Report was immensely popular. In polls conducted after its announcement, 86% of people said they thought it ought to be implemented, and only 6% not. The press welcomed it almost unanimously. It was one of the publishing successes of the decade, with 635 000 copies being sold.[34] Probably no other government white paper in history has ever aroused more interest, or a more favourable reception. Opposition to it there was, but overwhelmed by the contemporary clamour. The Chancellor of the Exchequer of the time, Sir Kingsley Wood, very much a Treasury man, thought it would be far too expensive. The right-wing *National Review* claimed that it would simply encourage everyone to stop working and draw the dole instead. A new free-enterprise pressure group, 'Aims of Industry', was set up to try to staunch the collectivist flow. None of these stood a chance.[35] Free market or *laissez-faire* capitalism was on the defensive, its believers marginalised, demoralised, at their lowest ebb for probably a hundred years. Churchill did not like Beveridge either, and tried at first to put off discussion of all these questions until the war was over. Later he came out with a few noises that could be construed as favourable towards the report, but only because of the pressure he was under, rather than any genuine change of heart.[36] That illustrates the strength of the pressure. Everyone was subject to it. The juggernaut was irresistible.

The reason for this was partly the war; but only because the war had come at a particular time. It followed 20 years of continuous failure – or perceived failure – for the freer forms of capitalism in Britain, especially with regard to employment; and another 50 years of decline before that. *Laissez-faire* had had its day. It had not lived up to expectations. The widely accepted explanation for this was that it was fundamentally flawed. Letting capitalists have their heads, and the market determine everything, did not conduce to welfare, or even to prosperity so far as most people were concerned. Nor did it conduce – as the international history of the last 30 years showed all too graphically – to peace. Of course that may not have been entirely fair. Capitalist enterprise had never been entirely free in Britain at any time over the past 70 years. It was less so elsewhere: in Germany, for example, and Russia, which could be said to have been the main breeding grounds of international conflict in the recent past. War and unemployment could well be the results not of a surfeit of capitalism, but of a lack of it. That no doubt was Aims of Industry's line. But it cut little ice generally. It was capitalism that had reduced people's wages in the recent past, and put them out of work. If that was the effect of capitalism on a long lead, the obvious answer was to make the lead shorter: not to let the animal run entirely free.

That was one way of meeting some of the domestic problems that had been increasingly besetting Britain for many years now. The war allowed Britain to do this. The contradictions of capitalism (as they appeared) were to be resolved by injecting some democracy and welfare into the joints where the friction was worst. That should save the system from collapse. The same approach was to be adopted in the colonial field. There the contradictions were if anything worse; and again resolvable – it was hoped – by a combination of self-government and 'development and welfare', to save the *empire* from collapse. It was a way of adapting to the destructive forces that Britain was being subjected to – not only the war, but also the ones inherent in her pre-war situation – in order to survive. Whether the form in which she survived would be satisfactory to those who had foretold the destructive forces in the first place, and tried vainly to avoid them, only time would tell. The Duke of Windsor, for one, was certainly not reconciled. In 1945, on a visit to the British embassy in Washington, both he and his wife, 'apparently oblivious to Nazi misdeeds', as the ambassador put it, were still regretting the fact that Britain had gone to war with Hitler at all.[37] By this time, however, they were completely out of touch.

Chapter 20

The People's Peace
(1945)

I

The after-effects of the war on Britain were profound, but mixed. It saved her from barbarism. That was the most important result. It also raised popular expectations, for a better society than she had had even before the threat of barbarism had loomed, and for a better world. That was probably the main reason for Labour's victory in the general election which was held shortly after the end of the European war: to the surprise of the Conservatives, who had thought Churchill's popularity would swing it for them. It did not, and so Labour romped home by 393 seats to the Tories' 213. 'The significance of the election,' wrote Aneurin Bevan, the new Health Minister, 'is that the British people have voted deliberately and consciously for a new world.'[1] Some of the younger Labour MPs, according to another minister, Herbert Morrison, thought they could build it in a day.[2] That, however, did not take account of some of the after-effects of the war; and in particular the damage it had done to Britain's economy, out of which – as the older and wiser heads in the Labour party knew – the materials to construct that new world would need to be forged.

The economic picture in July 1945 was almost as black as it could be. In the short run, of course, it was even blacker for the defeated powers, whose people were reduced to actual starvation for many months afterwards; but the harm done to Britain's situation was arguably more serious in the longer term. That was due to the structure of her economy, and in particular its reliance on foreign investment and trade. That, as we have seen, went back years: to the enormous expansion of her economy overseas in the early days of the industrial revolution, which by the twentieth century had left her uniquely dependent on her foreign markets for her prosperity, and even her very national life. It had also brought with it responsibilities, in the form of a colonial burden which was onerous at the best of times, but insupportable if the economic compensations that had used to come with it were taken away. That had been one effect of the war. To pay for it, Britain had had to divest herself of nearly every overseas asset she had. That came to about £4 billion worth of foreign stocks, and 40% of her markets abroad. Lord Keynes reckoned that the war had cost Britain at least a quarter of her total national wealth overall. Her outstanding war debts were £4.7 billion, or the equivalent of a whole normal year's income to the Treasury.[3] 'We'd used up all our resources. We'd allowed the Americans to have all kinds of export trades that we used to have. We'd emptied the till of our foreign investments even before the Americans came in. We'd had to sell out practically everything.' (This was the Prime Minister's assessment, afterwards.) In terms of assets, they were 'right down to the bottom of the barrel'.[4] Yet they still had the same obligations as when the barrel had been full: to their own people, in the empire, and elsewhere. On top of this they had further responsibilities, as victors. One was to keep the Germans from starving, in the interests both of humanity and of European stability. That cost £80 million in 1946.[5] In Britain's reduced circumstances at that time, this was clearly too much to bear.

And that was not the end of it. Britain's new situation left her not only poor and weak, unable to carry out the tasks that fell on her, but also vulnerable, to powers which had not been so damaged by the war, and for one reason or another wished to exploit the advantage this gave them over Britain to the benefit of either themselves, or an ideology, or both. That was exasperating. Having poured everything into defeating her enemy, Britain now found herself at the mercy of her friends. Some of those friends were unsympathetic. They seemed unaware of the scale of sacrifice Britain had made in the war. Chief amongst these ingrates was the United States of America under its new president, Harry Truman, who had succeeded the more Anglophile Roosevelt in April; and whose first bequest (almost) to the Labour government was to announce the end of 'lend-lease', under which the United States had furnished certain goods free to Britain for the duration of the war, less than a month after Attlee came to power. That was a shock. No one had expected it, or made contingency plans. It placed the country, as the Chancellor of the Exchequer, Hugh Dalton, put it, 'in an almost desperate plight'.[6] 'The Americans, I suppose,' speculated Attlee afterwards, 'didn't realise what it meant.'[7]

That was a relatively charitable view. Most of Attlee's colleagues suspected that there was more to it than that. The Americans had always mistrusted Britain's imperialism; now they had her socialism to take exception to as well. That clearly posed problems. America was committed to free enterprise. Some Americans seemed to think that that was what they had fought the war for: to extend capitalism in the world.[8] They resented giving money – or even lending it, later – for purposes which appeared to be in conflict with that ideal: wasting it on welfare, for example, or on building up a trade which competed 'unfairly' (that is, from within protective barriers) with the USA. Rather than risk that, they turned off the tap, leaving Britain in the position of a supplicant for charity on their terms. Those terms were spelled out shortly afterwards, when Britain did indeed supplicate, and America granted her a 50-year $3.5 billion loan only on condition that she stopped protecting sterling, and allowed full 'convertibility' with the dollar, within a year. That was seen in Britain as a ruse by America to subject Britain's weak economy to her strong one, and was greatly resented. The *New Statesman* called the arrangement a 'devastating appeasement of American capitalism'.[9] Even the considerably less radical *Economist* considered it 'aggravating to find that our reward for losing a quarter of our national wealth in the common cause is to pay tribute for half a century to those who have been enriched by the war'. Like nearly everyone else, however, *The Economist* accepted that there was no alternative to caving in. 'Beggars cannot be choosers. But they can by long tradition, put a curse on the ambitions of the rich.'[10] That was the only comfort that now remained to Britain, in the face of her new situation of dependence – some called it servility[11] – on her erstwhile ally.

American hostility also made things more difficult than they needed to be for Britain abroad. The trouble here was that Americans could never shake off their suspicion that everything she did in the world was for 'imperialistic' motives, when very often it was not. Attlee found this exasperating; especially in view of the fact that – as he saw it – the United States herself was not entirely blameless in this regard. (What, after all, was the winning of the West, and in particular the Mexican and Amerindian wars, if they were not imperialism? And could the Americans not see how imperialistic some of their own actions must seem 'in the eyes of Asia' now?)[12] Even when Britain genuinely intended to liberate her colonies – and she did so intend, in several cases – they would not credit it. They had no conception of the difficulties and complexities of the process of decolonisation, and interpreted delays as merely devices to enable Britain to hold on. (Dalton wondered whether pressure on the Democratic party from Irish-Americans might not have something to do with this.)[13] On India, for example, most of the advice Attlee got from America was 'very ill-informed'; the trouble was, however, that 'its strength' – with Britain in the condition she was in then – 'could not be denied'.[14] On Palestine, American opinion was even stronger, and partisan to boot. Palestine was Britain's most delicate and difficult colonial problem: fought over by two rival claimant peoples, with Britain trying to referee against all the odds. It is possible that a compromise solution which met at least a part of each of the rival claims could have been negotiated. That was the aim of Ernest Bevin, the new Foreign Secretary. Unfortunately for him the American government either did not perceive the genuine complexities of the situation, or ignored them, for domestic reasons of its own. 'There's no Arab vote in America,' as Attlee pointed out later; 'but there's a very heavy Jewish vote and the Americans are always having elections.'[15] All the pressure on Britain from that quarter, therefore, was pro-Zionist. It did not help.

If the Americans had offered to lend a hand themselves with some of these responsibilities it might have made up for this. But there was little sign of that. At one stage Britain suggested they take over her Palestine mandate from her, but they refused.[16] They were no more forthcoming in Europe. Britain worried terribly about her European neighbours: defeated, devastated, demoralised, and ripe therefore – as she thought – for plucking by an essentially imperialistic and consequently predatory Soviet Union. America initially did not share this concern at all. Her obstinate, almost obsessive association of imperialism with Britain may have had something to do with that too. Britain's warnings were seen as a pretence covering an ambition to 'return to the traditional practice of power politics in an attempt to restore a British sphere of influence in Europe... parallel to the recovery of the colonial empire.'[17] There was also some wishful thinking involved. The United States was anxious to disengage from Europe as soon as possible. Early on in the peace she insisted that her troops be brought home before Britain's, who had been fighting longer; and in British ships: which was another irritant between the two powers.[18] She needed to believe that was safe. Consequently she failed to perceive the threat from Russia. British ministers feared she was sliding into isolationism again, leaving Britain to carry the whole burden of European security, as well as all her other stresses and strains.

Britain was probably more alive to the Soviet threat because of the Soviets' attitude to her. From the beginning they seemed to single out Britain as their main enemy, leaving America alone. That was puzzling to some, but not when they reflected how *vulnerable* Britain was – especially in her empire – by contrast with the United States. There may have been another reason for it too. According to Marxist dogma full-blown capitalism was no real threat to socialism ultimately, because of its inherent contradictions, which would destroy it in the end. Social democracy, however, was something else. It modified capitalism, thus making it more tolerable, and confusing the proletariat. That, in the eyes of the Soviets' propaganda agency 'Cominform' in 1947, was precisely Attlee's and Bevin's crime. Their real function was to 'cover up the true rapacious essence of imperialist policy under a mask of democracy and socialist phraseology, while actually being in all respects faithful accomplices of the imperialists, sowing dissension in the ranks of the working class and poisoning its mind'.[19] (With a bit of editing here and there, one could imagine the Americans putting their name to that.) Hence the intense hostility displayed by Russia to Britain both when they met diplomatically – on one occasion, at a conference in Paris, Bevin and the Soviet minister Molotov apparently nearly came to physical blows[20] – and by her policies and actions nearly everywhere in the world. Bevin thought it might even lead to full-scale war between them: not because the Soviets wanted war, but because their resolve to 'stick at nothing' to get what they wanted in eastern Europe and elsewhere could get out of hand. 'The Soviet policy of expansion,' he wrote to Attlee in March 1946, 'has engendered its own dynamic which may prove too strong for him [Stalin] in spite of all his shrewdness and power. I don't think he's planning for war but he may be unable to control the forces he's started. We've always got to be prepared for that.'[21] Some of Bevin's cabinet colleagues felt his fears were exaggerated. Aneurin Bevan, for example, later called them 'hysterical'.[22] But they were genuinely felt.

What with both her great erstwhile allies now in their different ways gunning for her, these early post-war months were a difficult time for Britain. She had been on the winning side in the war, but it hardly seemed to matter now in any positive sense. She had none of the spoils of the war, which historically are usually associated with victory, but which in this case had gone exclusively to the USA and the USSR. She was as impoverished as she would have been if she had lost it, with the added disadvantages of having to satisfy certain expectations that were raised by her victory, and fulfil obligations (to her colonies, for example) which her victory had allowed her to keep. To these were added further burdens – in particular, the security of Europe – which she now had to shoulder in the face of direct opposition from one of the two allies who might reasonably have been expected to share them with her, and apathy from the other. It was a sorry outcome of the war: not sorry enough to make her regret that she had won it, obviously, but sorry enough to rub most of the gilt off her success.

Some of these initial difficulties were in a way fortuitous, and proved to be only temporary. In particular, the United States did not remain with its head buried in the sand for ever, but 'wakened up to the facts of life', as Attlee put it, eventually,[23] which relieved some of the diplomatic strain for Britain later. On the other hand there was a broader underlying logic to these events. They marked the culmination of a long-established trend: one that had begun (as we saw) in the nineteenth century, when Britain, in obedience to the laws of the market, had overstretched herself commercially, giving rise to tensions and contradictions – like imperialism – which were bound to cause her downfall eventually, whether or not the war had intervened. The war just hastened the process. It cruelly exposed Britain's systemic weakness, by the side of the far more resilient (because less extended, at this time) economies of her two great former allies. They now clearly overshadowed her. That should have been no great surprise.

Nor should it have been a surprise that they did not use that position to help her more than they did: to restore her, for example, to something like her former position in the world. Many Britons expected them to, out of a sense of community with them arising out of their shared experiences in the war; but that turned out to be a delusion. Neither the United States nor the Soviet Union had entered the war originally out of a sense of community. Any such sense forged during the course of it – and it was never without its stresses – was almost bound to fall apart once the war had ended, in view of the two powers' own very different interests and ideologies. The Soviet Union, as a socialist state, was unlikely to feel any sense of community with what it persisted in regarding as a capitalist power, and consequently a mortal enemy. Capitalist America, for her part, distrusted Britain's socialist tendencies, but even without this complication would have been unlikely to help. Capitalists do not usually help other capitalists, unless it is in their material interests so to do. They compete. That is their nature. It is what America resumed doing as soon as the war in Europe was over, without any compunction about exploiting Britain's misfortunes, which were regarded more as sources of opportunity than as calls on her charity. Hence the price – a proper commercial price – that was exacted for the American loan to Britain in 1946. It seemed heartless, ungrateful and unfriendly; but it really was an almost inevitable response from the kind of national economy America's was then. It was no use appealing to sentiment. Americans were blind to that. Britain's only real hope was to find some way of appealing to their own self-interest; which she managed to do a little later, with far happier results.

II

In the meantime the Labour government had to come to terms with the new situation, and build on the basis of it. There was a lot to come to terms with. Few ministers – or anyone else for that matter, of any political persuasion – managed to take it all in. Illusions abounded. The young Labour MP Michael Foot, in his maiden speech to the new Parliament of August 1945, claimed that 'Britain stands today at the summit of her power and glory', which in retrospect seems a little extravagant, unless he meant something else by 'power' than most folk did.[24] But he was not alone. Even Ernest Bevin, who was generally more realistic on these matters than most of his colleagues – as he was almost bound to be, directly confronted as he was as Foreign Secretary by the realities – still retained an elevated view of Britain's post-war role. 'I am not aware of any suggestion, seriously advanced, that, by a sudden stroke of fate, as it were, we have overnight ceased to be a great Power,' he told the House of Commons in May 1947. 'We regard ourselves as one of the Powers most vital to the peace of the world, and we still have our historic part to play. The very fact that we have fought so hard for liberty, and paid such a price, warrants our retaining this position.'[25] That was what parliament wanted to hear in the 1940s, on the Labour benches as well as the Conservative; and it was what both sides probably genuinely believed.

It is easy to mock these aspirations with hindsight. In fact, however, they were not quite so fantastic as they now seem. Most contemporaries, even those with the most high-flown notions of Britain's position in the world, made some concessions to cold reality. In claiming great-power status for Britain, for example, very few did so on terms of parity with the two 'superpowers'. That was clearly now beyond reach. Instead they went for something a little lower, and different: the *moral* leadership of the *rest* of the world, outside the USA and USSR. That seemed to be attainable in 1945. Britain after all had fallen behind in the world relative only to those two powers, and not to any others that mattered to her. However devastated she was in 1945, she remained better off than any of her European neighbours. Five years later she still held that position fairly comfortably: way behind the two leaders, but marginally ahead of the rest of the competition in production; national income; trade; foreign investment; and armaments.[26] These are crude measures of national 'greatness', and do not take account of Britain's obligations, on the other side of the balance sheet, which were always her real bugbear. Nevertheless they did seem to justify a fairly significant role for Britain at this time, as 'the chief of the smaller nations rather than the third of the giants', as Michael Foot put it 28 years later (rather more soberly than in 1945), and with 'her own individual contribution to make to the world'.[27]

'Individual' is the key word here. Britain would contribute now not through her strength or power – her ability to push other countries around, even benevolently – but through the exploitation in other ways of certain distinctive aspects of her situation in the world. To a great extent this revolved around the empire, which Labour (and especially Attlee) took great pride in, surprisingly perhaps, but entirely consistently with their general outlook. The empire really did mark Britain off from other nations, in many ways. It was bigger, more widespread and more diverse than any previous empire in the world's history. In years gone by it had been thought to be a fount of strength for Britain, though it has been argued in these pages that it was not in fact. Traces of that idea still lingered in Labour thinking occasionally. In 1943, for example, Attlee had argued in the war cabinet for maintaining 'the British Commonwealth as an international entity', in order to enable Britain to 'carry our full weight in the post-war world with the US and USSR'.[28] That delusion probably did not survive the first few months of the peace. Thereafter the empire continued to be valued, in a less grandiose way, for its economic benefits.[29] But that was not where Labour now placed its emphasis. Instead, it played up the moral aspects of an empire which it (in common, it has to be said, with many Conservatives) saw less as an agency of domination, than as a model of international co-operation, and an example to the world.

Only free peoples, of course, can co-operate. Britain's empire was not all free yet, but under Labour it was hoped that eventually it would be. The new government had plans for this. The process was to start with the Indian subcontinent, whose emancipation Attlee saw, significantly, as the 'fulfilment of our mission' there, the goal to which all the 'great men who have built up our rule in India and who did so much to make India united' had always had in view.[30] Other colonies were to be prepared more slowly for self-government: ostensibly because they were not so ready for it, but also, clearly, because they were less trouble than India to hold on to. Part of their preparation consisted in 'developing' them economically, to a point where they could survive as independent states.[31] Of course, Britain would benefit from this too. But it would not be at the expense of her colonial subjects. Everything was to be done for their 'welfare', in true Labour fashion, leading ultimately – as the Chancellor of the Exchequer, Hugh Dalton, suggested in November 1945 – to the creation of a great 'British Socialist Commonwealth'.[32] That was the ideal: a community of countries, spanning the globe, multi-racial, multi-cultural and multi-everything else, most of them independent, the rest ruled benevolently until they could reach that stage, and bound to each other and to the mother country by bonds of mutual help and friendship: the ideal international society.

The positive advantages of this to Britain were not likely to be of a material kind, and consequently were hard to measure. The most important was that it gave her a 'role'. Her Commonwealth provided her with a wealth of experience, and some influence, which she could use both to her own quite legitimate benefit, and also as a source of advice and help for the world. For a start, it broadened her national mind. Experience of first ruling and then dealing on more equal terms with so many different varieties of humanity gave her a wider degree of empathy and tolerance than other Western countries, which had not put themselves about quite so much. Attlee felt this was vital, especially in view of the rigid and potentially quite dangerous ideological differences that were dividing the superpowers at this time. In November 1945 he lectured the American Congress on this: on how 'essential' it was, 'if we are to build up a peaceful world, that we should have the widest toleration' of other peoples and systems.[33] It was also important, he thought, to see other people's points of view. That was something he felt the Americans were particularly bad at. 'The trouble was it was very difficult to make them see how the situation looked to other Asian peoples, which we knew because we have the great advantage of having Asian friends in the Commonwealth, which helps us to keep a world view.' In that particular instance Attlee was concerned to try to prevent the United States unwittingly turning the Korean imbroglio into something that might be perceived in the East as a race conflict between Europeans and Asiatics, with damaging results.[34] If he could get that over to the Americans, the Commonwealth would be worth its weight in gold.

More than this: it served as an example. In a world rapidly polarizing into two ideological extremes, it offered a way between. This was in spite of the fact that it was often associated with one of those extremes – capitalism – but wrongly, as we have seen. There was a connexion. The Commonwealth had *originated* with capitalism: but as one of its contradictions, a means of preserving capitalist interests in ways which undermined the ethos of the system.[35] It was run, as the empire before it had been, not by capitalists but by paternalists: men who had resisted – been bred to resist – the free entrepreneurial spirit of the time. That dissociated it from that extreme. It was dissociated from the other extreme – communism – by the political freedom it actively nurtured in the colonies. Both aspects appealed not only to Tory imperialist paternalists, but also to certain types of socialist, especially the Fabians, who had been working with the former for some time.[36] They also chimed in with Labour's aspirations on the domestic front, which were to achieve a different and freer form of socialism than the Russian sort, thus combining the best features – liberty and social justice – of the two extremes. The result would be to create an alternative model of human organisation for the world, between what Attlee characterised as 'downright capitalism and tyrannical communism',[37] so enabling Britain, in Bevin's words, 'to give the lead in the spiritual, moral and political sphere to all the democratic elements in Western Europe' – and by extension elsewhere – 'which are anti-communist and at the same time genuinely progressive and reformist, believing in freedom, planning and social justice – what one might call the "Third Force"'.[38]

The advantages of that were twofold. In the first place it would enable Britain and the Commonwealth, and any other countries which might like to join them in this social democratic 'Third Force' (western Europe, for example), to retain their ideological independence, at any rate, from the two great superpowers. Secondly, it might help all of them to buck history. In recent years that had seemed to be on the side of the communists. Capitalism was failing. Originally championed as the way of salvation for all sections of society, it was leaving huge portions of that society far behind. That was certainly true (claimed its critics) in Britain, the oldest industrial capitalist economy, which had been struggling for decades now: depression succeeding depression with dismal regularity, competition giving way to monopoly, poverty rife, unemployment endemic, and social tensions growing; just as Marx had predicted all those years before. All this was clearly to the advantage of the communists, whose membership burgeoned in Britain during the war years (from 17 756 to 45 435),[39] encouraged thereafter by the relentless advance of Sovietism westwards across Europe, and also in the Third world. It all seemed to be working out by the book. The only way to stop it before the next chapter, which promised either revolution or something worse, like war, was by intervening in the natural process to make capitalism more tolerable, or, by another way of putting it, socialism more democratic. ('Revolution,' wrote Bevan in 1952, 'is almost always reform postponed too long.')[40] That should staunch the flow.

This, then, was how the new government aimed to deal with the situation that faced it after the war. It did take account of at least some of the changes that the war had brought about, including the most adverse ones. It reflected a very positive outlook on Labour's part. They would respond to the challenges that confronted them by advancing in 'civilisation', as they liked to put it: away from narrow, selfish materialism on the one hand, or stifling tyranny on the other, towards 'a juster social order',[41] which they felt was ultimately the only 'hope for mankind'.[42] Britain would take the lead in this, as she had taken the lead in other ways before. That did something else for her. It sustained her national pride. 'The eyes of the world are turning to Great Britain,' Bevan proudly told a rally in Manchester, shortly after the launch of his contribution to the process – the National Health Service – in 1948. 'We now have the moral leadership of the world.' Within a few years they would have 'people coming here as to a modern Mecca, learning from us in the twentieth century as they learned from us in the seventeenth century'.[43] Now *there* was a thought; and a powerful ploy, too, if it really did succeed in harnessing British patriotism to such a radical cause.

III

Of course it would not be easy. Even this scaled-down role might be beyond Britain's grasp. Much of it depended on 'moral' influence; and no one yet knew how effective that could be when pitted against real power and wealth. Bevin, for one, always had his doubts about this. 'I have often heard him say,' recalled Attlee later, 'that a few million tons of coal at his disposal would have made all the difference' to some of his negotiations with the other powers.[44] That was one obstacle: Britain's poverty. Another was the burden of her responsibilities overseas, which drained away not only money, but also the manpower that was vitally needed to revive British industry, yet instead found itself still tied up in soldiering all over the world. Added to these were the two external complications: Russia's hostility, and America's unfriendliness. Britain's Labour government had a daunting task ahead of it, in the face of all that.

On the other hand, it had some advantages. The country seemed to be behind it. Twelve million Labour voters (48% of the total electorate) obviously were. So, it could be assumed, were most of the two and a quarter million who had voted Liberal (though with only 12 seats to show for it), on a similar programme to Labour's: full implementation of the Beveridge Report, and government takeovers of national monopolies. Even the Conservative manifesto in the election had gone along some way with Beveridge, and advocated 'co-operation' between industry and the State, which could be regarded as a half-way house to socialism.[45] There could be no reasonable doubt about Labour's mandate for these particular reforms. They reflected a consensus, a widespread measure of agreement across the country over broad lines of policy, which had not been seen in Britain since the great liberal consensus of 70 or 80 years before. Labour made much of this during its term in office. Its appeal to the electors in 1945, Attlee told them in an election broadcast, was not 'narrow or sectional'. Labour had used to be a class party, but was so no longer. Instead it was 'the one party which most nearly reflects in its representation and composition the main streams which flow into the great river of our national life'.[46] He also emphasised the narrowness of the gap that separated it from the other parties over the issue of social reform, at least. When the welfare state was formally inaugurated in July 1948, for example, Attlee made a point of thanking the two other parties for what he took to be their contributions to it in the past;[47] which was a clever way of bolstering the notion – or possibly myth, for there were some powerful exceptions, as we shall see – of national unity over this.

That consensus derived from two sources. One was the memory that people had of pre-war conditions, and in particular unemployment, which had disillusioned millions of them with free-market capitalism, whether justifiably or not. The other was the war. The war accustomed people to a different kind of social organisation entirely, in which the vagaries of the market, with all the muddle and iniquity it seemed to bring, were superseded by rational planning for the national good. In July 1945, when Labour took over, most of that planning was still in place. That was probably crucial; for if it had not been there already it would have been difficult to build it from nothing 'without something approaching a revolution', as Bevan put it.[48]

Even more important may have been the ethical transformation the war had brought about, in weaning people away from the politics of selfishness and on to what Attlee called 'a higher conception of social obligation'.[49] That was essential. If Labour, and Britain, were to succeed, it could not be on the basis of 'the niggling of the market and the compulsions of greed'.[50] People had to 'submerge all thought of personal gain and personal ambition in the greater and deeper desire to give our all to secure the future prosperity and happiness of our people.' (That was Stafford Cripps, the Trade Secretary, who equated this with 'Christianity'.)[51] In 1945 the people seemed willing to do that. Churchill had taught them all about 'blood, toil, tears and sweat' in 1940. If they thought they could let up on that after the war, Attlee soon disabused them. 'I do not seek to conceal from you that the post-war years will not be easy,' he told them on the eve of the election. 'They will require from the nation the same resolute spirit as was shown in war.'[52] So they knew what was coming. Most of them accepted it. That was likely to prove a source of strength, in the struggles that lay ahead of them; if it could only be sustained for long enough.

Chapter 21

Labour's Revolution (1945–51)

I

The Labour government of 1945–51 was a great success in many ways. Certainly it was in terms of its own aspirations and aims, and bearing in mind the problems that beset it. Its three major achievements were to repair the British economy after its wartime battering; to change the social face of Britain radically through its 'welfare state'; and to begin – at any rate – to build a distinctive new role for Britain abroad. At the end of their time in office most ministers were understandably proud. 'Here was a Labour Government,' Hugh Dalton wrote in his memoirs,

> supported for the first time in British history by a great and secure majority at Westminster which, in the lifetime of a single Parliament, beat all past records of legislative output, completed the whole very wide-ranging programme on which it had been elected, and brought in changes which, in the total, so changed the social and economic life of Britain that, at the end of those five years, a new Britain was emerging, not static, not finished, but an immense improvement on pre-war Britain and containing many seeds, sowed by us innovators, of future growth.[1]

According to Clement Attlee, in a speech he gave at North Berwick just before the fall of his government, 'in a world where there are many shadows' this had made Britain 'a beacon of light'.[2] It was an impressive record. Whether it was a sustainable one, however, or even a beneficial one to the country in the long run, remained to be seen.

On the economy it was a bumpy ride, but worthwhile in the end. Every now and then the vehicle looked as though it might come off the road, but was wrenched back by a bold bit of steering, which pointed it in the right direction again. The most serious skids were in 1945, 1947 and 1949. The first arose out of the ending of Lend-lease, and was corrected, as we have seen, by the negotiation in 1946 of an American loan. At the time many people felt that this had merely postponed the collision, not prevented it, because of the terms that had been attached to it, and in particular Britain's agreement to implement full sterling-dollar convertibility in a year's time. Her attempt to fulfil that commitment led to the second skid, in July–August 1947, when after the worst winter on record, with coal shortages, power cuts, factory closures and widespread unemployment, the lifting of exchange controls led to a haemorrhage of capital out of the country, and what Dalton called the 'looming shadow of catastrophe' again.[3] The government's response to that was to suspend the conversion, and introduce harsh new austerity measures: which did the trick. The third crisis originated in a sharp recession in the United States, which had the effect of depleting Britain's dollar reserves. That was countered, quite dramatically, by a massive devaluation of the pound against the dollar (by 35%) in September 1949. These were immensely worrying occasions. But they were all surmounted, with no lasting harm done.

They pointed a lesson, however. Britain's economy was vulnerable. In free-trade waters it was liable to be engulfed by the wash being thrown up by America's more powerful vessel, which was what made the latter's insistence that Britain put to sea in those waters so intolerable. The 1947 convertibility crisis proved that. Luckily, around the same time America was already changing her position on this, and becoming more flexible. Hence 'Marshall Aid', which began flowing to Britain and the rest of Europe from the end of 1948 onwards, had fewer strings attached. That helped enormously; 'it was like a life-line to sinking men,' Bevin told some American newspapermen in April 1949; '...The generosity of it was beyond our belief.'[4] In fact one reason for it may have been enlightened self-interest, once Americans had realised that it would hardly benefit their own economy to have its customers ruined. But Bevin was right about its being a lifeline. It gave Britain yet another breathing space to restore her economy; which she proceeded to do, in some blatantly interventionist – anti-free market – ways.

Her main priority was raising exports to the level required to reverse her existing balance of payments deficit, and wipe out her foreign debts. That she did by deliberately rigging the domestic market to discourage consumption, limit imports, and channel production into the 'export drive'. The means she used were mostly inherited from the war: in particular rationing, and controls over the supply of raw materials to industry. Rationing, in fact, got worse. In July 1946 it was extended to bread, which it never had been during the war, and bakers were compelled to use a higher proportion of the wheat grain in their loaves to economise further. That made the bread browner, which we know today makes it more nutritious, but in those days was associated with poor quality. After the sterling crisis of 1947 rations were reduced still further: to less than a pound of meat per person per week, for example; six ounces of butter; eight ounces of sugar; two pints of milk; and an egg.[5] Clothes and furniture were also rationed. Certain raw materials – mainly coal, steel and timber – were allocated directly by the government, with preference being given to export manufacturing industries. Imports were rigidly controlled, directly where the government itself was the importing agency – as it still was for two-thirds of all imports in 1946[6] – and through a licensing scheme for private importers. British tourists abroad were limited as to the amount of money they were allowed to spend there. All these controls fluctuated during the course of the period, and most of them were dismantled soon afterwards. Harold Wilson, President of the Board of Trade, announced a 'bonfire' of them on Guy Fawkes day, 1948.[7] They were also sometimes evaded, in a flourishing 'black market' which may have helped to relieve some of the pressures that a too rigid system would have caused. On the whole, however, they worked. The proof of that is the scale of Britain's recovery in the six years after the war.

That was remarkable in many ways. Industrial production, for example, increased by one-third between 1946 and 1951, to well above pre-war levels. That was an achievement. Exports trebled, invisibles leapt into the black, and the balance of trade more generally oscillated, but showed healthy profits in 1948 and 1950. Taxation was lower than in the war years (though higher than pre-war), earnings rose by 5.9%, and inflation was pegged to less than that. Most of Labour's budgets were 'balanced'. Almost full employment became the norm, for the first time ever.[8] These figures may have obscured underlying weaknesses, which would be revealed later: the failure of productivity to match higher earnings, for example, which had implications for Britain's competitiveness. Nevertheless they show that in what the government set out to do in 1945, it succeeded. By 1951 Britain had clearly recovered economically: with some help from outside, true, in the shape of the 1946 loan and Marshall aid; but mainly through her own efforts, and in her own interventionist (or 'socialist') way.

II

More than that: she was able to do all this, and weather the crises of 1947 and 1949, without ever greatly compromising Labour's *social* programme. That was sacrosanct, rather like Britain's military effort during the war: something to be tailored to a need, rather than to what the Treasury, for example, felt it could afford. Even when things were worst for Britain, with bankruptcy staring her in the face, ditching or even substantially curtailing the 'welfare state' was never an option that was considered seriously. Hence the latter's birth at what by some criteria must have seemed the worst possible time for it: when the country could least afford it economically, however politically desirable it seemed.

In fact the Attlee government was set on it. Plans for the welfare state went back to the war years, and even before. Not all of them were Labour inspired, as we have seen already. Lloyd George, a Liberal, had laid the foundations in 1906–11. Lord Beveridge, the original architect of the new building, was a Liberal too. The 1944 Education Act, which is generally included in the welfare legislation of the later 1940s, was devised by a Tory (R.A. Butler) and passed by the wartime Coalition. Later on however the whole scheme came to be associated with Labour, quite reasonably. It was Labour which built most of the structure, including its two great keystones, both laid in place in July 1948: the National Health Service (NHS), and a new National Insurance scheme. Health was a priority because it was the field, as Aneurin Bevan put it, 'in which the claims of individual commercialism come into most immediate conflict with reputable notions of social values'.[9] Bevan also thought it was an inappropriate field for charity: 'I have always felt a shudder of repulsion when I have seen nurses and sisters who ought to be at their work... going about the streets collecting money for the hospitals.'[10] So Bevan's new hospitals would be fully funded by the state, and open to everyone who needed them, whatever his or her financial means. The second measure, National Insurance, provided state benefits for everyone who was sick, unemployed or old. For families who were still in distress with these benefits, or without them, a National Assistance Act passed at the same time allowed their incomes to be supplemented from state funds. All this together was designed to relieve people from the fear of destitution or humiliation if they fell on hard times. By the same token, of course, it also relieved them from the necessity of planning to provide for those hard times themselves.

It was also more than that. Labour was not content with merely relieving distress. The welfare state was part of something greater than that. This is one thing that would have distinguished it from Liberal and Conservative versions, if the latter had ever been implemented. One of the objects of the welfare state was to bring about greater social equality: not merely by extending its benefits to everybody, both poor and rich – the principle of 'universality' – but also by the way it was financed. National insurance was funded mainly through separate contributions by workers; but the NHS and National Assistance came out of general taxation, which in the case of income tax was sharply 'progressive', meaning that the rich paid very much more than the poor. The same applied to public education, which was funded out of local authority rates, which were also 'progressive', albeit somewhat more crudely. The end result – a deliberate one – was a significant redistribution of effective wealth from the rich to the poor. At the poorer end of the social scale Labour also intervened directly to improve people's lot: subsidizing food prices, for example; building houses (though never as many as were needed); and eradicating serious unemployment by directing industries to 'development areas' where labour was spare. The effect of this was to augment the everyday lives of millions of people, at some expense to those whom the Labour party felt could afford it most.

Nationalisation – the Labour government's other main semi-revolutionary programme – had a similar aim in view, but one that was partially lost amidst a jumble of other considerations and motives. It was widely assumed that bringing industries into public ownership would benefit their employees. This was especially so in the case of coal, whose employ*ers* in the past had been a particularly bloody-minded lot. They had also, however, been a particularly inefficient lot, which may have weighed more. Most of the industries taken over between 1946 and 1951 – the full list is coal, electricity, gas, steel, civil aviation, cable and wireless, railways, road haulage and the docks – were in need of drastic reorganisation and massive investment after the war. In the cases of coal and the railways there were 'good grounds for doubting' that private ownership could furnish this.[11] Government control had worked well in many of these industries during the war. In some instances continuing that control was a more natural and less disruptive course of action than returning it to the private sector would have been. The other major purpose behind nationalisation was 'to gain freedom from the economic power of the owners of capital', and so enable the government to *plan* the economy with the needs of the whole nation in mind.[12] For this reason the very first 'industry' to be nationalised, in March 1946, was the Bank of England, which was thought to command the heights of the economy as no other agency did. Ministers claimed that none of this was done for 'ideological' reasons, presumably on the grounds that it had a practical end in view; though of course it could be said that that practical end was ideologically conceived. What they probably meant is that they did not want to nationalise everything, just for the sake of it. 'Private interest and public interest should be mingled,' wrote Attlee; '...we are not suggesting that the profit motive should not operate at all.'[13] Bevan saw the State's role as 'to create a framework within which private enterprise can operate efficiently'.[14] All ministers lauded what they called the 'mixed economy'. No doubt some of this was borne of alarm lest Labour lose middle-class voters if it appeared too 'extreme'; yet it was also the honest opinion of most of them. Nationalisation was not pitted *against* capitalism. It was supposed to be complementary to it.

This of course limited the extent of Britain's 'socialism' somewhat; but no one in the government lost much sleep over that. 'The victory of Socialism need not be universal to be decisive,' wrote Bevan, who was to the left of his party, if anything, on this. 'I have no patience with those Socialists, so-called, who in practice would socialise nothing, while in theory they threaten the whole of private property. They are purists and therefore barren.' So he was quite happy for 'the light cavalry of private competitive industry', as he called it, to continue galloping across the plains.[15] Even the heavy battalions – the nationalised industries – were not really socialist in any very profound sense. Most of them were run in much the same ways as before, except on larger scales: managed by men recruited from the private sector, for example, along ordinary commercial lines, and with little or no worker participation, which would have been something *really* socialist. (Later Attlee regretted Labour's resistance to this: 'A hangover from the past, I'm afraid'.)[16] Consequently they were not necessarily any freer than they had been in the bad old days from strikes by alienated employees, specially in the coal mines.[17] This was not a complete revolution. Capitalism still survived in a variety of forms, albeit controlled and limited more than it had used to be. But that was what most people seemed to want.

The same applied to the sphere of social welfare, where the principle of 'universality', for example, had its limits. The main one was that it never excluded other forms of welfare, some of which offended socialist principles quite fundamentally. In education the private sector still remained, allowing well-off parents a wider choice of schools for their children than poorer ones, and perpetuating distinctions by social class. As well as this, the state system itself discriminated between 'academic' children and others, who were separated at the age of 11 into different kinds of schools. Socialist educationalists regarded this as élitist and wrong. Socialist health workers did not mind their patients going to different hospital wards for different medical complaints; but they did object to the continuation of private practice in this field, mainly as a sop to the doctors, who were the doughtiest of all the opponents of the government's welfare measures, largely out of greed. In the field of personal insurance, too, private schemes still existed side by side with the state version. Again, the revolution was only a partial one. This had implications both for its own time, and for later on.

One of the contemporary implications was that it commanded widespread public approval, at least in the early years. There was little really committed parliamentary opposition to any of these measures, except iron and steel nationalisation: 'perhaps', suggested Attlee, 'because hopes of profits were greater here than elsewhere'.[18] Churchill used to rail against 'socialism' a great deal, but not all his followers went along with him on this; as was shown by an influential (albeit unofficial) Conservative 'Industrial Charter' published in May 1947, which went even further than Labour in some directions, such as its commitment to systematic planning of the economy.[19] On welfare the Conservative party was similarly split, with at least as many supporters of 'the broad principles', at least, 'of our social reform legislation' as ideological enemies.[20] The people more generally seemed satisfied, and willing to pay the price – rationing, shortages, controls, restrictions on consumer choice – which continued to be necessary to pay for their new welfare state. This probably shows that Labour had got it about right. It gave people as much socialism as they wanted, and no more.

Hence also the prevalent social calm that was another feature of these post-war years; contrasting markedly with the ferment that had followed the *first* world war, when Britain had looked to be on the edge of revolution, no less.[21] No one could think that now. British communism was in decline, with the CPGB's official membership falling to 38 853 in 1950, for example, and the communist *Daily Worker*'s circulation dropping away too.[22] In 1945 two Communist MPs had been elected (for West Fife and Mile End); by the end of February 1950, and for ever afterwards, there were none. Communists retained their influence in certain trade unions, mainly through the energy they displayed in their members' interests, and were blamed for the worst strikes of the period (in coal in 1947 and the docks in 1948 and 1949); but they were unable to sully the general industrial atmosphere at this time, which was one of peace. The average number of working days lost through industrial disputes between 1946 and 1950 was under two million a year, which was lower than any subsequent five-year span in British history before 1990, and much lower than most.[23] Serious crimes (murder, manslaughter, burglary, larceny) appear to have actually declined.[24] There was scarcely any rioting, hooliganism, or mass violence of any kind. It was a very safe time. Some people found it boring. American visitors, for example, used to comment on the 'universal greyness of the social climate' under Labour, which they took to be an indictment of socialism. Bevan, however, had an answer to this. 'If they had looked closer,' he wrote in 1952, 'they would have seen the roses in the cheeks of the children, and the pride and self-confidence of the young mothers,' which in his view more than compensated for any lack of the kind of 'meretricious glamour' these shallow critics hankered after.[25] People need security before they can enjoy the brighter, gaudier things of life; and the Labour government had given them that.

It also looked, very briefly, as though it had done much more. It had brought capitalism to heel. The problems and paradoxes that had dogged the latter for decades had finally been resolved. All its worst tendencies were contained. Capitalism could no longer impoverish people, put them out of work, deny them equal opportunities, deprive them of basic necessities like health care, or work against the interests of the whole body of society in other ways for the profit of a few. It had ceased being injurious, anti-social, increasingly more destructive of everything around it, as it had been before. Its sting had been drawn. As a consequence communism's sting had been drawn too. 'We had proved to all,' wrote Bevan afterwards, 'except those too blinded by prejudice to be able to see, how democratic institutions could be used to hold back Communism.'[26] It had done that by resolving, or bypassing, capitalism's internal contradictions, which in Marxist ideology were the factors that were supposed to culminate inevitably in the violent crisis which would spark the transition to the next, socialist, phase of history. Hence the social calm. Hence also the perplexity of many on the extreme left of British politics in this period, who did not know what to make of the mixed economy and the welfare state. They were not *predicted* features of late capitalism, which should by rights have grown more exploitative, not more accommodating, rougher, not gentler, as time went by and its contradictions bit. What was happening was all wrong. It diverted the train from its normal tracks. By doing so it would probably enable it to avoid the revolutionary buffers it would have smashed itself against otherwise. In other words, Labour had succeeded in cheating history, no less.

III

How long history could remain cheated, however, was uncertain. For a while it looked as though it might be for good. Most people seemed happy to accept Labour's compromise between the communist devil and the deep blue capitalist sea. To a non-Marxist it looked to be a much more natural resolution of Britain's past problems than any others that had been tried. There seemed no reason for this situation to end, and for the train therefore to return to the Marxist (or any other) rails. That, however, was to look at it purely in domestic terms, and to ignore Britain's susceptibility to certain international pressures, which were likely to be far less easy to cheat.

Those pressures have been described already.[27] They stemmed mainly from the rising power of the USA and the USSR, whose implications for Britain were aggravated by her poverty; her victory; and her inherited interests and responsibilities overseas. This bore on her domestic situation in a number of ways. Britain's poverty made her dependent on aid from America, which usually came – as we have seen – with domestic strings attached. The most serious strings were the ones that were meant to pull Britain back into the free world market with America, which in the view of many contemporaries would have exposed her fragile economy dangerously, and imperilled her nascent welfare state. That, of course, would not have been unwelcome to many Americans, who took the welfare state as proof that Britain 'had gone communist and mad'.[28] They also regarded her as 'imperialist', which made them reluctant initially to help her out with her problems abroad, even though in most of these places she was not being imperialist in the least. All her most serious problems arose either from the inherent difficulties of transferring power from the empire to the *indigènes* fairly and peacefully, or else from communist aggression, which ought to have concerned the Americans just as much. They involved Britain in enormous expense, which was balanced by no commensurate advantage, and drained away money which she would have preferred to spend at home. On top of this came her added responsibilities in Europe itself, as the one unambiguous western European victor in the war, feeding the vanquished, policing them, and protecting them too from Russian communist encroachment. She simply could not afford all this. Some members of the government – in particular Ernest Bevin, the Foreign Secretary – believed that even if she had been economically stronger the Russian threat, in particular, would have been too much for one medium-sized power to contain on its own. That meant seeking some arrangement – an alliance – with another power or powers; which again was likely to have ramifications, as alliances invariably do, on Britain's domestic scene.

The obvious ally, in Bevin's eyes, was the United States. An alternative sometimes mooted was a new western European federation, which however Bevin always discounted, firstly because he could never conceive it as being strong enough, and secondly because he did not trust the Germans not to revert to 'type'. ('I tries 'ard, Brian,' he once told the British military governor in Germany, General Robertson, 'but I 'ates them.')[29] So America it had to be. But there were two difficulties here. The first was that America might not play ball. For the first 18 months of the peace she seemed to want to turn her back on Europe, entirely oblivious of the danger from Russia that the British government felt was staring her in the face. That was a trying time for Britain diplomatically. She felt abandoned, in what Attlee called a 'No Man's Land'.[30] She also felt hard done by over Lend-lease, and over Palestine, which Bevin had wanted to partition equitably if he could, but was prevented from doing, as he saw it, by American obstructionism. It was in this period that Britain finally decided to develop an atomic bomb of her own, chiefly out of exasperation with the United States and concern at her unreliability. 'I don't mind for myself,' Bevin told the highly secret cabinet committee charged with this in October 1946, 'but I don't want any other Foreign Secretary of this country to be talked at by a Secretary of State in the United States as I have just had [*sic*] in my discussions with Mr. Byrnes. We have got to have this thing over here whatever it costs... We've got to have the bloody Union Jack flying on top of it.'[31] Later Attlee put it more soberly, in an interview. 'It had become essential. We had to hold up our position *vis-à-vis* the Americans. We couldn't allow ourselves to be wholly in their hands, and their position wasn't awfully clear always.'[32] It was a measure of desperation, borne of a feeling of deep mistrust of America. But of course it could not help with Britain's day-to-day problems, which simply became more and more onerous during this period of reluctant isolation, until eventually drastic measures were called for.

The most drastic measure Britain took was simply to throw in the towel, in certain of her areas of responsibility. George C. Marshall, the US Secretary of State, called it 'passing the buck'.[33] It happened early in 1947, Hugh Dalton's 'pig of a year',[34] in the midst of that terrible winter, and with a convertibility crisis looming. Attlee had been wanting to reduce Britain's responsibilities abroad for some months, especially in Greece and the Middle East, where he thought it was 'no good... pretending any more that we could keep open the Mediterranean route in time of war', which made Britain's presence there pointless.[35] The problems of 1947 allowed him to have his way. In February the government announced that it was withdrawing its troops from Greece and Turkey, and handing its Palestine mandate over to the United Nations. In the same month it set a date (June 1948) for India to be given her independence. The end results were mixed. India degenerated into communal (Hindu-Moslem) violence, with an estimated half-million people murdered,[36] before being partitioned into two new self-governing nations – India and Pakistan – in August 1947, even earlier than planned. Attlee reckoned the killings were not Britain's fault. Otherwise he regarded this as a great achievement, and with some reason, if it is an achievement to recognise the inevitable and bow to it gracefully. It was helped by the fact that in Britain, according to Dalton, not 'one person in a hundred thousand... cares tuppence about it' (India), apart from some unregenerate imperialists like Churchill, who made 'a great deal of hoot' about it, but to no avail.[37] Palestine was less easily presented as an achievement, with Britain playing no part at all in the final settlement, which was decided by sheer terrorist force to the advantage of the Zionists, who proclaimed their new state of Israel in May 1948. In Greece and Turkey the upshot was different. Britain's abdication there threatened to let the communists in. That seems to have stirred the Americans to a realisation of their obligations at last. In March 1947 President Truman proclaimed his famous 'Doctrine', pledging the United States to intervene anywhere in the world where the dragon of communism reared its head. Greece and Turkey were mentioned specifically. As Britain moved out of there, consequently, America moved in, making that little piece of the world safe for democracy; or for something.

That was the breakthrough. The Americans were back in the fold, though for how long no one knew: 'there was always the possibility,' as Attlee pointed out, 'of their withdrawing and becoming isolationist once again.'[38] For the moment, however, their resolve was further stiffened by some ominous events in eastern Europe over the next 18 months: with the Soviets tightening their grip over their 'satellites' there in clear contravention of the 1945 Yalta agreement; contriving a *putsch* in Czechoslovakia in March 1948 to get their man in; and then cutting West Berlin – a little Western enclave in communist East Germany – off from its lines of supply. That seemed belligerent. Some thought it presaged Russian designs on western Europe too, especially in Italy, where the local Communist Party was supposed to have Russian fingerprints all over it. That may have been alarmist. Italian communism was probably almost entirely indigenous, for example, and not master-minded from Moscow at all. Soviet moves in eastern Europe were as likely to have had a defensive purpose as an aggressive one. Russia had good reasons to feel threatened: with America clearly hostile to her ideologically, and armed with nuclear weapons (Russia only acquired hers in 1949); and with bitter memories of Allied intervention after the first world war, as well as of her own horrendous sufferings in the last. Most of her actions were as consistent with these motives as with more nefarious ones.[39] But the same had been said of Hitler at the time of Munich. That probably swung it. No one wanted to run the risk of being branded an 'appeaser'. Hence the resolute Anglo-American response to the Berlin blockade, for example: setting up a spectacular air-lift to relieve the city and keeping it going for three months until the Russians finally relented; and hence also the final, crucial confirmation of the United States' commitment to the cause of European security, which was the signing on 4 April 1949 of the North Atlantic Treaty between America, Britain, and nine other states, pledging mutual support if any of them was attacked.

That last is generally accounted a great British triumph – 'in foreign affairs the outstanding achievement of the Attlee government', as Attlee's biographer puts it[40] – which it surely was in many ways. But it also gave rise to problems. This was the second difficulty attaching to the American alliance. Not everyone in Britain was happy about it. It marked a worrying departure from precedent. It broke with what we have seen had been one of the main traditions of Britain's foreign policy over the past hundred-odd years: which was to keep clear of peacetime alliances wherever possible, in order to avoid Britain's being dragged into crises which did not directly concern her and preserve her freedom of diplomatic manoeuvre in other ways. It was also a very unequal alliance. 'Britain has never before been in a position,' wrote the American ambassador in London, Lew Douglas, in August 1948 (before NATO), 'where her national security and economic fate are so completely dependent on and at the mercy of another country's decisions.'[41] That did not go down well; even with Bevin, who was more responsible for the alliance than anyone. 'It is a very ignoble thing,' he confided to the TUC in September 1947, 'for any Foreign Secretary to deal with anybody upon whom you are dependent. Who wants that position?' On the other hand he believed it could not be avoided, at least until Britain

had rebuilt her economic base to a point where it could sustain a more dignified foreign-policy line. That was the main burden of his speech to the
TUC: 'to appeal to you to fight for our independence in the workshop, in
the mine, in the field'.[42] He thought that could be achieved, eventually. In
the meantime, hoewever, many on the Labour left were feeling increasingly uncomfortable at what they saw as the implications of Britain's
'subservience' to the United States.

In 1951 that discomfort broke out into open revolt. It was spearheaded
by Aneurin Bevan, the ex-Health Secretary (now Minister of Labour), who
resigned from the government over the issue with two junior colleagues.
The occasion was the budget of April 1951, in which charges were imposed
for the first time under the NHS for false teeth and spectacles, in order to
pay for increased expenditure on arms. The arms were needed to fight in
Korea, where Britain was now backing America (under United Nations
auspices) to defend the South against aggression by the communist North.
The link between foreign and domestic policy could hardly have been
pointed more plainly. Attlee referred to it in his new-year message to the
Labour movement at the beginning of 1951: 'but for the grave events
which have darkened the international scene', he said, 'we could certainly
have looked forward to an even wider extension of the great schemes of
social betterment which have been enacted since 1945'.[43] Instead, they
were having to retreat. It did not seem a very long retreat – making people
who could usually well afford it pay towards the cost of their glasses – but
it was over what Bevan saw as crucial, socialist ground. It just showed what
happened, he said in his speech on the budget, after his resignation, when
Britain allowed herself to be 'dragged too far behind the wheels of American diplomacy'.[44]

That was simplistic. NHS funding had been running into trouble before
the Korean war blew up. Britain was fighting in that war not only as a result
of American pressure, but mainly – Attlee and Bevin always insisted – out
of principle. Her role in the war was not entirely subservient, as was apparently demonstrated in December 1950, when a dramatic flight to
Washington by Attlee is supposed to have been influential in dissuading
the American president from using the atomic bomb in Korea. Korea was
not the only external restraint on Britain's domestic policy at this time, or
even the major one. Most of the others were entirely the results of her own
actions, usually long before: the legacy of her former 'over-commitment',
which she was now reluctantly but inescapably lumbered with. One example, just coming into prominence, was the Malayan 'emergency', sparked
off by a communist guerilla campaign against Britain and her preferred
successors which had begun in June 1948, and which was eventually to tie
up far more British troops than the Korean war, and for longer. All in all,

Britain at this time was much more a prisoner of her own past, than of America's present.

The extent of her imprisonment, however, was still not clear. She had had some disappointments. The main one was her failure to achieve the *distinctive* role in world affairs she hankered after. With Britain now so firmly committed to America's side in the 'cold war', there seemed little room for Bevin's (and others') idea of a 'Third Force'. This was not only sad for Britain; it was also – claimed the 'Third Force' advocates – potentially disastrous for the world, which needed a middle way between the extremes of capitalism and communism to heal its wounds and so stave off a third world war. As it was, the world was becoming dangerously polarised. Britain had been able to do nothing to stop that. On the other hand there was still time. She remained distinctive herself, in two ways: her particular brand of democratic socialism at home; and her interests overseas. She still had her welfare state, despite the blow that the Chancellor had dealt it recently; and she still had the Commonwealth, which so far seemed to be surviving the process of decolonisation remarkably well. (Of the four colonies that Labour emancipated between 1945 and 1951, three – India, Pakistan and Ceylon – elected to remain in the Commonwealth, with only Burma declining, and the Republic of Ireland leaving in 1949.) So there was still some hope for a British role in the world, apart from America and outside Europe; which is what most people in Britain seemed to want.

IV

Bevan's resignation came at a low time for the Labour government. It was racked with illness, much of it aggravated by the sheer strain of the years since 1945, on constitutions which in most cases were far from young. Dalton (64) was played out, unable to sleep, and plagued with boils. Cripps (62), his successor as Chancellor of the Exchequer, was in and out of a Swiss sanitarium during most of his last couple of years in office, slowly dying of a spinal infection. Ernest Bevin, whose heart had been giving him trouble for years, had to resign from the Foreign Office in March 1951 and died the following month, aged 70, just a week before Bevan's bombshell. Attlee (68) was in hospital undergoing treatment for a duodenal ulcer at that time; he always claimed afterwards that if he had been around he could have defused the Bevan row.[45] Morale in the government was poor. In February 1950 it had won a second general election, but with a reduced majority of votes and only a tiny advantage in seats. In October 1951 it again went to the country, polled more votes than the Conservatives – nearly 14 million, a record for any party before 1987 – but won fewer seats, enabling the Conservatives to come in with an overall majority of 17. It was a quirky result, and could reasonably have been regarded as 'unfair'.

'By this time, however,' as Denis Healey wrote afterwards, 'the Labour leaders were too tired even to complain.'[46]

It was not just a question of fatigue. Labour's momentum was faltering anyway. The reasons for this went deeper than mere questions of personal fitness or capacity. The processes of reform seemed to have reached a natural limit. Nationalisation is an example. All the obvious industrial and financial sectors – the most monopolistic and the most inefficient – had been taken over, leaving only competitive industries in Labour's line of fire. Its two most recent forays into that area – steel and road freight services – had already provoked far more controversy than any of the others. The next in line – the giant and generally efficient Imperial Chemical Industries (ICI) – would be sure to generate much more. That was why a majority in the cabinet preferred to leave it be for the present. That left them nowhere to go along that particular road. In the field of welfare, the constraints were of a different kind. Here there might well have been scope for further advance, if it had not been for the cost. The NHS was working well, and with massive public approval, but expensively. In 1949–50 – its first full year of operation – it cost £228 million; that leapt to £356 million in 1950–51, with higher rises predicted after that.[47] Herbert Morrison, Attlee's deputy, thought it was 'getting out of control'.[48] Others in the cabinet agreed. A few of them, claimed Dalton, had 'never been keen on the National Health Service' in the first place, though this may have been partly due to the personal antipathy that Bevan could sometimes arouse.[49] This suggests that the government had arrived at some kind of plateau in its climb towards social justice, too, at which it was natural to wish to rest awhile, and take stock.

They had, after all, made pretty good progress so far. The number of reforms they had carried through was unprecedented, capping the two previous greatest reformist governments in modern British history (1830, 1905), and rivalling – though they could not know it yet – the greatest subsequent one, of 1979. They had revolutionised Britain in many ways, and permanently, so far as they could tell. 'There will be no great change back,' wrote Dalton in his memoirs in 1962, 'from that main advance.'[50] That was because people's attitudes had altered. Individualism had been superseded, by the new 'higher' morality. That process had begun in wartime, when people had first learned the trick of pulling together for the general good, which was why they had won; it had continued afterwards, under the force of the momentum generated then; and it now looked to be established permanently. 'I am still,' said Stafford Cripps in September 1949, '...and shall remain, a persistent believer in the good of humanity, and all that has happened during the war and has happened since has only proved once again that it is not bribery but affection – affection for the family and for our people

– that constrains us to forego our immediate personal interests for the greater good of the community.'[51] In other words, socialism was natural. It was this that guaranteed that the revolution begun in 1945 would endure.

But would it? In fact not all the signs pointed that way in 1951. This may have been another reason for the government's loss of drive around then. People's social sense, which sustained all its policies, was faltering. Even the workers – Labour's prime constituency – could not be depended on. Repeated appeals to them to moderate wage demands out of 'public spirit-edness', for example, fell on deaf ears. Half the trouble here was that full employment and manpower shortages gave the trade-union side a decided advantage in the labour market, which it was reluctant to pass over. Government pleas were resented, as attempts to interfere with 'free collective bargaining'.[52] Unions pressed for higher wages regardless of what the government told them was the national interest, sometimes by calling strikes. The state's response, in several cases, was to bring in troops to blackleg, or even invoke the draconian Emergency Powers Act.[53] These were hardly 'consensual' things to do. They obviously disturbed ministers. Towards the end of their time in office one or two alighted on a possible explanation, or scapegoat, for the fact that the new social morality was not working better than it was. Russian communist subversives were at work, aiming – obviously – to scupper Labour's social democratic experiment.[54] That may have been a factor; or alternatively it may simply have been that the new morality did not come as naturally to folk as the socialists fondly hoped. Whatever the reason, however, it was clear that selfishness – the old morality – had not been vanquished yet.

It surfaced elsewhere, too, usually under different names: like 'individualism' (which is probably the most accurate), 'liberalism', or quite simply (but controversially) 'freedom'. The flourishing black market of the time is a clear if somewhat disreputable example: a 'free' economy operating clandestinely under the surface of the regulation-ridden official economy, where individual entrepreneurs (or 'spivs') could still shine. (One great centre of this trade, significantly, was Romford, in the heart of the territory which later became famous as the haunt of the highly individualistic *genus* 'Essex Man'.)[55] While there were still spivs around, no one could say that British initiative and enterprise were quite dead. Bevan once called private medical practice 'organised spivvery', which was immoderate, to say the least;[56] but medicine was nonetheless another area where old-fashioned individualistic principles ran strong. Hence the doctors' doughty battle against the 'National Socialism' – no less – that some of them claimed was implicit in Bevan's health reforms.[57] The same analogy was once used by Churchill, notoriously, in the 1945 election campaign, when he maintained that Labour's programme would require a 'Gestapo' to enforce it; which indicates how deep the feeling in certain quarters against the new morality went.[58] It also came out in debates in Parliament on some of the later nationalisation measures.[59] Individualists were not giving up without a fight. A number of new organisations were set up to help. Two of the most active, both formed at the very end of the war, were the British House-wives' League, which groused about rationing, having to queue in shops, and socialist controls generally; and Aims of Industry, which was the latest in what we have seen was a long line of private-enterprise-funded propaganda and pressure groups.[60] They also had a new guru: Professor Friedrich von Hayek, whose *The Road to Serfdom*, putting the case against state intervention in almost every area of life, enjoyed quite a vogue after its first publication in 1944. At the very least all this was something to cheer the spirits of downtrodden individualists as they languished in what for them was the prison of Labour's New Jerusalem. At best it might – who knew? – eventually suggest a means of escape.

On the other hand none of this may have had any significance at all. No revolution can expect to take everyone in tow. Some people will always resist, and so be left behind. If the revolution is successful in the long term, these folk will dwindle as time goes by. In the early 1950s most individualists saw themselves in this position: as a beleaguered group, battling against insurmountable odds. Even in their own minds their cause was lost. Collectivism, not freedom, appeared to be the way of the future.

Chapter 22

Churchill Again
(1951–55)

I

To a great extent people's attitudes to what had happened in Britain since 1945 depended on their views of the war itself. There were always two of these. One saw it as a 'People's War', testifying essentially to the strength of the democratic spirit of the ordinary Briton: the 'lion' to whom Winston Churchill, in his own vivid and touchingly self-deprecating phrase, had simply given 'the roar'.[1] That was what had sustained Britain in her time of struggle, and then carried her through into the happier days that followed, of welfare socialism, which represented essentially a continuation of the war spirit in time of peace. This was the first approach. The second was very different. It regarded the war as a triumph not of the 'people' particularly, but of certain rarer qualities in the British character, such as leadership, personal courage and initiative: Winston Churchill plus 'The Few'. *This* was what had won the war for Britain. Democracy had nothing to do with it. By the same token welfareism had nothing to do with it either, but rather the reverse. It was a travesty of the war spirit, eroding it dangerously, and dissipating all the gains that Britain had made in the war.

One person who shared that latter approach was Peter Fleming, brother of the thriller writer Ian; who shortly before the 1951 election published a novel of his own – *The Sixth Column* – which was meant to satirize this kind of thing. It is set in the near future, after a few more years of government under 'little Mr Goodbody' (obviously Attlee), whose effect has been to sap Britain's initiative, lose her the empire, and leave her a prey to the Soviets. The resulting transformation is startling.

A few years earlier the British had emerged with the status of heroes from a long and bitter war in which, but for their stubbornness and daring, the greater part of mankind would have lost their liberties... Of this interlude of greatness, all outward and some inward traces had been expunged... By processes which nobody really understood, the heroes, unarming, had converted themselves into mice – mild, well-regulated, apprehensive little creatures who scurried about in the commodious but perplexing bureaucratic cage which other and more knowing mice had built for them. As mice go, they were reasonably well off; and many of them accepted mousehood gladly enough, for it involved no risks of any kind, and although enterprise was frustrated and indeed penalised, the lack of it was perfectly *comme il faut*...

This is life under Labour. It gets worse. The nadir comes when the England cricket team is bowled out in a test match by West (*sic*) Africa for nine runs. The Soviets are poised to strike. Luckily at this point along comes a saviour: a hero in the old wartime mould, who manages to get rid of Goodbody by covert means and set Britain back on her feet just in time. This is the book's happy ending;[2] but in real life, of course, Fleming – who apparently intended all this seriously[3] – would not have been able to bank on that.

Shortly after *The Sixth Column* came out, however, it looked as though he might not need to. Little Mr Goodbody was removed by more conventional methods. That brought Winston Churchill and The Few to the helm again. The initial relief of people like Fleming was enormous. Field Marshall Montgomery, for example, wrote to Churchill straight after the election to 'Thank God' that 'At last we have you back again'. Cyril Garbett, who as Archbishop of York was presumably even closer to God than Montgomery, rejoiced that Britain could now be restored 'to the place she once had among the nations'.[4] A correspondent to *The Times* savoured the prospect of at last being able to put the years of 'sloth and complacency' behind them, and releasing the British economy from the 'shackles' that Labour had imposed on it, 'even if someone is hurt in the process'.[5] 'What we want are the fruits of victory,' proclaimed another contemporary spokesman for free enterprise, who clearly expected to get them.[6] The Road Haulage Association already had a plan prepared for the denationalisation of its industry, which it delivered to Churchill the day after he arrived back in Downing Street.[7] Another scheme that may have landed on his desk (though there are doubts about this) was one from a new, keen young Conservative MP called Enoch Powell to re-conquer India, no less.[8] The expectations of some at least of the reactionaries knew no bounds.

Superficially there was much to encourage them. Churchill's anti-socialist credentials seemed impressive. His anti-socialist rhetoric certainly was. 'A monstrous and imbecile conception which can find no real foothold in the brains and hearts of sensible people,' was how he had characterised socialism in 1908.[9] By the 1940s he appeared to have modified this view not one whit. 'I'll tear their bleeding entrails out of them,' he told his doctor, Lord Moran, in June 1946.[10] They were a 'vile faction'.[11] Britain's economic revival was being 'stopped, stifled, even strangled' by the regulations and restrictions they were placing on everything.[12] His election slogan in 1951 was 'Set the People Free'. Everyone knew what that was supposed to mean. Better than this – more promising, to anti-socialists – were his *actions* in the past: in 1926, for example, when he had engaged the General Strikers directly, and very effectively; and before that, in 1911, when he was reputed to have sent troops in to Wales to shoot trade unionists down, no less. He was also known to be deeply unhappy about Indian independence. Beyond and above all this, however, he was a hero, a man of resolute action, who had not flinched at danger when it had appeared in the form of the might of the German *Luftwaffe* over the Kent coast in 1940, and so was unlikely – surely – to appease any lesser threats. That was one way of reading the man.

Unfortunately, from the reactionaries' point of view, it was totally wrong. Churchill turned out to be a disappointment on almost every front. One reason for this was his personality, which was more complex than many of them perceived. It was larger, for a start: expansive, generous, warm, sympathetic. He was a sucker for sentiment, especially in his later years; apt to 'blub' a lot, as he put it, over many things: the condition of the world, the sufferings of the poor, even the political novels of Anthony Trollope, which as he himself told his doctor were not 'moving' works at all.[13] No one who cries can be a hard-line free marketist. Churchill had never been that. His early political reputation had been made helping to pilot through some of the social reforms of the Asquith government of 1908–16, which many extreme right wingers now regarded as the start of the socialist rot, but which he took enormous pride in, and used to boost his credentials with the working class.[14] He liked that class, too, or at least his conception of it: the decent, upright, patriotic, perhaps slightly *deferential* ordinary man and woman who had supported him so loyally in Britain's time of greatest need, and could be relied upon to do the same again, if they were appealed to 'without class or party bias'.[15] This affection extended to the trade union leaders of his time, whom he respected enormously: 'They are fine fellows. That is the element which has been the strength of England for a thousand years; responsibility, constancy.'[16] (He also denied strenuously that he had sent troops against them in 1911.)[17] The 'thousand years' is characteristic. Churchill – a historian himself on the side – viewed British history in broad sweeps, as befitted his nature. This may have been another thing preventing his falling into the narrow, dogmatic ways of thought which often breed ideologies like extreme free marketism. He was too big a man for that.

Personality is not always a crucial factor in politics. In Churchill's case it may have been so at this time, even more than during the war years, because of the aura his achievements during the war had bestowed on him. That made his position unassailable, even in a party he had no real commitment to ('a politician without a permanent address' is Paul Addison's happy phrase for him),[18] and many of whose members mistrusted him in their turn. They had no chance against him, even at his most apparently vulnerable: when felled by a stroke, for example, as he was in June 1953; or troubled in other ways by 'this old carcass of mine'[19] (he was 77 in 1951); or in one of his 'black dog' moods; or 'ga-ga', as his rivals and enemies used to put it around.[20] Somehow he survived all this, and the inevitable plotting that went on during the course of it, quite effortlessly; sustained by his by now almost mythical reputation, and by the strength he felt he drew from a constituency that far transcended the confines of the political party he had ridden to power on the back of, admittedly, but only because it was the only way *to* ride to power in Britain, even if – as in Churchill's case – you felt you really should be representing *everyone*. That was the pitch he made when he returned as prime minister in October 1951. What the nation needed now, he claimed in his first major Commons speech after the election, were 'several years of quiet steady administration, if only to allow socialist legislation to reach its full fruition'.[21] That must be one of the most magnanimous statements ever made by a victorious British prime minister, after a campaign which had been no less partisan, in the main, than these affairs generally are. It annoyed the reactionaries, of course, no end; but there was nothing at all they could do.

This was not only Churchill's doing by any means. The tightness of the election result also had much to do with it. In Harold Macmillan's view it represented 'a moral stalemate' at best.[22] *The Times* believed the Conservatives were honour bound to 'see themselves less as a party than as a national Government' after it.[23] No one thought it gave them a mandate to try to turn the tide back. People clearly had not rejected Labour's measures wholesale. Most Conservatives realised and accepted this, especially those engaged in policy formation at the Conservative Research Department, the party's main advisory body, which the 'progressive' Tory R.A. Butler had been steadily pushing in this direction ever since being put at the head of it in 1945. Almost everyone saw this shift as coming to terms with the *realities* of the age; an adjustment to 'post-war truths', as Anthony Seldon puts it: 'the welfare state, the mixed economy and full employment',[24] which all the signs suggested were there to stay. It would have been suicidal to try to swim against this current. Quite apart from anything else Labour was still powerful in the country, through the trade union movement, which was riding high in this period, and with a massive potential electorate (bigger than the

Conservatives', of course, on the last showing) just waiting to pounce on the Government, if it ever dared to venture very far beyond the bars of Peter Fleming's 'cage'.

II

The effect of all this was predictable. Churchill's government roughly speaking carried on where Attlee's had left off. One or two sops were thrown to the Conservative right, mainly in areas where it was widely felt that Labour had gone too far in any case. Legislation denationalising road haulage and iron and steel was passed in 1953, the latter, however, only partially. Commercial television was enabled – with safeguards to maintain standards – the following year. Various controls, regulations and subsidies were withdrawn gradually over the course of the whole parliament, leaving Britain much 'freer' in this sense in 1955 than she had been four years earlier; though it is only fair to point out that it was Labour that had begun this process, with Harold Wilson's famous 'bonfire' of 1948.[25] On the other side of the picture there were some public expenditure cuts early on; new health charges introduced in 1952; and a slight reduction of income tax (to 45% basic rate) in 1953, all of which went down well with the right. But that was it. Even taken all together it did not come to very much. It was hardly the great liberation of the economy and the nation from their postwar trammels that some right-wingers had been banking on. One or two bonds had been loosened, allowing a little more movement; but most of the old constraints were still in place. In the right's eyes this fell far short of *their* understanding of Churchill's resounding pledge during the 1951 election campaign, to 'Set the People Free'.

Indeed, for most of his time in office – while he was still able to give his attention to such things – Churchill seemed to take a positive pride in the way he was maintaining the structure Labour had bequeathed to him, and even improving on it at one or two points. Most of the newly nationalised industries stayed as they were. So did just about every important feature of Labour's welfare state: the National Health Service, National Insurance and so on. By the time of Churchill's departure, in fact, in April 1955, the government was actually spending more on social provision – both absolutely, and as a proportion of its overall budget – than Labour ever had,[26] which was probably the best proof of its commitment to the new way of doing things. It also managed to get built nearly twice as many houses: a particularly notable achievement in an area which Labour had always regarded as one of its own main strengths.[27] Full employment – the other great pillar of Labour policy in the 1940s – was not a serious problem for most of the time; but the new government had plans to tackle that, too, if it ever became one, involving schemes of public works, like the building of a Severn barrage, to soak up some of the unemployed.[28] In fiscal policy

Churchill scotched a plan to float the pound which his Chancellor, Butler, was keen on for a while, because of the risk of high import prices and unemployment that might follow, undermining the consensus he was so keen to preserve.[29] The result was that the new government's policies became almost indistinguishable from the last one's in this field as well as in most others. Hence the neologism 'Butskellite', coined in 1954 by *The Economist* to describe this convergence between Butler's outlook and that of his immediate Labour predecessor, Hugh Gaitskell; to the great irritation of the former, who knew himself – though he could not broadcast this at the time – how much he would have liked to have struck out on his own if he could.[30] But that was not Churchill's way.

Some people saw this as a kind of 'appeasement' on Churchill's part; which was the last thing, of course, anyone had expected of him. It was at its most apparent in the field of industrial relations, where it seemed to many that Churchill was never willing to stand firm even against the most importunate union demands, probably – Butler thought – because of the 'unhappy memories of the General Strike' he felt he had 'to live down'.[31] He himself explained that he did it for 'popularity'; not for himself, he hastened to add, but for his party: 'I hate giving way as much as I did in my hot youth, but I have come to know the nation and what must be done to retain power'.[32] He was also terrified of the effect on the economy of strikes in key industrial areas, like the railways, where a stoppage, as he told Moran in January 1955, could have brought the nation's factories to a halt in no time at all, by preventing coal from reaching the power stations.[33] He was not the only one to think like this. Lord Cherwell wrote to him in November 1951 to advise him that a coal stoppage then would be economically 'disastrous'.[34] Harold Macmillan used the same word to describe the rail strike that looked to be brewing in December 1954.[35] (Both disputes were settled on the unions' terms.) Most of the rest of the Cabinet were also behind him.[36] It may have been true that he was over-conciliatory in these matters – 'so brave in war and so cowardly in peace', as Butler put it to Harold Nicolson in 1952:[37] a little richly, one would have thought, coming from someone as easily swayed from his own convictions as Butler was – but if so he was in good company. He could also, of course, have been right. There were good arguments for paying certain groups of disaffected workers more in the 1950s, on political, social and even economic grounds. (It does not always make economic sense to give people as little money as you can.) This was not the same as Munich. The TUC was not the *Wehrmacht*. 'Appeasement', in these circumstances, may have been justified.

It did Britain no obvious harm in the short term. From what looked to be an almost desperate financial situation when Labour left office in October

1951 – Butler recalled his Treasury advisers talking ominously of 'blood draining from the system and a collapse greater than had been foretold in 1931'[38] – the national economy rallied well from the end of 1952 onwards, producing what could almost be called prosperity in the following year, just in time for the new Queen's splendid coronation in June. By 1955 – the year of Churchill's departure – industrial production was 16% higher than in 1951; exports were 11% up; Britain's net balance of payments looked healthy again after a frightening deficit in 1951; and her national income was 30% higher. Wages were increasing steadily, and unemployment was well under control. A million and a third more families had cars.[39] The impression was widespread – though of course this is unquantifiable – that people felt better, more confident, than they had done before. Fewer of them (marginally) seemed to be turning to crime.[40] Of course this was not entirely the current government's doing. Broad economic trends, in whatever direction, very rarely are. In this case much of it was the late-ripening fruits of Labour's original post-war achievement. Most of the healthiest developments merely continued Labour ones. In 1955 Churchill asked one bright young Treasury official, Robert Armstrong, for evidence to support his claim that his government had done better than Attlee's, only to be told that the best he could truthfully say was that it had done *as well* as Labour *since 1952.*[41] It was also helped greatly by factors outside its control entirely, like the dramatic upturn that took place after 1952 in international trade. All this takes some of the credit for the situation in 1955 away from the Conservatives. But it could not detract from the generally encouraging nature, in most contemporaries' eyes, of the situation itself.

That may have been an illusion. Since that time many commentators have detected endemic weaknesses in the British economy which were obscured by the revival of 1952 onwards, with the result that they were not tackled then in the way they should have been. Others have drawn attention to Britain's *relative* performance at that time. She recovered, but not so well as some other economies, and not nearly well enough to regain her former power and influence by the side of them. That was particularly galling to Churchill, who hated the idea that 'Lands and nations whom we have defeated in war or rescued from subjugation are today more solidly sure of earning their living than we, who have imparted our message of parliamentary institutions to the civilized world, and kept the flag of freedom flying in some of its darkest days'. He also resented Britain's new vulnerability (as he saw it) to economic forces outside her control: 'It does seem hard that the traditions and triumphs of a thousand years' – there is that 'thousand years' again – 'should be challenged by the ebb and flow of markets and commercial transactions in the swaying world.' That was at the height of Britain's economic difficulties, in June 1952, when Britain still seemed poised on what Churchill called 'the treacherous trap-door' of utter ruina-tion;[42] but it described a state of affairs that was bound to persist. Britain would always be shackled in this way. Churchill knew this. His Foreign Secretary Anthony Eden, he reckoned, did not, which may have been why he was so impatient to take over the premiership from him. (This was always understood; but Churchill rather hung on, to Eden's growing irritation.) 'I suppose he sees himself as the brilliant young leader who will change eve-rything,' Churchill told his doctor in August 1954. 'But there's no money, and without money, believe me, you cannot do anything.'[43] That was what spoiled things for Churchill, despite all his government's achievements on the domestic front. Two years later it also spoiled things for Eden, quite spectacularly, as we shall see.

III

Churchill's distress at the wider implications of Britain's penury was partly a reflexion of the old imperialist in him. The empire had always been one of his greatest loves, from the days of his youth, when it had furnished the stage for his earliest adventures; through his first government post, when he helped Lord Elgin to run it; and then into the middle stage of his long career, when his defence of the British *raj* in India against a rapidly turning tide gave him his pre-war reputation as one of the most antediluvian of imperial backwoodsmen. Even now, when the *raj* was lost – 'a great misfortune', as he saw it[44] – he was prepared to argue vigorously for it in retrospect; espe-cially against the criticisms of Americans, who he maintained did not understand it at all. 'I read with great interest all that you have written to me about what is called colonialism, namely: bringing forward backward races and opening up the jungles,' he wrote to the ultra-critical President Eisen-hower in August 1954. 'I was brought up to feel proud of much of what we had done. Certainly in India, with all its history, religion and ancient forms of despotic rule, Britain has a story to tell which will look quite good against the background of the coming hundred years.'[45] His final words to his cabinet when he stepped down from the premiership in April 1955 con-cerned the Empire.[46] It pained him enormously to know that Britain no longer had the resources to keep it up.

Possibly if he had thought she did have the resources he might have sought to re-conquer the parts that Labour had given away in the 1940s, taking up the offer that Enoch Powell is supposed to have made.[47] But that was clearly not on as things stood. Churchill was realist enough to know this. In this field, in fact, he made no change at all to the general thrust of policy he had inherited from Labour. He resisted appeals to go back into Persia to take back the British oil installations recently nationalised by Mossadeq's government, for example – the object of a furious onslaught by the Conservatives in Parliament when Labour originally allowed it to happen in July 1951. He also acquiesced in the policy of his Foreign Secretary to withdraw British troops from the Suez Canal Zone by the middle of 1956, even though he visibly hated it: 'he thinks Eden is throwing the game away', his private secretary noted in March 1952.[48] Indeed, on the latter issue he did more, lending his considerable authority on more than one occasion to try to tame his own Tory rebels – the 'Suez Group' – when they threatened to get out of hand. 'He gave them a tremendous wigging,' his wife recalled in October 1953. 'They knew that he was not a Little Englander, but he told them bluntly we simply could not afford to stay in Egypt.' Later he urged them to get a 'sense of proportion' over all this.[49] So far as the rest of the dependent empire was concerned he left it entirely in the hands of his Colonial Secretary, Oliver Lyttelton, whom he had originally chosen in preference to the other obvious candidate, Lord Salisbury, because he was less 'die-hard' than the latter, and who pledged from the beginning to carry on with Labour's aims.[50] There can be little doubt that Churchill was genuine in abjuring – albeit reluctantly – this kind of acquisitive imperialism in the 1950s. It is also understandable, however, in view of his oft-expressed feelings and past record, that others were sceptical of this; including (again) the Americans, who never were able to accept entirely his protestations that, when he asked for their help in Egypt to keep the Suez Canal going after the British troops left, for example, 'no question of British Imperialism or indeed of any national advantage to us, but only the common cause' was involved.[51]

That was a pity, because co-operation with the USA had by this time become Churchill's *substitute* for an imperial policy; a way of perpetuating what he saw as the main functions of the old British empire in the new conditions of the 1950s, with Britain having some sort of honourable input, though nothing approaching the leading role, of course, she had used to have. This, too, continued Bevin's line in the 1940s, though Churchill added one or two distinctive touches to it: including a degree of romantic idealism which the harder-headed Bevin would certainly not have brooked, and which may have led Churchill astray. He seemed terribly impressed by America's 'altruism', as he called it, in helping other nations so selflessly as she had in the recent past; the mere thought of which was one of the things that could be guaranteed to bring the tears to his eyes.[52] He also had a strong sense of Britain's consanguinity with the USA, their 'abiding fellowship and brotherhood',[53] which he saw as the strongest cement in a great 'English-speaking alliance' of the future which would take in the Commonwealth as well.[54] (This of course was an idea with a long history.)[55] In January 1953, dining with Eisenhower in Washington, he used an unusual metaphor to describe his vision. 'Winston said that a protoplasm was sexless,' recalled his private secretary, John Colville. 'Then it divided into two sexes which, in due course, united again in a different way to their common benefit and gratification. This should be the story of England and America.'[56] There is no record of what Eisenhower thought of that.

Leaving aside these sentimentalities, which may not have done Britain's cause all that much good in the long term, there were compelling practical reasons for keeping alive the American connexion in the 1950s. Unfortunately most of them were one-sided. Britain needed the Americans because she was weak and they were strong, and because the Soviet Union was strong and also menacing, which meant that Britain ultimately depended on America to defend her from attack. That situation was exacerbated, in Churchill's eyes, by recent advances in weaponry: in particular the invention of the atomic and thermo-nuclear bombs, which alarmed him, it seems, more than the majority of his contemporaries. (He himself speculated that this might have been simply because their implications were too dreadful for ordinary men and women to grasp. 'The people, including the well-informed, can only gape and console themselves that death comes to all anyhow, some time. This merciful numbness cannot be enjoyed by the few men upon whom the supreme responsibility falls. They have to drive their minds forward into these hideous and deadly spheres of thought.')[57] The H-bomb turned the risk of defeat by Russia into a risk of actual annihilation: 'the end of everything in the civilized globe that men had known and valued'.[58] Hence the need to ensure against defeat, or even attack, by calling on the assistance of the only power capable in its turn of annihilating Britain's enemy, and consequently also *deterring* her. That was why his final words to his *non*-cabinet colleagues on the day he left office in 1955 were: 'Never be separated from the Americans'.[59] That – far more than any residual imperial feelings – was the cornerstone of his foreign policy during the whole of his government.

It was *only* the cornerstone, however, and not the full edifice. On top of it Churchill built something much grander in his final years: a great scheme for a lasting world peace, free from the threat of these ghastly new weapons, leading eventually to what he called a new 'golden age'.[60] This was the other subject – together with English-speaking union – on which he waxed most lyrical at this time. His basic idea was a simple one: that if the boundless possibilities of modern science could be diverted from their present concentration on new ways of destroying people to more peaceful ends, the result could be a kind of heaven on earth for all: with abundance everywhere, and the sort of leisure that had used to be the exclusive prerogative of his own class in his early days now being extended to the 'masses' too. That was the other side of the nuclear coin.

These majestic possibilities ought to gleam, and be made to gleam, before the eyes of the toilers in every land, and they ought to inspire the actions of all who bear responsibility for their guidance. We, and all nations, stand, at this hour of history, before the portals of supreme catastrophe and of measureless reward. My faith is that in God's mercy we shall choose aright.[61]

That was said (magnificently) to the House of Commons in November 1953. By that time Churchill had already become convinced that this was to be the final task, and hopefully the ultimate achievement, of his career. The way to bring it about, he believed, was to bring the leaders of the great powers face to face with each other, to sort out their problems personally. 'You see,' he once said, 'the people at the top can do these things, which others can't do.'[62] He was the man to set this up. Indeed, he soon came to feel that he was the only man who *could* set it up.[63] Hence his desperate clinging on to power towards the end, long after everything else – including his own body – seemed to be telling him to call it a day. 'It is not that I want to hold on to office for a few weeks more,' he told Moran in June 1954. 'But I have a gift to make to the country; a duty to perform. It would be cowardly to run from such a situation.'[64] He still had to save humanity.

Moran by this time felt his patient was living 'in an imaginary world of his own making'.[65] Sir Evelyn Shuckburgh, of the Foreign Office, called his idea that everything would come right if only the top men could be brought together a 'sentimental illusion', which he attributed to 'the hubris which afflicts old men who have power'.[66] It was probably a lost cause in any case; but the particular factor that sank it was the hostility of the American government. Eisenhower and Dulles, his Secretary of State, obstructed Churchill at every turn. They saw no point in talking to the Russians; disapproved of Churchill's efforts to meet them; refused to accept that the Soviet Union might have grown slightly more amenable after Stalin's death in March 1953 (she was still 'the same whore underneath', claimed Eisenhower in one famous outburst);[67] and were not half so impressed by the overriding significance of the nuclear issue as Churchill was, which of course is what for the latter gave the whole issue its urgency. ('Whereas Winston looked on the atomic weapon as something new and terrible,' wrote Colville, 'he [Eisenhower] looked upon it as just the latest improvement in military weapons.')[68] The result was that Churchill's 'summit' scheme never got off the ground, before his time ran out, and Eden – who was also lukewarm about the whole idea – stepped into his boots.

Churchill in his exasperation tended to place the blame for this on the stupidity of the men at the head of affairs in the United States; especially Dulles, whose 'great slab of a face' he could not abide.[69] Eisenhower he thought mediocre, and entirely in Dulles's hands.[70] Harold Macmillan considered the whole American administration 'amateurish'.[71] These were just some of the kinder epithets. They came oddly from men who put so much emphasis on the 'fellowship and brotherhood' of the two peoples. In fact that may have been part of the problem. Churchill's wet-eyed view of the Anglo-American connexion blinded him to the significance of the differences between them: of outlook, culture, interest, strength. He was aware of the last of these, as he was bound to be; no-one with even half a dry eye could be ignorant in the 1950s of their huge disparity of power. 'Poor England!' he sighed to Moran in January 1952, on his way to meet the Americans; 'They have become so great and we are now so small.' He hated the deference that this forced on him: 'that England in her fallen state can no longer address America as an equal, but must come cap in hand, to do her bidding'.[72] There were no illusions here. On the other hand he did feel that Britain had some cards left. One was his own personal stature and experience in world affairs, which were unrivalled now that the two other great national leaders of the war years – Roosevelt and Stalin – were gone. Another was the character of the British nation itself: its long record in defence of freedom, its 'good sense', the 'institutions and way of life' which were, he believed, the 'envy' of millions beyond its borders;[73] all of which ought to have counted for something, surely, in the councils of the world, if only Eisenhower and Dulles had been intelligent enough to see it.

This was probably Churchill's greatest mistake: to overvalue Britain's moral credit. He himself *was* widely respected, and even adulated, especially in America, but not necessarily for his current views. His country was regarded much less. Quite apart from the common American misunderstanding (as Churchill saw it) over 'imperialism', Britain was rated low in other respects too. John Colville recounted how, at a dinner party in Washington in January 1953, Bernard Baruch, an influential American financier, told him that 'England now had three assets: her Queen ("the world's sweetheart"); Winston Churchill; and her glorious historical past.' Colville thought that was a rather insubstantial list, and suggested a further item: 'her unrivalled technical ability'; but without apparently eliciting much response.[74] Baruch's reduction of Britain to the status of a historical theme park – a kind of proto-Disneyland – was ludicrous, of course, but typical of a common American viewpoint. It reflected the fundamental irrelevance of Britain to the Americans now, except as what Churchill called an 'aircraft carrier' for her nuclear bombers;[75] the disparity of their cultures, especially during this continuing British welfareist stage; and of course the enormous lead that the USA had now opened up over Britain in material terms.

It was probably not an ideal basis on which to build a 'partnership'. Yet Churchill persisted in it; as well as most of his successors, in the years that followed his departure on 5 April 1955. It may have been a grave error, for many reasons. It was always an uncomfortable alliance; not only because of these intrinsic flaws in it, but also due to the fairly strong strain of anti-Americanism that was a continuous – and sometimes even violent – feature of British politics in these years. There were dozens of specific pretexts for that; most of which however boiled down to resentment (that the USA had not entered the last war earlier), jealousy (of her prosperity), and fear (lest she drag Britain with her into a nuclear war).[76] That made it a strain. It could also be said to be a distraction. By investing so much in her 'special relationship' with America, Britain neglected other relationships which might have been more valuable, and would certainly have been more dignified, in the longer term. The obvious one in retrospect is the European one. Churchill was not against European union, but only, as he put it once, 'for them' – the continentals – and 'not for us'.[77] In December 1951 he promised to 'work in true comradeship for and with United Europe', but not *in* it.[78] Joining it seemed out of the question to most government ministers at the time, because of Britain's very distinct *interests* from continental Europe's: not only her empire, but also the much wider spread of her trade and investment abroad; and also because she seemed to have this transatlantic alternative, which took away the need to seek accommodations nearer to home. In other words, the special relationship helped to obscure the stark truth of her post-war situation for Britain, and of the real choices before her, which it might have been better for her to have confronted earlier.

We shall be returning to this later. It was not only, or even chiefly, the work of Churchill and Eden, who in this regard, as well as others, merely carried on the work that Attlee and Bevin had begun. Labour acknowledged this too. In March 1956 Hugh Gaitskell, the new Labour leader, found himself talking to the Soviet minister Malenkov about these things. 'I explained,' he recalled, 'that there were some differences' between the two parties, 'but that they were far smaller than they had been before the war, and that to a large extent the Conservatives had taken over the policies of the post-war Labour Governments.'[79] That was true in most areas. Churchill had added a few things: a patina of sentiment; a certain nobility of style, especially in his oratory; and a breadth of vision that no Labour politician could ever compete with, and is probably the attribute that qualifies him for true 'greatness', even though the vision was occasionally hopelessly wrong. These things apart, however, there was very little to distinguish his government from Attlee's; both of which were therefore essentially parts of the same post-war phase of British history, when consensus – unaffected by the satirical pin-pricks of the likes of Peter Fleming, whose book incidentally was a publishing failure[80] – reigned supreme.

Chapter 23

The Last Paternalists (1955–64)

I

By April 1955, when Churchill left office, Labour's new dispensation had survived three and a half years of Conservative rule with scarcely a scratch. Britain remained then what Attlee and his colleagues had made her in 1945–51: a mixed economy, settled now at a comfortable mid-way point between the extremes of capitalism and socialism; cushioned domestically by an extensive system of social welfare; in the process of transforming her empire into a Commonwealth of free nations; and relying heavily for its defence on the United States. Churchill's departure made very little difference to this picture, for three reasons. The first was that the situation was still very widely accepted in the country, which made it difficult to change politically. The second was that Churchill's immediate successor, and the next two prime ministers after that, also went along with it, partly because they came from the same broad wing of the Conservative party as Churchill did: the soft, reformist rather than the hard, free marketist one, which *might* have tried to change things if *it* could have got its hands on the reins of power. The third reason – the most important one – is that the Attlee-Churchill system seemed to be working; which meant that there was no pressing need to change it, of the kind that was likely to be able to move public opinion and empower the free marketists.

That, of course, may have been misleading. There are certainly signs of this over the next nine and a half years, to October 1964, when this long stretch of Conservative government eventually came to an end. The system continued working, but not exactly smoothly; with periodic crises on just about every front of policy, and the widespread impression left afterwards that it had failed in the longer term. The period began and ended with scandals, of different kinds: the Suez adventure at the start, which was Britain's biggest diplomatic humilation in living memory; and the Profumo affair at the finish, which did not even have the saving grace of being about something important, but was merely sordid and sensational. Two of the prime ministers of the time were manifest failures (*as* prime ministers, that is), while the other – Harold Macmillan, who served the longest – possibly only avoided that reputation by being more plausible. He is best known for his phrase 'You've never had it so good', which is supposed to indicate his complacency in economic affairs; and for the cartoonist Vicky's portrayal of him as 'Supermac' (after the comic strip character 'Superman'): an image deliberately chosen for its obvious incongruity. That image also reflected another characteristic feature of the period in general, especially the latter part of it: the increasing cynicism of *young* people in particular about the whole world of high politics, expressed in the new satirical shows and journals of the time, like the BBC television series 'That Was The Week That Was' and *Private Eye*. While all this was going on Britain was lurching between deflationary ('Stop') and expansionary ('Go') economic policies; possibly storing up trouble for the future as a consequence; and going down in the world militarily and diplomatically. That is (roughly speaking) the reputation of the period in hindsight. It is not a flattering one.

Contemporaries would not have been surprised by it. This was not, by and large, a period of great illusions. People – most of them, at any rate – were well aware that Britain was declining, though their prescriptions for the disease – if they thought it was worth treating – varied considerably. This went for the politicians, too, who were not nearly so apathetic as some of them appeared; including even Macmillan, who was grotesquely slandered by the interpretation that was put on his 'never had it so good' utterance, which comes in fact from a speech whose whole burden was to warn his audience *against* the smugness it is supposed to exemplify. ('What is beginning to worry us,' he had gone on, 'is "Is it too good to be true?" or perhaps I should say "Is it too good to last?"'; in the light, that was, of looming wage inflation, which threatened to bring all their prosperity tumbling down.)[1] That was in July 1957. At other times he talked of the British economy's being balanced on a 'narrow knife-edge'.[2] Scarcely anyone disputed this, at any time during his premiership, except possibly trade-union leaders who needed to believe there was more wealth around for their members to share. This pessimism extended to other fields too. In foreign affairs there was no disguising Britain's loss of national power and ultimately also of status, particularly after Suez, even without the American Secretary of State Dean Acheson's infamous remarks in December 1962 about her being 'played out' and left without a 'role' in the world, which were mainly resented because they were felt to be gratuitous.[3] Even after ten years of Conservative government, Iain Macleod, the party chairman, admitted to a gathering of the faithful in April 1962, 'We are not as a nation confident of our future.' They did not need an American to tell them that.

None of this, however, necessarily meant that they were travelling along the wrong path. Macleod, who was very much on the 'soft' wing of the Conservative party, was adamant about that. 'One road for us,' he went on, 'is clearly marked "No Thoroughfare" – the road back. That way lies defeat. The modern Tory Party... has no future as a party of reaction.'[4] 'Reaction' at that time meant two things: imperialism of the old sort, involving ruling vast tracts of territory and trying to 'suppress the darkies by shooting them', as Harold Nicolson put it;[5] and a return on the domestic front to the economics of the free market – and specifically of mass unemployment – of before the war. They were impossible for a number of reasons. One was that they were, quite simply, wrong. A majority of people probably felt this, including many Conservatives, even imperialist ones, who genuinely believed in colonial self-government, for example, as 'the culmination of a set purpose of nearly four generations' of British tutelage, in Macmillan's words much later;[6] and in the emerging Commonwealth as a far better way of expressing Britain's moral purpose in the world than the old empire of white rulers and coloured subjects had been. Similarly, most of those who could remember it looked back on large-scale unemployment with revulsion, and took a moral stance against that too; including, again, Macmillan, who often acknowledged the 'indelible marks' that the sight of it in his old Teesside constituency in the 1920s had made 'upon my mind and heart'.[7] A second reason for rejecting reaction was that it was impractical. It would provoke resistance, among nationalists in the colonies and trade unionists at home, which Britain would find it difficult in her present parlous state to contain. If she tried it might have the effect of driving the resisters into the arms of the communists, which would make matters worse at a time when the communist threat was reckoned to be especially menacing, not only because of communist Russia's military build-up, but also in view of what appeared at that time to be her spectacular successes – far outstripping the capitalist West, many believed[8] – on the economic front. That was bound to make communism all the more attractive to colonial and working-class waverers; whom the government could not afford to alienate further, therefore, by depriving them of freedom, or of work.

There was also a third factor militating against structural change in the later 1950s and 1960s. That was that the alternative – keeping things roughly as they were – did not seem so very terrible. This may have been the crucial point. However much Britain was declining in almost every way relative to other nations in this period, the process did not appear to be affecting her people materially. They were doing better. National income was rising. Production and trade were increasing. There was still almost no unemployment: the figure averaged about 380 000 annually, which was not much higher than under Labour, for example, and was probably as low as was compatible with some degree of flexibility in the labour market. For those in work, earnings rose steadily, by about 27% in real terms between 1955 and 1964. Visible signs of affluence were all around: five million more new cars on the road in 1964 than ten years earlier, for example; television aerials on nearly every rooftop; holidays abroad for more and more people:[9] evidence, all of it, that 'life' was indeed 'better under the Conservatives', as the general election slogan of 1959 put it; whatever may have been happening to Britain as a world power, or to her economic position by comparison with other nations, or to her prospects for the future. None of these things, important as they may have been, felt quite so *tangible* as the new Morris Minor, or the latest Elvis Presley long-playing record, or the week in August on the Costa Brava; which were the criteria most people were bound to go by when they were asked to decide – at election time, for example – whether the system was working or not.

This was why there was so little fundamental change to the basic pattern of Britain's existence between 1955 and 1964: the mixed economy, the welfare state, the evolution of the new commonwealth, and the relationship with the United States. Change, it was felt, would be wrong, dangerous and unnecessary. These were compelling reasons for conservatism. So the ship sailed on, unaltered and unadapted, into the stormier seas which – though contemporaries could not reasonably be expected to know this – lay ahead.

II

The problems it encountered on its voyage may have been due to defects in the design of the vessel, or to the way it was skippered and crewed. This was a subject of some controversy at the time, and of much more later on. So far as the design was concerned, there were certainly some awkward features, which gave trouble at various times. The most awkward was undoubtedly the American alliance, which however desirable it may have been for Britain – Macmillan even went so far as to claim that the 'life of the free world' depended on it[10] – was always problematical.

This was because the United States had her own agenda, which was not always fully compatible with Britain's; and secondly because she was so much more powerful than Britain, which meant that that agenda had to take precedence. The most dramatic manifestation of this came during the Suez crisis of October–November 1956; though this was clearly an instance in which questionable navigation by Britain's leaders also played a part. The Suez crisis featured Britain and France invading Egypt in response to Nasser's (the Egyptian president's) unilateral seizure of the control of the Suez Canal in July 1956. The motives behind Britain's action were complex. Her material interests were at stake: the passage though the canal of her merchant ships, and especially those carrying oil from the Persian Gulf. Anthony Eden, the new prime minister, also felt that certain principles were involved: the sanctity of contracts, such as the one that had originally established the status of the Suez Canal company; and the general question of 'aggression'. His attitude to the latter principle was coloured by his memories of Britain's appeasement of Hitler's aggression in the 1930s, which he (together with Churchill) had been one of the bravest opponents of at that time. He probably went too far on this occasion in comparing Nasser directly with Hitler, which made even some of his loyal cabinet colleagues doubt his sense of proportion, and his opponents question his mental health.[11] He was also convinced that behind Nasser stood the Russians, who were using him as their tool to extend their empire over the whole of the Middle East, thus – among other things – destroying industrial Europe by cutting off its oil.[12] Consequently he felt the Americans should be with Britain on this. She was out to stop a 'megalomaniac',[13] staunch Soviet communist expansion, bring peace to a notorious trouble spot, help the Israelis and safeguard the interests of Western capitalism: all of these as much American as British interests, he reckoned, and consequently fully worthy of the Great Republic's encouragement and support. But that was not to see it from the American point of view.

It was partly a question of simple mistrust. Eden insisted that the British action over Suez was not 'imperialistic' – that its object was not to win territory for Britain, but simply to 'internationalise' an important waterway – but Eisenhower and Dulles were not convinced. Some of their scepticism may have been justified. Motives *were* very muddled on the British side. Those that were openly expressed seemed honourable enough, however mistaken some of them may have been; but they did not represent the whole picture. R.A. Butler pointed out how these kinds of arguments 'coalesced only too easily with less generous sentiments: the residues of liberal resentment at the loss of Empire, the rise of coloured nationalism, [and] the transfer of world leadership to the United States', which could muddy the scene somewhat.[14] When Macmillan (the Foreign Secretary) argued to the Americans that Britain had to take the action she did in order to avoid sinking 'into the rank of second-class nations', it may have given a similar impression: that the whole thing was partly, at any rate, a ruse to win back some imperial prestige.[15] As well as this, however, there was a certain amount of prejudice on the American side; some of which arose from the delusion – which Eden analysed quite perceptively in the volume of his *Memoirs* which covers this period – that just because the United States did not govern alien peoples, but merely exploited them, she was untainted by 'imperialism' and so free to criticise.[16] In this way, as Eden put it, 'The old spoor of colonialism confused the trail',[17] throwing the Americans off what he thought was the scent they should have been following. That was one thing that affected their agenda. Another was the interest they had – or believed they had – in cultivating the goodwill of other 'anti-imperialist' nations, which otherwise might go to the Soviet Union, whose anti-imperialist credentials were supposed to be (though of course they were not, any more than America's were) impeccable. That overrode everything, including the strict merits of Britain's Suez case. Again, it gave the two powers divergent interests.

Of course it may not have needed to. A case can be made for saying that Britain's action over Suez did not really conduce to her interests either, even if America's lack of support is disregarded; simply because Eden's analysis of the situation in the Middle East at that time – of the damage that Egyptian control of the canal was likely to do to Britain, Nasser's ambitions, and his relationship with the Soviets – was flawed. One can imagine another government coming to other conclusions, and dealing with the crisis in other ways, which would have allowed it to remain on good terms with the United States. That is where the navigation comes in. Alas, it was not to be. America and Britain fell out grievously over Suez; fatally for the fortunes of the campaign itself, which had to be aborted when sterling came under pressure, and the United States refused her backing for it unless Britain stopped fighting and then withdrew. (Eden tried to salvage a vestige of national self-respect by pretending that he had planned to stop then anyway, but that convinced scarcely anyone.)[18] It was a serious schism, and a worrying one if it was to last any length of time, in view of the crucial importance that Britain had placed ever since the end of the war on her hitherto 'special relationship' with America.

In fact the breach was soon healed; but that did not solve the underlying problems that the relationship was always bound to cause. The occasion for the healing was a meeting between Macmillan and Eisenhower in Bermuda in March 1957. (Macmillan had just succeeded Eden as prime minister, after the latter's resignation due to illness shortly after Suez.) According to the former the two of them got on famously – 'just exactly as in the old days' – which was a relief. They also negotiated a number of defence agreements, to do with the sharing of nuclear information; collaboration in intelligence; and the stationing of 60 American nuclear missiles in East Anglia. Macmillan hailed the last of these as 'a triumph of British diplomacy',[19] though its most obvious effect was to emphasise Britain's dependence on the United States.[20] Later that dependence increased, especially after Britain cancelled her own 'Blue Streak' missile-development programme in 1960 because of escalating costs, and consequently became reliant on America for the means of delivering her 'independent' nuclear deterrent. She negotiated that, too, later (some 'Skybolt' missiles originally, and then, when that programme was cancelled, the submarine-launched 'Polaris' system), in return for more American bases in Britain. It was a very unequal relationship, this; with Britain it seemed always in the position of supplicant, and able to contribute very little to it herself, beyond a few pounds of recycled plutonium, processed at Windscale in Cumberland, for America's warheads; some expertise in the intelligence field, for what that was worth; and great tracts of land or loch for the Americans to site some of their deadliest weapons on, with all the risks, of course, that this involved for Britain if the very worst befell.

There was, however, one thing more. Britain was no longer in the same league as the United States militarily, but she did have the wisdom that came from centuries of being in that position before. That could be useful to the Americans, new to this situation as they were, and consequently apt to be 'naïve and inexperienced', as Macmillan put it, in their dealings with foreign powers.[21] His opportunity came when when John F. Kennedy became President in January 1961: 'this splendid, young, gay figure', as he once described him,[22] whom he came to like enormously as he grew to know him over the next three years, and who – which was more to the point – seemed so much more willing than any other President he had known to take advice from the British. Lord Home, the Foreign Secretary at the time, described how when Kennedy first entered office he had rings run around him by the more streetwise Russian leader Khrushchev, and so was 'all the more grateful when the older Macmillan was so willing to place his wisdom and experience at his disposal'.[23] During the Cuban missile crisis of 1962, when for a time the world looked close to catastrophe, Kennedy apparently phoned Macmillan daily, and sometimes several times a day, at all hours, for advice. 'I think we played our part perfectly,' the latter recalled later. 'We were "in on" and took part in (and almost responsibility for) every American move.' This was his answer to those who made 'the accusation that there was no "special relationship" between London and Moscow'.[24] There clearly was; and a remarkably balanced one at that, if Britain's more cerebral contribution to it was given the weight it deserved.

Whether Kennedy saw it quite like that is uncertain. It is possible that in giving Macmillan this impression he was merely seeking to flatter him. In any case the relationship was not to last, as the murdered Kennedy was succeeded as President by Lyndon Johnson in November 1963, who turned out to be a different animal entirely: boorish, aggressive, and constantly interrupting their conversation to do underhand political 'fixes' over the telephone, when Macmillan's last Foreign Secretary, Butler, went to visit him in April 1964.[25] By this time, of course, Macmillan had gone as well. If there was a 'special relationship' it was clearly a very personal one, which could not survive the departure of the individual leaders concerned. Thereafter

– until perhaps Reagan met up with Thatcher in the 1980s – the relations between the two countries reverted to what seems to have been their natural state: somewhat ill-matched, and consequently uncomfortable, with frequent rows between them, for example over east-west trade (it was Britain's trade with Cuba which sparked off Johnson's ire against Butler); Britain doing most of the compromising; and a steady undercurrent of popular anti-American feeling in Britain, which occasionally flared into violence, over such issues as America's nuclear bases in Britain, and her own special brand of 'imperialism' in countries like Vietnam.

It may have had other drawbacks too. It certainly played a part in Britain's difficulties with Europe at this time. The American relationship was an awful lot of baggage for Britain to take with her into Europe, if she ever got serious about joining the 'union' of continental nations that was being floated then. Of course this was not the only obstacle. Others were poor judgment, especially on the part of the Foreign Office, which for years was highly sceptical about the whole prospects of the European movement;[26] simple xenophobia; very real disparities between the economies of Britain and most of the rest of Europe, especially with regard to agriculture and their foreign trading patterns, which were always going to be difficult to reconcile; and of course the Commonwealth, which Macmillan saw as overshadowing every other aspect of the problem 'politically, economically and, above all, emotionally'.[27] In the end, however, when all these hurdles seemed to have been overcome, and Macmillan made his decision to apply to the new 'European Community' of (originally) six nations in August 1961, it was the American connexion that stymied him. On 14 January 1963 the French President, Charles de Gaulle, announced that he would be resisting Britain's submission on the grounds that she was far too entangled with the United States to be a genuinely European power. Worse: to take Britain in would mean the whole of Europe succumbing to American domination eventually; the creation, as de Gaulle put it, of 'a colossal Atlantic Community under American dependence and leadership which would soon completely swallow up the European Community.'[28] The EC's formal rejection of Britain's application came just a fortnight afterwards.

Macmillan was devastated. 'We have lost everything,' he wrote in his diary; 'All our policies at home and abroad are in ruins.'[29] That was because *he* knew – even at this, the most euphoric, stage of his friendship with Kennedy – that the 'special relationship', flattering though it was in some ways, and necessary as it may have been in others, was not an adequate basis for power and influence in the modern world, which depended on something quite different. By the early 1960s he had come to the conclusion that what it depended on, so far as Britain was concerned, was a large free market, such as the expanded EC would have offered, in order to stimulate the economic growth which (as we shall see) he was continually pressing for at home, and believed was an essential prerequisite for British influence abroad.[30] This was another point, incidentally, at which British interests diverged from those of the United States, who because of her extensive domestic market needed foreign trade less; which was what was at the root of their many disputes over trade with the communists.[31] There was another aspect to this as well. Growth was necessary to strengthen the case for the efficiency of the capitalist system generally, against the rival claims – which we have seen appeared seductive at this time – of the command economies of the East.[32] This too had been jeopardised by the American connexion; or, to be more accurate, by the hostility it had evoked in the breast of the French President, possibly quite unreasonably.

So, what was left to Britain now? There was still, of course, her Commonwealth; but that was changing rapidly. Macmillan had no idea where it was going: 'Was I destined to be the remodeller or the liquidator of Empire?' he remembered wondering when he came to power in 1957;[33] and still at the very end was scarcely the wiser. During his premiership, which lasted just under seven years, 14 British colonies achieved their independence, which was more than in any other comparable period of British history.[34] That was quite a performance for what was supposed to be the party of Empire. Inevitably it provoked bitter opposition from the more reactionary sort of Conservative imperialist, led by the 5th Marquis of Salisbury, especially over the government's betrayal of the white settler communities which the dissidents believed had made colonies like Kenya and the Rhodesias what they were; but to little effect. When Salisbury himself resigned from the cabinet in March 1957 over the release of the Greek Cypriot leader Archbishop Makarios from prison, scarcely anyone noticed.[35] What was noticed, and widely applauded, was Macmillan's famous 'Wind of Change' speech to the South African parliament in February 1960, warning it of the irreversible force of black nationalism; which indicated the government's grasp of the realities of the time. Later Iain Macleod, who was the Colonial Secretary most responsible for this policy, admitted that they had gone rather faster with it than might have been thought to be ideal, from the point of view of preparing the new nations properly for self-government; but he insisted that 'any other policy would have led to terrible bloodshed'. That, he thought, was 'the heart of the argument'.[36] It meant, as his Under-Secretary put it afterwards, that whatever its other effects might have been, 'we did not leave behind us in Africa either a Congo or an Algeria'.[37] That was an important negative achievement. The positive side of it, however, especially from Britain's point of view, remained obscure.

Many people still harboured visions of a role for the Commonwealth, but not usually as grandiose as those that had gone before. It was clear that it would never become a 'third force' in the world, for example, of the kind that had used to be envisaged by imperialists of both main political parties until fairly recently. There were too many internal tensions for that; revealed first of all over Suez, which had been almost as divisive an issue for the Commonwealth as it was for Britain; and then over the issue of 'apartheid' in South Africa, which eventually forced the latter out of the club in 1961. Instead enlightened ex-imperialists now set their sights rather lower (or higher, by another way of looking at it): at the Commonwealth as a 'family', or a 'brotherhood', or a 'community', or a 'Council of Nations', or a 'bridge between East and West', or a 'moral influence in world affairs';[38] nothing quite so concrete and tangible as had been hoped for originally, but worthwhile all the same. Macleod's pet ambition, as he described it to his party's annual conference in October 1960, was to extend, if he could, the old Disraelian ideal of 'One Nation' to the Commonwealth, getting peoples and races to know, understand and help one another much more. 'If we can succeed in this, if we can begin to create One World abroad to match One Nation at home, Communism will seem irrelevant to the problems of the world.'[39] It was a worthy aspiration, very much in the spirit of the prevalent Tory outlook of that period, in home affairs too, as we shall see. But it still could not make up for what Britain had lost.

All the same, it demonstrated a remarkable capacity on the part of Britain to adjust. This needs saying. Sometimes during these years, and also afterwards, it was alleged that one of the reasons for her contemporary difficulties was that she insisted on clinging on to illusions of grandeur – and particularly imperial grandeur – inherited from her past. That was by and large not true. One of the most noteworthy features of this period, in fact, was the ease with which Britain was able to come to terms with the need to divest herself of her empire, and the little effect this had on her people, except at the margins of her political life. There were two reasons for this, both of which have been touched on before in this book: the paternalistic ethos which for some time now had infused the running of her empire, and left it open for imperialists at the end to claim that independence was its whole purpose; and secondly, the fact that, in British society as a whole, overtly imperialistic attitudes of any kind had never run very deep. Lord Salisbury and his ilk had always been marginal. The empire meant little or nothing to most people.[40] That was not Britain's major problem in these difficult mid-twentieth-century years.

Her major problem went deeper than this. It had to do with the patterns of trade and investment Britain had established in the world, going back to the nineteenth century, and their vital importance to her. These constituted her main material interest in the world, which the empire had merely existed to safeguard. In many ways it was – as we noted earlier[41] – a rather incongruous way of safeguarding those interests, because the paternalistic values attaching to it sat so uneasily with the commercial ones that had brought it into being; which may be another reason why the empire was relinquished so easily. By the end, what with colonial nationalism and all the rest, it was also creating more difficulties than it solved. Its dissolution brought an end to those difficulties. But it made no difference to the ones that lay underneath. Britain still remained more dependent on her foreign economic interests, especially outside Europe, than any other country in the world, and consequently distinct from everyone else. Hence her reliance on the United States, which was probably mistaken, but seemed at the time to be the only way of defending her extra-European interests now that her own imperial power had waned; her difficulties with her European neighbours, which were almost inevitable, quite apart from the row over the American connexion, in view of the enormous differences of economic interest between them; and the misunderstandings that bedevilled her foreign relations with just about every other power at this time, all of which were – it is only fair to point out – just as blinkered by the nature of their own interests as she was by the peculiar nature of hers.

III

At home the mass of people responded to these events fairly impassively. Two 'foreign' issues did provoke strong feelings among large minorities: the Suez adventure, on both sides of the debate, while the troops were still there in October and November 1956; and nuclear defence, which gave rise to the biggest popular protest movement in Britain for generations, the 'Campaign for Nuclear Disarmament', founded in 1958. At its height (*circa* 1960–63) CND attracted 100 000 people at a time to its rallies, while its more extreme offshoot, the 'Committee of 100', caused actual harm to military installations. 'The Bomb' did have a popular resonance, clearly because of its obvious (and horrific) domestic bearing. But none of the other great foreign, colonial and defence issues of the time did to anything like the same extent. Decolonisation went through almost on the nod. The American connexion only stimulated interest when the romantic young J.F. Kennedy visited Britain in 1963. The European Community, as Macmillan wrote regretfully in 1971, 'made little appeal to the imagination of our people' at any time.[42] This may seem surprising, in view of Britain's high international profile in the past, and her dependence on international events and trends in a dozen ways at this time. Or perhaps that was the reason for it. If the British could no longer dominate the world, they were blowed if they were going to take an interest in it.

There was nothing to make them really excited on the domestic scene, either. Little of importance happened. After Suez there were no great political crises – none, at any rate, worthy of the name – or economic catastrophes. The harm done to the Conservative party by Suez was soon repaired by Macmillan, who led his party to a third successive general election victory, with an increased parliamentary majority, in 1959. The Labour opposition was no match for him, especially divided as it was, over issues that did not really matter (a clause in the party constitution on public ownership, for example, which few members took seriously; and a minuscule difference over the nuclear issue), but which had the comrades at each others' throats nonetheless. As there was little to distinguish the two main parties in policy terms, with the Tories faithful to the post-war consensus throughout, this dissension on the left was probably the factor that made the difference electorally. People voted for stability. When they did eventually decide to change governments, in 1964, it was after a period of really quite startling blunders by the old government, under a faintly risible new premier, and even then by only the smallest of margins (four seats and 200 000 votes). The worst the Labour party could find to say about the Conservatives in that election was that they had 'wasted' – not mismanaged, or abused, or anything worse – their 13 years in office. In a way that could be read as a compliment, in its context; and a tribute to the moderation of the departing government.

Moderation was certainly Macmillan's aim. Eden and Home, the premiers who flanked him, were less wedded to it – more partisan and combative in their *rhetoric*, at least – but neither of them was in post long enough for this to make any difference. With Macmillan, moderation and pragmatism were everything. 'I was opposed to the over-regulation which comes with Socialism. I was equally convinced that, in the second half of the twentieth century, we could not revert to the *laissez-faire* of a hundred years ago.' In rather a good joke he adjured his hearers – this was in the budget debate of April 1956 – to 'let sleeping dogmas lie'.[43] 'Apart from any reasons of humanity,' he wrote later,

> it was clear that in modern conditions with the rigidity that had entered the economic system since the increased power of the trade unions and the buttressing forces of social benefits, which prevented the harsh pressure of poverty acting as it had in the past, some degree at any rate of state interference – or *dirigisme* – was both necessary and in conformity with traditional Tory philosophy.[44]

Hence his insistence throughout his time in goverment on what he liked to call 'the middle way'.[45]

That was a fair description of his government's economic practice, though the word '*dirigisme*' was perhaps a little strong. That implies, surely, governments taking an active role in the economy: directing invest-ment, for example, or helping infant enterprises. In Britain in the 1950s and early 1960s – unlike on the Continent – there was very little of that. By and large the country's economic development was left to go its own way – a kind of '*laissez-faire*' régime, in fact – but with two significant differences from what that term usually implies. In the first place it was a *laissez-faire* policy with a strong trade-union movement as part of the equation, com-prising one of the 'market forces' that determined levels of wages and employment. (Most classical *laissez-faire* economies postulate a more individual approach to wage bargaining.) Secondly, the state did intervene; but only to keep the ring, with a view to preventing the adversaries – employers and trade unions, high wages and competitiveness, expansion and a stable currency – damaging both one another, and the wider national economic interest. That – and little more than that, it seems – was the task of government in the economic sphere.

It was not a particularly heroic role, and it did not produce any dramatic results. In fiscal policy it was characterised by sudden switches in direction, between measures designed to expand the economy, which were always Macmillan's instinctive preference, and credit squeezes and public-spend-ing cuts to smother the inflation that this gave rise to; known at the time as 'Stop–Go'. Macmillan once described it as 'a policy of alternation between Benzedrine and Relaxa-tabs'.[46] He did not like it, but could not see any way to avoid it, short of galloping inflation on the one hand, and unacceptable levels of unemployment on the other. Similarly, in industrial relations a careful course had to be steered between allowing wages to fuel inflation and undermine competitiveness, and provoking equally damaging strikes. 'Above all,' Macmillan wrote in his diary for 10 April 1958, 'we must not "challenge" the Trade Unions as some... would like. We must appeal to the Unions.'[47] From 1955 to October 1959 that was Iain Macleod's job as Min-ister of Labour, before he moved on to the Colonies to apply his conciliatory skills there. 'We can afford strikes less than any other country in the world,' he told the Conservative party conference in 1956. 'We have got a knife-edge economy and the world is not going to wait for us while we squabble.'[48] He was keen to negotiate settlements where he could, therefore, usually in terms which disgruntled the employers slightly; though there were occasions – a busmen's strike in 1958, for example – on which he encouraged the employers to face the unions down. He turned out to be the perfect successor to Walter Monckton, Churchill's equally placa-tory Labour Minister; helping to continue the approach that had been laid down by Churchill in this field.

Macmillan claimed the policy was an enormous success, 'crowned', as he put it in a speech in 1962, 'by the dramatic change which had taken place in the happiness, comfort and wealth of the mass of the people' since the Conservatives had come to power.[49] It also had the effect, he reckoned, of neutralizing the war between the classes which had characterised British society in the pre-war years, so depriving the communists of the purchase that they had used to have on the latter.[50] (We have noticed this idea of the 'middle way' as a prophylactic against Marxism before.)[51] There was something in this. 'Happiness' and 'comfort' are difficult to quantify, of course; but there were fewer obvious signs of their *opposites* in Britain in this period than at most other times. There may have been other reasons for this: like the absence of wars, new labour-saving devices, wider consumer choice, developments in popular entertainment, or the sudden discovery (according to the poet Philip Larkin) of sexual intercourse in 1963;[52] but government policy will have had something to do with it too. 'Wealth' – the third of Macmillan's boasted achievements – *is* measurable, and can be shown to have increased in real terms for most people in the country, as we have seen.[53] In these ways life undoubtedly *was* better under the Conservatives. Which is not to say, of course, that it might not have been better still under some other and different régime.

There can be no doubt that there was room for improvement in Britain's performance. The most significant economic indicators of the time are not those that measure her absolute progress, or her progress by comparison with previous and subsequent years, both of which look fairly respectable; but the figures for her progress compared with her contemporary commercial competitors', which give a totally different picture. Britain's annual growth rate between 1955 and 1964 averaged 2.8% for example; Italy's for the same period averaged 5.4%; France's 5.4%; Germany's 5.7%; and Japan's 13.6%. Britain's share of world trade in manufactured goods fell from 19.8% in 1955 to 13.9% ten years later; and in 'invisibles' from 24.9% to 17.9% over the same period.[54] More and more countries began overtaking her in just about every area of economic activity, so that from being the second or third biggest producer in the world *per capita* around 1950, she had slumped to being the ninth or tenth by 1965.[55] It was an astonishing relative decline. Most of it had happened under Conservative governments. That was something, therefore, that had to be put on the other side of the scales, against Macmillan's alleged successes in the fields of happiness, comfort and individual wealth.

Ministers were not blind to this. They were conscious of the underlying fragility of the economy all along, as we have seen. Towards the end they could not help but be aware of it: with horrendous balance of payments deficits in 1960 and 1964, for example;[56] a bad year for strikes in 1962; and unemployment reaching 878 000 momentarily in February 1963, which for Macmillan brought back alarming 'memories of the past'.[57] For him the worst aspect of this situation was that the old remedy – a nudge on the 'regulator' – no longer seemed to be working; as if the economy had developed an 'immunity... such as the human body sometimes develops when it has become accustomed to a treatment too persistently applied'.[58] That called for new remedies. Macmillan tried three. One was to sack his Chancellor, Selwyn Lloyd, in July 1962 because of what he regarded as his 'lack of initiative'. (At the same time he sacked six other members of his cabinet, in what came to be called 'the Night of the Long Knives'; ostensibly in order – as he claimed – 'to mask the blow to the reputation' of one Minister: though to most onlookers it looked like an act of sheer panic.)[59] Lloyd was succeeded by Reginald Maudling, who was more of an expansionist. Macmillan's second new wheeze was an incomes policy: a freeze on public-sector pay first of all, in July 1961; followed by what was called a 'guiding light' of $2^1/2\%$ for increases in both public and private sectors in March 1962. That did not work ideally (dock workers were given 9% just six weeks after the guiding light was lit); but Macmillan retained enough faith in it to want to make it permanent.[60] His other remedy for Britain's economic ills we have mentioned already. One of his main reasons for wanting to enter the European Economic Community was the boost he believed it would give to foreign investment in Britain.[61] Denis Healey thought this motive betrayed 'a collapse of confidence' by the nation's rulers 'in their own ability to solve Britain's problems'.[62] Macmillan seems to have regarded it as his last throw of the economic dice. Hence the depth of his disappointment when the gambit failed.

By that time, disillusionment with the government was already becoming widespread. In March 1962 (while the British application to join Europe was still on the table) the Liberals won a famous by-election victory at Orpington in Kent, turning a Conservative majority of 14 760 into one for them of 7855. An opinion poll taken at the same time showed support for the Conservative party nationally down to 33%.[63] Macmillan thought that 'after ten years of unparallelled prosperity' the people were simply 'bored' with them;[64] but there was more to it than that. The government was looking jaded. The 'Night of the Long Knives' freshened it up a little, but not where it mattered, at the head. This became apparent shortly. The Profumo scandal was unimportant in itself (it involved a cabinet minister sharing a mistress with a Russian attaché and then lying to the House of Commons about it), but it showed Macmillan up as gullible (for having believed Profumo's lie) and out of touch (with the circles Profumo moved in). He was cruelly pilloried: by Malcolm Muggeridge, for example, who launched one particularly savage onslaught on his 'decomposing visage and somehow seedy attire', which went a good way beyond what had been generally accepted as the pale before then;[65] and by the new army of young satirists who were so fashionable and successful at that time. His government was also begrimed with rumours which associated nearly all of them with sexual or financial scandals of one kind or another, probably entirely undeservedly in most cases. By now there was also a strong element of class prejudice in the opposition, skilfully exploited by the new Labour leader, Harold Wilson, who in the main Commons debate on the Profumo case, on 17 June 1963, managed without any obvious mud-slinging to associate the sleazy upper-class world which the affair had uncovered – 'a diseased excrescence, a corrupted and poisoned appendix of a small and unrepresentative section of society that makes no contribution at all to what Britain is' – with what was wrong in Britain's government too.[66] Macmillan's choice of Lord Home to succeed him – the bluest-blooded of aristocrats, and the third Old Etonian in a row – was the worst possible in this situation: of very clear reaction against Britain's traditional but now utterly discredited ruling class.

Home's class, in fact, was never – after October 1964 – to rule again. That may not have mattered much in itself (classes can always find other classes to do their work for them); but it was symptomatic. The aristocracy represented two traits in British society whose time was past. The first was simple, undefinable 'old-fashionedness': resistance to change, and a lack of sympathy with modern trends. That may be best illustrated by the obvious unease that all four prime ministers of the 1951–64 period felt in the mere presence of economic problems, which they claimed had hardly troubled pre-war cabinets at all. Churchill, for example, was always grumbling that he 'was not brought up on such things': and that from a man who had been Chancellor of the Exchequer for four and a half years. Eden, Macmillan and Home all said the same.[67] Home told a journalist that he needed matchsticks to help him work out economic questions, which was meant as a joke, but was an unwise one in view of the way it reinforced what people suspected in any case. Macmillan tried to counter this kind of image by peppering his speeches with words like 'modern' and 'progressive', creating a new 'Ministry of Science' which he thought would be 'very good symbolically',[68] and setting up inquiries into the modernisation of everything under the sun, from the movement of traffic to higher education;[69] but none of this seemed convincing, coming from him. The point was that Macmillan did not look – and looks were coming to be important now, in the television age – a modern man.

The second trait that Macmillan and his ilk represented was paternalism. This was very important. For years the continued participation of the upper and public-school-educated classes in the government of Britain had had the effect, as we have seen, of softening the impact of capitalism on the lives of her people, by keeping alive certain values (like selflessness and service) which afforded them some protection against brute market forces. This was not those classes' doing alone. In part their role arose from contradictions within the capitalist system, which – as we have suggested – gave rise to these anomalies as a way of safeguarding capitalism against the self-destruction that might have resulted otherwise. This is why it is wrong to *blame* these classes and their values for British capitalism's limitations at this time. Another of these anomalies was the late nineteenth-century British empire, whose origin as the outcome of one particular contradiction of capitalism has been described already, and which, while it remained, constituted the paternalistic classes' main means of support, both materially and spiritually. As well as this, they had useful allies among the socialists, especially – though perhaps rather surprisingly – over the issue of the empire, where the notions of 'trusteeship' and 'welfare' (again, often in opposition to more crudely capitalistic ways of developing countries) furnished the basis for a common policy. That spilled over into the domestic field too, where socialists and paternalists found no difficulty at all in joining together to build and then maintain the welfare state. Hence the 'consensus' of these post-war years; which, however, depended very much on the ascendancy of this particular species of Conservatism within its own party to survive.

That ascendancy began to be shaken during Macmillan's final years. One reason for this may have been – though it is difficult to trace a clear connexion here – the emancipation of the empire, which took away the paternalists' main prop. Another was a very obvious practical problem: the sheer financial cost of supporting the welfare state, which had caused problems for Attlee's government too. The difference now was that some of Macmillan's colleagues appeared to see these problems also as opportunities, for modifying (at least) a system that their free market ideology told them was harmful anyway. One early manifestation of this was the resignation of Macmillan's own Chancellor, Peter Thorneycroft, in January 1958, together with two junior Treasury ministers, Nigel Birch and Enoch Powell, over the issue of public expenditure cuts. (They wanted to cut deeper.) As time went on Macmillan noticed this tendency growing in strength: especially among 'cold-blooded' academic economists, as he called them; the lower middle classes, who resented the way the workers were being mollycoddled and wanted (he claimed) to start up the class war again; and latterly in his cabinet, where on one occasion he was intrigued to find a 'quite deep divergence of view between Ministers, really corresponding to whether they had old Whig, Liberal, *laissez-faire* traditions, or Tory opinions, paternalists and not afraid of a little *dirigisme*'.[70] That, incidentally, was after Powell, who had used the interval to hone and perfect his free market ideology, was let back into the government. Later, during the Profumo affair, he was apparently the only cabinet minister to be left entirely untainted by innuendoes about his own personal life.[71] An analogy can be drawn here with the reputation for moral rectitude which the economics of the free market was also cultivating at this time, and which clearly added to its appeal among people of a certain puritan bent.

These were the ones, of course, who felt that the whole design of the vessel was wrong in the 1950s and 1960s; that Britain's problems were not simply due to the incompetence of its captains, but to the basic lack of seaworthiness of a boat laden down with welfare obligations and high taxation, and rendered sluggish in its movements – incapable of responding quickly to new winds and currents – by a culture that discouraged enterprise and hard work among its crew. There was a lot of this kind of feeling in 1964, but not yet enough to induce any government to go for another design. The position did not seem to be desperate enough. People still felt comparatively well off. Few of them were yet prepared to face the 'difficult things' that Enoch Powell was telling them would 'have to be done if the habits of this nation... are to become truly and fearlessly competitive'.[72] No one could be sure in any case that Powell's prescription – whatever the morality of it – was the right one. It was, after all, not the only one on offer. Labour held out a different alternative: roughly the same vessel – the mixed economy, welfare state and the rest – but 'modernised'. On 15 October 1964, that was what the British electorate – albeit only marginally – opted for.

Chapter 24

The Wilson Years
(1964–70)

I

'Modernity' was the keynote of Labour's appeal to the electorate in 1964. Its manifesto spelled it out grandiloquently. It promised 'A New Britain', no less: new not in a political or ideological sense – the Labour leadership had very little quarrel with the broad direction of British policy either at home or abroad over the past 13 years – but in its machinery, the cogs and pistons that drove the country on. The main agencies for this were to be science and technology, harnessed through 'our national wealth in brains, our genius for scientific invention and medical discovery', to a common end. In this way the 'decline of the 13 wasted years' could be reversed, and Britain given the opportunity 'to equal, and if possible surpass, the roaring progress of other western powers' over that period. It was a seductive message; the more so as it seemed to be politically neutral in most respects. Either party could have squared these general aims with its current philosophy. We have seen Macmillan making similar noises when in power.[1] But he had had his chance. You could not expect a languid Edwardian – let alone an ex-thirteenth Earl – to embrace these notions genuinely. 'The country needs fresh and virile leadership', Labour's manifesto concluded, pointedly.[2] Labour was much better tooled up for the task.

It was tooled up in a number of ways. It gave the impression of being younger and more vigorous than the Conservative leadership: though in fact in terms of literal age, Home's Cabinet was the sprightlier of the two.[3] It had a classless quality about it, with a mixture of working- and middle-class members, and a leader whom it was difficult to place exactly in social terms, except to say that he was certainly no aristocrat. Anthony Wedgwood Benn – who was also no aristocrat, though it had taken him a great constitutional battle recently to establish that – thought that this was rapidly turning Labour into 'a genuine national party' for the first time.[4] Its commitment to science seemed convincing, especially since Wilson's passionate advocacy of it in a celebrated speech to his party conference in October 1963, about the 'scientific revolution' that was to come, and the changes in Britain's economic and social life that would need to be made, or 'forged', in its 'white heat'. That last phrase really caught on. Wilson used it to indicate the potency of the new phenomenon. So far as he was concerned it overrode everything, including socialism in any of the ways it had used to be understood in the past. 'We are re-defining our Socialism,' he told Conference, 'in terms of the scientific revolution.'[5] In a way that served to depoliticise it; which was another thing that seemed to fit Labour for the times.

Of course it did have political implications. 'Modernisation' itself might be ideologically neutral, but the way it was proposed to be achieved was not. Mainly it was to be done through 'planning'. That was Labour's big new policy proposal in 1964: its solution to most of Britain's contemporary ills, and the thing that really distinguished it from the Conservatives, who still adhered to the free market as the ideal form of economic arrangement, even if most of them by this time had come to accept that it could never be perfect. Labour's emphasis was entirely different. 'We can no more win the battle of nuclear power, electronics and automation on the principle of *laissez-faire*,' said Barbara Castle, chairperson of the party, in 1959, 'than we could have won the last war on the same principle.'[6] Market forces were beneficial in many ways, but left entirely to themselves they did not always conduce to the best long-term interests of whole communities. They needed to be monitored, guided, restricted at certain points and assisted at others, in order, as Wilson himself put it, to make 'a more purposive use of our national resources for overcoming a national malady'.[7] The Conservatives could never have provided this. Their hearts would not have been in it. That was why a Labour government was necessary.

In the end the electorate accepted this, albeit by the smallest margin ever in British electoral history (0.7% of the popular vote); and so the planners got the chance to prove their point. They set about it with gusto. The centrepiece of the new government's policy was its National Economic Plan, designed – in the words of James Callaghan, Wilson's first Chancellor – as

> a framework for industrial development and production, whose object would be to increase exports and replace imports. The whole plan would be constructed on the potential capacity of each separate industry for production and export. Every industry would be able to see where it fitted into the national economy and would be able to make long-term plans more safely than hitherto in the expectation of steady industrial growth throughout the rest of the economy. This strategy would solve recurring balance of payments crises followed by the inevitable 'stop–go'.[8]

That last point was important: to get some *stability* into the performance of the British economy, away from the erratic lurching about – the result of relying too much on crude demand-management methods – that had been such a feature of recent years.

That was the general idea. It was also a genuine one. Some cynics at the time saw it as simply a 'gimmick', designed to win votes or to paper over Labour's cracks on other issues; both of which considerations certainly came into it,[9] but not necessarily to the exclusion of more principled ones. As soon as Labour came to power it began working on the details of its National Plan, which it then unveiled in all its quite impressive glory on 13 September 1965. The first thing the plan did was to set out targets for the British economy over the next five years. Growth, for example, was to increase by 25%; personal domestic consumption by slightly less; public expenditure by more; and investment by most of all: 38%.[10] That stated the government's priorities quite clearly: growth all round, benefitting everyone, including wage-earners, but with proportionately more going into fuelling further growth in the future, through capital investment in new plant and research in technologically sophisticated industries, and into state expenditure, in order to maintain – among other things – the just society. Everything else would need to fit around that. Industrial expansion would be nurtured, in areas where Britain was supposed to have advantages, such as the science-based ones. Those areas would be encouraged to become more efficient and competitive. Incomes would rise, but only in line with productivity, and after society had taken its cut for social and industrial investment. That was the blueprint.

New agencies were set up to implement it. The most famous was the Department of Economic Affairs, under Wilson's deputy, George Brown, the main purpose of which was to counter what was supposed to be the baleful influence of the Treasury – traditionally careful, deflationary, anti-growth – over the nation's economic affairs. It was the DEA which was charged with drawing up the National Plan. Less important initially, but to become very much more so later, was a new-fangled Ministry of Technology which Wilson set up under the trade union leader Frank Cousins in 1964, in order to encourage industry's modernisation along scientific lines. After a while it started calling itself 'Mintech', presumably because that sounded more modern than the whole mouthful. Later, under a new Minister, the dynamic young Anthony Wedgwood Benn, it swallowed up whole chunks of other Departments of State (Aviation, Power, the Board of Trade), to turn it into what was in effect a kind of Industrial 'Superministry'.[11] Another of the agencies it ingested was the Industrial Reorganisation Corporation, which had originally been formed in 1966 to encourage mergers between middling-size companies to make them more internationally competitive. Other departments also chipped in. Before he went to Mintech Benn was busy at the Post Office trying to make it more efficient and commercially orientated. The Ministry of Labour (later Employment and Productivity) devised structures for controlling wage rises. One was a new Prices and Incomes Board, set up in 1965, and chaired by a friendly ex-Conservative MP, Aubrey Jones. The Ministry of Education and Science did what it could to push technology at secondary and tertiary levels. Even the Treasury came up with some clever schemes for boosting home investment, and encouraging employment in productive as opposed to parasitic ('service') areas of the economy. Taken all round it was a considerable effort, on a broad front.

It had its successes. One of the earliest – though this may be a slightly cynical way of looking at it – was to win the government a more solid mandate, in March 1966 when Wilson went to the country again to strengthen his parliamentary position, and was rewarded with an overall Commons majority of 96. That was because people were impressed with Labour's plans. Some more solid achievements followed. One of the most impressive was the turn-around in Britain's balance of payments position that was effected between October 1964, when Labour inherited a record deficit of £800 millions, and the summer of 1970, when the country was in comfortable surplus again. 'No incoming Prime Minister... in living memory,' claimed Wilson shortly after his election defeat of that latter year, 'has taken over a stronger economic situation.'[12] A case could be made out for that. There were other triumphs too. The IRC helped push through some successful rationalisations, including one – ICL – which probably saved the British computer industry from strangulation at the hands of the American giants. The traffic between government and industry went both ways, with ministers like Wedgwood Benn, for example, eager to inject some of the 'drive and business sense' he associated with the private sector into nationalized concerns.[13] One prominent industrialist – Donald Stokes of British Leyland – was even brought in to advise the Ministry of Defence.[14] This unideological approach to the problems of industry undoubtedly brought benefits.[15] So did the enormous boost the government gave to technical education, largely through the new 'polytechnics' which sprouted up all over at this time. At a more superficial level the signs of 'modernity' in Britain were apparent: great new roads and bridges, like the Severn bridge, opened in September 1966, and the Almondsbury interchange leading to it, which reminded Barbara Castle of 'the highest forms of architectural expression of the past';[16] Concorde, which first flew in 1969; a clutch of spanking new nuclear power stations; parking meters; decimal currency. All this looked marvellous. At the same time Labour lived up to its social promises pretty well, with measurably more social equality at the end of its period of office than at the beginning,[17] and some famous (or notorious) achievements in the field of personal – especially sexual – freedom. This was regarded as tremendously 'modern', too.

Yet it did not seem enough. Towards the end of its period in office the first Wilson government was widely perceived as a failure. There were good reasons for this, as well as some bad ones. The government had certainly failed by its own standards: the ones set, for example, by the National Plan of 1965, whose projections of growth were probably always on the optimistic side – Anthony Crosland thought they made 'no sense' the moment he saw them[18] – and eventually turned out to be hopelessly wrong.[19] That failure more than anything else, writes one of Wilson's most sympathetic biographers, demolished 'Labour's short-lived reputation... as the party of efficiency and modernity.'[20] Its reputation for financial competency – if it ever had one – suffered even more. A month after it came to power it was rocked by the first of what turned out to be a succession of sterling crises, as money-dealers worldwide demonstrated their lack of confidence in the British economy by selling pounds. That did serious damage to the government's plans, as it was forced into public spending cuts in order to balance the books and to ingratiate itself with the people it needed to lend it money to tide it over the worst. In November 1967 it tried a different tack, devaluing sterling by 14%, which was thought to be a worse humiliation, with the pound, in Callaghan's words, having come to be regarded as 'a symbol of national pride, only somewhat lower than... the national flag';[21] and which did not seem to work – certainly not in the sense of staunching further gushes of sterling – in any case. As well as this the government always had problems controlling wage settlements, and found itself with higher inflation and unemployment rates at the end of its term than at the beginning. Lastly, few people felt that it had fully come to terms with the *underlying* problems of the British economy. Everyone knew the economy had some underlying problems by now. They were highlighted by the rising tide of industrial strikes that began to engulf the country towards the end of the 1960s, though that may not have been the root cause. In the face of this latter phenomenon, in particular, Labour seemed powerless. Almost its final major decision before it went to the country in 1970 was to abandon an Industrial Relations bill designed to deal with it, under pressure from intransigent trade unions, party malcontents and disloyalists inside the Cabinet. That was a clear sign – or appeared to be – of its general lack of economic grasp.

II

Whenever this sort of thing happens – frustration, disappointment, broken promises, thwarted hopes – it is normal for people to seek scapegoats. In this case there are a number of obvious ones to hand, and in particular the three leading members of the Labour government at the beginning of its time in office, all of whom displayed obvious character failings, mixed in with their undoubted qualities. George Brown, for example, was 'completely erratic and irrational and an impossible old boozer – rarely being sober after lunch', according to Tony Benn in 1964;[22] which was what underlay his eventual fall from office in 1968. Unfortunately this was the man who was given the job, central to Labour's strategy, of building up an entirely new Ministry (the DEA) to a position where it could override the centuries-long entrenched position of the Treasury: a task which probably required more sober abilities if it was to succeed. He was not helped by the fact that the Minister in charge of the Treasury, James Callaghan, who should have assisted in this, in reality seemed overawed by his department, and ended up a captive of it.[23] These two factors together helped ensure that what was called the 'Treasury view' of national economic affairs – broadly deflationary – eventually prevailed completely over most of the new thinking that Labour had wished to inject into this field. The DEA itself was formally dismantled in October 1969. Callaghan and Brown could be blamed for that.

They themselves either blamed each other; or the man at the head of the triumvirate, Harold Wilson, who has generally been people's favourite scapegoat since that time. He was also the favourite scapegoat then, especially at the hands of the press, which subjected him to what may have been the most sustained personal onslaught any serving prime minister has suffered this century.[24] Much of this was based on entirely false rumours, put about deliberately by his political enemies, including some people connected with the security services, which at one point he had tried to curb.[25] On the other hand there can be no doubt that he did have some enervating weaknesses. Barbara Castle probably hit on the most serious one in February 1968: 'Harold's trouble is that at bottom he just hasn't got faith in himself, despite all the air of bubbly india-rubber self-confidence'.[26] That made him more sensitive to attacks on him than was healthy, and over-suspicious of plots against him, not all of which were really going on.[27] He was said to be unprincipled,[28] which was not true, but probably arose from the fact that what he felt strongly about (racial tolerance, for example) did not always correspond with what his colleagues felt strongly about (like socialism); and from his propensity to settle and compromise wherever he could. He was a clever politician, who may have come to believe that clever politicking was all one needed to be a statesman. He was also prey to other self-delusions, such as the idea that he was uniquely equipped to settle the wider world's most pressing problems in much the same way.[29] Many of his colleagues complained that he did not take a decisive enough lead in Cabinet.[30] It is easy to see how all these personal factors may have contributed in one way or another to the relative economic failure of the governments of 1964-70. It is also easy to conceive, however, of critics taking refuge in this kind of explanation in order to protect them from the implications of rather more unsettling ones.

There were basically two of these: alternative explanations for the Labour government's failures, which would acquit the triumvirate of at least some of the guilt. The first was that ministers – some of Wilson's fiercest critics, certainly by the end – were really themselves to blame, by not properly fulfilling their Cabinet responsibilities to pull policy round to the direction they claimed they would have preferred. Wilson, Brown and Callaghan were, after all, only three people amongst 20-odd. They could have been outvoted. Why were they not? One reason may be that his colleagues trusted Wilson to win elections for them; which was not a very elevated motive, but must have been in the backs of their minds. 'Wilson is a bastard,' said Anthony Crosland once, 'but he's a genius. He's like Odysseus. Odysseus also was a bastard, but he managed to steer the ship between Scylla and Charybdis.'[31] There was also the problem that if he went, it would leave a messy succession problem behind. That basically was why none of the genuine 'plots' against his leadership succeeded. He was a magician; and there was no other prime ministerial candidate who commanded general assent.

There was also another excuse given for ministers' lack of clout. *They* complained that important decisions were made not by Cabinet, but by Wilson on his own; or Wilson and a few cronies; or even – this was a common complaint by nearly every Labour minister – by the Civil Service behind all their backs. There was some truth in this. One key government decision – to support sterling at its current parity ($2.80) in October 1964, and not devalue (possibly the most fateful of all its actions) – was taken by the triumvirate alone, together with their chief civil servants, before anyone else in the Cabinet knew what was going on. 'I didn't much like that,' Richard Crossman confided to his diary; but he had to go along with it nonetheless.[32] Afterwards devaluation – 'the Unmentionable' – was banned as a topic for discussion at Cabinets for most of the next three years.[33] This was despite the fact that a growing number of Ministers was coming round to the view that the root of their troubles was Wilson's insistence on the $2.80 parity. Budgets were the same: devised by chancellors and Treasury officials, and then simply presented to the Cabinet as *faits accomplis*. Probably only Wilson was privy to another key decision of his government, which followed from the resolve not to devalue: a pact he came to with the Americans in September 1965, promising general support for their Vietnam war policy (though not to the point of sending British troops, which Wilson always resisted); the maintenance of Britain's 'east of Suez' role, so as to relieve the United States of it; and no devaluation, which would hurt American exports; in return for American backing for the (high) pound.[34] That, too, was kept from the Cabinet, though several members suspected something of the kind. 'God knows what he has said to him,' said George Brown after Wilson had returned from one of his several trips to President Johnson. 'What did he pledge? I don't know: that we wouldn't devalue and full support in the Far East?'[35] He for one felt excluded and frustrated. Later (in March 1968) he resigned over this – what he called Wilson's 'presidential system' of government – though fortunately for the latter Brown managed to surround the issue with enough emotional and possibly alcoholic confusion to obfuscate it in most people's eyes.[36] Brown was also one of those who felt oppressed by the obstructionism of the Civil Service;[37] which Wedgwood Benn went so far as to claim vitiated parliamentary democracy altogether.[38] Ministers, in other words, had no real powers.

That may have been true; but it was also not the full story. The real obstacle to alternative economic policies in the 1960s was not presidential government, or secret diplomacy, or budget 'purdah', or the machinations of Whitehall, or Wilson's (or Brown's, or Callaghan's, or anyone else's) personal failings; but the objective situation of the time, and some underlying currents of history. Labour was in an unenviable position in 1964 in many ways. To the problems that would have faced any government at that time – the trade deficit, for example, and uncompetitiveness – was added the fact that few of the people it needed to trust it in order to solve them did. 'We had just got to face it,' Callaghan told Castle quite early on, 'that big business didn't like a Labour Government.'[39] That was broadly true (though there were some exceptions), and was *more* true then than it had been, for example, in 1945–51. That was where the historical current came in.

Ministers were continually frustrated by this. Wedgwood Benn, for example, was terribly unimpressed with the quality of most of the industrialists he had to meet with while he was at the GPO and Mintech – 'A typical British business board and not very impressive', he remarked of the English Electric Company directors in June 1965[40] – and also irritated by what he saw as their anti-Labour prejudices. 'I find it offensive meeting these big industrialists,' he wrote later, after another similar encounter, 'who live on Government work, who are financed by Government, and who are violently, bitterly anti-Government from beginning to end.'[41] It made him wonder on another occasion 'whether we were being hopelessly naïve in trying to work with industry, and whether we shouldn't just nationalise them'; except that he personally did not believe that nationalisation was 'efficient'.[42] If industry was hostile, the worlds of finance and banking were more so;

understandably, perhaps, in view of Harold Wilson's well-known antipathy towards them. (In the 1959 election campaign, for example, he had condemned the 'casino mentality' of the City, and called the Stock Exchange a 'spiv's paradise', which had not gone down at all well.)[43] One of the problems was that Labour wanted to tax the City and its profits, which upset it, quite naturally, but more, probably, than was reasonable. James Callaghan later recounted with some amusement how 'outraged City gents' reacted to the corporation tax proposals in his 1965 budget as if they were a ruse 'to upset the whole of the capitalist system' in Britain, and pledged themselves to 'fight like hell on the beaches' against the communist menace.[44] There was not much sense to be seen in that. It raised the question of how really rational the men and agencies Britain's financial stability depended on were; especially the international 'speculators', who were widely seen as responsible for the sterling crises that hit Britain periodically under Labour, with such damaging effect. Sometimes the sudden raids on sterling seemed to make no sense at all, especially those sparked off by political rumours that anyone with an ounce of common sense could see were ludicrous. 'God knew,' exclaimed an exasperated Callaghan on one such occasion, 'how the psychology of these people worked.'[45] The Conservatives seemed less prone to these attacks, mainly because they were seen as being on the City's side. It was a problem which afflicted socialists particularly, because of who they were.

Wilson tended to see all this in conspiratorial terms. The City was being *used*, he told an audience in Montgomery in July 1968, by 'a hostile and embittered Establishment... to do their dirty work for them'. The press – through its proprietors, millionaires to a man – were in on it too.[46] At one time Wilson also apparently suspected his own Chancellor, Callaghan, of being involved somehow. The idea of that 'plot' was supposed to be to oust Wilson and bring in a 'national' government, embracing all the parties, more to the City's taste.[47] At the same time as this, Wilson also believed he was being subverted from the left, through 'a tightly knit group of politically motivated men' in the Seamen's Union who had 'terrorized' its executive into striking against the government.[48] Much of this was probably true. There *were* plots going on, naturally; there always are in these circumstances. One very well attested one in May 1968 featured Cecil King, chairman of the company that owned the *Daily Mirror*, trying to interest Lord Mountbatten, no less, in taking over the government after a putsch.[49] Whether these were important, however, is another matter. Wilson probably allowed himself to be too affected by them – consumed by what many of his colleagues saw as a kind of 'paranoia' over them[50] – to a seriously disabling degree. They were not worth bothering with: not because they may not have been effective, to an extent; but because they could not have been effective on their own.

For a conspiracy to be accounted successful it really has to achieve something against the general trend. You can plot to swim with the current if you like, but it is not going to make much difference to anything. That is what these right-wing conspirators were doing: plotting outcomes that were bound to happen anyway, because history was moving in their direction. Of course they did not see it that way. If they had, they would not have bothered to plot. In their eyes everything was running against them: alarmingly so for many of them, who were at least as paranoid as Wilson, in the face of what they perceived as the danger from the communist left. Cecil King's appeal to Lord Mountbatten, for example, was couched in terms of the 'bloodshed on the streets' he saw coming if something were not done soon to stem the anarchy that threatened.[51] *The Times* saw revolution around every corner: especially when students gathered together in 'demos' against American Vietnam policy, one of which (October 1968) it claimed it had *proof* was going to be the occasion for an armed insurrectionary attack.[52] Deep in the dimmest crannies of MI5, the state internal security agency, some folk apparently seriously suspected the Labour party of being in the hands of the Russians, *via* Czech intelligence, which had penetrated it with countless 'moles'.[53] Fears like this were rife, and to a degree understandable, in view of certain other contemporary world events, like Russian aggression in Czechoslovakia, and the very left-wing and vocal worldwide student protest movement of 1968. But they were unnecessary. The Labour party was not a communist front. (Indeed, it is difficult sometimes to see it as a *socialist* front.) Britain was nowhere near revolution, or even anarchy, at any time. Capitalism was safe, from that direction at least; safer, in fact, than it had been for many years.

There were a number of reasons for that. One was the supranational dimension it was taking on these days, which left it effectively beyond anyone's power to undermine. The obvious example was multinational manufacturing companies, 'who operated dispassionately in any country and had no national loyalties', as Callaghan told Castle in August 1965, and whose operations it was consequently 'almost impossible to curb'.[54] Wedgwood Benn was first alerted to this problem when the great American-owned Ford Motor Company proposed to transfer its 'Escort' production line from Dagenham to Germany: 'the first big test', as he noted in his diary, 'of the conflict of interests between an international company with a plant in Britain and a nation state'.[55] Another example, of course, was the bankers, who were just as untouchable, because they too operated across national lines. For Britain this problem was compounded by the worldwide ramifications of her economy, and her relative poverty and weakness. She needed the bankers and multinationals – could not cut herself off from them, without crippling domestic repercussions – and so had to knuckle down to the policies (low taxes, low government spending, wage stability) they insisted on as the price of their help. There may have been alternatives, but they were not very dependable. Wilson claimed that he once called the bankers' bluff, by reminding them of the consequences if Britain refused to meet their terms, and so they allowed her to slide into bankruptcy, precipitating an *international* financial crisis which would be bound to drag them down too;[56] but that was a high risk strategy. The 1967 devaluation can also be seen as a blow for independence against these kinds of external restraints – Wilson talked of 'breaking free' as a result of it;[57] and it certainly had that effect in the short term, enabling Britain to turn down a loan in support of the old level of sterling whose terms even Callaghan felt were 'unacceptable',[58] and emboldening her to renege on her 'east of Suez' agreement with the Americans, to the latter's 'horror and consternation' according to George Brown, who was the one who had to break the news to them.[59] But it did not last. The economy stayed vulnerable to outside pressures: 'always near to the edge of the cliff,' as Roy Jenkins, who took over as Chancellor after devaluation, later recalled; 'with any gust of wind, or sudden stone in the path, or inattention to the steering, liable to send us over'.[60] One of the reasons why Wilson went to the country as early as he did in 1970, a good nine months before he needed to, was that he worried that the period of tranquillity Britain was enjoying then was too good to last, and that a new outbreak of bad weather emanating from the counting houses of the world might ruin things again if he delayed any longer.[61] That may have been craven; but it was also realistic, in view of international capitalism's abiding strength, in the face of the weaker forms of social democracy.

Capitalism's resilience was also reflected in the doubts that began to afflict nearly all Labour Ministers in the 1960s as they struggled with the broad practical effects of it. By the end of the decade the mood in the Cabinet was deeply pessimistic. On 8 May 1969 a *sotto voce* remark by Callaghan, that the only alternatives left to the government were to 'sink or sink', provoked a spirited attack on his 'defeatism' by Barbara Castle;[62] but it was an attitude shared by many of his colleagues. Wilson fell into it periodically: for example once in October 1969, when Crossman felt he had clearly 'lost his nerve', and was 'deeply depressed, trying to hold us for the catastrophe that was coming'.[63] By most other accounts, however, the main offender in this regard was Crossman himself: frequently relapsing into what Benn called his 'socialist-masochist', and Castle his 'Götterdämmerung' mood, prophesying defeat and destruction for Labour, and 'an extreme right-wing period' of government for Britain (and indeed the world) before very long.[64] At the time this seemed right over the top. But Crossman thought he had reason for it. Socialism 'wasn't and never had been popular with the voters'; they did not want to pay for it; they preferred 'the jingle of money in their pockets' – that is, high disposable incomes – to better social provision (this was originally Wilson's idea);[65] and in any case social welfare was incompatible with growth, so that if people wanted that they 'ought to accept Enoch Powell's *laissez-faire* doctrine' rather than what Labour was offering.[66] This was revisionism with a vengeance. It tied in with other trends of the time: persistent worries by Labour that its social base was being eroded by the security and affluence it was in part responsible for, for example; misgivings (like Benn's)[67] about nationalisation; and the new self-confidence that seemed to have come suddenly to the Conservative free marketist right. Labour felt itself to be on the defensive, probably because it really was.

Its 1970 election campaign bore this out. It was unadventurous, low-key, conservative. 'We did nothing,' complained George Brown, 'to show that we had fire in our bellies.'[68] Some of this was simple tactics: Wilson had decided some time before that people were basically 'not interested in politics and want to play tennis and clean their cars and leave things to the Government', and that Labour's best chance, therefore, was to have them vote for it out of apathy.[69] Developments in the enemy camp strengthened this line. In January 1970 the Conservatives came out with their 'Selsdon Park' programme, recommending a violent lurch away from welfare and state intervention and consensus, towards a market-orientated social philosophy that most Labourites assumed had gone out with the workhouse and the white slave trade. Wilson thought this had presented the election to Labour on a plate; that the 'skinheads of Surbiton', as he called the new Tory right, must frighten doubters back into the fold.[70] Most of his colleagues agreed. On the other hand a few also feared for what this approach said about their own morale and convictions. Barbara Castle saw it as a betrayal of socialism.[71] Wedgwood Benn, who took all this free marketist talk deeply seriously, and was especially impressed by a speech on the question Sir Keith Joseph made at around this time, remarked that 'the Tories seemed to be thinking of the seventies whereas the Labour Party looked as if it was just at the end of its period of office and didn't have much to say beyond that'.[72] That was yet another indication of the turning tide.

III

It was turning in another way too. The empire was rapidly disappearing. The Wilson government did not start this process, as we have seen, but it continued it steadily on. Fifteen colonies gained their independence in these years, including Kenya, Malawi, Zambia, Guyana and South Yemen. There was almost no controversy over this. The Conservatives accepted the inevitability of it. Labour positively welcomed it. Wedgwood Benn believed the end of the empire would remove what had been the main incubus on the British economy for nearly a century: ever since Britain had 'opted to become an imperial country instead of continuing as an industrial one'.[73] Get rid of the empire and they could really start modernizing. That seemed a reasonable viewpoint in 1966, when Benn used it as a main theme of speeches all over the country. What he could not foresee was what else would go when the empire went. One of the functions it had used to perform – as we argued earlier – was to bolster the paternalist wing of the Conservative party against its opposite, individualist tendency. In this way it contributed to the consensus of the time. Remove that bolster and there was nothing to stop the party being recaptured by the free marketists. The end of empire meant the resurgence not of modernity, as Labour understood it, but of no-holds-barred capitalism. It was all part of the same trend, with 'Selsdon Man' and the rest.

Of course it was not quite as tidy and straightforward as that implies. For a start Britain's retreat from empire – or from some of the trappings of empire – was a somewhat faltering progress, and contested at certain points. It was hard for many to give up their history. 'The past,' wrote one contemporary commentator, 'haunted this decade as few had ever been haunted before. Sometimes it seemed as though the ghosts would never be laid, the buried splendour never cease to shine out from the unquiet grave.' One prominent right-wing organisation of the time called itself the 'League of Empire Loyalists', even though by that time there was scarcely any empire left for it to be loyal to.[74] A few imperialist Tories – now increasingly coming to be known as 'backwoodsmen', because of their clear lack of modernity – made ritual protests at most of Labour's withdrawals, albeit with less and less conviction as time went on. But it was not only the right which clung on to its old, moth-eaten imperial ermine in this way. Labour, too, appeared to want to dig its heels in every now and then. It was Wilson's strong opinion, for example, stated to the Commons in December 1964, that 'we cannot afford to relinquish our world role'.[75] At that time this meant major troop deployments in Germany, Aden, the Persian Gulf, Malaysia, Singapore and Hong Kong. Fifteen months later Denis Healey, his Defence Secretary, assured an audience of journalists in Canberra that 'We have no intention of ratting on any of our commitments... We do intend to remain in the military sense a world power'.[76] Both would have denied that this was in any way an atavistic policy; Wilson, for example, was at pains to assure people that in his case he was 'moved more by thoughts of a contribution to international peace-keeping than by considerations of imperial splendour'.[77] But the implications were much the same.

One of those implications, of course, was the burden this entailed. Britain's defence expenditure in the middle of the 1960s came to around two and a half billion pounds. That was as much as was spent on the whole national education system, and three times the balance of payments deficit in 1964.[78] Many people felt it was too much, including the Cabinet, which decided early on on the need for drastic cuts. The ultimate target suggested was a round £2 billion.[79] Initially, however, that was to be done without abandoning any of Britain's responsibilities. The troops were simply to be spread more thinly, in what Healey called 'penny packages throughout the world'.[80] Most experts believed that was unrealistic, as it probably was. It also did not work. The £2 billion target was never achieved. Defence was always a drain.

But Britain did have a problem. It was not easy for her to give up her overseas position, just like that. Apart from the *amour propre* factor there were others, even more compelling. Britain was still uniquely dependent on wider-world markets and supplies, for example, for her commercial well-being.[81] This was not to change until after she entered the European Economic Community in 1973. That gave her an economic stake there. She also had a moral one. If she withdrew from certain parts of the world, or at least did so too precipitously, it was believed that anarchy or communist takeovers (or both) would inevitably result. This was a genuine dilemma. It can be seen most clearly in the case of Southern Rhodesia: which declared its independence from Britain ('UDI') in November 1965. In the ordinary course of things Britain would have welcomed this; but could not in this case because the ruling group was a white minority, and she felt a responsibility towards the blacks. That proved costly in commercial terms (with trade sanctions in force against Rhodesia), though not, as it happened here, militarily. (Wilson decided from the beginning that he would not use armed force to bring the Rhodesians to heel.) Elsewhere Britain's moral obligations may have been less clear-cut, but were nonetheless deeply felt. Michael Stewart, who was Wilson's Foreign Secretary for two separate spells, put it picturesquely. 'We were like a juggler who has a dozen plates circling in the air, and knows he cannot keep them going; but to fold his hands and let them crash would be irresponsible.'[82] It was also thought to be irresponsible in terms of Britain's commitments to the United States. The pressure from there was relentless.[83] There was, of course, a certain irony in this, which Denis Healey picked up: that America, 'after trying for thirty years to get Britain out' of these places, should now be 'trying desperately to keep us in.' (His explanation may be too cynical: that during the Vietnam war America 'did not want to be the only country killing coloured people on their own soil'.)[84] The pay-off for Britain, of course, was American support for the pound, as we have seen;[85] technical help with Britain's nuclear deterrent; America's commitment to the defence of western Europe; and the prestige that Wilson certainly felt accrued to Britain from being seen as such a special friend of the biggest boy in the playground. But the cost remained crippling.

In the end it became clear that it could not be sustained. That was what finally persuaded Callaghan, for example, another instinctive east-of-Suez man, to give in: 'I did not like to be brought up sharply against the costly realities of our worldwide role, but when I examined the figures I had to agree.'[86] The decisive moment came during discussions on the post-1967 devaluation public expenditure cuts, when it would have been difficult to argue that defence should remain sacrosanct at the expense of hospitals and schools. Having already cut it to the bone, the Cabinet accepted the logic of this further reduction, and decided to withdraw from all its east of Suez commitments by the end of 1971. The decision was announced on 16 January 1968: to the consternation of the professionals, who named the day 'Black Tuesday',[87] and of the Americans, as we have seen;[88] but to the unalloyed relief of the self-styled Little Englanders in the government, who thought this should have been done years before. Another supporter, incidentally, was Enoch Powell, shadow defence spokesman, who had used to be a terrific imperialist, as we saw,[89] but was now all for Britain getting out of the East: as of course one would expect of one of the new breed of free-market Conservatives, if he was being true to the logic of his faith.[90]

That decision was momentous. It marked an important stage in Britain's long 20th-century process of adjustment to her changing situation in the world. The adjustment was always a little behind the reality, as one would expect, bearing in mind the speed of the changes and the paraphernalia – inherited from previous stages – Britain carried with her, but it was handled with more skill by successive governments than they were sometimes given credit for. That was the negative side of the adjustment: the disengagement. The major problem came when she looked beyond that, to what should take the place of her old world-imperial role. The answer to that was not obvious: despite the insistence of some contemporaries – pro-Europeans, especially – that it was staring her in the face. Sometimes her failure to find the answer was blamed on the survival of old imperial illusions still; especially, again, by pro-Europeans, who tended to dismiss their opponents too easily in this way. In fact it arose from the inherent difficulty of the question, and the unsatisfactory nature, in reality, of all the alternatives.

The underlying difficulty should be a familiar one to the reader of these pages by now. It derived from the wide distribution of Britain's commercial and financial interests in the world, which should not be confused with the imperial responsibilities that had grown up around them over the past 200 years, and which still remained, as vital to her economic well-being as ever, after those responsibilities had been shed. This pattern of trade and investment was peculiar to Britain at this time, distinguishing her from every other country of the world, and in particular from the countries of continental Europe, none of which did a majority of *their* trade, as Britain did, *outside* Europe. The implication of this for Britain's relationship with the European Economic Community was obvious. A Community which was rational for them, in economic terms, was less rational for her; they were combining with their major customers, whereas Britain would be turning her back on hers. This was why Britain's entry to the EEC was always bound to be more difficult, require greater adjustments, than any other member's. It also explains why she sought as long as she could for alternatives.

Unfortunately they were rapidly disappearing at this time. There were three main ones. The first was to 'go it alone' ('GITA'), which most people thought was no longer viable, in age in which only large economic units would soon be able to compete economically with the giants. The second, the Commonwealth, had more or less run out of steam. Once the imperial factor was taken away it looked a rather arbitrary structure, without any real logic to it, apart from the historical accident that had brought it together in the first place. There were enormous disagreements within it: between India and Pakistan, for example, who actually went to war with one another in 1965; between Britain and the black African members over Wilson's attempts to settle with the white supremacists of Rhodesia in 1966 and 1968, though Wilson claimed he was only trying to wrong-foot the whites; and between the British government and liberals everywhere over restrictions the former placed on the immigration of Asians expelled from Kenya, even though they were technically British citizens, in February 1968. That went right against the old Commonwealth spirit. But one cannot build an economic federation out of 'spirit' in any case.

That left only the American connexion, which seemed to have a little more juice in it, but not much. Relations between Britain and the United States seemed close at this time. Harold Wilson thought this was because there was something special in the personal rapport he had with both the presidents of the period, Johnson and Nixon, whom he used to return home from visits to brimming over with an almost child-like delight at the way they got on. (In December 1965, for example, he told how had been asked to light the Presidental Christmas tree: 'the first time a PM has been asked to do this... since 1942'; in July 1966 Johnson compared him to Churchill at a White House dinner, which went down well; and in February 1970 he was particularly chuffed when Nixon took him along to a meeting of his holy-of-holies National Security Council.)[91] Sadly this did not fool his Cabinet, most of whom felt, as Benn put it in June 1967, that the Americans were simply laying on 'the trumpets appropriate for a weak head of state who has to be buttered up so that he can carry the can for American foreign policy'.[92] Others too felt that Britain's relationship with the USA was more demeaning than anything else; especially those hundreds of thousands of natural Labour supporters who as the 1960s wore on became deeply disillusioned with Wilson's abject support, as they saw it, for America's war in Vietnam. One of his reasons for that support, *he* claimed, was that it would enable him to broker a peace between the two sides: a task he invested a great deal of time, energy and optimism in. If he could have succeeded in that, it would obviously have vindicated his whole Vietnam line in retrospect; but he did not, and so he was left with only the obloquy. In the end this whole experience, together with all that business over America's support for sterling and the conditions she attached to it, only showed how impotent Britain was in these matters, and how dangerously unequal, therefore, any more formal relationship between the two countries – like a North Atlantic Free Trade Association (NAFTA) which was floated at one time – would be.

That left Europe as the only realistic option left: not a particularly desirable one, from Britain's point of view, and certainly not the 'golden opportunity' which was sometimes held out to her by the most zealous Europhiles; but simply the least bad choice. It was difficult to be enthusiastic about joining, but it had to be done. Wilson seems to have come to this conclusion some time in 1966, when he set about testing the water, with a series of visits to EEC capitals; and then got Cabinet approval (in May 1967) for a serious application. His line was – as it had to be, in view of Britain's genuine difficulties, and the divisions in his own Cabinet over the issue, which mirrored them – that he would only join 'if the conditions are right'.[93] The EEC had to make *some* allowances for Britain's radically different economic situation: safeguards for New Zealand imports; for example, and a modification of the EEC's current agricultural system, which was heavily weighted against Britain. In the end, however, it was not these demands that stymied Wilson's efforts, but de Gaulle's intransigence, rooted – as ever – in what George Brown called 'the American thing'.[94] Britain, thought the General, was still too tied to the United States' apron strings. Wilson tried to convince him that this was only because Europe was excluding her.[95] But it was pointless. While de Gaulle was there Britain had no hope of entry. In April 1969 he fell, and the path immediately became smoother. By that time, however, it was much too late for Labour to profit from it, and be given a reasonable chance of taking Britain into the EEC on terms that reflected her underlying interests, arising from her divergent historical development, as well as those of the original Six. That was one aspect of her 'modernisation' that would have to wait.

Part V
The Grain of Human Nature

Chapter 25

The Heath Government
(1970–74)

I

On the evening of Wednesday, 3 January 1973 Queen Elizabeth II, splendid in long dress, jewels and tiara, was greeted at the main doors of the Royal Opera House, Covent Garden, by her First Minister, Edward Heath. She was there to attend the opening concert in a series of events arranged to mark Britain's entry, at last, into the European Economic Community a few days before. It was an odd occasion, symbolic in many ways, not all of which had been intended by the organisers. As a demonstration of European unity, for example, or even congruence, it was not a great success. The programme consisted of a rag-bag of music and readings, few of which had a genuine European theme. The nearest to that was probably Leporello's catalogue aria from Mozart's *Don Giovanni* (sung by Geraint Evans), which lists the Don's sexual conquests in the various countries of what was later to become the EEC. Even that omitted Britain, where Giovanni's particular brand of Europeanism seems to have stopped short. Most of the recitations featured British writers or characters in fiction disparaging other European countries, or vice versa: Voltaire hating Greenwich, for example; Dr Johnson debunking Paris; or Dickens's Podsnap (impersonated by Laurence Olivier) boasting how much better it was to be English than anything else. That could have been taken as an omen. There were some other problems. Everyone who was anyone was invited, but some pointedly refused to attend, including the Leader of her Majesty's Opposition, Harold Wilson; and those who did were greeted with boos and even a few stink-bombs from a group of demonstrators as they arrived.[1] As a 'Fanfare for Europe' – which was the name given to the whole run of festivities – it was a disappointment; certainly unconvincing as any kind of national celebration, because of all the discordant notes.

This was scarcely surprising. EEC entry was the greatest – some would say the only – achievement of Edward Heath's government. But it was also a blemished one. It was highly controversial, with a majority of the British population opposing it most of the time,[2] and opinion divided finely in the Commons, leading government whips to resort (allegedly) to all kinds of dubious methods to force the enabling legislation through. 'I'm told,' claimed the leading Conservative dissident, Enoch Powell, afterwards, 'that those who went into Ted Heath's room in the week before the second reading came out looking more like ghosts than men.'[3] What made that even more difficult for some to stomach was Heath's earlier assurance that Britain would not go into the EEC without 'the full-hearted consent' of her 'Parliament and people', which this blatantly fell short of; though there were one or two who could be found to argue otherwise. ('Read in context,' Douglas Hurd, Heath's Political Secretary, wrote afterwards, 'the sentence clearly implies that the decision on entry would be taken by Parliament,... *conscious* of public opinion'; which was an eccentric interpretation of what to most other folk seemed a very plain form of words.)[4] Partly because of this, many anti-Marketeers refused to accept that the matter had been settled finally, and began agitating for a referendum on the issue, which was finally adopted as Labour party policy in October 1973. That made Britain's new place in Europe provisional, at best, and the fanfares possibly a little premature.

It was also arguable that the event was not worth celebrating in any case. There were all kinds of cultural reasons for welcoming it: this return, as it appeared to some enthusiasts, to the mainstream of the civilization that had nurtured Britain originally; but that was a sentimental way of looking at it. In hard material terms it was difficult to see many advantages. Opinions varied over its impact on ordinary people. Heath claimed that it would bring 'a great improvement' in their living standards;[5] but that was likely to be a long-term benefit, at most. In 1973 it was easier to see the drawbacks: an immense net contribution to the Community budget, for example; serious disruption of trade; increased competition; dearer food; and more bureaucracy. These were some of the immediate effects. Beyond them there were further dangers. The EEC was a train travelling in a certain direction: towards complete monetary union for one thing, and a federal political structure for another; both of which were its declared aims at the time when Britain boarded it. That had clear implications for every member's national sovereignty; which it was possible and indeed quite reasonable to welcome, of course, but not if – for example – you were a socialist, or a *laissez-faire* capitalist, who preferred other solutions than Community ones to the problems that beset the British part of the European economy. (For example, you could not devalue.) That was worth thinking about.

On the other side it may have been necessary. That is probably the best that can be said for it. Britain could not carry on as she was. The future lay with the large economies: superpowers like the USA and the USSR, or regional groupings of smaller ones, nurturing enterprises which could compete globally. It was a shame, and would have been a disappointment to the free-trade economists of the nineteenth century, who had looked forward to the day when the whole world was a single market, with no need for empires or federations or even effective nationalities at all;[6] but there it was. It was a requirement of the stage of development international capitalism had reached at that time. Britain, bereft of her empire, and no longer dominating the trade of the wider world as she had used to, needed to become part of something bigger to hold her own. Europe was the only viable possibility. It was a particularly uncomfortable one for Britain, as we have seen, with her entirely different commercial orientation from the rest of Europe (two-thirds of her exports still went outside the EEC in 1973, and a half beyond Europe more generally);[7] but the alternatives by now scarcely bore scrutiny. The Commonwealth was too scattered and disparate, the alliance with the United States too one-sided and degrading. Heath had none of his predecessors' regard for either in any case. He was always getting into trouble for his intolerance of what he regarded as the 'humbug' spouted by black African Commonwealth leaders, for example, especially over the sale of arms to South Africa;[8] and snapped the 'special relationship' with America – if that was possible, of a phenomenon that was so nebulous – almost the moment he entered office.[9] That left only Europe; which, if it had to be joined, had probably better be joined straight away.

That was Heath's unequivocal aim, as the existing members of the Community knew full well; which *may* have enabled them to settle on better terms for them, and worse ones for Britain, than if Britain's negotiators had been less obviously keen to get in. That was what the Labour opposition claimed, for example: that it could have negotiated better arrangements than the Conservatives did; though in its case there was more than a whiff of political expediency about this argument, in view of the deep divisions that rent the party over the very principle of entry at this time. Niggles over the 'terms' could paper those over for the time being. In fact the terms *were* bad, with the only substantial concessions being won on the *transitional* arrangement for Britain's entry; but that may have been inevitable in any case. One of the disadvantages of coming so late into the Community was that its rules had already been fixed to suit the existing members, and could not be fundamentally altered at that stage; especially the notorious Common Agricultural Policy (CAP), which hugely favoured the Six's (and especially France's) large agricultural sectors over Britain's small and more efficient one. When a new Labour government 'renegotiated' the terms in 1974-75 it could make no impact at all on that, and indeed managed to extract little more from its partners overall than Heath had done. That suggests that the high price Britain paid for entry was unavoidable.

All this was highly controversial, but only within a certain narrow band. This is worth emphasizing. It is another reason why the 'Fanfare for Europe' was so incongruous. Edward Heath believed that the Common Market was a vital issue for Britain; as did Enoch Powell and Peter Shore, who were the leading *anti*-Marketeers on the Conservative and Labour sides. But most people were bored by it. This, fundamentally, was why the legislation to make Britain a member of the EEC got through. The nation was apathetic. 'When it could have spoken,' wrote Powell shortly afterwards, it had 'stayed dumb; when it could have acted, it... remained idle.'[10] That was because Europe did not seem to have any very tangible implications for the way people lived in Britain – though this was a superficial view – by comparison with other much more immediate concerns.

II

There were a number of these in the early 1970s, though it is possible to see a common problem at the root of all of them. Which of them was most distracting depended on who you were, and where you lived. In Northern Ireland the problem was bloody political violence, which reached a ghastly crescendo during Heath's time in office, and particularly in the wake of 'Bloody Sunday' (30 January 1972), when 13 civil rights demonstrators were shot dead by an over-reactive soldiery in the mainly Catholic city of Derry. Three weeks later that was followed by the start of hostilities by the Provisional IRA on the British mainland, with the killing of five cleaning women, a gardener and a Roman Catholic padré by a bomb placed in the British Army barracks at Aldershot. Others suffered in different ways. Unemployment, for example, reached the million mark in January 1972, which was depressing for the unemployed, of course, but also worrying for those who feared that it might goad them to violence as well. Inflation was another problem, especially for those who did not have the bargaining power to keep their incomes floating above the rate of it, which by the end of Heath's term was approaching the unprecedented level of 25% annually.[11] That was also thought to threaten the social fabric. Then there were the strikes of the early 1970s, easily the worst and most disruptive since 1926, particularly those affecting the power industries: such as the great national coal strike which began in January 1972 (a bad month all round, this), bringing pitched battles in some places, such as the Saltley Coke Depot near Birmingham, where a brilliant new tactic – the 'flying picket' – gave 15,000 massed miners and their supporters a famous victory over their enemy (variously seen as their employers, or the state) in February. Ordinary people were affected by these events when their lights went out as a result of fuel shortages at the power stations, which happened more than once during this period. Some of those ordinary people were also affected – or felt they were – by another phenomenon of the time: black immigration, which had been causing unrest since the early 1960s, and is generally reckoned to have been a decisive factor in the Conservatives' election victory of 1970.[12] (Labour was seen as 'softer' on race.) These were the issues that people felt most strongly about.

Occasionally their feelings turned to physical violence against government ministers. Robert Carr, the Employment Secretary, for example, had his home bombed by a group called the 'Angry Brigade' in January 1971. A year later Edward Heath was threatened by the clenched fist of Dennis Skinner, the miners' MP for Bolsover, in the House of Commons, which must have been almost as alarming. On 30 January 1972 Home Secretary Reginald Maudling, a large man, was the target of a furious assault by the diminutive MP for Mid-Ulster, Bernadette Devlin, over Bloody Sunday. No one got quite so worked up as this about the EEC. Heath had a bottle of ink thrown at him as he was on his way to sign the Treaty of Accession in Brussels in January 1972 (that month again); but by a German woman, who was objecting not to the Common Market at all, but to plans for the redevelopment of Covent Garden. That was quite low on the list of popular grievances in Britain; but all these incidents seemed symptomatic of a new atmosphere of violence at this time.

This was an enormous worry to some. The Saltley episode was probably crucial here, especially in view of the interpretation which the flying pickets' leader, Arthur Scargill, placed upon it afterwards. 'Here was living proof,' he told journalists exultantly, 'that the working class had only to flex its muscles and it could bring governments, employers, society to a complete standstill.'[13] Encouraging as this was to him, it sent a tremor through the clubs, common rooms and messes of the contemporary 'Establishment'. A chasm opened beneath them. 'The lights all went out,' remembered Brendan Sewell, a Treasury adviser, afterwards, 'and everybody said that the country would disintegrate in a week. All the civil servants rushed around saying, Perhaps we ought to activate the nuclear underground shelters... because there'll be no electricity and there'll be riots in the streets.'[14] Two years later, in the middle of another miners' strike, Sir William Armstrong, head of the home civil service and Heath's closest adviser, became quite overcome by the prospect, muttering darkly of communists everywhere – 'They might even be infiltrating, he said, the room he was in' – and seeming 'really quite mad at the end... lying on the floor and talking about moving the Red Army from here and the Blue Army from there', before he was gently removed to Lord Rothschild's villa in Barbados for a well-earned rest.[15] His was an extreme case, but not an uncharacteristic one.

In fact things were probably never anything like as bad as Armstrong feared. He and his kind had very little contact with ordinary people, and consequently could not know how stable and unrevolutionary the vast majority of them were. Either that, or he overestimated the capacity of the small revolutionary minorities which did exist in Britain to subvert them regardless. (This was a common miscalculation on the political right at this time.) Nevertheless he was right to be worried in a general sort of way. Something was fairly seriously wrong. Economics was at the bottom of it. The system that had been running for a quarter of a century now – a mixed economy with social responsibilities – seemed to be badly faltering. Full employment – one of those social responsibilities – had already slipped. Rising individual living standards, which were another post-war expectation, were under threat. Welfare provisions were becoming more and more of a burden to a national economy which was no longer furnishing a sufficient surplus to pay for some of them. All this was creating a novel situation. For the first time in ages, significant numbers of people were experiencing economic decline. The decline was not new, of course, at least in relative terms; but the experience of it was. Men and women *saw* their situations deteriorating. To counter this they demanded higher money incomes to keep them ahead, and struck in support of them if they had the muscle to. One result of that – according to most contemporary pundits – was to fuel the price inflation which pushed those who did not have the muscle further behind. This clearly accounted for the industrial tensions; and may also have contributed in a minor way to some of the other troubles of the time: resentments against black competitors for jobs and houses, for example; and even the horrors of Northern Ireland, which also happened to be the region of the United Kingdom with the highest percentage of unemployed.[16]

III

The Conservative government's response to these problems looked at one time as though it might be radically different from its predecessors', but turned out not to be. Edward Heath in the period surrounding the 1970 election made much of the fundamental changes he intended to bring about: 'a revolution so quiet, and yet so total', he told his party conference in October, 'that it will go far beyond the programme for a Parliament'; which was widely taken to mean something along the lines of the Selsdon Park manifesto of earlier that year.[17] 'Change will give us freedom...,' he went on; 'Free from intervention, free from interference... Free to make your own decisions, but responsible also for your mistakes.'[18] What else could that be but a coded reference to the agenda of the new Conservative right: rolling back the state, cutting down on welfare, encouraging self-reliance and enterprise? But that was misleading. It was probably not deliberately so.

Heath made a great play in the 1970 election of the need for 'honesty' in politics, in order to distance himself from the more devious Harold Wilson, whom he despised.[19] *Pretending* he was Selsdon Man in order to buy right-wing votes would have been far too Wilsonian. The mistake was the right-wingers'. They had simply got him wrong. Heath was never one of them. A truer guide to his thinking was his statement on the steps of 10 Downing Street before he entered it on 19 June 1970: 'Our purpose is not to divide but to unite, and, where there are differences, to bring reconciliation';[20] which sounds platitudinous, and in other mouths might have been hypocritical, but in Heath's case was probably quite genuine.

His main approach to the crisis that seemed to be engulfing Britain in the early 1970s was to seek to repair the old system, rather than to destroy and replace it, as the Selsdonites advised. Originally he thought that this could be done in a *laissez-faire* way in some areas, which explains all the rhetoric about 'freedom', and the hopes the right wingers continued to repose in him for several months into his government. In fact he was never as dogmatic about these things as they were. Industry, he felt, needed to be liberated – released from government supervision, encouraged to be profitable, stimulated by initiatives, allowed to follow the call of the markets rather than the dictats of Whitehall – but with a broader aim in view. That aim was social. Only a prosperous economy could afford the social provision he – in common with all his predecessors over the past 25 years – believed was necessary for a civilized national existence. Hence the enormous increases in social expenditure that were sanctioned during his administration (amounting to 4.3% of GNP); especially – it has been pointed out many times – by two of his ministers, Sir Keith Joseph at Social Security and Margaret Thatcher at Education, who were to become the most zealous of Selsdonites later on.[21] The Cabinet was united on this. All of them, recalled Agriculture Minister Jim Prior later, 'were strongly committed to the post-war economic consensus in which the basic goal of economic policy was full employment' within 'an improved Welfare State'.[22] There was no break here. The only difference was that Heath believed initially that this could best be afforded by removing the shackles from industry. Later on he changed his mind on that.

In fact he changed his mind on a lot of things. This was a source of great embarrassment to him later, especially in view of another great play he had made during the 1970 election campaign: which was that a government under him would not indulge in the 'endless backing and filling' that had characterised the Wilson years, but would have the 'courage', as he put it, to 'stick to' policy decisions once they were made.[23] There can be no doubt that this was what he intended. Unfortunately for him it proved difficult to live up to. Heath's government backtracked on at least as many decisions as its predecessors had, and on many of the same issues: sterling, industrial strategy, trade-union reform, prices and incomes policy. (Whether this led Heath to come to regard Wilson's alleged 'deviousness' in a more charitable light is not known.)

The reason behind these 'U-turns', as they came to be called, was that persisting in the policies which ministers had originally determined on was found to undermine consensus, and so endanger the social fabric. A clear example was the government's Industrial Relations Act, which came into operation in August 1971, and was intended to be consensual, in the sense of guaranteeing and strengthening trade union rights as well as modifying the right to strike in certain circumstances, but was abandoned (or, rather, 'put on ice') when massive union opposition defeated its ultimate object, which was to create industrial harmony. Another policy decision, to resist legislation on incomes (written unequivocally into the 1970 Manifesto: 'We utterly reject the philosophy of compulsory wage control'),[24] was abandoned when Heath's preferred alternative, *voluntary* restraint, failed at the end of 1972. The purpose of that U-turn, as he put it himself, was to protect 'the interests of the community as a whole'.[25] Similar motives impelled the government to abandon its non-intervention policy for industry with almost indecent haste, just a few days after its Trade Secretary, John Davies, had delighted the right with some ringing words in Parliament about the folly of rescuing 'lame duck' businesses with public money: when Rolls-Royce was bailed out with a grant of £42 millions. One consideration there was patriotism: 'We just couldn't imagine Rolls-Royce going – the name had prestige, like the BBC', as one junior minister put it later.[26] More telling in the next significant rescue, of Upper Clyde Shipbuilders in February 1972, seems to have been a report from the Glasgow Chief Constable that he could not guarantee to be able to control the civil strife that he thought would erupt there if the yard was closed down. 'Of all the places where death was in the air it was Glasgow', recalled a Cabinet minister somewhat apocalyptically later. So UCS was propped up too; against the best economic advice of the time, which was that it would soon be pointless trying to compete in shipbuilding with the low-wage economies.[27] This was one of those situations in which social considerations were thought to have precedence over accountancy.

But it went deeper than this. Part of Heath's problem was that he did not trust British industry to deliver the goods even where the accountants said they should. This was another thing that distanced him from the Selsdonites. They claimed that the economy would recover when the right – 'free' – conditions were restored. Heath reckoned he had restored those conditions, and it had not worked. The main problem was industrial investment, which was far lower in Britain than in any other major industrial country. In the summer of 1973 he visited the Institute of Directors, and berated them for this.

> When we came in, we were told there weren't sufficient incentives to invest. So we provided the inducements. Then we were told that people were scared of balance of payments difficulties leading to stop–go. So we floated the pound. Then we were told of fears on inflation; and now we're dealing with that. And still you aren't investing enough.[28]

Heath's exasperation with the business community was another characteristic he shared with Harold Wilson. (Industrialists used to remark on how he often sounded 'more like a Labour politician than a Tory'.)[29] In his view, it had let him down.

Whether this was entirely fair is questionable. British industry was certainly inefficient, poorly led (with some exceptions) and undercapitalised at this time. That however was the result of an ethos and a system that had consistently favoured the financial sector of the economy over manufacturing for years. The latter was bound to find it difficult attracting investment, therefore, when there were so many more profitable opportunities around. Serious as this situation already was in 1970, the new government made it worse by allowing the Bank of England to 'liberalise' its credit regulations in the following year, giving rise to an extraordinary speculative boom in the non-productive sector, especially property and secondary banking, again to the detriment of manufacturing. (It also stimulated inflation, incidentally, by boosting 'M3', which was the measure of the money supply that included credit.) To blame industry and the banks for this was slightly wide of the mark. For them the decision to invest in other areas was a rational one. Looked at dispassionately, the real villain of the piece was the pull of the free market, whose cold, impersonal logic at that stage of Britain's development seemed to be decreeing that she no longer needed a significant industrial base.

One obvious implication to be drawn from that was that if the government nonetheless wanted a significant industrial base, it would need to intervene *against* the force of the market in certain ways. That, of course, had long been the Labour party's line. By 1972 the Conservative government seemed to have come round to it. In the spring of that year it unveiled what it called its 'Industry Bill', designed to encourage industrial development in positive ways, partly through an 'Industrial Development Executive' which, though purporting to be new, bore an uncanny resemblance to the previous government's Industrial Reorganisation Corporation,[30] whose abolition had been one of the Heath government's first acts in its quasi-Selsdon phase. According to one Treasury official later, 'when... the wraps came off it was a very great shock to some of the other members of the government', especially 'those who were most committed to the market economy philosophy'.[31] When Wedgwood Benn hailed it as 'spadework for socialism' in the House of Commons in May 1972, they must have been even more discomfited.[32]

That was just the start. In the spring of 1973 the government set off on what was called its 'dash for growth' (or sometimes the 'Barber boom', although Anthony Barber, the Chancellor, was not so responsible for it as Heath was):[33] a programme of massive state spending on roads, housing, welfare and a host of other projects in order to galvanise the economy. By this time Heath appears to have been desperate, both to get Britain into some kind of shape to face the European competition that was coming,[34] and to do something about unemployment, which he shared all his post-war Conservative predecessors' horror of, both on moral grounds and because it was supposed to lose Conservatives elections.[35] 'Every government,' he told the Institute of Directors in June, 'has to go for full employment – no government could exist on any other terms.'[36] Benn must have been bemused by that too; spending for growth was what the Labour left had been urging on Wilson and Callaghan for nearly six years, only to be told then that it would be irresponsible. Eventually Heath's government came to that conclusion too, and slammed the brakes on at the end of the year; but only after a series of what it regarded as unlucky accidents. The worst of these was the aftermath of the Arab-Israeli war of October 1973, which quadrupled the price of oil coming into Britain, thus adding to her trade deficit, increasing production costs, and giving the coal miners – with whom the government was in dispute again during the winter of 1973–74 – a strong argument in favour of their demands: 'Why can't you pay us for coal what you are willing to pay the Arabs for oil?'[37] All this fuelled inflation, which was the great danger of the 'growth' strategy in any case; and so the 'dash' was brought to an end, *possibly* just before it had a chance to prove itself.[38] That at any rate was the government's excuse.

It was not however a universal way of looking at it. Some economists thought that the Barber 'boom' was bound to 'bust' whatever the circumstances.[39] The oil crisis had simply hastened the day. Others were unhappy about the government's strategy more generally. They even apparently included one or two ministers, although because they did not speak out it is difficult to know. (Sir Keith Joseph blamed his departmental work: 'I failed to lift up my eyes.')[40] On the Conservative backbenches there were certainly some doubters: free-market theorists who winced at every state intervention, like Enoch Powell, who once asked Heath whether he had 'taken leave of his senses' in trying to impose a statutory wages freeze;[41] and less ideological Tories who simply objected to the government's 'giving in' all the time. That was understandable. By the end of 1973 the list of people the government had given in to did seem rather long. At the top came trade unionists, welfare scroungers and French farmers (over the EEC). Then there were the 28 000 Ugandan Asians the Home Secretary let into Britain after President Idi Amin had expelled them from their country in 1972. For some Conservatives the most abject surrender was to the republicans in Northern Ireland, where William Whitelaw, the Secretary of State (a new post), even agreed to meet the IRA face-to-face on one occasion,[42] and ended by forcing the Unionist majority into a 'power-sharing executive' with the Catholics, after 50 years of lording it over the province on their own. It was all concession; very little standing firm.

This may have been one of the factors behind Heath's determination *not* to give in on one last occasion: the miners' dispute of 1973–74. Unfortunately for him that turned out to be his downfall. The problem here was that the miners did have a good case, even in 'market' terms, with coal at a premium and thousands of miners leaving the industry because of the pay; the government's own Pay Board looked like recommending a high settlement; and the TUC had offered to dissuade its members from citing that as a precedent. Whitelaw, who was called in at the last moment to try his conciliatory skills on the miners, wanted to go along with this. On this occasion, however, his advice was disregarded. When the government not merely resisted, but also decided to call an election on the issue, a year and a half before its full term was up, many people failed to see the point of it. 'It will be an election,' wrote one, 'to decide which party is to sell out to the miners.'[43] In an effort to emphasize the seriousness of the occasion ministers gave out energy-saving advice to people: to clean their teeth in the dark, for example (though that particular tip, by Patrick Jenkin, rather fell flat when a picture of his home with every light blazing was published in the press);[44] and – on 13 December 1973 – put all factories on to a three-day week. No one blamed the miners for that, as they were supposed to; and in fact many quite welcomed the time off, especially when it was discovered that it made scarcely any difference to the level of production.[45] Conservative activists in the constituencies loved all this: 'large sections of the Tory Party', wrote Prior later, were never so happy as when they felt they were bashing the unions';[46] but for others the tactic fell flat.

Some ministers tried to broaden the issues. Anthony Barber claimed that the choice before the electorate was between his government on the one hand, and 'chaos, anarchy and a totalitarian or Communist régime' on the other; which was certainly broader, but seemed far-fetched.[47] (For one thing the miners were behaving themselves this time, with only peaceful picketing, and their extremists kept well muzzled.) Heath tried 'firmness with fairness' as a slogan, but found his Conservative audiences only cheering the 'firm' bits – a proposal to take social benefits away from strikers' families, for example – and lukewarm towards the rest.[48] In any case 'fairness' was generally seen as Labour's territory. Hurd claimed afterwards that what Heath was *really* fighting the election on was not the miners' strike at all, but the oil crisis, and the implications this was bound to have for government policy over the next few years;[49] but if that was so it was too subtle a message to sound above the clamour from the pits. Hence the government's defeat in the election when it came, on 28 February: unexpectedly and narrowly (it actually polled more popular votes than Labour), but decisively nonetheless.

That was a shock and a disappointment to most Conservatives, though not to them all. Enoch Powell for example – who considered the election to be 'fraudulent', refused to stand in it, and advised his supporters to vote Labour (because Labour might take Britain out of the EEC) – described afterwards how he celebrated the result by singing the *Te Deum* in his bath.[50] Others on the right may have had similar feelings, or at least mixed ones, because of their frustration too over Heath's 'betrayal' of so many of the hopes they had reposed in him at the beginning. This defeat at least gave them the chance to make a fresh start, with a new leader, and a return to the principles of Selsdon Park.

At this time, however, this seemed a tall order. The forces arrayed against the dissidents looked formidable. There was still, for example, the potential 'muscle' of Arthur Scargill's working class, flexed so menacingly and effectively two years before at Saltley, and clearly still a force to be reckoned with if a Conservative government was minded to cross it again. For those of a conspiratorial cast of mind there was something even worse to fear: the threat of covert communist subversion in Britain, which some influential people (including apparently Lord Rothschild, who ran Heath's 'Think Tank') believed had already made deep inroads into the trade unions and the Labour party.[51] That would need special vigilance and clever handling, which – as we shall see later – it by and large got.[52] Lastly – and probably more significantly – there was another obstacle: a kind of natural law of British politics, by which parties seemed to converge to the centre as they stayed in office. That was the conclusion, for example, of the authors of the main academic study of the February 1974 general election, who deduced from the experience of the previous decade that 'whatever a party may say in opposition', once in government 'the facts of life and the conventional wisdom of the public service lead it to tackle the problems of inflation and national growth in very similar ways'. Heath's three and a half years in office certainly seemed to bear that out. (If so, of course, it let him off the hook for his U-turns.) The real masters of events were not parliaments, or governments, or prime ministers, but what one 'Whitehall mandarin' called 'ongoing reality'.[53] That exerted far more power than Scargill and the communist moles in the Labour party ever could; which was reassuring in one way, but not in another: if the policies you wished to implement were not convergent, for example, and consequently flew in the face of this all-powerful 'reality'. That was how things looked on 4 March 1974, when – after a short interregnum, because of the uncertainty of the political situation after the election, with no party having an overall majority – Harold Wilson returned to No. 10. If the 'convergence' theory was right, few people should notice much difference.

Chapter 26

The Collapse of Consensus (1974–79)

I

One difference Labour certainly hoped for when it came to power again in 1974 was that consensus ('convergence') could be made to *work*. Barbara Castle felt there was a chance of this. 'I don't think it is euphoria,' she wrote in her diary on 6 March, '...but I have a hunch things are going to be very different this time. We *could* turn out to be the most successful Labour government in history.'[1] They had a number of things in their favour: like their experience, which Wilson pointed out was greater than any other incoming government's that century;[2] and their sheer ability. Most of them were a good deal wiser now than they had been the first time round, from the lessons both of Heath's debacle, and of their own failures in 1964–70. Wilson had clearly learned a lot in the intervening years about his own style of leadership, which was quite transformed. This time, he told his Senior Policy Adviser Bernard Donoughue, there was to be none of that 'presidential nonsense', no hogging the limelight, no playing in every position on the field; instead he was content to adopt a lower profile, delegating more to his Ministers, and taking the 'deep-lying centre-half' role.[3] He was also, remembered Denis Healey afterwards, 'no longer plagued by the demons of jealousy and suspicion which had tormented him in his first two governments',[4] which was more relaxing for everyone. These were some superficial grounds for confidence.

A more substantial one was thought to be Labour's close relationship with the trade-union movement, which gave it the particular strength that Heath had so disastrously lacked. He had tried to impose pay restraint on the unions. Labour had a better way. It could *persuade* them. If Labour ministers told them that low settlements were necessary for the economic health of the nation, they were more likely to take it from them than from the allies of the capitalists. Labour could also ensure that their sacrifice was compensated for in other ways. Hence the 'Social Contract', so-called; an arrangement – dreamt up during the election – whereby the Government agreed to consult the unions over social priorities, in return for their acknowledgement (as Callaghan put it) 'that they had a wider loyalty to the community and were not simply seeking to increase their members' wages irrespective of the consequences'.[5] 'If there is an answer to this country's problems,' Barbara Castle wrote in January 1975, 'it lies in this inchoate union between our Government and the unions.'[6] That would really be consensus in action, if it worked.

For a time it looked as though it might. Trade-union leaders seemed anxious to make a success of it. Wilson had cleverly given them Michael Foot, a left-winger whom they trusted, as Employment Secretary to act as go-between. Some of his civil servants complained that he was too soft on them – 'his only policy', claimed one of them, 'is to find out what the unions want'[7] – but he managed to broker some remarkable agreements nonetheless. These hardened the Contract up, made it less 'inchoate'. Both sides delivered, to an extent. The unions got the hated Industrial Relations Act repealed, a clutch of new employment-protection Acts passed, an increase in what was called the 'social wage' (state benefits and so on), tax cuts at the bottom end of the scale, and some input into the machinery for wage restraint to make sure it was 'fair'. One way to make it fair was to protect the lowest paid. That was done by setting a flat-rate limit for pay increases rather than a percentage one. In July 1975 the rate was £6 per week, which everyone under a ceiling of £170 could claim: those for whom it made the difference between starving and surviving, and those who would scarcely notice it. That was entirely voluntary, so far as the workers were concerned, though some steel was put into it by the threat of sanctions against employers who *conceded* more than the £6. That side-stepped the risk – highlighted in Heath's time – of taking unions to court, but not very effectively. The success of the policy really depended on the latter's goodwill. By and large that was forthcoming. Average pay settlements fell steadily between mid-1975 and mid-1976. Over the next 18 months, following a second agreement with the unions in May 1976 – this time for a £4 or 5% limit – they fell again, to less than 5% on average. Price inflation also plummeted, from a peak of 26.9% in August 1975 to 8% in the summer of 1978.[8] It was natural to assume that the two trends were connected. Inflation had been tamed by pay restraint. This was exactly what Heath had sought but failed to achieve in 1974. That was because he had tried to bully the unions into it, instead of proceeding, like Wilson (and later Callaghan), by 'leadership, agreement and consensus'.[9]

That was how things looked in the summer of 1978. Up till then there could be little doubt that the Labour government – relative to most other governments of the post-war era – was a success. Not only was inflation down, but other indices were also encouraging. Production was growing, exports were increasing, the balance of payments was in credit, and sterling – so often in the past Labour's tender spot – looked safer than for years. There was more to look forward to; especially with North Sea oil just beginning to flow significantly now, providing more than half Britain's domestic needs in 1978, for example, for the first time.[10] That neutralised the effect of the Middle Eastern oil hike of 1973. This seemed a moderately pleasing position, at the very least, especially in view of what the government had had to go through to get there. For a start it had inherited a horrendous situation from the Heath years: rising inflation and unemployment, a record balance of payments deficit, the pound under daily threat; all in all probably the worst economic mess any new British government has ever faced since the war,[11] although as Wilson himself pointed out, with some justice, Labour was getting used to this sort of thing – coming in after the Conservatives had come to grief in a reckless expansionary dash – by now.[12] Then it had been afflicted by its old enemies the speculators again, behaving like 'a screaming crowd of schoolgirls at a rock concert', as Callaghan put it,[13] in a series of raids on sterling early on which was only finally repulsed by a massive ($3.9 billion) credit from the International Monetary Fund in January 1977, in return for public-expenditure cuts, which stabilised things. That was perhaps the government's lowest point on the economic front before the winter of 1978–79: Chancellor Denis Healey, for example, described the four months of this particular sterling crisis as 'the worst of my life';[14] though later it was found that, due to a rather large error (£2 billion) in the Treasury's estimate of the following year's public sector borrowing requirement, the loan – and hence the conditions – may have been unnecessary after all. (Healey wondered whether the Treasury was not doing it on purpose, to force him into cuts he might otherwise not make.)[15] To come out of this gloomy, menacing valley into the sunny uplands of the summer of 1978 must have been exhilarating. Alas, the sunshine was not to last.

In fact the clouds were never far away. The most visible and threatening one was unemployment. That seemed to be scarcely affected at all by the recovery, averaging about 1.4 million throughout 1978,[16] which at that time was considered intolerably high. Other problems were only slightly less apparent. The government's pay policy, successful as it was in the short term, was known to be gestating 'anomolies' which would stir up trouble later on. The main one was the narrowing of 'differentials' between the rewards given for different kinds of work and skills, which a flat-rate-increase limit was bound to produce. Well-paid workers liked to keep a distance between

themselves and the unskilled. *Very* well-paid workers – higher civil servants, for example – were even keener on this, and, because they were closer
to the fonts of largesse that were available, managed by and large to insu-
late themselves from the effects of the government's constraints.[17] 'Top
people', for example, were given a special rise of up to 100% (in two
stages) in June 1978, partly apparently because of worries about a shortage
of *judges* at the current rate of remuneration for them.[18] That can have done
little for the continuing self-restraint of those beneath them. There were
other breaches too. One was a rise of 17% granted to the power workers in
March 1978, which was a compromise on the 30% they had originally
demanded, but was still too high. These were exceptional cases, not really
seriously threatening the general success of the policy at that time; but they
augured worse. In the autumn of 1977 TUC leaders warned the prime minister that they might not be able to hold the line very much longer. 'This
was a blow', commented Callaghan afterwards.[19]

The heavens finally opened in the winter of 1978–79. The government
had announced a limit of 5% for the next round of pay increases, but this
time without the blessing of the TUC. In the autumn of 1978 both the TUC
and the Labour Party annual conferences rejected not only that figure but
also the whole philosophy of pay restraint, by large majorities. That of
course destroyed the Social Contract, which had been Labour's main shelter from the hostile elements until now. The rains came down relentlessly
from then on. Unions queued up with claims for increases way over the
5%, which some firms conceded, if they reckoned they could afford them,
or at least could afford them better than strikes. In one case the government
considered using its reserve powers to impose sanctions, against the Ford
Motor Company which had just conceded 17%, only to have that last
weapon dashed from its hands by a revolt of its own left wing in the House
of Commons on 12 December 1978. That left it entirely defenceless, during the infamous 'winter of discontent' that followed; a nightmare period
for the Labour government, with its erstwhile trade-union allies turning
against it quite viciously, in a rash of strikes, especially in the public sector
and among the low paid, accompanied in some instances by what David
Owen, the Foreign Secretary, characterised as plain 'thuggery'.[20] This may
have been atypical, but it set its mark on the whole episode from a public-
relations point of view. One television image that burnt deep was of coffins
remaining unburied because council workers refused to dig the graves for
them; another was of an ambulance drivers' leader telling an interviewer
that if their refusal to carry patients to hospitals 'means lives must be lost,
that is how it must be'.[21] The effect of all this, exploited to the full by a
popular press whose sympathies were generally anti-union in any case, was a
public revulsion against trade-union power of a kind that the Conservatives

could have done with, but had failed to get, in the winter of 1973–74. This time it worked for them. At the height of the 'discontent' the government was forced (by a Commons defeat on another issue entirely) to go to the country. The election took place on 3 May 1979. Its result was predictable: a comfortable win for the Conservatives; largely as a result of the unburied corpses and the dying patients, and of the collapse of 'consensus', or 'convergence', that lay beneath that.

II

No one was surprised by this outcome, unlike the last three times, when a lot of people (including public opinion pollsters) got the results of the elections quite badly wrong. It was not only the 'winter of discontent' that made this one predictable. The government had been teetering on a knife edge for ages. For most of its time in office it had not had an overall majority in the Commons, having come to power as a minority government in March 1974, and then when it went to the country in October to try to improve this situation only squeezing in by a majority of four, which was whittled away to nothing again by deaths and defections in April 1976. That it survived as long as it did – five years and two months – was regarded by Callaghan as 'little short of a miracle'.[22] Towards the end this was only achieved by means of arrangements with minority parties, and a certain amount of parliamentary legerdemain. The main thing that kept it going from March 1977 was a 'pact' with the Liberals, by which the latter agreed to co-operate with the government, in return for really very little.[23] There was also another, rather shadier, understanding with the Ulster Unionists, of all people, promising them increased representation in Parliament: 'one of the Government's least attractive commitments', as Bernard Donoughue admitted later.[24] The Liberal pact came to an end in August 1978. Thereafter the government had only the ingenuity of Michael Foot – now translated to Leader of the House – to keep it alive, sometimes by means of tactics which had Conservative MPs accusing him (over-excitedly) of 'fascism'.[25] This was demoralising.

The government had other problems. It was not the happiest conceivable cabinet. At least one of its members probably should not have been there. Roy Jenkins already considered himself 'a closet Liberal' at this time, and had actually privately wanted Labour to lose the February 1974 election.[26] He was always uncomfortable, and made his colleagues more so. Some of them suspected him – not unreasonably, by his own admission later[27] – of hankering, if not actively plotting, for a 'national' or coalition government, which obviously would have involved the destruction of the one he was serving in. That smacked of disloyalty. Wilson called Jenkins 'semi-detached'.[28] The same epithet could be applied to Tony Benn, as he now liked to be called (rather than *Wedgwood* Benn, or 'Wedgie'), who –

belying the normal tendency of folk as they grow older – had moved perceptibly to the left since the last time he had been in government, and was now, if not the most socialist member of the cabinet, at least the most *provocatively* socialist one. Colleagues saw him as 'more preoccupied with leading the left wing in the country than with contributing to the Government's success in Whitehall and Westminster'; an impression which is borne out by his published diaries for this period.[29] As a result he always felt 'isolated' in cabinet, and justifiably so.[30] Wilson apparently – and very uncharacteristically, for such a mild-mannered man – regarded him with a 'hatred' bordering on the 'hysterical'.[31] Even those of his colleagues 'who are on his side on policy', noted Barbara Castle on one occasion, soon got 'sick' of his 'determination to strike attitudes publicly... regardless of our old friend collective responsibility'. They saw this as a sign of ambition.[32] It meant that yet another cylinder of the government machine was not firing efficiently.

Luckily it had Harold Wilson for its first two years to keep it on the road nonetheless. This was a considerable achievement, which it 'galled' Wilson himself to be dismissed – as it often was at the time – as mere 'deviousness': 'in my view a constant effort to keep his party together, without sacrificing either principle or the essentials of basic strategy, is the very stuff of political leadership.'[33] That was what Wilson did. The most remarkable example of this was his bridging of his party's rift over Europe. That was enormously divisive, with the cabinet about equally split over whether Britain should remain a member of the Community or pull out, and the Labour party at large favouring the latter option. Jenkins and Shirley Williams threatened to resign from the government if that one was chosen. Wilson's way around this was to oppose not Britain's membership *per se*, but the terms on which Heath had secured it, and to promise to 'renegotiate' those terms, in order to improve them, and then put the whole matter before 'the people', probably in a referendum. That was exactly the kind of thing that was excoriated as 'devious' by those who believed that 'leadership' consisted in taking a strong line on one side of a question and then sticking to it; but it could also be regarded as reasonable, and democratic. Even some Europhiles admitted that 'the UK really did have a lousy deal', as David Owen put it, from the existing EC arrangements,[34] and also – in a different way – from Heath's reneging on his 'full-hearted consent' pledge of 1970.[35] Wilson's approach promised to soothe both these sores. His 'renegotiation' secured a minimal concession on Britain's contribution to the Community budget, but enough of one to allow him to recommend that Britain stay in Europe, when the referendum was held, on 5 June 1975. The result of that was a two-to-one majority in favour. That was ideal. It meant that his Europhiles had no excuse to resign, and his Europhobes no cause – surely –

to complain. So it kept the party together, and exorcised a daemon. (The EC was scarcely mentioned at the next Labour party conference, four months afterwards.)[36] It also avoided the trauma and disruption that a withdrawal would undoubtedly have caused. All these considerations were far more important than the merits of the question itself, which Wilson had always regarded as 'marginal' and 'finely balanced',[37] not worth the risk of wrecking any vehicle on. Directly afterwards he claimed this as one of the proudest achievements of his whole period in office. (The other was the Social Contract.)[38] There was much to be said for that.

Nevertheless it took a lot out of him. 'I'm sick of pulling this Party back from the brink,' he told Barbara Castle after another cabinet row in January 1976. 'If this goes on I shall throw in my hand – and then see how some of you will get along.' Castle noticed that his eyes were 'baggy'.[39] He felt oppressed in other ways too. He had always had a touch of paranoia about him, usually directed in the past against people in the party he believed to be plotting against him. He was more relaxed about that threat now, mainly because he was not so fussed about hanging on in any case. (As early as March 1974 he had decided that he would retire on his sixtieth birthday, which was just two years off at that time.)[40] But now other shapes loomed into his ken, originating elsewhere entirely. One took the form of the South African secret-service agency BOSS, which he told Barbara Castle in March 1976 he had 'conclusive evidence' was involved in a plot against the Liberal leader Jeremy Thorpe, who was just then on the point of resigning over an alleged homosexual scandal. BOSS, he thought, was gunning for him too.[41] He also had his doubts about MI5, which was awkward, because in the ordinary course of things it would be MI5 that he would rely on to protect him from this kind of thing.[42] It was possible that agencies like this were behind the stream of rumours that appeared throughout his term of sexual, financial and political improprieties by him and other leading members of his government; accompanied by mysterious burglaries, presumably searching for materials that were incriminating or could be made to appear so (Wilson's tax papers were among the stolen items, for example), and by some ingenious forgeries, such as letters purporting to connect Labour MPs with the IRA, and Swiss bank accounts implying that Edward Short (among others) had some ill-gotten gains to salt away.[43] Whatever the source of this campaign may have been, it was relentless, and entirely unprecedented (on this scale) in British history; which was dispiriting and enervating for those members of the government who were directly targeted by it.

It certainly seems to have got Wilson down; which is why his resignation, when he eventually announced it publicly on 16 March 1976, will have come as a relief to him. (It was a complete surprise to others, fuelling even more speculation that there must be some great scandal brewing to have forced it on him; which might have had some credence were it not for the facts that it was not really as sudden as it seemed, having been planned – and vouchsafed to his close confidants – some time previously; and that it is easily explicable on other, more innocent grounds.) That undoubtedly weakened the government thereafter. James Callaghan, Wilson's successor, had many qualities, but lacked Wilson's political agility ('Footwork is my strong point', as the latter once boasted to Barbara Castle),[44] which was greatly missed, for example, in the weeks leading up to the 'winter of discontent'. It is of course impossible to be certain; but it is difficult to imagine Harold Wilson being quite so *rigid* about the 5% pay limit as Callaghan was then, which might possibly have saved the government, albeit at the cost of more sneers about Wilson's lack of 'firmness' and 'leadership'. Healey attributed that 5% limit to the sin of 'hubris'.[45] Wilson, whatever his other faults, had very little of that.

None of these circumstances helped. A minority government, plagued by divisions and disloyalty, assailed from without, subverted – possibly – by its own servants, and faced at the beginning of its term by a serious economic crisis not of its own making, was bound to struggle somewhat. It would be easy to attribute its ultimate failure solely to this. But there was more to it. Many of these factors were not so much reasons for the failure in themselves, as symptoms of some more fundamental causes underneath. Just before polling day in May 1979 Callaghan told Donoughue that he sensed 'a sea-change in politics', of a kind that happened about every 30 years in Britain, and was impervious to anything a politician like him could say or do.[46] Callaghan may not have been quite as sensitive as Wilson to the day-to-day nuances of politics, but his antennae were pretty well tuned in to the longer term. A sea-change there was. No government could have resisted it. Both Labour and Conservatives had struggled against it for a decade, but without success. In May 1979 the country at last decided to allow it to wash over it. The result was the end – for the foreseeable future – of the postwar 'consensus', and of the hopes that for 35 years had ridden on it.

III

One of those hopes, as we saw earlier,[47] was that Britain might avoid the extremes of capitalism or communism – or the extreme of capitalism *followed* by communism – which had seemed to be the direction that history had been pushing her in before 1945. That had been every government's underlying purpose – in different degrees, and more explicitly in some cases than in others – since then: under Attlee, Churchill, Eden, Macmillan, Home, Wilson, Heath and Callaghan. That was the purpose of 'consensus': to allow the country to steer a moderate course between the rocks, avoiding the sirens stationed on each one. Now that hope was looking somewhat tattered. The rocks were crowding in, and Britain's chosen course becoming more turbulent. That may have been because the latter was not a viable long-term option in any case. This was what the extremists had always argued, of course. The significance of the events of the year 1979 is that it seemed to prove that they – and not the moderates – were right.

'Extremism' – in the sense of simple and absolutist sets of political beliefs – had been on the rise throughout the 1970s. On the left it was manifested in a recrudescence of Marxist (or neo- or pseudo-Marxist) zealotry in a bewildering variety of forms, on university campuses, for example, and on the edges of the mainstream Labour movement, mainly among the young. On the right it took two main forms, which sometimes coalesced: nationalism in several different guises, including racism; and free marketism taken to hitherto undreamt of lengths. Both these tendencies made inroads into the two major political parties, but deeper on the Conservative side than on Labour's. Labour always had its troublesome left wing, especially among constituency activists, represented by the 'Tribune group' in Parliament, which is what had brought about the government's defeat over pay-policy sanctions in December 1978, for example;[48] but it was always a minority at that level, and an even smaller one in Cabinet. (Benn was the only real zealot among ministers.) The Conservative party was the mirror-image of this at the beginning of the decade – extremer in the constituencies than in government – but later proved more pervious at the higher level, especially during its years in opposition. The ousting of Edward Heath as leader by the more free-marketist Margaret Thatcher in February 1975 was a crucial stage in the rise of that particular extreme, although this was not fully apparent at the time. (The extent of Thatcher's zealotry crept up on the country by stages.) By 1979, therefore, the 'mush of consensus', as Benn called it,[49] was being unpleasantly squeezed by harder ideologies on both sides of it, but especially on the right.

The right had a number of advantages. It was better organised than the extreme left, and much better funded. One of the reasons for this was that some very rich people were associated with it; more than could be found to support socialism, for obvious reasons. It also received subventions from the American CIA,[50] which will have compensated – at the very least – for the subsidy which the British far left is known to have received from the KGB.[51] As well as this it was more vigilant than the left, partly because it fell for the latter's propaganda, which tended to be more triumphalist than was justified. This was one of the left's grossest miscalculations during the 1970s: its confidence in its strength – Scargill's 'the working class had only to flex its muscles...', for example[52] – and in its inevitable ultimate victory, which turned out to be entirely misplaced. This was one of the factors that led it to overplay its hand so disastrously during the 'winter of discontent'.

It had the opposite effect on the right. It scared it into powerful counter measures: propaganda on a massive scale, some of it 'black' (i.e. false) or 'grey' (half true), put out by a number of private agencies; and covert activities of various kinds, in which a rogue element of MI5 – which affected to believe, incredibly, that Harold Wilson was really a secret Russian 'mole' – may have been involved.[53] All this was done to plug a gap that right-wingers believed existed in Britain's official defences against subversion;[54] but in fact the state was pretty well prepared against left-wing threats as well. In 1972, for example, a new 'Civil Contingencies Unit' was set up to be able to respond at an hour's notice, if need be, to strikes in essential industries and domestic crises of other kinds.[55] The army, too, was looking at ways in which it could help with what it called 'counter-insurgency' operations if it was called upon by a government under seige; or even possibly on its own initiative, according to some whispers that came to the ears of Lord Carver, Chief of the Defence Staff from 1973 to 1976, from 'fairly senior officers at the Army's headquarters' during the 1974 miners' strike.[56] At around the same time MI5 proper – that is, the less rogue element – apparently shifted the main focus of *its* attention away from foreign spies and towards home-grown left-wing 'subversives', in response to the mood of the time.[57] All this represented a formidable array of weaponry, which the Left could not hope to compete with, at least in kind.

How effective it was is difficult to say. Extremists on both sides tended to place great emphasis on it: right-wingers in order to puff their own part in the Great Victory against Socialism, and left-wingers to show how underhand that victory was. (It can sometimes be a comfort, if you have lost a contest, to believe that it was only because your opponents were cheats.) Right-wing trickery against Labour in the 1970s must have had some impact, just as the Zinoviev letter did in 1924; but it was probably not a crucial one, in view of other more fundamental political and economic trends of that period, as we shall see. It was more important as a symptom: of the political polarisation of the time, for example; the growing pessimism; the decline of liberalism, except in its narrow economic sense; and a certain amoralism that was entering politics, especially on the right (though the right often claimed that it was only in response to the amorality of the left), which had not been there to this extent before.

More significant, however, was what was happening closer to the mainstream of British politics, and especially in the Conservative party, which was to become the chief temple of the new free-marketist flame in the 1980s, just as Labour had been the cathedral of the old religion in the years before. The Conservatives, of course, had always had some old religionists among them too: worshippers at the altar of the mixed economy and social justice, which is what had enabled the 'consensus' to survive so long. But they were never so firmly established there. They were a curious sect: a throwback to an earlier age of Tory paternalism, which is where their feeling for social justice derived from, but drawing sustenance during the course of the first 60 or so years of the twentieth century from the empire, which was in many ways – as we saw – Tory paternalism writ large. The empire was vital. Without it there was no need for Tories to be paternalists; and without paternalism there was no other reason for them to cohabit, as they had done for so long, with socialists. By the mid-1970s most of the empire had gone. The paternalist tradition in the Conservative party consequently declined. It took some time to do this, as Tories who had been brought up as paternalists were not going to change their whole way of thinking the moment they stopped being able to be imperialists (unless they were Enoch Powell); but it was bound to happen in the end. The Conservative party slowly changed its character. Its social conscience withered on the vine. The free-marketist, individualist, nationalistic tendency, which had always been there, but overshadowed by the grapes until now, grew sturdier. The transformation can be traced in the social and occupational composition of the party, with upper-class gentlemen being gradually replaced by middle-class estate agents and advertising executives at every successive election in the 1970s.[58] This was Margaret Thatcher's constituency. Hence the collapse of one of the two props that had supported consensus in the post-war years; without which neither it, nor the institutions which *it* was supporting (like the welfare state), could hope to survive for very long.

That, however, was still not the bottom of it. The main reason why consensus collapsed at the end of the 1970s was that it was no longer holding up economically. If it had done so more Tories could surely have been found to support it, empire or no. But it simply was not working. Unemployment was the clearest sign of this: averaging well over a million for four full years by 1979, and so beginning to look chronic, which ran right against one of the main pillars of the post-1945 settlement. There were still gross inequalities, which ran against another; and which were inevitably highlighted at a time of recession, which helps explain the particular bitterness of the low-paid element in the rebellion against the government's incomes policy in the winter of 1978–79. A third pillar, welfare provision, was still standing, but was under pressure (especially from international creditors) because of the sheer and growing expense of it. One answer to that, of course, would have been to increase taxes; but people were becoming resistant to this. That was another signal that Harold Wilson's antennae had picked up some time before: that given the choice, many of them preferred 'the jingle of money in their pockets' to a decent 'social' wage.[59] One of the reasons for this may have been that a new generation of Britons had come on stream, which had no memories – as Heath and Callaghan for example had – of the suffering that a jingle-in-the-pocket economy could cause. (In this way welfareism could be said to have directly benefited free-market capitalism, by wiping out its previous sins.) That eroded the fourth pillar of the post-war settlement: middle-class guilt. Taken all together these signs were ominous for consensus, which appeared to be buckling under the double weight of its own inadequacies, and of the very nature – individualistic, selfish, anti-social, enterprising, acquisitive – of human kind.

Of course it would have been easier if Britain's general economy had been healthier. One of the reasons why unemployment was so high, for example, and welfare such a burden, was that Britain's growth rate was still worryingly sluggish at this time, even making allowance for a world-wide recession which affected nearly every other country too. In 1974–79 Britain's economy grew by only 1.05% per annum in real terms, compared with Germany's 2.4%, France's 2.9% and Japan's 4.1%.[60] The main factor behind this was the continuing relative decline of her manufacturing base. That had been a problem for very many years now – possibly even as many as a hundred, if the economic historians were right[61] – without anyone having hit on an agreed solution as yet. Management laid it all at the door of the unions, which looked plausible in the winter of 1978–79. The Labour party tended to blame 'inadequate investment', and an 'innate conservatism which made us reluctant... to adopt new techniques of production'; together with 'a financial system which discourages long-term borrowing' and made it 'more profitable to invest abroad than in Britain'.[62] Hence the vital need – in its view – for government intervention; which during Wilson's second term was mainly channelled through a new 'National Enterprise Board' (the successor to Heath's Industrial Development Executive, and Wilson's earlier Industrial Reorganisation Corporation: more evidence of the 'convergence' of the times); which had 'more success than it was credited with by a biased media', according to Bernard Donoughue, but on much too small a scale, as he himself acknowledged, to make any serious impact.[63] It was also handicapped by having to take charge of 'lame duck' companies, like British Leyland and Chrysler UK, which the government felt obliged to prop up in order to save the jobs that were threatened if they collapsed; and by the fact that Tony Benn, who was put in charge of the Ministry which oversaw it, from the very start conceived his main role there as 'to look after our people' – that is, the trade unions – which went down predictably badly with the other side.[64] Even when he was removed from the Industry Department by Wilson in June 1975, however (he swapped posts with Eric Varley at Energy; Joe Haines, Wilson's press officer, called it 'castling'),[65] it made little difference. Manufacturing industry, and the economy generally, failed to respond.

This marked another failure for economic interventionism, to add to all the other industrial planning and incomes policy debacles of the recent past. Whether these were avoidable or not is debatable. It could be that the interventionists simply did not try hard or skilfully enough. Another push, and they might have succeeded. At the time, however, that looked unlikely. The pressures against them were too powerful: from reactionary and prejudiced industrialists, for example; anarchic trade unionists; a myopic Treasury; and bankers who were basically not interested in British industry. The *Zeitgeist* was also unfavourable. Margaret Thatcher, the Leader of the Opposition, noticed this early in 1977: that 'The tide is beginning to turn against collectivism, socialism, statism, *dirigisme*, whatever you call it', in almost every part of the world. Her view was that this was happening because it had to; because socialism (or whatever) was bound to fail.[66] If that was true it meant that intervention was pointless. There was no bucking the market, and no escape for Britain ultimately, therefore, from whatever fate a much 'freer' form of capitalism had in store for her.

Thatcher might have been intrigued – to put it no more strongly – to be told that this standpoint of hers allied her with the Marxists; who also believed that *Labour*'s version of socialism, at any rate – this feeble attempt to forestall a proper revolution by mixing capitalism with some more palatable, pseudo-socialist ingredients – was doomed to collapse. The difference between them, of course, was that Thatcher was confident that things would improve for everyone under free-market capitalism, whereas the Marxists looked forward to their getting worse. Time would reveal which was the more accurate prognosis of the two.

IV

In the meantime things had manifestly been getting worse recently on a number of fronts. The economic situation – unemployment, industrial decline, poor growth, the vulnerable pound sterling – we have noticed already. But these were only part of the picture. The 1970s were years of decline in many other ways. Some of them went to the core of Britain's national character and identity. For the first time in perhaps 400 years her people were uncertain who and what they were.

Strictly, of course, they should have been Europeans by now. The referendum was supposed to have established that. 'It was a free vote, without constraint, following a free democratic campaign,' as Wilson pointed out directly afterwards; consequently it ought to have meant that '14 years of national argument are over.'[67] Not every anti-marketeer agreed, however; like Douglas Jay, ex-President of the Board of Trade, who refused to accept the verdict as final because of the unfair propaganda advantage he believed the pro-Market side had enjoyed during the campaign – with eight times the funds of the antis, for example, and just about every national newspaper on their side – whose effect in his view was to 'overturn the natural balance' of opinion in the country. So far as he was concerned the result was 'a historical tragedy'.[68] This sort of attitude was not uncommon. At bottom it derived from something we have remarked on before: Britain's objectively divergent historical experience and interests from those of the original 'Six', which were bound to make them uncomfortable bedfellows.[69] At the very least it seemed unreasonable to expect Britain to renounce other liaisons entirely. Heath's government, claimed Callaghan in the February 1974 election campaign, had 'banked everything on our relations with Europe. The time has come to cultivate the rest of the world once more.' As Foreign Secretary, therefore, Callaghan was at pains to return America, Russia and the Commonwealth to Britain's ambit.[70] That prolonged Britain's confusion about her role.

The confusion did not begin at her shore line. The later 1970s were also the time when Britain nearly broke up internally, with Scottish and Welsh nationalisms rampant, and the government caving in to demands for at least a limited degree of 'devolution' to them. In the event it never came to this, because insufficient Scots and Welsh voted for devolution in the referenda that were held for them, and the government was toppled (on this very issue) before the matter could be taken any further. But it was unsettling to find the Union, which had always been considered a model for other similar multi-national states, even questioned after all these centuries. (Benn saw it as 'part of the collapse of confidence of the English establishment'.)[71] Northern Ireland, the fourth main constituent of the United Kingdom, was more problematical. Torn between two rival nationalisms, a solution to its by now endemic blood-letting seemed entirely out of reach. A referendum would certainly not settle it. Heath had tried bringing the parties together to 'share' power, in a joint executive; but that experiment collapsed shortly after Labour came to office, wrecked by a political strike masterminded by 'Loyalists' in May 1974. After that politicians simply despaired of doing anything for Northern Ireland, apart from trying to keep terrorism contained. 'While it may have seemed negative, almost defeatist,' Wilson wrote afterwards, 'the Government inevitably had no new proposal for the future of the Province... No solution could be imposed from across the water. From now on we had to throw the task clearly to the Northern Ireland people themselves.'[72] In fact it was not quite like that, because Northern Ireland was directly ruled from Westminster by this time, and policed by British troops. That may have provoked one side, and stiffened the other. (If you are being protected by guns you do not need to settle.) On one occasion apparently the Cabinet secretly considered withdrawing altogether,[73] but decided against it, presumably because of the risk of unleashing an all-out civil war. So the wound continued suppurating, feeding the ambiguity that had long existed in that part of the Kingdom about the real extent of Britain's national identity.

It also raised questions about its *nature*. Northern Ireland had always represented something of an anomaly from this point of view: fiercely 'loyal' to the British connexion, so far as its Protestant majority were concerned, yet with dominant values and an ethos which were very different from those which, by and large, characterised the mainland to which they were so sentimentally attached. Some of this had to do with the nature of their religion; but more was probably due to their material situation in Ireland, as a minority (taking the island as a whole) among a population they regarded as alien. (South African whites had a similar outlook.) In particular Northern Ireland had never been a notably 'liberal' place, for example politically, partly because it could not afford to be, especially latterly in view of the Republican terrorist threat. During the 1970s that threat pushed it to greater lengths of illiberalism: with people being imprisoned ('interned') simply on suspicion of terrorism, for example; law courts dispensing with juries; interrogations accompanied by torture; and the security services resorting to what normally would have been considered quite unacceptable practices – planting evidence, agent-provocateuring, blackmail, assassination, even on one occasion *possibly* setting off a car-bomb themselves in Dublin (on 17 May 1974) in order to fool the Irish Republican government that it was under threat from the IRA as well as Britain[74] – in their efforts to come to grips with an even less scrupulous foe. All these practices directly contradicted principles which for years – centuries in some cases – had been considered essential attributes of 'Britishness'. Again, the national identity was being thrown into doubt.

So long as this was confined to Ireland most Britons put it out of their minds, as a way of insulating their view of themselves as a broadly liberal people; as they had used to do, in fact, on comparable occasions (1880s, 1910s) in the past. It was difficult to sustain that, however, when the virus spread. That happened in two ways. Firstly, as the terrorists extended their activities on to the British mainland they triggered the same sort of responses there. In October 1974 the IRA began a campaign of bombing crowded public houses in urban areas of Britain, the worst of which – in the Mulberry Bush and Tavern in the Town pubs in Birmingham on 21 November – killed 21 innocent people and maimed 182 more. The official reaction to that carnage was to rush through Parliament the most illiberal security measure – the Prevention of Terrorism Act – seen in Britain in peacetime since 1820; and (at a much lower official level) to arrest, 'fit up' and incarcerate the wrong men for the actual crime. The other way the virus spread – though we cannot be so certain about this – was *via* the British secret intelligence community, whose 'plots' against the Labour government in the mid-1970s – such as they were – seem to have originated in Northern Ireland, at least in part. (They also targeted Thorpe, and – while he was still Conservative leader – Edward Heath. The best guess is that they were provoked by power-sharing.)[75] If nothing more, this made the political atmosphere in Britain uglier than it had been. It was another symptom of a change in the national character; by one way of looking at it, a decline.

It certainly marked a decline of *liberalism* in Britain, in the generally understood sense of the word (not, that is, the narrowly economic one). Northern Ireland was only one manifestation of this. That was a case where a liberal approach seemed inappropriate, irrelevant, even impossible. There were others. Britain was becoming a more violent society domestically, with crimes of violence doubling during the course of the 1970s, for example;[76] racist attacks in immigrant areas; picket-line battles; various cultural expressions of a new positive liking, even, for aggression and anger (action films, the fashion for militaria, body-building, close-cropped hair styles, 'Punk rock' popular music); and, on the far-right edges of the political world, a recrudescence of Nazi-style fascism in the guise of the burgeoning 'National Front'. Little of this probably affected more than a minority of people directly and materially, but it created an atmosphere which liberalism found it difficult to breathe. A good litmus paper of this was Roy Jenkins, who was Home Secretary twice: first in the 1960s, when he became celebrated as *the* great liberalising minister, the chief enabler of the 'permissive revolution' of the age of the Beatles; and then again in 1974, when he found he had to behave entirely differently, concentrating almost exclusively on the grimmer task of maintaining 'the authority of the state'.[77] That marked the extent of the change.

All this had implications for mainstream politics. Society was becoming colder, harder, tougher in its outlook. It craved – or a significant part of it did – colder, harder, tougher policies: an end to prevarication; facing reality, whatever the consequences; reasserting the primacy of laws of all kinds, including economic ones; and taming those – like the unions – who were perceived as having brought Britain to the state she was in in 1979. It also favoured a different approach to political authority: no longer the gentle, moderate, conciliatory, *appeasing* style of former years, but a more resolute and aggressive one. This was why Wilson's idea of 'leadership' fell so much out of favour, for example; because it tended to emphasise bringing people together and avoiding confrontations,[78] whereas 'real' leadership required one to stamp one's own authority on people and events. Gentler politicians found it hard to adjust to this. David Steel, who after Thorpe's disgrace in 1976 became the leader of the gentlest of all the parties, the Liberals, had a shot at it in September 1977, when he called on his followers to become 'militants for the reasonable man'; which was a good try, but not really convincing.[79] The fact that he felt he needed to dress his party's moderation up in this way was significant. It showed that he, too, sensed that the time for overt moderation – or 'consensus', or 'convergence' – was passing fast. In the spring of 1979, after the events of the previous winter, only one political tendency was likely to benefit from that.

Chapter 27

Thatcherism
(1979)

I

The Conservatives came to power in May 1979 on a wave of revulsion against the trade unions, and of frustration at the perceived inadequacies of consensus politics. That was enough to win them the election fairly comfortably. The problem for them was that it might be merely a temporary, fickle movement of opinion, which would swing back again when memories of the 'winter of discontent' had faded. This would not have mattered for a government which intended to pursue moderate, 'consensus' policies; but that was not what Margaret Thatcher, the new prime minister, had in mind. She wanted a radical change of direction. Some of this had been spelled out in the Conservative election manifesto (though it was naturally sugared there, to hide its full bitterness): trade-union reform, tax relief for the rich, cuts in public spending, and tougher police powers.[1] Whether beneath the wave of May 1979 there was a deeper surge that would sustain all this seemed doubtful initially. Most contemporary commentators, for example, were convinced that Thatcher would be forced to compromise eventually. It had happened before, most notoriously in Heath's time. The 'ongoing reality'[2] would get through to her, too, in the end.

Thatcher's ultimate success in the face of this prospect has been widely ascribed to her determination and willpower; but it was also a tribute to her perception of what the 'reality' of that time really was. She was in a minority here, but she was right. She claimed afterwards that she had always known instinctively that socialism was bound to fail eventually, which is what had sustained her 'through the bleak years of socialist supremacy'.[3] Towards the end of those years she sensed that the tide was on the turn.[4] After a short time in office she knew it was ebbing fast. History, she told an international group of right-wing politicians in June 1983, was definitely on the capitalists' side.[5] Later everyone came to see this; but it was her distinction, and indeed genius, to see it before most of them. All she had to do then was to ride the beast to victory.

The signs were there. The struggles of Britain's mixed economy and welfare society in recent years seemed to be one. In the early days it was possible to put them down to bad luck, or poor management, or irrational factors like group insanity among foreign 'speculators';[6] but as time went on these excuses began to wear thin. The problems were just too persistent: recurrent sterling crises, forcing round after round of public spending cuts; continual trouble over wages; growing unemployment; inflation rising to unprecedented levels: and all with apparently no end in view. It was a depressing cycle, provoking understandable impatience among the electorate; and looking more and more as though it might be symptomatic of a basic disfunction underneath. The system was not working. It was costing too much. Britain was both taxing and paying herself more than she could afford, if she expected to survive in the increasingly competitive international commercial environment that was forming around her at this time. It could not last. 'The cosy world we were told would go on for ever, where full employment would be guaranteed by a stroke of the Chancellor's pen, cutting taxes, deficit spending – that cosy world is gone,' the Labour prime minister, James Callaghan, told his party conference in 1976.[7] If he – a socialist – had come to this conclusion, it must be true. It was shortly after this that Britain went over to what was called a 'monetarist' economic policy, when Callaghan's Chancellor, Denis Healey, began publishing monetary targets (though he later insisted that they were merely estimates dressed up as targets) every year.[8] That was when the old consensual (or 'Keynesian') economic system effectively came to an end in Britain; before Thatcher arrived on the scene, be it noted; which proved it had nothing essentially to do with her.

Attitudes had also been shifting recently. In Britain growing affluence in the 1960s, for example, had made people more acquisitive. That fostered an individualist ethos rather than a social one. (Harold Wilson had also spotted this: hence his 'jingle of money in their pockets' gibe.)[9] Other contemporary developments had encouraged this: the spread of private home ownership, for example, from 29% of the housing stock in 1951 to 55% in 1980;[10] and a huge rise in the number of private cars, from 2.26 million in 1950 to 15 million in 1980.[11] These were both anti-social trends, in a way. The car revolution, for example, freed people from the need to travel together, on buses and trains. Television meant they did not need to rub shoulders with each other to be entertained. At the same time the numbers of the working classes – traditionally the most socially-minded section of the community – were shrinking, in line with the decline of manufacturing industry, and to the advantage of the middle classes, who had always been the chief guardians of the individualist grail.[12] These were powerful influences on political behaviour. They undermined the sense of common interest between people, and consequently the commitment folk had to structures (trade unions, the welfare state) which grew out of that. The mortar that bound the bricks of society together – all except Carlyle's 'cash nexus'[13] – was drying out and crumbling. This – again – was long before Thatcher began poking at it.

Add to this the effect of the end of the empire, whose contribution to the maintenance of the social reformist consensus in Britain from the beginning of the century has been described already,[14] and the strength of the new tendency is easily understood. It was as if it was the *natural* way of human development, only held back hitherto by artificial obstacles, and now – as the obstacles were removed – suddenly released. In Britain the main obstacle had been the perpetuation of a set of pre-capitalist, paternalist values which in the normal course of things would have been extinct by this stage, but had been bolstered (especially in the Conservative party) by the needs of the empire. Elsewhere the obstacles had been very different, but equally unnatural. In eastern Europe it was sheer political tyranny, which was the only thing sustaining the communist system in Russia and her satellites. A little later, when that was removed, the same thing happened as in Britain – the return of free-market capitalism – but even more dramatically, because of the size of the dam holding the river back there. It was a mighty tendency, this great primal force of nature; and a tremendous ally, therefore, for Thatcher to have on her side.

That makes her task sound easy. In fact it was not, certainly at the beginning. Few people around her gave much for her chances. Her own confidence faltered more than once. One particularly bad time was the spring of 1981, with soaring unemployment, rioting, and some dreadful opinion poll results.[15] 'You know, Alan,' she told one of her advisers (the monetarist economist Alan Walters) at the time, 'they may get rid of me for this.'[16] It needed courage – or obstinacy – to stick to her task in the face of all that. Most people expected her to give in at least a little. Some may have been genuinely misled by her first words on entering 10 Downing Street as prime minister (attributed to St Francis): 'Where there is discord, may we bring harmony',[17] which suggested that she was a conciliator at heart. When she saw the discord her rigid application of monetarist policies was provoking, she would surely need to trim.

But she did not. One of the reasons for this was that she kept insisting she would not. That made the prospect of trimming more humiliating than it would have been for more of a pragmatist. (Edward Heath had already been through this.) Despite the 'Herculean task' that lay ahead of them,

Thatcher told the guests at her first Lord Mayor's banquet, in November 1979, 'we are not faint-hearted pilgrims. We will not be deflected by a stony path.'[18] Later this was famously translated into 'the lady's not for turning', at the Conservative party conference of October 1980.[19] After that it was inconceivable that she could change tack. Besides, she was a zealot. If people had listened beyond the first item in the catechism she had quoted outside Number 10 on 4 May 1979 they would have realised this. 'Where there is error, may we bring truth', was the second item; followed by 'Where there is doubt, may we bring faith'.[20] Truth and faith are altogether harder, less tolerant objectives than 'harmony'. For Thatcher they were far more important. That made it doubly inconceivable that she could alter course. The truth, as she saw it, could not be compromised. Hence her willingness to face defeat, rather than submit to the clamour of the faithless. If that happened, as she told Walters, 'At least I shall have gone knowing I did the right thing.'[21] That was where the determination and willpower came in.

There were also darker forces abetting her. The secret conspiratorial right, for example, which had always mistrusted her predecessor (and may possibly have been influential in removing him),[22] backed her to the hilt. Thatcher valued its advice, and probably welcomed its help in other ways, though to what effect is difficult to say.[23] She was also – according to one of her ministers – 'positively besotted' by her *official* security services,[24] whose activities against those she chose to regard as her internal political enemies are only now partially (and unreliably) coming to light.[25] She had the overwhelming support of the 'press barons', five out of seven of whose national daily papers (representing 70% of readers) rooted for her in 1979, which was more than Edward Heath had ever been able to command.[26] She cultivated the black art of advertising more than any previous party leader, apparently successfully. (The most notorious example was the Conservatives' 'Labour isn't working' poster of 1979, with its snake of Saatchi & Saatchi employees simulating a dole queue; somewhat ironically, as it turned out later, in view of her own government's record on unemployment.) She tolerated these techniques mainly because of her sensitivity – unusual at her level – to the danger of communist 'subversion', whose effect she believed was to distort the normal democratic processes; which could be said to justify trying to distort them back.[27] The darkest force of all on her side, however, may have been sheer good fortune, especially at the beginning of her period in office, though it was less significant in the middle, and deserted her eventually. These factors all helped, and were significant in other ways, as we shall see. But they do not need to be called up to explain the main trend of events in Britain in the 1980s; which had much more to do with the direction history was galloping in in any case, and the determined way Thatcher let it have its head.

II

That determination stemmed, famously, from her sense of 'conviction', which she saw as one of the great strengths of her character, though it could also of course be regarded in other ways. The conviction itself came from her early upbringing, as the daughter of a small shopkeeper-cum-local-politician in a provincial town. The economic principles she imbibed then – a simple and extreme version of free marketism – were never modified subsequently.[28] Nor were the *passions* she picked up a little later, which were very different from her immediate predecessors'. That owed much to her age. It gave her no direct or even vicarious experience – none that made any impression, anyway – of unemployment. Where Macmillan and Heath, for example, had been seared by the sight of stunted and wasted lives in the great depression years, Thatcher had to wait until the later 1940s before she experienced anything so feelingly. That turned out to be post-war austerity: the horrors of 'snoek, Spam, and utility clothing', and the 'petty jealousies, minor tyrannies, ill-neighbourliness and sheer sourness' that were associated with them, apparently, in Grantham.[29] (Elsewhere, as we have seen, people's responses were different.) It was this that fired her hatred – as opposed to mere disapproval – of socialism; which filled the place in her emotional make-up that hatred of injustice, or poverty, or the deeper forms of suffering took in other Conservatives'.

Although Thatcher was aware of this conditioning she preferred to ascribe her main impulses to 'instinct', which sounded more basic and pure. She depended on this a great deal. If she made mistakes, it was because she ignored her instincts: as for example when she had gone along with Heath's profligacy in the early 1970s.[30] Her problem then was that she had failed as yet 'to develop these instincts into a coherent framework of ideas or into a set of practical policies for government'.[31] That was to come later, partly under the influence of Sir Keith Joseph, Heath's other main high-spending minister, who underwent something of a Damascan conversion to 'true' Conservatism in April 1974.[32] Between then and May 1979 the two of them, with the help of some like-minded academics, and a new right-wing 'Centre for Policy Studies' set up in 1974 to challenge the ideological authority of the existing (and more pragmatic) Conservative Research Department, built up a formidable intellectual case for their intuitive views. That was not difficult, in view of those views' inherent plausibility, especially – as we have seen – at that particular point in time. They seemed logical, as the ideology of the free market always has done; and in tune with Britain's experiences recently.

One of the professed intentions of the New Right (as it came to be called) was to restore Britain to her situation before those experiences. In this sense it was reactionary, aiming to turn the country back; though only in order – the New Right maintained – to rediscover the path, abandoned long before, that led to true modernity. This was where History was brought in to help: to show how well free marketism had worked until socialism, and before that Tory paternalism, had knocked the country off its course.[33] Thatcher's own contribution to this was her theory of 'Victorian values', which according to her had been the key to Britain's greatness in the nineteenth century. They comprised hard work, thrift, self-reliance, personal responsibility and patriotism.[34] Most professional historians were rather snooty about this, partly no doubt through resentment at this trespass into their specialism,[35] but also because it gave, in fact, a very skewed view of Victorian times, as attentive readers of the early chapters of this book will know. That however hardly mattered, firstly because no one took any notice of the professionals, and secondly because 'Victorian values' were really intended to make a moral rather than a historical point. This reflected another of Thatcher's instinctive feelings: that capitalism was somehow the *virtuous* path. (Later, in a lecture to the General Assembly of the Church of Scotland in Edinburgh in May 1988, she even equated it with Christianity.)[36] In this, of course, she *was* accurately reflecting at least a minority Victorian view.

In others she was not. There were some significant differences between this new manifestation of free-market ideology, and its Victorian model. The main one related to the state. Mid-Victorian free marketists had believed that the state's control over people's affairs should be minimal. That applied to the political as well as the economic field. It was not thought to be difficult, because it was natural. Political freedom would be an inevitable concomitant of the economic kind. As the benefits of the free market filtered down, profiting everyone, and abolishing poverty and hardship, people would not need to be restrained or controlled. The state therefore would wither; if not quite to nothing, then to a purely 'night watchman' role. In the meantime it should be kept on the tightest possible rein. For many contemporaries, as we have seen, this *justified* the free market: its compatibility, that is, both with social justice, and with the widest degree of political liberty, defined as the freedom of people from an intrusive and overbearing government.[37]

What was missing from the new, late twentieth-century version of free market ideology was that kind of naïve hope. The New Right still believed that free marketism was 'natural' to people: the Conservatives' 1979 election manifesto promised that if elected they would work 'with the grain of human nature', for example;[38] but not that this made it unnecessary to *enforce* it. One reason for this was that people could no longer be trusted to go with the grain, act automatically in their own self-interest; especially after their experience of socialism, which the Victorians of course had not known, and which clearly demonstrated how irrationally – unnaturally – folk could behave if they were subjected to powerful enough subversive pressures. Another was that few New Rightists were as sanguine as the Victorians had been about the ability of the market to deliver social justice. That meant that resistance was always likely, which gave a continuing – even increasing – role to the state.

That was probably 'Thatcherism's' most original and characteristic feature: this new conjunction between the free market, and what came to be called the 'Strong State'.[39] It was not, of course, entirely unheralded. We have traced its earlier development already: beginning with the revolt of the Whigs against the first signs of weakening of the Liberal party's free-marketist faith in the 1870s and 1880s, which set off the long process by which economic liberalism eventually severed its connexion with political liberalism altogether, and came to lodge on the right. Free marketism had been a Conservative creed for some time now, although until recently – as we have seen – not the only one. It became that (virtually) under Thatcher. The result of this switch in polarities was to change its political aspect entirely, so that instead of being an almost anarchistic doctrine it was now a profoundly statist one. In Thatcher's time it was associated with centralisation, for example; tough laws; strong policing; national self-assertion ('jingoism'); and all the other characteristic nostrums of the right. It was this that mainly distinguished it from its Victorian model; that, together with its pervading 'realism', or pessimism, which contrasted sharply with the mid-Victorians' bright confidence; and (thirdly) the zeal with which it was extended to areas of British life that the 'hybrid' Victorians would never have admitted were its proper concern. It was a kind of economic and political 'post-modernism', this new revival, like much of the architecture of the period: a pastiche of what had gone before, but with little sense of the spirit that had informed that style originally. Which is not to say, of course, that it might not have a perfectly valid spirit of its own.

That, essentially, was 'Thatcherism'. It was a product of its time, and not for example of an earlier one, as it sometimes pretended to be, or of some ageless, immutable principle of human affairs. It had grown out of the collapse of the British version of socialism, which was probably inevitable in the face of the pressures on it both from outside and within (its 'internal contradictions'), and which had the effect of returning Britain to the capitalist track she had been travelling along before she had taken that diversion. This statement, however, needs to be qualified. When Britain returned to the capitalist rails, it was not to the same place she had left them, but quite a bit further down the line. That explains the form free marketism took at that time, and the ethos that surrounded it. Capitalism evolves, like every other human institution, responding both to changing circumstances outside and to an internal dynamic of its own. In the mid-nineteenth century it had taken one particular form for Britain. Later on it changed; not altogether beneficially in the opinion of many people, which was why they had sought to cushion some of its impact by means of 'socialism'. By the time that ruse had failed, and Britain set about returning to full-blooded capitalism in 1979, it had moved on further. It was larger-scale, more widespread, 'multinational', 'managerial', differently financed, and far more cut-throatedly competitive. These changes had obvious implications for the political environment surrounding it, which needed to adapt to meet its needs. Hence the rise of the right.

By the very end of the 1980s – to anticipate a little – the train had moved on further still. It seemed to be passing through a bleaker, gloomier landscape, with capitalist Britain thriving no better than she had before, and indeed suffering much worse so far as a large minority of her population was concerned, in a world economy which was suffering similarly, if not always to the same extent. This may have been a temporary set-back, merely 'cyclical'; or it may have been a symptom of something worse. A century and a half earlier some people – Karl Marx most notoriously, but also some rather more respectable English commentators – had worried about the prospects for capitalism if it were left unfettered, because of what they perceived to be certain contradictions within it, deriving from the tendency of competition to drive down profits, consequently wages, and consequently purchasing power. The end result, they feared, would be escalating decline, poverty, unemployment and civil unrest.[40] Marx predicted that out of this would arise true socialism, like a phoenix from the flames; but it is not necessary to accept that to appreciate the plausibility of the rest of the scenario. It was in order to prevent this, as we have seen, that Britain turned to socialism. The fact that *that* was destroyed by internal contradictions does not mean that the *capitalist* contradictions it was designed to counter were not there too. This may be what Britain returned to in 1979, in fact: a train hurtling its way along an increasingly dangerous track, without a brake any more, towards ultimate wreck, perhaps; or revolution; or simply everlasting struggle, suffering and the 'Strong State'. Alternatively it was possible that things might get better, as world capitalism recovered, and realised its full potential for human progress, well-being, happiness and liberty later on. There were theories to support both of these versions. In the end, however, only time would tell.

III

There can be little doubt, therefore, that Margaret Thatcher was a tool of history to some extent: more than she herself credited, and more than her obvious qualities of character led many others to assume. (That tends to happen, incidentally, with people who are mainly driven by 'instinct', which quite often turns out to be a *Zeitgeist* in disguise.) But she was by no means a passive tool. Without her Britain would have had to accommodate to the new trend anyway, but not necessarily with the enthusiasm she brought to it. Before her time Wilson and Callaghan had found themselves accommodating to it perforce, for example; but reluctantly, and in ways designed to protect the most vulnerable sections of society from its effects. Thatcher's approach was entirely different. She embraced the current spirit unreservedly. For her the market could do no wrong. That made a difference. What others tolerated as a necessity, she regarded as a positive virtue. It certainly did not require people to be protected against it (except to ensure they did not actually starve). Instead of being merely carried along by the tide of the revolution, therefore, she rode it exultantly. This had a huge effect on the extent and nature of its impact on people, and also – although less tangibly – on the 'ethos', or moral climate, of her time.

One way it influenced the latter was by infusing it with the values of the market place. That was deliberate. One of the prime tenets of New Right historiography was that Britain's economic decline had begun with the growth in the later nineteenth century of a pervasive anti-capitalist culture, for which the the aristocracy, schools, ancient universities, professions, civil service and English pastoral poets were chiefly to blame.[41] This was by no means an implausible explanation, though it has been argued in this book that it was a very incomplete one.[42] It could only be remedied, according to its afficionados, by a calculated policy of rehabilitating entrepreneurial values at every level, and in almost every sphere. The obvious places to start were education and the media, two of the main transmitters of public values, and leading offenders – according to the New Right – in recent years. (Teachers and broadcasters were widely regarded in these circles as a kind of socialist fifth column.) But there were also other routes to the national soul. One was by changing people's working environments; most obviously through 'privatisation' (a new word), but also by introducing business methods and objectives into institutions that could not be privatised (or not yet). Nearly every area of professional activity became subjected to one or other of these influences during the 1980s: railways, for example, where 'passengers' became 'customers'; hospitals, now run as 'trusts' by accountants and small businesspeople; schools, turned into fund-holders; universities, whose professors suddenly found themselves called 'senior management'; the Civil Service, threatened with competitive tendering; the arts, commercially subsidized; and the great public utilities, privatized to the last litre, amp and therm. The primary motives for all this were efficiency and economy; but it also had a cultural dimension. By familiarising people with the language (at least) of modern business practice, it was hoped that they would also become imbued with the entrepreneurial spirit, which was so necessary – in the New Right's eyes – to turn Britain into a dynamic capitalist economy again.

This sort of approach was unprecedented in Britain, certainly in modern times. Labour governments, for example, had never tried to propagandize the people to this extent. (If they had, it would probably have been called 'brain-washing'.) It exemplified a number of features of Thatcher's style of government: its zeal, obviously; its extremism, in a literal (and not necessarily pejorative) sense; and a certain desperation that seemed to lie behind it all, to persuade a government that it needed to go to quite such lengths to establish its policy. It also illustrated something else. The government's efforts were relentless, but they did not completely succeed. Thatcher suffered a number of setbacks, for example, in her attempts to impose what she regarded as a sound 'National Curriculum' on the schools (including in history).[43] She also found the Church of England a hard nut to crack. Britain could not be entirely won over. There were still pockets of resistance. That was clearly why the New Right felt it had to try so hard.

It may also help explain its combativeness. That was unprecedented too. Thatcherites were never mealy mouthed on issues they felt strongly about. Opponents were attacked mercilessly. Sometimes a real rancour crept in. The best personification of this was probably Norman Tebbit, one of Thatcher's closest ministerial colleagues for a while, and famous for the crude venom of his contributions to debates. There seemed to be a genuine hatred there, not seen in British politics since Bevan's notorious 'vermin' gibe against the Tories in 1948.[44] Thatcher also clearly seethed with hostility and contempt towards a number of people: socialists obviously, but also Conservative 'traitors' like Edward Heath;[45] cabinet 'wets', as she dubbed her more pragmatic colleagues; 'grandees', or upper-class Tories; and the usual right-wing gallery of bogeypeople: social workers, intellectuals, *Guardian* readers, pacifists, doubting vicars, European bureaucrats, and the closet communists who ran the BBC. Some of this arose from a simple love of conflict on her part, which she acknowledged; fuelled by the increasingly violent mood of the times, and the call from some quarters, which we have noticed already, for 'leadership' defined in this kind of way ('the smack of firm government').[46] Another factor was a build-up of resentments and frustrations over previous years among the class (the lower-middles) Thatcher particularly represented. Beneath all this, however, may have lain a degree of insecurity and even fear for the prospects for capitalism, which is curious in the light of what we have seen were its real strengths at this time, but not if we remember its beleaguered position previously. For 50 years or more prior to 1979 the free-market system had felt itself to be on the defensive, against the on-rushing hordes of a triumphalist foreign communism, riding what *they* believed was the tide of history, and the slower but apparently solid advance of a smugly satisfied welfareist consensus which thought it had found the way to hold those waters back. That was enough to discourage anyone. It turned some people into paranoiacs, seeing socialist conspiracies everywhere; a habit of mind which it would take more than a mere turn of the tide to erase. Hence the mood and spirit that became associated with free marketism in the 1980s: cold, aggressive, ungenerous; again in marked contrast to 150 years before.

Add to all this Thatcher's own personal sense of conviction, that what she was doing was right, and you had a powerful potion. Conviction, in fact, may have been the magic ingredient. It was certainly a novel one. Most other British prime ministers in history have been amenable to argument to some extent. Even Gladstone was sometimes afflicted by doubts. If Thatcher ever was, she kept them well hidden. When pressed she would sometimes admit to some tactical errors, but not that she was ever 'wrong about the fundamental things'.[47] Her beliefs about these, she claimed, had never faltered since her childhood days.[48] She clung to them even against the most clamorous opposition, on the grounds that 'If I were the odd one out and I were right, It wouldn't matter, would it?'[49] Fixed as she was in her own beliefs, she was intolerant of irresolution in others. One anecdote attests to this. In the summer of 1975, shortly after becoming Tory leader, she visited the Conservative Research Department, in the middle of a seminar paper being given by a moderate. 'Before he had finished...,' recalled a member of the staff of the CRD later, Thatcher 'reached into her briefcase and took out a book. It was Friedrich von Hayek's *The Constitution of Liberty*.' (Hayek was one of the leading gurus of the New Right.) 'Interrupting our pragmatist, she held up the book for all of us to see. "This," she said sternly, "is what we believe," and banged Hayek down on the table.'[50] It must have been an electric moment. It was also significant. The action was almost as telling as the words. It was the combination of absolute certitude with aggression that marked Thatcher out as a truly new kind of personality in modern British politics. It was also, incidentally, what probably set most academics – for whom certitude is almost the most cardinal of sins – against her; to her slight disadvantage in one or two situations, such as when academic historians came to write about her in their books.

Chapter 28

Serving Britain Right
(1979–90)

I

Nothing like Margaret Thatcher had ever been seen before in British politics. This may partly explain her early success. She was so novel that hardly
anyone believed in her. This included many of her ministers. 'Those of us
in Cabinet who were out of sympathy with Margaret's views grossly underestimated her absolute determination... to push through the new right
wing policies,' wrote Jim Prior, her Employment Secretary, afterwards.[1]
That was probably based on past experience. It was a fatal mistake. It gave
Thatcher and her closest allies (Sir Keith Joseph, Sir Geoffrey Howe) a
head start. They were several yards down the track before the 'wets' even
knew there was a race on.

The new government set off, indeed, at a cracking pace. From the beginning its approach was deeply ideological. The key to prosperity, its 'dries'
believed, was economic 'freedom'. Britain was over-regulated. The first
task, therefore, was to put this right. Joseph, the Industry Secretary, began
by announcing the abolition of the Price Commission, cuts in regional aid,
and the run-down of the NEB. The Chancellor – Howe – followed this up
by scrapping exchange controls at a stroke in October 1979. At the time
that was regarded as particularly brave. Exchange controls (restrictions,
that is, on the export of capital) were what had protected Britain's balance
of payments position for more than 40 years. Howe himself admitted that
this was the only decision of his life that had caused him to lose a night's
sleep. Michael Heseltine, the Environment Secretary, warned that it would
lead people to 'buy villas in the south of France rather than invest in productive assets at home'.[2] In fact it made little immediate difference to the overall
picture: but only because Britain's off-shore oil industry, which (as Labour
had always feared) had come on song just in time to help the Conservatives,

was now sucking foreign money in.[3] (That was their first piece of luck.) How long this would last was impossible to say. The potential was always there for this decision to exacerbate what for years had been one of Britain's major economic problems – the lack of investment in her domestic industry. For the time being, however, the Jeremiahs seemed wide of the mark. The drawbridge had been lowered, the portcullis raised, and no harm had come to the castle as a result.

In any case ideology also provided the answer to the Jeremiahs' fears. If capital did flee the country under a more liberal régime it would be because British industry was not worth investing in. The solution to that was to free it some more, to make it efficient and competitive. One obvious shackle to be removed was the penal top rate of taxation, which was supposed to be a major disincentive to enterprise. 'Unless people are able to earn and keep sufficient reward for [their] investment and effort,' claimed Howe, '...they are just not going to be interested.'[4] True to his word, he knocked three pence off income tax in his first budget in June 1979. That was not to be repeated until several years later; but it stood as a token of intent. Secondly, industry had to be liberated from the state. The government got off the mark quickly with that too. The first beneficiaries, announced in July 1979, were British Airways, British Aerospace and BNOC (the state oil-drilling enterprise). Soon afterwards Joseph announced that the Post Office's telephone side would be separated off, prior to 'privatization' there as well. That would force these concerns to sharpen up their acts. Another motive was to create a more capitalist 'culture' in the country, by encouraging wider share ownership, which would hopefully then invigorate other parts of the economy too. Lastly, the labour market needed liberalising. Overpowerful trade unions were an obvious (in 1979) source of industrial inefficiency. They had to be curbed. That was probably the government's most difficult task. It was certainly thought to be. Prior's approach was to try and do it 'gradually, with as little resistance, and therefore as much by stealth, as was possible'.[5] His opening shot was a new Employment bill in December 1979, limiting picketing and the 'closed shop', and encouraging ballots before strikes. It was a small step, but a definite one, towards a truly free market in human labour, too. Then the economy would really be on its way, and investment would flow in.

So long – that was – as the money invested held its value. That was the government's other main economic preoccupation from the start. Inflation was almost as pernicious as state control. It, too, sapped initiative and energy: what was the point of making money if later it only bought less? *The Times* even regarded it as 'immoral', far more so than unemployment, for example, or poverty: 'It is a concealed tax levied on any holder of cash through higher prices... All inflation is theft.'[6] The government agreed, and decided early on that 'the conquest of inflation, and not the pursuit of growth and employment,... should be the objective of macroeconomic policy';[7] though it usually also insisted that low inflation would conduce to higher growth and employment too in the end. The means by which it intended to achieve this was 'monetarism': limiting the growth of the money supply, that is, rather than trying to influence prices and incomes directly, on the grounds that, as Thatcher put it later, 'price rises were a symptom of underlying inflation, not a cause of it', and that 'Inflation was a monetary phenomenon which it would require monetary discipline to curb.'[8] That too met with some dissent in cabinet. Prior, for example, found that the New Right's reliance on monetarism began to 'stick in the gullet' after a while. 'As a Tory, I instinctively reacted against the dogmatic or simplistic answers to what I believed were very complex and deep-seated problems.'[9] But the government ploughed on.

It was a bold programme; especially as the real, committed advocates of it were probably in a minority in the cabinet at this early stage. 'Even during Margaret's ascendancy,' wrote another dissident, Peter Walker, later, 'there was never a large, dedicated right-wing or Thatcherite group. This is little understood.'[10] So how did the right prevail? They held the key economic posts, of course (First Lord, Exchequer, Industry); but still they could have been outvoted theoretically. Prior blamed himself and his more moderate colleagues for not being 'subtle' or 'clever' enough. He was also, as we have seen, rather slow to read the signs until it was too late. (Howe's first budget, he later wrote, came as 'an enormous shock'.)[11] Walker had a horror of 'party groups expressing organised opposition' within the Conservative party, and could certainly never bring himself to lead such a one.[12] When Francis Pym, another relative liberal, did so later, the attempt fell pathetically flat.[13] Walker attributed this to the wider parliamentary party's penchant for loyalty: few Tory MPs were particularly right-wing, or indeed ideological in any sense at all – 'instinctively many shrink from doctrine' – but 'if leaders with the ability of Keith Joseph and Margaret Thatcher say the right thing is to adopt a monetary policy, which involves the volume of money supply as defined by M3, they think they are clever, nice people and it may be right.'[14] That was an advantage the Conservatives had always had over Labour, which the New Right now exploited to great effect.

On the other hand Walker may have underestimated the extent of genuine support among Conservatives for Thatcher's views. The technical arguments for and against monetarism were probably beyond most of them (as they are beyond most of the rest of us); but the general ethos that was seen to lie behind it – economic 'discipline', a word much used by Thatcher – was not. They responded to that. Discipline would beat some efficiency into the lazy British economy at last. Any hardships on the way would be worth it to that end. Some rightists – Denis Healey called them 'sado-mon-etarists'[15] – thought those hardships were a good thing *per se*. They also, in common with many in the centre and on the left of the party, went along wholeheartedly with most of Thatcher's other attitudes, at least in princi-ple: on taxation, for example; privatization; trade unions; and the 'freedom' thing generally. Some of them had shied away from these policies in the past on the grounds that they were impractical, but that was all. Thatcher seemed to show them otherwise. That was at least as powerful a reason for the support she got as blind, unthinking loyalty.

By the same token, however, this kind of support was dependent ulti-mately on success. That seemed a long time coming. The first two or three years of the new policy gave few signs of it. The economy as a whole actu-ally shrank during the course of them, despite all the government's brave measures, plus North Sea oil, and against the trend abroad. Manufacturing output declined. Unemployment more than doubled, to over three million in January 1982. Bankruptcies soared. Even in its priority areas the govern-ment seemed to be failing, with both public expenditure and taxation rising, for example, and Howe less successful in controlling the money supply than his Labour predecessor had been, which was ironical to say the least.[16] There were serious urban riots in Bristol in 1980, and Brixton (London), Toxteth (Liverpool) and Moss Side (Manchester) in 1981. Of course it was possible to find excuses for most of this. The riots were the fruit of simple wickedness, probably born of 1960s permissiveness, and fuelled by agita-tors. The economic situation was the result of Labour's legacy. The bankruptcies and unemployment were part of a necessary shake-out, of inefficient and excess economic capacity, which would make the patient sparer and fitter in the end. 'After almost any major operation,' Thatcher told the nation in a political broadcast in February 1980, 'you feel worse before you convalesce. But you do not refuse the operation when you know that, without it, you will not survive.'[17] The government was winning the battle against inflation, despite its failures with the money supply. Strikes were becoming fewer.[18] It simply needed more time for the remainder of its measures to start paying a dividend. That sort of reasoning calmed some nerves, but not others. One really needed to have a great deal of faith in Thatcher and her ideology to stick with them through all this.

By the winter of 1981–82 there were signs of deep concern, if not panic, in the Tory ranks. The government was plummetting in the opinion polls, which boded ill for the next election. Conservative MPs might be loyal, but they were not lemmings, and would not follow any leader over the edge of a cliff. Two former prime ministers, Macmillan and Heath, were predicting 'disaster' if Thatcher went on as she was doing then.[19] She ignored them, and stayed resolute, publicly contemptuous of those she felt lacked the 'backbone' for the struggle, some of whom she sacked or rid herself of in other ways,[20] but without staunching the growing dissent. Backbench rebellions forced government retreats on petrol tax (April 1981), local government reform (December 1981) and unemployment benefit (March 1982). Unemployment was the main worry. Few people believed that any government could stay afloat for long politically with these three millions of human ballast in its hold. In December 1981 the cabinet announced a 'Youth Opportunities Programme' to try to alleviate the situation, but without any obvious political gain. A Gallup poll published at the end of March the next year put the Conservatives in third place behind the two other major parties in public esteem, with only 31 percentage points.[21] The government looked becalmed. That was the position in the spring of 1982; just before the storm blew up from the south Atlantic that was to fill its sails again, and set it back on course.

II

Fortune does not always favour the brave; but it did on a couple of occasions in Thatcher's case. The Falklands conflict was probably her greatest piece of good fortune. It was almost entirely unexpected, partly through official incompetence. It came at an ideal time for the government, when its fortunes were at their lowest. It may have saved Thatcher's political bacon. It certainly revived her reputation, and saw her through a difficult patch. All this, it should be emphasized, was because of the way she responded to the crisis; another, weaker leader could quite easily have been destroyed by it. Thatcher rode her luck courageously and cleverly. The political gain she reaped from it was, in this sense, merited.

It was a remarkable episode in several ways. Thatcher's decision to resist utterly Argentina's invasion of the Falklands (2 April 1982) took many people by surprise, including clearly the Argentines themselves. The invasion was a gross act of aggression, and so deserved this response; but another leader might have weighed other factors before going in quite so strongly as Thatcher did. Britain's historical and legal title to the islands was not indisputable. Her possession of them made no practical sense in modern conditions. Her material interest in that part of the world was minimal, and arguably less than the benefits that better relations with Argentina would have brought. The Argentines had some reason to suppose that Britain felt lukewarm over the islands, especially after the recent withdrawal of almost the entire British naval presence in the area (an ice-patrol vessel called HMS *Endurance*), with Thatcher's full knowledge and approval, despite warnings at the time that it would send the wrong signals out, as indeed it did. Reconquering the islands did not look an easy task initially, from 8000 miles away, in rough waters, and with the southern winter approaching. Opportunities for negotiation and hence a face-saving compromise were

there. The whole thing seemed irrational, for a market-oriented government. People at the time sometimes regarded the Falklands campaign as a
reversion to nineteenth century 'imperialism' or 'gun-boat diplomacy'; but
it is difficult to imagine the harder-headed Victorians expending quite so
much relative effort and treasure, and at such a risk, for so small a material
return, if the situation had ever arisen then.[22]

Thatcher however had other considerations in mind. 'We were defending our honour as a nation, and principles of fundamental importance to the
whole world – above all, that aggression should never succeed.' That was
one. Secondly, she felt that this was an ideal opportunity to exorcise what
she called the 'Suez syndrome', or the *feeling* of decline that had afflicted
Britain ever since the Egyptian debacle of 1956, and so restore the nation's
reputation and importance in the world.[23] These were far nobler aims. In
Thatcher's view they amply justified the 255 British lives lost and £5 billion of money expended[24] in winning the war; which was achieved
eventually – with great military skill and bravery, plus some brutality – on
14 June 1982. It was well worth it. A principle had been upheld. Prestige
had been restored. 'We have ceased to be a nation in retreat,' Thatcher
proudly told an audience in Cheltenham a couple of weeks afterwards. 'We
rejoice that Britain has rekindled that spirit which has fired her for generations past and which today has begun to burn as brightly as before.'
'Everywhere I went after the war,' she remembered later, 'Britain's name
meant more than it had.'[25] That was a real, solid benefit, was it not?

It may have been. The trouble was – as it usually is with questions like
this, where 'prestige' is involved – that it was difficult to quantify. So far as
deterring aggression was concerned the Falklands lesson was certainly not
sufficient on its own. Aggressors continued aggressing, often with impu-
nity. The world generally was no more secure after 1982 for the stand
Thatcher took then, mainly because simple aggression is not the most common cause of international *in*security. Britain was undoubtedly regarded
differently, but not necessarily with any more respect. Ronald Reagan, the
American president, admired her for the Falklands episode, but there were
doubts about his grip on reality. If other national leaders shared his feelings
they rarely showed it, or allowed it to make much practical difference to the
way they treated Britain. So far as her European partners were concerned,
their regard was more than a little tinged with irritation, at Thatcher's high-
handed and hectoring treatment of them, especially after 1982. (Thatcher
never concealed her dislike for the EC.) To many her whole attitude to foreign affairs, exemplified by the events of that year, appeared arrogant,
bullying and xenophobic. If this elicited respect for her from foreigners, it
was not necessarily the best or most useful kind.

Further than that the Falklands war had no discernable influence on Britain's 'place in the world'. How could it? The relative strength and importance of modern nations are not governed by such things as military victories in marginal theatres, still less by the 'spirit' that is 'fired' by them. Other long-term factors had brought Britain to the position she was in in the 1980s, and were to keep her there: her economic capacity (which did not change), her responsibilities in the world (which did, but only slightly), and the position of the superpowers. These confirmed her as a minor power still, with less influence over her own destiny, let alone the world's affairs, than Thatcher seems to have believed. Two other foreign policy events of her term exemplify this: her government's final capitulation to the black Marxists of Rhodesia (now Zimbabwe) in 1980; and its agreement in 1984 with China over the return of Hong Kong. That was more like the old Britain: *appeasing* others, from a position of weakness, and in the face of what appeared to be the realities of the time, just as a succession of British governments had done for decades past, in the course of adjusting to the implications of their nation's decline, and usually wisely, though of course there had been some notable exceptions to that. By all accounts Thatcher was unhappy with both these decisions, which were initiated and executed in detail by the harder-headed Foreign Office, but she was powerless to prevent them.[26] That said more about Britain's real situation in the world than the Falklands aberration did.

In fact that situation may actually have declined under Thatcher. It depended on how one regarded her relationship with Reagan's America, which was the keystone of her foreign policy, mainly for reasons of ideology. The United States in the 1980s, under the influence of its own 'New Right', was almost Thatcher's model polity; it was also the strongest bulwark in the world against the threat of Soviet communism, which made it the obvious ally for as virulent an anti-communist as she. There was also another consideration. Thatcher's ideology put her against other *kinds* of relationship with other countries than straight alliances. She despised the United Nations, for example, and the Commonwealth; partly because of what she saw (understandably) as their hypocrisy, but also because of their co-operative and consensual aspects. (The very words 'common wealth' must have struck a discordant note.)[27] The European Community was open to the same objections. All offended against her sense of individual – in this sphere elevated to *national* – independence, by their tendency to subsume it in something larger. Alliances were different. They were the equivalent of 'contracts' at the lower level: arrangements entered into freely, and with limited and closely-defined purposes, preserving therefore the essential independence (or 'sovereignty') of both (or all) sides. NATO was just such a creature, and consequently the only form of international organisation for which Thatcher had any time.[28] That, of course, provided Britain's main formal link with the USA. Whether it really was as free and equal a partnership as Thatcher assumed must be open to doubt. For all Thatcher's personal superiority, in terms of intellect and force of character, over the almost ludicrously inadequate Reagan, it was clear that America's was the dominant role. She defended Britain; Britain in return gave support in various forms, the most visible of which were the highly controversial American 'cruise' missile bases at Greenham Common in Berkshire and Molesworth in Cambridgeshire; and the facilities Thatcher gave the US Air Force to launch its notorious punitive raid on Libya on the night of 14-15 April 1986. That even had the local middle classes – who feared retaliation – protesting against her.[29] These were somewhat passive contributions to the common cause. A more positive one was the moral strength Thatcher was supposed to have given Reagan and then his successor George Bush at critical moments, like when Iraq invaded Kuwait in August 1990: 'Maggie puts the beef into Bush', as one newspaper headline had it;[30] but Bush himself may not have seen it quite like that. At other times in the recent past this kind of relationship between a British prime minister and an American president – Macmillan and Kennedy, for example, or Wilson and Johnson – had been widely regarded as demeaning and distracting for Britain. The same could be said of this one, and quite often was, at the time.[31]

III

'Prestige' is a chimera if it is not founded on solid material strength. (Gladstone had always known that.)[32] Thatcher's claim to have raised Britain's prestige in the world in the 1980s was questionable at best, and probably meaningless in practical terms. Nevertheless it may have had an effect domestically. Many Britons *felt* she had raised their national reputation, and behaved accordingly. Some manifestations of this were less attractive than others: the excessive jingoism of the actual time of the Falklands war, for example, particularly in the tabloid press; and a certain arrogance among some species of British traveller abroad, which lingered. Elsewhere it simply restored people's self respect, which was no bad thing, and may have been a positive benefit, if Thatcher was right in believing that one of the roots of Britain's problems in the past had been a defeatist attitude of mind. She herself felt that a tangible dividend could come of it. In speeches around the country after the war she repeatedly argued that what she called the 'spirit of the South Atlantic' was something that might inspire them in their industrial activities, too. (The first time she made this point was in order to shame railwaymen into calling off a projected strike.)[33] There is no evidence that this ever worked; but on another level the Falklands 'spirit' clearly had a tremendous influence on the home front. In the first place the success of the war repaired the Conservative government's popularity almost overnight, and pretty solidly, with the result that it won the next general election, in June 1983, by a landslide. Secondly, it had an immense personal impact on Thatcher. It was the first major test of her fighting qualities, and of her combative approach to problems. She passed it magnificently. That encouraged her to apply the same approach to other issues, including domestic ones, which in the past had not generally been considered to be the domain of warfare, but which Thatcher treated as if they were.

The major example was the miners' strike of 1984–85, which Thatcher regarded in much the same way as the Falklands invasion: as an act of aggression that needed to be uncompromisingly put down. 'Mr Scargill's insurrection' was what she called it later in her memoirs: Arthur Scargill had been the brains behind the 'flying pickets' that had been so successful in the 1972 miners' strike,[34] and was now President of the main mineworkers' union (the NUM). According to Thatcher his ultimate aim now was to 'impose a Marxist system on Britain'. Hence the need for him to be defeated thoroughly, in order that 'the use of strikes for political purposes' should be 'discredited once and for all'.[35] It was a battle on two fronts, just as the Falklands war had been: against the 'enemy within', as she dubbed the militants (or perhaps *all* the strikers – it was not made clear at the time) in July 1984;[36] and against those on her own side who wished to appease them, either out of a misplaced sense of moderation, or for short-term economic advantage – to get the mines working again and so staunch the loss being caused by the strike. Her own hand-picked National Coal Board chairman, a Scots-American called Ian MacGregor, had to be restrained more than once from settling on terms that would have saved some face for the NUM. He regarded this as unwarrantable interference; but then, as Thatcher commented, 'He was a businessman, not a politician', and could not realise the broader significance of the struggle from a national point of view.[37] That made this a political conflict, whether or not the NUM had really intended it as such originally. It also turned it into a war to the finish, which the government side decisively won. The striking miners returned to work, proudly – marching behind their banners – but still comprehensively beaten, on 5 March 1985; after which the wholesale closure of 'uneconomic' pits which the strike had ostensibly been called to prevent began.

That was Thatcher's most important and characteristic victory. She had others, but none of them was quite so sweet. Some were pyrrhic. By the time the Greater London Council – another of her arch-enemies – was abolished in 1986, most people had considerable doubts about the wisdom of leaving Britain's largest city without a unitary authority, simply because it tended to be left-wing. The defeat in 1987 of the newspaper print unions, whose restrictive practices were insufferable by almost any criteria, was marred by the fact that the main victor in this particular battle – the Australian press tycoon Rupert Murdoch – was almost the quintessential capitalist amoralist, and so not widely liked himself. (Thatcher's respect for the judgments of the market gave her some odd allies, for so outwardly moralistic a woman.) In 1984 workers at the secret Government Communications Headquarters at Cheltenham were deprived of the right to join a trade union, whose obvious implications for fundamental civil liberties left a bad taste even in some Conservatives' mouths. In 1989 Thatcher achieved one of her most cherished aims, when she succeeded in replacing the – roughly progressive – local-authority domestic-rates system by a flat-rate 'community charge', against vociferous objections from almost every quarter, including many in her own camp. That however was the shortest-lived of her successes, and also the most self-destructive; for it was the unpopularity of the new 'poll tax' (as it was almost universally called) which largely brought about her ultimate fall.

Apart from that critical failure, however, Thatcher succeeded in nearly everything she set out to do. She tamed the Argentines, the trade unions, left-wing local councils, schools, universities, and the BBC. She devastated the opposition parties; though not without a great deal of help from them, which was her third (and last) great piece of luck. (Labour was reckoned to be almost unelectable, due to the 'extremism' of its left wing, and then the defection of its other wing to form the 'Social Democratic' party in 1981, crucially splitting the anti-government vote.) Under her there was a significant shift of economic power in Britain away from the state and towards private enterprise, partly through the withdrawal of trade-union privileges, and partly through a 'privatisation' programme that gathered strength and speed with every passing day. As a result the 'market' became the predominant influence in British human affairs again, in a way it had not been for 50 or perhaps even a 100 years. Another success was to reverse the recent (albeit slow) trend towards greater equality in Britain, by means of huge tax reductions at the top end of the salary scale, together with the erosion of the 'social wage', compounded by unemployment, at the other. In 1979 for example the best-paid 10% of the population earned four times as much as the bottom 10%; by 1989 this proportion had risen to five and a half.[38] This was deliberate. (The argument for it on national economic grounds was that it was the rich who created jobs for the rest, so long as the latter did not price themselves out of them.) Thatcher herself was in no doubt about her overall achievement. 'My colleagues and I,' she boasted 18 months after she left office, 'turned round the whole philosophy of government.'[39] That – if we allow for some exaggeration of her and her colleagues' personal part in this – was largely true.

IV

Philosophy, however, is not everything. In government what usually matter more are its practical effects. In this case those were problematical. Thatcher had succeeded in her aims, but not – to use a management-derived distinction fashionable at the time – in her objectives. Those were to bring 'harmony', 'truth' and 'faith', remember; and – on a more concrete level – to revive Britain's prosperity and strength. In none of these areas was her achievement unequivocal.

'Harmony' was a clear failure. Thatcher's combative style of government was incompatible with that. One compelling image of the 1980s was of large bodies of police in 'riot gear' counter-attacking even larger rabbles of strikers or demonstrators, with truncheons flying, amidst clouds of tear-gas smoke. The worst pitched battles (after 1982) were at Greenham in 1983, with anti-nuclear demonstrators; at the Orgreave coke works in 1984; in various inner-city areas (Handsworth, Brixton, Tottenham) in the summer of 1985; outside Murdoch's new union-breaking printing works in Wapping in 1986–87; and finally at the gates of the very heart of government, in Whitehall, in March 1990, when police engaged poll-tax rioters in what was probably the bloodiest civil conflict seen in London since the 1880s. That was quite apart from Northern Ireland, where Thatcher's firm stand against terrorism did nothing to stem the by now endemic violence there. The latter was brought home to her in a very direct way on the night of 12 October 1984, when the hotel she was staying in for that year's Conservative party conference in Brighton was blown up by an IRA bomb. Her fortitude on that occasion was much admired. But any emollient qualities she may have had were not much in evidence.

The 1980s were an inharmonious decade in other ways too. There was a great deal of social distress, naturally, and the alienation that usually stems from that. That appeared in various manifestations. One was – or seemed to be – crime, which rose unprecedently during Thatcher's term of office.[40] On the surface it appeared logical to associate that with joblessness; though government spokespeople vehemently denied this, and there is, in truth, no sure way of proving that poverty – as opposed to lack of parental discipline, for instance, or the decline of religion, or sheer wickedness – was primarily responsible. In much the same way ministers preferred to blame the marked deterioration of health that afflicted those who lost out most by the government's policies not on that, but on individual fecklessness;[41] though there was still a case to be made for the alternative view. (In fact the two sides in these arguments may have been talking about different things.) Among the better-off there was also some suffering, though of a different order and kind: fear of crime, for example; stress from over-work caused by the contraction of labour forces; worries over job security; and demoralisation (especially in the public sector) arising from the government's clear lack of respect for what certain workers did. 'If you people were any good,' Thatcher is reported to have told a group of British Rail executives once as they were welcoming her to a working lunch, 'you wouldn't be here. You'd all be working in the private sector.' That may be apocryphal, but it rings true.[42] All these things made Britain in the 1980s not a very *happy* country. Few Conservatives bothered to deny this. Their line was that if it had been happy before, it was because people had been living in a fool's paradise. Now they had been dragged into the 'real world' (a favourite expression of theirs), which was, objectively, not a happy place.

A certain amount of suffering was also thought to be necessary to rouse the country from its lethargy. People needed to be galvanised into self-reliance, by showing them what the natural and stark alternative was. Then the country would benefit too, as productive energies were stimulated and channelled (by the market) into the most profitable areas. That was supposed to be the point of the whole exercise; though in some cases, as we have seen,[43] there must be a suspicion that the *moral* lesson this inculcated was thought to be sufficient on its own. This may be why Thatcher – who was essentially a moralist rather than an economist – persisted in believing that her government had been a great triumph overall, when in fact its economic record was mediocre, to say the least. Greater individual 'freedom' – in this sense – did not bring about any significant improvement in Britain's economic performance or comparative standing in the world. Which suggests either that this was not the solution; or that it had not been taken far enough; or that the patient was simply too far gone to be cured even by the right medicines.

The government had some successes. One was the defeat of inflation, which peaked at 18% (for the year) in 1980, but then began a somewhat erratic course downwards, until it reached the remarkable figure of 2%, shortly after Thatcher left.[44] Ministers were delighted with that. They also took pride in the new dynamism that deregulation (the 'Big Bang') gave to the City of London after 1986, enabling it to maintain and extend its leading international role. Some of them got very excited around 1986-88, when they persuaded themselves that they had a genuine German-style economic 'miracle' on their hands. That was short-lived, however, and may have been illusory. Its main effect was to give people a sense of false confidence, which led them to over-extend themselves financially, often with disastrous results. That was one contributor (though not the only one) to the recession that followed: the second of Thatcher's reign (which is a lot of recessions for one government), and the worst since World War II.

Looking back from that time it was difficult to discern the really solid recovery that Thatcher's medicine had been supposed to promote. Industry was certainly not a beneficiary. In 1979 manufacturing had represented 28.4% of Britain's gross domestic product. Ten years later this had fallen to 22.2%.[45] In some products Britain simply stopped competing, and left it to foreigners. In 1981 a symbolic watershed was reached when for the first time in her history she imported more manufactured goods from abroad than she sent there.[46] That was partly the reverse side of the rise of the City, which throve on high interest rates, whereas industry, of course, likes them low. This may not have mattered. The vacuum left by manufacturing was filled by other things: banking, insurance and stockbroking, for example, and what were called the 'service industries', like retailing and the hotel trade. Committed free marketists assumed that if this was the way nature (the market) was pushing Britain, it must be all right. Lord (David) Young, Thatcher's Employment Secretary from 1985 to 1985, believed it would take up at least some of the jobless slack eventually, if only northerners (especially) could be brought to see the value of it. The problem here, as he told the House of Lords in May 1985, was 'that too many people thought that "service" was somehow the equivalent of "servile". The profession of waiter was honourable... I argued that a hotel was the equivalent of a factory, earning foreign exchange from overseas visitors the same as exports and creating wealth by employing people just as a factory would. The hotel might even last longer than a factory.'[47] That was almost an admission of defeat on the manufacturing front. It may have been realistic. But it did not impress people who all their lives had been used to *making* things; least of all the tens of thousands of unemployed ex-steel workers and coal miners for whom – even if they had managed to conquer their prejudices – there were simply not enough pinnies to go around. Waitering was no compensation, either materially or spiritually, for the loss of the mills and the mines.

On balance, therefore, the British economy fared no better under Thatcher than it had under any other government in the post-war period. Growth rates remained low; indebtedness high; the trade balance precarious; unemployment at record levels, possibly even for the century; and taxation – if everything was included: indirect as well as direct taxes – comparable to under Wilson at his most swingeing.[48] That had to mark another failure, to put beside the conflict and violence and other stresses of these years.

On the other hand the government was probably not *responsible* for them. It certainly did not originate any of this: neither the country's economic problems, which long pre-dated Thatcher; nor the social disharmony, which we saw rearing its head in a number of guises during the 1970s, and even before. These things almost certainly reflected deeper trends. The main one was the progress of the global capitalist economy at this stage. That seems now to have been inexorable, as was shown by the collapse of non-capitalist systems nearly everywhere in the world at the end of the 1980s; unless you believed – as Thatcher appears to have done in her final, megalomaniac phase[49] – that she was personally responsible for that as well. It also, however, brought problems in its train. They may have been inevitable too. Every capitalist economy experienced them: the newest ones most acutely, as might have been expected, but also the strongest systems – Japan, Germany, the USA – and middling-strength free economies like Britain. The symptoms were similar everywhere: recession, bankruptcies, mass unemployment, casualization of labour, poverty, intolerance, social and national conflict, violence. Some of these were undoubtedly transitory phenomena – trans*itional*, probably, in the case of the ex-socialist economies – but others appeared ominously permanent. Few analysts, for example, held out much hope for a significant easing of the world unemployment situation before the end of the century, if then. High human wastage seemed to be an endemic feature of free-market capitalism at this stage of its development. Now that Britain had rejoined the main stream of that development she could not expect to escape these effects. It was not the government's – or Margaret Thatcher's – fault. It was simply the way nature worked.

That seemed to be confirmed by later events. On 22 November 1990 Thatcher resigned as prime minister, reluctantly and bitterly, after failing to garner enough cabinet or backbench support to repulse a leadership challenge convincingly. The main grounds for her party's abandonment of her were the issue of Europe, the unpopularity of the 'poll tax', and her increasingly domineering manner; all of which were believed to make her an electoral liability. In her place, the Conservative party chose someone who was thought to be the very antithesis of her, certainly in 'style' – John Major seemed a friendly, moderate, compromising sort of fellow – and possibly in other ways too. That did the trick. Against many odds, and most predictions at the time, including the opinion pollsters', the Conservatives won the next election under him (in April 1992), albeit with a much reduced majority. But it made little difference to the broad current of events. Those who had hoped that government policy would now be different in substance were to be disappointed. The poll tax was withdrawn. That was no longer supportable. But otherwise the 'Thatcherite' juggernaut careered on: extending privatisation, for example; continuing the dismantling of the welfare state; and obstructing European Community efforts to protect workers from the harshest effects of market forces (the 'social chapter'). The recession deepened, then 'bottomed out', but never showed any sign of solid recovery: to an extent that would fulfil the promise that free-market capitalism had used to hold out to people, for example, of general prosperity. Abroad things were no better. (That was part of the trouble: recession abroad shrank Britain's

market, and hence her chances of recovery.) The face had changed –
Major's engaging smile replacing Thatcher's forbidding glare – but not
the underlying reality. Major was as much a prisoner of his time as
Thatcher had been; no less, and no more.

Chapter 29

Full Circle?
(1990)

I

Britain had been here (or somewhere like it) before. Then her reaction had been to do what she could to get away. That was because of the contradictions in her situation, which appeared intrinsic to free-market capitalism in its mid-nineteenth-century form. They included poverty, which capitalism had been supposed to eradicate, but did not; the enormous powers it gave to certain human beings over others, which seemed inconsistent with the system's proclaimed ideal of individual 'freedom'; the opportunities for 'exploitation' (in the worst sense) it afforded unscrupulous capitalists, especially of weak and unsophisticated foreigners; and the discontent these factors gave rise to in their turn, both at home and overseas, leading sometimes to violent protest, which necessitated stronger methods of state repression than the original free marketists – who were also usually political liberals – felt comfortable with.

It was for these reasons that Victorian Britain, despite its later reputation, had never been a model free-market society. In an earlier chapter we described it as 'hybrid' – a mixture of old and new – and attributed its survival and stability to this. Towards the end of the nineteenth century – to recapitulate one of the arguments of this book – that hybridity became more pronounced, as the 'contradictions' bit deeper, and forced further compromises on two fronts: at home in the form of state intervention in the interests of social reform (later social*ism*); and abroad in the guise of a highly paternalistic version of imperialism. That was how Britain effected her escape from the contradictions of capitalism then.

Unfortunately her life on the outside was not to last long. That was because it too was beset by contradictions. (Probably every form of society is.) The most glaring ones arose from the disparities between Britain's strength and her responsibilities abroad, which are what destroyed her empire in the end. The end of socialism followed; partly because of its *dependence* on empire, which has been described above, and which consequently left it with one important prop missing when the latter went; and partly through the force of its own internal contradictions, which were becoming glaringly obvious by the 1970s, even to some socialists. The result was Britain's return (in the company of much of the rest of the world) to the path she had strayed from all those years before. That relieved the particular contradictions she had been suffering from recently. But it also threatened to bring the old ones back.

II

In fact it did not bring them back altogether; but only because free marketists' expectations had altered over the past hundred years. We have covered that change, too, in previous chapters: the process by which free marketism was prised away from its previous association with liberalism, and came to be lodged in the opposite camp. That solved a lot of problems, simply by making them less problematical. Latter-day free marketists, for example, did not *mind* that the market did not seem to conduce to equality, or social justice, or even progress, which were less fashionable concepts than they had used to be. Nor were they particularly worried by its implications for civil liberties. 'The trouble about a free market economy,' wrote one perceptive commentator in 1985, 'is that it requires so many policemen to make it work.'[1] He might have added that some of them were *secret* policemen. The mid-Victorians would have hated that. It struck at their whole conception of the relationship between the free market and government. So did another related tendency: which was the late twentieth-century free marketists' cavalier disregard for popular participation in government, if it seemed to them to conflict with market efficiency, as democracy, of course, very often does. The emasculation of local government, especially, under the new régime would have hurt them very sorely indeed. The replacement of representative bodies in a host of areas by officially-appointed 'quangos' would have astounded them. All these trends would have set up unbearable tensions for the earlier, liberal brand of free marketist. Their late-twentieth-century disciples, however, having cast aside all this idealistic paraphernalia, scarcely flinched.

The new free marketism produced many similar discrepancies. Some of them were philosophical, and so could perhaps be disregarded. They turned on the concepts of 'freedom' and 'choice', which free marketists made great play of, but were – one would think – at least slightly vulnerable on. 'Freedom' was a problem because giving more freedom to some people, by releasing them from the constraints of the state, delivered other people into their grasp. The 'right to manage', for example, which became something of a slogan in Britain in the early 1980s,[2] involved a corresponding obligation to *be* managed by those lower down the line. That did not extend freedom. At best it redistributed it. Some of its implications were almost indefensible: such as the dilemma faced by National Health workers who in the later 1980s were instructed by their new-style market-orientated 'managers' that they owed their loyalty solely to their institutions, and so must not reveal shortcomings which affected the public good. The reason why that was so tyrannical was that it undermined the public's freedom, too. This arose directly from each institution's need to compete, and so present a good appearance. It was intrinsic, in other words, to the market situation. It could be corrected; but only by modifying that situation to some extent.

'Choice' was another problem area. Theoretically there should have been far more of it under capitalism than under socialism, which was widely pictured as grey and uniform. To a large extent this was so. No one in a position to compare a Moscow department store with a London one before 1990, for example, could be in much doubt about this. Capitalism did offer more variety. The revival of it in Britain in the 1980s certainly extended the range of people's choice. But there were limits. Certain choices were ruled out if they were ideologically suspect: like some vaguely socialist municipal enterprises, however many municipal voters had chosen them. An example was the old Greater London Council's overwhelmingly popular – and environmentally beneficial – policy of subsidising public transport ('Fare's Fair'), which was outlawed because it offended against competitive principles. A more startling example, because it did not involve socialism and affected *individual* choice, was the 'privatising' – with government encouragement – of the Victorians' beloved Trustee Savings Bank[3] in 1985, because it was non profit-making; thus restricting the range of the *kinds* of bank people could choose, which was clearly an impoverishment. In other areas one effect of market forces seemed to be to cater only for majority tastes. Commercial radio stations only played popular music; all television sets were black (or whatever was the fashion at the time); shopping 'malls' all over the country were franchised to the same stores, obscuring regional differences. Grey uniformity had been replaced by a more garish kind. The arts were particularly vulnerable to this, as a minority taste. Left to the mercies of the market, *that* area of choice would probably have dried up altogether for most people, just as it had (effectively) in Victorian times.[4] 'Serious' music, for example, was kept alive only by state and municipal subsidies, and the non-commercial BBC. (The new 'Classic FM' commercial radio station, started up later, confined its patronage mainly to dead composers' more tuneful bits.) In the 1980s both these sources of government funding came under threat from free-market ideologies. Had the latter won, there can be little doubt that the effect would have been a further erosion of choice.

Another source of tension was in the field of morality. Capitalism is a peculiarly amoral system. Many capitalists have disputed this, including Victorian ones, who used to like to think that it conduced to morality by rewarding virtue, encouraging self-reliance, and punishing laziness; but that was never a wholly convincing proposition even in their time. Then, insofar as capitalism was conducted ethically (and it was not entirely), it was mainly because of the influence of extraneous factors: like Christianity, and gentlemanly rules of conduct inherited from pre-capitalist times. Later, as these restraints – and others, like socialism – weakened, the amoral tendencies of the system showed through. Financial success became the main criterion for conduct, for example, elevated above honesty, integrity and truth. The effects were seen everywhere where the competitive ethos was allowed to dominate: especially in business, of course, where financial corruption and scandal appeared to reach a new high in the 1980s, but also in public life and government, where standards of probity definitely declined. That was a puzzle for the naïver free marketists, and a worry to the wiser ones.

By the 1980s, however, these negative aspects of the system were less damaging than they would have been considered once. Free marketism could easily survive in the new harsh conditions of the later twentieth century without morality, real liberty, and certain kinds of choice. (It could certainly survive without art.) Other inconsistencies, however, may have been more serious. Some of them struck at the vitals of the system. One of these was the *expense* of it, which was a crucial consideration. A free market was supposed to be cheap. That was absolutely necessary. The central idea was that individuals made better and more profitable use of their monies than the state possibly could. Hence taxation should be as low as possible, to leave more cash in people's pockets, where it could (as Gladstone had put it) 'fructify'. That may have been fine in theory, but it proved difficult to implement. One problem was the cost of unemployment, which benefitted the system in one way (by keeping wages low), but also cost the state dear, in lost taxes and social payments to the unemployed and their families. (You could not let them starve. That would be imitating nature rather *too* closely.) Other effects of unemployment, like poor health, social protest and crime, also bore on public funds. Policing, for example, was not cheap. Hospitals were horrendously expensive. Hence the continued heavy burden of taxation in Britain throughout the 1980s, despite the government's keen desire to cut it drastically. Add to this the considerable increase in the necessary costs borne by employed people as a result of government policies – bigger insurance premiums to cope with the crime wave, private health and dental treatment to compensate for a perceived deterioration of state provision in these fields, and higher transport costs because of the withdrawal of subsidies – and there must have been little if any extra disposable income left. That rather spoiled the object of the exercise.

There were also doubts about the value of the use that was made of any money that was released into the private sector in this way. It was not immediately apparent that it was spent more beneficially, from the whole community's point of view, than it could have been by a moderately competent and far-seeing state. There was a great deal of waste, for example, which was probably inevitable, and even acceptable under a system in which risk played an important and necessary part, but often seemed excessive. Millions were lost in bankruptcies. Large-scale fraud and corruption cost billions more. Those who gained most from the new dispensation, even legally, were not necessarily the most productive members of society. One typical example was supposed to be the *genus* 'Essex Man': 'young, industrious, mildly brutish and culturally barren', according to the newspaper which discovered him in 1990, who made most of his money through selling 'used motors', or 'underpriced shares in British Telecom'.[5] These were not a very convincing vanguard for a revival of Britain's economic fortunes in the world. Higher up in the financial firmament, where the big-money deals were made, the charge was usually that they only sought short-term profits, to the detriment of what was sometimes called the 'real' economy (especially native British industry), which required a more solid commitment from its backers than this. Certainly industry's major post-war problem since the War, of chronic under-investment, was not helped at all by the device of allowing the river of money to follow its natural course. At the same time industry suffered as the infrastructure (railways, education, training) was starved of funds. If this is fair (and it is contentious), then it means that the system may even have been self-destructive in some of its tendencies.

There was another contradiction. This related to the public sector. Free marketists tended to devalue – even despise – public service; but they also needed it. (Any form of government except a truly anarchist one does.) Unfortunately their attitude undermined it. Many well-intentioned educational reforms, for example, may have been neutralised by the clear lack of regard that government ministers showed for teachers and their professional judgments, and the managerial-style changes they foisted on them as a result. In other public sectors too morale plummetted measurably during the 1980s. This even affected government. Most 'insider' accounts of Thatcher's cabinets testify that the atmosphere in them was never happy.[6] Much of this bad feeling emanated from the attitude of their head. Thatcher often spoke and acted as if she despised most of the ministers under her. That probably derived from this same prejudice. (Contemporaries tended to assume it was because they were men.) What were ministers doing ministering, when any man with real talent and initiative would have been out there in the market, making his money work? The only exceptions – her two favourite ministers – were atypical, men with entrepreneurial credentials, after a fashion: Sir Keith Joseph, who had once been chairman of his father's building firm; and David (Lord) Young, who was brought into her government from a fairly successful career in property development. 'Other people come to me with their problems,' Thatcher told the *Financial Times* in 1984; 'David Young comes to me with his achievements.'[7] That was the mark of a businessman. Non-businessmen were inherently less capable. That was why Thatcher thought so little of them. In the end most of them lived down to her expectations; as they were almost bound to, in the eyes of someone who rated public service – even at this level – so low.

III

Nineteenth-century society had also had its contradictions, as we saw. Some of them were similar to these late-twentieth-century ones, though not all. (There was not the same disdain for public service, for example.) There were also other differences. The most crucial one had to do with ethos. In the nineteenth century people had thought their contradictions were resolvable. They had hopes. Free traders for example believed that things would get better if free trade was persisted with; dissidents thought they would improve if it was modified, or overthrown. That made the nineteenth century an optimistic time for most folk.

The same could not be said of the later period. Then, pessimism ruled. This was almost the biggest difference between the two times. Even the newly victorious free marketists were nowhere near as confident as their predecessors had been. There could be no relaxation of the fight against socialism, thought Thatcher; lower one's guard, and the creature would be at one's neck again. Hence the need for constant vigilance, suspicion, distrust of people; for a strong army, the nuclear deterrent, powerful police forces, covert surveillance of anyone who might mean you harm. The opposition was no more sanguine. How could it be? Every form of resistance against full-blown capitalism, from the mildest and most democratic to the most tyrannical, had failed. Marx had been proved wrong. So had Keynes, Beveridge, Attlee, Bevin, Bevan, Benn: all the politicians who had wished to steer a compromise course between both kinds of excess. Most of the signs at the end of the 1980s were ominous, including events at the heart of capitalism's most recent triumph, the ex-Soviet Union, and its former satellites. Here and in other places the breakdown of government –

for that was what the collapse of socialism entailed – had played into the hands of crooks, gangsters, warlords, zealots; smaller tyrannies than the great one that had been dismantled, but no less terrible. Elsewhere the capitalist world had a recession to cope with, plus escalating crime rates, and a collapsing environment, caused by over-exploitation. No one, of any political persuasion, could be happy in the face of all that.

There seemed little that any person or party in Britain could do about it. People were powerless. Certain people seemed less powerless than others; but only because they went along with the broad tide of events. Thatcher was like that: effective only because she did not try to buck history, but submitted to its imperatives. It was those imperatives that had brought Britain to where she was now: a train of events originating in the early nineteenth century, developing out of each other by their own internal logic, which had taken her from the high libertarian hopes of 1851, *via* the contradictions implicit in that to the experience of empire and socialism, and on to the collapse of both these solutions to the contradictions, due to *their* internal contradictions, to what appeared to be irredeemable decline. Thatcher had had no effect on that broad picture. Whether any alternative leader could have resisted more effectively was doubtful, to say the least. The best that he or she could have done was probably to cushion some of the weakest members of society against the worst effects of the trend.

Of course that trend – the imperative – might change. There were some small signs of that happening in 1990. Thatcher's removal was one. That made no immediate significant difference, as we have seen, but it did highlight some of the contradictions the tendency she represented had brought in its train. The problems the Conservative party encountered in finding a suitable successor to her were one. They showed up the difficulty free marketism was bound to have in recruiting competitive leaders from its own ranks. The widely-perceived inadequacies of Major's government in its early years, therefore, were no accident. Nor was the horrendous financial situation it presided over after the 1992 election, which was – in part at least – an outcome of another of the internal contradictions we have already described. There were others. Crime, corruption and the well-publicized sexual adventures of a handful of Conservative MPs continued to mock the free marketists' ethical pretensions. A couple of arms-sale scandals, going back to Thatcher's time but only coming into the open afterwards, served to reveal one clear discrepancy between the pursuit of market gain on the one hand, and morality and national interest on the other. (In one case the government had used overseas aid, which was meant to be altruistic, as a carrot for lucrative military contracts; in the other it had approved the arming of a murderous dictator who – unluckily – was to become its enemy later on.) More to the point for most people, however, were the continuing poverty and unemployment of the early 1990s, which undermined the free marketists' economic claims. That was probably the most significant of the period's 'contradictions'. Twelve years of struggle and sacrifice seemed to have been in vain, for the majority of people at least. That might have been expected to turn things around. Whether it would, however, depended on whether there was still any room for Britain to manoeuvre, at this stage of her national economic development, and in the stormy and crowded ocean she was bobbing about in then. That remained to be seen. In 1990 no one could be sure of anything.

One thing *was* certain, however. The new situation would have gravely disappointed the Victorians. Many of the fundamental things they had craved and worked for had come about, but without the benefits they had confidently expected from them. Most of the world was capitalist; free trade between nations was increasing; national barriers – in this sense – were now almost meaningless. The great natural law of the market had at last asserted itself, almost universally. The outcome, however, was mixed at best. Poverty, unemployment, alienation, crime, immorality and war (especially war) continued worldwide. Most people seemed less free. Nearly everyone was a good deal less contented. That would have been a shock. (It probably should not have been. The truth is that the 'law' of the market is no more benevolent than any other law of nature, when left unmodified by man. Look at earthquakes, disease, baby birds starving to death in the winter, buck rabbits eating their own broods. Why anyone should have supposed that *this* natural law would be any different is odd.) Britain's situation would have shocked the Victorians even more. We have already indicated how. It was a terrible fall, from the hopes (not necessarily the achievements) of the mid-nineteenth century to this pass. Britons in the nineteenth century had expected much more of their own.

The fall was mirrored in a number of ways. One was particularly striking. Buildings can be very redolent of their times. This book opened by describing one of them, the Crystal Palace of 1851 in Hyde Park, London, which certainly was. It was a triumph of British engineering, as well as of architecture; housing an exhibition of Britain's impressive industrial and commercial achievements; and pored over by a (mainly) confident and hopeful populace. It was also a feast of light, gaiety, openness and activity. That reflected the confidence of the time. At the end of our period two new buildings dominated London, which similarly symbolised *their* time. The first was the Canary Wharf tower: the huge centrepiece of a great new financial development built on the now derelict site of London's great dockland – which in itself could be said to reflect the shift in the British economy that had taken place since 1851. At the end of the 1980s the company that sponsored it collapsed, which could also be seen as symbolic.

The second building was the new headquarters of MI6 (the secret intelligence service) going up at this time a few miles up the Thames, near Vauxhall Bridge. That represented the other side of the Thatcherite equation: the 'strong state' (stronger and far more intrusive than ever in Victorian times) which was thought necessary then to shore up the 'free economy'. Both these buildings were designed in the fashionable 'post modernist' style of the period, and were (to this critic, at least) particularly aggressive and soulless examples of it. They had windows which the inhabitants could see out of, but no one could see through from the outside. The contrast with the Crystal Palace, in this respect as in others, was striking. But then so was the contrast between Britain as a whole, in 1851, when our period began, hopefully; and in 1990, when it ends.

Notes

Chapter 1

1 Anon., *The World's Fair; or Children's Prize Gift Book of the Great Exhibition of 1851* (London, [1851]), p. 99.
2 C.R. Fay, *Palace of Industry, 1851* (Cambridge, 1951), p. 47.
3 *The World's Fair*, p. 99.
4 *Dickinsons' Comprehensive Pictures of the Great Exhibition of 1851* (1854), quoted in Fay, op. cit., p. 23.
5 *The World's Fair*, pp. 99–101.
6 Queen Victoria's journal, quoted in Fay, op. cit., pp. 46–8.
7 C.H. Gibbs-Smith, *The Great Exhibition of 1851* (London, 1981), pp. 10, 12
8 Robert Payne, *Marx* (London, 1968), pp. 234–40.
9 Bernard Porter, *The Refugee Question in Mid-Victorian Politics* (Cambridge, 1979), pp. 86–87.
10 *Daily News*, 2 May 1851.
11 *Official Descriptive and Illustrated Catalogue of the Great Exhibition of the Works of Industry of all Nations, 1851* (London, [1851]), part IV, p. 987.
12 Ibid., part I, *Introductory*, pp. 16–19.
13 Ibid., part II, *passim*.
14 [Samuel Prout Newcombe], *Little Henry's Holiday at the Great Exhibition* (London, 1851), pp. 135–7.
15 Bernard Porter, '"Bureau and Barrack":Early Victorian attitudes towards the Continent', in *Victorian Studies*, vol. 27 (1984), pp. 419–21.
16 Speech at Manchester, 15 January 1846; reproduced in John Bright and Thorold Rogers (eds.), *Speeches on Questions of Public Policy by Richard Cobden* (London, 1870), vol. I, pp. 362–3.
17 *Official Descriptive and Illustrated Catalogue*, vol. I, p. 35.
18 [Newcombe], op. cit., p. 119.
19 *The World's Fair*, pp. 3–4.
20 Fay, op. cit., p. 47.
21 *Official Descriptive and Illustrated Catalogue*, vol. I, pp. 3–4.
22 Gibbs-Smith, op. cit., p. 24.

Chapter 2

1 *The Annual Register, or a View of the History and Politics of the Year 1851* (1852), p. 104.
2 Statistics to support these and other similar generalisations can be found in B.R. Mitchell and Phyllis Deane, *Abstract of British Historical Statistics*

(Cambridge, 1962); and in B.R. Mitchell, *European Historical Statistics 1750–1970* (1975).

3   The workhouse population in England and Wales in 1853 was 104,000. *Statistical Abstract for the United Kingdom... 1852–1866* (London, 1867), p. 118.

4   *Annual Register... 1851*, p. 180; Mitchell and Deane, op. cit., p. 427.

5   Mitchell and Deane, op. cit., p. 397.

6   *Annual Register... 1851*, p. 181.

7   See Bernard Porter, '"Bureau and Barrack": Early Victorian Attitudes towards the Continent', in *Victorian Studies*, vol. 27 no. 4 (1984), pp. 424–45.

8   *Hansard*, 3rd series, vol. 119, cc. 511–12 (Commons, 1 April 1852).

9   Bernard Porter, *The Refugee Question in Mid-Victorian Politics* (Cambridge, 1979), pp. 58–9, *et passim*.

10 Mitchell and Deane, pp. 283, 333, 366.

11 Sylvaine Marandon, *L'image de la France dans l'Angleterre Victorienne* (Paris, 1967), p. 102.

12 C.B. Elliott, Letters from the North of Europe (London: 1832), pp. 293, 368; John Murray, *Hand-book for Northern Europe* (London, 1849), p. 398.

13 See Pierre Tucoo-Chala, *Pau: Ville Anglaise* (Pau, 1979.

14 Bernard Porter, '"Monstrous Vandalism": Capitalism and Philistinism in the works of Samuel Laing (1780–1868)', in *Albion*, vol. 23 (1991), pp. 253–68.

15 Charles Babbage, *The Exposition of 1851; or, Views of the Industry, the Science, and the Government, of England* (London: 1851).

16 Anon., *The World's Fair; or Children's Prize Gift Book of the Great Exhibition of 1851* (London, [1851]), pp. 80, 85.

17 Mrs Gaskell, *Mary Barton* (1848) and *North and South* (1855); Charles Kingsley, *Alton Locke* (1850); Charles Dickens, *Hard Times* (1854); Henry Mayhew, *London Labour and the London Poor* (1851); Augustus Mayhew, *Paved with Gold* (1857); Friedrich Engels, *Condition of the Working Classes in England* (London, 1845).

18 Mitchell and Deane, op. cit., pp. 50, 64.

19 J.S. Mill, *Principles of Political Economy* (2nd edn, London, 1849), book II chapter I section 3.

20 E.g. Samuel Laing, *Journey of a Residence in Norway* (1836), pp. 38, 176, 331–32, 481.

21 Mitchell and Deane, op. cit., p. 349.

22 Ibid., p. 7.

23 *Annual Register... 1851*, 'Chronicle', pp. 197–99.

24 There are no reliable homicide figures until the later 1850s: see V.A.C. Gatrell, B. Lenman and G. Parker (eds.), *Crime and the Law* (London, 1980), p. 343. For the other statisics, see *Annual Register... 1852*, 'Chronicle', p. 214; *Annual Register... 1851*, 'Chronicle', pp. 202–3.

25 F.B. Smith, *The People's Health* (1979), pp. 210–11; J.R. Vincent, *The Formation of the British Liberal Party* (New York, 1966), p. 209.

26 *Annual Register... 1855*, 'Chronicle', p. 107.

27 Charles Greville, *A Journal of the reigns of King George IV, King William IV and Queen Victoria* (new edn., ed. Henry Reeve, London, 1896–98), vol. IV, p. 423.

28 R.W. Seton Watson, *Britain in Europe 1789–1914* (Cambridge, 1955), pp. 286–88.

29 *The Times*, 10 November 1851.

30 Reproduced in Bernard Porter, *The Refugee Question in Mid-Victorian Politics* (Cambridge, 1979), p. 166.

31 Robert D. Storch, 'The Plague of Blue Locusts. Police reform and popular resistance in northern England, 1840–1857', in *International Review of Social History*, vol. 20 (1975), pp. 62–90.

32 John Saville, *1848. The British State and the Chartist Movement* (Cambridge, 1987), pp. 200–229.

33 Porter, *Refugee Question*, pp. 151–52.

34 Mayne to Waddington, n.d. [but after 5 June 1851], in Metropolitan Police Papers, Public Record Office, MEPO 2/92.

35 J.A. Gallagher and R.E. Robinson, 'The Imperialism of Free Trade', in *Economic History Review*, 2nd series, vol. VI, no. 1 (1953), pp. 1–15.

36 Mitchell and Deane, op. cit., p. 60.

37 J.F.C. Harrison, *Early Victorian Britain* (1971; new edn., London, 1979), p. 46.

38 J.M. Bourne, *Patronage and Society in Nineteenth-Century Britain* (London, 1986), p. 134 *et passim*.

39 W.O. Aydelotte, 'The House of Commons in the 1840s', in *History*, vol. 39 (1954), pp. 249–62.

40 D.C.M. Platt, *The Cinderella Service British Consuls since 1925* (London: 1971), pp. 2, 20, 51, 239; Bernard Porter, *Britain, Europe and the World 1850–1982* (London: 1983), ch. 1.

41 David Ricardo, for example, and E.G. Wakefield.

42 Bourne, op. cit., pp. 133–35.

Chapter 3

1 B.R. Mitchell and P. Deane, *Abstract of British Historical Statistics* (Cambridge, 1962), pp. 115, 129, 182, 188, 196, 199, 218, 225–26, 283, 333–34, 367.

2 *Annual Register...1866*, pp. 183–85.

3 Mitchell and Deane, op. cit., pp. 64, 129, 283, 343–44.

4 David Jones, *Chartism and the Chartists* (London, 1975), p. 182.

5 Brian Harrison, *Peaceable Kingdom: Stability and Change in Modern Britain* (Oxford, 1982), ch. 4.

6 John Saville, *Ernest Jones: Chartist* (London, 1952), pp. 80–81.

7 Patrick Joyce, *Work, Society and Politics. The culture of the factory in later Victorian England* (Brighton, 1980), p. 71.

8 Ibid., p. 148; and see chs. 4 and 5, *passim*.

9 Ibid., pp. 134, 183–4.

10 H. Oliver Horne, *A History of Savings Banks* (London, 1947), pp. 41, 388.

11 Sir Spencer Portal, 'Foreword' to ibid., p. vii.

12 Below, p. 387.

13 Trygve R. Tholfsen, *Working Class Radicalism in Mid-Victorian England* (London, 1976), *passim*; Neville Kirk, *The Growth of Working Class Reformism in Mid-Victorian England* (Urbana, Illinois, 1985), *passim*.

14 Bernard Porter, '"Bureau and Barrack"', in *Victorian Studies*, vol. 27 (1989), pp. 407–33.

15 Bernard Porter, *Plots and Paranoia. A History of Political Espionage in Britain 1790–1988* (London, 1989), pp. 95–6, and ch. 5 *passim*.

16 John Stevenson, *Popular Disturbances in England 1700–1870* (London, 1979); Donald Richter, *Riotous Victorians* (Athens, Ohio, 1981); Sheridan

Gilley, 'The Garibaldi Riots of 1862', in *Historical Journal*, vol. 16 (1973), pp. 697–732.

17   Reprinted in Peter Keating (ed.), *Into Unknown England 1866–1913* (Manchester, 1976), pp. 33–54.

18   Ibid, 'Introduction'.

19   B.R. Mitchell and P. Deane, op. cit., p. 410.

20   John Stuart Mill, *Autobiography* (new edn.: Oxford, 1979), p. 138.

21   Alan Lee, 'Ruskin and Political Economy', in Robert Hewison (ed.), *New Approaches to Ruskin* (London, 1981), p. 83.

22   Charles Dickens, *Hard Times* (1854; new edn., London, 1958), p. 20.

23   [Lady Charlotte Campbell], *Conduct is Fate* (Edinburgh, 1822), vol. I, p. 76.

24   [Felix McDonagh], *The Hermit Abroad* (London, 1823), vol. I, pp. 257–58.

25   Matthew Arnold, *Culture and Anarchy* (1869; new edn., London, 1932), p. 50.

26   William Woodruff, *Impact of Western Man* (London, 1966), pp. 314–16.

27   Ibid., p. 304.

28   Kirk, op. cit., ch. 7.

29   Royden Harrison, *Before the Socialists* (London, 1965), ch. 3.

Chapter 4

1   I have been unable to trace the source of this reference.

2   Oliver MacDonagh, 'The nineteenth-century revolution in government', in *Historical Journal*, vol. III (1960).

3   John Vincent, *The Formation of the Liberal Party* (London, 1966), *passim*; and see Anthony Trollope's political novels, *Phineas Finn* (1869) and its sequels.

4   Donald Southgate, *The Passing of the Whigs 1832–1886* (London, 1962), p. 303.

5   Robert Blake, *Disraeli* (London, 1966), p. 434.

6   Robert Strewart, *The Foundation of the Conservative Party 1830–1867* (London, 1978), p. 310.

7   W.L. Langer, *European Alliances & Alignments 1871–1890* (2nd edn., New York, 1950), p. 18.

8   B.R. Mitchell and P. Deane, *Abstract of British Historical Statistics* (Cambridge, 1962), p. 397.

9   Bernard Porter, *The Refugee Question in mid-Victorian Politics* (Cambridge, 1979), pp. 58–59.

10   Karl Marx and Friedrich Engels, *Articles on Britain* (Moscow, 1975), p. 203.

11   G.B. Henderson, *Crimean War Diplomacy and Other Historical Essays* (Glasgow, 1947), pp. 238–41.

12   V.J. Puryear, *England, Russia, and the Straits Question, 1844–56* (Berkeley, 1931).

13   A.J.P. Taylor, *The Troublemakers* (London, 1957), ch. 2.

14   W.E. Mosse, *The European Powers and the German Question, 1848–71* (Cambridge, 1958), p. 183.

15   Sir Charles Wood, quoted in Blake, op. cit., p. 436.

Chapter 5

1   F.B. Smith, *The Making of the Second Reform Bill* (Cambridge, 1966), p. 40.

2   I have been unable to trace the source of this quotation.

3 Francis Herrick, 'The Second Reform Movement in Britain 1850–1965', in *Journal of the History of Ideas*, vol. 9 (1948), p. 190.
4 T.R. Tholfsen, *Working-Class Radicalism in Mid-Victorian England* (London, 1976), p. 317.
5 F.B. Smith, op. cit., p. 2.
6 Sotheron Escourt, quoted in Robert Stewart, *The Foundation of the Conservative Party 1830–1867* (London, 1978), p. 311.
7 D. Southgate, *The Passing of the Whigs* (London, 1962), p. 321.
8 Royden Harrison, *Before the Socialists. Studies in Labour and Politics 1861–1881* (London, 1965), p. 83.
9 Ibid., pp. 111–2.
10 Ibid., p. 121.
11 Ibid., p. 114.
12 P. Smith, *Disraelian Conservatism and Social Reform* (London, 1967), p. 103.
13 Walter Bagehot, *The English Constitution*, Introduction to the Second Edition (1872); new edn., London, 1986, pp. xx, xxii–xxiii, xxix.
14 Below, p. 163.
15 P. Smith, op. cit., p. 185.
16 Ibid., ch. V *passim*.
17 C.L. Mowat, *The Charity Organisation Society 1869–1913* (London, 1961), ch. 1.
18 Ibid., p. 26.
19 Above, p. 31.
20 *The Times*, 24 September and 27 October 1871.

Chapter 6

1 Quoted in R.J. Moore, *Liberalism and Indian Politics* (London, 1966), p. 25.
2 R.W. Seton-Watson, *Britain in Europe 1789–1914* (Cambridge, 1955), p. 574.
3 Quoted in Robert Blake, *Disraeli* (1966), p. 577.
4 Gwendolen Cecil, *Life of Robert Marquis of Salisbury*, vol. II (London, 1921), p. 171.
5 Quoted by W.N. Medlicott, 'Bismarck and Beaconsfield', in A.O. Sarkissian (ed.), *Studies in Diplomatic History and Historiography in honour of G.P. Gooch* (London, 1961), p. 250.
6 David Landes, *The Unbound Prometheus. Technological Change and Industrial Development in Western Europe from 1750 to the Present* (Cambridge, 1969), p. 221.
7 William Woodruff, *Impact of Western Man. A Study of Europe's Role in the World Economy 1750–1960* (London, 1966), pp. 300-32.
8 D. Grant and others quoted in C.A. Bodelsen, *Studies in Mid-Victorian Imperialism* (Copenhagen, 1924), p. 82.
9 Edward Ingram, *The Beginning of the Great Game in Asia 1828–1834* (Oxford, 1979), p. 135.
10 Quoted in Richard Millman, *Britain and the Eastern Question 1875–1878* (Oxford, 1979), p. 285.
11 B.R. Mitchell and P. Deane, *Abstract of British Historical Statistics* (Cambridge, 1962), pp. 284, 64.
12 See Earl Granville in House of Lords, 10 August 1885, in *Hansard*, 3rd series, vol. 300, cc. 1537–40.

13 Martin J. Wiener, *English Culture and the Decline of the Industrial Spirit 1850–1980* (Cambridge, 1981), p. 14.
14 Paperback edition (Harmondsworth, 1969), p. 161.
15 Ralph E. Pumphrey, 'The Introduction of Industrialists into the British Peerage', in *American Historical Review*, vol. 65 (1959).
16 Above, p. 33.

Chapter 7

1   *Daily Chronicle*, 1 April 1881, p. 4.
2   *The Times*, 15 January 1881 p. 10; 18 March 1881 p. 8.
3   *Annual Register... 1881* (1882), 'Chronicle', p. 11.
4   See K.R.M. Short, *The Dynamite War. Irish-American Bombers in Victorian London* (Dublin, 1979).
5   *Annual Register... 1878* (1879), 'History', pp. 294-95; 'Chronicle', p. 52.
6   *Annual Register... for the Year 1881* (1882), 'History', pp. 270–71, 397–98.
7   Sir Algernon West, *Recollections 1832 to 1886* (London, 1899), vol. II, p. 194; and see Bernard Porter, *The Origins of the Vigilant State* (London, 1987), pp. 31–34.
8   Sir William Vernon Harcourt to Gladstone, 28 December 1883 (copy), in Harcourt papers, Bodleian Library, Oxford, box 696, ff.181-82.
9   Hyndman played for Sussex in 1863–64 as a right-hand middle-order batsman, making 309 runs in all (highest score 64) at an average of 16.26. Benny Green, *Wisden Book of Obituaries* (London, 1986), under 'Hyndman'.
10 [Andrew Mearns], *The Bitter Cry of Outcast London* (1883); reprinted in Peter Keating (ed.), *Into Unknown England 1866–1913* (London, 1976), p. 94.
11 B.S. Rowntree, *Poverty: A Study of Town Life* (London, 1901); reprinted in Keating, op. cit., p. 200.
12 Quoted in M.E. Townsend, *Origins of Modern German Colonialism* (London, 1921), p. 18.
13 Harcourt to Queen Victoria, 30 June 1885 (copy); in Harcourt papers, Bodleian Library, Oxford: box 692 f.249 (punctuation added).
14 *Annual Register... 1880* (1881), 'History', p. 109.
15 William Morris in *Commonweal*, 5 May 1890; quoted in A.L. Morton (ed.), *Political Writings of William Morris* (London, 1973), p. 220.
16 William Morris, 'The Hopes of Civilisation', 1885, quoted in ibid., p. 175.
17 K.S. Inglis, 'English Nonconformity and Social Reform 1880–1900', in *Past and Present*, no. 13 (1958), p. 78.
18 *Royal Commission on the Depression in Trade and Industry*, Final Report, PP 1886 xxiii; minority report by G.A. Jamieson.
19 C. Cunliffe Lister, quoted in Benjamin H. Brown, *The Tariff Reform Movement in Great Britain 1881–1895* (New York, 1943), p. 30.
20 Sir Edward Clarke, *Public Speeches 1880–1890* (London, 1890), p. 239.

Chapter 8

1   Quoted in L.P. Curtis, *Coercion and Conciliation in Ireland* (Princeton, NJ, 1963), p. 72.
2   Quoted in Medlicott, *Bismarck, Gladstone and the Concert of Europe* (London, 1956), p. 10.

3   W.E. Gladstone, third Midlothian speech, printed in *Political Speeches in Scotland, November and December 1879* (London, 1879), pp. 115–17.
4   Ibid., loc. cit.
5   W.L. Langer, *European Alliances and Alignments 1871–1890* (New York, 1931), p. 308.
6   'General Act of the Conference of Berlin', printed in *Parliamentary Papers*, 1886 xlvii pp. 97ff.
7   J.R. Seeley, *The Expansion of England* (London, 1883); J.A. Froude, *Oceana, or England and her Colonies* (London, 1886).
8   William G. Hynes, *The Economics of Empire. Britain, Africa and the New Imperialism 1870–95* (1979), *passim*.
9   Above, p. 46.
10 In 1880, Ireland had one seat for every 51 000 people; Britain had one for every 53,490. After 1885 the disproportion increased. Calculated from Chris Cook and Brendan Keith, *British Historical Facts 1830–1900* (London, 1975), pp. 103, 232.
11 H.C.G. Matthew (ed.), *The Gladstone Diaries*, vol. IX (Oxford, 1986), Introduction, p. lxxv.
12 Ibid., pp. lxxvii–lxxviii.
13 H.C.G. Matthew (ed.), *The Gladstone Diaries*, vol. X (Oxford, 1990), Introduction, pp. cxiv–cxv.
14 *Annual Register... 1881* (1882), p. 91.
15 John Morley, *Life of Gladstone* (London, 1903), vol. III, p. 57.
16 Ibid, vol. III, p. 189.
17 Bernard Porter, *The Origins of the Vigilant State* (London, 1987), p. 36.
18 Morley, op. cit., vol. III, p. 58.
19 *Annual Register... 1881*, p. 91.
20 Below, p. 100.
21 Donald Southgate, *The Passing of the Whigs* (London, 1962), pp. 428-31.
22 Ibid., p. 367.
23 *Annual Register... 1880* (1881), p. 92.
24 Southgate, op. cit., p. 368.
25 J.L. Garvin, *The Life of Joseph Chamberlain*, vol. I (London, 1932), pp. 392–93.
26 *Annual Register... 1885* (1886), pp. 3–4; C.H.D. Howard, 'Joseph Chamberlain and the "Unauthorised Programme"', in *English Historical Review*, vol. 65 (1950), pp. 477–91.
27 Southgate, op. cit., p. 367.

Chapter 9

1   Figures in *Annual Register... 1886* (1887), p. 215.
2   *Hansard*, 3rd Series, vol. 305, cc. 616–22 (Commons, 10 May 1886).
3   *Annual Register... 1886*, p. 148.
4   Gordon L. Goodman, 'Liberal Unionism: the Revolt of the Whigs', in *Victorian Studies*, vol. 3 (1959), p. 183fn.
5   *Annual Register... 1885* (1886), pp. 144-46.
6   Goodman, op. cit., pp. 180–81.
7   Above, p. 98.
8   Donald Southgate, *The Passing of the Whigs 1832–1886* (London, 1962), p. 370.
9   W.H.G. Armytage, 'The Railway Rates Question and the Fall of the Third Gladstone Ministry', in *English Historical Review*, vol. 65 (1950), pp. 18–51.

10 Ibid., p. 41.
11 Southgate, op. cit., p. 391.
12 Ibid., p. 414.
13 Gregory D. Phillips, 'The Whig Lords and Liberalism, 1886–1893', in *Historical Journal*, vol. 24 (1981), pp. 168–69.
14 Southgate, op. cit., p. 367.
15 Ibid., p. 391.
16 Quoted in Helen Merrell Lynd, *England in the Eighteen-Eighties: Towards a Social Basis for Freedom* (Oxford, 1945), p. 107.
17 Armytage, op. cit., p. 40.
18 Above, p. 57.
19 A.D. Elliott, *Goschen* (London, 1911), vol. I, p. 161.
20 [Henry Reeve], 'The Parting of the Waters', in *Edinburgh Review*, vol. CLXII (1885), p. 298.
21 Ibid., pp. 293, 299–300.
22 John Roach, 'Liberalism and the Victorian Intelligentsia', in *Cambridge Historical Journal*, vol. 13 (1957), pp. 58–81; Goodman, op. cit., p. 186.
23 N. Soldon, '*Laissez-Faire* as Dogma: The Liberty and Property Defence League, 1882–1914', in Kenneth D. Brown (ed.), *Essays in Anti-Labour History* (1974), pp. 208–33.
24 John Galsworthy, *The Man of Property* (1906; new edn. Harmondsworth, 1951), p. 154.
25 [Henry Reeve], op. cit., pp. 295–6.
26 Bernard Porter, *The Origins of the Vigilant State* (London, 1987), ch. 3 *et passim*.
27 [Henry Reeve], op. cit., p. 288 (italics added).
28 D.G. Hoskins, 'The Genesis and Significance of the 1886 "Home Rule" Split in the Liberal Party', Cambridge Ph.D. Dissertation, 1963, Ch. 1.

Chapter 10

1 H.E. Manning, 'The Condition of Labour', in *Dublin Review*, 3rd series, vol. 26 (1891), pp. 153–67.
2 William Booth, quoted in *Review of Reviews*, vol. 2 (1890), p. 130.
3 Florence Fenwick Miller, 'Insect Communists', in *National Review*, vol. 15 (1890), pp. 392–403.
4 'Ouida', 'The State as an Immoral Teacher', in *North American Review*, vol. 153 (1891), pp. 193–204.
5 J.R. Buchanan, 'The Coming Cataclysm of America and Europe', quoted in *Review of Reviews*, vol. 2 (1890), p. 239.
6 E.g. the *New Review*, vol. 4 (1891), pp. 1–28, 41–51, 100-18.
7 W.T. Stead, 'The Progress of the World', in *Review of Reviews*, vol. 2 (1890), p. 317.
8 B.R. Mitchell and Phyllis Deane, *Abstract of British Historical Statistics* (Cambridge, 1962), p. 72.
9 W.T. Stead, 'The Progress of the World', in *Review of Reviews*, vol. 3 (1891), p. 329.
10 N. Soldon, 'Laissez-Faire as Dogma: The Liberty and Property Defence League, 1882–1914', in Kenneth D. Brown, *Essays in Anti-Labour History* (London, 1974), p. 223.
11 Mitchell and Deane, op. cit., p. 64.
12 November 1894; quoted in Gwilym Gibbon and Reginald W. Bell, *History of the London County Council 1889–1939* (London, 1939), p. 96.

13 C.A. Whitmore, 'The Prospects of Conservatism in England', in *Quarterly Review*, vol. 172 (1891), p. 272.

14 Rowland Blennerhassett, 'Ethics and Politics', in *Fortnightly Review*, vol. 54 (1890), pp. 224–37.

15 G. Rome Hall, 'Public Health and Politics', in *National Review*, vol. 14 (1890), p. 615.

16 Frederick Greenwood, 'The Revolt of Labour', in *New Review*, vol. 4 (1891), pp. 41–51.

17 Miss Cobbe, quoted in *Review of Reviews*, vol. 3 (1891), p. 77; Mrs Emily Glode Ellis, 'The Fetish of Charity', in *Westminster Review*, vol. 135 (1891), pp. 373–84.

18 W.T. Stead, 'The Progress of the World', in *Review of Reviews*, vol. 3 (1891), p. 222.

19 Henry Pelling, *Origins of the Labour Party* (1954; 2nd. edn., Oxford, 1965), p. 109.

20 Sydney Webb, 'The Moral of the Elections' in *Contemporary Review*, vol. 62 (1892), pp. 272–87.

21 Sydney Webb and G.B. Shaw, 'To Your Tents, O Israel!', in *Fortnightly Review*, vol. 60 (1893), pp. 582-83.

22 Quoted in D.A. Hamer, 'The Irish Question and Liberal Politics 1886–1894', in *Historical Journal*, vol. 12 (1969), p. 528.

23 T.W. Heyck, 'Home Rule, Radicalism, and the Liberal Party, 1886–1905', in *Journal of British Studies*, vol. 13 (1974), p. 85.

24 Michael Barker, *Gladstone and Radicalism: the Reconstruction of the Liberal Party in Britain 1885–94* (Brighton, 1974), p. 250.

25 W.T. Stead, 'The Progress of the World', in *Review of Reviews*, vol. 5 (1892), p. 328.

26 *Review of Reviews*, vol. 12 (1895), p. 6.

27 Barker, op. cit., p. 248.

28 Reproduced in *Review of Reviews*, vol. 8 (1893), p. 355.

29 Frederick Greenwood, 'Britain Fin de Siecle', in *Contemporary Review*, vol. 58 (1890), p. 312.

30 James Bryce, 'An Age of Discontent', in *Contemporary Review*, vol. 59 (1891), pp. 15

31 See Paul Kennedy, *The Rise of the Anglo-German Antagonism 1860–1914* (London, 1980), part 4 *passim*.

32 Salisbury speech at Lord Mayor's Banquet, 9 November 1891: *Annual Register... 1891* (1892), p. 200.

33 G.E. Buckle (ed.), *The Letters of Queen Victoria*, 3rd series, vol. 1 (London, 1930), p. 615.

34 Professor R.H. Thurston, 'The Borderline of Science', in *North American Review*, vol. 150 (1890), p. 76.

35 'Federative moves' in the Balkans are mentioned in *Review of Reviews*, vol. 4 (1891), p. 10. W.T. Stead looked forward to a 'United States of Europe' in ibid., vol. 1 (1890), p. 258 and vol. 4 (1891), p. 110. Lord Rosebery floated the idea of an Anglo-US union as early as 1884: Marquess of Crewe, *Lord Rosebery* (London, 1931), vol. I p. 209. An anonymous article in the *Westminister Review*, vol. 136 (1891), pp. 113–23, predicted world federation.

36 M. Shepard in *Nouvelle Revue*, 1 March 1891, summarised in *Review of Reviews*, vol. 3 (1891), p. 372.

Chapter 11

1   Bernard Porter, *The Lion's Share: A Short History of British Imperialism 1850–1983* (2nd edn, London, 1984), pp. 150–51.
2   Ibid., pp. 175–77.
3   Quoted in A.L. Kennedy, *Salisbury 1830–1903: portrait of a Statesman* (London, 1953), p. 277.
4   I.F. Clarke, *Voices Prophesying War 1763-1984* (London, 1966), *passim*.
5   David A.T. Stafford, 'Conspiracy and Xenophobia: The Popular Spy Novels of William Le Queux, 1893-1914', in *Europe* (Montreal), vol. 4 no. 2 (1981), pp. 173–75.
6   See Bernard Porter, 'The Edwardians and their Empire', in Donald Read (ed.), *Edwardian England* (London, 1982), pp. 134–35.
7   *Census of the British Empire, 1901*: PP 1905 CII, pp. xxv, 1.
8   There were 11 881 200 males over 15 years of age in England, Wales and Scotland in 1901. To these one should add about half a million adult male protestants in Ireland, and subtract probably a larger number of foreigners, Catholic Irish, pacifists, infirm and elderly living in Britain. Calculated from B.R. Mitchell and Phyllis Deane, *Abstract of British Historical Statistics* (Cambridge 1962), pp. 12–13.
9   Quoted in R.J. Sturdee, 'The Ethics of Football', in *Westminster Review*, vol. 159 (1903), p. 181.
10 Letter to *The Times*, 1900, quoted in Bentley B. Gilbert, *The Evolution of National Insurance in Britain* (London, 1966), p. 72.
11 John St Loe Strachey, 'The Problems and Perils of Socialism', in *National Review*, vol. 49 (1907), p. 960.
12 T.J. Macnamara, 'In Corpore Sano', in *Contemporary Review*, vol. 87 (1905), p. 248.
13 Lord Milner, *The Nation and the Empire* (London, 1913), p. 139.
14 Porter, *The Lion's Share*, pp. 129–33; and 'The Edwardians and their Empire', *passim*.
15 Anon., 'Imperial and Foreign Affairs: A Review of Events', in *Fortnightly Review*, vol. 91 (1909), p. 607 (italics added).
16 Calculated from Mitchell and Deane, op. cit., pp. 283, 367.
17 Porter, *The Lion's Share*, p. 121.
18 Quoted in Bernard Semmel, *Imperialism and Social Reform* (London, 1960), p. 16.
19 'St Barbara', 'Admiralty and Empire', in *National Review*, vol. 51 (1908), p. 376.
20 Lord Curzon, 'The True Imperialism', in *Nineteenth Century*, vol. 63 (1908), pp. 157–58.
21 Speech at Chesterfield, 16 December 1901; quoted in Marquess of Crewe, *Lord Rosebery* (London, 1931), vol. 2, p. 571.
22 G.B. Shaw, *Fabianism and the Empire* (London, 1900); Bernard Porter, *Critics of Empire. British Radical attitudes to colonialism in Africa 1895–1914* (London, 1968), pp. 109–23.
23 John Springhall, *Youth, Empire and Society* (London, 1977), *passim*; John Mackenzie, *Propaganda and Empire* (Manchester, 1984), *passim*.
24 M.D. Blanch, 'British Society and the War', in Peter Warwick (ed.), *The South African War* (London, 1980), pp. 210–38.
25 Richard Price, *An Imperial War and the British Working Class* (London, 1977), *passim*.

26 Andrew Porter, *The Origins of the South African War* (Manchester, 1980), chapter 2.
27 'Calchas', 'Will England last the Century?', in *Fortnightly Review*, vol. 75 (1901), p. 24 (italics added).
28 Anon., 'England after the War', in *Fortnightly Review*, vol. 78 (1902), p. 2.
29 John Galsworthy, *In Chancery* (1920; new edn., Harmondsworth, 1962), pp. 217–18.
30 Chris Cook and John Stevenson, *The Longman Handbook of Modern British History 1714–1980* (London, 1983), pp. 212, 214.
31 Mitchell and Deane, op. cit., pp. 389, 427–28.
32 Quoted in J.A. Spender, *The Life of the Right Hon. Sir Henry Campbell-Bannerman* (London, 1923), vol. 1, p. 336.
33 J.A. Hobson, *Imperialism: A Study* (London, 1902).
34 Supra, p. 121.
35 Salisbury to Cranbrook, 1 January 1895; quoted in Robert Taylor, *Lord Salisbury* (London, 1975), p. 145.
36 See David Dilks, *Curzon in India*, vol. 1 (New York, 1969), p. 128.
37 B. Porter, *Critics of Empire*, pp. 44–47.
38 J.A. Schumpeter, 'The Sociology of Imperialism', in *Imperialism and Social Classes* (New York, 1951).
39 Charles Wilson, *History of Unilever* (London, 1954), vol. 1, pp. 166–67.
40 S. Wolpert, *Morley and India* (Cambridge, 1967); M.N. Das, *India under Morley and Minto* (London, 1964); L.M. Thomson, *The Unification of South Africa 1902–10* (Oxford, 1960).
41 Bentley B. Gilbert, *The Evolution of National Insurance in Great Britain* (London, 1966), *passim*.
42 J. Ellis Barker, 'The Future of Britain', in *The Nineteenth Century*, vol. 60 (1906), p. 704. Barker was a naturalized Briton, original name 'A.O. Eltzbacher'.

Chapter 12

1 B.R. Mitchell and Phyllis Deane, *Abstract of British Historical Statistics* (Cambridge, 1962), pp. 398, 428–29.
2 Above, pp. 123.
3 Henry Pelling, *A Short History of the Labour Party* (London, 1961), p. 16.
4 Kenneth Morgan, 'Edwardian Socialism', in Donald Read (ed.), *Edwardian England* (1982), p. 94.
5 See Bernard Barker (ed.), *Ramsay MacDonald's Political Philosophy* (London, 1972), *passim*.
6 L.T. Hobhouse, *Liberalism* (London, 1911), ch. 4.
7 'Introductory' article in *Progressive Review*, vol. 1 (1896), pp. 1–9.
8 Peter Clarke, *Liberals and Social Democrats* (Cambridge, 1978); M. Freeden, *The New Liberalism* (Oxford, 1978).
9 Priscilla E. Moulder, 'The Coming Race and Moral Depravity', in *Westminster Review*, vol. 163 (1905), pp. 678–81; G.B. Lissenden, 'Racial Suicide. The Reply of the Masses', in *ibid.*, vol. 172 (1909), p. 267.
10 Lord Meath, 'Have we the "Grit" of our Forefathers?' in *Nineteenth Century*, vol. 64 (1908), pp. 421–22.
11 Madge Barry, 'Women and Patriotism', in *National Review*, vol. 53 (1909), p. 303.
12 Clara Jackson, 'Housekeeping and National Well-being', in *Nineteenth Century*, vol. 58 (1905), p. 298.

13 Sir Theodore Martin, *Queen Victoria as I Knew Her* (1908), p. 69.

14 Ben J. Wattenburg (ed.), *The Statistical History of the United States from Colonial Times to the present* (New York, 1976), pp. 164, 224–25, 240.

15 'Yolet Capel', 'England's Peril', in *Westminster Review*, vol. 157 (1902), p. 163; 'Calchas', 'Will England last the Century?', in *Fortnightly Review*, vol. 75 (1901), p. 25.

16 See Bernard Porter, 'The Economic Interpretation of Imperialism', in *Themes in British and American History: A Comparative Approach, c. 1760–1970* (Milton Keynes, 1984), pp. 14–22.

17 Mitchell and Deane, op. cit., pp. 334, 283–84.

18 P.L. Payne, 'The Emergence of the Large-scale Company in Great Britain, 1870–1914', in *Economic History Review*, vol. 20 (1967), pp. 519–42.

19 W.D. Rubinstein, *Men of Property* (London, 1981), Ch. 2.

20 Andrew Carnegie, 'The Advantages of Poverty', in *Nineteenth Century*, vol. 29 (1891), p. 370.

21 A.J. Taylor, 'The Economy', in S. Nowell-Smith (ed.), *Edwardian England* (London, 1964), p. 105.

22 Mitchell and Deane, op. cit., pp. 130 (steel), 65 (unemployment).

23 *Statistical Abstracts for the United Kingdom... 1899 to 1913* (London, 1914), p. 433.

24 Mitchell and Deane, op. cit., pp. 344–45, 367–68; Wattenburg, op cit., p. 164.

25 Leo Chiozza Money, *Riches and Poverty* (London, 1906), p. 328.

26 'Calchas', op. cit., p. 25.

27 C.W. Radcliffe Cooke, 'The Invasion Scare – a New View', in *Nineteenth Century*, vol. 61 (1907), p. 398.

28 [J. Ellis Barker], 'The Economic Decay of Great Britain – II', in *Contemporary Review*, vol. 79 (1901), p. 787; and see Bernard Porter, 'The Edwardians and their Empire', in Donald Read (ed.), *Edwardian England* (1982), pp. 131–33.

29 V.I. Lenin, *Imperialism, The Highest Stage of Capitalism*, in V.I. Lenin, *Selected Works* (Moscow, n.d.), p. 773; and see above, p. 124.

30 J.A. Hobson, *Imperialism: A Study* (London, 1902), ch. 6.

31 A. Cuthbert Medd, 'The Judgment of Posterity', in *National Review*, vol. 40 (1903), p. 1004.

32 Bernard Porter, *Critics of Empire* (London, 1968), pp. 67 *et passim*; Searle, op. cit., pp. 25–26 *et passim*.

33 George Trobridge, 'The Decay of Morals', in *Westminster Review*, vol. 163 (1905), p. 609.

34 H.G. Wells, *Tono-Bungay* (1909; new edn, London, 1933), pp. 87, 241.

35 Harry Hodgson, 'A National Crisis', in *Westminster Review*, vol. 157 (1902), p. 408.

36 G.R. Searle, *Corruption in British Politics 1895–1930* (Oxford: 1987), pp. 10ff, 52ff, ch. 8.

37 Ibid., ch. 7.

38 T.R. Nevett, *Advertising in Britain: A History* (1982).

39 Paul Kennedy, *The Rise of the Anglo-German Antagonism 1860–1914* (London, 1980), p. 362.

40 I have been unable to find the source of this quotation; which however chimes in with Massingham's general views, retailed in Alan Lee, *The Origins of the Popular Press 1855–1914* (London, 1976), pp. 219–21.

41 Trobridge, op. cit., p. 609. The term 'cash nexus' to describe the characteristic capitalist relationship was first used by Thomas Carlyle, in *Chartism* (1839; new edn, London, 1895), pp. 36, 41 (ch. 6).
42 Eric Midwinter, *W.G. Grace: His Life and Times* (London, 1981), p. 133.
43 Martin J. Wiener, *English Culture and the Decline of the Industrial Spirit 1850–1980* (Cambridge, 1981), *passim*.
44 Calculated from Mitchell and Deane, op. cit., p. 60. See also Harold Perkin, *The Rise of Professional Society in England since 1880* (London, 1989).

Chapter 13

1 *Illustrated London News*, 16 December 1911, p. 1035.
2 Kenneth Rose, *King George V* (London, 1983), p. 132.
3 *The Times*, 13 December 1911, p. 9.
4 Alastair Service, *Edwardian Architecture* (London, 1977), p. 187.
5 *The Times*, 13 December 1911, p. 8.
6 Rose, op. cit., p. 133.
7 Ronald Hyam, *Elgin and Churchill at the Colonial Office 1905-8* (London, 1968), pp. 237–62.
8 Above, p. 131.
9 W. Schlote, *British Overseas Trade from 1700 to the 1930s* (1952), pp. 162–63; Lance E. Davis and Robert A. Huttenback, *Mammmon and the Pursuit of Empire. The Political Economy of British Imperialism, 1860–1912* (Cambridge, 1986), p. 42.
10 Davis and Huttenback, op. cit., *passim*.
11 Above, p. 130.
12 Below, p. 167.
13 *The Times*, 13 December 1911, p. 10.
14 *Annual Register... 1911* (1912), p. 145. Dr Nicholas Hiley told me about the news-reels.
15 *Annual Register... 1911*, p. 217.
16 B.R. Mitchell and Phyllis Deane, *Abstract of British Historical Statistics* (Cambridge, 1962), pp. 71–72.
17 Standish Meacham, '"The Sense of an Impending Clash": English working-class unrest before the First World War', in *American Historical Review*, vol. 77 (1972), p. 1346.
18 Mitchell and Deane, op. cit., p. 68.
19 Meacham, op. cit., p. 1347.
20 Basil Thomson, *Queer People* (London, [1922]), p. 263.
21 Ibid., p. 265.
22 Randolph Churchill, *Winston S. Churchill*, vol. II, *Companion*, vol. 2 (London, 1967), p. 1274.
23 Public Record Office, HO144/1553–54/199768.
24 Harold Brust, *In Plain Clothes. Further Memoirs of a Political Police Officer* (London, 1937), p. 60. (The archaic 'feminity' is *sic*.)
25 Jerrold Northrop Moore, *Edward Elgar. A Creative Life* (London, 1984), p. 621.
26 David French, 'Spy fever in Britain, 1900–1915', in *Historical Journal*, vol. 21 (1978), pp. 355–70.
27 Paul Kennedy, *The Rise of the Anglo-German Antagonism 1860–1914* (London, 1980), pp. 370–71, 375.
28 Robert Baden-Powell, *Scouting for Boys. A Handbook of Instruction in Good Citizenship* (4th edn., London, 1911), p. 19.

29 Ibid., p. 291.
30 See Richard Soloway, 'Counting the Degenerates', in *Journal of Contemporary History*, vol. 17 (1982), pp. 137–64.
31 See above, p. 130.
32 A.V. Dicey, *Lectures on the Relation between Law and Public Opinion in England during the Nineteenth Century*, Introduction to second edition (London, 1914), p. liii.
33 Ibid., pp. liii–lxx.
34 Kenneth D. Brown, 'The Anti-Socialist Union, 1908–49', in *Essays in Anti-Labour History* (London, 1974), p. 248; Barbara Lee Farr, 'The Development and Impact of Right-Wing Politics in Great Britain 1903–1932', Ph.D. thesis, University of Illinois, 1976, pp. 52–3, 64.
35 Farr, op. cit., p. 99.
36 Bernard Porter, *Plots and Paranoia. A History of Political Espionage in Britain 1790-1988* (London, 1989), p. 121.
37 Kennedy, op. cit., p. 374.
38 Bernard Porter, *The Origins of the Vigilant State* (London, 1987), ch. 11 *passim*.
39 Above, pp. 132, 154.
40 Richard Popplewell, 'British intelligence and Indian "subversion": the surveillance of Indian revolutionaries in India and abroad, 1904–1920', Cambridge Ph.D. thesis, 1988, ch. 3 *passim*.

Chapter 14

1   12 January 1896; quoted in C.H.D. Howard, 'The Policy of Isolation', in *Historical Journal*, vol. 10 (1967), p. 79.
2   E.g. 'Calchas', 'Will England Last the Century', in *Fortnightly Review*, vol. 75 (1901), p. 30; Charles Tupper, 'The Problem of Empire', in *Nineteenth Century*, vol. 61 (1907), p. 716.
3   Above, p. 159.
4   A.V. Dicey, *Lectures on the Relation between Law and Public Opinion in England during the Nineteenth Century*, Introduction to second edition (London, 1914), p. lxxxvi.
5   Bernard Porter, *The Origins of the Vigilant State* (London, 1987), pp. 167, 169.
6   Michael MacDonagh, *In London During the Great War* (London, 1935), p. 91.
7   John Bourne, *Britain and the Great War 1914–1918* (London, 1989), p. 202.
8   E.g. Sidney Felstead, *German Spies at Bay* (London, 1920), pp. 201–2.
9   MacDonagh, op. cit., pp. 15, 64, 112.
10 Thomas Howarth, *Charles Rennie Mackintosh and the Modern Movement* (2nd edn, London, 1977), p. 196.
11 MacDonagh, op. cit., p. 32.
12 Bourne, op. cit., pp. 212–13.
13 Ibid., p. 209.
14 Gloden Dallas and Douglas Gill, *The Unknown Army* (London, 1985), pp. 66–81.
15 Bourne, op. cit., p. 213.
16 Ibid., p. 223.
17 Ibid., pp. 212–13.
18 Ray Challinor, *John S. Clarke, Parliamentarian, Poet, Lion-tamer* (London, 1977), pp. 42–45.

19 Nicholas Hiley, 'British internal security in wartime: the rise and fall of P. M.S.2, 1915–17', in *Intelligence and National Security*, vol. 1 (1986), p. 405.
20 Bernard Waites, *A Class Society at War. England 1914–1918* (Leamington Spa, 1987), p. 202.
21 Colin Lovelace, 'British press censorship during the First World War', in G. Boyce, J. Curran and P. Wingate (eds.), *Newspaper History: from the seventeenth century to the present day* (London, 1978), p. 315.
22 MacDonagh, op. cit., pp. 25, 55.
23 J.M. Winter, *The Great War and the British People* (London, 1985), pp. 92ff.
24 Bernard Waites, 'The Government of the Home Front and the "Moral Economy" of the Working Class', in Peter Liddle (ed.), *Home Fires and Foreign Fields. British Social and Military Experience in the First World War* (London, 1985), pp. 175–93.
25 Bourne, op. cit., p. 209.
26 Winter, op. cit., *passim*.
27 MacDonagh, op. cit., p. 196.
28 Ibid., p. 312.
29 B.R. Mitchell and Phyllis Deane, *Abstract of British Historical Statistics* (Cambridge, 1962), p. 70.
30 John Turner, 'The Politics of "Organised Business" in the First World War', in John Turner (ed.), *Businessmen and Politics. Studies of Business Activities in British Politics, 1900–1945* (London, 1984), pp. 33–37, 47.
31 Barbara Lee Farr, 'The development and impact of Right-wing politics in Great Britain 1903–1932', Ph.D. thesis, University of Illinois, 1976, ch. 5.
32 Nicholas Hiley, 'Counter-espionage and security in Great Britain during the First World War', in *English Historical Review*, vol. 101 (1986), p. 118.
33 Phillip Knightley, *The Second Oldest Profession: The spy as Bureaucrat, Patriot, Fantasist and Whore* (London, 1986).
34 Basil Thomson, *Queer People* (London, 1922), pp. 282–83, 302; and *The Scene Changes* (London: 1939), p. 375; Christopher Andrew, *Secret Service: The Making of the British Intelligence Community* (London, 1985), p. 228.
35 W.H. Thompson, *Guard from the Yard* (London, 1938), p. 91.
36 C.E. Carrington, 'The Empire at War', in *Cambridge History of the British Empire*, vol. 3 (Cambridge, 1959), p. 605.
37 Ibid., pp. 641–42.
38 Ibid., pp. 606, 642.
39 Calculated from Mitchell and Deane, op. cit., pp. 318–26.
40 Carrington, op. cit., p. 632; Nicholas Mansergh, *The Commonwealth Experience* (London, 1969), pp. 174–76.
41 W.K. Hancock, *Survey of British Commonwealth Affairs*, vol. II part 1 (Oxford, 1940), pp. 106–8.
42 Max Beloff, *Imperial Sunset*, vol. 1, *Britain's Liberal Empire 1897–1921* (London, 1969), p. 214.
43 Beloff, op. cit., pp. 214–16; Carroll Quigley, *The Anglo-American Establishment from Rhodes to Clivedon* (New York, 1981), *passim*.
44 Beloff, op. cit., p. 224.
45 Mansergh, op. cit., pp. 168–69.
46 Carrington, op. cit., p. 616.

47   Richard Popplewell, 'British intelligence and Indian "subversion": the surveillance of Indian revolutionaries in India and abroad, 1904–1920', Cambridge Ph.D. thesis, 1988, pp. 103–13, 161–68, 192–202.
48   Edwin Montagu, *An Indian Diary* (London, 1930), p. 66.
49   S.R. Mehrotra, *India and the Commonwealth 1885–1929* (London, 1965), p. 102.
50   Montagu, op. cit., p. 238.
51   William Roger Louis, *Great Britain and Germany's Lost Colonies 1914–1919* (Oxford, 1967), p. 77.

Chapter 15

1   Leopold Amery in House of Commons, 30 July 1919: *Hansard*, 5th series, vol. 118, c. 2175.
2   Trevor Wilson, *The Downfall of the Liberal Party, 1914–1935* (London, 1966), p. 136.
3   Peter Hart, '"Operations Abroad": the IRA in Britain, 1920–1923', unpublished paper.
4   See J.A. Gallagher, *The Decline, Revival and Fall of the British Empire* (London, 1982), pp. 91–94.
5   B.R. Mitchell and P. Deane, *Abstract of British Historical Statistics* (Cambridge, 1962), pp. 284, 398, 403, 429.
6   C.E. Calwell, *Field-Marshall Sir Henry Wilson* (London, 1927), vol. II, pp. 240–1.
7   Ralph Isham to General C.C. Lucas, D.A.G. Great Britain, 24 March 1919; in Isham papers, Yale University Library (copy shown me by Dr Christopher Andrew).
8   Kenneth Morgan, *Consensus and Disunity. The Lloyd George Coalition Government 1918–1922* (Oxford, 1979), pp. 77–78.
9   Basil Thomson, *The Scene Changes* (London, 1939), p. 375.
10   Mitchell & Deane, op. cit., p. 72.
11   Christopher Andrew, *Secret Service: The Making of the British Intelligence Community* (London, 1985), p. 236.
12   David Omissi, *Air Power and Colonial Control: the Royal Air Force 1913–1939* (Manchester, 1990), chapter 2, *passim*.
13   Morgan, op. cit., pp. 97, 244, 249; Gallagher, op. cit., p. 96.
14   Above, p. 128.
15   Briton Cooper Busch, *Britain, India and the Arabs, 1914–1921* (Berkeley, Cal., 1971), p. 380.
16   Morgan, op. cit., p. 134.
17   E.g. H. Nield in House of Commons, 3 November 1921: *Hansard* (Commons), 5th series, vol. 147, cc. 2050–51.
18   Quoted in A.P. Thornton, *The Imperial Idea and its Enemies* (London, 1959), p. 168.
19   *Statistical Abstract for the United Kingdom... 1913 to 1927* (London, 1929), pp. 106–8.
20   Omissi, op. cit., p. 41.
21   David Butler and Jennie Freeman, *British Political Facts 1900–1960* (London, 1964), p. 122. Strictly speaking 13 million is the difference between the new electorate, and that at the previous general election, in 1910.
22   Above, p. 57.
23   Butler and Freeman, op. cit., pp. 122–23, 128.

24 Thomson, op. cit., pp. 387, 393.
25 Nicholas Hiley, 'Counter-espionage abd security in Great Britain during the First World War', in *English Historical Review*, vol. 101 (1986), p. 124.
26 Bernard Porter, *Plots and Paranoia. A History of Political Espionage in Britain 1790–1988* (London, 1989), chs. 7–8 *passim*.
27 Keith Jeffery and Peter Hennessy, *States of Emergency. British Governments and Strikebreaking since 1919* (London, 1983), pp. 50–53.
28 Gerald D. Anderson, *Fascists, Communists, and the National Government. Civil Liberties in Great Britain, 1931–1937* (Columbia, Missouri, 1983), pp. 15–18.
29 M.L. Sanders and Philip M. Taylor, *British Propaganda during the First World War, 1914–18* (London, 1982), p. 248.
30 Jeffrey and Hennessy, op. cit., p. 66.
31 Sir Donald Maclean in House of Commons, 2 December 1920: *Hansard*, 5th series, vol. 135, c. 1541.
32 Above, p. 189.
33 Morgan, op. cit., pp. 83–84.
34 Philip Abrams, 'The Failure of Social Reform, 1918–1921', in *Past and Present*, no. 24 (1963), pp. 64.
35 Morgan, op. cit., p. 175.
36 Keith Middlemass and John Barnes, *Baldwin: A Biography* (London, 1969), p. 72n.
37 J.M. McEwen, 'The Coupon Election of 1918 and Unionist Members of Parliament', in *Journal of Modern History*, vol. 34 (1962), pp. 294–306.
38 Mitchell and Deane, op. cit., pp. 272, 284, 429.

Chapter 16

1 *Hansard*, Commons, 5th series, vol. 161, c. 2473 (20 March 1923).
2 Ibid., cc. 2474–85 and 2491–2506 *passim*.
3 D.H. Aldcroft, *The Inter-War Economy. Britain 1919–1939* (London, 1970), p. 18.
4 B.R. Mitchell and P. Deane, *Abstract of British Historical Statistics* (Cambridge, 1962), pp. 345, 368.
5 Ibid., pp. 66–67, 132, 134, 181, 222, 284.
6 W.J. Reader, *Imperial Chemical Industries: A History*, vol. II (London, 1975), p. 497.
7 *Hansard*, loc. cit., cc. 2482, 2493–94.
8 Ibid., c. 2498.
9 Ibid., cc. 2494, 2499.
10 L. Urwick (ed.), *The Golden Book of Management* (London, 1956), pp. 72–79; Keith Middlemas, *Politics in Industrial Society* (London, 1979), p. 179.
11 F.W. Taylor, *The Principles of Scientific Management* (New York, 1911), p. 7.
12 E.g. Anthony Jay, *Management and Machiavelli* (1967; new edn, London, 1987), pp. 17–18, 35–36 *et passim*.
13 E.H. Phelps Brown, *The Growth of British Industrial Relations* (London, 1959), pp. 96–98.
14 *Hansard.*, loc. cit., c. 2494.
15 Mitchell and Deane, op. cit., pp. 69, 72.
16 David Butler and Jennie Freeman, *British Political Facts 1900–1960* (London, 1964), pp. 123, 126, 128. The March 1923 figure is made up of

142 elected in the general election of November 1922, plus two added in by-elections since.

17   Trevor Wilson, *The Downfall of the Liberal Party, 1914–1935* (London, 1966), p. 138.

18   G.R. Searle, *Corruption in British Politics 1895–1930* (Oxford, 1987), ch. 15.

19   Keith Middlemas and John Barnes, *Baldwin, A Biography* (London, 1969), p. 123.

20   John Ramsden, *The Age of Balfour and Baldwin 1902–1940* (London, 1978), pp. 182, 194.

21   Ibid., p. 189.

22   Above, p. 57.

23   L. Chester, S. Fay and H. Young, *The Zinoviev Letter* (London, 1967), *passim*; Christopher Andrew, *Secret Service* (London, 1985), pp. 301–15; John Ferris and Uri Bar-Joseph, 'Getting Marlowe to hold his tongue: the Conservative Party, the Intelligence Services and the Zinoviev Letter', in *Intelligence and National Security*, vol. 8 (1993), pp. 100–37.

24   Ramsden, op. cit., p. 265.

25   Middlemas and Barnes, op. cit., p. 6.

26   Ramsden, op. cit., p. 265.

27   Middlemas and Barnes, op. cit., pp. 296–97; Patrick Renshaw, 'Anti-Labour Politics in Britain, 1918-27', in *Journal of Contemporary History*, vol. 12 (1977), p. 699.

28   Above, p. 186. The expression 'Red Friday' was invented by the Labour *Daily Herald*.

29   Middlemas and Barnes, op. cit., p. 411.

30   Patrick Renshaw, *The General Strike* (London, 1975), pp. 190, 199–209.

31   Keith Jeffery and Peter Hennessy, *States of Emergency. British Governments and Strikebreaking since 1919* (London, 1983), pp. 114–15; Jane Morgan, *Conflict and Order. The Police and Labour Disputes in England and Wales, 1900–1939* (Oxford, 1987), pp. 123, 125, 211.

32   L.J. MacFarlane, *The British Communist Party. Its Origin and Development until 1929* (London, 1966), pp. 74, 119, 137–38, 166.

33   Harriette Flory, 'The Arcos raid and the rupture of Anglo-Soviet relations, 1927', in *Journal of Contemporary History*, vol. 12 (1977), pp. 707–23.

34   Renshaw, 'Anti-Labour Politics in Britain, 1918–27', pp. 703–04.

35   Mitchell and Deane, op. cit., p. 72.

36   MacFarlane, op. cit., p. 302.

37   See Douglas Hyde, *I Believed. The Autobiography of a former British Communist* (London, 1951), ch. 5.

38   Above, p. 136.

39   *Hansard*, loc. cit., cc. 2482–83.

40   Michael Freeden (ed.), *Minutes of the Rainbow Circle, 1894–1924* (London, 1989), *passim*, especially pp. 341–46.

41   Quoted in Middlemas, op. cit., p. 177.

42   Mitchell and Deane, op. cit., p. 66.

43   Robert Skidelsky, *Politicians and the Slump. The Labour Government of 1929–1931* (London, 1967), p. 366.

44   Butler and Freeman, op. cit., p. 123.

45   E.g. Ramsden, op. cit., p. 284.

46   Ibid., p. 331.

47   Middlemas and Barnes, op cit., p. 453.

48 Middlemas, op. cit., p. 209.
49 Wyndham Childs, *Episodes and Reflections* (London, 1930), p. 209–10.
50 Andrew, op. cit., p. 362; Ramsden, op. cit., p. 235; Economic League, *Fifty Fighting Years* (London, 1969), p. 4; Arthur McIvor, 'A Crusade for Capitalism: the Economic League, 1919–39', in *Journal of Contemporary History*, vol. 23 (1988), pp. 631–55.

Chapter 17

1 Paul Kennedy, *The Rise and Fall of the Great Powers* (1988; paperback edn, London, 1989), p. 414.
2 G.P. Gooch, 'British Foreign Policy, 1919–39', in *Contemporary Review*, vol. 158 (1940), p. 624.
3 Speech to Royal Empire Society, 1928, quoted in L.S. Amery, *My Political Life*, vol. II (London, 1953), pp. 471–72.
4 B.R. Mitchell and P. Deane, *Abstract of British Historical Statistics* (Cambridge, 1962), pp. 284, 478; W. Woodruff, *Impact of Western Man* (London, 1966), p. 313.
5 Woodruff, op. cit., p. 313.
6 W. Schlote, *British Overseas Trade from 1700 to the 1930s* (Oxford, 1952), pp. 156–59.
7 M. Barratt Brown, *After Imperialism* (London, 1963), p. 110.
8 McDonnell in House of Commons, 27 July 1925: *Hansard*, 5th series, vol. 187, c. 172.
9 W.K. Hancock, *Survey of British Commonwealth Affairs*, vol. II part 1 (Oxford, 1940), pp. 123–23; and see D.J. Morgan, *The Official History of Colonial Development* (5 vols., London, 1980).
10 Ronald Henderson in House of Commons, 17 July 1929: *Hansard*, 5th series, vol. 230, c. 526.
11 See Bernard Porter, 'Fabians, Imperialists and the International Order', in Ben Pimlott (ed.), *Fabian Essays in Socialist Thought* (London, 1984), pp. 62–64.
12 Penelope Hetherington, *British Paternalism and Africa 1920–1940* (London, 1978), p. 61.
13 David Omissi, *Air Power and Colonial Control: the Royal Air Force 1913–1939* (Manchester, 1990), pp. 13–16, 50–52.
14 Above, p. 179.
15 A. Montgomery Hyde, *Lord Reading* (London, 1967), p. 382.
16 H. Stephens, *Political Transformation of Tanganyika* (London, 1968), p. 30.
17 A.B. Keith, *Speeches and Documents on the British Dominions 1918–31* (Oxford, 1932), pp. 161–70.
18 Nicholas Mansergh, *The Commonwealth Experience* (London, 1969), p. 237.
19 Trevor Reese, *The History of the Royal Commonwealth Society 1868–1968* (Oxford, 1968), p. 156. See also John M. MacKenzie, *Propaganda and Empire. The manipulation of British public opinion 1880–1960* (Manchester, 1984), *passim.*
20 Amery, op. cit., vol. II, p. 340.
21 Reese, op. cit., pp. 156–57.
22 R. Graves and A. Hodge, *The Long Weekend* (London, 1941), p. 251.
23 R. Payne, *The Life and Death of Mahatma Gandhi* (1969), p. 404; House of Commons, 29 March 1933 and 11 February 1935, in *Hansard*, Commons, 5th series, vol. 276, cc. 1035, 1038, 1058; vol. 297 cc. 1651, 1654.

24 Frederick, 2nd Earl Birkenhead, *F.E.: The Life of F.E. Smith, First Earl of Birkenhead* (London, 1960), p. 506.
25 Payne, op. cit., p. 404.

Chapter 18

1   B.R. Mitchell and P. Deane, *Abstract of British Historical Statistics* (Cambridge, 1962), pp. 66, 272, 284, 335, 368.
2   John Ramsden, *The Age of Balfour and Baldwin 1902–1940* (London, 1978), pp. 355–56.
3   Mitchell and Deane, op. cit., p. 239.
4   For example, Walter Citrine of the Electrical Trades Union, and Arthur Pugh of the Iron and Steel Trades Confederation, both in 1935.
5   David Butler and Jennie Freeman, *British Political Facts 1900–1960* (London, 1963), pp. 123–24, 128.
6   *Colin Cross, The Fascists in Britain* (London, 1961), p. 60.
7   Above, p. 212.
8   Oswald Mosley, *My Life* (London, 1968), p. 267.
9   George Orwell, *The Road to Wigan Pier* (London, 1937; new edn., Harmondsworth, 1962), p. 186.
10 Above, p. 211.
11 Keith Middlemas, *Politics in Industrial Society* (London, 1979), p. 230.
12 John Charmley, *Chamberlain and the Lost Peace* (London, 1989), p. 109.
13 Above, pp. 48.
14 Middlemas, op. cit., p. 260; and see George Peden, *British Rearmament and the Treasury 1932–9* (Edinburgh, 1979).
15 Martin Gilbert and Richard Gott, *The Appeasers* (London, 1963), pp. 14, 85.
16 See Richard Cockett, *Twilight of Truth. Chamberlain, Appeasement and the Manipulation of the Press* (London, 1989); Benny Morris, *The Roots of Appeasement. The British Weekly Press and Nazi Germany during the 1930s* (London, 1991).
17 Charmley, op. cit., p. 140; C.L. Mowat, *Britain Between the Wars* (London, 1955), p. 619.
18 Butler and Freeman, op. cit., p. 132.
19 D.C. Watt, *Personalities and Policies* (1965), p. 91.
20 Ibid., ch. 8 *passim*; Ritchie Ovendale, *'Appeasement' and the English-Speaking World* (Cardiff, 1975).
21 Charmley, op. cit., p. 147.
22 Gustav Schmidt, *The Politics and Economics of Appeasement* (Leamington Spa, 1986), p. 248.
23 Lionel Kochan, *The Struggle for Germany 1914–45* (Edinburgh, 1963), p. 64 (taken from a German account of their conversation).
24 Robin Higham, *Armed Forces in Peacetime* (London, 1962), pp. 326–27.
25 Charmley, op. cit., p. 209.
26 Quoted by Philip Howard in *The Times*, 1 January 1971, p. 10.
27 Michael Glover, *Invasion Scare 1940* (London, 1990), ch. 8.
28 Scott Newton, 'The economic background to appeasement and the search for Anglo-German detente before and during World War 2', in *Lobster*, no. 20 (1990), p. 29.
29 Ibid., p. 30.
30 See Martin Gilbert, *Finest Hour. Winston S. Churchill 1939–41* (London, 1983), pp. 469, 767, 951.
31 Frances Donaldson, *Edward VIII* (London, 1974), p. 377.

Chapter 19

1 Frances Donaldson, *Edward VIII* (London, 1974), chs.30–31.
2 David Butler and Jennie Freeman, *British Political Facts 1900–1960* (London, 1963), p. 161; B.R. Mitchell and Phyllis Deane, *Abstract of British Historical Statistics* (Cambridge, 1962), p. 368; B.R. Mitchell, *British Historical Statistics* (Cambridge, 1988), p. 603.
3 Rita Hinden, *Empire and After* (London, 1949), pp. 143–44.
4 W.D. McIntyre, *The Commonwealth of Nations, Origins and Impact* (Oxford, 1977), pp. 264, 345, 443.
5 J.A. Gallagher, *The Decline, Revival and Fall of the British Empire* (Cambridge, 1982), p. 142.
6 Lord Elton, *Imperial Commonwealth* (London, 1945), p. 521.
7 Malcolm MacDonald in House of Commons, 21 May 1940, in *Hansard*, 5th series (Commons), vol. 361, c. 42.
8 W.K. Hancock, *Argument of Empire* (London, 1943), p. 7.
9 Above, pp. 217–18.
10 *Margaret Cole, The Story of Fabian Socialism* (London, 1961), pp. 281–88.
11 *Hansard*, 5th series, Commons, vol. 391, c. 48 (13 July 1943).
12 *Hansard*, 5th series, Commons, vol. 361, cc. 42–43, 45 (21 May 1940).
13 Paul Addison, *The Road to 1945. British Politics and the Second World War* (London, 1975), p. 72.
14 J.W. Wheeler-Bennett, *King George VI. His Life and Reign* (London, 1958), p. 473.
15 Angus Calder, *The People's War. Britain 1939–45* (London, 1969), pp. 464–68.
16 Hugh Thomas, *Hess: A Tale of Two Murders* (London, 1988), argues that 'Hess' was in fact a double.
17 David Englander and Tony Mason, 'The British Soldier in World War II', *Warwick Working Papers in Social History* (Warwick, n.d.), p. 7.
18 Addison, op. cit., p. 102.
19 Calder, op. cit., p. 136.
20 Peter Fleming, *Invasion 1940. An Account of the German preparations and the British counter-measures* (London, 1957), p. 204.
21 John W. Wheeler-Bennett, *King George VI. His Life and Reign* (London, 1958), pp. 468–70.
22 Addison, op. cit., p. 130.
23 Ibid., p. 72.
24 Calder, op. cit., pp. 115, 395.
25 Addison, op. cit., p. 118.
26 Calder, op. cit., p. 263.
27 Keith Middlemas, *Politics in Industrial Society* (London, 1979), ch. 9.
28 Mitchell and Deane, op. cit., p. 66.
29 Calder, op. cit., pp. 115, 331, 351, 385, 388.
30 Addison, op. cit., pp. 247–48; Englander and Mason, op. cit., pp. 13–14.
31 Henry Pelling, *The British Communist Party* (London, 1958), p. 192.
32 Calder, op. cit., p. 259.
33 Addison, p. 232.
34 Ibid., pp. 217–18; Calder, op. cit., p. 528.
35 Addison, op. cit., pp. 220, 231; Calder, op. cit., p. 530.
36 Addison, op. cit., pp. 173, 227–28.
37 Donaldson, op. cit., p. 377.

Chapter 20

1 Michael Foot, *Aneurin Bevan: a Biography*, vol. 2, *1945–1960* (London, 1973), p. 18.
2 Lord Morrison of Lambeth, *Herbert Morrison, an Autobiography* (London, 1960), p. 250.
3 Alec Cairncross, *Years of Recovery. British Economic Policy 1945–51* (London, 1985), chapter 1 *passim*.
4 Francis Williams, *A Prime Minister Remembers. The War and Post-War Memoirs of the Rt. Hon. Earl Attlee* (London, 1961), pp. 94, 134.
5 Hugh Dalton, *High Tide and After. Memoirs 1945–1960* (London, 1962), p. 166.
6 Ibid., p. 71.
7 Williams, op. cit., p. 129.
8 Alan Bullock, *Ernest Bevin, Foreign Secretary 1945–1951* (London, 1983), p. 13.
9 Ben Pimlott, *Hugh Dalton* (London, 1985), p. 437.
10 Bullock, op. cit., p. 203.
11 Dalton, op. cit., p. 62.
12 C.R. Attlee, *As it Happened* (London, 1954), p. 210; Williams, op. cit., p. 238.
13 Dalton, op. cit., p. 58.
14 Attlee, op. cit., p. 210.
15 Williams, op. cit., p. 181.
16 Bullock, op. cit., p. 172.
17 Ibid., p. 16; and cf. Williams, op. cit., p. 132.
18 Williams, op. cit., pp. 120–24.
19 Bullock, op. cit., p. 485.
20 Ibid., p. 282.
21 ibid., pp. 234–35.
22 Foot, op. cit., p. 344; and cf. Pimlott, op. cit., pp. 499, 567–68.
23 Williams, op. cit., p. 172; and see below, p. 263.
24 *Hansard*, 5th series, Commons, vol. 413, c. 340 (20 August 1945).
25 *Hansard*, 5th series, Commons, vol. 437, c. 1965 (17 May 1947).
26 D.H. Aldcroft, *The European Economy 1914–1970* (London, 1978), ch. 4; Paul Kennedy, *The Rise and Fall of the Great Powers. Economic Change and Military Conflict from 1500 to 2000* (London, 1988), pp. 475, 495.
27 Foot, op. cit., p. 33.
28 Bullock, op. cit., p. 64.
29 E.g. ibid., p. 517.
30 Kenneth Harris, *Attlee* (1982), p. 382.
31 Attlee, op. cit., p. 223.
32 Dalton, op. cit., p. 65.
33 Harris, op. cit., p. 281.
34 Williams, op. cit., p. 237.
35 Above, pp. 80.
36 Above, pp. 241.
37 Harris, op. cit., p. 309.
38 Bullock, op. cit., pp. 513–14.
39 Henry Pelling, *The British Communist Party* (London, 1958), p. 192.
40 Aneurin Bevan, *In Place of Fear* (London, 1952), pp. 151–52.
41 Harris, op. cit., p. 436.
42 Foot, op. cit., p. p.335.

43 Ibid., p. 236.
44 Attlee, op. cit., p. 197.
45 Angus Calder, *The People's War. Britain 1939–45* (London, 1969), p. 575.
46 Harris, op. cit., p. 257.
47 Ibid., p. 424.
48 Bevan, op. cit., p. 10.
49 Harris, op. cit., p. 436.
50 Foot, op. cit., p. 286.
51 Colin Cooke, *The Life of Stafford Cripps* (London, 1957), pp. 355, 360.
52 Williams, op. cit., p. 79.

Chapter 21

1   Hugh Dalton, *High Tide and After. Memoirs 1945–1960* (London, 1962), p. xii.
2   Kenneth Harris, *Attlee* (London, 1982), p. 489.
3   Dalton, op. cit., p. 221.
4   Alan Bullock, *Ernest Bevin, Foreign Secretary 1945–1951* (London, 1983), p. 405.
5   K.O. Morgan, *Labour in Power 1945–1951* (Oxford, 1984), p. 369.
6   Alec Cairncross, *Years of Recovery. British Economic Policy 1945–51* (London, 1985), p. 339.
7   Paul Addison, *Now the War is Over. A Social History of Britain 1945–51* (London, 1985), p. 53.
8   Cairncross, op. cit., pp. 18, 41–2, 201; Morgan, op. cit., p. 182.
9   Aneurin Bevan, *In Place of Fear* (London, 1952), p. 73.
10 Michael Foot, *Aneurin Bevan: A Biography*, vol. 2, *1945–1960* (London, 1973), p. 134.
11 Cairncross, op. cit., p. 471; and cf. Dalton, op. cit., p. 94.
12 C.R. Attlee, *As it Happened* (London, 1954), p. 189.
13 Harris, op. cit., p. 339.
14 Morgan, op. cit., p. 121.
15 Bevan, op. cit., p. 118; Foot, op. cit., p. 259.
16 Francis Williams, *A Prime Minister Remembers. The War and post-War Memoirs of the Rt. Hon. Earl Attlee* (London, 1961), p. 93.
17 Cairncross, op. cit., pp. 467, 494.
18 Attlee, op. cit., p. 192.
19 Paul Addison, *Churchill on the Home Front 1900–55* (London, 1992), p. 394.
20 Attlee, op. it., p. 191.
21 Supra, pp. 186–87.
22 Morgan, op. cit., p. 295; Henry Pelling, *The British Communist Party* (London, 1958), pp. 190, 192.
23 Chris Cook and John Stevenson, *The Longman Handbook of Modern British History 1714–1980* (1983), p. 154.
24 *Annual Abstract of Statistics*, No. 89 (London, 1952), p. 60.
25 Bevan, op. cit., p. 168.
26 Ibid., p. 125.
27 Above, pp. 251–54.
28 Nicholas Davenport, quoted in Ben Pimlott, *Hugh Dalton* (London, 1985), p. 491.
29 Bullock, op. cit., pp. 90, 618, 763–64.
30 Ibid., p. 340.

31 Ibid., p. 352.
32 Williams, op. cit., p. 118.
33 Bullock, op. cit., p. 470.
34 Dalton, op. cit., p. 292.
35 Ibid., p. 101.
36 Vincent A. Smith, *The Oxford History of India* (Oxford, 4th edn, 1983), p. 849. The figure is for the Punjab only.
37 Ibid., p. 211.
38 Harris, op. cit., p. 119.
39 Cf. the very full and fair account of the Russian government's point of view telegraphed to London by the British Ambassador in Moscow in December 1945, paraphrased in Bullock, op. cit., pp. 199–200.
40 Harris, op. cit., p. 312.
41 Bullock, op. cit., p. 602.
42 Ibid., p. 454.
43 Harris, op. cit., p. 468.
44 Foot, op. cit., p. 335.
45 Attlee, op. cit., p. 239; Williams, op. cit., p. 245.
46 Denis Healey, *The Time of My Life* (London, 1989), p. 131.
47 Morgan, op. cit., p. 161.
48 Lord Morrison of Lambeth, *Herbert Morrison, an Autobiography* (London, 1960), p. 263.
49 Dalton, op. cit., pp. 364–65.
50 Ibid., p. 3.
51 Colin Cooke, *The Life of Stafford Cripps* (London, 1957), p. 396.
52 E.g. Harris, op. cit., pp. 419–20.
53 Keith Jeffery and Peter Hennessy, *States of Emergency. British Governments and Strikebreaking since 1919* (London, 1983), ch. 6.
54 Ibid., ch. 7; and cf. Harris, op. cit., p. 458.
55 Addison, op. cit., p. 45; and below, p. 389.
56 Foot, op. cit., p. 238.
57 Ibid., pp. 142, 194.
58 Martin Gilbert, *Churchill: A Life* (London, 1991), p. 846.
59 See D.N. Chester, *The Nationalisation of British Industry* (London, 1975), pp. 55–61.
60 Addison, op. cit., pp. 40–44.

Chapter 22

1 Churchill, speech of 30 November 1954, quoted in Martin Gilbert, *'Never Despair.' Winston S. Churchill 1945–1965* (London, 1988), p. 1075.
2 Peter Fleming, *The Sixth Column. A Singular Tale of Our Times* (London, 1951), pp. 27–28, 164 *et passim*.
3 Duff Hart-Davis, *Peter Fleming. A Biography* (London, 1974; 2nd edn., Oxford, 1987), p. 328.
4 Gilbert, op. cit., p. 649.
5 Letter from Eric MacFadyen, *The Times*, 30 October 1951, p. 5.
6 John Birch, chairman of the National Council of Passenger Vehicle Operators' Association, at a dinner in London on 29 October: in ibid., p. 2.
7 Ibid., loc. cit.
8 Patrick Cosgrave, *The Lives of Enoch Powell* (London, 1989), p. 115. Cosgrave attributes the tale to R.A. Butler's Cambridge high table gossip, after he retired from politics to become Master of Trinity.

9   Paul Addison, *Churchill on the Home Front 1900–1955* (London, 1993), p. 435.

10 Lord Moran, *Winston Churchill: The Struggle for Survival 1940–1965* (London, 1966; new edn, 1968), p. 339.

11 Addison, op. cit., p. 398.

12 Ibid., p. 391.

13 Moran, op. cit., pp. 442, 455, 468; Harold Macmillan, *Tides of Fortune 1945–55* (London, 1969), p. 363.

14 Paul Addison, *Churchill on the Home Front* (London, 1992), p. 230.

15 Speech at Newcastle, 16 October 1951, quoted in Gilbert, op. cit., p. 647.

16 Moran, op. cit., p. 628: diary entry for 7 September 1954.

17 Addison, op. cit., p. 403.

18 Ibid., p. 434.

19 Moran, op. cit., p. 532: diary entry for 3 December 1953.

20 E.g. Gilbert, op. cit., pp. 961 (Harry Crookshank), 964 (Anthony Eden).

21 Speech of 6 November 1951, quoted in Gilbert, op. cit., p. 659.

22 Macmillan, op. cit., p. 361.

23 *The Times*, 27 October 1951, p. 7.

24 Anthony Seldon, *Churchill's Indian Summer. The Conservative Government 1951–55* (London, 1981), p. 57.

25 Above, p. 264.

26 Addison, op. cit., p. 419.

27 *Annual Abstract of Statistics*, No. 93 (London, 1956), p. 61.

28 Gilbert, op. cit., pp. 734–35.

29 Lord Butler, *The Art of the Possible. The Memoirs of Lord Butler, K.G., C.H.* (London, 1971), pp. 158–60; Addison, op. cit., pp. 410–12.

30 Anthony Howard, *RAB. The Life of R.A. Butler* (London, 1987), p. 203; Butler, op. cit., pp. 159–60.

31 Butler, op. cit., p. 164.

32 Moran, op. cit., p. 552.

33 Ibid., p. 658.

34 Addison, op. cit., p. 413.

35 Seldon, op. cit., p. 204.

36 Ibid., p. 207.

37 Harold Nicolson, *Diaries and Letters 1945–62* (London, 1968), p. 224

38 Butler, op. cit., p. 157.

39 *Annual Abstract of Statistics*, no. 93 (1956), pp. 103, 127, 216, 232, 243.

40 David Butler and Jennie Freeman, *British Political Facts 1900–1960* (London, 1964), p. 237.

41 Gilbert, op. cit., p. 1138.

42 Ibid., pp. 732–33: speech of 11 June 1952.

43 Moran, op. cit., p. 622.

44 Churchill at the Bermuda Conference, 7 December 1953, quoted in Gilbert, op. cit., p. 934.

45 Ibid., p. 1040.

46 Ibid., p. 1123.

47 Above, p. 279.

48 John Colville, *The Fringes of Power, Downing Street Diaries*, vol. II, *1941– April 1955* (London, 1985; new edn, 1987), p. 298.

49 Gilbert, op. cit., pp. 903 (October 1953), and 1037 (July 1954).

50 Seldon, op. cit., pp. 16, 348–77 *passim*.

51 Churchill to Eisenhower, 25 February 1953, quoted in Gilbert, op. cit., p. 804.
52 See Moran's diary entries for 10 January 1952 and 5 July 1954, in Moran, op. cit., pp. 386, 607.
53 Speech in Glasgow, 17 April 1953, quoted in Gilbert, op. cit., p. 816.
54 Speeches of 25 February, 8 and June 1954, cited in ibid., pp. 954, 992, 1011.
55 Above, pp. 117–18.
56 Colville, op. cit., p. 318.
57 Churchill to Eisenhower, March 1954, quoted in Gilbert, op. cit., p. 960.
58 Moran's diary for 26 June 1954, in Moran, op. cit., p. 591.
59 Gilbert, op. cit., p. 1123.
60 Ibid, p. 700 (House of Commons, 11 February 1952).
61 Ibid, p. 908 (House of Commons, 3 November 1953).
62 Moran, op. cit., p. 477 (diary for 16 August 1953).
63 Ibid., pp. 432, 525, 591 (diary for 25 June and 10 November 1953, and 26 June 1954).
64 Ibid., p. 583 (diary for 10 June 1954).
65 Ibid., p. 530 (diary for 2 December 1953).
66 Evelyn Shuckburgh, *Descent to Suez: Diaries, 1951–1956* (London, 1986), p. 61 (diary for 24 July 1953).
67 Colville, op. cit., p. 348 (diary for 10 December 1953).
68 Ibid., p. 350 (6 December 1953).
69 Ibid., p. 321 (7 January 1953).
70 E.g. ibid., p. 324 (12 January 1953); Moran, op. cit., p. 536 (7 December 1953).
71 Macmillan, op. cit., p. 532 (diary for 25 June 1954).
72 Moran, op. cit., pp. 377, 381 (4 and 7 January 1952).
73 Churchill to the Queen, 18 April 1955, quoted in Gilbert, op. cit., p. 1128.
74 Colville, op. cit., p. 318 (diary for 5 January 1953).
75 Ibid, p. 289 (note dated 25 November 1951).
76 There is an able contemporary analysis of this by Hugh Gaitskell, printed in Philip M. Williams (ed.), *The Diary of Hugh Gaitskell 1945–1956* (London, 1983), pp. 316–20.
77 Quoted in Michael Charlton, *The Price of Victory* (London, 1983), p. 137.
78 Gilbert, op. cit., p. 670.
79 Williams, op. cit., p. 485.
80 Hart-Davis, op. cit., p. 329.

Chapter 23

1   Harold Macmillan, *Riding the Storm: 1956–59* (London, 1971), pp. 350–51.
2   Harold Macmillan, *Pointing the Way: 1959–61* (London, 1972), p. 324.
3   *The Times*, 6 December 1962, p. 12.
4   Nigel Fisher, *Iain Macleod* (London, 1973), p. 215.
5   Harold Nicolson, *Diaries and Letters 1945–62* (London, 1968), p. 369.
6   Macmillan, *Pointing the Way*, p. 117.
7   Harold Macmillan, *At the End of the Day: 1961–63* (London, 1973), p. 61.
8   See for example Ben Pimlott, *Harold Wilson* (London, 1992), pp. 198, 218, 230, 276.
9   *Annual Abstract of Statistics*, No. 102 (1965), pp. 107, 191, 211, 250.
10 Macmillan, *Riding the Storm*, p. 196.

11 Lord Avon, *The Memoirs of the Rt. Hon. Sir Anthony Eden, K.G., P. C., M.P.: Full Circle* (London, 1960, p. 431; Lord Butler, *The Art of the Possible. The Memoirs of Lord Butler, K.G., C.H.* (London, 1971), p. 188.
12 Avon, op. cit., pp. 338–39, 465, 498; Lord Home, *The Way the Wind Blows. An Autobiography* (London, 1976), pp. 288–89.
13 Avon, op. cit., p. 431.
14 Butler, op. cit., p. 189.
15 Macmillan, *Riding the Storm*, p. 104.
16 Avon, op. cit., pp. 500–1. This concept, of course, – 'neo-colonialism' – is usually associated with the Marxist point of view.
17 Ibid., p. 459.
18 Avon, op. cit., pp. 557, 577; and cf. Macmillan, *Riding the Storm*, p. 166.
19 Macmillan, *Riding the Storm*, pp. 246, 250.
20 David Reynolds, *Britannia Overruled. British Policy and World Power in the 20th Century* (London, 1991), p. 213.
21 Macmillan, *At the End*, p. 335.
22 Ibid., p. 453.
23 Home, op. cit., p. 155.
24 Macmillan, *At the End*, pp. 194, 198–99, 214.
25 Butler, op. cit., pp. 256–57.
26 E.g. Sir E. Hall Patch to Eden, 8 July 1952, in R. Bullen and M.E. Pelly, ed., *Documents on British Policy Overseas*, Series II, vol. 1 (London, 1986), pp. 898–903.
27 Macmillan, *At the End*, p. 7.
28 Reynolds, op. cit., p. 221.
29 Macmillan, *At the End*, p. 367.
30 E.g. Macmillan, *Riding the Storm*, p. 86; and below, p.
31 See, for example, Harold Macmillan, *Tides of Fortune: 1945–1955* (London, 1969), p. 651; and *Riding the Storm*, p. 318.
32 E.g. Macmillan, *Pointing the Way*, p. 310.
33 Macmillan, *Riding the Storm*, p. 200.
34 Listed in Bernard Porter, *The Lion's Share. A Short History of British Imperialism 1850–1970* (London, 1975), p. 335.
35 Macmillan, *Riding the Storm*, pp. 222–30.
36 Fisher, op. cit., p. 142.
37 Ibid., p. 198.
38 Fisher, op. cit., pp. 145, 202; Macmillan, *Riding the Storm*, p. 596; Home, op. cit., p. 118; Philip M. Williams (ed.), *The Diary of Hugh Gaitskell 1945–1956* (London, 1983), p. 621; Lord Wigg, *George Wigg* (London, 1972), p. 261.
39 Fisher, op. cit., p. 155.
40 On this see Bernard Porter, 'Jingoism, Imperialism, and Soames Forsyte', in E. Serra and C. Seton-Watson (eds.), *Italia e Inghilterra nell'età dell'imperialismo* (Milan, 1990), pp. 215–28.
41 Above, p. 131.
42 Macmillan, *Riding the Storm*, p. 83.
43 Ibid., p. 43.
44 Macmillan, *At the End*, pp. 398–99.
45 Macmillan, *Riding the Storm*, p. 351.
46 Macmillan, *Pointing the Way*, p. 221.
47 Macmillan, *Riding the Storm*, p. 711.
48 Fisher, op. cit., p. 112.

49 Macmillan, *At the End*, p. 61.
50 Ibid., p. 60, and Macmillan, *Pointing the Way*, p. 15.
51 Above, pp. 253, 269.
52 Philip Larkin, 'Annus Mirabilis', in *High Windows* (London, 1974), p. 34.
53 Above, p. 294.
54 M.W. Kirby, *The Decline of British Economic Power since 1870* (London, 1981), pp. 146, 149, 155; W.W. Rostow, *The World Economy. History and Prospect* (Austin, Texas, 1978), p. 262.
55 Sidney Pollard, *The Development of the British Economy 1914–1967* (2nd edn., London, 1969), pp. 434–60 *passim.*
56 Ibid., p. 450.
57 Macmillan, *At the End*, p. 387.
58 Ibid., p. 85.
59 Ibid., p. 92.
60 Ibid., pp. 105, 109.
61 Ibid., p. 364; Fisher, op. cit., p. 218.
62 Denis Healey, *The Time of My Life* (London, 1989; this edn. Penguin, 1990), p. 210.
63 Fisher, op. cit., p. 214.
64 Macmillan, *At the End*, p. 60.
65 A. Koestler (ed.). *Suicide of a Nation? An Enquiry into the State of Britain Today* (London, 1963), p. 10.
66 Pimlott, op. cit., p. 296.
67 Lord Moran, *Winston Churchill: The Struggle for Survival 1940–1965* (paperback edn., London, 1968), p. 378; Avon, op. cit., p. 276; Macmillan, *Riding the Storm*, pp. 704–705; Home, op. cit., p. 218.
68 Macmillan, *Pointing the Way*, pp. 17–18.
69 See Fisher, op. cit., p. 227.
70 Macmillan, *Pointing the Way*, p. 218; *Riding the Storm*, p. 711; *At the End*, pp. 55, 58.
71 Patrick Cosgrave, *The Lives of Enoch Powell* (London, 1989), p. 182.
72 Enoch Powell in 1965, quoted in ibid, p. 134.

Chapter 24

1 Above, p. 306.
2 Ben Pimlott, *Harold Wilson* (London, 1992), p. 348.
3 Average age 51.9 years in October 1964, compared with the Labour Cabinet's 56.5 years.
4 Tony Benn, *Out of the Wilderness. Diaries 1963–67* (London, 1987; paperback edn, 1988), p. 399 (1 April 1966). Benn's campaign to renounce the peerage that came to him on the death of his father, Lord Stansgate, in 1960 is summarised in *ibid.*, p. 2.
5 Pimlott, op. cit., p. 304.
6 David Horner, 'The road to Scarborough: Wilson, Labour and the scientific revolution', in R. Coopey, S. Fielding and N. Tiratsoo (ed.), *The Wilson Governments 1964–1970* (London, 1993), p. 57.
7 Harold Wilson, *The Labour Government 1964–70* (London, 1971; paperback edn, Harmondsworth, 1974), p. 17.
8 James Callaghan, *Time and Chance* (London, 1987), pp. 152–53.
9 Horner, loc. cit., pp. 61–62.
10 Clive Ponting, *Breach of Promise. Labour in Power 1964–1970* (London, 1989; paperback edn, London, 1990), p. 118.

11 Richard Coopey, 'Industrial policy in the white heat of the scientific revolution', in Coopey, Fielding and Tiratsoo, op. cit., pp. 112, 114.

12 Wilson, op. cit., p. 993.

13 Benn, op. cit., p. 239 (29 March 1965).

14 Denis Healey, *The Time of My Life* (London, 1989; paperback edition, London, 1990), p. 275.

15 For two moderately favourable assessments of Labour's achievement in this sphere, see Nicholas Woodward, 'Labour's economic performance, 1964–70', and Richard Coopey, 'Industrial policy...', in Coopey, Fielding and Tiratsoo, op. cit., pp. 72–122.

16 Barbara Castle, *The Castle Diaries 1964–1976* (London, 1980, 1984; one-volume edn, London, 1990), p. 78 (22 July 1966).

17 Ponting, op. cit., pp. 391–92.

18 Richard Crossman, *The Diaries of a Cabinet Minister*, 3 vols (London, 1975, 1976, 1977), vol. I, p. 301 (3 August 1965).

19 Ponting, op. cit., p. 118.

20 Pimlott, op. cit., p. 364.

21 Callaghan, op. cit., p. 200.

22 Benn, op. cit., p. 382 (3 February 1966).

23 See, for example, Crossman, op. cit., pp. 154 and 244 (11 February and 4 June 1965).

24 Pimlott, op. cit., p. 508.

25 He forbad MI5 to tap MPs' telephone lines without his personal permission. Stephen Dorril and Robin Ramsay, *Smear! Wilson and the Secret State* (London, 1991), chapter 9 *et passim*.

26 Castle, op. cit., p. 190 (23 Feb); and see Benn, op. cit., p. 428 (14 June 1966)

27 See below, p. 317.

28 E.g. Healey, op. cit., p. p.331.

29 See below, pp. 325.

30 E.g. Crossman, *Diaries*, vol. I, p. 244 (4 June 1965); Healey, op. cit., p. 331.

31 Susan Crosland, *Tony Crosland* (London, 1982), p. 172.

32 Crossman, *Diaries*, vol I, p. 28 (22 October 1964).

33 Castle, op. cit., p. 142 (22 July 1967); Crosland, op. cit., p. 128; Healey, op. cit., p. 334.

34 Ponting, op. cit., ch. 3 *passim*.

35 Crossman, *Diaries*, vol. I, p. 574 (18 July 1966); and see ibid. pp. 316–17, 455–56, vol. II, p. 156 (1 September 1965, 14 February and 9 December 1966); and Castle, op. cit., pp. 76 and 80 (18 and 31 July 1966).

36 George Brown, *In My Way. The Political Memoirs of Lord George-Brown* (London, 1971; paperback edn. Harmondsworth, 1972), pp. 161–77; Wilson, op. cit., pp. 641–48.

37 Brown, op. cit., p. 119.

38 Benn, *Out of the Wilderness*, p. 459 (21 July 1966).

39 Castle, op. cit., p. 30 (31 August 1965).

40 Benn, op. cit., p. 268 (2 June 1965).

41 Tony Benn, *Office without Power. Diaries 1968–72* (London, 1988), p. 102 (18 September 1968).

42 Ibid., pp. 64–65 (6 May 1968).

43 Pimlott, op. cit., p. 223.

44 Callaghan, op. cit., pp. 181–82.

45 Castle, op. cit., p. 30 (31 August 1965).

46 Wilson, op. cit., p. 687.

47 Crossman, *Diaries*, vol. II, p. 588 (22 November 1967); Callaghan, op. cit., p. 205.
48 *Hansard*, 5th series, vol. 730, col.42 (20 June 1966); Wilson, op. cit., pp. 307–08.
49 Dorril and Ramsay, op. cit., ch. 24.
50 E.g. Benn, *Office without Power*, p. 63 (30 April 1968); Castle, op. cit., pp. 87–88, 234 (27 September 1966, 24 June 1968); Healey, op. cit., pp. 336, 339.
51 Dorril and Ramsay, op. cit., p. 179.
52 *The Times*, 26 October 1968, p. 1.
53 Dorril and Ramsay, op. cit., ch. 27.
54 Castle, op. cit., p. 30 (31 August 1965).
55 Benn, *Office without Power*, p. 129 (25 November 1968).
56 Wilson, op. cit., pp. 65–66.
57 Castle, op. cit., p. 163 (16 November 1967).
58 Callaghan, op. cit., p. 211; Wilson, op. cit., p. 577.
59 Crossman, *Diaries*, vol. II, pp. 646–47 (12 January 1968).
60 Roy Jenkins, *A Life at the Centre* (London, 1991), p. 220.
61 Castle, op. cit., p. 389 (8 March 1970).
62 Castle, op. cit., p. 329 (8 May 1969); Benn, *Office without Power*, p. 166 (8 May 1969).
63 Crossman, *Diaries*, vol. III, p. 706 (30 October 1969).
64 Benn, *Out of the Wilderness*, p. 474 (14 September 1966), and *Office without Power*, p. 151 (25 February 1969); Castle, op. cit., p. 335 (29 May 1969).
65 Benn, *Out of the Wilderness*, p. 503 (8 June 1967).
66 Ibid., p. 453 (17 July 1966); Benn, *Office without Power*, pp. 62, 70 (28 April and 22 May 1968).
67 Above, p. 312.
68 Brown, op. cit., p. 254.
69 Benn, *Out of the Wilderness*, pp. 422, 436 (7 and 21 June 1966).
70 Wilson, op. cit., p. 908; Benn, *Office without Power*, p. 232 (2 February 1970); Castle, op. cit., pp. 382–82 (2 February 1970); Crossman, *Diaries*, vol. III, p. 945 (14 June 1970).
71 Crossman, *Diaries*, vol. III, p. 800 (2 February 1970).
72 Benn, *Office without Power*, p. 232 (2 February 1970).
73 Benn, *Out of the Wilderness*, pp. 461–62 (27 July 1966).
74 Bernard Levin, *The Pendulum Years. Britain and the Sixties* (London, 1970; paperback edn, London, 1972), p. 234.
75 Phillip Darby, *British Defence Policy East of Suez 1947–1968* (London, 1973), p. 284.
76 Ibid., p. 296.
77 Wilson, op. cit., p. 276.
78 *Annual Abstract of Statistics*, No. 108 (London, 1971), p. 297.
79 Darby, op. cit., p. 286.
80 Crossman, *Diaries*, vol. II, p. 156 (9 December 1966).
81 *Annual Abstract of Statistics*, No. 102 (London, 1965), p. 220.
82 Michael Stewart, *Life and Labour. An Autobiography* (London, 1980), p. 144.
83 Darby, op. cit., pp. 295–96; Ponting, op. cit., ch. 3.
84 Healey, op. cit., pp. 280–81.
85 Above, p. 315.

86 Callaghan, op. cit., p. 169.
87 Darby, op. cit., pp. 322–26.
88 Above, p. 319.
89 Above, p. 279.
90 Darby, op. cit., p. 292.
91 Castle, op. cit., p. 38 (21 December 1965); Wilson, op. cit., p. 342.
92 Benn, *Out of the Wilderness*, p. 501 (1 June 1967); and cf. Crossman, *Diaries*, vol. III, p. 807 (5 February 1970).
93 Wilson, op. cit., p. 283.
94 Castle, op. cit., p. 100 (20 December 1966).
95 Wilson, op. cit., pp. 129, 518–25.

Chapter 25

1 *The Times*, 4 January 1973, pp. 1, 10.
2 George H. Gallup, *The Gallup International Public Opinion Polls: Great Britain 1937–1975* (New York, n.d.), vol. II, *passim*. Surveys of opinion on the EEC were taken almost monthly in this period. The only times when there was a marginal majority in favour were November 1971, February 1972 and January 1973 (pp.1157, 1166, 1219).
3 Phillip Whitehead, *The Writing on the Wall. Britain in the Seventies* (London, 1985), p. 68.
4 Douglas Hurd, *An End to Promises. Sketch of a Government 1970–74* (London, 1979), p. 60 (italics added).
5 John Campbell, *Edward Heath. A Biography* (London, 1993), p. 436.
6 Above, p. 8.
7 Calculated from *Annual Abstract of Statistics*, No. 117 (London, 1980), pp. 317–20.
8 Lord Carrington, *Reflect on Things Past* (London, 1988), p. 253.
9 Campbell, op. cit., pp. 341–42.
10 Douglas E. Schoen, *Enoch Powell and the Powellites* (London, 1977), p. 88.
11 N.F.R. Crafts and Nicholas Woodward (eds.), *The British Economy since 1945* (Oxford, 1991), p. 120.
12 Schoen, op. cit., pp. 55–66.
13 Whitehead, op. cit., p. 76.
14 Ibid., loc. cit.
15 Ibid., p. 110; Campbell, op. cit., p. 539.
16 *Annual Abstract...* (1980), p. 159.
17 Above, p. 320.
18 Martin Holmes, *Political Pressure and Economic Policy. British Government 1970–1974* (London, 1982), p. 10.
19 Ibid., p. 37.
20 Campbell, op. cit., p. 290.
21 Morrison Halcrow, *Keith Joseph. A Single Mind* (London, 1989), p. 51.
22 Jim Prior, *A Balance of Power* (London, 1986), p. 71.
23 Heath's Introduction to the 1970 Conservative Party Manifesto, quoted in Holmes, op. cit., p. 37.
24 Hurd, op. cit., p. 21.
25 Holmes, op. cit., p. 19.
26 Ibid., p. 41.
27 Ibid., pp. 44–45.
28 Whitehead, op. cit., p. 96.

29 Campbell, op. cit., p. 452.
30 Above, p. 311.
31 Sir Leo Pliatsky, quoted in Whitehead, op. cit., p. 83.
32 Campbell, op. cit., p. 453.
33 Whitehead, op. cit., p. 84.
34 Holmes, op. cit., p. 78; Campbell, op. cit., p. 412.
35 Holmes, op. cit., p. 46; Campbell, op. cit., pp. 410–11; Prior, op. cit., p. 74.
36 Whitehead, op. cit., p. 96.
37 Lord Armstrong reporting an NUM delegate at No. 10 Downing Street, quoted in Holmes, op. cit., p. 107.
38 Campbell, op. cit., p. 526.
39 E.g. Peter Jay in *The Times*, May 1973, quoted in Whitehead, op. cit., p. 97.
40 Halcrow, op. cit., p. 46.
41 Schoen, op. cit., p. 96.
42 William Whitelaw, *The Whitelaw Memoirs* (London, 1989; paperback edn, London, 1990), pp. 128–29.
43 David Butler and Dennis Kavanagh, *The British General Election of February 1974* (London, 1974), p. 266.
44 Whitehead, op. cit., pp. 106–7.
45 Peter Walker, *Staying Power. An Autobiography* (London, 1991), p. 124.
46 Prior, op. cit., p. 87.
47 Holmes, op. cit., p. 113.
48 Butler and Kavanagh, op. cit., p. 122.
49 Hurd, op. cit., pp. 135–36.
50 Whitehead, op. cit., p. 113.
51 Peter Wright, *Spycatcher. The Candid Autobiography of a Senior Intelligence Officer* (New York, 1987), pp. 366–67.
52 Below, p. 362.
53 Butler and Kavanagh, op. cit., p. 4.

Chapter 26

1   Barbara Castle, *The Castle Diaries 1964–76* (London, 1990), p. 429 (6 March 1974).
2   Harold Wilson, *Final Term. The Labour Government 1974–1976* (London, 1979), p. 17.
3   Bernard Donoughue, *Prime Minister. The Conduct of Policy under Harold Wilson and James Callaghan* (London, 1987), pp. 47–48; Wilson, op. cit., p. 17.
4   Denis Healey, *The Time of My Life* (London, 1989; paperback edn, London, 1990), p. 388.
5   James Callaghan, *Time and Chance* (London, 1987), p. 417.
6   Castle, op. cit., p. 549 (20 January 1975).
7   Conrad Heron, quoted in ibid., p. 491 (30 July 1974).
8   Calculated from *Monthly Digest of Statistics*, no. 370 (October 1976), p. 156; no. 371 (November 1976), p. 153; no. 384 (December 1977), p. 151; no. 396 (December 1978), p. 157; and no. 406 (October 1979), p. 163.
9   Wilson, op. cit., p. 119.
10 *Annual Abstract of Statistics*, No. 117 (London, 1980), p. 215.
11 Martin Holmes, *The Labour Government, 1974-79. Political Aims and Economic Reality* (London, 1985), p. 1.
12 Wilson, op. cit., p. 22.

13 Callaghan, op. cit., p. 428.
14 Healey, op. cit., p. 428.
15 Ibid., pp. 381, 402, 432-33; and see Joe Haines, *The Politics of Power* (London, 1977; revised edn, London, 1977), pp. 41-42 *et passim*.
16 *Annual Abstract of Statistics*, No. 117 (1980), p. 160.
17 E.g. Donoughue, op. cit., pp. 71, 181.
18 Joel Barnett, *Inside the Treasury* (London, 1982), p. 161.
19 Callaghan, op. cit., p. 469.
20 David Owen, *Time to Declare* (London, 1991; revised edn., London, 1992), p. 408.
21 Phillip Whitehead, *The Writing on the Wall. Britain in the Seventies* (London, 1985), p. 283.
22 Callaghan, op. cit., p. 309.
23 David Steel, *Against Goliath* (London, 1989), pp. 129–45; and see Owen, op. cit., pp. 288–90.
24 Donoughue, op. cit., p. 159.
25 Simon Hoggart and David Leigh, *Michael Foot: A Portrait* (London, 1981), p. 191.
26 Roy Jenkins, *A Life at the Centre* (London, 1991), pp. 364, 367.
27 Ibid., pp. 425–25.
28 Ibid., p. 371.
29 Donoughue, op. cit., p. 50: Tony Benn, *Against the Tide. Diaries 1973–76* (London, 1989; paperback edn, London, 1990), p. 115 (5 March 1974).
30 Benn, op. cit., p. 118 (10 March 1974).
31 Healey, op. cit., p. 446; Benn, op. cit., p. 156 (19 May 1974).
32 Castle, op. cit., pp. 464, 474 (11 June, 4 July 1974).
33 Wilson, op. cit., p. 234.
34 Owen, op. cit., p. 245.
35 Above, p. 330.
36 Callaghan, op. cit., p. 326.
37 Castle, op. cit., pp. 597–98 (26 April 1975).
38 Ben Pimlott, *Harold Wilson* (London, 1992), p. 684.
39 Castle, op. cit., p. 714 (21 January 1976).
40 Wilson, op. cit., p. 227.
41 Castle, op. cit., p. 734 (9 March 1976).
42 Stephen Dorril and Robin Ramsay, *Smear! Wilson and the Secret State* (London, 1991), p. 291.
43 Reproduced in Paul Foot, *Who Framed Colin Wallace?* (London, 1988), pp. 292–98.
44 Castle, op. cit., p. 425 (3 March 1974).
45 Healey, op. cit., p. 398.
46 Donoughue, op. cit., p. 191.
47 Above, p. 269.
48 Above, p. 345.
49 Benn, op. cit., p. 119 (11 March 1974).
50 Brian Crozier, *Free Agent. The Unseen War 1941–1991* (London, 1993), pp. 65–68 *et passim*.
51 See the *Guardian*, 15 November 1991, for evidence of Soviet financial support for the CPGB, 1958–79.
52 Above, p. 333.
53 Peter Wright, *Spycatcher. The Candid Autobiography of a Senior Intelligence Officer* (New York, 1987), pp. 368–72. Wright later modified

his testimony on this: see ¬The Wilson Plot', *Panorama* (BBC TV), 13 October 1988.
54 Crozier, op. cit., pp. 138, 144.
55 Keith Jeffery and Peter Hennessy, *States of Emergency. British Governments and Strikebreaking since 1919* (London, 1983), pp. 237–38.
56 Dorril and Ramsay, op. cit., pp. 211, 231.
57 Wright, op. cit., p. 359.
58 The changes in MPs' occupations are charted in the books by David Butler about successive British general elections, cited above. The shift in Conservative MPs' educational backgrounds is analysed in Martin Burch and Michael Moran, 'The changing British political élite, 1945–1983', in *Parliamentary Affairs*, vol. 38 (1985), pp. 4–6.
59 Above, p. 320.
60 Calculated from figures in D. H. Aldcroft, *The European Economy 1914–1990* (3rd. edn., London, 1993), p. 197.
61 E.g. D.H. Aldcroft, 'The Entrepreneur and the British Economy, 1870–1914', in *Economic History Review*, vol. 17 (1964).
62 Healey, op. cit., p. 405.
63 Donoughue, op. cit., p. 149.
64 Benn, op. cit., pp. 122, 170 (19 March and 10 June, 1974).
65 Haines, op. cit., p. 31.
66 Hugo Young, *One of Us. A Biography of Margaret Thatcher* (London, 1989; revised edn, London, 1990), p. 123.
67 Wilson, op. cit., p. 108.
68 Douglas Jay, *Change and Fortune. A Political Record* (London, 1980), pp. 480, 484–87.
69 Above, pp. 298, 323–24.
70 Callaghan, op. cit., pp. 295–96.
71 Castle, op. cit., p. 546 (17 January 1975).
72 Wilson, op. cit., p. 78.
73 Benn, op. cit., pp. 137–38 (10 April 1974).
74 See Kevin Kelley, *The Longest War: Northern Ireland and the IRA* (London, 1982), p. 215; Paul Foot, op cit., p. 78.
75 Paul Foot, op. cit., *passim.*
76 *Annual Abstract of Statistics*, no. 117 (1980), p. 101.
77 Jenkins, op. cit., p. 376.
78 Above, p. 347.
79 Steel, op. cit., p. 134.

Chapter 27

1 David Butler and Dennis Kavanagh, *The British General Election of 1979* (London, 1980), pp. 155–57.
2 Above, p. 340.
3 Margaret Thatcher, *The Downing Street Years* (London, 1993), p. 13.
4 Above, p. 354.
5 *Guardian*, 25 June 1983.
6 Above, pp. 317, 344.
7 James Callaghan, *Time and Chance* (London, 1987), p. 426.
8 Denis Healey, *The Time of My Life* (London, 1989; new edn, London, 1990), p. 434.
9 Above, p. 320.

10 David Butler and Gareth Butler, *British Political Facts 1900–1985* (6th edn., London, 1986), p. 334.
11 B.R. Mitchell, *British Historical Statistics* (new edn., Cambridge, 1988), p. 558.
12 See E.J. Hobsbawm's essay in Martin Jacques and Francis Mulhern (eds.), *The Forward March of Labour Halted?* (London, 1981), pp. 1–19.
13 Above, p. 148, 407n. 41.
14 Above, pp. 123 *et passim*.
15 Below, p. 374.
16 Hugo Young, *One of Us. A Biography of Margaret Thatcher* (London, 1989; revised edn, London, 1990), p. 215.
17 Ibid., p. 136.
18 Ibid., p. 192.
19 Ibid., p. 209.
20 Ibid., pp. 136–37.
21 Ibid., p. 215.
22 Above, p. 348.
23 Brian Crozier, *Free Agent. The Unseen War 1941–1991* (London, 1993), ch. 10.
24 Nigel Lawson, *The View from No. 11. Memoirs of a Tory Radical* (London, 1992; paperback edn, London, 1993), p. 314.
25 Bernard Porter, *Plots and Paranoia. A History of Political Espionage in Britain 1790–1988* (London, 1989), pp. 219–27.
26 David Butler and Dennis Kavanagh, *The British General Election of October 1974* (London, 1975), pp. 166–67; and *The British General Election of 1979*, p. 232.
27 E.g. Crozier, op. cit., pp. 127–28.
28 Thatcher, op. cit., p. 11; Young, op. cit., pp. 3–10; George Gardiner, *Margaret Thatcher, From Childhood to Leadership* (London, 1975), ch. 1.
29 Thatcher, op. cit., p. 12.
30 Ibid., p. 13; and above, p. 335.
31 Ibid., p. 14.
32 Morrison Halcrow, *Keith Joseph. A Single Mind* (London, 1989), ch. 8.
33 E.g. Lord Young of Graffham, *Enterprise Regained* (London, 1985).
34 The original idea came from the television interviewer Brian Walden, on 'Weekend World' (LWT), 16 January, 1983, reported in *The Times*, 20 January 1983; but Thatcher afterwards made it her own.
35 See Brian Harrison, 'Mrs Thatcher and the Intellectuals', in *20th Century British History*, forthcoming (1994); Bernard Porter, 'Thatcher and History', in *Durham University Journal*, forthcoming (1994).
36 The full text of what some contemporary theologians rather flippantly referred to as the 'Sermon on the Mound' is published in Jonathan Raban, *God, Man and Mrs Thatcher* (London, Chatto & Windus, 1989).
37 Above, pp. 6–7.
38 Butler and Kavanagh, *British General Election of 1979*, pp. 155–57.
39 See Andrew Gamble's (critical) *The Free Economy and the Strong State. The Politics of Thatcherism* (London, 1988).
40 Above, p. 24.
41 Early academic backing for this theory was provided by Martin J. Wiener, *English Culture and the Decline of the Industrial Spirit 1850–1980* (Cambridge, 1981).
42 Above, pp. 70–71.
43 Thatcher, op. cit., pp. 595–97.

44 Michael Foot, *Aneurin Bevan: A Biography*, vol. 2 (London, 1973), p. 238.
45 Young, op. cit., p. 223.
46 Above, pp. 357–58.
47 Interview with Hugo Young in *Guardian*, 10 July 1986.
48 Young, op. cit., p. 207.
49 Interview with Hugo Young in *Guardian*, 9 July 1986.
50 John Ranelagh, *Thatcher's People* (London, 1991; paperback edn, London, 1992), p. ix.

Chapter 28

1 Jim Prior, *A Balance of Power* (London, 1986), p. 118.
2 Nigel Lawson, *The View from No. 11. Memoirs of a Tory Radical* (London, 1992; paperback edn, London, 1993), p. 40.
3 David Smith, *From Boom to Bust. Trial and Error in British Economic Policy* (London, 1992), pp. 22–23.
4 Judy Hillman and Peter Clarke, *Geoffrey Howe. A Quiet Revolutionary* (London, 1988), pp. 134–35.
5 Prior, op. cit., p. 158.
6 *The Times*, 20 May 1985.
7 Lawson, op. cit., pp. 414–15.
8 Margaret Thatcher, *The Downing Street Years* (London, 1993), p. 33.
9 Prior, op. cit., p. 104.
10 Peter Walker, *Staying Power. An Autobiography* (London, 1991), p. 137.
11 Prior, op. cit., pp. 118–19; above, p. 370.
12 Walker, op. cit., p. 134.
13 Pym launched his 'Centre Forward' group in May 1985. It gathered hardly any support. *The Times*, 13 May 1985, p. 1.
14 Walker, op. cit., p. 137.
15 Denis Healey, *The Time of My Life* (London, 1989; paperback edn, London, 1990), p. 491.
16 Figures from Christopher Johnson, *The Economy under Mrs Thatcher 1979–1990* (London, 1991), pp. 265–66, 274, 278, 292, 315, 317; and Smith, op. cit., pp. 236–37.
17 Hugo Young, *One of Us. A Biography of Margaret Thatcher* (London, 1989; paperback edn, London, 1990), p. 202.
18 Johnson, op. cit., pp. 280, 312.
19 E.g. Lord Stockton in House of Lords, 13 November 1984: *Hansard*, Lords, 5th series, vol. 157, cc. 234–42; Edward Heath in House of Commons, 27 November 1980: *Hansard*, Commons, 5th series, vol. 994, cc. 602–606; and Heath speech at Manchester, 4 October 1981: *The Times*, 7 October 1981, p. 6.
20 Thatcher told Prior he had no 'backbone' in 1979: Prior, op. cit., p. 114. He was shunted off to Northern Ireland, unwillingly, in September 1981. Sir Ian Gilmour, another 'wet', resigned at the same time. Before that, in January 1981, she had sacked Norman St John Stevas, her Leader of the House.
21 David Butler and *Dennis Kavanagh, The British General Election of 1983* (London, 1984), p. 21.
22 The Crimean war? But there was more at stake there, and less at risk. And the free marketists of the time disapproved of it anyway.
23 Thatcher, op. cit., pp. 8, 173.
24 G.M. Dillon, *The Falklands, Politics and War* (London, 1989), pp. 237–42. This figure includes the cost of the post-war 'Fortress Falklands' policy.

25 Thatcher, op. cit., pp. 173, 235.
26 See David Reynolds, *Britannia Overruled. British Policy and World Power in the 20th Century* (London, 1991), pp. 261–64.
27 See Bernard Porter, 'Wealth or Commonwealth? The History of a Paradox', in Richard Maltby and Peter Quartermaine (eds.), *A Common Culture?* (Exeter, 1984), pp. 28–30.
28 Thatcher, op. cit., p. 12.
29 *Observer*, 27 April 1986.
30 *Daily Express*, quoted in *Guardian*, 11 August 1990.
31 E.g. Hugo Young, 'A terrible price to pay for the love of Ronnie', in *Guardian*, 18 October 1986. A popular radical poster of the time, modelled on the one for the film *Gone with the Wind*, depicted Thatcher in Reagan's arms, with the caption underneath: 'She promised to follow him to the end of the earth. He promised to organise it.' Reproduced in Ronald A. Smith, *The Premier Years of Margaret Thatcher* (London, 1991), p. 122.
32 Above, p. 85.
33 Speech at Cheltenham, 3 July 1982, quoted in Young, op. cit., p. 281. Similar exhortations were made at the Conservative Party Conference on 8 October, and the Lord Mayor's Banquet on 13 November 1982: ibid., p. 290.
34 Above, p. 332.
35 Thatcher, op. cit., pp. 339, 364.
36 Ibid., p. 370.
37 Ibid., p. 364. Ian MacGregor's own account, in *The Enemies Within. The Story of the Miners' Strike 1984–5* (London, 1986), pp. 244, 282, is at odds with this. He claims that he and Thatcher saw eye to eye, but that Walker, the Energy Secretary, did intervene, usually in favour of settling.
38 Johnson, op. cit., p. 313.
39 Margaret Thatcher, 'Don't undo what I have done', in *Newsweek*, April 1992; reprinted in the *Guardian*, 22 April 1992.
40 J. Young, *The Rise in Crime in England and Wales 1979–1990* (1992), showed crime to have increased by 32% annually during the 1980s, or twice as fast as under any previous government.
41 Eg. lecture by Edwina Currie in Newcastle upon Tyne, 23 September 1986, reported in *The Times*, 24 September 1986. In 1980 the report of an inquiry chaired by Sir Douglas Black which attributed poor health directly to social deprivation was suppressed – i.e. made deliberately hard to obtain – by the Government. See Peter Townsend and Nick Davidson (eds.), *Inequalities in Health* (Harmondsworth, 1982).
42 *Observer*, 15 August 1993.
43 Above, pp. 364, 372–73.
44 David Smith, op. cit., pp. 232–33; *Annual Abstract of Statistics*, No. 130 (London, 1993), p. 331.
45 Johnson, op. cit., p. 268.
46 *Annual Abstract of Statistics*, No. 127 (London, 1990), pp. 226, 228.
47 Lord (David) Young, *The Enterprise Years. A Businessman in the Cabinet* (London, 1990), pp. 44, 144–45; *Hansard*, Lords, 5th series, vol. 464, c. 320 (22 May 1985).
48 David Smith, op. cit., pp. 232–33.
49 See Thatcher, 'Don't undo what I have done': loc. cit.

Chapter 29

1   Neal Ascherson, 'Law and order in the market place', in *Observer*, 26 May 1985.
2   See, for example, Ian MacGregor, *The Enemies Within. The Story of the Miners' Strike 1984–5* (London, 1986), p. 236.
3   Above, p. 30.
4   Above, p. 15.
5   'Maggie's Mauler', in *Sunday Telegraph*, 7 October 1990.
6   E.g. Jim Prior, *A Balance of Power* (London, 1986), p. 134.
7   Lord (David) Young, *The Enterprise Years* (London, 1990), p. 112. The popular press version of this substituted 'solutions' for 'achievements'.

Index